WEAVERS, SCRIBES, AND KINGS

WEAVERS, SCRIBES, AND KINGS

A NEW HISTORY OF THE ANCIENT NEAR EAST

AMANDA H. PODANY

OXFORD
UNIVERSITY PRESS

OXFORD
UNIVERSITY PRESS

Oxford University Press is a department of the University of Oxford. It furthers the University's objective of excellence in research, scholarship, and education by publishing worldwide. Oxford is a registered trade mark of Oxford University Press in the UK and certain other countries.

Published in the United States of America by Oxford University Press
198 Madison Avenue, New York, NY 10016, United States of America.

Library of Congress Cataloging-in-Publication Data
Names: Podany, Amanda H, author.
Title: Weavers, scribes, and kings : a new history of the ancient Near East /
by Amanda H. Podany.
Other titles: New history of the ancient Near East
Description: New York, NY : Oxford University Press, [2022] |
Includes bibliographical references and index.
Identifiers: LCCN 2022010837 (print) | LCCN 2022010838 (ebook) |
ISBN 9780190059040 (hardback) | ISBN 9780190059064 (epub) |
Subjects: LCSH: Middle East—Civilization—To 622. |
Middle East—Social life and customs.
Classification: LCC DS57 .P63 2022 (print) | LCC DS57 (ebook) |
DDC 939/.4—dc23/eng/20220524
LC record available at https://lccn.loc.gov/2022010837
LC ebook record available at https://lccn.loc.gov/2022010838

DOI: 10.1093/oso/9780190059040.001.0001

Printed by Sheridan, United States of America

For my mother
Margaret Graham Hills
with love and thanks

Contents

PART V. THE OLD BABYLONIAN PERIOD, 1792–1550 BCE

PART VI. THE LATE BRONZE AGE, 1550–1000 BCE

PART VII. THE FIRST MILLENNIUM, 1000–323 BCE

Introduction

A few years ago, the world discovered Ea-nasir. An article by an archaeologist named Kristina Killgrove in *Forbes* magazine was titled "Meet the Worst Businessman of the 18th Century BC."[1] Killgrove detailed the financial problems of a merchant, Ea-nasir, who lived in a big house in the city of Ur in what is now Iraq. She made a strong case for his ineptitude, quoting from letters that he had received from unhappy customers, people who were at their wits' end, trying to get him to send products they had been promised or refunds for goods he hadn't delivered. Killgrove quoted one letter in full. It had been written by a man named Nanni, and it reads like an angry diatribe to a complaints department. In the middle of his letter, Nanni wrote, "Who am I that you are treating me in this manner—treating me with such contempt? . . . I have written to you to receive my money, but you have neglected [to return] it."[2]

The remarkable thing about this frustrating case of incompetence is that both of the men involved have been dead for many thousands of years. Ea-nasir lived almost 3,800 years ago. Just think how long ago that is; it's hard to wrap your mind around. He lived 2,400 years before the time of Mohammad and the beginning of Islam, 1,300 years, even, before the *founding* of the Roman Republic. And yet, as the article showed, we recognize Ea-nasir—he's the vendor who fails to reply to our emails and phone calls, and any of us might have written Nanni's letter. We just wouldn't write it in cuneiform script on a clay tablet.

The article clearly resonated with readers and it enjoyed a flurry of interest on social media. Any number of my friends and students sent it to me. Other posts about Ea-nasir appeared, and the long-dead merchant suddenly rose to the top of the news cycle and became (if briefly) a household name. Suddenly something in my obscure field of expertise made sense to people who had been mystified about what I actually study, about what is written on the clay tablets I write and teach about.

But Ea-nasir's file of complaint letters wasn't a new discovery when the article appeared. The tablets were found a century ago during excavations at the ancient city of Ur in the 1920s and have been in the British Museum ever since. By the time the *Forbes* article came out, Ea-nasir had been discussed in at least twenty scholarly articles, the earliest in 1931.[3] Already in 1967, the letter from Nanni was translated into English and included in a book called *Letters from Mesopotamia*.[4] Ea-nasir was well known in the field of Assyriology, but he had escaped public notice, so he seemed to be a revelation. Who would have guessed that someone living so very long ago could have been so incompetent in such an ordinary way?

Here's another surprise, though: he was not alone. There were hundreds, maybe thousands, of Ea-nasirs. I don't mean that everyone in the ancient Near East was incompetent—Ea-nasir was a standout in that respect—just that they were very human and, cumulatively, they left behind hundreds of thousands of documents to prove it. If you could have listened in at any doorway in Ur, or any door in any ancient city in the Near East during ancient times for that matter, you would have heard stories that strike a familiar note. People would have been talking about promising business deals, complicated wedding plans, long-planned trips, unfair bosses, and crazy uncles; you'd have heard arguments over dinner and lullabies at bedtime.

In this book I will take you behind many of those doors to listen in on men and women from the very ancient past. Some of them were famous in their time and wanted to be remembered; they would no doubt be delighted to know that their names have lived on so long after their deaths. Others had no way to make a mark on history; they were illiterate and powerless, subject to the whims of their employers and leaders or the vagaries of the climate and agricultural pests. But we know about them anyway.

This is because scribes wrote about the things that mattered, the things they were asked to write about. Scribes were professionals who had mastered the cuneiform script after years of training; most other people couldn't read or write. Some of the highest-ranking scribes wrote out royal inscriptions and proclamations at the command of kings and queens—documents that were composed with an eye to impressing the gods and people in the future—but those made up just a tiny percentage of what was written. Most scribes kept track of administrative details for bureaucratic purposes. They made lists of the names of workers and the rations or monthly payments they received, names of taxpayers and the amounts of their contributions, numbers of soldiers called up for a campaign and where they came from, numbers of sheep dedicated for a particular festival, and on and on. Other scribes were hired to record contracts and write down letters, like the ones sent to Ea-nasir.

In some eras of ancient Near Eastern history we know a great deal about the political world of the leaders: kings and queens, priestesses and priests. In some eras we know very little about the rulers and their achievements, glimpsing them only tangentially. An important diplomatic mission may be revealed to us only because of the survival of an administrative text recording the requisition of a gift for a foreign ruler. In this document, the main actors are the artisan who made the gift and the functionary who requested it. In such a situation I couldn't write a history of the dynasty if I tried—no one could. For all eras in the ancient Near East, the common people named in the lists, contracts, and letters wildly outnumber the kings and queens (though, admittedly, often the names of those commoners are all we know about them).

Ancient Near Eastern history is therefore more of a weathered mosaic than a grand narrative. Parts of it are rich with detail, others frustratingly blank. We are, no doubt, completely unaware of any number of major wars, diplomatic embassies, palace coups, and royal achievements. Our only sources of knowledge are the random documents that have been recovered from archaeological sites, and the physical contexts in which they were found. They shine a bright light on odd corners of the ancient Near Eastern world, but we often can't even guess what might be in the documents that did not survive or have not been found yet. So I can't claim that this book covers all the most influential people and events. Instead, we will travel through 3,000 years of history knocking on doors and settling in for a while with individuals whose lives tell us something about the time in which they lived. Some of those individuals were political and religious leaders, some were officials and scribes, and some were weavers, brickmakers, and brewers. Between them, they will help you to see the history of the ancient Near East in a more intimate way than classic political history allows.

Each of the dozens of people whose lives we will visit, in his or her own way, changed the world, from the most powerful king or priestess to the poorest tenant farmer. A direct line can sometimes be traced from their original decisions and innovations to the world we see around us now. They figured out how to live together in cities, how to bake bricks, how to keep track of the calendar, how to make sense of the night skies, how to survey a field, how to examine evidence in a court case, how to negotiate a peace treaty, how to brew beer, how to write, how to trade over long distances, how to create a school curriculum, and so much more. These things happened in other places as well, and I am not claiming that the people of the ancient Near East were the only ones who changed the world, but they were very early to the party and had a tremendous impact. In many cases these innovations were never forgotten; they were passed down from generation to generation.

You may have heard of some of the individuals you will meet in this book but, unless you are a scholar in the field of ancient Near Eastern history, I am quite sure that many of them will be completely new and surprising to you. Many of them were completely new to everyone in the modern world until recently, when ancient texts mentioning them were discovered and read. The lives of these ancient individuals were far from dull; they (like people in all eras) cared passionately about the events of their times, having no idea what the future held, and the humanity they share with us can be disarming.

It is astonishing just how much we know about some people of the ancient Near East and how deeply we can dive into their world, but it is also striking how little this knowledge has penetrated into the wider consciousness of educated people today. In contrast, other ancient cultures that shared the same general region of the world—Egypt, Israel, Greece, and Rome—are thoroughly familiar and are well represented in books and documentaries about ancient times. This disparity didn't always exist. In the mid-twentieth century, several books captured the attention of a wide public with their evocative representations of ancient Near Eastern history and archaeology. These included *Ur of the Chaldees* by Charles Leonard Woolley,[5] *History Begins at Sumer* by Samuel Noah Kramer,[6] and *Treasures of Darkness* by Thorkild Jacobsen.[7] The ancient Near East deserves our attention now more than ever because of the extraordinary discoveries of the past few decades, to which I will introduce you in the coming chapters.

This book begins in the city of Uruk, in southern Iraq, around 3500 BCE. Uruk was the first true city anywhere in the ancient Near East, and probably the largest city on Earth at the time. It was also where the region's wedge-shaped cuneiform writing was invented, and where scribes first began to learn to read and write in scribal schools. We have scribes to thank for so much. Not only did they write the practical documents on clay tablets that have survived—still thoroughly legible—as both mementos and records of the eras in which they were written, but generations of scribes in school also copied important works of literature, hymns, and royal inscriptions that would otherwise be lost to us. Every document that I quote in this book, and the record of every person that we know by name and can spend time with, exists entirely because scribes wrote them down at some point and because the tablets and other written works have been discovered in the ground by archaeologists. It is lucky for us that they wrote on clay and stone, which have endured far better than the papyrus and parchment documents of some other ancient cultures.

The chapters move forward in time from Uruk in 3500 BCE, right through to the fourth century BCE, and as we arrive in each new era, we will stop to meet different people. In the earliest periods, when literacy was monopolized by the great institutions—the temples and palaces—many of the men and women we meet will be kings, queens, officials, and priestesses. As time went on, more and more people hired scribes, fell within the orbit of the great institutions, or became literate themselves, so that we can begin to visit with brickmakers, slaves, soldiers, merchants, musicians, translators, sculptors, diviners, gardeners, brewers, and people in many other professions. Each person's story becomes a window into their era. Imagine that you could sit down with each of them over a beer (which was the drink of choice for almost everyone), in their house or at a local tavern, and could talk about their lives. You would learn so much more about their world than is possible from a general description in a survey. I hope that I have re-created the lives of each of them well enough to give you the same feeling.

Archaeology is also a crucial contributor to our understanding. The archaeological evidence—pottery, tools, ovens, jewelry, walls, canals, food remnants, anything at all that has survived in the ground—richly complements textual evidence as scholars reconstruct the past. For that matter, the cuneiform documents themselves are archaeological evidence, every one of them having been found buried after being lost and forgotten for thousands of years.

As you might imagine, much changed over the 3,000 years of history covered by this book. One language after another dominated the various regions; people migrated; technologies changed; temples and palaces lost and then regained their prominence in the economies; kingdoms came and went; cities and sometimes entire regions were abandoned but later repopulated; climate crises caused droughts and famines; epidemics ravaged populations but eventually subsided; kings presented themselves sometimes as kind shepherds and sometimes as terrifying warlords. This is not a story of progress; history never really is. For example, women had more prominence and power in society in the third millennium BCE than they did 2,000 years later. Chariots became more maneuverable but treatment of defeated enemies became harsher. A great many examples come to mind—life got better, and then it got worse, and then it got better again, and never for all groups in society at the same time.

But certain things stayed more or less the same and provide threads running through the cultures, like the strands on a loom.

One continuity was the writing system and the system of scribal training. I am limiting the regions covered in this book to those that used cuneiform writing; that is, ancient Iraq (Mesopotamia), Syria, parts of Turkey (Anatolia), northern parts of the Levant (the eastern Mediterranean coastal lands), and parts of Iran (Elam and later Persia). Occasionally cuneiform spread to other regions, such as Egypt, Bahrain (Dilmun), the Lake Van region (Urartu), and the southern Levant, in which cases these regions will make brief appearances. Scribes writing in cuneiform, mostly on clay tablets, will be our guides every step of the way.

Another continuity through the eras was people's passionate trust in family as the bedrock of society. For most of the time, men and women had little interest in pigeonholing their friends, neighbors, or (in the case of kings) their subjects as members of particular social classes. Identification with a particular group, city, or state came and went. But one's family was always crucial. Family also served as a metaphor for many other relationships, such as with bosses, subordinates, allies, and rulers, and it helped define hierarchies, which were always important in this era and region.

A third continuity is found in what we now think of as religion. The ancient gods and goddesses who were worshiped in Uruk when it first grew to be a city were still being worshiped when Alexander of Macedon conquered the region more than 3,000 years later. Across the Near East, almost all peoples considered everyone's deities to be real and powerful. But they didn't think of the deities as being part of anything that they could separate, in their minds, from the rest of life. They had no abstract concept of religion. To them, the gods and goddesses existed, they were real, they controlled everything, and they made non-negotiable demands of their human subjects. Much of life was spent discerning what they wanted, providing for them, and not getting on their bad side. Oaths provided a way to call on the gods to assess the truth of a claim and to hold people to their promises; oaths were never taken lightly. This system of thought made perfect sense and fit with the evidence of their senses. The world offered no other explanation. Government could not be extricated in even the smallest way from the world of the gods: kings ruled because the gods wanted them to and they had to expend a great deal of energy and wealth on the gods' needs. Throughout ancient Near Eastern history, temples were home to the gods (in the form of statues) and homes to statues of the kings who worshiped them. Those temple homes often stayed in exactly the same places in the cities for thousands of years, rebuilt from time to time but almost never moved.

The kings provide a fourth continuity across time. The people of the ancient Near East believed that the gods wanted them to be ruled by kings, and in three millennia no viable alternate system of government ever developed. The kings were sometimes advised by councils, or assemblies, or high officials, and those individuals could have considerable clout, but in almost every place and time one can identify a king who was at the top of the administrative hierarchy. Theirs was a world dominated by powerful men, most of whom had inherited their power from their fathers. That said, it was also a world with plenty of powerful women, including queens who advised or even ruled with their husbands or sons. Priestesses, in particular, oversaw many of the human interactions with gods and gained authority and wealth by running vast estates belonging to temples.

We will encounter other continuities as well. Justice was always sought and corruption condemned. One reason so many documents survive is that contracts had to be drawn up for a wide variety of purposes, just in case anyone involved in a transaction needed to go to court. The ownership and use of real estate played a profound role throughout the ancient history of the region, as did the employment and payment of vast workforces by the great institutions. Wide disparities of wealth separated rich court officials from tenant farmers and manual laborers. Slavery existed in all eras (as was true in so many ancient societies), but the economies were not based on slavery. And the weavers mentioned in the title of this book played an important role in all eras. Textiles represented many things: a commodity created by workshops in palaces and temples, a valuable export, a fine art, and a lifelong occupation for just about every woman. Even those who were not professional textile workers spent many of their waking hours spinning thread for their families' clothing. Anywhere people were living, some of them (usually women) were weaving.

Contrary to popular misconceptions, the ancient Near East was not a perpetually violent place. Wars certainly happened; in some eras they must have seemed endless to the people living through them. But diplomacy was almost always attempted before military conflicts were declared, and combatants almost always sought peace. Conquering forces often treated defeated armies and their leaders harshly but, within cities and communities, people were remarkably civil to one another. Courts existed to prevent vigilante justice, judges weighed evidence carefully, and people accepted their decisions. Laws might have prescribed harsh punishments for crimes, but most actual punishments (as reflected in written accounts of court cases) took the form of monetary fines. Throughout the millennia, random crimes against strangers seem to have been rare, happening mostly in situations outside the context of cities, for example when merchants might be robbed when traveling. Even then, the incensed kings who represented the merchants insisted on justice from the rulers of the land in which the robbery took place.

In sum, you will find that you will be visiting an unfamiliar but exciting, innovative, and generally civil and humane place in this book (excepting, that is, the behavior of some of the more brutal individuals, who seem to show up throughout history). It was a place and time that has had a huge influence on the cultures that followed it. The people of the ancient Near East developed diplomacy around the same time that they developed organized warfare, they wrote legal contracts almost as soon as they could write anything, and for the most part, they cared about their fellow humans. And they wanted to be remembered. I'm pleased to be able to play a small part in making that last wish a reality for a few dozen ancient people who had not even the vaguest notion of the future world in which their names would indeed be remembered. They deserve our attention.

A few additional notes before we go on: first, almost all the dates in the book are BCE, or Before the Common Era, also referred to as BC. Of course, the people of the time had their own ways of identifying years. Sometimes they named the years, either by a great event or the name of a high official. Sometimes they numbered the years within a particular king's reign. The correlation between their dates and our years BCE is not set in stone; scholars are still working on perfecting the chronology. I am using dates in the so-called Middle Chronology, which is widely used and increasingly seems likely to be correct. The earliest dates in the book are the least certain, but they gradually become more reliable as one approaches the first millennium BCE. The relative order of events that historians have reconstructed is reliable, and dates in the last four chapters of the book are mostly not disputed. I have provided regnal dates for kings in parentheses after their names, if these dates are known.

Second, ancient words seem to have been pronounced pretty much the way they are spelled. I have simplified spellings in this book. For example, I haven't distinguished between two types of "s" sound (written as "s" and "ṣ" in scholarly works), nor between two types of "t" sound (written "t" and "ṭ"). Many of the ancient Near Eastern languages included a sound similar to the "ch" in the Scottish word "loch" and written "ḥ." It's represented just as "h" here, except in a few cases where conventional spelling of a name has it as "kh." An "e" at the beginning or end of a word was not silent and (at the end of a word) it did not change the sound of any earlier vowel. "E" was pronounced like the sound "ay" in "bay." So, for example, the name of the god that was spelled Ea was pronounced "Ay-a."

The ancient names may seem unfamiliar and perhaps difficult to remember, but I encourage you to try saying them aloud so as to get used to them. There is a cast of the main characters at the back of the book in case you need a reminder of who someone was. A few ancient Near Eastern individuals were already known from writings by Greek, Roman, or biblical authors before records from their own times were recovered. In these cases, for simplicity, I use the more familiar names, rather than the ones the individuals used during their lifetimes.

Third, I have quoted from ancient sources throughout the book so that the ancient voices can come through and tell their own tales. But because they wrote on documents that are now often fragmentary or abraded, there are places where words are missing. Such breaks in the original are identified with square brackets. Ancient words that are not translated appear in italics,[8] and words in parentheses within a quote have been added to help explain the meaning.

Fourth, I should note that other cultures in adjoining regions also had rich histories with profound impacts on world history, and they were periodically in contact with the peoples on whom this book focuses, especially through trade. This included not just Egypt, Nubia, and much of the Levant, but also the Jiroft culture of Iran; the Harappan culture of the Indus Valley and later cultures of South Asia; the Minoan, Mycenaean, and later Greek cultures of the Aegean; and Magan, along with the Qedarite and other cultures of Arabia. These regions did not, however, use cuneiform as their main medium of written communication, so I made the choice not to include them in this book. This has allowed me to focus on individuals and their lives, and to trace continuities through cuneiform history. But the web of connections among ancient peoples was profound and long-lasting, with influences flowing in all directions.[9]

And, finally, no, Ea-nasir is not among the people featured in this book. He has had his moment in the sun—feel free to look him up online. Other ancient Near Eastern individuals were just as engaging, as you will find.

PART I

The Uruk Period,
3500–2900 BCE

Chapter 1
Builders and Organizers

Around 3500 BCE a huge change began to take place in southern Mesopotamia, one that had ramifications for the rest of human history: large numbers of people began to live in densely packed communities with thousands of other people, namely, cities. And once they began to live in cities, a whole lot of changes followed, in the ways people interacted with one another, the ways they were governed, the types of technology they used, and any number of other aspects of life.

By this time, humans had been living on the planet for millions of years, modern humans (*Homo sapiens sapiens*) for around 200,000 years. They had been speaking fully developed languages for at least tens of thousands of years. They had migrated and settled across the planet. Throughout all these millennia, people were on the move, seasonally following their sources of food as animals migrated and plants ripened in different areas. Archaeologists find burials, cave paintings, intricate stone and bone tools, and small sculptures—tantalizing evidence of people with sophisticated technologies and ideas, and certainly with religious beliefs and explanations of the world they saw around them.

These hunters and gatherers sometimes created extraordinary monuments that would challenge people of any era to build, especially without modern technology. The best known is at Göbekli Tepe in southeast Anatolia (now Turkey), but there must have been others like it. Twelve thousand years ago, hundreds of people gathered at Göbekli Tepe to create a series of circles of engraved T-shaped standing stones, the largest of which weighed 16 tons. The incised images are of animals of prey, such as lions, scorpions, vultures, and snakes. This must have been a place of great importance for the people who built and visited it. But because writing didn't develop until 7,000 years after it was built, we can only guess at its meaning.

Around the same time as the construction of the monument at Göbekli Tepe, humans in a few places in the Near East first settled in small communities that they occupied year-round. Initially, people living in these communities supported themselves by hunting wild animals and gathering plants that were available locally. It was no coincidence that in the Near East early villages were often located near stands of wild wheat and barley that, after being harvested, could be stored over long periods to feed a settled population. Only after they had settled did people begin to farm. This transformation has sometimes been called the "agricultural revolution," but people living through it would have experienced nothing revolutionary. Farming and herding seem to have crept into the economy, only very gradually coming to replace hunting and gathering. This period is called the Neolithic, and in the Near East it lasted from around 10000 BCE to around 5300 BCE.

During the Neolithic, people in the Near East traded for goods they needed, and luxury goods they wanted, over vast areas and for a very long time. Shells spread out from the Red Sea, passing from person to person and being treasured in many places. Obsidian, a volcanic glass that was particularly sharp and useful for stone tools, spread from central Anatolia— modern Turkey. Other beautiful stones were transported all the way from Afghanistan to Mesopotamia—modern Iraq.

By 6500 BCE, some of the finest pottery in all of history was already being manufactured by specialists. People lived in neatly built rectangular brick or stone houses with plaster floors. Most Neolithic communities were small— just a few dozen people—but a few grew to considerable size. Çatalhöyük, in what is now Turkey, boasted a remarkably large population of between 3,500 and 8,000 people in the mid-seventh millennium BCE.[1] Its population seems to have been egalitarian, with an equal distribution of wealth, and the city was not dominated by monumental buildings like later cities. Although Çatalhöyük can be described as a city, based on its population size, it didn't give rise to an urban culture in its region.

As the Neolithic came to an end, people had moved into southern Mesopotamia. The coast of the Persian Gulf was considerably farther north than it is now (though scholars disagree about where it was actually located),[2] and the Tigris and Euphrates Rivers, with their origins in what is now Turkey, took their separate winding courses across the hot, almost rainless flood plain of southern Iraq, eventually reaching marshland and spilling into the Gulf. People settled there in the fifth millennium BCE, north of the marshlands, in an area that was ideal for their needs—the soil was rich from the silt carried down by the rivers; the water was fresh, not salty, and it spread out across the landscape in fans of small channels.[3] These fans could be managed so that the land they passed through could hold on to floodwater for longer. People began to construct banks and dams to create basins to achieve this.[4] This is called basin irrigation, and it provided enough water for annual crops of barley and wheat. The communities in which the people settled grew larger than villages, larger than towns.

All of which is to say that, by the mid-fourth millennium BCE, the world was already a sophisticated place with plenty of history and tradition, and, in spite of the hot, dry climate, southern Mesopotamia was an excellent place to live.

People at the time had interests and skills, they no doubt talked about fascinating things, they loved their families, they worried about the crops, and they had expertise that most of us have long since lost. They knew how to store their grain so that it would be safe from vermin and insects. They knew how to spin flax into linen thread using a spindle whorl and how to weave the thread into fabric. They knew how to create a perfect blade by chipping a flint block just so.

Cities developed independently in other regions of the globe, of course, but, as far as we can tell, in 3500 BCE the largest city on Earth, and one of the earliest, was in southern Mesopotamia. The city's name was Uruk. It was situated by the Euphrates River, right in that ideal area where basin irrigation produced abundant crops, around 120 kilometers (75 miles) from what was then the coast of the Gulf.[5]

For this first chapter I can provide you with no names for the inhabitants of Uruk whose lives interest us. The people of the middle of the fourth millennium BCE certainly had them, each one a phrase or sentence that had meaning in their language, but they are all lost to us. In later periods, scribes wrote letters, lists, inscriptions, contracts, and many other types of documents that provide us with evidence about the people who lived at the time. But until the late fourth millennium BCE, writing had not yet developed. We face much more of a challenge to see the world through their eyes without more detailed texts to help us. So, as we begin to look at what life was like in Uruk, before writing came along, we will explore other types of evidence of individuals who lived around 3500 BCE and experienced some of the biggest changes in all of human history as they accustomed themselves to urban life.

At that time, perhaps as many as 40,000 of the newly urbanized people lived in Uruk. A gathering of that many people today at a football stadium would be unremarkable, and a town of 40,000 is not a big place in the modern world. But for the fourth millennium BCE, it was astounding. The world had never seen anything like it. In fact, a city that big continued to be a rarity for millennia. Uruk was 2.5 square kilometers (a square mile) in extent, and was on a completely different scale from its neighbors: ten times the size, in fact, of the next biggest city in the region.[6] Uruk was already the same size as Athens in 500 BCE, 3,000 years later.[7]

Uruk in the fourth millennium BCE was altogether a remarkable place to be. People living there experienced a style of life that had never existed before. It created the mold for all Mesopotamian cities to come.[8] This period also saw the creation of the artistic style of the Mesopotamians. It saw the development of a system of accounting and of weights and measures that placed subsequent Mesopotamian economies on a sound footing. It saw the invention of a writing system that allowed information about their culture to pass down through the ages. Incredibly, after this abrupt and almost uncanny start, these institutions and others continued for thousands of years and had an impact on the surrounding cultures as well.

Uruk had existed as a smaller community for at least a thousand years before this,[9] but now that it had grown so large, its people faced new challenges. For one thing, the city needed organizing. We tend to assume that any large group of people in premodern times must have had a powerful man in charge. After all, once monarchy developed in any region, that system of government tended to become deeply established and pretty much unassailable. Uruk had no clear royal palace at this time, however, and no names of kings are preserved once they began to write, and yet some person—or some group of people—must have been running the place. Archaeologists and historians of this era have gone in search of these individuals. Who were they?

Excavations at Uruk

When the first archaeologists came to dig at Uruk in 1913, they encountered a site that was vast and unexplored. Not much was known about the beginnings of urban culture back then; the discoveries at Uruk and those of other archaeologists in southern Iraq vastly expanded the world's knowledge of early cities. Over the decades, the German team heading the excavation returned year after year (with interruptions for world wars and local conflicts) and they discovered temples, palaces, and walls that had been built over about a 5,000-year period, from the fifth millennium BCE to the fifth century CE. Imagine: one city stood on exactly the same spot for 5,000 years, at the *end* of which the Roman Empire was still around. What we lump together as ancient history lasted for a very, very long time.

In fact, Uruk lasted long enough that, over centuries, the city had grown higher and higher in elevation above the floodplain. This was true of all ancient cities in the Near East. The debris that was generated just by living—the broken walls and abandoned floors and forgotten trash— was rarely swept away. The debris just stayed where it was and, time and again, was incorporated into new floors and streets as new buildings were constructed. The giant mounds that formed are now, and were then, called "tells." Even the word is ancient.

The German archaeologists at Uruk dug down through many layers of occupation; the city remained important long after the fourth millennium. In 1928 they began to excavate the levels that were laid down during the fourth millennium BCE, and what they found were buildings and artifacts of unanticipated and stunning sophistication. The archaeologists assigned Roman numerals to these levels of occupation, starting at I for the top, most recent, level, then II, III, and so on for the earlier levels; these level numbers are still in use. A little confusingly, the numbers therefore get smaller as one moves forward in time, so that the city of Uruk level VI existed before Uruk V, which existed before Uruk IV, which existed before Uruk III.[10] Together these levels (VI through III) constitute what is called the Uruk period, named for the city because Uruk seems to have taken the lead in technological and social innovation, providing a model for other cities across the Near East.

A Visitor to the Stone Cone Temple

Two great temple complexes dominated the city in the Uruk period. We know from later eras that one was dedicated to the god An, the god of the heavens (the sky), and the other to the goddess Inana, who controlled love and warfare. Inana's temple complex was called the Eanna, the "house of the heavens."

Within the Eanna stood a truly remarkable building. We often describe things offhandedly as "unique" while knowing that it's not really true, but this building was exactly that. Nothing remotely like it has ever been found. It was constructed during what the excavators called Level VI, around perhaps 3500 BCE. The archaeologists discovered only its foundations and the layers of debris from when it was abandoned, but it's possible to reconstruct what it would have looked like when newly built and to explore some of the extraordinary innovations that the architect or architects introduced into it.

A man from another ancient town, let's say the town of Ur to the south, might have come to visit the Eanna during Level VI, arriving in Uruk at a southern gate in the wall of the city. Turning around to survey the countryside before entering, the visitor would have been struck by the flatness of the landscape. The Euphrates River flowed next to the city, a wide band of water heading for the Lower Sea (the Persian Gulf, to us) beyond the horizon. Reed boats with high prows sailed southward, following the current. Boats going north could be seen being towed with ropes by people walking along a riverside path. As far as his eye could see and beyond—the whole of southern Mesopotamia—was a wide river valley. Off to the east, though not visible from Uruk, flowed the Euphrates's twin river, the Tigris. Between them, these two great rivers had laid down a vast landscape of silt. This dominating feature provided the origin of the name given to the region by the ancient Greeks. It was "between"—*meso*— "the rivers"—*potamia*.

Fields surrounded by banks stretched out along natural channels around the base of the tell on which Uruk stood, and farmers would have been at work everywhere. Their towns and villages dotted the landscape as well, the bigger towns raised from the plain on tells of their own. In the region around Uruk, archaeologists have found the remains of many smaller communities, which would have been dependent on the city. Next to the riverbank and the riverside path stood orchards of date palms, planted slightly higher than the fields, growing on the natural levees that had built up on the edge of the Euphrates.

The visitor entered Uruk and made his way toward the city center. It was a very different experience to live in a city than in a village or small town. People on the streets were mostly strangers, even to other residents of Uruk.

Any given person could have been acquainted with only a small fraction of the city's population. Living in such proximity to so many strangers was an unusual experience at this point in human history, though in any given neighborhood people probably lived close to family members. This was true throughout Mesopotamian history; family bonds were very tight.

The visitor walked on along the dusty streets, which were lined with windowless mudbrick houses, without breaks between them. (The excavators didn't explore the neighborhoods of Uruk, but we have a sense of what they would have been like from excavations of other towns and cities of the same era.) Some houses opened onto pleasant internal courtyards, others had long central halls with rooms opening off them, but every house kept its secrets from people in the street. There were no front yards or spaces between houses—adjoining houses shared walls.[11] The man visiting from Ur probably kept close to the walls to take advantage of their shade; the weather in southern Mesopotamia was hot for most of the year, and the sun unforgiving.

We moderns take living in cities for granted—we expect services like trucks that haul away our trash, pipes that bring clean water, sewerage systems that whisk away our waste, grocery stores that provide fresh food, and hospitals that help us when we're ill, all of which make life in a densely packed community manageable. The people of Uruk shared with us many of the same needs but had none of the conveniences. They needed water and food, along with oil to light their homes, wool to make their clothing, bricks and clay to repair their houses. All these had to be carried into the city. Meanwhile, they produced all kinds of waste and trash, which they either threw into the street or dropped from the edge of the tell. They must have been annoyed by the loud noises of animals and people in the street, and they must have been vulnerable to diseases that could have spread easily in such a close community. Altogether you might imagine life there to have been a sort of bedlam. Old village hierarchies based on families, which would have kept the peace in villages, wouldn't have worked to contain the whims, plans, and passions of tens of thousands of people. So, was living in Uruk dangerous and chaotic? It seems not. The evidence suggests that it was a well-run place and that people lived there not under duress but voluntarily. Studies of skeletal remains have shown that, not just in Uruk but throughout Mesopotamia at this time, people were less likely to be struck in the head than in surrounding regions.[12] It was not an especially violent place.

From a distance, the visitor would have spotted the most prominent feature on the Uruk skyline: a temple raised on a platform. It was probably dedicated to the god of the heavens, known as An, who was worshiped in a temple on that spot for many centuries to follow. The platform and temple had been built and rebuilt over centuries, and the temple itself was plastered and would have gleamed a bright white in the sunshine. The excavators called it the White Temple.[13]

The visitor chose not to go there—his destination was the Eanna temple to the goddess Inana (Fig. 1.1). As he approached he would have noticed a long, plastered wall that seemed, from a distance, to have been painted with dark vertical stripes. On drawing closer it would have become clear that the stripes were the shadows of dozens of vertical buttresses, evenly spaced along the walls surrounding a rectangular enclosure. He would not have been able to tell (because of the plaster coating), but this wall was built from limestone, not the usual mudbrick that had been used in construction for centuries.[14]

For most Urukians, this was probably the extent of their access to this sacred spot, but let us say that our visitor was a high-ranking person who was allowed inside the wall. There he encountered a dazzling courtyard space gleaming with bright colors in regular geometric patterns. The inside face of the enclosure wall, and the walls of the impressive temple that it surrounded, were all decorated in mosaics (Fig. 1.1). Various geometric, symmetrical, blue and yellow-green patterns appeared on the surrounding wall,[15] while red, white, and black mosaic diamond shapes decorated the walls of the building inside the enclosure.[16]

All the stone for the mosaics on the temple had been carefully carved into innumerable small cones, each about ten to thirteen centimeters (four to five inches) long. Only the circular, flat ends of the cones made up the mosaics; their sharp points were set into the wall. They are the earliest known mosaics anywhere. Someone had worked out a way to keep the cones in place: archaeologists found thousands of rectangular clay plaques, each about 21 centimeters (8 inches) long, with curved ends and small holes at each end. They had been set in horizontal rows, sticking out from the walls, between each layer of building material. Perhaps a grid was threaded through the holes, providing a support structure for the small but heavy stone cones and to make sure they were placed accurately, like knots in a giant stone carpet.[17]

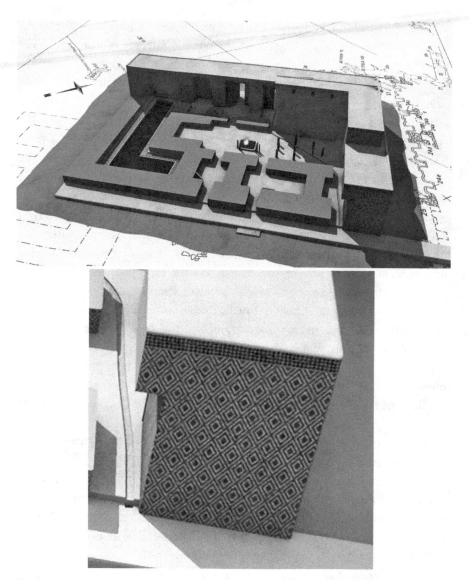

Fig. 1.1 A reconstruction proposal of the Stone Cone Temple with close-up showing the mosaic pattern of stone cones on the walls c. 3500 BCE. This image was made in 2012. (© artefacts-berlin.de; Material: German Archaeological Institute)

The German archaeologists who excavated the building called this the Steinstifttempel or Stone Cone Temple, but the ancient visitor would not have been aware of the cones, only of the beautiful diamond patterns in brilliant colors that their polished circular ends formed on the walls.[18] They gave the whole building the look of a giant jewel box.[19]

Perhaps the strangest feature of the Stone Cone Temple was the composition of the walls that supported the mosaics. For thousands of years, people in the Near East had been building structures out of reeds and mudbrick, or of stone if they lived near a source of building stone. (Note, though, that until the time of the Stone Cone temple, stone had almost never been used for building in the southern stretches of the Mesopotamian river valley because it didn't occur there naturally.) In some regions, plaster was often used as a coating on the walls and floors. It was created by burning limestone at around 600 degrees C (more than 1100 degrees F) to turn it into a dry powder. As with modern plaster of Paris, water was then added to the dry powder, which made it malleable or spreadable. Once the plaster dried, it became hard and water-resistant.

People had been making lime plaster this way for more than 4,000 years before the Stone Cone Temple was constructed; it even predated the invention of pottery. In the eighth and seventh millennia BCE in regions of the Levant, plaster had briefly been tried as a medium for vessels and sculpture,[20] but clay had proved to make superior pots (the plaster ones disintegrated over a fire), and stone made longer-lasting sculptures, so their plaster equivalents had long since gone out of fashion.

Nevertheless, someone involved in the planning of the Stone Cone Temple had a bright idea about plaster. Perhaps, this person thought, burned lime combined with crushed bricks might make a new and sturdy building material.[21] It could be poured into molds in layers and would set hard.[22] The archaeologists who dug up the temple recognized the walls as being made of a form of concrete, used in a confoundingly early historical context.

Most ancient innovations can be traced over a long period of development and they continued to be perfected, so it's hard to imagine a single mind behind them; there are almost no ancient Thomas Edisons. But the walls of the Stone Cone Temple are so strange that they suggest the existence of an anonymous inventor trying a new experimental building technique.

The architects must have been aware of the structural complications of the weight of the concrete walls of the Stone Cone Temple, along with the weight of the cones themselves.[23] The building has a much more substantial limestone and clay foundation than was normal, and this seems to have been added specifically in order to support the extra weight of the building.[24] Scholars have also calculated that the Stone Cone Temple was much more costly, in terms of the effort involved to construct it, than any other comparable monumental building of the Uruk period, even though it wasn't the largest.[25]

Our visitor to the temple would not, however, have been aware of the deep foundations or the concrete walls, which were invisible under the stone mosaics. Inside the temple, in the relative cool of the high-ceilinged rooms, the diamond-shaped mosaic patterns continued on the walls. The core of the temple was a long room flanked by smaller rooms on both its long sides. This three-part design has been dubbed the "tripartite temple" form, and it became the classic template for temples in the Uruk period (though subsequent tripartite temples were built of mudbrick).

Yet again, though, the Stone Cone Temple broke the mold and was unlike any other tripartite temple. This is because it contained a large L-shaped pool that was 13.7 meters (45 feet) long and 0.8 meters (2.5 feet) deep and took up an entire room.[26] The pool had been created to be watertight, and it was not the only room for which this was true. The floors of the whole temple were waterproofed with imported bitumen. In the long central room, the bitumen was, in turn, coated with a waterproof lime plaster, and a channel crossed its floor diagonally to allow water to flow.[27] In fact, *everything* about the Stone Cone Temple was designed to be waterproof—even the stone cones themselves would not have been affected by long exposure to water.[28] So perhaps water was not confined to the pool; it could have covered the floor and flowed from the doors into the courtyard during some rites or festivals.[29] Unlike clay cones, stone ones would not have eroded in water, and the concrete walls would have fared much better than mudbrick.

The floor of the central hall was imprinted with postholes into which two-meter-tall bronze rods would have been placed. Perhaps they supported a canopy under which a statue of the god (or a priest) would have been seated.[30] These rods were later preserved—buried all together in a brick hut in the courtyard, with lime plaster from the floor of the hall still stuck to their ends.[31]

Had our visitor arrived on a festival day, he might have witnessed a ceremony in which the whole complex became a giant reflecting pool, mirroring the bright mosaics of the walls and the blue of the sky. Bronze standards stood at the doorway to the structure,[32] and the god himself (in the form of his statue) could perhaps have been seen under a canopy in the central hall. The god of water, named Enki, was often portrayed in just this way on cylinder seals.[33]

What, though, was the use of the L-shaped pool? No one knows, but water certainly played a big role in the life of the temple. The goddess Inana, to whom this temple complex was dedicated in later historic times, wasn't a water deity, so this building probably wasn't hers.

About a century later, the Stone Cone Temple was ritually destroyed,[34] and then, as though it had been an important person, it was, in a way, buried in a brick monument.[35] This was a square, subterranean, doorless structure built right into a corner of the ruins of the Stone Cone Temple.[36] It looks like a tomb, but no body was found inside.[37] This smaller, newer structure, conservatively built of mudbricks rather than concrete, was filled with all manner of treasures, from copper and stone vessels to jewelry, weapons, furniture, and storage jars, and also with animal bones.[38] These had been piled more than two feet high in a corridor, and covered in matting. The "burial" of the Stone Cone Temple was then completed as the remaining spaces in the rooms of the newer building were filled with debris from the earlier structure. A fire that torched and discolored the walls of the central chamber of the tomb might have been accidental or it might have been ceremonial. Robbers looted some sections of the "tomb" in ancient times, but many of the rich goods that had been interred were untouched. One wonders who left them there and why the Stone Cone Temple was so important as to deserve this treatment.

Construction of the Stone Cone Temple

Although so much is mysterious, the planning behind the Stone Cone Temple can be guessed at; it proves to be remarkable and tells us a lot about this earliest of cities. The very existence of the structure shows that innovation was supported by whoever was in charge and also shows that people of Uruk worked (by the thousands) to create truly glorious monuments for their gods. The temples, in turn, may have attracted more residents to Uruk, the presence of the deities providing divine protection to the population. The workers were almost certainly called up from among the free population, as a labor duty to the state, known as corvée labor. Just as a man might be drafted to serve in the military, so he might be drafted to construct a building. Corvée workers toiled on state projects throughout ancient Near Eastern history.

Once plans had been finalized and workers enlisted (by whoever had this authority), the construction materials had to be obtained, and most of these came from regions far from Uruk. Had it been a normal mudbrick temple like the ones that had come before it, or like the contemporary temple to the god An in a nearby neighborhood, the brick making could have commenced right there in the city, but the builders of the Stone Cone Temple were more ambitious. Fortunately, the Urukians didn't live in isolation from the world beyond their city—they knew where to find the building materials they needed.

The limestone for the enclosure wall and the foundations, and to burn for the concrete, could be imported from relatively close by; there was a source about 50 kilometers (31 miles) away to the west.[39] Scholars have calculated the quantities of every material used in the temple,[40] and they estimated that the walls required about 1,400 cubic meters (almost 49,500 cubic feet) of concrete and the foundations and enclosure wall used almost 1,300 cubic meters (46,000 cubic feet) of limestone. Each cubic meter of limestone weighs 2,711 kilograms (5,977 pounds), so the weight of stone in the walls and foundations can be estimated to have been 3,795,400 kilograms (7,770,100 pounds or 3,886 tons). That doesn't include the limestone for the concrete walls.

The transportation of such a large amount of limestone overland was no simple matter. Wagons may not have been in use yet—the wheel had been invented and was used in Mesopotamia by the Uruk period, but there's a lot to building a successful cart and it's unlikely that they had one yet, let alone one that could support the weight of large amounts of building stone. So the limestone may have been dragged on sleds, and 50 kilometers is a long way when you're dragging heavy stones. Thousands of workmen were probably involved in the quarrying and transport.

The source for the bitumen was about 400 kilometers (250 miles) north of Uruk on the Euphrates,[41] and the colored stones for the decorative cones and the long timbers necessary for roofing the interior spaces had to travel much farther, all the way from the mountains far to the north.[42] The bitumen and stone would have been transported on boats, and the logs could be floated downstream, tied together as rafts, but someone first had to travel to the places where they were available and negotiate for the large quantities required. These natural resources lay in settled areas and were certainly not free for the taking to anyone who showed up. Once the deal had been struck, an official probably also oversaw the quarrying and logging, and watched to see that everything was loaded properly. It has been estimated that the Stone Cone building required around 50 cubic meters (1,766 cubic feet) of bitumen, 40 cubic meters (1,413 cubic feet) of fine colored stone for the cones, and more than 100 cubic meters (more than 3,500 cubic feet) of timber.[43]

After the materials arrived, the corvée laborers (almost certainly men, who formed the workforce for hard labor in all later eras of Mesopotamian history) must have burned limestone in kilns, mixed in crushed bricks, and waited to add water until just the right time so that it set when it was supposed to. Others manufactured and fired the terracotta plaques that were to be laid between layers of concrete. Still others spent their days carving and polishing colored stones to create the thousands of cones (Fig. 1.2).

When construction started, each phase of the process must have been carefully planned. The materials had to be at the building site and available to the workmen who needed them. The concrete had to be poured in the wall molds and allowed to set at just the right moment; the cones had to be placed in meticulous arrangements before the concrete dried, presumably following a grid marked into the wall.

All the workmen employed on the project also needed plenty of water to drink in the hot climate, along with food to eat. These must have been provided by the administration that enlisted them. It seems likely that there was nothing about this whole operation that was unplanned. The obvious conclusion from all of this must be that someone, or some group of people, was in charge.

Organizing the Workforce

The excavators at Uruk estimated that the construction of a mudbrick terrace in the Eanna precinct involved 1,500 men laboring ten hours a day for five years.[44] But many more structures were being built than just a single terrace. The demands for labor must have been fairly constant. How were

Fig. 1.2 Stone cones used for mosaics in the Uruk period, mid-fourth millennium BCE. (Metropolitan Museum of Art)

the workers paid? Who paid them? Who organized their work shifts and how? All of this took place before writing was invented, so how did anyone keep track of all the materials, crew, building schedules, and provisions? For these questions, happily, we have more than guesswork. Scholars have taken fragments of evidence and pieced together a picture of how it all worked.

In the ruins of the Stone Cone Temple, archaeologists found some rather prosaic objects that helped provide answers: clay balls, clay tokens, and broken pottery.[45] The clay balls, often called bullae, might be unimpressive to look at, but they represented an ingenious way of keeping track of commodities and perhaps people (Fig. 1.3).

Suppose someone wanted to record a quantity of bitumen that was being sent to Uruk, and to make sure that all the bitumen arrived, with no theft along the way. The shipper made small clay tokens in a shape that was agreed upon to represent jars of bitumen (the tokens look a little like game

Fig. 1.3 Clay bulla with tokens from Susa, c. 3300 BCE. (© RMN-Grand Palais/ Art Resource, NY/Art Resource)

pieces), and then placed them inside a ball made of clay that had not set hard. He sealed the ball, baked it in the sun, and sent it along with the shipment. When everything arrived, the official in Uruk could count the number of jars in the shipment and check it against the number of tokens. If they matched up, all was well. If not, he would have had questions for the shipping agent. There were plenty of other uses for the tokens and bullae, for record-keeping and to aid in remembering numbers of commodities and people; they had been in wide use right across the Near East long before Level VI at Uruk. In fact, sixteen bullae were found under the foundations of the Stone Cone Temple—those had been used and discarded before it was even constructed.[46] Other tokens were found in the debris of the ruined temple, and in the memorial structure that was built for it. They represented a very useful administrative tool.

The outsides of the bullae were not necessarily blank. Some of the ones under the Stone Cone temple had been sealed.[47] Perhaps the agent shipping bitumen from the region to the north wanted to make sure that no one cheated by breaking the bulla, taking out a couple of tokens so as to hide his theft of jars, and making a new one enclosing fewer tokens. The shipping agent could ensure against such tampering by rolling his cylinder seal across the surface of the original bulla. As long as the receiving agent in Uruk recognized the seal impression, he could be sure that the shipment had arrived intact.

Whereas bullae and clay tokens were old news by 3500 BCE, cylinder seals were relatively new. Stamp seals had existed for thousands of years,[48] so the concept of sealing was a familiar one, but a cylinder seal had the advantage that it could seal the whole surface of a bulla. To make such a seal, an artisan carved a scene or intricate pattern in reverse relief onto the surface of a cylindrical bead so that, when it was rolled on clay, the impression could be as long as needed, repeating over and over. At this time, each cylinder seal seems to have been controlled either by a particular person or, more likely, by an office,[49] so that the sealing could be "read," identifying who had sealed the bulla and enclosed the tokens and therefore was responsible for the shipment.

People started sealing other things as well, rooms and jars in particular. Clay was ubiquitous, so it was easy enough to place a lump of it on a closed jar or on a closed door-latch and to roll a cylinder seal across the clay. Anyone could see if the seal was broken, and the seal impression identified who had last been in the room, or who had sealed the jar. Like the bullae and tokens, the sealings created a message that could be understood later, and by people who didn't have to speak directly to the original sealer.

The pottery fragments found in the ruins of the Stone Cone Temple hint at how workers in the Eanna precinct, including all the workers constructing the temple itself, were provided for. Pots in the Uruk period were mostly of two kinds. About one-fifth of the potsherds found in the Uruk period levels came from wheel-made ceramics. These marked a significant technological advance in that they could be made more quickly than the carefully coiled handmade pots of previous eras; a type of mass-production of good quality ceramics had become possible. The other four-fifths of the potsherds—the vast majority—were from coarse, shallow, cone-shaped bowls with thick walls and a beveled rim, which could be made even more quickly than those created on a pottery wheel (Fig. 1.4).[50] They were manufactured simply by pressing clay into a mold and baking the resulting bowl,[51] and each held approximately a liter of a dry substance.[52] (They were porous so would have been useless to hold liquids.) Unlike so many objects from the Uruk period, these beveled-rim bowls were not made carefully or neatly. On the other hand, they are so ubiquitous in Uruk period sites across the Near East that it's clear that they were both essential and disposable—the Starbucks cups of their era. One scholar calculated that a single family could have thrown away as many as 280 such bowls a year.[53]

Fig. 1.4 Beveled-rim bowl from Nippur, late fourth millennium BCE.
(Metropolitan Museum of Art)

Scholars disagree about whether the beveled-rim bowls were containers
for daily grain rations for workers[54] or were bread molds.[55] Either way, they
were associated with food. We know this because the symbol for bread
and food in the later cuneiform writing system was exactly the shape of
this type of bowl,[56] and the symbol for "to eat" was a head with just such
a bowl to its lips. Whether they were for grain or for bread, an institution
(almost certainly a temple) seems to have made the bowls and used them
to distribute rations to workers, including those who labored in all the
construction jobs on the Stone Cone Temple. This system predated the
temple—the bowls were already found hundreds of years earlier, in level X
at Uruk[57]—and for all that time, large numbers of people had been provided
with food both fairly and efficiently.

The trash found in the ruins of the temple therefore tells us a great
deal: that workers were provided with food in cheap, standardized bowls;
that records of materials being used were kept using clay tokens sealed in

bullae; and that accountability for stores and shipments was improved with cylinder seals impressed on clay.

On the whole, though, and in spite of efforts at understanding its construction, the Stone Cone Temple is a glorious enigma. We don't know what happened inside it, why it had its unique features, and why it later warranted its own tomb, but it obviously meant a lot to the people. It also seems ultimately to have been judged to have been an engineering failure. For one thing, it's clear that the beautiful stone cone mosaics were not securely held by the lime plaster, and whole sections of them fell off the wall.[58] And the people of Uruk don't seem to have tried building with this type of concrete again.[59] There's really nothing else like Stone Cone Temple anywhere.

The Priest–King of Uruk

The cylinder seals also have another story to tell that goes beyond their administrative applications. The scenes engraved on them provide miniature windows into life in Uruk more than 5,000 years ago. With surprising naturalism (especially given the tiny scale of the seals), the artisans who made them revealed quotidian details, such as scenes of animals grazing in pastures, and people farming, irrigating their fields, fishing, and weaving.[60] The choice of design may not have been arbitrary; it may have reflected the office or person for whom the seal was made.[61] So, for example, a number of seals show women lined up together, weaving on looms, apparently working in some kind of a textile workshop.[62] The owner of this seal might have been the supervisor of such a workshop.

In later eras, inscriptions on the seals identified the owners, but in this era, before writing, it makes sense that the figures and activities depicted were expected to do the same thing. If so, the seals could represent a form of recorded communication.

Some of the most intricate seals found in early levels at Uruk were carved with ritual scenes, and in these you can often pick out a particular object that had a deep symbolic significance to the Urukians: a tall reed bundle with a ring at the top and a streamer hanging down. This was the symbol of the great goddess of the land, Inana. A drawing of the reed bundle became the way to write her name. The Eanna, as we have seen, was Inana's temple complex.

The ritual scenes on seals also often show a man who seems to have held an important position. He was generally portrayed the same way each time, wearing specific clothes. We are getting closer here to being able to create a mental image of a leader who may have managed the complicated machinery of administration at Uruk.

You can see this man on a cylinder seal that is currently in the British Museum[63] and another in the collection at Yale (Fig. 1.5).[64] He is bearded and wears a headband and a robe made of some sort of open netting that falls almost to his ankles.[65] The artist has managed to depict the delicate weave of the net over the man's legs and body. In this seal he holds out two branches to a group of animals and, in the scene on the British Museum seal, the artist also included three of the reed bundles representing Inana.

In a group of five other cylinder seals that were found together at Uruk, the same figure, again in the net robe, is shown with the goddess herself (recognizable again by the reed bundles). Between the two figures stand two tall conical baskets filled with offerings.[66] One way or another, the man in the net robe is often shown with some association with Inana;[67] when a ritual offering is taking place, he provides food to the goddess.

Fig. 1.5 Uruk period cylinder seal showing a priest-king of Uruk wearing a net skirt, accompanied by animals. (Yale University, Peabody Museum)

In other seals, however, a man with the same characteristics is shown hunting, sometimes with no sign of the goddess at all. A few fighting scenes on seals represent him with a long spear, accompanied by victorious soldiers, who are standing, along with vanquished soldiers, who are naked and cowering on the ground, their hands tied.[68] This suggests that warfare was already an organized pursuit, led by the same man who had a priestly role. He has, therefore, been dubbed the "priest-king" of Uruk.[69]

The priest-king doesn't just appear on cylinder seals. One of the most remarkable works of art found by archaeologists in the Eanna temple complex was a narrow alabaster vase, more than a meter tall, which was carved with scenes that wrap right around it, almost as though it had been impressed with enormous cylinder seals. It's known as the Uruk Vase (Fig. 1.6). The priest-king appeared here too. The uppermost scene, just below the rim, bears a strong resemblance to the ritual scenes on cylinder seals.

Fig. 1.6 The Uruk vase showing offerings to the goddess Inana, Uruk period. (bpk Bildagentur/Vorderasiatisches Museum/Staatliche Museen/Berlin/ Germany/Art Resource, NY)

Just as on the seals, Inana is shown on the right-hand side of the scene, next to her reed-bundle symbol. She has the same long hair and plain robe with a band along the bottom that is seen in the cylinder seals. In front of her, again, you see a conical basket full of offerings, as on the seals, but this time it's carried by a naked male figure (Fig. 1.7). On the left, the priest-king in his net skirt stands facing toward Inana, just as he does on the ritual cylinder seals. Unfortunately, on the vase, most of the figure of the priest-king is broken—his image may have been cut out of the vase on purpose. All that is left are his feet and the bottom of his net skirt. But it's clearly him. In the vase he even has a long-haired attendant behind him, holding up what seems to be a sash to his net skirt.

This top register of the vase includes some details, on the right, that aren't found on cylinder seals: behind Inana and the two reed bundles, which would have marked the entrance to the sanctuary of the goddess, are some items that would have been found inside. These include two more conical baskets, two tall vases (much the same shape as the Uruk Vase itself, in fact), and two small animals.

Fig. 1.7 Close-up of Inana and her symbols on the Uruk vase, Uruk period. (bpk Bildagentur/Vorderasiatisches Museum/Staatliche Museen/Berlin/Germany/Art Resource, NY)

The strangest objects in this group, though, are two small figures standing on pedestals, which are, in turn, set on the backs of bearded rams. The figure at the back is accompanied by Inana's reed bundle symbol, whereas the one in front carries a flat box with a stack of what look like beveled-rim bowls. And here's the most striking thing about those piles of bowls: they became a sign in the early pictographic writing system that looked exactly the same. It was read "*en*," which meant "lord" or "priest." It's almost as though the artist of the Uruk Vase was giving us captions for his two main characters. One was Inana, identified by her pictogram (the reed bundle) and the other was the *en* priest-king, identified by his pictogram (the pile of bowls).

Three more scenes adorn the Uruk Vase, in registers below the one showing the *en* priest-king and Inana. Water, in the bottom register, is represented by two wavy lines. When writing was invented, the word for water—"a"—came to be expressed by two wavy lines.[70] Above the water comes a row of plants: date palms and flax.[71] The date palm—as you might have guessed—looks very much like the later written symbol for "date palm." It's unclear whether early writers borrowed their symbols from artworks like the Uruk Vase, or whether the artist of the vase was using signs already in the writing system to "caption" the scenes. We will come back to the writing system in the next chapter.

One more level up on the Uruk Vase you find a procession of ewes and bearded rams, walking toward the right. Here are the products of the land in simplified form—animals that produced meat and wool, plants that produced dates and linen. Right below the scene of the *en* priest-king and Inana, a procession of identical naked men walk to the left, each carrying an offering such as a conical basket of food, or a vase. The raw materials from the animals and plants shown below have, in this register, been turned into products for the goddess to consume. The men carrying them are not only naked, they are bald and beardless. This was a sign of ritual purity and they may represent men who were employed in the temple.[72] The naked figure carrying the basket on the top row, between the *en* and Inana, is clearly at the head of the procession of gift-givers.

The artist has told a story, just as though this were a picture book. Later Mesopotamian artists often did the same, using horizontal registers full of images that are to be read from the bottom to the top. It's a story about the wealth of Uruk, the authority of the *en* and his nurturing relationship to the goddess, and the glory of Inana. Other images of the *en* priest, or priest-king, a few war scenes notwithstanding, are mostly peaceful and ritualistic, as here on the Uruk Vase. Perhaps this reflects that his role was not that of an oppressive tyrant but of an organizer of the economy and the population, and an intermediary with the gods. Uruk in this era may, therefore, not yet have transcended the structures of kinship and household that bound earlier, smaller communities together; it was not run by an impersonal bureaucratic administration.[73] The *en* was simply the head of a household—the household of the goddess—and a father to his population. But Uruk *was* a city. Just because it doesn't match some of our modern expectations for what a city should be, it was no less extraordinary as a development.

These early Urukians have told us so much about their world without, at this point, having written a word. Almost everything they did, in the end, was for Inana and the other gods. In the next chapter we'll see how things changed as writing came into wide use.

Chapter 2
Colonizers, Scribes, and the Gods

When planning was underway for the Stone Cone Temple and wood had to be acquired to roof its wide hallways, it's possible that the Urukians were not dealing with foreigners when they negotiated to buy the logs. Yes, the providers of the timber lived hundreds of miles away—far to the north up the Euphrates, near the modern border between Turkey and Syria—but they may have lived in a city that would have felt just like home to someone from Uruk. They may, in fact, have lived in a colony that had been founded by southern Mesopotamians, a place now called Habuba Kabira (its ancient name isn't known). This may sound like science fiction—how could a people without a writing system, without any form of long-distance communication except heading out in person—have come up with the idea of colonizing a distant land hundreds of miles from home? But that is just what happened, and not just at Habuba Kabira. In the first half of the fourth millennium BCE, all across the Near East, people from Uruk were not just trading with distant lands but they were showing up, in person, and settling in.

Uruk Expansion

Habuba Kabira seems to have been an unoccupied place next to the Euphrates with no local settlement at the time the Urukians got there.[1] What was built on that empty land was a mini-Uruk, a rectangular city with an imposing (and presumably effective) city wall that was studded with square defensive towers. The two main gates on the east side of the city had guardhouses on both sides, so the colonists were well protected. They lived

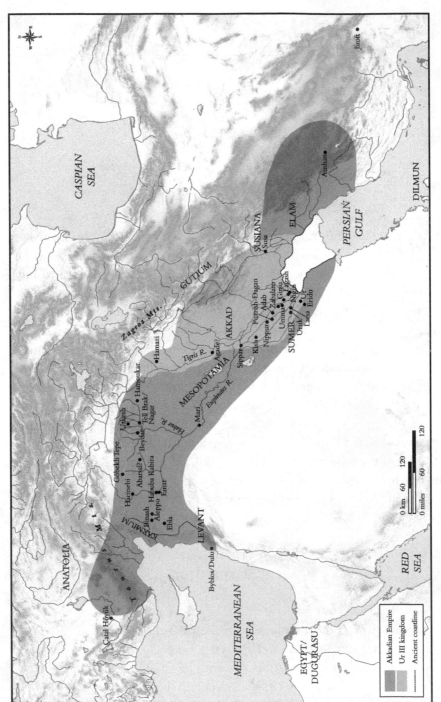

Map 1 The Near East, third millennium BCE

in tripartite-style houses that seem to have packed the area inside the walls, where they ate their meals from Uruk-style pottery, received their bread or rations in beveled-rim bowls, rolled their Uruk-style cylinder seals on clay bullae containing tokens, and even decorated some of the walls of public buildings with clay cone mosaics.[2] Their city was nothing like the local settlements nearby. They were strangers there, perhaps sent specifically by the government of Uruk to set up a post on the Euphrates and to facilitate the acquisition of goods like timber and metal ores from regions farther north and west.[3]

Other people from Uruk chose to settle not in new colonies but in existing cities. During the previous millennium, the fifth millennium BCE, towns had flourished across the Near East during what is called the Ubaid period. These towns all had distinct local traditions in buildings, stamp seals, and some other objects, but they already were in contact with one another—the pottery of the Ubaid period was similar everywhere. So, some of the places where Uruk colonists wanted to live were already occupied, and by people with whom they probably already had relationships.

The city of Susa, to the east of Mesopotamia in what is now western Iran, was something of a twin to Uruk. There, as in Habuba Kabira, the public buildings were adorned with vertical niches and clay cones, and archaeologists found Uruk-style cylinder seals, clay bullae with tokens, beveled-rim bowls, and other Uruk-style pottery.[4] It seems likely that some people from Uruk had crossed the marshy expanse that separated the Mesopotamian river valley from Susiana (the land around Susa) and had settled, bringing their material culture with them. But, unlike Habuba Kabira, Susa had existed for centuries before the Urukians got there, and after they left, the people of Susa returned to their local culture and the city remained an important metropolis for millennia afterward. The Susians were enthusiastic adopters of ideas and technologies from Uruk, but only for a limited time.

In other communities that were distant from southern Mesopotamia, a little enclave of Uruk colonists can be made out in the midst of a town; you can see them insisting on their familiar architecture and housewares, even their cone mosaics and cylinder seals, but surrounded by people who lived differently.[5] And in some communities, the beveled-rim bowls or bullae with tokens that were found may just be the result of Uruk's powerful influence, rather than a sign of the presence of actual colonists.

This explosion of Urukian culture wasn't an empire. There's no sign that the *en* of Uruk—the net-skirted priest-king who seems to have played such an important role there—was ruling these far-flung regions directly. It seems, instead, to have represented an era when the people of Uruk looked outward and set off in search of the raw materials they needed and desired, settling in areas and communities that would be useful and, ideally, not hostile to them.

On the other hand, colonization was not exclusively a peaceful process and, not surprisingly, the Urukians may have been unwelcome in some regions. In northern Syria, two cities, Tell Brak and Tell Hamoukar, seem to have been attacked right before the Uruk people settled there, around 3500 BCE. The attacks were quite possibly by their prospective colonizers.[6] Both cities were thriving beforehand, with city walls and a very distinct local culture. Tell Brak at this time is well known for flat little stone figurines with schematic shoulders and giant eyes. They look like cartoon renditions of space aliens (though without noses or mouths), and they're called "eye idols," but no one is entirely sure whether they represent gods or not.

The Uruk colonists (if that is who attacked) fired clay balls over the wall at Hamoukar—1,200 small ones, and 120 more the size of softballs. Then they burned the buildings. They built their Uruk-style structures on top of the ruins.[7] Or did they? The clay balls were pretty soft—could they have been ready for some duller purpose, such as administration? Could the fire have had another cause? It does seem telling, though, that much of the local culture was replaced after the fire.

The farthest reach of the people of Uruk seems to have been—incredibly—to Egypt. Egypt was flourishing and had already developed its own architectural and pottery styles, burial traditions, economy, and so on. This was still 1,000 years before the construction of the Great Pyramids, and the Egyptians were moving on a parallel course with the Mesopotamians toward urbanism, kingship, and writing. But during a period known as the Naqada II phase (which lasted from around 3500 to 3200 BCE), clear signs of contact with Mesopotamia began to appear in Egypt. In an ancient community at a site now called Buto, near the Mediterranean coast, colored clay cones in red, black, and white were apparently used to make mosaics.[8] They could have obtained these by trade; there's not much else in northern Egypt to suggest contact with Uruk. But farther south along the Nile the connections are clear. People in several towns adopted cylinder seals, using imported ones from Mesopotamia or making their own. They began building with mud bricks, which had not previously been a tradition in Egypt, and using them to create Mesopotamian-looking monumental buildings with lines of vertical niches. The classic façade of an Egyptian palace retained these niches for centuries.

Some Egyptian artisans even incorporated Mesopotamian motifs into artworks—a man flanked by two rearing animals, for example, or a high-prowed Mesopotamian boat.[9] No Uruk colony has been found among the Egyptian sites, but it does seem likely that Urukians were living there somewhere, if temporarily, as they did in other cities across the Near East. A fascinating, but perhaps unlikely, theory is that people from Uruk sailed their high-prowed boats south down the Euphrates, continuing through the Persian Gulf and right around Arabia, then north along the Red Sea, disembarking somewhere on its western shores and trekking across the desert to Upper Egypt.[10] This is an almost incomprehensibly long and difficult sea journey for such an early period, but it would at least explain how Uruk period objects wound up in the Nile river valley while leaving the northern part of Egypt unaffected (other than those few clay cones from Buto). Perhaps it is more likely that the influence on Egypt came through western Syria, rather than directly from Uruk.[11] In this scenario, Urukian goods from Habuba Kabira passed westward to the Syrian coast, were traded south through the Levant (the lands that border the eastern shores of the Mediterranean) to Egypt, and from there up the Nile.

No matter how it happened, or what exact form the various colonies and communities took, the people of Uruk had a tremendous impact on people living all across the Near East and into Egypt during the same few centuries that their hometown was growing into an impressive city.

The Eanna in Later Centuries

At the beginning of Level IV at Uruk, many new monumental buildings were constructed in the sacred precinct of the Eanna in the heart of the city.[12] By now, the complex was immense; it covered about 9 hectares (22 acres).[13] To give you a sense of scale, that is an area about three times larger than the much later acropolis in Athens. The buildings in the temenos area were designated by the excavators as Building A, Building B, Building C, and so on, but it's unclear which were temples, which (if any) were palaces, which (if any) were open to the public, and which were private—just for priests and officials.

At this point, around 3300 BCE, a visitor might have approached the new structures by walking past the brick tomb that incorporated the ruins of the Stone Cone Temple. Many of the buildings featured crisp buttresses separated by niches that created the same striped exterior appearance as the wall around the earlier Stone Cone Temple. These types of buttresses were a distinctive feature of Mesopotamian temple architecture for centuries to come. Everything was now built of mudbrick; there was not a concrete wall or a stone cone to be found.

A visitor might have been struck by how accessible it all seemed. There were, for example, three or more doorways on each of the long sides of every building—and once you ventured inside a building, into the shady interior, multiple doorways allowed entry into the main hallway, one from each of the side rooms.[14] The builders don't seem to have been preoccupied with defending the structures. Although the temple precinct as a whole was walled, within it, people could move easily between one building and another, and there were many entry points to the heart of each structure. Unlike later Mesopotamian temples, each of which had a holy shrine usually accessed by just one door and open to only a few high-ranking priests and priestesses, the Eanna buildings, including whichever one was the main temple, seem to have been open and inviting.

Many of them were decorated with the same type of cone mosaics first created in the Stone Cone Temple. But the builders had found that they could create the same dazzling visual effect, which had previously been achieved with stone cones, by using baked clay cones with painted ends. (These, sadly, have faded over the millennia and don't retain the vivid colors of the stone cones or the glazed cones of the Stone Cone Temple.) In one courtyard area, a row of large columns with no spaces between them each had a different mosaic design, alternating big diamonds, then zig-zag lines, then small triangles, back to big diamonds, and so on. The effect would have been almost dizzying.[15]

The entire complex was beautifully designed. Nothing about it was slipshod or incomplete; details had been considered carefully and executed with masterly artistry. The complex was an appropriately spectacular home for Inana, and she continued to live there for thousands of years.

Beginning of Writing

As the Level IV buildings rose, and their halls filled with priests, priestesses, artisans, workers, and administrators, all the work of running the Eanna must have become a growing headache for those in charge. The people who worked for the temple and its estates had to be provided with payment or rations, and any number of administrative details had to be committed to memory: the amounts of crops produced by the fields, the numbers of animals in the herds, the quantities of goods to be presented to the goddess, and countless other details. At some point, someone in power came up with a system to help keep track of things. Clay tablets used for this system were found in Uruk, within the Eanna, discarded in trash heaps after they were no longer useful.

With the benefit of hindsight, we moderns herald these clay tablets as representing the first writing (and the tablets found in the Eanna do indeed seem to have been the earliest in the Near East). It seems like a great leap forward. People were beginning to commit words to written form! But the truth is that this early system had little in common with what writing later became. It did not, in fact, represent an attempt to record language, nor was it a system used to express ideas.[16] The signs did not even appear in the order in which words were spoken. They had more in common with clay tokens and bullae than with the words on this page that you are reading. The system the Uruk people created has been dubbed "proto-cuneiform," because the later script is known as cuneiform, but the people who developed it had no idea that their innovation was "proto" anything, that it would develop further in the future. It was simply a useful tool that one could use to keep track of commodities, and it worked fine.

The date when those first proto-cuneiform tablets were written is unclear; we only know that they were thrown away as useless trash at a time when the Stone Cone Temple was no longer in use but the later Eanna temples were thriving. Scholars have suggested that the first ones might have been written as early as 3500 BCE,[17] or as late as 3200 BCE (though the latter seems too late, given the level in which they were found).

Whatever the date, the new system for recording administrative details met a pressing need. In an influential book published in 1992, Denise Schmandt-Besserat, a professor at the University of Texas at Austin, proposed that the tokens and clay balls of earlier periods were precursors to writing, that administrators had moved from placing clay tokens inside bullae, first to creating the same record by pressing the clay tokens on a clay lump without it having to be hollow, and next to pressing the end of a stylus onto clay to indicate numbers and drawing pictures (sometimes pictures of the tokens) with a sharp point, to indicate nouns.[18] It's an ingenious theory that has influenced scholars in this field for decades. Archaeologists working at the site of Tell Sabi Abyad, far from Uruk in north Syria, have found tokens used as some kind of counting device as early as 6000 BCE, though they didn't see any sign of them evolving or increasing over time.[19] What is clear is that, by the early Uruk period, the way administrators thought about numbers and commodities when using tokens was very similar to the way they thought about numbers and commodities when using proto-cuneiform.[20] Neither system really had anything to do with language.

On the earliest proto-cuneiform tablets, the administrators included numerical signs impressed with a stylus, in various shapes, with no indication of what was being counted. After a while, they began to divide up the surface of the clay tablet with incised lines, and to add pictograms to identify commodities (see Fig. 2.1). Each box on the front of the tablet—the obverse—usually contained a number and a picture. Some of these were little sketches of the thing being tracked—a fish, a stalk of grain, or a pot, for example—and some reproduced the shape of a token that had been used for a commodity, such as a circle with a cross in it, to represent "sheep." Signs sometimes also indicated the profession or name of a person, perhaps the one receiving the things listed. The back of the tablet usually featured nothing more than the sum total of the goods shown on the front.

The vast majority of proto-cuneiform tablets found in the debris at Uruk comprised administrative lists of goods and people, lists that were produced during the day-to-day running of the temples. Most recorded a single set of transactions, and a few combined information from several of the smaller tablets into a larger ledger.[21] The tablets aren't completely deciphered yet, but it's clear that the mechanisms of the administration were already quite sophisticated.[22]

The goods listed can tell us quite a bit about life in the temple storerooms, and more broadly in the city of Uruk during this period. Not surprisingly, wheat and barley are mentioned a great deal, and a lot of it was distributed as rations for workers employed by the temple.[23] The ration system took a

Fig. 2.1 Proto-cuneiform tablet with seal impressions, recording the distribution of barley, c. 3100–2900 BCE. (Metropolitan Museum of Art)

person's status into consideration: supervisors received more than ordinary male workers, who in turn received more than women. The temple also dealt with dairy products[24] and with meat.[25] Higher-ranking individuals again got preferred treatment in distributions of meat, which seems to have been provided for feasts. A striking revelation from these apparently dull lists is just how centralized the economy seems to have been at such an early time. The temple employed and provided for a great many people and must have had a lot of food stored in granaries and warehouses.

Not all of the tablets pertained to food and animals, though. Many others recorded the production of textiles made of wool. Each of fifteen different types of sheep was identified with its own pictogram, including one that was specified to be the "wool sheep."[26] Over time, as you will see in later chapters, cloth became one of the most important exports from Mesopotamia. Already, right at the beginning of urban culture, its production was at least partly controlled by the temples, and it was essential to the Mesopotamian economy.[27] Prior to the Uruk period, linen seems to have been more commonly used as a fabric, but it was more labor-intensive to make than wool, and it was made from flax plants that had to be grown in fields that could otherwise have produced food. Sheep, in contrast, could graze in lands that weren't at all suitable for agriculture, so once some types of sheep had been bred to produce wool that could be spun and woven, cloth production switched overwhelmingly to wool.[28]

Fortunately for us, all of this production was being tracked by officials, using clay tablets impressed with proto-cuneiform pictograms and number signs. Without them, we would know little about the remarkable mechanisms that had been created to make everything work smoothly.

Who were the people of Uruk? A pictogram can be read in any language, so it's impossible to be sure of the language spoken by the users of proto-cuneiform. Over the centuries that the signs were in use, the pictograms gradually became less like drawings. The reed stylus that they used in order to write had a tip much like the square end of a modern mass-produced wooden chopstick. If you press the edge of the square end into clay it makes a sharp line, with a little triangle at the top, and if you press the corner into the clay it just makes the triangle. Hurried scribes found that they could make the shapes of the pictograms out of straight lines and triangles by pressing the stylus into clay in this way. At some point, the signs, each made of combinations of lines and triangles, were no longer recognizable as anything at all. They were no longer pictograms.

The thing that strikes a viewer most about these more developed signs is the omnipresence of the triangle shapes. They give the script a rather extravagant look, like a medieval manuscript on steroids—there seem to be triangles everywhere. But they were not unnecessary curlicues. They were all needed in order for signs to be distinguished from one another. In the late seventeenth century of our era a German physician and world traveler named Engelbert Kämpfer spent time in Persia and produced a beautiful copy of an example of this wedge-shaped writing (though one written long after the Uruk period). The script wasn't deciphered in his lifetime, so he never knew what it recorded, but he came up with a name for it: "cuneiform," because "cuneus" means wedge in Latin. The term stuck.[29]

The users of proto-cuneiform seem to have managed well with their system, even though it was very limited in its range of expressions. Number-noun-person, number-noun-person, number-noun-person. Total. Person responsible. This was enough to relieve the administrator of the burden of memorizing innumerable details, and of making vast numbers of tokens and clay balls.

There were a few words that they needed to record, though, that were not nouns. One was the verb "to return," but there's no obvious way to draw "return." For this, the administrators ingeniously began to use the sign that meant "reed." And once they did this, we can detect the language hiding behind the script. This tiny detail tells us that they were thinking and speaking in the language known as Sumerian, because the word for "reed" in Sumerian was "*gi*," and that was also the word for "to return."[30] They used the sign for the sound of the word here, not the meaning of the picture, and this marked the start of writing words phonetically.

Later written documents reveal that Sumerian was the native tongue of most people in Uruk and throughout southern Mesopotamia—the area they called Sumer—during the late fourth millennium BCE and through most of the third. It continued to be the language of religion and learning long after that; Sumerian was considered to be a singularly prestigious and important language for thousands of years. Sadly, though, it left no descendants and is unrelated to any modern language.

In the proto-cuneiform system, writers used a huge number of individual signs—around 1,500.[31] About a third of these have been found only once on any of the tablets, which means that these signs were used very, very rarely, because about 6,000 tablets are known. It's possible that these singleton signs may have been made up on the spot by an official needing to record some obscure commodity. But about 100 of the signs were in frequent use, each showing up more than 100 times, and another 370 signs appear between 11 and 100 times.[32] So although some signs seem to have been invented somewhat spontaneously, it's clear that many signs formed a shared system and that the writers had learned these ones so that they could communicate with other people.

The signs that recorded numbers were also consistent—remarkably so. They were ordered in complicated numerical systems. We will come back to Mesopotamian mathematics in a later chapter, but for now you should know that it was based on the number 60, and is therefore referred to as a sexagesimal system. The main units were at what we would designate 1, 10, 60, 360 (60 × 6), 3,600 (60 × 60), and 36,000 (60 × 60 × 10). A separate numerical sign existed for each of these numbers.[33] This sounds confusing, but we still use it, in a way. There are 360 degrees in a circle, 60 seconds in a minute, and 60 minutes in an hour, because the Mesopotamians came up with this system and, in a long and convoluted way, we inherited it. The sexagesimal system works particularly well for fractions. The number 60 can be divided evenly by 1, 2, 3, 4, 5, and 6, and since the Mesopotamians dealt with commodities in large numbers, fractions were in constant use and no decimal points were needed (which was good, because they hadn't invented them). The weird thing is that, in proto-cuneiform, the sexagesimal system was used for keeping track of some things—but not for everything. Some other items were counted using a bisexagesimal system, with the units at 1, 10, 60, 120 (60 × 2), 1,200 (60 × 2 × 10), and 7,200 (60 × 2 × 60), again with separate signs for each. It got even more complicated, because different signs were used depending on what type of countable object was being counted, so that *thirteen* different systems of counting goods and people were in use at the same time.[34]

Kushim: Controller of the Barley Warehouse

The people whose names appear in the proto-cuneiform tablets from Uruk are a little like the everyday people who posed for some of the earliest photographs, thousands of years later. Suddenly, there they are, fellow humans, named, but the mark they have left on history is almost vanishingly faint. We can't even be sure how to pronounce their names. But their appearance on the clay tablets testifies to the fact that they were real people who lived more than 5,000 years ago, that they were as real as you and I are, and that they were the first named individuals in history.

One such man seems to have been named Kushim—at least that's how the signs in his name would have been read later on, when Sumerian was definitely the language being represented. Scholars were able to reconstruct some details of Kushim's professional activities and to analyze the tablets he drew up.[35] He was a high-ranking temple administrator with the official title "*sanga*," who worked in the Eanna complex around 3000 BCE. We don't know which building housed the rooms where he worked, but one can imagine him, at home in that immense complex, talking with other officials, counting jars of goods, writing and sealing tablets, and thinking through how he could get his deliveries completed.

Eighteen of the proto-cuneiform tablets found at Uruk were "signed" by him (that is, his name appears at the end) and tell us a little of what occupied his days. Kushim had a role in the distribution of ingredients for an all-important item of the Mesopotamian diet: beer. Specifically, he oversaw a warehouse and kept track of the malt and cracked barley that were kept there. Large deliveries came and went on a regular basis and had to be recorded—and almost all the grain in his domain was destined to become beer, which was essential to life, in the Mesopotamian view.[36] His tablets show that beer was not just brewed at home by farmers; it was produced by the temple and was integral to the city's economy.[37]

Beer had been brewed and drunk in the Near East long before scribes began writing about it, possibly as early as the Neolithic.[38] Fermentation made beer safe to drink, free from the germs and impurities that could infest river water, and the alcohol content of most beers (though not all) seems to have been lower than today; people drank beer a lot. As in colonial America, and in many other places and times, low-alcohol beer was safe to drink and considered to be an important part of a meal.[39] It's possible that some Near Eastern beers had no alcohol content at all, though some types certainly were associated with drunkenness, as plenty of later tales confirm.[40] We know from images on early cylinder seals that a favorite social event involved arranging chairs around a big pot of beer, gathering friends or family members together, and drinking it through long straws (see Fig. 2.2). Kushim might well have done this himself, though presumably not when he was working. Their beer must have tasted very different from its modern equivalents because it was brewed without hops but with a number of aromatic herbs and, sometimes, date syrup.[41]

Charged with keeping track of the vital ingredients in his warehouse, Kushim carefully wrote lists of the amounts of cracked barley and malt that were being distributed to particular individuals. Sometimes these amounts were vast. One tablet refers to a delivery of 135,000 liters of barley.[42] Another, written by a scribe who worked for Kushim, detailed the ingredients that were needed for eight different types of beer, and for nine other products made of cereals. In this tablet alone, the scribe used five of the different number systems.[43] Kushim's job extended to the distribution of finished

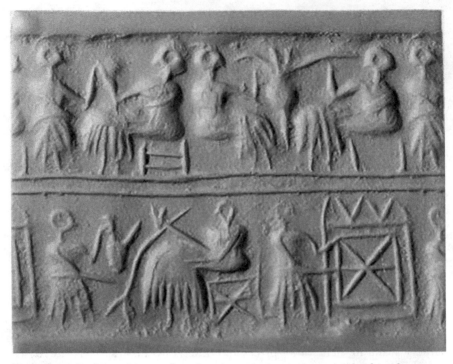

Fig. 2.2 Cylinder seal impression showing people at a banquet drinking beer through straws, c. 2600–2350 BCE. (Metropolitan Museum of Art)

beer, as well; one tablet notes that his office delivered thirty-five jars of beer, of three different types, to a single person.[44] Kushim did have an Achilles heel, though. He was a powerful man, but he wasn't necessarily at his best when it came to mathematics. He made quite a few mistakes in the totals that he recorded on his tablets.

Kushim, along with other administrators and scribes, must have been educated. His mathematical mistakes notwithstanding, he had learned to add, subtract, divide, and multiply, presumably in all thirteen of the different numerical systems. He had also learned to copy and memorize the hundreds of commonly used pictographic signs and numerals and to create records that could be understood by others. This would have been a lot to pick up on the job, so schools almost certainly existed to prepare aspiring administrators for their work.[45] The schools might in fact have been the institutions that had systematized the script and decided on the signs that would be used in the first place.

Luckily for us, the very few tablets that weren't written in service of the administration seem to have been products of these schools, and they provide some clues about the curriculum.[46] They show that students had to write and memorize long lists of the nouns they would need during their careers; these are known as lexical lists. One of these tablets was found in Level IV of the Eanna temple complex and featured a list of professions.[47] It's small, just 8.7 by 6.1 centimeters (3.4 by 2.4 inches) in size, but was divided into four vertical columns on each side, with nine or ten boxes per column, and each box included the number one, followed by the sign for an occupation. These are listed in hierarchical order from the most important functionaries to the least. At the top, where you might have expected to find the *en*, the most powerful man in Uruk, is instead the *nameshda*, who seems to have been the top-ranked official.[48] Curiously, the title of *en* doesn't appear. Perhaps his exalted role was in a different category entirely from those of temple officers. It's unclear, though; the term *nameshda* was later equated to the word for "king," so it could already have been one of the *en*'s titles.

This is far from the only known copy of this list of professions, but it is the earliest. Scribes in schools continued to copy the standard list of professions for hundreds of years after this, long after most of the professions they had to memorize were completely obsolete. Schooling, like many things in the ancient Near East, was marked by a deep conservatism, or at least this was the case after the explosion of new ideas and institutions that occurred during the Uruk period.

The same was true of the accounting system, which seems to have appeared at Uruk, almost fully realized, during Levels IV and III. For thousands of years after this, scribes kept on performing the same routine: they recorded exact amounts of goods in a particular consignment, along with the name of the person they would be delivered to or were being received from, and (later) the use to which they would be put, then they totaled them up, sealed the tablet, and sometimes dated it. Groups of small tablets like this were stored together. Periodically, scribes transferred the information from the small tablets to big ledgers, which were then archived.

Admittedly, not everything stayed the same as in the Uruk period. In later centuries most of the byzantine numerical schemes were simplified so that the same number signs could be used for many different weights and measures and many different goods, and the number of cuneiform signs in regular use dropped to around 600, following a fairly quick abandonment of all the eccentric, one-use-only signs. But the basic system invented by the Eanna administrators was sound. It provided Mesopotamia with the foundation for an economic system that functioned effectively for a very long time. (I should add that most subsequent administrators did better than Kushim at adding up quantities of goods.)

The Fields of the *En*

The earliest tablets from Level IV at Uruk have no parallels elsewhere. But tablets like the ones from Level III, which started to be written around 3100 BCE—the ones with numbers, commodities, and possible names—have shown up at a number of ancient cities, including places hundreds of miles from Uruk.[49] One late Uruk period tablet from a site called Jemdet Nasr has been singled out in particular as among the most important documents in all of Mesopotamian history.[50] It's not exactly a literary masterpiece, though. It's a list of fields, and for each field, the scribe provided its dimensions— the length, the width, the perimeter or the area of the field—along with the profession of the person who controlled it. They were all important officials. At the end, of course, is a total of all the land listed.

The first five fields listed were rectangular, of about the same large size, and three times as long as they were wide. Throughout Mesopotamian history, fields were generally long and narrow.[51] The landscape seems to have been divided up pretty regularly, even at this remarkably early date. A centralized authority hides behind this fact; the division of the land was not organic or arbitrary. But this isn't the main reason for the tablet's importance. Those first five fields, between them, make up only one-third of the allocated land. The other two-thirds of the land are listed in a separate box, and the cuneiform sign used to identify their owner is the one that looks like a tray holding a pile of beveled rim bowls: the sign for "lord"—the *en*.[52] This was our friend the priest-king, the man who, in Uruk, was so closely associated with the goddess Inana. In Jemdet Nasr, we see that the man in the same role controlled ten times as much land as any of the first five individuals.

This tablet provides some of the earliest proof of power and wealth being consolidated by one man, the *en*, in each city, and of the dramatic social stratification that was a feature of the new urban world of the Uruk period.

It's also interesting to note that among the recipients of the other fields—who included men with the titles "chief exchange agent," "equid herder," "chief justice," and "priest"—was the "wife of the *en*." Queens played a major role in Mesopotamian history, as you will see in future chapters. Although the "wife of the *en*" seems to have controlled only a tenth of the land of her husband, she was clearly an important public figure.

A whole lot of developments had been taking place at Uruk and other cities in Mesopotamia in the years leading up to 3100 BCE. We've already seen their advances in monumental architecture, organization and provisioning of workers, management of the economy, division of the landscape, development of a writing system, use of the wheel (and of the pottery wheel), creation of cylinder seals to identify individuals or offices, imports of large amounts of raw materials from distant lands, and development of an artistic style with figures shown in registers, as on the Uruk Vase. We've also seen changes in society, such as an increased separation between rich and poor, and consolidation of power by the *en* priest-king. But there were even more innovations. The plow was in wide use: it's pictured on cylinder seals. Metalworking had become more sophisticated. Objects of gold, silver, and especially copper have been found in the Uruk period levels of a number of sites—metalworkers were casting utensils, tools, vessels, jewelry, and statuettes.[53] To see so many changes in a relatively short time is extraordinary given the slow pace of change in culture before the Uruk period and, surprisingly, after it as well.

There's a reason that the focal point of much of this activity was the Eanna temple complex. Many of the innovations at Uruk, probably most of them, were in the service of the goddess Inana.

How They Understood Their World and Their Deities

On the surface, life in Uruk was surprisingly similar to life today. The buildings of the Eanna would be impressive even to modern visitors if we could have visited them in their original condition. We, too, recognize the impulse to make a glorious space for the divine—a temple, church, or mosque, for example. We share a surprising number of other life experiences with people who lived in Uruk five and a half thousand years ago. We have inherited many of the same institutions: farming, trade, marriage, and taxation, for example. Like us, people in the Uruk period lived in rectangular houses that opened onto streets. Although houses haven't been excavated at Uruk itself, we know from other Mesopotamian cities of the same period that their houses had rooms, furniture, doors, and windows (though without glass, which had not yet been invented). They cooked their meals in ovens and ate from pottery bowls. Their diet was based on bread, fish, vegetables (they loved onions and garlic), fruits, and some meat (beef, pork, lamb, goat). They drank beer. They wore clothes made of wool and linen. Sometimes their community, as a whole, got into a dispute with another one, and sometimes these disputes led to warfare. In all these ways, life hasn't changed dramatically from earliest times. I suspect that it will change a great deal more in future and that "ancient history" will come to be seen as everything up to about the beginning of the eighteenth century CE when technology began to leap forward.

On the other hand, the ancient Near Eastern conception of the universe was completely different from ours. They would not have understood how we think, and it's very difficult for us to understand them. Partly this is because modern science has provided us with an explanation for almost every natural phenomenon, but there's more to it than that. How the Mesopotamians explained their world is usually termed their "religion," but most modern religions are so different from ancient ones that we need to shed our preconceptions about religion in order to try to grasp their conceptions of the divine.

Some of what they experienced in life was predictable, even beautiful, in its regularity and orderliness, such as the way the sun rose, without fail, every morning; the way the moon waxed and waned, without fail, every 29½ days; the way the seasons reliably shifted through the year; the way the rivers provided an endless source of fresh water to sustain crops. On the other hand, the people of Mesopotamia during the Uruk period—actually, the people of the whole Near East throughout ancient history—were confronted with any number of inexplicable phenomena, many of which could cause them immense grief and loss. Flood damage, dust storms, epidemics, crop diseases, swarms of locusts, earthquakes, droughts—humans did nothing to bring these on. How could they be explained? How could they be prevented? In every family, loved ones got ill and died, sometimes in infancy, sometimes in old age, or at any time in between. Why?

The answer to all these questions was so obvious to them that it didn't need a book or a creed to explain it. The peoples of the ancient Near East didn't even have a word for religion; the source of all these phenomena was as much a part of the observable world as was a tree or a river. Think of it this way: people could see causes and effects in the things they themselves did every day; a human could plant crops in a field, tear down a house, or eat a meal. The outcomes of these actions were obvious—plants grew, walls fell, hunger was satiated. So, something, or someone, must be causing the phenomena that humans didn't control, and it was clear that this someone (or someones) lived longer than any human and had vastly more power. It was also clear to the people that there were many of these powerful beings. The one that provided water for their crops was not the same one that caused the sun to rise in the eastern sky every morning, and so on. These powerful beings were real and they were everywhere. They also seemed to have human characteristics—love, anger, generosity—and at some point before the Uruk period they had been anthropomorphized and imagined to be human in temperament and even in appearance.

To a Mesopotamian, family was all-important, as was respect for hierarchy. Parents cared for their children; children obeyed and respected their parents; siblings watched out for one another and could be relied upon to be there when needed. A workplace emulated a family, with the supervisor as the father. So, later, did a state, but with the king as the father. It's not surprising, then, that gods and goddesses (because that is what the powerful beings obviously were) had families—husbands, wives, and children—and that some had more clout than others. It was the gods' universe, and humans represented nothing more than a cosmic afterthought, far down in the hierarchy, as slaves to the immortals. The gods and goddesses had created the universe for themselves. Humans could enjoy its gifts, taking advantage of the food, water, and raw materials available to them, but their lives were subject to the whims of their unseen masters. And when these masters decided to unleash erratic storms of chaos from time to time, humans just had to ride them out and try to survive.

Throughout the ancient Near East, a few gods were worshiped almost everywhere. Four of the most important deities were just what you might expect: the heavens (called An, in the Sumerian language), the sun (Utu), the moon (Nanna), and the storm (Ishkur). They weren't just gods of these phenomena—they *were* the phenomena. Each divine name was the same as the word for the realm that god controlled. There was no way to say that the sun rose without saying that the god of the sun rose. There was no way to say that a storm might be coming without invoking the name of the storm god. Not surprisingly, we have no evidence of atheists. One could no more deny the existence of the sun god than the existence of a sheep or a goat. Another major god, Enki, embodied fresh water, which was imagined to fill a great underground sea, the Abzu, and to seep up through the ground in springs. His name, curiously, does not mention water; it seems to have meant "lord of earth." Enlil, the king of the gods, has a name that seems to mean "lord of air" though he wasn't associated with the air or wind, at least by the time writing developed. Among the greatest of the deities, only one was female. This was Inana, to whom the Eanna temple in Uruk was dedicated. Her name seems to have originally been Ninana, meaning "Lady of Heaven,"[54] hence the name of her home. Eanna meant "House of Heaven" (*e* meant "house," *ana* meant "of heaven").

The deities had areas of expertise, just as a human might. The sun god, Utu, was the god of justice. The storm god, Ishkur, was a warrior. The moon god Nanna helped bring fertility to animals. The freshwater god, Enki, was considered the wisest of the gods and perhaps the kindest to humans, and so on. To the north of Sumer, in central Mesopotamia, the gods had different names but the same attributes. Inana was known as Ishtar there, Utu's name was Shamash, Nanna was Sin, Ishkur was Adad, Enki was Ea, but no one seems to have thought of these as different gods, just different names for the same familiar figures. Much later, the Greeks and Romans worshiped similar gods—anthropomorphic, related to one another in families, each having control over some specific aspect of the cosmos. In their time, too, the deities had different names in Greek than in Latin, so, for example, the god of the sea and storms was called Poseidon in Greek and Neptune in Latin.

Other gods and goddesses had local followings in the cities in which they resided. Their existence wasn't denied by people from other regions—all deities were regarded as real—they just weren't all that important outside their home area.

Caring for the Gods

Let us return to the Eanna temple complex, in Level IV, around 3200 BCE. Inana's own personal shrine was not a gathering place for the people of Uruk to worship her; the goddess would not have wanted all that fuss and noise.

It was the goddess's home, and she was physically present there. Commoners might have had access to some areas, but not to the goddess herself. This was true of all major temples. Unfortunately, we can't be sure where exactly, in the Eanna, Inana was housed. She was associated with the planet that we know as Venus, but she was present not only in the night sky. Somewhere in the Eanna was a statue of her that embodied her power, that *was* her, right here on Earth. The statue would have been a life-size representation of a woman, probably seated on a throne, wearing sumptuous clothes, and bedecked in jewelry. Her face was probably carved from marble.

Although we can read of countless statues of gods and goddesses that resided in temples across the Near East, and across the three and a half millennia of ancient Near Eastern history, almost none of them has survived. Except, that is, for the face of the oldest of them all, that of Inana in the Eanna temple (see Fig. 2.3). Excavators found a life-size marble face during

Fig. 2.3 Uruk head, made of marble with missing inlays, late fourth millennium BCE. (Photo 12/Alamy Stock Photo)

the excavations there that is surely too carefully made to be anything but a representation of the goddess herself.[55] It now resides in the National Museum of Iraq in Baghdad: a strikingly naturalistic marble representation of a woman whose eyes, eyebrows, and hair would have been inlaid with gold and semi-precious stones (though these inlays are lost). Her body would have been made of wood or precious metals.

When a priest or priestess set eyes on this figure, he or she was in the actual presence of the mighty, immortal goddess. Inana ruled over many realms—sexual love, warfare, and violence—she was volatile, and she was feared. A visitor would have brought her an offering and said a prayer. People visiting or working in the Eanna didn't see her as a lifeless statue because, to them, the gods were absolutely real. She watched and listened. She appreciated gifts. She got hungry and thirsty. She would have been angry if she had been neglected, and no one wanted to witness what might happen then.

An unquestioning belief in the divine was the only way to account for pretty much every occurrence in one's world. The deities caused everything from dreams, to luck (or lack thereof), to thunderstorms, to the fertility of sheep, to the movements of flocks of birds. These were shared beliefs, over the entire region.

Suppose a priestess had arrived in Uruk, having traveled from northern Mesopotamia, or Iran, or even Anatolia or Egypt. Even she would not have doubted the power of Inana. Back at home, this goddess probably had a different name, or she might not even have been worshiped at all, but this didn't make Inana a false deity in the mind of the visiting priestess. No gods were false; all were members of a single community of gods that extended to all lands. They could not be separated from the world they controlled, and the products of that world all existed, primarily, to satisfy their needs.

For these reasons, religion, politics, society, and economy were not separate institutions in the ancient Near East; they were all bound together, because the service of the gods was all-important.[56] All the deities (taking the form of their statues) needed housing, food, drink, clothing, praise, and riches, just like very demanding humans. Everyone knew this. These were some of the central demands, not just of the belief system, but of life; all people were servants of the gods, all the time. One's role, as a human on Earth, was to serve them, placate them, provide for them, try to divine their needs, and then meet those needs. That was pretty much it.

On the other hand, the ancient Near Eastern people seem to have been unconcerned with what we would call spirituality, and it didn't occur to them that they might be rewarded in the afterlife for virtuous acts during their lives. They believed that the gods could (and did) punish people for doing evil, but also that the gods could punish people for no reason at all, and neither of these types of punishments had anything to do with the afterlife. We will come back to the afterlife later; but whatever they may have believed about it, it was not a heaven.

Perhaps because the gods could unleash such chaos on the world, the people seem to have craved structure in their lives. They could never control disease, they could never predict weather, they could never anticipate a devastating flood, and they could die apparently for no reason at any time. What we talk about as their "religion" was an ongoing, lifelong attempt to try to tame, or at least influence, the gods and goddesses by providing for them.

They also believed that the gods planted clues about their plans in the world around them, which constituted a form of advice for humans. Specially trained diviners could decipher the clues. By following this advice and providing for the gods, the people hoped that the gods would, in return, be kind, or at least leave them alone. We will come back to diviners as well, in a later era when their activities can be traced in the documents they wrote.[57]

It followed that, as Uruk grew and prospered, the people who lived there would have seen its prosperity as a sign of divine favor, specifically from the goddess Inana and the god An who lived right there in the city among them. Every city had a resident god who was particularly venerated and whose temple was also his or her physical home. Uruk had these two resident deities, An and Inana, probably because two earlier villages had merged to become a single city.

The people were compelled to share their prosperity by creating ever bigger and grander homes for the two deities and working to expand the gods' estates and wealth. In a way, they had no choice. The Eanna was more than Inana's temple, more than the complex of shrines and buildings created for her in the center of the city; it was a vast economic and social institution, supported by its farms, herds of animals, orchards, and fisheries, and run by hundreds of workers, from shepherds to plowmen, weaving women to cooks, brewers to barbers.[58] It's possible that some land in the territory of

Uruk was privately owned, but the evidence suggests that the gods were the main landowners and employers in the city. To Urukian minds, this was as it should be. The people believed that the gods had originally constructed the city and its temples for themselves, long before humans were even thought of. It was their land; humans only lived there because they were useful to the gods.

PART II

The Early Dynastic Period,

2900–2300 BCE

Chapter 3
Kings and Subjects

In southern Mesopotamia, it's unlikely that anything dramatic happened around 2900 BCE. The people alive at the time presumably didn't suddenly feel themselves to have entered a new era. They kept right on farming and making pottery and weaving and working for the temple and doing all the things they had been doing during the Uruk period. But several things *did* change around this time. One was that more and more people began to live in cities and those cities grew larger and larger. Another is that these city populations needed more farmland than basin irrigation of natural channels could provide. The people began to take more control of the rivers on which they depended and to create canals of increasing size and complexity to bring water to their fields.[1] They did this probably by enlarging and adapting existing natural channels.[2] A third innovation, the one that gives this era its name, was that the powerful men who ruled each of the various major cities became yet more powerful, taking personal credit for monumental buildings and irrigation projects that they commissioned.[3] These men were now recognizably kings, so this new era is known as the "Early Dynastic period." Unfortunately, one looks in vain for the cuneiform documents to tell us about the first halting steps from priest-kings to kings whose roles were different from those of priests, if they were indeed halting steps.

Ushumgal and Shara-igizi-Abzu: A Priest and His Daughter

It is in the Early Dynastic period that we can begin to learn more about the specific lives of individuals. The writing system had developed beyond proto-cuneiform, as scribes began to use the signs phonetically to reflect the sound of a word. When they did this, we can begin to think of their system as writing in the conventional sense—as an attempt, in a limited way at this point, to record the sounds of a language.[4] The language it represented was Sumerian, which had a couple of features that coincidentally lent themselves to syllabic writing: it featured a lot of one-syllable words and a lot of homonyms. As in the case of the sign "GI," which could be read as "a reed" or "to return," plenty of other Sumerian words sounded alike, with at least one of the meanings having already been turned into a pictogram, so that the pictogram could be used whenever that sound was needed.

By now, the signs no longer looked anything like pictures; the script from this era onward is called "cuneiform." In the Early Dynastic period, a few people began to use cuneiform to write about themselves—not often, and not in much depth—but we get clearer glimpses of them in the cuneiform texts. Although 90 percent of documents were still written for administrative purposes,[5] a few inscriptions extolled the achievements of powerful people, and a few recorded legal transactions. You might expect that kings were the only ones to take advantage of this new use of writing, but that's not the case. Two of the earliest individuals whose activities were described in something resembling a narrative form lived at the beginning of the Early Dynastic period and were not kings. They were a man named Ushumgal and his daughter Shara-igizi-Abzu. They lived in the city of Umma in southern Mesopotamia.

Although they do not seem to have been royalty, they were also not commoners. Ushumgal was a *pab-shesh* priest who served a god named Shara. His daughter Shara-igizi-Abzu had a profession too, she was an *esh-a*, though we don't know what this meant. Shara was the chief god of the city of Umma, so Ushumgal was one of the most powerful religious leaders in the community. As in the Uruk period, as a priest he would have overseen the administration of temple properties. In later centuries, *pab-shesh* priests kept track of grain, received special garments for festivals, and poured libations when other priests were chanting.[6] The same might well have already been true for Ushumgal.

We not only know the names of these two people, we even know what they looked like, or at least how they were represented by an artist who knew them.[7] Ushumgal had long hair and a beard; he wore an ankle-length skirt with a fringe at the bottom and a wide rope-like band at the top, along

Fig. 3.1 Figure of Ushumgal, on the stela of Ushumgal and Shara-igizi-Abzu, c. 2900 BCE. (Metropolitan Museum of Art)

with a cape of some kind over one shoulder. His feet were bare (see Fig. 3.1). Shara-igizi-Abzu wore her hair braided around her face and bound up in a bun in the back. Her dress was long and simple, without a fringe or belt, and the fabric looped over her left arm (see Fig. 3.2).

One curious feature of Early Dynastic art is that artists usually depicted women with straight, almost male physiques. In contrast to so-called fertility figurines from earlier in human history, Early Dynastic artists rarely included any suggestion of breasts or hips under the depiction of clothing, which might have distinguished the women from the men. Only their clothes and hairstyles mark them as women. This is true of the depiction of Shara-igizi-Abzu. Often women's names were also ambiguous, so it is not always possible to tell whether a text was written about a woman or a man. Names consisted of phrases or sentences, most of which were expressions of piety. Only a few of them were particular to women at this time.

Fig. 3.2 Figure of Shara-igizi-Abzu on the stela of Ushumgal and Shara-igizi-Abzu, c. 2900 BCE. (Metropolitan Museum of Art)

The reason that the artist immortalized Ushumgal and Shara-igizi-Abzu is that they were involved in a transaction so important that a record of it was carved onto a stone boulder, complete with pictures of the main parties. The roughly drawn cuneiform signs that litter the sides of the boulder, and even extend over the figures themselves, record that this transaction pertained to animals, land, and houses, in large quantities: 450 *iku* of fields are mentioned (about 158 hectares or 392 acres), along with three houses and some bulls, donkeys, and sheep.[8] Unfortunately, the inscription suffers from a dire shortage of verbs, which would have been useful in determining what exactly was going on.

Some other people were involved as well, and four of them were portrayed on the boulder next to the two main parties. These other four, even though they too were apparently important people, are dwarfed by the large figures of Ushumgal and Shara igizi-Abzu. One, a woman who, like Shara-igizi-Abzu, served as an *esh-a*, was also the daughter of another priest. The three others were men: the chief of the assembly, the foreman of the assembly, and the chief herald. These movers and shakers of the Umma community had been brought together to do something, or to witness something, that pertained to the animals, houses, and fields. No price was listed, which argues against its being a record of a sale, but it does seem likely that the property was changing hands.[9] One possibility is that Ushumgal was giving all the real estate and animals to his daughter.[10]

The boulder is all that is left to attest to a solemn moment, almost 5,000 years ago, when these people gathered, decided on a course of action, and transferred property. An oath was even sworn, according to the inscription, which suggests that it represented a legal document. Some kind of a judicial system must already have been in place to enforce it, hundreds of years before laws began to be written down.

The artist, whose name is given as Enhegal,[11] must have spent considerable time immortalizing the occasion. When the carving was finished, the stone monument, or stela, was probably set up in a temple as a permanent record. That same permanent record is now on display in a gallery at the Metropolitan Museum of Art in New York.

Although this boulder is one of the earliest examples of individuals being portrayed and named, it illustrates several deep Mesopotamian traditions, mentioned in the Introduction, that will recur throughout this book. One is that real estate was viewed as extremely important and the people felt that changes in the ownership of, or rights to, land and houses needed to be recorded, not just remembered. The records were maintained and stored and passed down through generations. Whereas wills and letters and lists might be thrown away after the deaths of the people to whom they pertained, real estate contracts and deeds tended to be carefully preserved.

Another long-lasting tradition seen here for perhaps the first time was that it was always best to get the gods involved when humans were doing potentially contentious things such as transferring property. In the ancient Near East, oaths never lost their power to rein in natural impulses; the fear of the gods remained a powerful restraint on greed and corruption for thousands of years.

A third tradition seen here was less resilient but still lasted for millennia. Although men held powerful positions as kings, princes, and priests, their female counterparts—queens, princesses, and priestesses—could at times be just as powerful and were not denigrated for their sex. A powerful woman was to be feared and obeyed, no less than a powerful man. Shara-igizi-Abzu was not portrayed on this stela just because she was the daughter of Ushumgal—she was there playing a major role. She was even depicted as just a little bit taller than her father.

The city of Umma, where they lived, was presumably ruled by a king, though at the beginning of the Early Dynastic period there is very little written evidence from anywhere in Mesopotamia for kings, or for anything else, for that matter. Ushumgal and Shara-igizi-Abzu emerge from the general anonymity of the era like beacons in a fog, reminding us that hundreds of thousands of people in the Near East were busily getting on with their lives; we just do not know about almost any of them.

The city of Umma was watched over by the god Shara, whose temple was one of the most impressive in all of Sumer.[12] The ruler of Umma controlled not just the city itself but several smaller cities and towns,[13] along with the villages and lands around the city—it was a city-state. Sumer was dotted with city-states, each home to at least one city god or goddess and each with its own government. (The same was true of the region of Akkad, which lay to the north of Sumer.) Directly to the east of Umma was its neighbor, the city-state of Lagash, with which it is always associated, as though they were ancient twins (though very argumentative twins).

Lagash seems to have had a ruler at the beginning of the Early Dynastic period, around the same time that Shara-igizi-Abzu and her father were alive. He was portrayed on a stone stela, in a style not unlike that used by the artist Enhegal to portray the priest Ushumgal.[14]

Like Ushumgal, the ruler of Lagash wore his hair long and had a beard, and his skirt extended to his ankles. Unlike Ushumgal, though, his skirt resembled those of the Uruk period priest-kings. It seems to have been made of net, represented by cross-hatching on the sculpture, and he had two feathers in his headdress. He was shown grasping one of two tall maces. The symbolism of all this is lost on us—what did the maces imply? Why was he in a feathered headdress? We do not even know his name; only the name of the god of Lagash, Ningirsu, is given. Some scholars think that he may even represent a god, not a ruler, though gods tended to be shown with horns on their heads, not feathers.

In these early centuries of Sumerian kingship, hints have been found of alliances between southern cities, with perhaps as many as twelve of them forming some sort of a network, perhaps for trade.[15] Meanwhile, the rulers of a city-state called Kish, at the very northern edge of the Sumerian-speaking area in what is now central Iraq, were becoming more aggressive than their southern neighbors. An alabaster rectangular plaque bearing what is apparently the earliest historical inscription ever found was published in 2013.[16] Perhaps we should not be surprised that it records not a peaceful alliance but the capture by the city of Kish of 36,000 prisoners from at least twenty-five places. Although no king's name appears in the preserved section, we do know the name of the scribe who wrote the inscription—a man called Amar-Shid. He had carefully inscribed the name of each community and the number of people taken from it, in neat text boxes in rows, to be read from right to left and from top to bottom. On the opposite side of the stone from the inscription, a sculptor had carved two bearded men holding weapons. Those tens of thousands of prisoners were put to work, according to the inscription, with"filling the threshing floors (with grain) and the making of grainstacks."[17] These prisoners, put to work for the palace or temples of Kish, were among the first of many, many men and women in the ancient Near East who were captured in war and forced to labor for their captors.

Over the course of the Early Dynastic period (c. 2900–2300 BCE), the Sumerian city-states went back and forth between these opposing poles of peaceful alliance and armed conflict. To protect themselves in the case of conflict, they built walls around their cities, but to pursue alliances, they developed mechanisms of diplomacy.

As the centuries passed in Umma and Lagash, scribes created more inscriptions, and the rulers of the two city-states shook off that enveloping fog of anonymity. They become known to us as people—people who for generations squabbled and sometimes battled with one another. The point of contention between the two city-states was a stretch of land known as the Gu'edena, which was claimed by both.[18] A ruler of either Umma or Lagash would no sooner have set up a boundary stone to mark the border than his counterpart would be outraged at its placement and would remove it, claiming the land for himself. This was an act of war and the troops of the two lands would launch a campaign to fight for control. It happened again and again. This all started very early on, in the reign of a king of Lagash named Ur-Nanshe.

King Ur-Nanshe of Lagash: Creating the Model of the Pious King

Ur-Nanshe (mid-third millennium BCE) ruled so early in the history of the city-state of Lagash that we do not know who he was, exactly, or for how long he reigned.[19] Luckily for us, though, he created inscriptions that included more narrative than was found in the terse list of captives from Kish. Ur-Nanshe was one of the first rulers to come up with the novel idea of using writing to record something about himself. In some cases, this new use for writing was largely a matter of labeling people on relief sculptures, much as Ushumgal and Shara-igizi-Abzu had done some time before, but King Ur-Nanshe did tend to add a few words about his achievements as well.

A limestone plaque produced by one of his court artists shows the king in two poses, looking a little cartoonish to modern eyes (see Fig. 3.3). His face is in profile, and a huge, surprised-looking eye and triangular nose dominate his clean-shaven, bald head. His head is too big for his body, making him seem childlike; his torso faces the viewer but his feet point sideways; and he is twice the size of the other people who line up in front of him. These individuals have their names written across their skirts or in front of them—and they almost all have the sign "DUMU" after their names. The Sumerian word *dumu* is usually translated as "son" but it also meant "child." Here, then, were King Ur-Nanshe's children, and one of them— the tallest one, standing at the front of the line—was clearly a daughter, as she was dressed in women's clothing.[20] Her name seems to have been Abda. The seven other children were all sons, one of whom eventually took the throne after the death of his father.

But at the time this plaque was made, that sad moment was off in the future and royal succession seems not to have been at the forefront of the king's mind. What he wanted to memorialize on this plaque were three pious acts. He had the stone carver write that he had "built the temple of the god Ningirsu; built the Abzu-banda (building) (and) built the temple of the goddess Nanshe."[21] These words were squeezed in next to one of

Fig. 3.3 Limestone plaque showing King Ur-Nanshe of Lagash and his family, mid-third millennium BCE. (Renée Lessing-Kronfuss/Art Resource)

the images of the king—appropriately enough, one that showed him with a basket on his head, as though carrying bricks to a building site. These buildings that he boasted of constructing would of course have been the work of many corvée laborers, called up from the population for the purpose and provided with rations and perhaps accommodations.

There is one other achievement that he thought to include, this one next to the second image of the king: he "had ships of Dilmun submit timber as tribute from foreign lands (to Lagash)."[22] Dilmun was hundreds of kilometers to the south of Lagash on the shores of the Persian Gulf, in what is now Bahrain. It seems improbable that Lagash controlled Dilmun, so the "tribute" may have been something more in the nature of trade, but evidence from Bahrain confirms that it was serving as a trading center for the whole region and was indeed in contact with the Mesopotamian city-states at this time.

This plaque is not all we know of King Ur-Nanshe; he left us plenty of evidence of his reign, including at least thirty-seven inscriptions. He had them written on figurines, on objects made of stone—limestone, diorite, and onyx—and on bricks, door sockets, and copper nails, but never, apparently, on anything so prosaic as a clay tablet. He frequently boasted about constructing public buildings, and on seven occasions he repeated his assertion about the ships from Dilmun bringing timber for Lagash. In other inscriptions he listed many statues he had dedicated to (or perhaps of) various gods, along with a number of canals he had commissioned. Once he noted that he had distributed a truly vast amount of barley to a temple, presumably for its staff.[23] Another time he noted that he had chosen someone to be a "spouse" of the goddess Nanshe, probably as a priest of some sort.[24] All of these activities benefited his people, and he comes across in his inscriptions as a public-spirited and pious king.

Surprisingly, in the surviving inscriptions, Ur-Nanshe rarely mentioned war or conflict—only twice, in fact. In his longest inscription he wrote that he "went to war against the leader of Ur and the leader of Gesha" and that he "defeated and [captured] the leader of Ur" and "defeated the leader of Gesha."[25] Gesha was used as another name for Umma, the city-state that neighbored Lagash. This was the start of the long hostilities between the two kingdoms. He fought farther away, as well, in Elam, to the east of Lagash in what is now western Iran.[26] Elam, which was to become one of the great powers of the Near East, was at a low point in the mid-third millennium. The city of Susa, its capital, had shrunk in size and was soon to be abandoned, though not for long.[27] Ur-Nanshe's campaigns, to both Umma and Elam, must have been major undertakings, requiring his soldiers to be armed and provisioned, and involving scouts and camp followers, donkeys, chariots, and considerable quantities of bows, arrows, and spears. Unfortunately, though, we know almost nothing about his wars or what the purpose might have been for his expedition to Elam. He certainly wasn't preoccupied with recording their specifics for posterity. Later kings of Lagash provided many more details.[28]

It's a little unclear, in fact, for whom Ur-Nanshe commissioned his inscriptions. They clearly were not for his subjects. For one thing, the Mesopotamians were mostly illiterate and, for another, the inscriptions probably were not set up in public places. They were in temples or palaces, accessible only to a few high-ranking people. The ones written on bricks would have been hidden from everyone's view, covered up by other bricks. The frequent focus on his construction of temples for the gods suggests that gods themselves may have been the main audience. As a result of Ur-Nanshe's inscriptions, the gods would be reminded forever that the king had taken good care of them.

That was a great thing about writing: a message conveyed this way did not have to be repeated over and over. It didn't die when the king did—not like his spoken words. The gods lived forever and this message to them—carved on stone, or brick, and set in a holy place—might live forever too. We are so used to this fact about the timelessness of the written word that it doesn't even occur to us as worthy of note. But it must have been magical to the Early Dynastic kings to realize that words, which had previously been as ephemeral as the wind in the trees, could be pinned down and preserved on stone.

Ur-Nanshe's inscriptions may not prove to be eternal, but they are doing pretty well, having already lasted about 4,500 years. It is just possible that the king was writing to the future as well as to the gods. His sense of the future would not have included us, of course, as we examine the plaque that shows him with his family, by enlarging it on a computer screen. But he might have written on those bricks to let future kings know who first built the structure that they were, perhaps, remodeling.

After Ur-Nanshe, later kings often actually addressed their successors in their inscriptions, asking them to preserve the images and the words (and sometimes adding curses on anyone who defaced the inscriptions). Written words, they realized, could transcend time and the physical world, reaching unseen gods and as yet unborn successors. They provided a measure of immortality for the kings themselves.

No matter why the kings commissioned them, the important thing for us is that the royal inscriptions existed and that kings in the Near East continued to write them throughout ancient history. Their preoccupations stayed much the same over time—building projects, statues, water management, trade, alliances, appointments of priests and priestesses, and wars. These came up over and over. The kings' words provide us with a skeleton of political events on which we can begin to hang a narrative about their world. Never mind that their accounts were certainly biased, probably exaggerated, and clearly self-serving. In them we find the names of people and places, and accounts of joys and troubles. It has always been easier to study society, religion, and economy in the ancient Near East than to study politics, but it is helpful to have a general sense of what was going on politically in order to give a framework to the rest.

The origins of kingship are unclear but, once invented, monarchy clung on tenaciously. Perhaps it seemed natural in Mesopotamia because the population had become accustomed to priest-kings running things during the earlier Uruk period. Having a powerful man in charge was not new. Perhaps kings were accepted by their subjects because they gradually began to claim that the gods had chosen them for their role (though Ur-Nanshe did not mention this; it seems to have been a concept that developed after his reign). Perhaps it was because kings got their start as military leaders and presumably had the loyalty of their troops. And perhaps it was because the role of king became hereditary, like just about every other job in Sumer. The chosen crown prince got plenty of training so that he could take over his father's position smoothly. Whatever the reason or reasons, the Mesopotamians embraced monarchy and came to believe that the gods had given it to them as the ideal form of government. Who were they to question the gods?

Ur-Nanshe, like other Early Dynastic kings, was probably assisted in his role by a town assembly and a council of elders.[29] Although divinely ordained, the Sumerian idea of monarchy was not absolute. Ur-Nanshe was a contemporary of the kings of the Fourth Dynasty in Egypt, but his power over his subjects was much less sweeping than theirs, and his little kingdom was a fraction of the size of Egypt. The Fourth Dynasty Egyptian kings in Ur-Nanshe's era could (and did) command the construction of what are still among the biggest and heaviest monuments ever constructed on Earth: the Great Pyramids. Nothing in Mesopotamia at this time was remotely comparable.

People often now speak of ancient Egypt and ancient Mesopotamia in the same breath. They shared a fairly small region, at least to modern eyes, and were the earliest two urban cultures on Earth. As we have seen, during the Uruk period they were in contact with one another, trading and sharing influences. It's possible that the Mesopotamians were influenced by Egypt in adopting the idea of having kings to rule their urban states. By Ur-Nanshe's time, though, the two civilizations seem to have fallen out of regular contact with one another, and it is entirely possible that the king of Lagash knew nothing of his contemporaries along the Nile. Egypt is never mentioned in texts from Early Dynastic Sumer—at least not those that have been found.

Ur-Nanshe used the title *lugal,* which meant, literally, "big man" (*lu* meant "man"; *gal* meant "big" in Sumerian), and *lugal* is almost always translated as "king." His successors in Lagash chose instead the title *ensi.* In later times an *ensi* was a governor and therefore lower in rank than a king, but in this early era the two terms seem to have been synonymous. Ur-Nanshe's successors continued not to focus on grand demonstrations of superhuman power like their contemporaries in Egypt; instead they became increasingly preoccupied with their battles with neighboring Umma over control of the Gu'edena lands.

Ur-Nanshe is one of the very earliest kings on Earth whose name is known to us, but he certainly did not think of himself as being at the beginning of history. No one in what we call the ancient world did. Their culture was, at the time, the most modern the world had ever seen, advanced in technology, developing hitherto impossible connections with other cultures, proud of its accomplishments.

The people of Ur-Nanshe's era had no memory of a time before their cities had been built or kings had ruled. When, a few centuries later, scribes created a document called the "Sumerian King List" to capture their understanding of the past, they wrote (concerning the time before what we call the Early Dynastic period), "In five cities eight kings reigned for 385,200 years."[30] They believed that this period was followed by a flood, after which a further "23 kings reigned for 23,310 years" in the city of Kish, and then more besides, all before we get to approximately the era of Ur-Nanshe (who was not named in the list). One of the kings of Uruk in this mythical early period was "Gilgamesh, whose father was a ghost" who "reigned for 126 years."[31] Gilgamesh came to be one of the great heroes of Mesopotamian literature, but if he was a real king we have no evidence of his existence from his own time. We will come back to the epic poem about him later.[32]

Obviously, the alleged reigns in the Sumerian King List were absurdly long and lay in the realm of legend, not history, but they tell us that the people of Early Dynastic Sumer probably believed themselves to be living at the endpoint of more than 400,000 years of civilization. To their minds, their culture was almost inconceivably old and well established. They would have been astonished to know that we see them as having been right at the beginning.

Before we move on, I should note one other fact about Ur-Nanshe, his successors in Lagash, and kings of many other Early Dynastic city-states.

They did not rule alone. The queen—the principal wife of each king—played a considerable role. Ur-Nanshe did not just depict his sons and daughters on his relief sculptures; his wife Min-bara-Abzu appeared as well.[33] After the time of Ur-Nanshe, much more is known about the queens and their responsibilities.

King Eannatum of Lagash

Sometime in the twenty-fifth century BCE, Ur-Nanshe's grandson Eannatum came to power in Lagash. He continued to fight against the city-state of Umma, the perpetual enemy of Lagash, but he also claimed to have fought and won battles against distant lands such as Mari, far to the northwest on the Euphrates in Syria, and (like Ur-Nanshe before him) against Elam, to the east. These military campaigns don't seem to have enlarged his kingdom at all, however.[34] The main reason for his importance to history is the impressive stone stela that he set up in his capital city of Girsu to commemorate his victories over Umma. It's known as the "Stela of the Vultures," and its surviving fragments measure 180 centimeters (almost 6 feet) tall by 130 centimeters (4 feet 3 inches) wide. It might have been even taller when it was complete.

The stela gets its modern name from a rather gruesome scene at the top of the back, showing vultures pecking at the heads of dead soldiers, but the vultures were incidental to the main scenes. On the front (see Fig. 3.4), a standing god dominates everything, taking up about two-thirds of the height of the monument. In his hand he holds a huge net containing a mass of naked, dead soldiers, all piled together, limbs intertwined. The viewer would have had no doubt that these were the men of Umma who had been defeated by Eannatum and that the god was responsible for the victory.

On the back (see Fig. 3.5), the artist showed scenes from a battle that Lagash had won. Only fragments survive, but there's enough of it for the main points to come across clearly. In four scenes, or registers, stacked on top of one another, enemies from Umma (again naked and dead) are shown sprawled on the ground, sometimes literally underfoot. In at least two of the registers, Eannatum, larger than life, leads his troops to triumph. The troops of Lagash line up behind him, armed with helmets, shields, and spears, the model of discipline. In the second to the top register (the small top register

Fig. 3.4 Front of the Stela of the Vultures showing the god Ningirsu holding prisoners in a net, twenty-fifth century BCE. (Renée Lessing-Kronfuss/Art Resource)

just shows those ominous vultures), the soldiers' weapons are drawn as they march in phalanx formation, spears pointing out between their matching rectangular shields. Eannatum marches ahead of them. In the scene below this, the troops have their weapons stowed over their shoulders, while Eannatum rides alone in his chariot at their head, a lance in his hand, poised to strike someone or something—the relevant part is missing. The general impression one gets is that Umma didn't stand a chance of victory. It's also interesting to note that the army of Lagash was obviously well trained to fight as a unit, and that the soldiers were equipped with standard arms, cloaks, shields, and helmets. All this must have been organized and paid for by the palace.

Eannatum claimed in the accompanying inscription on the stela that he was the physical son of the local god Ningirsu—that his birth resulted

Fig. 3.5 Back of the Stela of the Vultures showing King Eannatum of Lagash leading his troops in battle, twenty-fifth century BCE. (Renée Lessing-Kronfuss/ Art Resource)

from "semen implanted in the womb by the god Ningirsu."[35] Although he stopped short of claiming to be a god himself (Mesopotamian kings rarely did), he went into more detail about his close ties to the gods, and then moved on to an account of the battle with the king of Umma over their shared border, presumably the one shown in the scenes on the back of the stela.

Eannatum then noted that he had required the king of Umma to swear to support him and never, in the future, to encroach on the lands controlled by Lagash. The king of Umma swore oaths in the names of six different gods, and much of the text on the stela is taken up with them. The first oath was in the name of the king of the gods, Enlil: "Eannatum gave the great battle net of the god Enlil to the leader of Gish[a] (i.e. Umma) and made him swear to him by it."[36] The king of Umma then made the same promise to the goddesses Ninhursag (a fertility goddess of the mountains) and Ninki (goddess of plants and daughter of Ninhursag), and to the gods Enki (god of fresh water), Sin (god of the moon, also known as Nanna), and Utu (god of the sun).

Oaths like this, and like the one sworn by Ushumgal years before in the somewhat indecipherable stela from Umma featured at the start of this chapter, continued to be crucial to the resolution of disputes. Only the gods could be trusted to hold a king (or anyone else) to his word. The king of Umma could expect all six deities to punish him if he attempted to move the border in the future.

King Enmetena of Lagash: Warrior, Diplomat, and Benefactor

The oath sworn by the king of Umma may have worked to discourage aggressions for a short time, but a few decades later King Enmetena of Lagash (c. 2450 BCE) was still fighting against Umma over the same territory. Fortunately for historians, he wrote a long summary of the conflict, setting his own actions against the context of decades of what seem, in retrospect, to have been rather futile wars. This is one of the earliest attempts anywhere at writing a history of events. It was certainly also a work of propaganda and self-promotion, but it must have involved some research into past engagements between the two lands, perhaps even looking at old inscriptions.

He started his history not with the life of his great-grandfather King Ur-Nanshe, but with the gods. According to King Enmetena, it had been the god "Enlil, king of all the lands, father of all the gods" who had "fixed the border (between the god) Ningirsu and (the god) Shara," meaning the border between the kingdoms of Lagash and Umma.[37] The border had not been created by men; it had been the work of Enlil himself, the greatest of all gods. This obviously meant that it had to be maintained just where the god had set it and it had to be protected from movement. And so, as he described it, one Lagash king after another had attempted to do just that, against what they saw as the dastardly incursions of the kings and armies of Umma. No doubt the kings of Umma saw things differently.

During Enmetena's reign, his counterpart in Umma was King Il, a former temple administrator who had somehow ascended to the throne. The two men disagreed over more than the position of the border between them. There was also the question of an unpaid loan in barley. King Il was supposed to repay the barley to Enmetena with interest. The quantities listed are staggering—beyond anything remotely possible. The 1,866,240,000 liters that Il had supposedly paid to Enmetena were not enough![38] There is something wrong with these numbers—this amount of barley would fill about 750 Olympic-size swimming pools—so we can ignore the quantity and just note that, to Enmetena's mind, the payments made by Umma did not cover what was owed.

Here is where the inscription gets even more interesting. The scribe wrote that "Enmetena, ruler of Lagash, sent representatives to Il" to deal with the issue of the loan payments and the border with Umma. In a way, this makes perfect sense. Of course, the two kings had to send representatives to one another; they could not have gone in person without losing face. Someone had to demand the loan payments and bring the barley back on their behalf. Someone had to let the king of Umma know that the king of Lagash was unhappy with the position of a new boundary channel that had been dug by the men of Umma. The representatives seem to have presented their king's cause to the king of Umma, and to have done some negotiating. They were, in a word, diplomats.

In this case, the king of Umma was unwilling to accede to Enmetena's demands. He shouted at the envoys from Lagash: "The boundary-channel of Ningirsu and the boundary-channel of Nanshe are mine!"[39] and he swore to move a levee to a location more advantageous to his own kingdom. We do not know whether the envoys returned home with a letter from the king of Umma or whether they just memorized the message. Either way, they provided the means for a conversation to take place between the two kings.

King Enmetena must have used diplomacy at another point in his reign as well. He recorded in a different inscription that "Enmetena, ruler of Lagash, and Lugal-kinesh-dudu, ruler of Uruk, established a brotherhood (pact) (between themselves)."[40] Brotherhood, *nam-shesh* in Sumerian, referred to a formal alliance, and this is the first known mention of it in

Mesopotamian history. Probably the two kings swore an oath not to attack one another and to regularly send envoys between their courts. Diplomacy had a very long history in the region after this; as you will see, kings often preferred to be at peace than at war, and in times of war they liked to have allies—"brother" kings—in other states. It would be fascinating to know what inspired the king of Lagash and the king of Uruk to agree to this alliance. Who proposed it? What were the terms? What did each gain? Had they fought one another in the past? Did they jointly fight against other city-states, such as Umma? We do not know, but Enmetena was ahead of his time. Friendly kings created formal alliances and referred to one another as brothers for centuries after this.

He was ahead of his time in another way as well. As he put it: "He cancelled obligations for Lagash, restored child to mother and mother to child. He cancelled obligations regarding interest-bearing grain loans."[41] This action was just what it sounds like: Enmetena canceled debts for the people of Lagash and reunited mothers with their children who were serving as debt slaves, and vice versa. Can you imagine a more popular act? Interest rates in Sumer were crippling, and few people who had borrowed grain could ever hope to repay both the principal and the interest. A final resort of the borrower was to serve, sometimes with his family members, in the household of the creditor as slaves until the loan was considered to have been paid. Enmetena, in one sweep, restored hope to such people in his city-state. The weight and worry of their unpaid loans were lifted, families were reunited.

The term in Sumerian that we translate as "freedom," *amar-gi*, literally meant "return to mother." It's a sad and touching image. Where we refer to freedom as an abstract ideal, they envisaged the concrete situation of a child moving from a place where she or he was enslaved, back to the safety and comfort of home and mother. Enmetena boasted that he provided this kind of freedom to debt slaves in Lagash.[42]

He probably decided on this action for several reasons. Popularity might have been one of them. It didn't hurt to be appreciated by one's subjects, even in a monarchy. But it might also have been good for the economy. The temples that made most of the loans could afford to absorb the loss, and the interest payments made by borrowers could have been taking wealth away from the court's own income. Whatever the reason, Enmetena was creating the mold of a conspicuously kind monarch, one whose public face was not that of a warrior or taskmaster, but a generous benefactor of his people. Who would want to overthrow such a man?

In his inscriptions, Enmetena also often listed the temples he had built in his kingdom and noted that he had constructed "for the god Ningirsu, the master who loves him, his (Ningirsu's) brewery."[43] Perhaps a brewery is not the first thing you would expect a deity to need, but everyone in Mesopotamia drank beer, the gods included. You may remember that Kushim, who controlled the beer supplies in the Uruk temple complex centuries before this, was one of the first people to be named on a document.

And then there was Enmetena's statue, about which one could write a whole biography of its own (see Fig. 3.6). It was carved of diorite, a hard

Fig. 3.6 Diorite statue of King Enmetena of Lagash, found in Ur, c. 2450 BCE. (Osama Shukir Muhammed Amin FRCP (Glasg))

stone imported from what is now Oman, and it stands 76 centimeters (30 inches) tall. Enmetena wears a flounced wool skirt pulled up almost to his chest, his feet are bare, and his hands are folded over his bare chest in prayer. Unfortunately his head is missing, but an inscription survives on the statue, and it tells us not just that the figure represents King Enmetena, but even the name of the statue and where it was placed: "At that time Enmetena fashioned a statue of himself, named it 'Enmetena (is the) Beloved of the god Enlil' and set it up before the god Enlil in the temple."[44] The statue could stand in for the king, perpetually praying in front of the greatest of the gods. He continued, calling on his personal god to also put in a good word constantly with Enlil: "Enmetena, who built the E-ada (temple)—may his personal god, the god Shul-utul, forever pray to the god Enlil for the sake of Enmetena."[45]

This sounds a little like a cheat—Enmetena could get on with his life and not worry about praying to Enlil. His statue and his personal god could take care of this for him. But if you look more carefully you see that the statue inscription actually gives us an insight into a bigger idea, one that is alien to us in the modern world. The statue was not just a representation of the king. To the mind of a Mesopotamian, a statue contained some part of the very being of the person it represented. Enmetena was not avoiding prayer—he would now be doing it all the time because the part of him that resided in the statue was perpetually praying on his behalf. The statue could also receive offerings. It had a life force of its own that even outlived the king. After his death it became a focus of rituals, as we will see.

At some point, probably long after Enmetena's death, someone decided to rob the statue of its power—to kill it, in a way—by lopping off the head. And then perhaps it lay in the ground for centuries. Ultimately, archaeologists found the statue on the citadel in the city of Ur, not Lagash, and not in an Early Dynastic building but in a much later occupation level, one that dated to the Babylonian king Nabonidus who ruled this region almost 2,000 years after Enmetena.[46] It may have been a museum object, of sorts, in the Babylonian king's personal collection. He liked to collect objects that were already very ancient, even in his time. We don't know where Nabonidus found Enmetena's statue before bringing it into his collection. It is now on display in the Iraq Museum in Baghdad.[47]

Royal Tombs of Ur

Enmetena's tomb has not been found, nor have the tombs of any of the kings of Lagash or Umma. But royal tombs from this era were excavated in the nearby city of Ur and they were extraordinary. Ur was southwest of Lagash, on the coast of the Lower Sea (the Persian Gulf), and it seems to have been subject to Lagash at some points during the Early Dynastic period.

The tombs at Ur were excavated in the 1920s, and they made for sensational news at the time. They were excavated by a team led by a British archaeologist named Leonard Woolley. He employed many workmen on the site at Ur, who uncovered literally thousands of tombs during their excavations. Of those, about 660 were burials of people from the Early Dynastic period.[48] Most were simple graves whose occupants took little with them in death—some jewelry, some pots, a dagger, that sort of thing. They were almost all buried in a flexed position with their hands near their mouths, and most of them held a cup.[49]

Sixteen of the tombs, though, were much more elaborate, and Woolley decided that they were the tombs of royalty. Although there have been plenty of arguments over the century since he found them, about whether the deceased were indeed kings and queens, most of the evidence does support Woolley's original conclusion.[50]

Many of the royal tombs had been robbed extensively in ancient times, but some of them still retained many of the luxury gifts that had been buried with the monarchs, so Woolley was very careful as he uncovered them. He and his wife Katherine did most of the excavation of the royal tombs by themselves. They were so careful, in fact, that Woolley admitted to finding the work tedious at times, as he lay on the ground, meticulously brushing away dirt from tiny beads and fragile pieces of gold and shell.[51] Fortunately, the Woolleys kept surprisingly careful records and photographs in comparison with some other excavations of the same era.

The finds in Ur were newsworthy in part because of the vast quantities of gold and other precious goods that were found, and for historians they were important because very few royal tombs had been discovered in Mesopotamia. (This remains true.) Unlike their Egyptian counterparts of the same era, the Mesopotamian kings did not place giant monuments over their tombs, so they are not easy to find.

Two of the earliest of the royal tombs at Ur were constructed a few decades before the time that Ur-Nanshe ruled in Lagash. The dead rulers in these earliest tombs spent the afterlife in elaborate buildings with thick plastered stone walls and vaulted ceilings over each room, both houses featuring four rooms connected by doorways.[52] The main entry doors were topped with stone arches. They looked like expensively constructed houses that happened to be underground. Stone was not easily obtained, so its use marked these structures as important.

Both of these tombs had been thoroughly robbed in ancient times, leaving the rooms empty except for a few objects and some glittering fragments on the floor that hinted at the riches that must have been buried with the ruler. A few earrings and pins survived in these mausoleums, along with leaves made of gold, a silver gaming board, and some cups. If the robbers thought that these riches were trifles worth abandoning, what must they have stolen? The possibilities boggle the mind.

Woolley found, however, that one corner of the farthest room in one of the buildings had somehow escaped the robbers' attack.[53] In it, he discovered the skull of a man who had been buried wearing a cap decorated with thousands of tiny lapis lazuli beads. Next to his head was one of the most dramatic finds from any of the royal tombs: a narrow wooden box decorated with a mosaic of shell and lapis lazuli.[54] It came to be known as the "Standard of Ur," though its original purpose is uncertain. It is diminutive, each face not much bigger than a sheet of legal-sized paper, 47 centimeters (18.5 inches) in length and just 20 centimeters (8 inches) high. It is hard to imagine it being carried into battle as a standard around which the troops might rally, as Woolley proposed. At the top of a pole one would not necessarily even be able to make out the tiny figures on it. Another possibility is that it was the soundbox of a musical instrument.

On both long sides of the box, the rectangular scenes are divided into three levels, or registers, like the earlier Uruk Vase or the Stela of the Vultures, with pale figures laid out in single file against the rich blue of the lapis lazuli. On one side the artist created an image of a time of peace (see Fig. 3.7). Rows of men and animals (donkeys, sheep, goats, and cattle) walk on the lower two registers, some of the men carrying bags or bearing packs on their backs. In the top register is a banquet attended by seven men. The tallest among them was almost certainly the king and was probably the same man with whom the object was buried. Here he presides over the

Fig. 3.7 Peace side of the Standard of Ur, found in the Royal Tombs of Ur, mid-third millennium BCE. (© The Trustees of the British Museum)

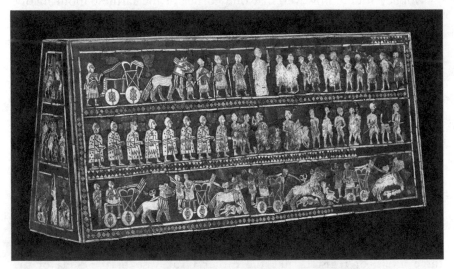

Fig. 3.8 War side of the Standard of Ur, found in the Royal Tombs of Ur, mid-third millennium BCE. (© The Trustees of the British Museum)

richness of his land, which is a place of music, feasting, abundance, tame animals, dutiful servants, and orderly behavior.

On the other side, the three registers tell a different tale (see Fig. 3.8). The bottom register depicts four matching chariots and their charioteers. Like a graphic novel, read from left to right, the first chariot is moving slowly, the second, in front of it, is going more quickly, the third faster still, and the fourth at a gallop, the donkeys' front legs raised up, their heads straining against the harnesses. Beneath the feet of the front three chariots lie the naked, bleeding figures of the enemy dead. The second register shows Sumerian soldiers outfitted in identical capes and helmets, each carrying a spear in both hands, along with prisoners of war, some of them naked, some bleeding, being led in a miserable procession that continues onto the top register where they are presented to the king, now standing and facing them, a mace in his hand. His importance is underscored by his considerable height and by the floor-length robe that he wears. Behind him stand four attendants, along with his waiting chariot.

In these two scenes, and with no writing, the artist has told a tale of a leader who is dominant in both war and peace and whose world is orderly, even in the aftermath of a bloody battle. Every man seems to know his role. And they are indeed all men, with the possible exception of one of the musicians at the banquet whose long hair might indicate a woman, though the figure's clothes seem male. In spite of the prominence of women in the courts and the temples at this time, which we will explore in the next chapter, this was certainly a society in which men were dominant.

This king of the royal standard was not the only inhabitant of his tomb. A rectangular depression in the floor of one room would have held another coffin,[55] as did a similar depression in another room.[56] And scattered in disarray were other human bones. Woolley estimated that there were perhaps five bodies near the entryway,[57] one skull in one room,[58] and four bodies in another,[59] though two of them were missing their skulls. To judge from what seem to have been three main burials in three of the four rooms, this early tomb seems likely to have been constructed for more than one member of the royal family, serving as a family burial place and reused over several generations.

Tombs like this have been discovered at a site called Tall Ahmad al Hattu, but from an earlier period than the tombs at Ur.[60] At Tall Ahmad, as at Ur, elite people had been buried in houses for the dead. Successive burials had taken place in a single underground building, with the previous occupants swept unceremoniously aside to make space for the latest burial.[61] One burial chamber there boasted eleven skulls and assorted long bones, presumably moved out of the way when a new funeral took place.[62] Does this explain the skulls and partial skeletons in the four-chamber tomb at Ur? Perhaps.

But after these first two multiroom tombs, the slightly later burials of Early Dynastic kings and queens at Ur included many more skeletons, and it is clear that, in these tombs, they were not the result of successive individual burials. The bodies were all buried at the same time. This might sound macabre, and it probably was. The conclusion seems inescapable that people, sometimes dozens of people, were killed and buried during the course of the royal funerals at Ur.

The details of these deaths, though, are hard to discern, as are the rituals of the funerals. Eight of the tombs, in addition to the two I have already discussed, included buildings to house the dead monarchs underground.[63] The later built tombs were considerably smaller, however, than those in the first two burials. They did not have four rooms—usually just one room was built. It contained the coffin of the dead king or queen, along with sumptuous gifts (some of which escaped the tomb robbers). Unlike the earlier tombs, some of these tombs had been built in a corner of a larger pit which could contain more gifts . . . and people.

Woolley believed that the people were court attendants who had walked, alive, into the tomb pits (possibly singing and playing music), and had then drunk poison in order to voluntarily die with their ruler, ready to assist him or her in the afterlife. However, a team of researchers has done CT scans of two of the attendants' skulls (from two different tombs), and these paint a very different picture.[64] Both of the victims had been hit in the head with a sharp pointed object, and each had been hit hard enough for the weapon to have punctured his or her skull. It seems that the skeletons in the royal tombs did not provide evidence for a peaceful group suicide, but rather a mass murder.

The original funeral of the king or queen might well have included music and feasting, as Woolley had proposed, and the people who ended up in the tomb with the king or queen might even have been part of that ceremony. But the killing of the attendants might have happened days or even weeks later. After the attendants had been killed, their bodies were dressed in fine clothes and arranged in the tomb like mannequins, posed as though playing music, leading oxen, or standing guard. Tellingly, the skulls showed signs of having been heated and treated with mercury, both of which would have delayed putrefaction of the bodies and made for a more convincing tableau.[65]

Strangely enough, Woolley and the excavators also found five burial pits that seem to have included only attendants, apparently without any sign of the person they were supposed to have attended.[66] Woolley thought that there had been tomb chambers and dead monarchs with these victims and that these must have been destroyed by later tombs. But perhaps these pits were additions for one of the other burials. Or perhaps the dead king or queen, priest, or priestess was indeed among the other skeletons, remarkable only for the extravagance of his or her dress.[67]

Woolley called one of these group burials the "Great Death Pit," which certainly made for a lot of publicity.[68] In it were seventy-four skeletons, most of them women dressed in what must have been elaborate gowns (though those had disintegrated) and decked out in jewelry—pins, necklaces, earrings, and hair ribbons made of gold, silver, carnelian, and lapis lazuli, all of which had been imported from great distances and would have been worth a fortune. The bodies were lined up in neat rows on the floor of the pit. Three lyres were also placed in this pit, ready to be used by the dead women to provide music in the afterlife.

One skeleton in the Great Death Pit (number 61, as designated by Woolley) stood out from the others—although she had not been placed in a built chamber, she was distinguished in several ways from the women around her. For one thing, the cup she held was made of silver while those of the other individuals were made of clay, and she was adorned with more jewelry than anyone else.[69] A cylinder seal found on another of the skeletons might have identified her profession. It read "Child of the Gipar."[70] The Gipar was the name of the palace in Ur that was occupied by the high priestess of the god Nanna, the moon god who made his home in Ur. Perhaps skeleton 61 had been the high priestess.

A number of the rulers for whom these burials were staged were queens. One of them can be identified by her cylinder seal. She was named Puabi and she had one of the most extravagant burials of all, accompanied in death by twenty people, along with two oxen and a cart. She would have been contemporary with one of the earlier Lagash royal couples, perhaps King Ur-Nanshe and Queen Min-bara-Abzu.[71] Might the earliest royal couples in Lagash have engaged in the same kind of funerary practices as the rulers of Ur? Might they, too, have had attendants killed to join them in the afterlife? Until their tombs are found, if that ever happens, we have no way of knowing.

Scholars have come up with many theories to account for the presence of the dead attendants in the early Ur royal tombs, but they have reached no consensus. It may not, in the end, be something that even needs a specifically Mesopotamian explanation. The earliest kings of Egypt did the same thing, as did the earliest kings in Nubia (at a later date), along with some Chinese kings during the early Shang dynasty, and others later still in the New World in Panama and Peru.[72]

The practice never seems to have lasted long in any of these places. Perhaps the murder of attendants at the death of a ruler was a symptom of a time when kingship was relatively new in each region and the limits of royal power had not been completely set. If one needed servants in this life, surely one needed them in the next life as well. Having courtiers killed and buried conveniently close by in one's own tomb assured that they would be right there for eternity.

More telling, perhaps, is the fact that the practice stopped. It cannot have been a particularly popular tradition among those selected for death, or for their families, and it might also have handicapped the heirs to the ruler, who may have lost a considerable amount of court expertise—which died along with the attendants to the previous king or queen. In Egypt and China, murdered attendants were replaced by models or paintings of people who could miraculously come to life in the netherworld. That does not seem to have been true in Mesopotamia.

Perhaps the latest of the royal tombs at Ur was of a king or prince named Meskalamdug.[73] His coffin had disintegrated but the impression of the wood remained in the clay around it when Woolley was excavating.[74] Both inside and outside the coffin, Woolley found a staggering quantity of goods, including ceremonial weapons such as a gold dagger and electrum axes. Both would have been useless in battle, but they provided gleaming evidence of the man's power and prestige. His name was engraved on a lamp and a gold bowl. Woolley wrote that "The offerings outside the coffin were bewildering in their number."[75] Objects of gold, silver, bronze, copper, lapis lazuli, diorite, and shell filled the burial shaft. There were no people with him, and there were also no models of people. Meskalamdug was going to the afterlife alone, dependent, perhaps, on his heirs to supply him with food and drink to keep him going through eternity in the netherworld.

The scribes of the Early Dynastic period didn't let us know what people believed about the afterlife during this era. To judge from the burials, though, they thought that you could take your wealth and power with you when you died. Even poor people were optimistic enough to include small treasures and pots of food for the dead in their tombs. Oddly enough, this concept seems to have been replaced by one in which the people believed that the dead lived on only in a dark, underground, comfortless world where kings had no more power than anyone else. This, at least, was the way the netherworld was described in two later literary works, the Epic of Gilgamesh and the Descent of Ishtar.

The scribes did not let us down, however, when it came to leaving a record of the economy of the era. Tablets continued to be covered with details of Early Dynastic palace and temple administrations, which we will explore in the next chapter.

Chapter 4

A Queen, a Reformer, and Weavers

King Enmetena of Lagash, whom we met in Chapter 3, was succeeded by his son, whose reign was short,[1] and who proved to be the last of the dynasty founded by Ur-Nanshe. The throne then passed to a man named Enentarzi, who had been a priest during Enmetena's reign.[2] His reign was also brief—just five years. The six-year reign of Enentarzi's son, Lugalanda, was barely longer than those of his immediate predecessors, but we will pause here, because the life and career of his wife Baranamtara is particularly well documented and provides a vivid picture of an Early Dynastic royal estate and its personnel.

Queen Baranamtara of Lagash: An Administrator, Diplomat, and Religious Functionary

When Lugalanda took the throne in Lagash, around 2400 BCE, queen Baranamtara did not immediately take over control of the queen's estate, as might have been expected. Instead, her mother-in-law, the Queen Mother Dimtur, continued to control the E-Mi (literally the "house of women") for another year.[3] Perhaps during that time Baranamtara was learning from her mother-in-law, so that she would be able to take over the whole administrative machine effectively when the time came.

Meanwhile Baranamtara commissioned a new cylinder seal to be carved for her with an inscription suitable to her new rank: "Baranamtara, wife of Lugalanda, ruler of Lagash."[4] It's a big seal, with three registers of images, each of them showing heroes flanked by rearing animals (see Fig. 4.1). This type of imagery was reserved for the seals of people with power.

The E-Mi palace was located in the city of Girsu, which was the capital of the city-state of Lagash at this time. The E-Mi had traditionally been a temple estate, dedicated to the goddess Bawa, but the queen had taken over the management of the estate at some point before Baranamtara's time. Running the E-Mi must have been a full-time job once Baranamtara took it over. Although it was called a "house" (the word was "*e*" in Sumerian), the E-Mi constituted much more than just a physical building. It owned 4,465 hectares (more than 17 square miles) of fields.[5] These fields produced vast quantities of barley. During her husband's reign as king, Baranamtara's name appeared on records concerning all aspects of the grain production of the E-Mi. She oversaw the sowing of the seed, harvesting (which took a large workforce), storing the grain, and grinding it into flour. To provide

Fig. 4.1 Impression of the seal of Queen Baranamtara of Lagash, c. 2400 BCE. (Erich Lessing/Art Resource, NY/Art Resource)

water to the fields, canals stretched throughout the E-Mi's territory, and those required regular maintenance. More land was allocated to reed beds, vegetable gardens, and orchards. About 100 fishermen also worked for the queen.[6] The palace owned sheep and goats, cattle and pigs, and supported workers who cared for the animals. A vast workforce of about 700 people answered to Baranamtara.[7] Among them, about 250 men in senior positions were awarded the use of subsistence fields as their payment, though they also received payments in barley four or five months a year. The other 450 lower-ranking workers were provided with barley allocations every month.[8]

Among these lower-ranking workers, a large cohort at the E-Mi was involved in producing textiles from the wool of the estate's sheep; this was a source of wealth for the queen and for the kingdom. The women who worked in spinning and weaving were assigned to teams of twenty, each with a supervisor. The supervisors were mostly women, though men could also be found in these positions.[9] We will return to them later in this chapter. The workforce of the E-Mi grew considerably during the time that Baranamtara was in control.[10]

It is odd, really, how rarely the king, Lugalanda, is mentioned in the 1,800 tablets that survived from the E-Mi. Did the royal couple live separately from one another in their respective palaces? We don't know. They certainly worked separately, with dominion over their respective estates, neither needing to supervise the work of the other. King Lugalanda's palace archive has not been found, but we have to assume that its contents would be similar to those of his wife's estate. The one difference is that there is no evidence for a military role for the queen, whereas the king certainly was responsible for the troops of Lagash, like his predecessors. (Lugalanda did not, though, leave any royal inscriptions that mentioned military campaigns, so perhaps his short reign was not marked by warfare.)[11]

Baranamtara was the mother of at least two princesses, named Munus-saga and Geme-Bawa,[12] whose births were cause for great celebration. Offerings were made of sheep and goats both to living relatives and dead ancestors on the day of a daughter's birth, and a scribe kept track of the details. For one of the baby girls, it is just about possible to figure out her birthday based on clues in the text, but this was rare.[13] Mesopotamians didn't keep track of their birthdays or their ages.

King Lugalanda and Queen Baranamtara also maintained separate diplomatic relationships.[14] An important alliance for Baranamtara was with the queen of the city-state of Adab, which lay just upriver of Lagash; the two states shared a border. Adab was independent of Lagash, with its own ruler, whose wife was named Nin-gishkimti. She and Baranamtara kept in touch and on good terms by sending their agents back and forth between their palaces. Nin-gishkimti's agent was given no professional title—not messenger or scribe or merchant. He was just "her man."[15]

The agents probably relayed messages (though the queens' letters have not survived) and brought along gifts, which were recorded in the archives. The agents of the two queens traveled together; this was a practice that was to continue for more than a thousand years, as the same types of diplomatic ties formed, generation after generation, across the Near East.

We know of three occasions when the agents traveled between the two cities with gifts from one queen to the other, but it is likely that they made many more visits.[16] On one occasion, two messengers arrived in the land of Lagash with gifts for Queen Baranamtara from Queen Nin-gishkimti.[17] You might think that the goods in each land would be pretty much identical, given how close they were to one another geographically, but Lagash was a center for the copper trade, which meant that the queens had different gifts for one another. The agent from Adab brought ten female donkeys, a footstool, and two female figurines, one made of wood and the other of ivory, from his queen for Baranamtara.[18] In return, Baranamtara sent the queen of Adab 120 minas (43 kilograms, 120 pounds) of copper, along with 5 minas (2.25 kilograms, 5 pounds) of tin-bronze. Baranamtara also generously provided a personal gift to the agent from Adab: she gave him two garments and a jar of scented oil. Likewise, when Baranamtara's agent delivered her gifts to Nin-gishkimti, the queen of Adab gave him a set of clothing.[19] These types of rewards for messengers and envoys who maintained the diplomatic contacts between kingdoms also had a long life; a millennium later, a man carrying a letter and gifts to a foreign court could still expect to receive a valuable gift when he arrived.

Baranamtara's diplomatic ties extended farther afield as well, and this helps to explain how she had access to copper to give to her ally, Queen Nin-gishkimti. The land of Dilmun, located on what is now the island of Bahrain in the Persian Gulf, was an important trading partner for Lagash. This had probably already been true all the way back in the reign of

Ur-Nanshe, but for this era more evidence survives. This includes a letter between two officials, pertaining to a gift from the queen of Dilmun to the queen of Lagash.[20] The latter might have been Baranamtara. The queen of Dilmun sent 120 minas (pounds) of copper—just the same amount sent by Baranamtara to the queen of Adab, in fact—along with some more personal gifts, namely fifteen baskets of dates and three linen garments.[21] Dilmun was famous for its delicious dates, and no doubt linen garments would have been a delightful change from the hotter woolen clothes that were the norm in Mesopotamia.

Other documents found at Lagash show that regular trade, not just the gift exchange between the royal families, took place with Dilmun. Lacking a common currency, merchants from each land paid for goods in materials that they had in abundance. When a Lagash merchant named Urenki traveled to Dilmun (which he did at least once for Queen Dimtur, Baranamtara's predecessor,[22] and several times for King Lugalanda[23]), he took with him barley, wheat, lard, and flour, which were local products, along with cedar, which had been imported from the hilly lands far to the northwest, and perfumed oil, which required imported plants for its scent. Urenki traded these items in Dilmun in exchange for hundreds of pounds of copper.[24]

To put this in perspective, Dilmun was about 850 kilometers (530 miles) from Lagash, and Urenki would have traveled most of that way, if not the whole way, by boat. Seaworthy boats had been built long before cities developed, though their captains probably stayed within view of the coast as they traveled. It would have been a difficult journey, but evidently was worth the risk. Copper was needed everywhere for making bronze. The copper was not mined in Dilmun, though. It had come from even farther away, from what is now Oman (ancient Magan), where archaeologists have found evidence for extensive mining and smelting.[25] Dilmun had become an international center for trade, with goods and merchants meeting there from regions to the south and east, as well as from Mesopotamia and the cedar forests to the north. The rich Mesopotamian fields produced more food than was needed for the local population, so it could be used to trade for materials that they did not have.

It would be interesting to know more about the figurines that the queen of Adab sent to Baranamtara. Figurines and statues were not just works of art in the minds of the people of Early Dynastic Mesopotamia; they had a kind of built-in power and often bore inscriptions attesting to this. We

have already seen this in the case of the statue of Enmetena, the earlier ruler
of Lagash, which was placed in the temple to pray eternally for the king's
well-being.

Even people who were not members of the royal family could commission
such statues (see Fig. 4.2). A cache of twelve of them was found in a temple
at a Mesopotamian site called Tell Asmar, apparently put there for much the
same reason.[26] Several of these figures, which were created at the beginning
of the Early Dynastic period, held cups in their hands to pour libations to
the gods on behalf of the donors whom they depicted.[27] Other figures in
this group had their hands clasped in prayer, in the style of the statue of king
Enmetena. Perhaps the queen of Adab sent a figurine of herself to pray on
her behalf in a temple in Baranamtara's city.

Fig. 4.2 Alabaster statue of a praying woman, c. 2600–2500 BCE. (Metropolitan
Museum of Art)

Baranamtara's role as queen extended beyond administration and diplomacy; she was also an important figure in the local religious rites. At festivals for the gods during this time, it was usually Baranamtara, not her husband the king, who was responsible for making the sacrifices. A typical text recording the expenses of a festival ends with the statement "At the festival of eating malt of (the goddess) Nanshe, Baranamtara, wife of Lugalanda, ruler of Lagash, made the sacrifice."[28] Festivals were held throughout the year and each one took several days. The gods were provided with meat (from sheep and goats), fish, beer, oil, dates, bread, garlic, and flour[29]—essential ingredients for an elaborate meal. Baranamtara did not stay only in the capital city of Girsu for these festivals; sometimes she traveled to other parts of the city-state as well. Although she was not described as a priestess, she took care of the gods and goddesses all the same.

The festivals of the goddess Nanshe seem to have been of particular importance to the people of Lagash, and Baranamtara's role in them was extensive. The largest of the festivals was the curiously named "festival of eating malt of Nanshe."[30]

The festival lasted a full eight days[31] and took place at the beginning of the agricultural growing season.[32] On the first day, Baranamtara traveled from the capital city Girsu to the city of Lagash, bringing with her a sacrificial sheep for the god Ningirsu in his temple. Presumably she traveled with a large entourage, and she may have been transported in a chariot. On the second day, she dedicated more offerings—one was brought by a chariot to "the canal of the marsh," while others went to three other deities in three temples in Lagash. Then Baranamtara moved on to the third great city of the kingdom: Nigin, seven kilometers (4.3 miles) southeast of Lagash.[33] A text notes that "The woman who came from Lagash (the queen) went through the gate of (the temple) E-Pa and brought a lamb. (It was) the second day."[34] Even more offerings to even more gods took place in Nigin on the third day. Some of the offerings were also given to statues of past kings and queens of Lagash. It was not until the fifth day that Baranamtara returned to Lagash; on this day the offerings were made to the great god of Lagash, Ningirsu. Little is known about the rest of the festival, but by the eighth day Baranamtara presumably had returned home to her city of Girsu.

By making this journey around the kingdom, Baranamtara was doing more than appeasing all the gods and goddesses and providing them with food and drink, though that was certainly important. She was reminding the people of the kingdom of her legitimacy as queen and bringing her subjects together in a shared celebration.

Baranamtara commissioned the creation of a statue of herself during her lifetime, which later received offerings during festivals. The royal statues must have taken up considerable space in a temple. Eight are mentioned by name as receiving individual offerings, and others were grouped together and received collective offerings. Besides the statue of Enmetena, there was one representing King Ur-Nanshe (who founded the dynasty), both of which received offerings, as did a statue of Enmetena's wife Nin-hilisud. After Baranamtara's death, her statue joined this group, along with a statue of her husband Lugalanda.

Shasha, the queen who later took over control of the E-Mi from Baranamtara, also came to be represented by a statue that joined this group, and, remarkably, she made offerings to her own statue during her lifetime.[35] One did not need to be dead, apparently, to warrant such attention. And the statues were not just of queens and kings; other important figures from the past also had statues that received offerings, even including a temple administrator from Enmetena's reign, an influential man named Dudu.[36] The royal and elite statues received food and drink on a regular basis.

Although these dead royals were not called gods, in the minds of the people of Lagash, the distinction between immortal gods and mortal monarchs might have been a little hazy. Statues of royal family members stood in temples, just like statues of gods. Both the statues of dead monarchs and those of gods needed food, drink, and clothing.

It is often argued that most Mesopotamian royals were not divine, in contrast to Egyptian kings who were, but the hard-and-fast line between god and human that we perceive now was probably a lot more porous in the mind of an ancient Mesopotamian. The average person might have had trouble distinguishing between the divinity of deities and deceased royals. It's clear that queens were in the same category as kings in this regard—both required offerings. In fact, there were almost as many queens as kings among the venerated statues.

This was not an "ancestor cult," not only because the statues were not exactly worshiped, but also because many of the statues were not of ancestors of Lugalanda. The dynasty started by Ur-Nanshe had ended before this time, but the kings of the dynasty were still venerated. The last of the queens to maintain offerings to the dead elites, Queen Shasha, was not a descendant of any of the people whose statues she cared for.[37] The statues were, however, of people who in the past had led the kingdom of Lagash, and this seems to have been the reason why they were important—not necessarily because of a blood relationship. If treated well, the dead kings and queens, in the form of their statues, could help the kingdom continue to prosper.

The Funeral of Baranamtara

The royal leaders, male and female alike, also received lavish funerals. It's not clear how Baranamtara died, but it must have been during the reign of her husband's successor. Her funeral was planned with the attention owed to a great leader, so there seems to have been no hostility between the two successive royal couples. Two records have survived listing the people who were paid rations by Shasha, the next queen, in honor of her predecessor. The names on the list were described as "people (who) were mourning in the death rituals for Baranamtara," and more than 300 of them were present on both days of the funeral.[38]

   Of great importance were *gala* priests, who were specialists in lamentation. They played the lyre and sang at funerals. No fewer than seventy-two of them attended the first day of Baranamtara's funeral, and ninety-two of them were present on the second day. Imagine a massed choir of ninety-two singers accompanied by the sound of their lyres; the music must have carried across the city. The *gala* priests received payment in bread and beer for their participation: three and a half loaves each on the first day, and three more loaves and a jug of beer on the second day. Joining them on the second day was the highest-ranking member of their group, the chief *gala* priest, who received sixteen loaves of bread for his participation. *Gala* priests were men, who were sometimes married and had children, but they were often classed with women in ration lists, and their songs were apparently sung in Emesal, a dialect of Sumerian that was associated with ritual but also considered to be a women's language. The *gala* priests seem not to have been constrained by normal expectations of gender that prevailed at the time for most of the population.[39]

An Early Dynastic sculpture of a musician named Ur-Nanshe (not to be confused with the king of the same name), which was discovered in the ancient Syrian city of Mari, may have represented a person who might now be described as gender nonconforming (see Fig. 4.3).[40] The inscription on the statue is clearly written about a man: "For Iblul-Il, king of Mari, Ur-Nanshe, the great musician, has dedicated his statue to the goddess Inana-[...]."[41] But the statue's gender is ambiguous; the musician has a somewhat feminine physique, his face has no beard, but he wears male clothing. Some scholars believe that he may have been castrated,[42] though others disagree. Although he does not describe himself as a *gala* priest, Ur-Nanshe may well have been one.

Fig. 4.3 Statue of a musician named Ur-Nanshe, from Mari, Early Dynastic period. (Renée Lessing-Kronfuss/Art Resource)

Women of a particular status or behavior were often associated with the *gala* priests at funerals. They were usually referred to as "crying old women," though at Baranamtara's funeral they were called "wives of the elders"—seventy of them present on the first day and forty-eight on the second.[43] They were provided with bread and beer as though they were paid professional mourners. Although this suggests a detached attitude to the queen, if these eminent women had worked with her during her lifetime, they might well also have been sincerely mourning her death. The same is probably true of Baranamtara's ten "brothers by birth" who came to the first day of the funeral and were also paid. The people named may have been a mix of paid professional mourners, relatives, and friends.

Also listed were slave women—148 on the first day and perhaps more on the second day, each of them provided with three loaves of bread and some beer on both days. Enslaved people in ancient Mesopotamia included prisoners of war, debtors paying off their loans, people sold as children by their impoverished parents, and individuals born into slavery—we will return to the subject of slavery later.[44] The enslaved women at the funeral might well originally have been prisoners of war. Baranamtara's funeral was probably an even bigger event than these texts suggest. Many more people would have attended than just those being paid to be there. Thousands might have gathered,[45] drawn by the music and the wish to witness a dramatic and unusual ceremony, and to pay their respects to their former queen, who would have been a familiar figure in their lives.

The dead queen was sent to the afterlife with elaborate gifts. There is no record of these for Baranamtara's funeral, but lists survive from the Syrian city of Ebla at around this same time. There, the gifts for a queen's funeral were similar to the ones she received for her wedding.

A list of gifts that Baranamtara and her husband had previously provided, either for a royal funeral or wedding, was found at Girsu and it gives a sense of how a queen or princess might be buried (or perhaps married) in style. These goods had been accumulated by the royal couple, and the recipient was their son's wife.[46] We just do not know if they were celebrating a marriage or mourning a death at the time.

The wealth that Baranamtara and Lugalanda provided on this occasion was impressive—eight items of clothing, a team of donkeys, a slave girl, several large wooden items including a sledge, a bed, a chair, and a footstool, plus plenty of small, valuable items made of stone, copper, silver, gold, carnelian, wood, and ivory. These included eleven pieces of jewelry, eight containers of various kinds, a mirror, and a pot of perfumed oil. These sound, of course, like the types of things a princess would need during life, rather than after death. They would make up a sensible and generous gift to a new daughter-in-law to help her in her married life and her new role in the royal family. With these items, she would now have the kinds of clothing and jewelry appropriate to her status, along with some fine furniture and vessels for her household. The donkeys and slave girl seem as though they would be much more useful to the couple in life than after death. The problem is that the term for the event when they were sent is ambiguous, and some scholars do think these were funerary gifts. The riches buried in the royal tombs at Ur show that members of the royal family could be sent to the afterlife with exactly these types of goods. If so, what should we make of the slave girl who is mentioned in the text?

It does not seem likely that she was sacrificed. By Baranamtara's time, the practice of killing attendants and placing them in royal tombs seems to have stopped in Ur, and there is no mention of it in the funerary texts from Lagash. The servants and enslaved women who were named as receiving bread when they were mourning for Baranamtara fortunately do not seem to have ended up dead themselves.

King Urukagina: A Reformer

Baranamtara was a widow when she died, her husband Lugalanda having predeceased her. She had seen some remarkable changes in her later years, because the king who had taken the throne was a reformer; he seems to have been the first individual in Mesopotamian history to boast of his efforts to curb corruption among his officials and civil servants.

Unfortunately, we really do not know how to pronounce this king's name. It was written in one way in cuneiform, but it is transcribed in many different ways by modern scholars. The king may have been named Urukagina, Uruinimgina, Irikagina, Erekagina, or even Eri'enimgennak![47] The first two signs in his name, URU and KA, can be read in a number of different ways, resulting in different possible meanings for the name, hence the confusion. Since there is no consensus, I will call him Urukagina here.

In any event, he was not the son of Lugalanda, but he doesn't seem to have overthrown his predecessor in a violent way.[48]

Urukagina (mid–twenty-fourth century BCE) wanted life in Lagash to go back to the way it had been in the past, or at least to the way he imagined it had been, in some earlier, less decadent time. This would be a way of life that would restore (as he saw it) an appropriate respect for the state god Ningirsu, who would no doubt approve of his actions. Urukagina claimed, using the third person about himself, that "he (re)established the norms of old; the commands which his king the divine Ningirsu had commanded him."[49] Many people, he believed, had been getting rich at the expense of the state and the temples; those people were to be removed from their positions, and even his own royal court was to become a religious institution. "He put the house of the ruler (and) the fields of the ruler in (the hands of) the divine Ningirsu his king."[50]

These reforms had an impact on Baranamtara's palace, the E-Mi, as well. Urukagina determined that it should be dedicated to the goddess Bawa (as perhaps it had been in the past): "he put the house of the E-Mi (and) the fields of the E-Mi (into the hands of) the divine Bawa, his queen." So the E-Mi would no longer be the "house of women," it would be the E-Bawa, or "house of (the goddess) Bawa." But the records found there show that, after the reforms were enacted, nothing much changed in practice. After Baranamtara's death, the queen in charge of the queen's palace, now Urukagina's wife Shasha, continued to administer the estate with its fields, canals, orchards, flocks of sheep and goats, and dozens of weavers.

Zum, Igi-bar, and Emete: Weaving Supervisors at Girsu

Among the hundreds of workers listed on the ration lists drawn up by the queen's scribes were three women named Zum, Emete, and Igi-bar. (Actually, the last woman's full name was Igi-barluti, but the scribes often referred to her as Igi-bar, so I will do the same.) They were all weavers and we can follow their careers as they moved up in the hierarchy of the textile workshops thanks to the work of several scholars who have recently analyzed the administrative tablets in creative ways.[51]

Weavers in the E-Mi were assigned to teams of up to twenty women (the weavers there were all women). Some worked in wool, some in linen. The members of each team presumably sat there together at the horizontal looms (known as ground-looms) in the palace workshops, day in, day out, making the bolts of cloth for which southern Mesopotamia was famous (see Fig. 4.5).[52]

They received monthly wages that varied in amount. Some women always received more than others, some could be suddenly paid less, then the amount went up again, for reasons we can only guess at. Some of the women had small children and were given more, so as to provide for them. Girls worked on the looms next to grown women and were paid for their efforts—perhaps they had been in the workshops since infancy at their mothers' sides, or perhaps they were orphans.

In any event, the weavers would have known one another well. Zum was one of the wool weavers and, when we first hear of her shortly before Urukagina took power, she was on a team of twenty women overseen by a man named Malga. Zum was at the top of the list when the wages were recorded. Lists were almost always hierarchical, so Zum must have been the most senior or influential woman on her team. She would have been seen as a relatively important person within the world of the textile workshops of the palace. Zum was also paid more than the rest of the women. Whereas the other women on her weaving team received a monthly allotment of 18 silas of barley, Zum was paid 24 silas.[53] A sila was about a liter, so this was not a great deal of food on which to live for a month, but 24 silas certainly would have helped her family's livelihood. Men who worked for the E-Mi in other roles were paid considerably more than women (usually 48 silas per month in this period),[54] and children received 12 silas of barley, so a family could bring in plenty of wages between them.

Unlike some of the other women, Zum had no young children to feed at this point—no sons or daughters were listed next to her name. Perhaps her children had grown by now and were working independently. It's likely that she did have children; almost every woman did, whether biological or adopted. Zum also probably had a husband (unless he had died before this), but the women's husbands weren't named on the lists.

Zum's overseer, Malga, was probably in charge of assigning the weavers to particular projects, weighing and measuring out the wool that they would use, and keeping an eye on the quality of the weaving. Spinning the wool was the responsibility of a different department in the E-Mi, and it was a time-consuming activity. It has been estimated that one piece of cloth the size of a modern sheet for a single bed would have required 47 kilometers (29 miles) of woolen thread, which, using the hand-spinning technology of the third millennium BCE, would have taken 1,382 hours to spin.[55] A team of twenty spinners could have produced this much woolen thread in sixty-nine hours. Spindle whorls are common finds on ancient archaeological sites; spinning thread was a form of specialized work that many women did constantly, not just as workers for the palace but in their own homes, in order to produce clothes for their families.

Malga's was not the only team of weavers who worked for the E-Mi at this time. Another twenty women worked for a man named Nanshe-danumea.

After four years, the supervisor Malga left his position and Zum got a new boss. This time it was a woman, Nin-kazida. We do not know where she came from; this is the first time her name appears in the archives from the E-Mi, but presumably she had experience in weaving at another institution in the city of Girsu. It would be fascinating to know how Nin-kazida was hired. Did someone from the E-Mi ask around at other temples and palaces for good prospects, once Malga left?

The other supervisor, Nanshe-danumea, stayed on, continuing to oversee his team for all of the eight years covered by the surviving records. But during the reign of King Urukagina and Queen Shasha, the workforce of the E-Mi began to increase and more supervisors were needed. The monarchs seem to have been particularly interested in textile production, increasing the number of teams of weavers from two, when Urukagina took power, to four in his second year on the throne.[56] Two of the teams had male supervisors, and two had women in that role. One of the women was Zum's supervisor Nin-kazida, the other was named Igi-bar.[57]

Igi-bar and Nin-kazida had all the same responsibilities as the two male supervisors (though they were paid less well), and, just like the men, their workshops were named for them. For example, at one point, timbers were needed by all the weaving houses, though it is unclear what they were to be used for. All four of the supervisors received a specified number of these timbers and took responsibility for whatever it was that would be done with them. The list noted that thirty-nine timbers "were deposited in the weaving house of Igi-bar,"[58] whereas "the weaving house of Nin-kazida" received twice as many: seventy-eight timbers. The supervisors also sometimes were given lump quantities of flour, wheat, and wool that they were charged with distributing evenly to their workers.[59]

King Urukagina and Queen Shasha kept on expanding the number of workshops so that, by the king's sixth year, six weaving houses were making woolen textiles, and three weaving houses were making linen, with a workforce of 138 women and children serving on these teams.[60] These women made up the largest group of workers of any kind on the queen's estate.

Many workers came and went from the weaving teams during this time of growth and restructuring of the weaving workshops. At the end of the eight years, only five of the women on Nanshe-danumea's original team were still working for him; some had switched to other teams and some had left palace employment. This suggests that the women weren't enslaved or tied to the palace household; they were free to leave if they chose.[61] But Zum had stayed on with her team even when other women had moved on, and perhaps she stood out as someone who was hard-working and organized.

When the palace administrators needed three supervisors for new teams of weavers that they were creating, they promoted Zum into one of these spots. In fact, they put women at the heads of five of the six teams of wool workers. Nin-kazida, Zum's old boss, kept her position as supervisor, as did Igi-bar. Zum led her own team, and two other women became supervisors. One of them, like Zum, had been listed at the top of her team previously, receiving higher wages than the rest.[62] Another had come over from the spinning workshops.[63] Outstanding weaving women were clearly being rewarded through promotions and increases to their salaries. All three of the linen weaving houses had women in charge.[64] Nanshe-danumea was by then the only male supervisor in the palace textile workshops.

The scribes who listed the weavers and their payments on the monthly accounts henceforth made a distinction between the wool weavers who had been there all along (who were described as being "from former times") and the ones who had been brought in to staff the new teams. The new women were paid, though not well, and none of them was listed as having had children. Some scholars think they may have been slaves.[65] Either way, they probably had a harder life than that of the older generation of weavers. Zum was now in charge of twenty of these presumably young women. If they had little experience with weaving, as seems likely, she would have been training them as well as supervising them.

A woman named Emete might well have been the most senior of all the supervisors. Even before she took control of one of the weaving workshops, she was the "head of female royal servants"[66] and therefore presumably a close advisor to the queen. Unlike any of the other women who supervised the weavers, but like the male supervisors, she was not just paid in grain but was also given the use of fields that she could cultivate herself.[67] Given how consuming her career must have been, she no doubt hired laborers to farm her fields. She took on other typically male roles as well, such as providing a sacrificial goat for a ceremony and being formally recognized as a gift-giver to others.[68]

Unfortunately, after the sixth year of Urukagina, no more records from the E-Mi survive. The brief, shadowy glimpses of these weavers and supervisors come to an end. But we can guess a little about their life outside the palace. Although she spent her whole life weaving textiles, a weaver like Zum (before she became a supervisor, at least) probably only owned one or two garments for herself. Wool for clothes was expensive and she was not paid particularly well. She would have paid for anything she needed to live—wool, salt, oil, and so on—out of the surplus barley that she was paid and that her family did not need for food each month. Presumably she (and her possible husband and older children) lived in a house elsewhere—it is highly unlikely that the palace contained barracks for all its hundreds of workers.

Month after month the workers received their wages, and each month the scribes created a big ledger-sized tablet on which they listed all the workers' names, the amount of barley each person received, the number of young children each woman had, and the team and workshop that employed her. These tablets were stored in an archive room and must have been consulted from time to time, perhaps when the administrators were called on to account for all the barley that had been spent.

The lists include many other workers besides those in the textile workshops (see Fig. 4.4). There were men and women who worked as millers, brewers, and swineherders.[69] These teams of workers had remained more stable than had the weavers during Urukagina's reign, without big increases in staff and without much turnover of personnel either.[70] One orphan girl who served as the "assistant to pigs in the pasture" was paid 24

Fig. 4.4 Cuneiform account of workers from Umma, c. 2400–2350 BCE. (Yale University, Peabody Museum)

Fig. 4.5 Cylinder seal and impression showing two weaving women operating a loom, a third woman holding a skein of thread. (Yale University, Peabody Museum)

silas per month.[71] This was a higher amount than many women, perhaps because she had no family to help support her.

The palace seems to have made a point of integrating the children of their workers, even orphaned children, into the system of work and wages. This had the advantage of giving them a salary and a place to belong (working with their mothers, if those women were alive), and it kept orphaned children off the streets.[72] Of course, the palace also benefited from their labor, and it never seems to have occurred to them that children should not be put to work—child labor laws were thousands of years off in the future. Many, perhaps most, of the children born to palace workers became palace workers themselves.

Wages weren't equitable; that was a fact of life. A male senior official could be paid eight times as much barley as a female manual laborer.[73] But in spite of this, and although the work was hard, one does not have the sense that the E-Mi palace was a cruel place. King Urukagina even emphasized in his royal inscriptions that his goal was to make sure that weaker members of society were treated fairly. He had his reforms listed and copied out on large clay cones, along with clay "nails"—smaller conical objects—and on at least one clay plaque.[74] He wrote that he "made a compact with the divine Ningirsu that the powerful man would not oppress the orphan (or) widow."[75] Of course, one has to take royal inscriptions with a pinch of salt; they were propaganda for the king as he tried to impress the gods. But at least it seems that the gods approved of kindness, and Urukagina aspired to please them.

The weavers in Lagash had their counterparts in other cities. We may not know their names or be able to trace their careers everywhere, but women with similar lives and responsibilities produced textiles in Umma, Ur, Uruk, Adab, and all over Sumer, as well as in cities to the north in Syria.

Given that the natural environment in Sumer provided its people with no mineral ores for metalwork, wood for building or carpentry, hard stones for sculpture, or other luxury goods to trade, it makes sense that they created something precious from one resource that they had in abundance—wool. The spinners, dyers, weavers, and embroiderers must have pushed themselves to create fabrics of unmatched quality. Although the textile workers were paid in similar amounts of barley as millers and brewers, their work must have matched the artistry of jewelers and sculptors. This was true throughout Mesopotamian history. Imagine if robes and carpets from this period were hanging in museums today; it would be so much more obvious why they were sought out in lands far from home. We would no doubt be dazzled at the fineness of the weave or the stitches or the intricacy of the designs.

Early Dynastic Sumer was a patriarchal society. Men were in charge of most aspects of the society and economy. But in some cases, women did the same work as men, in supervising weavers and in some other positions, such as doorkeepers, rope-makers, and barbers.[76] Children growing up in the society would have heard about powerful men, like the reforming king Urukagina, and also about powerful women like Baranamtara, with her responsibilities for administration, diplomacy, and ritual. Many women worked outside the home for monthly pay in barley and could expect to be provided with additional amounts if they had children to support. And perhaps it did not escape people's notice that the region's most valuable export, the textiles that were sold and given as luxury gifts, were made by women. Women were not considered to be the equals of men, but they were central to politics, society, religion, and the economy, and seem to have been regarded with respect.

Sumer was rich and prosperous during the Early Dynastic period. The kings and queens of its city-states practiced diplomacy, managed vast estates, and benefited from trade with distant lands. The period of time when attendants were buried with monarchs was short-lived, and wars, though violent, were not constant. It is unlikely that people lived in perpetual fear. The kings seem to have decided not to terrorize their populations into submission but to try to endear themselves to them and to emphasize that the gods had chosen them to rule. Many of the same strategies were adopted by their contemporaries to the northwest, in Syria. This is seen, especially, in the remarkable finds from the city of Ebla, which will be our focus in the next chapter.

Chapter 5

Royal Couples, Divine Couples, and Envoys

The cuneiform tablets found at the site of Ebla didn't give up their stories easily.[1] In 1974, when Italian excavators first discovered the main archive room in the ancient palace,[2] the sight of the clay tablets must have been almost overwhelming. As the archaeologists carefully removed the dirt, thousands of cuneiform tablets appeared, piled on the ground, some still in exactly the order in which they had been placed 4,300 years ago, before the palace burned down (see Fig. 5.1).

The intact ones, 1,727 of them,[3] looked for all the world like stacked roof tiles but were covered in careful columns of ancient script. Others had tumbled against one another, most of them in pieces, some in minute fragments. The potential knowledge contained in those rooms was incredible. Ultimately, 17,000 artifacts with cuneiform script were uncovered and they proved to be parts of at least 3,500 tablets,[4] ranging from large square documents the size of a laptop computer to small memos that would easily fit in your hand. These tablets promised to reveal a previously unknown world. Until that moment, historians had almost no textual evidence at all from Syria in the third millennium BCE, during the same time as the Early Dynastic city-states of southern Mesopotamia. (There are still almost no Syrian documents for the previous period, from 3100–2600 BCE.)[5] But now, for the mid-third millennium BCE, they had more evidence than anyone could have dreamed of. One gets such a sense of connection to the people of Ebla just from seeing these tablets, let alone reading them. The scribes who wrote them and stacked them on shelves and in baskets had lives, interests, and families. They also had very human frustrations—one small tablet in the archive had been balled up, perhaps in anger, while it was still

Fig. 5.1 Ebla tablets when discovered in the ruins of the palace, c. 2300 BCE. (© NPL—DeA Picture Library/Bridgeman Images)

soft. The imprints of the scribe's fingers (even his fingerprints) are clearly visible where he squeezed the tablet in his hand before tossing it aside.[6]

There was just one big obstacle to overcome in writing history based on the palace archive—a lack of royal inscriptions. The vast majority of the tablets recorded lists of administrative details about the day-to-day running of the palace. These are not unlike the tablets from the E-Mi in Girsu, only the people of Ebla didn't speak Sumerian. Their language has been dubbed Eblaite; it was a Semitic language, so it is distantly related to languages such as Arabic and Hebrew. The scribes used a lot of Sumerian cuneiform signs, but it's clear that the language they were thinking in was Eblaite. The history contained in these tablets wasn't there to be picked up and read; even the names of the kings and queens had to be fathomed through their mentions in lists that were not intended for posterity.

The scribes seem to have been largely preoccupied with recording the production and distribution of textiles, which was clearly just as important here as it was at Lagash, if not more so; 543 of the documents consist of monthly registers of endless amounts of clothing and cloth of different types (see Fig. 5.2). Fortunately, when these textiles were distributed, the

Fig. 5.2 Administrative tablet from Ebla listing textiles, clothes, and jewelry, 2350–2300 BCE. (Erich Lessing/Art Resource, NY)

scribes would note the reason why they were being given out or to whom they were being given. From this, we get glimpses of life beyond the textile warehouse. Other administrative lists that pertain to metals, agriculture, herds of animals, and palace revenues add to the picture.

And, fortunately, the big archive room also included some other documents that the scribes had deemed worth keeping, including a few ritual texts, hymns, and incantations, dictionaries and lists of words, and a few royal decrees, letters, diplomatic reports, and agreements with other states.[7]

Tabur-damu and Ishar-damu of Ebla: A Royal Couple

When a young woman named Tabur-damu became engaged to King Ishar-damu of Ebla around 2300 BCE, the kingdom was flourishing. Ishar-damu ruled from a sprawling and finely built palace in the capital city, a little more than 54 kilometers (33 miles) south of the already important city of Halab (now Aleppo).[8] The palace, which archaeologists uncovered, was spread out over 2,400 square meters (almost 26,000 square feet)[9] on an acropolis overlooking the city. The city wall would have been visible in the distance, surrounding the 60 hectares (148 acres) of densely packed buildings that made up Ebla. Fields and countryside extended in all directions beyond.

During Ishar-damu's reign, Ebla was one of the major kingdoms of his era; it included at least twenty cities that recognized him as their king, it was home to more than 700 villages that were mentioned in the archives,[10] and it stretched at least 200 kilometers (125 miles) from east to west across northwest Syria. The kingdom of Ebla bordered other powerful kingdoms of the day, Nagar to the east in the Habur River region, and Mari to the southeast along the Euphrates. Both were homes to major kings and both were thriving. The three kingdoms were not always at peace with one another, however. Ebla and Mari had a particularly contentious relationship.

King Ishar-damu did not rule alone. Not only was he assisted by his queen, like the kings of the Sumerian city-states, but Ebla had a long tradition of the king sharing power, at least to some extent, with a vizier. The vizier's title, confusingly, was written with the Sumerian word "*lugal*," which in the south meant "king." When the Ebla tablets were first being read, this led to some early speculation that these *lugal*s were also kings. But, although viziers led many military campaigns, it soon became clear that they were subordinate to the king. The two men worked together, but it was Ishar-damu who was the king, and his "*lugal*" was a man named Ibrium who served him as vizier. A collection of notable men known as "lords" provided input as well.

At the time of his betrothal to Tabur-damu, King Ishar-damu had already been on the throne for at least thirteen years. This was a normal amount of time for a complete reign for a king in this era, but Ishar-damu was still a young man when he got engaged. He had been just a child when his father died and he had come to power. And therein lies a story, so before we get to know Tabur-damu and follow her through the elaborate royal wedding, it might be good to pause for a moment to get to know more about the family she was about to enter.

Dusigu: Queen Mother

Ishar-damu's father was King Irkab-damu (c. 2325 BCE), who ruled Ebla for eleven years. But Ishar-damu wasn't his oldest son, and he wasn't a son of his father's queen (known as a *maliktum* in the local Eblaite language), whose name had been Keshdudu. In fact, Ishar-damu's mother had no title.[11] People in the palace at the time of his birth might not have given him much thought at all. But to dismiss his future prospects would be to overlook the formidable qualities of his mother, Dusigu. When she joined the court, Dusigu was just one of the "king's women." A king's secondary wives and concubines were all called the "king's women," lumped together in this category along with his mother's sisters and his own daughters. They didn't even all live in Ebla. At one point, an Ebla king had as many as twenty "king's women" in his Ebla palace, along with five at palaces elsewhere in his kingdom.[12]

So Dusigu was initially one of the king's women, one of many. But then Irkab-damu's queen Keshdudu died, perhaps soon after they married, and Irkab-damu never married another *maliktum*. Dusigu seems to have spotted an opportunity, or perhaps she was the king's favorite secondary wife and it was his preference for her that propelled her up in the ranks of the women. In whatever way it happened, from that time on, she became increasingly prominent in lists of the king's women.[13]

In spite of having no official title, Dusigu acquired considerable power and must have been a brilliant woman; King Irkab-damu came to depend on her. Like Baranamtara in Lagash, who lived around the same time, she took a role in diplomatic relations with other kingdoms and participated in rituals, and she moved up through the ranks of the royal women at court until her name was listed first among the women in important documents.

When her son (the future king Ishar-damu) was born, Dusigu employed a wet nurse to feed and take care of him. As an important woman at court, Dusigu could not be tied to the fusses and whims of a young baby. The wet nurse, Kisadu, could take care of all that. Wet nurses made public life possible for many prominent women in ancient Near Eastern history. In time, the baby prince was weaned, but Kisadu stayed on at court. In fact, she lived there throughout her life.[14] Her own son was about the same age as Ishar-damu and they may well have been playmates. Perhaps his nurse Kisadu continued to be one of Ishar-damu's confidantes, even when circumstances propelled him to take the throne at a young age.

King Irkab-damu's death must have been traumatic for the kingdom, especially given that there seems to have been no obvious heir to the throne. His queen probably hadn't lived long enough to give birth to an heir, so any of the sons of secondary wives and concubines might have become king.[15] Prince Ishar-damu was not the oldest among his brothers; he might even have been the youngest. But Dusigu was the most powerful woman in the palace, and somehow she maneuvered her young son Ishar-damu onto the throne.[16] He might have been only four years old![17]

Such a young boy was in no position to administer a great kingdom. You may not be surprised to hear that those same hierarchical lists that were kept by palace scribes sometimes listed Dusigu's name before that of her young son Ishar-damu, even after he became king.[18] His mother was certainly advising him and helping him make decisions in his early years, and she may well have been serving as his regent, effectively running the country.[19] And, at last, she had a title. She had never been queen—*maliktum*—but, with her husband's death and her son's ascension to the throne, she became the "great mother of the king."[20] It must have been gratifying.

When it came time for King Ishar-damu to marry, he needed advice. Marriage was a very big deal for a king of Ebla; the woman he married would become the *maliktum*, who would play a vital role in the kingdom and hold significant power. She oversaw a host of servants, advised her husband, and helped run the court. Princes and kings in ancient Mesopotamia don't seem to have married for love (a truth in almost every era of history); a candidate for queen had to come from a family of the right social status and, in Ebla, she had to show promise as a leader herself. For suggestions of whom to marry, King Ishar-damu turned, as you might have already guessed, to his mother.[21]

Dusigu had someone in mind. Her own late husband, King Irkab-damu, had a brother, and that brother had a daughter, Tabur-damu, who fit the qualifications for queen nicely. First-cousin marriages were not frowned on in the ancient Near East; in fact, they were often seen as ideal because property stayed within the family. It might not have hurt that Dusigu already knew her niece well and must have realized that Tabur-damu would probably be willing, as *maliktum*, to take second place among the women, beneath the "great mother of the king," Dusigu herself. The *maliktum* was traditionally the most powerful woman in the court and some other prospective brides might not have been inclined to allow Dusigu to retain her power.

It turns out that Dusigu wasn't the only one who supported the match; the gods also agreed. The king ordered omens to be read when his mother proposed that Tabur-damu should be *maliktum*, and they came back positive. Certainly Ishar-damu would never have gone ahead with the marriage if the gods had been against it.

The Marriage of Tabur-damu and Ishar-damu

Now Tabur-damu had been chosen; she was to become the *maliktum*. Perhaps she found this to be an intimidating prospect, or perhaps she was thrilled. There's no way to know. No matter how she felt, her life was about to change dramatically, starting with the wedding ceremony itself and the month of rituals that followed it. Every step during this transition was carefully planned and had to be performed just so, in exactly the way that it had been performed by royal couples in Ebla for as long as anyone could remember. The ceremony was so important that it was recorded on ritual tablets that were kept in the palace archives. These weren't generic; one had been written out when King Ishar-damu's father, Irkab-damu, went through the ceremony with his queen,[22] and one would be written out to record the exact proceedings that Ishar-damu and Tabur-damu would go through.[23] The documents recorded almost exactly the same movements and devotions each time, but the court archivist in Ebla apparently felt the need to have a separate record of each.

The traditional marriage ritual had been designed, in part, to introduce a queen from a foreign land to the people of Ebla. But Tabur-damu was not from a foreign land, nor was she marrying a stranger. She had grown up in the same city where she would reign. It was familiar. She spoke the language, she understood the rituals, she worshiped the local gods. No doubt she could easily find her way around the grand palace, with its workshops and storerooms, and its vast courtyard with a dais for the king's throne. Tabur-damu presumably didn't need to be introduced,[24] but she had to go through all the stages of the ceremony anyway. Only then would she truly be seen—by the gods, the divine former kings and queens, and the people of Ebla—as queen.

By the time the marriage ritual day arrived, the palace administration had been planning the ceremonies for some time. The royal wedding symbolized not just the initiation of the new queen but a rebirth and renewal for the king as well. He was finally old enough to truly take power and would now rule with the queen at his side.

Although kings and viziers ruled and administered the land of Ebla, many of the significant events in Ebla had something to do with royal women. These were the moments that stand out among the administrative records. They were when the biggest expenditures were made, such as when a prince or princess was born, when a princess married a foreign king, when a princess was initiated into the priesthood, or when a royal woman died (whether in Ebla or elsewhere).[25] Queens and other royal women were revered, both in life and after death, and they were active in all aspects of the life of the court. As in the southern city-states at the same time, no one would have dreamed of restricting their movements to a separate area of the palace, secluded from the men. The only palace activity that fell outside the purview of the royal women was warfare.[26]

Everyone in the court at Ebla, male and female, had a clear sense of their place in the pecking order, and their names were listed on administrative texts according to this hierarchy. Various royal women, perhaps secondary wives and concubines of the king, ranked lower than the queen, as did princesses, along with wet nurses of the royal children.[27] Tabur-damu must have known, though, that Dusigu, the queen mother, had been at the top of the list for many, many years. Tabur-damu would be in second place until her mother-in-law died.[28]

First Day of the Wedding

When the first day of the wedding ceremonies arrived, Tabur-damu wasn't in Ebla.[29] She was at her father's estate somewhere outside the city.[30] This first day wasn't a public event but a private one. In this way, it was probably not unlike the beginning of a wedding for any couple at the time. The father-in-law or the groom himself (if his father was deceased, as in the case of Ishar-damu) traditionally came to the bride's house with gifts for her and for her family.

The term for these gifts is often translated as the "bride price," but this gives the wrong impression. The groom was not buying the woman from her parents. Gifts were exchanged in both directions. In cases when the father of the royal groom was still alive, he was showered with presents by the bride's parents, as was the groom himself. On one occasion, a princess from Ebla married the heir to the throne of the powerful kingdom of Nagar. The groom was offered a set of three garments that made up a standard package (his official representative got the same), along with 1 mina and 20 shekels (627 grams or 1.4 pounds) of gold plate. But the king of Nagar, father of the groom, received more. In addition to the standard garments, he was given several gold vessels—a gold plate weighing 2 minas; two gold vessels, called *bur-kak* (these were used in the wedding ceremony) weighing more than 1 mina; and various other gold vessels totaling 45 shekels. This represented 1.9 kilograms (more than 4 pounds) of gold. The gold that circulated in Ebla in vast quantities was imported from Anatolia.[31] The king of Nagar wasn't deprived when it came to silver, either, which also came to Ebla from Anatolia.[32] His gift included 50 minas of silver—23.5 kilograms (almost 52 pounds)![33] All these were provided by the Ebla king, the father of the bride. No one ever refers to these as a "groom price," but they served the same purpose as what is sometimes termed the "bride price." People who had given and received gifts had an ongoing obligation to one another, and this would be true of Ishar-damu and Tabur-damu. He was not paying for a bride and taking her away; he was tying himself to her family. Her family was doing the same.

In addition, the father of Tabur-damu provided considerable wealth for his daughter's dowry and trousseau. These goods belonged to her, not to her husband, for the rest of her life.

The palace would have distributed gifts lavishly to officials of the court and their families, just to mark the occasion. We don't have a list of these gifts for Tabur-damu's wedding, but one does survive, a generation later, for the wedding of her daughter, Keshdut (who was called "daughter of the queen"),[34] to a prince of the kingdom of Kish, which was far to the southeast of Ebla.[35] The gifts are listed on a big tablet; it records a considerable and generous distribution of palace wealth in the form of hundreds of textiles and articles of clothing. Not only did the vizier of Ebla receive a gift at this time, but so did six of his sons, twenty women of his family, and nineteen men in the family of the previous vizier. "Elders," religious leaders, and traders also benefited. The vizier provided gifts, as well as receiving them. Notably, he gave the queen of Kish seventy-four items made of cloth, and he gave her husband a set of the three items of clothing that were always grouped together, and two gold and lapis lazuli bracelets. The list goes on and on, including gifts to fifty-five high-ranking women, including Tabur-damu herself, as mother of the bride. Even dignitaries who happened to be in Ebla at the time, visiting from towns that had nothing to do with the royal marriage, all benefited from the largesse associated with the wedding. Gift-giving on a grand scale was an important part of diplomacy and power throughout ancient Near Eastern history. Outdoing one's neighbors in the number and quality of one's gifts was a sign of importance and wealth.

On that first wedding day, King Ishar-damu would have brought a large number of animals for his father-in-law (who was also his uncle), along with other gifts for Tabur-damu's family members.[36] For his new wife he brought a bracelet, a gold chain, and the all-important ceremonial clothes that she would wear on her wedding day: a dark red garment, a yellow-orange one, and a multicolored item.[37] Unfortunately, we really don't know the exact translations of the terms used for these articles of clothing, but it seems likely that one was a dress, one a veil, and one a band of some kind. Tabur-damu was strictly forbidden to wear these until later.[38]

It was also crucial that the groom should bring two sheep to sacrifice to the gods. Some sort of divination might have been involved, as one sheep was sacrificed to the sun god and the other to the god of his wife's family.[39] A reference to these two sheep shows up again in the ceremony later; it seems likely that their wool was eventually used to make some sort of item for the couple, or perhaps swaddling for a future baby.[40]

Presumably Tabur-damu's family shared meals with their new son-in-law over the course of the day. Given that he was a king, Ishar-damu certainly didn't arrive alone; the events might have been closed to the public, but Tabur-damu's family house was no doubt full of people that day.

At some point during the day, King Ishar-damu anointed Tabur-damu's head with oil. This tradition had incredible staying power in Syria; for more than a thousand years it continued to mark the symbolic moment when an engagement was formalized. From that time on, the two were considered to be a couple. No matter how long it took for them to reach the date of the marriage ceremony, they were legally husband and wife once the woman had been anointed.

Second Day of the Wedding

In Ebla, it took almost no time at all between the anointing and the actual wedding. The couple slept apart that night and, early the next morning, Tabur-damu made her way to Ebla. This portion of the ceremony seems to have been hers alone, without her husband present, and the citizens of Ebla would have been well aware that it was happening. She arrived at the Kura

Gate of the city, perhaps at the northwest end of the town.[41] The gate must have been one of the biggest and most important entrances to Ebla, as it was named for the city god. The gate opened and she entered, bringing with her gifts for the gods. She was in civilian clothes; she still wasn't allowed to wear her marriage robes just yet. It's likely that everyone in Ebla had the day off work for this once-in-a-lifetime celebration and that the streets were lined with cheering people, some of them scrambling onto walls or rooftops to get a look at their new queen.[42] Had Tabur-damu not been a native of Ebla already, this would have been her introduction to her new city. It's hard to imagine a more dramatic moment, but perhaps it was also a joyful one. She was apparently not veiled; she could see the faces of the people around her. They were no doubt thrilled to have a new queen.

Tabur-damu took a ceremonial route through the city to reach the temple of the god Kura, following in the footsteps of generations of queens before her. The temple was near the king's palace, on the "Saza," the acropolis of the city of Ebla.[43] The entrance to the Saza has been excavated in modern times and it was impressive, with a portico and monumental steps up to the acropolis, extending for 22 meters (72 feet). As she climbed the stairs, Tabur-damu was coming close to one of the most important moments in the day.

As she entered the Saza, Tabur-damu had to present a gift related to those two sheep who had been sacrificed the day before: she handed over their wool, which would later be woven into a special garment.[44] Near the temple, she came to a place called the *marasum* where her husband seems to have been waiting. *Marasum* means "cultivated land," but if it were literally that, it would be an odd thing to find inside a temple complex. It was probably an open space adjoining the temple. Here she stopped. She was finally allowed to don her wedding garments. The ritual text specifies that "the queen enters the Cultivated Land and her red, yellow-orange and embroidered garments are presented to her, and her golden chain is presented to her in the Cultivated Land, and the queen is dressed with them in the Cultivated Land, and the king veils the queen and they enter the temple of Kura."[45] Everything about her garments, including the colors and shapes, had symbolic importance. One robe was called a *dururu* and it could only be worn by married women (and married goddesses).[46] The robing seems to have been a public event, and some scholars think that this action, when she was veiled by her husband, was the crucial moment, the moment when Tabur-damu became queen.[47]

As the king and queen entered the temple, their eyes would have taken a moment to adjust. It was dark—in stark contrast to the sunny courtyard—and the statues of the gods resided in the holy cella at the center of the building. There the royal couple presented gifts to Kura and his divine wife Barama, and to three other gods of Ebla.[48] The marriage was complete; the gods approved.

This wedding didn't happen in isolation. Kings and officials all over the Near East would have received messages from Ebla informing them about it and, in response, they sent valuable gifts. An alabaster lid with an inscription from the reign of King Pepy I of Egypt was found in the palace at Ebla; this (and the container it belonged to) might well have been a wedding gift to Ishar-damu and Tabur-damu from the pharaoh.[49] Marriages were gift-giving extravaganzas, providing an opportunity for wealth to flow into and out of Ebla on an epic scale.

At some point, perhaps on this second day, the members of the court and the family of Tabur-damu enjoyed a huge banquet of bread, meat, and other dishes, along with wine and beer. Singers and musicians provided music for the guests. The food was prepared by the chefs of the palace, of whom there were at least thirteen, all of them women.[50] Tabur-damu and Ishar-damu would have presided at the dinner—the king with his new queen, enjoying their last day in Ebla before their (for lack of a better word) honeymoon.

There is plenty of evidence at Ebla for banquets associated with weddings, though not for Tabur-damu's wedding in particular. When one diplomatic marriage took place between a high-ranking Ebla woman (a niece of the vizier) and the king of the land of Dulu (which might have been an ancient name for Byblos on the Mediterranean coast), records were kept of many different kinds of breads served at the banquet.[51] Another tablet records forty-two jars of wine sent from Ebla to the king of the land of Nagar when he got married.[52] No doubt even more wine was needed for the banquet at the wedding of the king of Ebla himself. Wine was produced in Ebla and also imported from its allies;[53] the weather was more suitable for grapes in this part of Syria than in Sumer. As for the singers and musicians, they appear in just about every representation of a banquet throughout Mesopotamian history (see Fig. 5.3). And when the prince of Nagar later traveled to Ebla to marry a local princess, he brought six singers with him (along with eighty other people from his homeland).[54] The Mesopotamians loved music.

Fig. 5.3 Limestone plaque showing a banquet with a harpist in the upper registers. Early Dynastic period. (Scala/Art Resource, NY/Art Resource)

Beginning of the Honeymoon

Once the wedding ceremonies in Ebla were complete, the new couple prepared to set off on their four-week honeymoon. But they weren't going somewhere pleasant to relax and take a romantic break. They actually spent a great deal of their honeymoon in a building with the gloomy name of the "House of the Dead"—a mausoleum. This was an obligation that they had to fulfill to the gods and to their ancestors for vital reasons. It was no doubt a grueling experience, but it was also essential, transforming the couple and blessing their reign.

The couple didn't travel alone. Several officials accompanied them on the honeymoon, along with, remarkably, the cult statues of the divine couple Kura and Barama.[55] These statues embodied the gods, and the gods protected Ebla, so they rarely left their temple home. The actions the gods took during the honeymoon were so critical that the priests and the people of Ebla were willing, perhaps even eager, to let them leave. They must also have been very well protected along the way. Statues of gods in Ebla were made of precious materials—lapis lazuli, silver, bronze, and gold—formed over a wooden core, and they were dressed in the finest clothing.[56] It's not that the priests and priestesses would have feared that anyone would steal the statues for the value of their materials, though. Everyone, including bandits and highwaymen, feared the gods; it would have been unthinkable to melt down the faces or hands of their statues. The gods would have been swift in their punishment. Everyone believed that. But the statues of city gods made for very valuable hostages if seized by enemy forces. Fortunately, the honeymoon travel was entirely within the borders of the Ebla kingdom, so the gods were unlikely to be threatened en route.[57]

The royal couple, gods, and officials had one more obligation before leaving Ebla. They performed a sacrifice, dedicating a sheep to the deity of the sun, and another to a royal ancestor, King Ibini-Lim, who had ruled long, long before, as the tenth king of Ebla. Dead kings of the Ebla kingdom figured prominently on the honeymoon. This wasn't the last sacrifice to Ibini-Lim on this journey; he was clearly considered one of the great kings of the past.

After the sacrifice, the procession left Ebla and seems to have traveled northeast, in a meandering journey that stopped in six towns over four days. Each town was a place of pilgrimage, and in each they performed sacrifices to gods and to one or more past kings.[58]

The final destination of the honeymoon procession was a place called Binash.[59] This holy place was where at least three former Ebla kings had been buried,[60] and here the Ebla delegation settled in for a three-week stay in the House of the Dead. During this time King Ishar-damu and Queen Tabur-damu were consecrated to the city gods, Kura and Barama.[61]

Deified Former Kings of Ebla

The kings and queens of Ebla seem to have been particularly aware of their genealogy—more so than rulers in some other places and times in Mesopotamia—and equally aware of the power of their dead ancestors to intercede in the living world. The former kings were gods now, deified after death. The names of these earlier kings of Ebla, sadly, mean nothing to us. We have just a list of them, carefully recorded, passed down by scribes over generations, and found in the excavation of the palace.[62]

There are twenty-six names on the list, but documents only survive from the reigns of the last four to rule before the destruction of the kingdom—Kun-damu, Igrish-Halab, Irkab-damu, and Ishar-damu—and the vast majority of the tablets that were found in the excavations at Ebla date to just the last two of those.[63] Those other kings on the list—they're just names without stories. Some of them would no doubt have been as familiar to the people of Ebla as George Washington or Abraham Lincoln are to Americans today. The people might have told stories about the great victories or reforms of these kings, they might have known which of them first built a palace on the acropolis in Ebla. They would have known, perhaps, why many of them were not buried in Ebla proper but in other places in the kingdom with names such as Irad, Uduhudu, and Lub.[64] The town of Binash might well have been a place of pilgrimage for Eblaites not just during the royal honeymoon. As the resting place of deified kings, it might have attracted worshipers and petitioners. As far as the people of Ebla were concerned, these kings continued to influence events on Earth and they required a lot of attention.[65]

The tablets found during the excavations of the palace at Ebla were written over about a fifty-year period.[66] If that was a typical span for the combined reigns of four successive kings, then the kings on the rest of the list would have stretched back as much as 325 years before the destruction of the palace at the end of the reign of Ishar-damu. The first among them, back in the twenty-seventh century BCE, were some of the earliest kings anywhere. A king named Sagisu, for example, might have ruled 225 years before the time when the royal couple Ishar-damu and Tabur-damu showed up to pay homage to him.

The House of the Dead

When Tabur-damu and Ishar-damu arrived in Binash, the whole procession entered the House of the Dead there. It must have been a relatively big place, but there's nothing like it that has survived from

Mesopotamia or, at least, that has been recognized as such, so it's hard to envision it. Was it above ground or underground? Were the tombs of the kings under the floor? Were guards or priests employed to protect them? It seems likely that the tombs themselves weren't visible, but that the deceased kings were felt to be present because of the proximity of their graves, and because they were probably represented in the House of the Dead by statues.[67]

Once the members of the entourage were inside, a purification ritual took place, and a priest presented offerings to the gods and the dead kings. The description of what happened next is curious and a little hard to decipher. It records that "the divine couple, [the gods] Kura and Barama, come to the house of the dead and enter the chamber. And they remain there."[68] So it seems that the statues of the city gods of Ebla were set up in the House of the Dead, where they would live for the next three weeks. As for the royal couple, "the king enters his chamber and the queen enters her chamber." Were these rooms in the House of the Dead where the royal couple lived during this time? It seems so. We know that they stayed in the mausoleum at night, apparently in these separate chambers.

While the ancestral king Sagisu was being honored, with offerings of two sheep and "one silver bird,"[69] two more statues were being added to the crowd of sculptures in the chamber: images of Ishar-damu and Tabur-damu themselves. These had been brought along for the entire journey from Ebla. The scribe wrote, "While the new king (Ishar-damu) offers the sheep in the temple of the god of Sagisu, the ancestor, then they placed that statue of the king . . . , (and) that of the queen . . . the young carvers made them."[70] These statues were valuable. Their expense had been calculated in silver (though they probably were not made entirely of silver). An administrative text records that "305 g (almost 11 oz) of silver" was the "value of one statue, which is that of the king and the queen, for Binash."[71]

A statue, as we have seen, was much more than a representation, in the minds of the people of Mesopotamia in this era. It didn't necessarily look anything like the person, in fact. But it had a magical connection with its subject and it had a life force. The statues of Ishar-damu and Tabur-damu joined statues of former kings and queens in an unearthly community here in the House of the Dead. Free from the constraints of time, they could communicate among themselves, worship, and be worshiped. And all the statues, like the demanding men and women they represented, expected to be provided with food, drink, clothes, and gifts. Having the god and goddess, Kura and Barama, temporarily among them in the form of their statues made this a supremely important event. It was as though the gods were introducing the new couple to their ancestors.

A night passed. Did Tabur-damu manage to sleep? Would the presence of the images of all those dead kings and queens just outside the door (and of their remains beneath the floor) have been reassuring or unnerving?

The ritual text reports that, next, "When those of the cloth arise, the king and the queen depart and sit on the thrones of their fathers and await the presence of the sun god." Apparently, the royal couple woke up before dawn to watch the sun rise, while seated on thrones. It continues, "When the sun (god) rises, the invocation priests invoke and the lamentation priests intone the laments of when the birth goddess Nintu was angered."[72] It has been proposed that the whole marriage ritual was focused on the fertility of the royal couple[73] and the presence of the birth goddess in this episode does seem to support that suggestion.

The birth goddess continued to play a crucial role, as Nintu "makes an announcement, and the announcement that Nintu makes is that there is a new god Kura, a new goddess Barama, a new king, a new queen."[74] Somehow, the royal couple and the divine couple were both made "new" after these laments and incantations to the birth goddess. It was perceived to be a real and radical transformation. Ultimately what resulted was that the king and queen acquired the authority to rule. Another document referred to preparations for this event as "the purification of the mausoleum of Binash for the enthroning of the king . . . (on the occasion of) the king's attaining sovereignty."[75] Although Ishar-damu had already ruled Ebla for thirteen years, only now was he old enough to marry and to go through the consecration ceremony, to become truly powerful. He shared his authority with Tabur-damu, his queen, his *maliktum*. They were both legitimate in the eyes of the gods.

You might think that just one morning of these invocations would have been plenty, but the process continued for twenty-one days—three programs of ceremonies of seven days each—with the royal couple continuing to offer libations and sacrifices during the days, while sleeping at night in the House of the Dead.[76]

Before the entourage left to return to Ebla, they made sacrifices one more time, and this time they added one for King Igrish-Halab. He was not a distant ancestor like the others, he was Ishar-damu's grandfather. He may not have been buried in Binash, but he could receive gifts and sacrifices there.[77]

Return to Ebla

Finally, the ceremonies of the House of the Dead were over and the group could return to Ebla, trusting that the gods and the dead kings would bless the reign of Ishar-damu and Tabur-damu. The royal couple didn't go straight to the palace, however. Their first stop was in the temple, where the gods Kura and Barama were restored to their normal places and where the king and queen ate a meal of offerings that had been provided to them. The royal couple then spent the night in the temple. The ritual text specifies that "in that day the king lies in the temple (of Kura) on a linen sheet. And also the queen lies in the temple of the gods of the king."[78]

The whole process was, in a way, one huge rite of passage for Tabur-damu. She had come so far since the first day of her wedding. From now on, Tabur-damu was allowed to eat ritual meals that were reserved for royalty. She had gone from being a civilian (albeit one from a branch of the royal family) to a queen, the *maliktum* of Ebla, deserving of offerings in her own right.

As time passed, Tabur-damu no doubt grew comfortable living in the palace. She would have had her own quarters, her servants and ladies-in-waiting,[79] but for three years after her marriage to Ishar-damu, Tabur-damu continued to be outranked by the queen mother, Dusigu.

Death of Dusigu

The queen mother Dusigu died three years after the wedding of Tabur-damu and Ishar-damu, in the fourth year of the vizier Ibbi-zikir,[80] and her devoted son must have been heartbroken. He named the year to commemorate her death.[81] Everyone in the kingdom would have realized her importance. Gifts flowed into the palace on the occasion of her funeral.[82]

And now Tabur-damu was the highest-ranking woman in the land; she was the mother of royal children, including the crown prince Irak-damu and the princess Keshdut.[83] Tabur-damu ruled with her husband as *maliktum*, and her name at last appeared at the top of the lists of women.

But Tabur-damu still had a responsibility to Dusigu, even after her mother-in-law's death. The statue of Dusigu that sat among the statues of the ancestors, and held some part of the dead queen's life force, continued to require offerings and respect. This relationship between the living and dead queens was illuminated in a surprising way. During the excavations of the Ebla palace, a group of artifacts was discovered that came from a single object: a kind of tableau of small sculptures that would have been mounted at the top of a pole as a standard that could be carried in ceremonies.[84] Such things are portrayed in relief sculptures from other places and eras in Mesopotamia; it seems entirely likely that they would have existed in Ebla as well.

This tableau features two women (see Fig. 5.4). One is tall, standing, and has one hand on her waist and the other balled into a fist and held against her face. Her long dress is made of a smooth fabric without ornamentation except for the fringe around the edge. She wears nothing on her head. The other figure is much smaller, seated, and wears an old-fashioned fleeced cloak that completely swamps her. On her head is a turban. Between them stands a bronze incense burner. The scene seems to depict the younger woman as a living figure, worshiping a less-than-lifesize statue depicting the older woman. Paolo Matthiae, director of the Ebla excavations, has a persuasive explanation for this scene. The smaller figure, he says, is Dusigu, after her death, in the form of her funerary statue. The younger figure is Tabur-damu, paying homage to her mother-in-law.[85] The choice of this image for a royal standard might have been designed to make the case that Tabur-damu was now the equal of her late mother-in-law. But it might instead have indicated that Tabur-damu was still in the inferior position; perhaps it was made to mark Dusigu's deification.[86]

Textiles in Ebla

At Ebla, as we have seen, textiles were always foremost among the luxurious goods distributed as gifts, both at home and to distant kingdoms. Silver and gold featured as well, but those weren't native products. The only way for the land of Ebla to obtain silver and gold was from other lands, mostly in Anatolia. And the only way to obtain them from other lands was through

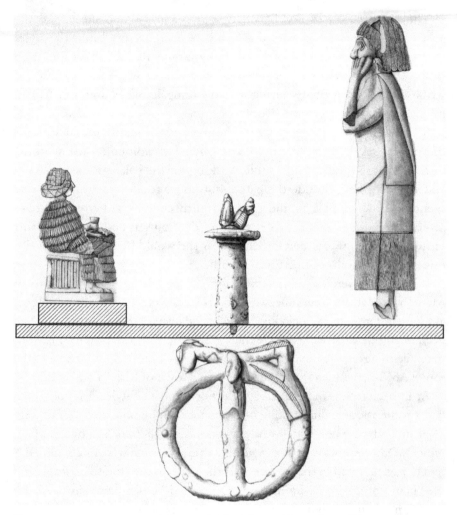

Fig. 5.4 Reconstruction of the standard of the *maliktum* from Ebla, c. 2300 BCE. (Copyright Missione Archeologica Italiana in Siria. Republished with permission of Walter de Gruyter and Company, from "The Standard of the *maliktum* of Ebla in the Royal Archives Period" by Paolo Matthiae, *ZA* 99 (2008); permission conveyed through Copyright Clearance Center, Inc.)

trade or luxury gift exchange. As in Lagash (and throughout Mesopotamia and Syria), textiles were the obvious choice of export or luxury gift. The evidence for this in Ebla is even clearer than in Lagash—all those hundreds of records of distribution of clothing and fabrics reflect the engine of the kingdom's economy.

The king of Ebla owned between 80,000 and 136,000 sheep,[87] so the palace had vast stores of wool that could be manufactured into the styles that were most appealing. Even so, the records show that wool was imported from other regions as well—from Mari and elsewhere[88]—and textiles and wool were seized as booty during military campaigns. The industry had an insatiable need for ever more wool.

It was distributed in many ways. The majority of textile production for the palace was done by hired workers (men and women), some working directly for the royal women, some working for the palace more generally, and some working outside the palace but under royal oversight.[89] Anyone spending time in Ebla in the twenty-fourth century BCE couldn't have avoided discussions about textiles; their production was ubiquitous. A court visitor would know, for certain, that he or she would be going home with one or more lengths of fine Eblaite cloth.

But textiles weren't just reserved for the people in power. Unlike in Mesopotamia at the same time, wool and textiles were used, along with food, as payment for workers (including weavers and dyers).[90] Even a man who had been hired by the palace to buy textiles in faraway Kish was paid for his work in textiles! The relevant text reads as follows: "I *gu-mug* textile, I *ib*-textile to the son of Abadan, the merchant, who goes to the town of Kish to buy textiles."[91]

At Ebla, cloth was made in a bewildering number of styles, each of which had a name, though almost none of the names can be translated. Some were of plain, undyed wool, which came in gray, black, spotted, and (rarest of all) white.[92] Others were dyed using vegetable dyes, and some were multicolored.[93]

They were stored in special rooms in the palace—the "house of wool" and the "house of textiles"—from which they could be distributed as needed.[94] As in a modern rug shop, these rooms were probably piled high with folded lengths of fabric—tall piles of red garments here, piles of gossamer-thin yellow-orange ones there. The administrative tablets account for thousands of textiles on hand in these rooms at a given moment. The storeroom must have been as securely guarded as a treasury; those garments and fabrics represented decades of man-hours (or, more often, woman-hours) of work, and immense wealth.

Diplomatic Letters and Treaties in Ebla

Given the prominence of textiles in so many moments of gift-giving at Ebla, it comes as a surprise that the one diplomatic letter that survived in the palace archive listed no textiles at all; the gifts from Ebla were of ropes and wagons. The letter was addressed to an envoy of the distant land of Hamazi, hundreds of miles to the east. The letter wasn't from the king of Ebla; it was sent instead by his steward, a man named Ibubu. Ibubu assured the Hamazi envoy that they were equals:"I am (your) brother and you are (my) brother."[95] Their kings were also allies. Ibubu wrote that "Irkab-damu, the king of Ebla is the brother of Zizi, the king of Hamazi."[96] Just as the queen of Lagash and the queen of Adab had exchanged gifts, so did the high officials of Ebla and Hamazi. Ibubu asked for "the finest quality equids," noting that in exchange he was sending his counterpart "ten (wagon) ropes, and two boxwood wagons." No doubt similar exchanges took place between the kings themselves, and probably between their queens as well. To judge from the administrative documents, expensive gifts seem to have been forever on the move between allied lands, but this letter is the first example of diplomatic correspondence that accompanied them.

The letter shows that the diplomatic system was well established, though sadly we have no evidence for its inception. As in Sumer, "brotherhood" referred to a formal relationship between allied states, and that alliance was maintained through the regular exchange of letters and gifts, carried across long distances, often far beyond Ebla's borders, by messengers and ambassadors. The same diplomatic system also left its imprint on other documents in the archives—records of goods sent out and received, and messengers dispatched.

The messengers and envoys who conveyed the letters and gifts were protected in their work by formal treaties between the states they represented. Even the source of their food was designated by the ever-meticulous diplomats who had drawn up the agreement. Only one such treaty survives from this early period, but it seems likely to have been typical; nothing about it suggests that it was the only one of its kind. It, too, was found in the Ebla palace, and it governed Ebla's relationship with a vassal state to the east, Abarsal. The treaty includes these clauses: "Arriving messengers will stop as long as ten days and will eat their travel provisions. But if you want them to stay (longer), you will give them travel provisions. . . . Messengers receiving a gift will not be given travel provisions: they will come back without travel provisions."[97] If a king insisted on detaining another king's envoy or messenger for longer than the standard ten days, he had to either provide him with food for the return trip, or he had to give him a gift. One can imagine a messenger from Ebla waiting, day after day, for a letter to take back to his king, all the while reminding his counterpart in Abarsal (no doubt politely) that he was owed travel provisions. His own king didn't have to pay for the delay. Appropriate treatment of the king's representatives was essential in this diplomatic world.

Enar-Lim and Ruzi-malik: Merchants Traveling between Ebla and Dugurasu

Two men, Enar-Lim and Ruzi-malik, made some of the longest journeys from Ebla, traveling all the way to a distant place called Dugurasu. The gifts they carried to the king there were particularly extravagant. Two historians, Maria Giovanna Biga and Piotr Steinkeller, have recently made a startling assertion: Dugurasu was in Egypt.[98] This is extraordinary because one of the striking omissions from surviving cuneiform documents of this era has always been any reference to Egypt. As we've seen, the Sumerians of the Early Dynastic period seem to have been completely unaware of the existence of the spectacular civilization with which they are now so often compared. But the kings of Ebla were not only in contact with Egypt, they sent men there regularly.

The scholars make a fascinating case: the goods that envoys brought back from the "king of Dugurasu" included linen, elephant ivory, hippo teeth, copper, bronze, and monkeys—exactly what one would expect from Egypt.[99] As we have seen, a lid of a stone container from Egypt has been found at Ebla.[100] And at least a little of that gold in Ebla could well have come from Egypt, as it did a thousand years later when close ties were again forged between Egypt and Syria.[101]

Dugurasu was definitely a major power and it was far away. The king of Dugurasu never came to Ebla (unlike the vassal kings and some of the neighboring kings who came to pledge their support for Ishar-damu), and he was the only foreign king to whom the king of Ebla sent large amounts of tin, lapis lazuli, and silver.[102]

There's another clue about the location of Dugurasu, this one from Egypt itself. An autobiography of an Egyptian official named Iny shows the other side of the relationship; he traveled to Byblos and on farther into Syria, right at this same time, in the reign of Pepy I (whose alabaster vase lid was found in the Ebla palace). What did he bring back to his king? Silver, tin, lapis lazuli, and oil—exactly the goods that Ebla sent to Dugurasu.[103] Biga suggests that the name of Dugurasu may have come from an Egyptian town in the eastern Nile Delta, but presumably references to the "king of Dugurasu" were to the king of Egypt.

One document from the Ebla archive records the travel provisions and gifts allocated to Enar-Lim and Ruzi-malik when they were bound for Dugurasu during the reign of Ishar-damu.[104] The two men were not Ebla natives. They lived in the land of Kakmium, on the coast, to the northwest of Ebla, and they worked for a merchant there named Ilum-Bala.[105] Merchants from Ilum-Bala's firm in Kakmium almost always accompanied envoys from Egypt (assuming that this was the location of Dugurasu) when they traveled to or from Ebla.[106]

Enar-Lim and Ruzi-malik must have spent some time preparing for their travels once they arrived in Ebla from their hometown. They were paid by the palace, splitting the standard allocation of money between them for their journey (each of them received five shekels of silver—a substantial sum).[107] They each also received a double set of clothes. They needed to make a good impression on arrival—the king of Dugurasu was an important man. Presumably someone in the delegation was also given a letter for him (perhaps one not unlike the letter to the envoy of Hamazi) in which Ishar-damu greeted the king of Dugurasu as a brother and asked him to send goods that were needed in Ebla. In the letter, King Ishar-damu would also have listed the gifts that the Egyptian envoys, accompanied by Enar-Lim and Ruzi-malik, were bringing with them.

These gifts were extravagant; we know that from the administrative list. They included items produced in Ebla, which were listed first: the king of Dugurasu received the standard set of three garments that were the trademark of Eblaite gift-giving (and certainly of the finest quality), and a dagger decorated with gold, no doubt fashioned in an Ebla palace workshop. The other gifts that they brought for the Dugurasu king were raw materials derived from lands to the east and north of Ebla—they had been obtained as a result of trade and gift exchange and were being passed on—4 minas (1.88 kilograms, 4 pounds) of silver (probably from Anatolia), 4 minas (1.88 kilograms, 4 pounds) of tin, 13 minas (6.11 kilograms, 13 pounds) of lapis lazuli (both probably from Afghanistan), and a "stone" that was not described further, but may have been a standard stone weight.[108]

The merchants from Kakmium, Enar-Lim and Ruzi-malik, were employed by the court in Ebla to accompany six representatives of the king of Dugurasu on their journey. These six men were responsible for transporting the gifts from Ebla to their king, just as they had been responsible for bringing their king's gifts to Ebla in the first place. The representatives from Egypt weren't named in this text, but one of them would have been the chief envoy, who was often listed as a man named Awa.[109]

The Egyptian men were also given clothes by the Ebla administration, though they didn't receive the payment of silver. No doubt the cost for their travel was supported by their king. All eight of the travelers, from both Kakmium and Dugurasu, also received gifts from the Ebla treasury. The Egyptian men were given a bag, along with a silver and gold bracelet weighing ten shekels, and Enar-Lim, the merchant from Kakmium, received a copper and gold bracelet weighing thirty shekels. Ruzi-malik seems to have been senior to Enar-Lim, to judge from the gifts he received. Besides getting the clothes, the five shekels of silver, and the same kind of bracelet as his companion, he also received a white bag, a foot band, and a silver dagger.

Not every object carried by the men was a gift. Some of the Ebla documents imply that the men traveling on these journeys may well have taken objects to trade for personal gain as well. The merchants from Kakmium might have brought wine or timber from their homeland to sell in Ebla,[110] and the envoys and deputies from Egypt sometimes received payments in Ebla, apparently for goods that they were selling. These were probably the same types of items that had been sent by their king as gifts: elephant and hippopotamus ivory, beads made of semiprecious stones, copper, and linen textiles.[111]

One has the sense that the journey back and forth between Ebla and Egypt would have been a familiar one to these men who were traveling together. The first leg of the journey from Ebla took them to the Mediterranean coast at Kakmium. From there, they traveled south, either on foot or by boat, with a stop at the coastal city of Dulu, which was almost certainly an ancient name for Byblos. Archaeology shows that Byblos already had a long history of trade with both Egypt and Syria, and the tablets show that Dulu was one of Ebla's most reliable trading partners, providing many of the same goods that came from Dugurasu. The expedition then continued on from Dulu to Egypt—Dugurasu.

They would have traveled about 1,370 kilometers (850 miles) to get there, a journey that would have taken them about two months. With a stay when they got there and the return journey to follow, Enar-Lim and Ruzi-malik were leaving Syria for at least six months. One can't help wondering what the merchants thought of the lands they visited, and all the varying landscapes and cities they encountered along the way.

The roads in the kingdom of Ebla and beyond it were well traveled. The people of Ebla knew that a wide world extended beyond their immediate domain, and the mechanisms of diplomacy were well established. Formal gift exchange with distant kings may, in fact, have been more reliable than trade in providing luxury goods for the court.

Pilgrimages

Sometimes the king couldn't send an envoy in his place; sometimes he had to leave Ebla and travel himself. The reasons for these expeditions were usually religious. In fact, the king and the crown prince made a pilgrimage of some kind every single month, which meant that they regularly spent days away from the capital city.[112] They had rituals to perform in shrines that were as much as a four-day journey away from home. Although the purpose of the travel was to maintain good relationships with the gods across the kingdom, it must also have had a unifying effect on the people. The king's procession was no doubt a sight to see as he and his attendants made their way on a regular circuit of towns and villages. He was not distant and secluded, locked up in his palace. He was right there, out among his people, on a regular basis.

It was not just men who traveled. Princesses and queens journeyed around the kingdom as well. In fact, many of the adult daughters and sisters of the king had moved away from Ebla to live elsewhere. Some of them had married leaders of city-states or powerful foreign kings, and they moved to the courts of their husbands. These types of diplomatic marriages were a fixture of Mesopotamian diplomacy, and we'll look into them in more detail later. The princesses from Ebla who became queens of other lands weren't forgotten by their families; they continued to receive gifts from home on a regular basis, especially, of course, after giving birth. On this happy occasion, many textiles and jewels arrived, not just for the mother but also for her baby.[113]

The princesses could come home, too. Tisha-Lim was a queen of the city of Emar (one of the cities within the Ebla kingdom, though quite a long way away from the capital), and she shows up regularly on the administrative lists: she was in Ebla frequently. It seems likely that she had been born in Ebla and found plenty of reasons to come home to visit.[114]

Other Ebla princesses were inducted as priestesses of gods or goddesses whose shrines were in other towns. King Ishar-damu's sister Tinib-dulum, for example, became a priestess of the agricultural god Adabal. Adabal had three main centers of worship; Tinib-dulum's assignment was to his main temple in the distant city of Luban, far away in the mountains near the Antioch plain.[115] When inducted, she traveled there in style; she took five princes with her, probably to carry her there in a sedan-chair.[116] And she was provided with rich gifts (mostly textiles, of course) when she was inaugurated, in this case by the "lords"—the elders who advised the king.[117]

Once she had settled in Luban, Tinib-dulum would not have been deprived of the company of people from the capital city. She no doubt took attendants with her from the court, and her new home of Luban was a popular site of pilgrimage. Once a year, a group of pious and powerful young men from Ebla made a thirty-nine-day journey to thirty-six holy places associated with the god Adabal, starting with the great temple at Luban. They traveled there during the same month each year,[118] the month of the great festival for the god. The group was made up of between five and fourteen men, and sometimes the king, Ishar-damu—priestess Tinib-dulum's brother—was among them.[119] We don't know how formal or informal the visits to Luban might have been. Certainly the men had religious rituals to attend to when they were there, sacrifices and libations to make, and prayers to offer. It seems likely, though, that the royal brother and sister had a chance to see one another and to talk.

Queen Tabur-damu traveled across the kingdom too, even though, as a native Eblaite, she had no other "home" to travel to. Most importantly, she and her husband King Ishar-damu returned to the House of the Dead at Binash on their wedding anniversary each year for a ceremony that pertained to what was called "their dressing."[120] They were clothed in particular garments made of black and white wool that had been made for the occasion. Black wool was common, but, as we've seen, white wool was rare. It was reserved for royalty.

Like the men traveling to the shrines of Adabal, Tabur-damu had a religious reason to travel, not just to Binash but also to visit the sanctuary of the goddess Ishhara. Unlike the priestess Tinib-dulum, Tabur-damu probably wasn't carried in a sedan-chair on the journey, but she had her own chariot.[121] Her mother-in-law Dusigu did the same thing, though perhaps the two royal women didn't visit Ishhara's temple together. It would be fascinating to know whether Tabur-damu and Dusigu got along well, and how they each advised King Ishar-damu. Regrettably, administrative texts shine no light on this at all.

Destruction of Ebla

Queen Tabur-damu and King Ishar-damu must have consulted oracles when they chose a son who would inherit the throne of Ebla on the death of his father, and they had also possibly started negotiations for an appropriate wife for the crown prince, a future *maliktum*. But it was not to be. Ishar-damu and Tabur-damu turned out to be the last of their dynasty. Ebla had probably been a great power for more than 300 years and must have seemed, to its subjects, stable and eternal. But the kingdom of Ebla was about to fall victim to the same political storm that would bring an end to the dynasty in Lagash. Someone attacked, plundered, and burned the Ebla palace to the ground, inadvertently preserving all the clay records that immortalized their era. That someone was a king from a distant region of central Mesopotamia called Akkad, which we will visit in the next chapter.

PART III

The Akkadian and Ur III Periods,

2300–2000 BCE

Chapter 6
A Conqueror and a Priestess

One day, around 2300 BCE, a man was working in a storeroom in the city of Ur, probably surrounded by jars of foods or beer. He fixed a small piece of clay to the top of a terracotta pot and rolled his cylinder seal across it, so that anyone who later came across the pot would know who had last opened it. He was performing a responsibility that had stayed much the same for 1,200 years, ever since the invention of cylinder seals around 3500 BCE in Uruk.[1] Sealing shipments of various kinds of goods was a very mundane thing for an official to do; it happened all the time. Within a day or two, or perhaps within hours, the man had no doubt forgotten that he had sealed this particular jar. But, in the odd way that things happen, the resulting clay sealing survived in the ground for thousands of years and is the only witness to his presumably illustrious career (see Fig. 6.1).

Kitushdu: A Scribe and His Cylinder Seal

The man's name was Kitushdu, and this little piece of clay bearing the impression of his seal is, in fact, the only evidence that he existed at all. Leonard Woolley found it during excavations at Ur in 1928, in the same area as the royal tombs (though it was from a later period). Woolley described the sealed piece of clay in a note in his excavation records and later had it transported to the British Museum in London, where it was catalogued and put in a drawer. But it is not hidden from public view—you can see it pictured on the museum's website.[2] The sealing is tiny—just a little more than 2.5 centimeters (1 inch) by 4 centimeters (1.6 inches) in size.

Fig. 6.1 Impression of the cylinder seal of Kitushdu, scribe, mid-twenty-third century BCE. (© The Trustees of the British Museum)

Kitushdu's seal was nevertheless impressive; it bore a beautifully sculpted water buffalo and an inscription in honor of the princess for whom he worked, which reads as follows:

> Enheduana,
> daughter of Sargon
> [ ]-Kitushdu,
> the scribe,
> (is) her servant.[3]

Kitushdu and his seal make a good starting point for our study of his era, the twenty-third century BCE, because of the people mentioned, the artistry of the seal itself, and the animal portrayed on it.

Let's start with the people. Kitushdu shows in his seal inscription that he was in close contact with the most powerful family in Mesopotamia of his time. He was a scribe, and presumably a high-ranking one, to judge from the quality of his seal and the words written on it, and he was a "servant" of a princess named Enheduana. The term translated "servant" also meant "slave" and was used by anyone who was lower in rank to refer to their relationship to a member of the royal family—and everybody was lower in rank than the royal family. When used in a cylinder seal inscription in association with a king or princess, the person described as a "servant" was a member of the royal court. There's a good chance that Enheduana had personally given him the seal. We'll come back to her shortly. Her father is listed as Sargon; and he was someone who was very influential, a man who transformed the Mesopotamian concept of what a king could be and do.

Sargon of Akkad: A Legendary Conqueror

Sargon (c. 2316–2277 BCE) is the earliest Big Name in Mesopotamian history. Few people today have heard of Ur-Nanshe, Enmetena, or Ishar-damu, let alone Baranamtara or Tabur-damu. But Sargon is familiar. He is even sometimes known as "Sargon the Great"—the world's first empire builder, the first man to unite Mesopotamia from the Persian Gulf to the Mediterranean. He shares his epithet with later imperialistic conquerors like Cyrus of Persia and Alexander of Macedon but I have no idea who first dubbed him "the Great."

He would no doubt have approved of the epithet, and later Mesopotamians felt that way about him too.[4] Sargon's story just got bigger over time, his feats more impressive, his parentage more divine. One legend, composed centuries after his death, has Sargon speaking in the first person, weaving a story of a magical birth and miraculous survival:

> My mother was a high priestess, I did not know my father. . . .
> My mother, the high priestess, conceived me, she bore me in secret.
> She placed me in a reed basket, she sealed my hatch with pitch.
> She left me to the river, whence I could not come up.
> The river carried me off, it brought me to Aqqi, drawer of water.
> Aqqi, drawer of water, brought me up as he dipped his bucket.
> Aqqi, drawer of water, raised me as his adopted son.
> Aqqi, drawer of water set (me) to his orchard work.[5]

The only explanation of Sargon's sudden ascent to the throne, in the legend, was that "during my orchard work, (the goddess) Ishtar loved me,"[6] after which, just like that, he was king. Obviously, none of this is likely to have been true. None of these details of Sargon's supposed biography were even mentioned until hundreds of years after his death, but it does make a great rags-to-riches story.

The rest of the legend recounts Sargon's valiant expeditions and victories. It makes no mention of an army. Sargon, a third-millennium BCE superhero, did it all himself:

> I was wont to ascend high mountains.
> I was wont to cross over lower mountains.
> The [l]and of the sea I sieged three times.
> I conquered Dilmun, I [ ]
> I destroyed [Ka]zallu and [ ] . . .[7]

For centuries after Sargon's death, kings thought the world of him, anxious to emulate his glory. Some of them borrowed his name or those of his descendants, or adopted their titles.[8] They honored him in rituals for centuries.[9] Around 1,800 years after his reign, a broken head of Sargon was found by an awestruck Babylonian king in the ruins of a temple at Sippar. He reverently set it up on a pedestal and dedicated offerings to it.[10]

Sargon's name and achievements were therefore familiar to people in the region for about 2,000 years, and we hear about him a lot from their later writings. Curiously, though, if the only clues we had were documents and objects that were created in Sargon's own time, he might seem inconsequential—just one of hundreds of kings whose reigns came and went without leaving much trace.

Kitushdu's seal impression might be just a small piece of clay, but its inscription is one of only nine short inscriptions that survive from Sargon's own time that mention him at all. Most of the others are similarly unimpressive and tangential to Sargon's life. Two other servants of the princess Enheduana, daughter of Sargon, live on as a result of their seals. A man named Ilum-palil who served as her hairdresser owned a valuable lapis lazuli seal; the seal itself, not just an impression, was excavated at Ur in 1928.[11] Her steward Adda also used a cylinder seal that identifies him as her servant.[12] Both of these mention Sargon only because he was Enheduana's father. The other inscriptions comprise a short dedication by the estate administrator who worked for Sargon's wife,[13] and two objects dedicated to the god Shara by a temple administrator "for the well-being of Sargon, king of Agade."[14] Three short inscriptions do seem to have been commissioned by Sargon himself, but they say nothing much at all, just that he dedicated a stone mace head and a vase to a god, and that he wanted the gods to curse some future person for something. That inscription reads, "may they tear out [his foundations] and take away his seed."[15] And that's it. They give no facts at all about Sargon's achievements or his reign. We have no lengthy royal inscriptions commissioned by Sargon on stone sculptures or vases, unlike the Early Dynastic kings of Lagash whose inscriptions are abundant. And his image is preserved only in a worn monument found in Susa, in which he is shown in profile marching at the head of some soldiers. His face has been flattened with time and erosion, but one can make out his long beard and outstretched arm.[16]

Fortunately, though, we have more than legends from which to learn about Sargon's life. Later scribes sought out and copied inscriptions that they saw on sculptures of the king and on relief sculptures of his battles. We'll come back to scribes and their educations later in this book.[17] We have them to thank for a lot of our knowledge of the literature, religion, and political history of the region. Scribes even sometimes noted where they had found the text they had copied. For example, about 500 years after Sargon's death, a scribe transcribed an inscription that he found on a stone sculpture that had been commissioned by Sargon. He copied it onto a clay tablet and noted at the end that the "inscription was written on the socle in front of Lugalzagesi."[18] An image of this king, Lugalzagesi, must have featured on Sargon's monument, and it is Lugalzagesi to whom we turn now, because he laid the groundwork for Sargon's empire.

Lugalzagesi: First King to Dream of Empire

Before Sargon began his imperialistic campaigns, Lugalzagesi, king of Umma (c. 2320 BCE), was busily uniting (and laying waste to) much of southern Mesopotamia. The city-state of Umma was, as we have seen, the perpetual nemesis of the city-state of Lagash. They had battled for so long over their shared border that inhabitants of both city-states must have viewed the feud as some kind of fact of life. Soldiers from each state must have assumed that they would forever be sent out by their king with spears, bows, and arrows to fight for their god—Ningirsu (for Lagash) or Shara (for Umma)—to reclaim control of the lands of the Gu'edena. But King Lugalzagesi brought an end to the feud, conquering both Umma's rival, Lagash, and the ancient city of Uruk, to which he then moved his capital.

By Lugalzagesi's time, approximately 1,200 years had passed since Uruk had emerged as the first great city of Mesopotamia. It was as venerable as some of the very oldest mosques and cathedrals are to us today. But the Sumerians believed that Uruk was much older than that. With their expansive view of the deep roots of cities and kings in the region, the creators of the Sumerian King List (writing a couple of centuries later) recorded that kings had first built and ruled Uruk a very precise (though wildly mistaken) 8,077 years before Lugalzagesi's reign. But even this was all relatively modern history in their view, given how many hundreds of thousands of years they believed had passed since the beginning of kingship.

Lugalzagesi cast himself as a new kind of king. He was not a king of a single city-state, but "king of the land."[19] The people didn't have a name for Mesopotamia yet. It was, to Lugalzagesi, simply "*kalam*"—"the land." In the same inscription, he created new language for this vast space over which he claimed to rule, and he did it by defining the extreme edges of the world. The kingdom stretched "from the Lower Sea, through the Tigris and Euphrates, to the Upper Sea" (that is, from south to north, to the seas in both directions that bounded the world) and "from the sunrise to the sunset" (that is, from east to west).[20]

This was an exaggeration, but we have to give him credit (or possibly blame) for his new idea. Lugalzagesi dreamed bigger than his predecessors. He must have known that there were many areas over which he did not, in fact, rule. He would have been aware that traders came and went from Dilmun in the Lower Sea, and from the lapis lazuli mountains beyond Afghanistan, and the cedar mountains far to the north in Syria, and that he had no jurisdiction over these places at all. But he created a fantasy that inspired Mesopotamian kings for thousands of years after his death, though they didn't know to credit him. He invented the power-crazed concept of a vast empire, perhaps even the whole world, ruled by just one man.

When it came to actually naming the lands that he ruled, the reality of Lugalzagesi's state proved to have been far more modest than his bombastic titles suggested. He listed six former city-states and described their joy and pride at being subjected to his wondrous rule:

> At that time, Uruk spent its time rejoicing,
> Ur, like a bull, raised high its head,
> Larsa, the beloved city of (the god) Utu, made merry,
> Umma, the beloved city of (the god) Shara, lifted its huge arms,

Zabalam cried out like a ewe reunited with its lamb,
Kian raised high its neck.[21]

This was still a significant achievement—not the rejoicing and merriness,
but the very fact of the regional state that he had created (and the good
cheer seems highly suspect, given that these cities had just been defeated
and were forced to pay tribute to the leader whose troops had killed many
of their young men). It must have taken innovative administrative structures
to organize and tax the people of such widely spread, and presumably
resentful, cities.

Would Sargon have dreamed up (and eventually fought to construct) his
empire, had it not been for Lugalzagesi's earlier attempts? Historians can't
"what if" about the past—if any one event had been different there is no
telling what else would have changed—but clearly Lugalzagesi's rhetoric
influenced Sargon. Sargon even borrowed the same phrases. He, too, claimed
to rule from the Lower Sea to the Upper Sea.[22] The main difference is that
Sargon apparently was more successful in this than Lugalzagesi had been,
and Sargon's grandson Naram-Sin (2254–2218 BCE) was more successful
still. Had Lugalzagesi not come up with that enticing image of world
domination, Sargon might have been content to stay closer to home. But
it is impossible to know what might have been, because what happened,
happened.

In any event, it's unclear where Sargon came from or why he got it into
his head to become a king, let alone an emperor. He grew up in Akkad,
the region to the north of Sumer, in central Mesopotamia, and his native
language was the local Akkadian. His name was a fiction. It meant "the king
is legitimate"—just the kind of name you'd want if you actually were not
a legitimate king at all.

Those inscriptions that Sargon authorized and that were copied by later
scribes all start with him already in power, leading troops. He never named
his father, almost certainly because his father was not a king. Instead he
launched into the close relationships he had with gods, using their Akkadian
names—he was the "emissary for Ishtar (the goddess of love and war, Inana
in Sumer), . . . attendant of Anu (god of the heavens), chief governor for
Enlil (the king of the gods)"[23]—and in the next breath, he was attacking
Lugalzagesi's city of Uruk. He "conquered the city of Uruk and destroyed
its walls. He was victorious over Uruk."[24] This happened around 2292 BCE.[25]

What had happened before this was that, somehow or another, Sargon had seized the throne, probably of the city-state of Kish, and had built himself an army. He must have hired experienced military leaders to train the men. He must have taxed his new subjects to pay for arms and armor. One suspects that militarism and imperial ambition were built into Sargon's reign from day one, and that he had immediately set his sights on Lugalzagesi, the most powerful king in Sumer. Perhaps diplomats shuttled between Kish and Uruk as they had in earlier centuries, seeking ways to defuse the situation. Or perhaps the two war leaders with such similar dreams relished the idea of clashing on the battlefield. When they did, Sargon was victorious. He gloated in one of his inscriptions that he "conquered fifty governors with the mace of (the god) Ilaba."[26] Better yet, to his mind, he "captured Lugalzagesi, king of Uruk, and brought him to the gate of Enlil in a neck-stock."[27] For Lugalzagesi this would have been more humiliating than death on the battlefield. And this was the scene that must have been depicted on the missing sculpture, the one on the base of which this inscription was also carved and copied by a helpful scribe.

According to the royal inscriptions that were copied, Sargon did a lot of campaigning; he "was victorious in thirty-four battles"[28] over the course of his reign, and he claimed that the god Enlil "gave him the Upper Sea (the Mediterranean) and the Lower Sea (the Persian Gulf)."[29] It's unclear how successful he was in controlling the more distant regions in these lands—notwithstanding Enlil's wish for him to rule them—but one can argue that Sargon deserves the title of the world's first emperor.[30] He may even have been responsible for the destruction of the city of Ebla, though that might have been the work of his grandson, Naram-Sin. Both claimed to have conquered this region, as they fought their ways to the Mediterranean.

The realm Sargon controlled was populated by people of many different cultures and languages. But to judge from the number of campaigns that he and his successors launched to try to maintain this empire, it was not exactly an auspicious start for the whole imperialistic venture. The logistics were almost impossible. How could one king rule lands that took weeks of travel to reach? How could he convince people to pay taxes to him when there was no clear benefit to doing so? How could he maintain a military large enough to be available to put down rebellions whenever they broke out?

He created systems to try to address these ongoing crises. One of them was to try to cow his subjects into submission through force, destroying the walls around cities that could have continued to protect them, and emphasizing his fierce bravado over and over in his inscriptions. Sargon, as he boasted, "showed mercy to no one."[31] Another strategy was to set up civilian and military governors in cities around the empire. He wrote that "men of Agade hold governorships all the way from the Lower Sea."[32] We are told in one inscription (again, copied by a later scribe) that "5,400 men eat daily before him."[33] That tiny fragment of a sentence has been used to conjure a standing army, paid by the king, or a huge personal bodyguard. "He washed his weapons in the sea."[34] Was he washing off the blood of his many battles? Or was he plunging the weapon into the sea as though to claim it for himself? Did he do this at all?

At some point in his reign Sargon built a new capital city at a place called Agade. A later legend recalled Agade as immeasurably rich, its people dining in cosmopolitan style on "the best of food" and "the best of drink."[35] The storehouses were full of gold, silver, copper, tin, and lapis lazuli, and music played in the streets: "There was drumbeat in the city, winds and strings without. Its harbor, where ships tied up, hummed cheerfully."[36] Unfortunately, there is no way to know if any of this was true because Agade has not yet been found. Archaeologists do know where to look, though—Sargon's new capital probably was built somewhere near the confluence of the Tigris and Adhaim Rivers, north of what is now Baghdad.[37]

A giant fragment of an over-lifesize statue of a man made of basalt was found there at a site called Qadasiyah—it would have been a statue appropriate for a capital city (see Fig. 6.2). When complete, the figure stood about 2.75 meters (9 feet) tall, bigger than anything else known from this era.[38] Was this Sargon? It might have been. All that is left are his bare feet, which are inset and protected from what seem to be hammer marks that pit the surface of the rest of the sculpture. Julian Reade, a curator at the British Museum, aptly described the sculpture as looking like "cheese or ice cream that has been attacked with a scoop."[39] It seems that at some point an angry mob may have set upon the statue and that it later may have spent some time, maybe a very long time, in the river. Ironically, for a king whose memory overshadowed that of so many others, no definite statue of Sargon survives. But perhaps this figure was of him and perhaps it was once a towering presence in Agade. The city is one of the great lost sites of the ancient world; if it is identified and excavated in the future it may prove to

Fig. 6.2 Fragment of an over-lifesize basalt sculpture of a man from Qadasiyah, possibly early twenty-third century BCE. (© The Trustees of the British Museum)

contain archives and inscriptions that will finally bring Sargon out of the haze of legend.

Trade and Innovation in Sargon's Time

We return now to Kitushdu's seal, in order to appreciate the artistry of the depiction of the water buffalo (see Fig. 6.1). Its head tilts upward, the muscles in its back and legs taut as it strides forward. Sargon's reign and the reigns of his successors—that is, the Akkadian period (named for Sargon's homeland of Akkad)—was a time of extraordinary creative innovation in cylinder seal designs; the unnamed artists created one miniature masterpiece after another.[40] In later periods of Mesopotamian history, the scenes became more standardized and many seals looked very much like one another, but the Akkadian period seal carvers observed their world and experimented. They depicted remarkably naturalistic people and animals, with their limbs and muscles convincingly doing the right things. When you consider that the artists carved these on a miniscule scale, without the help of magnification, in reverse relief, and on the curved surface of a hard stone, their skill becomes hard to fathom and all the more impressive.

The stones they used for the seals were imported. We don't know what Kitushdu's seal was made of because only its impression survives, but Akkadian seals were often carved from serpentine, diorite, rock crystal, jasper, or lapis lazuli.[41] These types of stones had been used in earlier times as well. The trade in lapis lazuli from the Hindu Kush mountains had been taking place for thousands of years, since the sixth millennium BCE.[42]

But Sargon was not content with the traditional trading mechanisms; he initiated a new era of trade by inviting foreign traders and their boats directly to his capital. He boasted in one inscription that boats from Magan, Dilmun, and Meluhha docked at the harbor in Agade.[43] These boats brought not only precious goods but also animals that the Mesopotamians had never seen before, animals that the seal carvers captured in their work. The water buffalo on Kitushdu's seal, with its huge horns, was an import from the Indus Valley—ancient Meluhha. Even Indian elephants were later said to have made the long trip to Mesopotamia. The world was opening up, and the artisans wanted to show off these fantastic creatures in their designs. It almost seems as though some people of the Akkadian period saw themselves as different from those who had come before them, living in a new and exciting age.

Innovations were happening all over the place. Metalworkers developed the ingenious technique of lost-wax casting to use bronze more efficiently— a sculpture could be lighter and could be made with less metal because the resulting object was hollow.

Scribes figured out how to use cuneiform to write the Akkadian language of central Mesopotamia as well as Sumerian, and Sargon took the radical step of making Akkadian the language of administration. Like Eblaite, Akkadian was a Semitic language. In histories from the early twentieth century of our era, Sargon's conquest of Sumer was sometimes portrayed as an invasion by foreigners with a different culture—Akkadian troops attacking Sumerian cities. But Akkadian speakers had lived in Sumer (and Sumerian speakers had lived in Akkad) at least since writing was invented. Beyond the difference in language and in the names given to the gods, the cultures of the two regions were almost indistinguishable.

Sargon also tried to standardize administrative practices across his realm. Weights and measures, for example, had always been subject to regional variations. Sargon wanted a *"gur"* measure to be the same everywhere in the empire, for example. He wasn't entirely successful in this attempt at standardization, but again it was a break with the past.

Sargon even decided to use a new (and self-promoting) way to identify the years of his reign. The Mesopotamians never numbered the years from a fixed date in the past the way we do now. Sargon decided to name the years; at the end of each year, he chose one of his recent great achievements to be the name of the year that was beginning. Scribes were supposed to use this year-name whenever a date was needed on a document. It was Sargon's cunning way of reminding his people of his power, and it created a precedent. Mesopotamian kings regularly used year-names as a form of propaganda for more than 700 years after his reign and, in a few states, kings even continued to name their years for at least three more centuries after that. Since so few documents survive from Sargon's reign, we know of only four of his year-names. None of them can be assigned to specific years in his reign, but all of them boasted of his military victories. They were the years in which "Sargon went to Simurrum," "Sargon destroyed Uru'a," "Sargon destroyed Elam," and "Mari was destroyed."[44] Remember that his throne name was already propagandistic, so anyone mentioning the name of a year couldn't help repeating two ideas that Sargon wanted to reinforce—his legitimacy and his military might. Hence, a farmer might say, "I first grew barley in this field during the year when 'The king is legitimate' destroyed Elam."

Sargon's grandson, King Naram-Sin, also named most of his years for military victories, but a few year-names referred to achievements that were not related to warfare. He named a year for his construction of a temple to Ishtar in Agade,[45] for example, and another was the "Year in which Naram-Sin chose the *en*-priestess of Nanna by means of the omens."[46]

And this takes us back, once again, to Kitushdu's seal, because Enheduana, the princess whom Kitushdu served, was also an *en*-priestess of Nanna.

Enheduana: Princess, High Priestess and Poet

Enheduana was, as Kitushdu's seal impression makes clear, the daughter of Sargon, but she was not his only child. He had at least five children, and he was married to at least one wife: Tashlultum. As with so many aspects of Sargon's life, his wife's memory survives because of just one small fragment of an inscription, in this case, one that was carved on an alabaster bowl. The bowl was dedicated by her estate administrator, whose name is lost, but it records that he worked for "Tashlultum, wife of Sargon."[47]

Sargon's reign stretched for at least forty years (he was sometimes even credited with a fifty-five-year reign), so he lived to see his sons and daughters grow up and have children of their own. After his death, two of his sons succeeded him: first Rimush, who ruled for only seven years (c. 2276–2269 BCE), and then Manishtusu, who ruled for another fifteen years after that (c. 2269–2254 BCE). Manishtusu, in turn, was followed by his son, Naram-Sin, who ruled for at least thirty-seven years. Between them, these three generations of kings dominated Mesopotamia for more than a century.

King Manishtusu's name means "Who is with him?," which sounds like something a startled midwife might have cried out when attending the birth of twins (in their world, as through most of history until modern times, the number of babies in the womb wasn't known before birth). This explanation of Manishtusu's name is probably wrong, given the Mesopotamian propensity for naming babies with pious messages about the gods, but I like it anyway. Sargon must have lived to see the childhoods of plenty of his grandchildren, and perhaps, late in life, he already saw promise in Manishtusu's young son Naram-Sin, who ended up, in some ways, exceeding his grandfather's achievements.

Enheduana is sometimes described as the daughter of Sargon and Tashlultum,[48] but that's just speculation. Her mother could have been a different royal wife or concubine. Like Sargon's other children, she was no doubt given an Akkadian name at birth, though we don't know what it was. Unlike most girls—unlike most children, for that matter—she seems to have learned to read and write, and it's likely that she stood out in the royal family as exceptional. When she reached adulthood, she was an obvious candidate for a singularly important role in her father's empire, as the *en*-priestess in the city of Ur.

Sargon had conquered Ur, in southern Mesopotamia, in the course of building his empire. It had been the capital of one of the great Sumerian city-states, home to the moon god, Nanna, and Sargon seems to have encountered some trouble from his new subjects there. It would hardly be a surprise if the locals resented Sargon's conquest. After all, in his own inscription Sargon had boasted that he "vanquished Ur in battle and smote the city and destroyed its fortress."[49] The proud citizens of Ur must have been crushed to see their fortifications in ruins and were hardly in the mood to feel affection toward the man responsible. So, Sargon seems to have decided that he needed a family member in a powerful position in Ur, someone he could trust to keep an eye on the locals, plead his case with the city god, and perhaps even endear herself to the population.

In Naram-Sin's year-name about the appointment of a later *en*-priestess of Nanna, he claimed that she was chosen "by means of the omens,"[50] and this was true of Enheduana as well. The king asked the gods for their advice on whom to choose. Naturally occurring omens could take many forms, from the appearance of comets, to the movements of flocks of birds, to the passage of the five visible planets through the constellations in the night sky. The gods could appear with messages in dreams as well, or they could speak through the internal organs of sacrificed animals. We will explore these in more detail later.[51] No matter how they sent their messages, the gods spoke cryptically, which meant that specially trained diviners were required to decipher what they meant. Diviners were always literate and, over time, they developed a body of writings—lists of past omens and their outcomes—which they could consult to be sure that they were not misunderstanding the gods' intentions.

As a result of some omen or another, Enheduana was "chosen for the pure rites"[52] and sent to Ur. There, she went through elaborate installation rituals and took on her new name in the local Sumerian language: Enheduana, which meant "*en* (priestess), ornament of the heavens."[53] If she wasn't already bilingual beforehand, she presumably learned to speak Sumerian soon after her arrival, in addition to her native Akkadian.

Although Enheduana is the earliest *en*-priestess whose name we know, the same position may well have been held, about a century earlier, by one of the women buried in the royal tombs of Ur. This was the lady of the "Great Death Pit" we encountered in Chapter 3, who had been surrounded in death by female attendants.[54] Like the earlier woman, Enheduana would have taken up residence in the Gipar, the palace of the priestess, located on Ur's citadel near Nanna's temple. And, also like her earlier counterpart, she was no doubt provided with riches; she would have taken her meals and drinks from silver bowls, and worn fine jewelry of gold, carnelian, and lapis lazuli.

A short inscription carved during her lifetime and apparently commissioned by the priestess herself gives us a little more information:

> Enheduana, the *zirru* of Nanna, the spouse of Nanna, the daughter of Sargon, king of the world, in the [temple of the goddess Ina]na-ZA.ZA of Ur, she erected a plinth (and) named it: "the dais, the table of the god An of the heavens."[55]

The term *zirru* was also used to refer to the moon god's divine wife, the goddess Ningal. Enheduana seems, in some way, to have embodied Ningal.[56] This is supported by the next phrase, in which Enheduana also claimed to be the god's "spouse." Priestesses were viewed as the wives of gods (just as priests could be the husbands of goddesses) throughout this era. Mesopotamians tended to think of all relationships as somehow having a basis in the family, even if a relationship was between a human and a deity.

Enheduana emphasized her tie to her father just as a crown prince or new king might have done; it helped to legitimize her authority. And, in proper royal fashion, she also boasted that she had built and named a new plinth or dais in a temple. Oddly, though, although Enheduana was the priestess of the moon god, the dais was not in his temple, but in the temple to Inana-Zaza, a form of the goddess of war and love. Enheduana was particularly fond of Inana, as was her father, who venerated the same goddess but called her Ishtar, the Akkadian equivalent of Inana.

This inscription was carved onto a 25 centimeter (10 inch) alabaster disk, which was found in the Gipar palace where Enheduana lived.[57] The inscription wasn't, however, the main attraction of the disk (though it is very helpful to historians). On the other side is a relief sculpture showing four people and an altar (see Fig. 6.3). The disk is fragmentary, and, many years ago, restorers reconstructed the missing parts as best they could. Right in the middle of the scene is a female figure, who clearly represents Enheduana herself, overseeing an offering being made at an altar. Enheduana is taller than the men behind and in front of her, her head extending right up to the top of the relief, much like the standing king in the Standard of Ur, and

Fig. 6.3 Front of the disk of the *en*-priestess Enheduana, made of calcite, mid-twenty-third century BCE. (Courtesy of the Penn Museum, image 295918 and object B16665)

she wears a flounced, pleated robe and a distinctive headdress.[58] Her hair is braided, with a lock of hair looping down in front of her ear.

It is a little unclear how old Enheduana was when she arrived to take her position in the Nanna temple. She was described in one source as "the pure *en* of Nanna."[59] That adjective "pure" suggests that she took a vow of chastity and therefore was young, perhaps in her late teens, as Mesopotamians would expect a virgin bride to be (even a bride of a god). On the other hand, the dramatic events of her life mostly took place in later decades, not during the reign of her father but of her nephew, king Naram-Sin.[60] Some scholars have proposed that she was not appointed until Naram-Sin's reign,[61] but it seems more likely that she was appointed by her father and lived on, serving as priestess, through the reigns of her brothers and into that of her nephew.

As a high priestess, Enheduana's responsibilities were extensive. She performed many rituals in the temple, such as purifications, initiations, and divinations, along with providing food offerings to the god.[62] The reason you may have heard of Enheduana, though, isn't the fact that we have an image of her, or that she was the daughter of the first empire builder, or that she was a powerful priestess. It's that she's considered by many to be the world's first identified author: the first person to put her name to a work of literature.[63] Because of this, she is one of the most familiar names in ancient Near Eastern history.[64] Enheduana wrote a number of hymns— perhaps as many as six—one of which she composed in the first person as "I, Enheduana."[65] No examples of her hymns survive in copies from her own time. Once again, as is true of Sargon's inscriptions, later scribes preserved them for us.

Her writings were considered important enough to be venerated and studied generation after generation. They included literary works, two of which mentioned Enheduana's name, along with a collection of hymns. The latter was apparently embellished and adapted over time. It ends with the statement that "The compiler of this clay tablet is Enheduana."[66] Yes, but modern scholars have noted that the tablet includes hymns to two temples that were built after her death.[67] Some scholars have gone so far as to assert that this shows that she probably did not write any of the works herself.[68] It is true that she clearly couldn't have written or even compiled those particular verses about the later temples, but Enheduana may well have put together the original collection and subsequent scribes added to it, without changing the credit at the end. I see no reason to strip her of her authorship of all her works or to speculate that she had a ghost writer.

Interestingly, the focus of Enheduana's devotion in most of her writing wasn't Nanna, the god to whom she was ostensibly married by virtue of being his priestess, but Inana, her family god with whom she seems to have felt a deep, almost passionate, connection. Her best-known hymn was the autobiographical one. It was called "*Ninmesharra*" in Sumerian, which literally means "Queen of all Cosmic Powers," but it is more commonly known in English as "The Exaltation of Inana."

One scholar, maybe 500 years after her time, carefully copied the hymn in meticulous cuneiform onto three identically sized tablets, including fifty-one lines of the hymn on each (see Fig. 6.4).[69] He probably kept this copy in his personal library. Dozens of other ancient copies of the hymn survive, excerpted in school exercises. The hymn was one of ten texts that advanced scribes learned in school when studying Sumerian, centuries after her lifetime, around 1740 BCE.[70] Presumably the words of the hymn were familiar to others too. Enheduana's emotion jumps off the page when you read it. Even in translation from Sumerian—a very dead language—and even after the passage of more than 4,000 years, Enheduana's voice rings through. It is, though, a singularly unhappy voice.

She began the hymn by extolling Inana's great powers, especially in times of war, which she likened to a great storm:

At your battle-cry, my lady, the foreign lands bow low. When humanity comes before you in awed silence at the terrifying radiance and tempest, you grasp the most terrible of all the divine powers. . . . In the van of battle, all is struck down before you. With your strength, my lady, teeth can crush flint. You

Fig. 6.4 Copy of "The Exultation of Inana" by Enheduana written on a series of three tablets, Old Babylonian period. (Yale University, Peabody Museum)

charge forward like a charging storm. You roar with the roaring storm, you continually thunder with (the storm god) Ishkur. You spread exhaustion with the stormwinds, while your own feet remain tireless.[71]

The language about battles and storms was apt when Enheduana was writing, because it was a chaotic and terrifying time of revolt in her adopted land of Sumer. Her nephew Naram-Sin had taken the throne after the death of his father only to face a massive rebellion around 2230 BCE, known as the "Great Revolt."[72] Upstart kings declared themselves to be in power in the ancient Sumerian cities of Uruk and Kish; each formed a league of cities, and both rejected Akkadian rule and claimed independence.[73] One of the rebels who joined them was a man named Lugal-ane, who was mentioned, along with self-proclaimed kings of Uruk and Kish, in another document from the time.[74] Lugal-ane was the man who turned Enheduana's life upside down. He led troops in a campaign against her adopted home of Ur.

It may seem from this chapter that the Sumerian cities were under constant attack. You might suppose that the residents would have been inured to violence by now. But that's just an illusion, because whole lifetimes get compressed into paragraphs here. In fact, most of the adults who had witnessed Sargon's conquest of the city would have been dead by the time Lugal-ane appeared with his forces. People who had been children when the Akkadian army first arrived might still be alive, but they would barely have remembered living through it.

Meanwhile, Enheduana must have been quite old by now. Presumably she was comfortable in her role as priestess, well known and probably well respected by the hundreds of people who worked for the Nanna temple in Ur. But Lugal-ane's invasion changed everything. Enheduana vividly described the destruction he wrought in a temple, along with his blasphemous attitude toward the god:

In connection with the purification rites of holy An, Lugal-ane has altered everything of his, and has stripped (the god) An of the E-ana (temple). He has not stood in awe of the greatest deity. He has turned that temple, whose attractions were inexhaustible, whose beauty was endless, into a destroyed temple.[75]

Then Lugal-ane turned on Enheduana herself. As aunt to the current king, and daughter of the hated Sargon, she was an obvious target of the rebel leader's ire. Lugal-ane marched into the temple of the moon god Nanna, took Enheduana's crown, deposed her from her position, and forced her into exile:[76]

> He (Lugal-ane) stood there in triumph and drove me out of the temple. He made me fly like a swallow from the window; I have exhausted my life-strength. He made me walk through the thorn bushes of the mountains. He stripped me of the rightful crown of the *en*-priestess. He gave me a knife and dagger, saying to me "These are appropriate ornaments for you."[77]

Those thorn bushes in the mountains—you can almost feel them tearing her fine clothes, as she grew weaker and weaker, searching for a place of refuge far from the flat river valley surrounding Ur. Perhaps the knife and the dagger were "appropriate" because Lugal-ane wanted her to commit suicide. Or perhaps he simply was making a comment about exiles: like others in her position, Enheduana would have to defend herself.[78]

It's remarkable that she survived this incident. Left to wander, apparently alone, in rebel-held territory, the living embodiment of the oppressive Akkadian regime, she might well have been killed. In her telling, it was the goddess Inana who saved her. Switching to the third person, the poem ends with Enheduana's salvation by Inana: "The powerful lady (Inana), respected in the gathering of rulers, has accepted her offerings from her (Enheduana). Inana's holy heart has been assuaged."[79] She was saved because Naram-Sin had succeeded in putting down the rebellion. He claimed to have done so in just one year, and to have killed 95,340 men in the process[80] (though numbers like this in royal inscriptions are always suspect). Lugal-ane, who seems to have briefly called himself "king of Ur,"[81] disappears from the story. Naram-Sin's aunt, Enheduana, gratefully returned to her position in Ur.

What more do we know of the *en*-priestess of Nanna? The hymns she wrote recall a living, vibrant person. If only we had some of her correspondence with her family, or administrative texts attesting to gifts sent or received, or to her role in managing the estates of the temple, we would have a clearer sense of her life. But these documents are lost. In my view, the evidence is in her favor—that she did write the hymns attributed to her (or most of them) and that she had a rare literary gift for capturing the tumultuous emotions of her era. After Enheduana's death, King Naram-Sin appointed her replacement as *en*-priestess at Ur: his daughter Enmenana.

He also installed other daughters as high priestesses in the cities of Nippur and Sippar.[82]

It may not have escaped your notice that these first chapters have introduced you to as many prominent women as men—from Shara–igizi-Abzu as one of the first people to be named on a relief sculpture, to Queen Baranamtara of Lagash, to Queen Tabur-damu of Ebla, to the *en*-priestess Enheduana in Ur. This is simply because women had prominent roles in the third millennium BCE in government and religion. One can't write a history, even a political history, without them. No woman ruled a kingdom by herself—the society was certainly patriarchal—but it was the royal couple, not the king alone, that was central to the official cult. Many cylinder seals from the Early Dynastic and Akkadian periods show the royal couple, often seated and facing one another, or engaging in ritual activities together. The king was not shown as taller or more prominent than the queen; they were equals in this context.[83]

This began to change after the Akkadian period. Royal women continued to be powerful in many ways, but they no longer appeared in artworks as equals to their husbands in depictions of festivals and rituals.[84] At that point, the world of the third millennium BCE, the one in which Ishar-damu's wedding to Tabur-damu was more important to his position than was his coronation, had passed.

Naram-Sin of Akkad: Divine King

To return to the political context of Enheduana's later life: after crushing the rebellion, Naram-Sin started making claims that no Mesopotamian king before him had ever made. He began placing a cuneiform sign looking like a star ahead of his name whenever it was written. Only gods—actual gods—got this privilege. The star sign, representing the Sumerian word "*dingir*" (god), was written before a name to tell the reader that the word coming next was that of a deity. It had never before been appropriated by a human.[85] Did Naram-Sin really think he was divine, more so than his grandfather Sargon or any other king before him? Perhaps.

Naram-Sin explained in an inscription how he acquired this new status. He said that he had "secured the foundations" of Agade, which made the people of the city so grateful to him that they asked the gods of many great cities to make him a god too—a god of the city of Agade.[86] It was after he crushed the rebellion that this request for his deification was supposedly submitted to the great gods. The image of a king had changed a great deal since Early Dynastic times. The Akkadian kings presented themselves as conquerors who terrified their opponents; powerful (even divine) rulers who had no use for city assemblies or councils of elders; and kings of the "Four Corners of the World."[87]

Around this time, King Naram-Sin commissioned a large stone stela that shows him, victorious in battle, striding up a mountain (see Fig. 6.5).[88] He's followed by his own proud troops; they echo his pose while

Fig. 6.5 Victory Stela of King Naram-Sin of Akkad, found in Susa, twenty-third century BCE. (© RMN-Grand Palais/Art Resource, NY/Art Resource)

staring admiringly up at him and stepping over crumpled, dead and dying troops of the enemy. Naram-Sin certainly looks godlike: he is much bigger than anyone else, young, and athletic. And then there's his helmet: it has horns on both sides. These too were reserved for gods. He was the first king to appropriate these symbols. But he wasn't to be the last.

The Akkadian Empire didn't last long after Naram-Sin's reign, and his son and successor didn't claim to be divine. Very little is known about this son, in fact, but it's clear the empire went into decline during his reign. This is hardly surprising; the lands of the Near East had not been unified before Sargon's conquests, and the whole period of Akkadian rule had been marked by rebellions and repeated military attempts by the Akkadian kings to bring the conquered cities properly under control. The people clearly hadn't taken kindly to the idea of being ruled by a distant emperor, especially one who took control of temple lands for his own use, as the Akkadian kings had done. Although the kings had developed many innovations that continued after the end of their era, the empire was not long-lasting. Many books and articles have been written about the reasons for the collapse of the Akkadian Empire, but in a way it is more surprising that it stayed together for any time at all.

That said, the most obvious reason for the collapse was that a people called the Gutians invaded Akkad from the Zagros mountains to the east. Even the ancient Mesopotamians recognized this, though, oddly, they didn't think the Gutians were to be blamed for their actions. They thought that gods were responsible for the invasion, but not the gods of the Gutians. In the Mesopotamians' understanding, their own gods—and especially their great god Enlil—were evidently angry at them and used the Gutians as a tool by which to take their revenge on the people and kings of Agade. This was the reason given for the invasion, in a later hymn called the "Curse of Agade," and it probably represents the opinion of the people of Akkad at the time.

Modern scholars are, of course, unconvinced that Enlil's anger was the reason for the fall of the Akkadian dynasty. They credit, instead, the Mesopotamian cities' long-standing distrust of the Akkadian leaders (as witnessed by all those rebellions), combined with a climate crisis that hit the region around 2200 BCE. It was a time of drought, perhaps caused by volcanic eruptions in Anatolia. These conditions may even have helped bring about the end of the Old Kingdom in Egypt that happened around the same time.[89]

After the Gutian invasion, cities that had been subject to the kings of Agade shook off imperial rule and reinvented themselves as city-states for a while. But that power-hungry seed had been planted in some rulers' minds—they could now aspire to be like Sargon or Naram-Sin and to unify Mesopotamia, even to become a god.

Chapter 7
Brickmakers, Litigants, and Slaves

After the Gutians had conquered Agade and helped bring an end to the Akkadian Empire, no one could claim to be king of the whole land. Even the author of the Sumerian King List, who normally valiantly maintained the fiction of a united Mesopotamia, despaired of making any sense of this era. "Who was king? Who was not king?" he wrote.[1] This period was mystifying to the ancient writer and remains so to us.

Gudea of Lagash: A Peaceful King

One of the few stable kingdoms that emerged around this time was in Lagash. Its principal king—the man who dominated a brief period of renewal for Lagash—was named Gudea (c. 2144–2124 BCE). He projected a meditative calm in the many statues that he commissioned of himself.

He was portrayed in prayer, his boyish face solemn beneath his kingly cap (see Fig. 7.1). Gudea's image is one of the best known in Mesopotamian history, not because he was especially influential, but because so many of his statues have survived. He chose to have them carved of stone, rather than cast in bronze or silver: "For this statue nobody was supposed to use silver or lapis lazuli, neither should copper or tin or bronze be a working (material). It is (exclusively) of diorite."[2] He had a good reason for doing this: "Nobody will forcibly damage (the stone)."[3] He was at least somewhat correct about that; many of his statues did survive. But his sculpted head is often found without his body, and vice versa—someone did, at some point, forcibly damage them. Unlike the metal statues of other kings, however, they could not be melted down. Gudea, even when headless, is still recognizable.

Fig. 7.1 Seated diorite statue of King Gudea of Lagash in prayer, twenty-second century BCE. (Metropolitan Museum of Art)

His many inscriptions are almost as tranquil as his sculpted face and are written in elegant Sumerian. In striking contrast to the Akkadian kings who came before him, Gudea rarely mentioned military conflicts; just one sentence in a single extant inscription noted that "he defeated the cities of Anshan and Elam and brought the booty therefore to (the god) Ningirsu in his Eninnu (temple)."[4] That was it for conquests. He named his years for religious activities and construction projects and filled his inscriptions with details of the buildings he commissioned.[5] He traded with foreign lands to obtain materials for them: cedar from the Levant, stone slabs from the northern mountains, copper from Magan (Oman), diorite and gold from Meluhha (the Indus Valley). Many kings boasted of the temples they built, but Gudea actually depicted himself in one sculpture with the blueprint (or its ancient clay equivalent) for a temple laid out on his lap. He also prided himself on the order he brought to his land, a welcome balm after the furies of the late Akkadian period and the Gutian invasion. Like Enmetena long before him, he canceled debts and promoted kindness. "No one was lashed by the whip or hit by the goad" during his reign, he wrote, "no mother would beat her child."[6]

Gudea's wife's sister, Enanepada, served as the en-priestess of the moon god at Ur, like Enheduana more than a century earlier.[7] She resided in the Gipar palace and assumed all the rituals and responsibilities associated with her high office. It seems likely, therefore, that Lagash controlled Ur at that time, though its kings were soon to lose that great city.

Meanwhile the Gutians hadn't all left. They seem to have taken control in much of southern Mesopotamia for several decades, until a man named Utu-hegal (2119–2112 BCE) claimed the throne in Uruk. He rallied an army of local men to drive the Gutians out, and he took over Ur as well.

Ur-Namma of Ur: Builder and Lawgiver

Utu-hegal's successor had a significant impact on world history, and we can examine life in his realm through the eyes not just of the royal family and others in power but of some of the poor and dispossessed as well. About a decade after the death of Gudea, Ur-Namma (2112–2095 BCE) took power in the city of Ur. He seems to have been the brother of King Utu-hegal, and he had served under him as the military governor in Ur. When Utu-hegal died, Ur-Namma succeeded him, but he chose to rule from Ur rather than Uruk, founding a new dynasty there. This was more than 300 years after the time of Ur's extravagant royal burials and about 150 years after Sargon's daughter Enheduana had been installed as high priestess.

At the start of Ur-Namma's reign, the kingdom was small. But Ur-Namma had caught Sargon's empire-building bug, and over the course of his life his realm expanded to encompass much of Mesopotamia and even areas to the east in what is now Iran. Unfortunately, he provides us with few insights as to how he did it. Some scholars think he might have achieved this feat through diplomacy rather than warfare, but he didn't brag about that either. Unlike Sargon and Naram-Sin, with their bombastic accounts of destroying walls and washing their weapons in the sea, Ur-Namma seems to have striven for peace. Perhaps he followed the lead of Gudea of Lagash. He focused, in his year-names and inscriptions, on the priestesses he appointed, the walls and temples he built, the canals he dug, and the gods he provided for. His only year named for a military victory is one in which "the land of Guti was destroyed."[8]

The dynasty that Ur-Namma founded is known as the Third Dynasty of Ur, and the era that his family dominated generally goes by an abbreviation of this: it was the Ur III period. You will look in vain, however, for references to an Ur I or Ur II period. The first and second dynasties of Ur didn't give their names to whole eras because they didn't have a big impact on history. The conventional divisions of ancient Mesopotamian history are, in a way, like the streets of the ancient city of Ur—they grew up organically as scholars discovered new kingdoms and translated new texts, and, unfortunately, they have none of the reassuring regularity of ancient Chinese or Egyptian dynasties.

Thus far, we have discussed the Uruk, Early Dynastic, and Akkadian periods. These all fell in the Early Bronze Age, the first era of the Bronze Age, which is so called because bronze began to be used widely for tools and utensils in the Uruk period and continued to be the dominant metal until around 1200 BCE, when iron came into wider use. The Early Bronze Age in the Near East ended around 2100 BCE, that is, around the beginning of the Ur III period. The Middle Bronze Age began at that point and ended in 1550 BCE, but these distinctions represent an entirely modern creation—a way for us to structure chronology. Ancient Near Eastern historians tend to refer to the names of the periods (Uruk, Early Dynastic, Ur III, and so on) until they come to 1550 BCE, at which point they refer to the era that began then as the Late Bronze Age. The dates of the various Bronze Ages of other parts of the world are different depending on when these metal technologies came into use.

In any event, Ur-Namma was self-consciously a Sumerian king. The era that he began has sometimes been called the "Sumerian Renaissance" because in so many ways he and his successors looked backward in time for their inspiration, past the preceding Akkadian period to the Early Dynastic city-states of Sumer. They reinstated the Sumerian language for their administration and proclamations, in place of Akkadian, which had been used during Sargon's dynasty. Artists created works in careful horizontal registers, copying the Early Dynastic style that had been used in the Standard of Ur, and in the Uruk Vase from a thousand years before. And, at least during Ur-Namma's reign, the king of Ur was a man who was devoted to the gods, not a man who considered himself to be one.

Ur-Namma commissioned an enormous stone monument to be set up in the temple complex that was dedicated to the moon god Nanna, making a clear visual statement about what kind of king he was (see Fig. 7.2).[9] The round-topped stela was originally more than 4 meters (13 feet) tall and 1.5 meters (5 feet) wide, and it weighed more than a ton.[10] It was divided into five old-fashioned horizontal registers on each side. Unfortunately, when it was excavated by Leonard Woolley, it was found in fragments, and big sections of it have never been recovered. Still, what survives tells us a lot. Ur-Namma had himself portrayed much more like an Early Dynastic king than like the Akkadian king Naram-Sin. He was not striding up a mountainside in victory, but standing in prayer before the gods.

Ur-Namma (seen in the middle of the bottom register of the fragment in Fig. 7.2) wore a round hat with a wide brim, which had been the standard headdress of kings for centuries, and a long, fringed cloak that hung over his

Fig. 7.2 Fragment of the stela of King Ur-Namma of Ur, late twenty-second century BCE. (Courtesy of the Penn Museum, image 152349 and object B16676.14)

left shoulder and left arm and wrapped under his right arm, leaving the arm and his right shoulder bare. The gods still wore the tufted, layered tunics of the Early Dynastic period (gods always tended to be depicted in clothes that had gone out of fashion), but the kings had adopted a more modern style. To judge from the stela, Ur-Namma had a long beard, though his hair seems to have been short—it didn't extend out under his round cap.

Unlike Naram-Sin, Ur-Namma had no horns on his cap and demanded no star-shaped *dingir* sign to be written before his name. He was not claiming to be a god. He was, instead, a pious man who was shown praying and pouring libations to various seated gods and goddesses. In one scene, the seated moon god Nanna reaches toward the king to hand him a rod and a coil of rope.[11] These were measuring tools that an architect needed in order to lay out the plan of a building. Ur-Namma was telling his subjects that the temple in which they stood when viewing the stela was his own work and had been authorized by the god Nanna himself.

Ur-Namma was not just claiming to be the architect of buildings for the gods; according to what remains of the third register of the stela, he helped build them himself. We see the king following the god in a procession, preparing to go to the building site[12] with an axe and hoe, along with a measuring compass and basket, all slung over his right shoulder.[13] A clean-shaven assistant walks behind him, adjusting the basket. The register below is almost completely destroyed, but it clearly included a brick wall that was under construction, with men on ladders and carrying bricks.

Did the king really participate in construction like this? Would anyone have ever seen Ur-Namma carrying the tools of a workman? It's unlikely, unless he was going to the third-millennium BCE equivalent of a formal groundbreaking ceremony. The actual construction was the work of hundreds, possibly thousands, of workmen. But you may remember King Ur-Nanshe of Lagash who, hundreds of years earlier, had shown himself in a relief sculpture with a basket of bricks on his head. Ur-Namma was making the same claim: he was a builder, not a destroyer; and his building project was spectacular. Someone standing in front of this stela had only to look up to witness the glory of this building. Ur-Namma had created, within the temple complex of Nanna, the largest structure that had ever been built in Mesopotamia up to that time.

It was called a ziggurat, a massive stepped tower made of mudbrick that was built at the heart of the temple complex dedicated to Nanna. It must have been visible across the city, standing around 30 meters (100 feet) high, with a grand three-part stairway leading to the top of the first level. One stairway extended straight out from the front of the structure, the other two hugged the sides of the ziggurat on either side, with all three staircases meeting at a single landing at the center of the first terrace. There was no practical reason for building three stairways to exactly the same point; perhaps they were used for dramatic ceremonies in which groups of people mounted them at the same time. Further stairways would have led to the higher levels, but those don't survive. There were certainly two, and probably three, more levels (see Fig. 7.3).

The base of the ziggurat measures 62.5 by 43 meters (205 by 141 feet),[14] covering almost 2,700 square meters (almost 29,000 square feet). It would have been about the size of Westminster Abbey in London, had anyone been able to enter it, but that was impossible. The ziggurat was made of solid mudbrick; it had no rooms inside. Unlike almost any other Mesopotamian monument from this period, one can visit the Ur ziggurat in southern Iraq today. The first level still stands and has been reconstructed with a modern brick facing.

The ziggurat at Ur was not the only one planned by Ur-Namma. He also had ziggurats built in Uruk (for the goddess Inana), Eridu (for the god Enki),

Fig. 7.3 The ziggurat at Ur photographed soon after excavation, Ur III period, early twenty-first century BCE. (Courtesy of the Penn Museum, image 8735b)

and Nippur (for the god Enlil), with all four structures under construction simultaneously. The ziggurat design was revolutionary and impressive. Once the plans were made, as was always the case for the construction of monumental buildings, a huge workforce had to be summoned, organized, trained, provisioned, housed, and put to work, not just in Ur but in the other three cities as well.

A Brickmaker for the Ziggurat at Ur

A man called up to work on making bricks for the ziggurat was assigned to a team of ten men, who answered to an overseer, and five of these teams formed a group that had its own supervisor.[15] The brickmakers didn't work in the city itself; their worksite was located in and around the pits where the clay was obtained, which would have been next to a river or canal.[16] Men dug the clay from the ground, mixed it with straw in large basins, added water, shaped it in brick molds, laid the bricks out in yards to dry, then stacked the bricks ready for use.[17] We know from tablets written at the time that each man was expected to manufacture approximately 240 bricks per day.[18] Eventually they transported the stacks of bricks to the building site in the sacred complex in the heart of Ur.

Our laborer made bricks in two shapes: rectangular ones of around 25 × 16.66 centimeters (c. 10 × 6.5 inches) and square ones, which came in several sizes. A common type of brick was 33.33 centimeters (13 inches) on each side.[19] The rectangular bricks were mostly put out in the sun to dry, whereas the square bricks were usually baked.[20] Baking would have involved many kilns and a phenomenal quantity of fuel. Again, this must have taken place outside the city—the brick-firing yard would have been a loud, smoky facility.

Before the bricks were fired in the kiln, workers stamped some of them with an inscription that read: "Ur-Namma, king of Ur, the one who built the temple of the god Nanna."[21] Others bore a longer inscription: "For the god Nanna, his lord, Ur-Namma, king of Ur, built his temple (and) built the wall of Ur."[22] Each stamp had a handle on the back and was created with the cuneiform inscription in mirror writing so that it would appear the right way round on the finished brick. The workman who stamped the bricks didn't need to be able to read or write to impress the pious message.

The message wouldn't even have been visible in the finished building; it was imprinted on the flat side that would have been covered by other bricks. The point was that the gods would know of Ur-Namma's devotion, as would any future king who might have been tempted to claim the temple's construction as his own.

One day, as one of these bricks was drying in the sun, a dog walked across it, leaving clear paw prints in the clay (see Fig. 7.4). Was this a feral dog wandering through the brickmaking yard? No one knows. Dogs had been domesticated in the Near East thousands of years earlier, perhaps as early as 13,000 BCE,[23] and they would have been a familiar sight in the city. No doubt this one was unwelcome and was shooed away before causing any more damage. The brick was baked, taken to the building site, and positioned in a wall, after which it rested there for thousands of years. It was eventually excavated by Leonard Woolley, transported to the United States, and placed in the collection of the University of Pennsylvania Museum, where the brickyard's canine trespasser is immortalized forever.[24]

Fig. 7.4 A brick from the walls of Ur with an inscription of King Ur-Namma of Ur and paw prints, late twenty-second century BCE.

A scholar has calculated that the first level alone of the ziggurat at Ur would have required the manufacture of a staggering 7,595,100 baked and sun-dried bricks.[25] Our brickmaker would have spent months, perhaps years, doing nothing during his days but mixing clay, molding bricks for this building, and stacking them on their sides to harden. He would have been out in the hot sun for much of that time, with clay caking into the skin of his hands and lodging under his fingernails. It was no doubt exhausting work.

You might suppose that the work of brickmaking and construction would have been entirely done by men, and through most of ancient Near Eastern history that does seem to have been true. But for the Ur III period this is belied by tablets from a place called Garshana in the province of Umma where, around 2030 BCE, a major construction project was taking place, involving a number of buildings and a surrounding wall.[26] During this project, three women were responsible for supervising some of the construction teams.[27] More surprising still, women made up two-thirds of the free laborers there, and seem to have done almost all the work of hauling bricks to the building site.[28] Although the female laborers were paid less than their male counterparts (3 liters of grain per day, compared to 5 or 6 for a man), the women who supervised the workers received more than men in the same positions, perhaps because the women oversaw twice as many people.[29] It's possible that women were more prominent in the workforce of manual laborers than we currently suspect in other Ur III cities as well.

The bricklayers who set the bricks in place in the building may have had an even harder job than the brickmakers. To judge from the images on Ur-Namma's stela, they used ladders to reach the top of the terrace as it grew, while balancing baskets of bricks or mortar on their heads. Like the brickmakers, they would have been organized in teams of ten, and groups of five teams, with overseers at every level keeping an eye on their work. The construction of the first stage of the Ur ziggurat required about 145,700 man-days of work, just to make and place the bricks.[30] Depending on the size of the workforce, this may have taken several years.

New technologies had been developed to allow the ziggurat to stand securely, and these technological advances affected the builders' work. Only the exterior bricks were baked. Inside a 2.4 meter (8 foot) thick façade of baked bricks set in bitumen, the core was built up of layer after layer of sun-dried bricks. Even after baking in the sun, these would not have completely dried out, so engineers developed a way to cope with the moisture that might otherwise have threatened the ziggurat's integrity and to make the whole structure stronger. They ingeniously realized that reed mats laid between the layers of bricks increased the building's structural stability, and "weeper holes" cut into the baked brick facing could allow moisture to escape as the bricks continued to dry. They also designed drains to rid the terraces of rainfall (which, though rare in this area, could be torrential). All these had to be incorporated as the building process continued. Once the bricklayers had completed a layer, work on the bricks halted while reed mats were spread across them. Other workers spread layers of mortar and bitumen.

All of the materials needed, other than the bricks—including bitumen, palm leaves, and reeds—had been acquired and processed or woven, as the case may be, and the tools, brick molds, baskets, and other containers used by the workmen must have been continually manufactured and maintained. The men (and perhaps women) would all have received rations, if they were slaves or corvée laborers, or monthly pay in barley, if they were free and had been hired,[31] and these were distributed regularly. So one has to add scribes and granary supervisors to the list of people employed in ziggurat construction. The work team, made up of many residents of Ur and its surrounding towns, must have been huge and very visible in and around the city.

As during the construction of the Stone Cone Temple about 1,400 years before, but on a much larger scale, someone also had to keep track of where and when each team was working, of ordering the correct amount of building materials, making sure the materials arrived on time, and determining where they should be sent on the building site. Mathematical problems found from later eras show that the scribes learned how to calculate the number of bricks necessary for a building of a particular size, and even to take into account that only five-sixths of a wall was made of bricks; the rest was mortar.[32] Although mathematical calculations are attested a thousand years before, in the Uruk period, these more sophisticated techniques must have developed by the Ur III period.

Fortunately, after so many centuries of practice, the Mesopotamians had a highly efficient system for managing a workforce. A group of men who shared the title "*shidim*" were in charge of these bigger organizational challenges, and they, too, were overseen by a boss, a "chief of the *shidims*."[33]

Presumably the *shidim*s talked to one another regularly and the chief of the *shidim*s reported to the king on the progress of his ziggurat.

You may be wondering what the point was of building the ziggurat, given that it was a solid pile of brick. Honestly, scholars wonder too. Unlike an Egyptian pyramid, it wasn't built to cover a tomb, and it didn't have smooth sides—a ziggurat rose in several giant steps. Although pyramids had been constructed in Egypt for centuries before Ur-Namma built his ziggurats, the Mesopotamians didn't necessarily borrow even the shape of the structure from Egypt. In any ancient land, a tall building was, of necessity, triangular in cross-section, with much less weight at the top than the bottom. Otherwise the structures would have fallen down. Mesopotamians had been building temples on top of platforms since the Uruk period; maybe the ziggurat was just a much larger platform than before. It was, though, only a fraction the size of the Great Pyramid in Egypt, which was 230 meters (756 feet) on each side, four times as long as the longest side of the ziggurat at Ur.

The ziggurat did not replace the shrine where the god Nanna lived, which was located next to it. It may, though, have had another shrine at the top, and it was probably a place of ritual, where participants ascended high above the rest of the ceremonial complex, perhaps to be closer to the gods in their celestial forms. Also, the view of the night sky was unobstructed from the top of the ziggurat, which would have allowed priests and priestesses to observe the movements of the stars and planets.

Incredibly, the ziggurat was not the only new building that Ur-Namma erected in the sacred precinct at Ur. He was also responsible for starting construction on a large square building called the E-hursag, which may have been a palace,[34] and for building a thick buttressed enclosure wall, faced with baked bricks, around the whole sacred area.[35]

Ur-Namma's Laws

If you had heard of Ur-Namma before this, outside of specialized books and articles, it is probably not because of his ziggurat or the expansion of his kingdom, but because he was the first known lawgiver in history, though even that title is often awarded, mistakenly, to Hammurabi of Babylon. Ur-Namma's laws were inscribed on stone stelas, but these are all, unfortunately, lost.[36] We have instead a fragmentary clay cylinder from the Ur III period that was inscribed with the laws,[37] along with five partial copies of the laws on broken cuneiform tablets, written centuries later, by scribes in school. These do not have the same impressive effect as the seven-foot-tall stela on which the later king Hammurabi inscribed his own laws, but Ur-Namma's laws predate Hammurabi's by more than 300 years.

Ur-Namma promulgated his laws at the height of his reign, after he had, as he noted in an inscription, "liberated Akshak, Mirad, Girkal, Kazallu, whatever (territories) were under the subjugation of Anshan."[38] This was one of his few references to military action. The cities listed were to the north of Ur, in the region of Akkad, whereas Anshan was about 800 kilometers (about 500 miles) to the south and east of Ur, near modern Shiraz in Iran. Anshan seems to have taken advantage of the disarray that followed the Gutian invasion to take control of the region of Akkad, so in a way Ur-Namma *was* "liberating" these regions, as he claimed, though he seems to have taken control there in Anshan's stead.

It seems that Ur-Namma didn't intend this inscription to record a brand-new innovation—he didn't conceive of himself as inventing the idea of law. The laws appear only after a 170-line account in praise of his own great deeds, almost as though the laws were an afterthought.

We refer to that first section of the inscription as the "prologue," but it was important in its own right. Ur-Namma wanted to make a good impression in it. Right off the bat, he emphasized his piety by listing the "regular offerings" of barley, sheep, and butter that he set up for the gods. He continued with a list of ways in which he had improved life for his people, especially with regard to the economy: he had re-established trade with Magan (Oman), rooted out corruption, standardized weights and measures, regulated boat traffic on the rivers, and made the roads safe for travelers (including building inns for them).[39] In this, he might remind you of King Urukagina of Lagash, several centuries earlier, in the Early Dynastic period, who had also presented himself as a reformer. Ur-Namma was the anti-Sargon, to hear him tell it. He made a special note of how good he was to people who were otherwise oppressed: "I did not deliver the orphan to the rich. I did not deliver the widow to the mighty. I did not deliver the man with but one shekel to the man with one mina (i.e. 60 shekels). I did not deliver the man with but one sheep to the man with one ox."[40] Ur-Namma then summed up the essence of his reforms: "I eliminated enmity, violence, and cries for justice. I established justice in the land." It sounds a little like a campaign advertisement, but kings didn't run for office, and of course he was already king. It didn't hurt, though, to be loved, and capitalizing on the Mesopotamians' love of order and dislike of violence and enmity was a good strategy to discourage anyone who might be thinking of usurping the throne. Mesopotamian kings always needed the support of their people;[41] Ur-Namma clearly was aware of this.

After the self-congratulatory prologue, the inscription then segues into a series of laws, introduced only by the statement "At that time:" They don't read like modern laws, though. Each one is conditional. It begins with "If a man . . ." (or "If a male slave," or "If the wife of a young man," and so on) and then describes a crime or transgression of some sort, and ends with the fine or punishment that should be imposed.

The most complete copy of the inscription includes eighty-five laws, most of which are fairly complete.[42] Forty-five of the laws pertain to crimes, ranging from murder, theft, and bodily harm to neglecting a field or losing a sheep in a sheepfold. Fifteen of these look, at first glance, similar to the biblical "eye-for-an-eye" type of laws (known as *lex talionis*), but Ur-Namma's equivalents were mostly "monetary-fine-for-an-eye" laws, which reflect a very different idea of punishment. So law 23 reads "If a man causes the loss of another man's eye, he will pay thirty shekels."[43] In fact, monetary fines were imposed more often than any other penalty; a fine was mandated in twenty-two of the criminal laws. These ranged from two shekels of silver for cutting another man in some way (the term for the afflicted body part is missing)[44] to a hefty sixty-shekel fine for fracturing another man's bone with a weapon.[45] Ur-Namma recommended the death penalty for only seven crimes, including murder, banditry, rape of a betrothed woman, and beating a woman to death.[46] A free man could also be put to death for marrying the widow of his elder brother or for falsely claiming to have lost property, and an enslaved man could be executed for marrying his mistress.[47] The laws were not comprehensive; most crimes that one might think of were not mentioned.

Thirty-six of the others—almost half the extant laws that can be made out—represent attempts to fix wages, rents, prices, and interest rates, and to mandate inheritance practices and divorce provisions. One suspects the price controls were ineffective.

Even though he wrote down the first laws, Ur-Namma didn't invent the judicial system. Enmetena of Lagash had called himself the "King of

Justice,"[48] so the idea of justice was centuries old already. Contracts with lists of witnesses had been written long before Ur-Namma's time; even the Ushumgal inscription back in the Early Dynastic period (with its depictions of the priest Ushumgal and his daughter Shara-igizi-Abzu) seems to have been a contract of some kind.[49] Before Ur-Namma's laws were written, judges had presided over courts, considered evidence, and pronounced verdicts for a very long time. You don't need laws to have a judicial system. In fact, the proclamation of these "world's first laws," which we see as earth-shaking in their importance to world history, doesn't seem to have been regarded as a major event at the time. Ur-Namma might simply have collected some legal precedents and added them to his inscription to further burnish his image and provide concrete evidence that he had indeed "established justice," as he claimed. There's no clear evidence that the laws were followed.

Geme-Suen and the Wife of Ur-lugal, the Head-Gardener: Adversaries in Court

The court in the city of Umma was the setting for a dispute between two women. The name of one of the women is unknown; she was described in the record of her court hearing only as the wife of a man named Ur-lugal. The other woman was named Geme-Suen.[50] Court records like theirs give us a vivid sense of how the judicial system worked. In the Ur III period, many court records were drawn up in the city of Umma.[51]

We don't know exactly where this court proceeding took place, but it was probably close to a temple. A scribe kept track of what happened, and it is his record that is to be found in the British Museum on a tablet that is just a little more than 5 centimeters (two inches) wide and 7.6 centimeters (three inches) tall.[52]

The discussion began with Geme-Suen stating that the wife of Ur-lugal had borrowed two minas of silver from her, and that she still owed some of the money. Two minas represented a large amount of wealth, even for a relatively rich person. One shekel of silver was equivalent to 300 liters of barley,[53] and a manual worker was paid 60 liters of barley per month;[54] therefore a shekel of silver represented five months of pay. Sixty shekels made a mina, so the two minas that Ur-lugal's wife had borrowed were equivalent to 120 shekels, or fifty years' pay for a worker. It's unclear what Ur-lugal's wife needed it for, but Geme-Suen must have been a wealthy woman to have had that amount on hand and available to lend. Ur-lugal was described as the head-gardener, so his wife would not have been poor either.

It's possible that a contract had been drawn up at the time that Geme-Suen had lent the silver to Ur-lugal's wife. Contracts were widely used by this time to create formal records of such things as loans or sales. It would have been written by a scribe, in the presence of witnesses, and the interest rate might have been listed. Usually, for loans of silver, this was steep—20 percent. Some loan contracts also listed a time when the loan had to be repaid.[55]

Back in the court room, the wife of Ur-lugal had an answer to Geme-Suen's demand for the rest of the loan to be repaid. "Ki'ag closed my case,"[56] she stated, presumably speaking to the judge who was presiding. She meant that this case had already been tried and decided in her favor. She did not owe anything. The man named Ki'ag, who had overseen the previous trial, seems to have been present for this new one as well. He was one of three known judges at Umma who presided in court cases,[57] so he would have been well known to the judge to whom the wife of Ur-lugal was speaking. We know from other sources that Ki'ag had also donated animals for sacrifice at the city's New Year's festival,[58] and on one occasion he had administered an oath to someone in his own house.[59] He was an eminent man of Umma.

The wife of Ur-lugal continued to speak in her own defense, by identifying another powerful man who would support her claim: "Lu-Suen was my commissioner in the concluded case," she said.[60] Commissioners, with the title "*mashkim*," oversaw court cases in the Ur III period. They prepared everything in advance of the trial, recorded the outcome, and are mentioned frequently in the documents.[61] In this instance, the judge decided to check her story. He called on Lu-Suen to confirm that the wife of Ur-lugal was telling the truth, but it turned out that she'd made a mistake in mentioning him. Lu-Suen didn't help her. The record states that "he declared: 'It is a lie.'"[62]

What seems to have happened next is that, interestingly, Ki'ag, the judge from the first case, got involved.[63] He asked all five of Ur-lugal's children to swear an oath, presumably to confirm that their mother had been telling the truth. But they decided not to support her and refused to swear. Had they agreed, they would all have been required to go to the temple so that the oath could be taken in the presence of the god.[64]

At this point, Ur-lugal's wife decided to back down. Neither the commissioner from the previous trial nor her own children were willing to lie for her. She acknowledged that, yes, she still owed ten shekels of silver to Geme-Suen. Not only that, but one of her sons admitted that he also owed five shekels.

The court case doesn't say anything else, except to list five witnesses who attended the court proceeding. Records like this almost always ended with the oath, whether or not the people involved decided to swear it, because the oath (or refusal to swear it) often determined the judge's decision.[65] In this case Geme-Suen won the lawsuit, and the wife of Ur-lugal had to pay back the rest of the silver.

This little slice of life in Umma reflects several aspects of the legal system there, which are confirmed by other court cases as well. First, unlike in most other Mesopotamian cities and other times, each case in Umma was tried by one judge. Elsewhere, a whole panel of judges—as many as seven of them—was needed.[66] No one at this time was a judge by profession; men like Ki'ag who took on the role from time to time were literate and important in the city, but they had other jobs as well.[67] Second, the judge cared about evidence and wanted to make sure that the parties to the case were telling the truth. That was why he questioned Lu-Suen, and that was what the oath would have been for—judge Ki'ag tried to get Ur-lugal's children to swear in support of their mother so that he could determine whether she was being truthful.

The original statements in a trial were rarely made under oath, but oaths often came in later in the proceedings and were seen as potent legal tools throughout ancient Near Eastern history. Oaths brought the power of the gods into the lawsuit. They're mentioned in Ur-Namma's laws as well. One law states that "if a man appears as a witness, but retracts (his) oath, he will make compensation for whatever was the matter in that trial."[68] The children of Ur-lugal had not presented themselves as witnesses—they had been called up by the judge—and they were wise not to take that oath. Apparently they refused because their mother was lying and they knew they would have perjured themselves. It would not have been worth it: they could have been responsible for the silver due in the case. Another nagging concern no doubt prevented them from lying under oath: the gods would have known they had done so and the gods had no patience with humans who swore false oaths in their names. The children would have believed that the gods' punishment was likely to have been much worse than paying an amount of silver. So, refusing to take an oath was a way of telling the judge that you would be lying if you did so. This helped him determine the truth of the case.

A third feature of this court record that you might have noticed is that no lawyers were mentioned. There simply were no lawyers; the profession didn't exist yet. Men and women of all classes (including slaves)[69] represented themselves in court and were expected to provide their own witnesses and evidence. There was no jury; the judge or judges made the decision alone.

In two other laws in Ur-Namma's list, he mentions another way of getting at the truth of a case—beyond taking statements from the main parties, examining contracts, and putting witnesses under oath—namely, the River Ordeal. It was especially useful in cases involving accusations of adultery and witchcraft, for which impartial evidence was hard to find; there were rarely any witnesses and there certainly weren't any contracts. One law reads as follows: "If a man accuses someone of sleeping with a betrothed woman, after the river clears him, the man who made the accusation will pay 20 shekels of silver."[70] We know from other sources that the River Ordeal provided the judges with a way to learn the truth of a situation, in a sense by asking the gods to rule on the case. If no one could find witnesses to a crime, the accused would be required to jump into the river. If this person drowned, the gods had indicated that he or she was guilty, and conveniently carried out the death penalty at the same time. Surviving the ordeal, on the other hand, was an indication of innocence and, in this case, resulted in a fine being imposed on the man who made the false accusation.

This wasn't perceived to be superstition; everyone believed that the gods knew the truth and would reveal it. Better still, the sincerity of this belief actually often resulted in the truth coming out. If someone agreed to leap in the river, trusting in the gods that he or she would survive, that person was obviously innocent; on the other hand, a guilty person would often confess rather than submit to their inevitable fate of being drowned in the river. Either of these responses from an accused person prevented the Ordeal from being necessary; it seems often to have been canceled. In spite of the existence of Ur-Namma's laws that invoke it, the River Ordeal is never mentioned in any of the surviving court records of the Ur III period, so it must have been rare, though some administrative texts do refer to people going to or returning from the River Ordeal.[71]

Many of these legal practices seem to have predated Ur-Namma's laws and don't seem to have been particularly affected by them. Very few of the court cases even pertain to crimes covered by the surviving laws, and they don't mention judges consulting the laws, either. The laws didn't comprise a "law code" the way we think of such a thing today. The term "code" suggests an attempt at providing a comprehensive and binding collection of laws, and that is not what Ur-Namma did. Judges may have been aware of his laws, but they decided cases based on their own analysis of the evidence and their own conclusions about the suitable punishment.

In the case of Geme-Suen v. Ur-lugal's wife, the judge decided in favor of the richer, more powerful of the two women, but this wasn't a result of the judicial system favoring the rich. The court records reflect surprising transparency in the legal system, and a genuine desire for justice to prevail. Had Geme-Suen been at fault, it's clear from other cases that she would have been the one who would have had to pay. It's also clear, not just from the laws but also from records of court cases, that fines were by far the most common form of punishment.

Waifs, Prisoners, and Lu-Nanna, an Escaped Slave

The courts were available to anyone who needed them, it seems. In one instance, a man who had been released from slavery was accused of lying about his freedom. He went to the judges with the contract for his manumission in hand as evidence, and his freedom was confirmed.[72]

But the courts upheld the social and political system, and slavery was part of that system in this era. The story of an enslaved man named Lu-Nanna reflects this.[73] He lived in the city of Umma, subject to a man named Uda. A court record relating to him notes that "Uda appointed (Lu-Nanna) for service as 'bowman.'"[74] It's unclear exactly what this meant. Did Lu-Nanna perform Uda's military service for him? What was Uda's profession? How had Lu-Nanna become a slave in the first place? None of these questions is answered by the court record, but it's possible that Lu-Nanna was sold into slavery by one or both of his parents. Sale contracts from the Ur III period show that this was a known practice, though the majority of such sales were of daughters.[75] Some parents sold one or more of their children into slavery apparently because the family was desperately poor and could not afford to support them. The very existence of such slave sale contracts shows that this was seen as an acceptable (if tragic) way for a family to cope with poverty.

It was not the only way to become a slave, however. Adults were sometimes enslaved to men and women to whom they owed money or barley, so perhaps Lu-Nanna had landed in slavery because of debts that he wasn't able to pay back to Uda. It's unlikely that he had been captured as a prisoner of war; such men and women were apparently enslaved by the great households—the temples and palace.[76]

In any event, according to the court record, Lu-Nanna had two sons, both of whom had also been enslaved with him, but Uda had freed them, while keeping Lu-Nanna captive. But then Uda died, and Lu-Nanna seems to have decided that, during this chaotic time for his owner's family, he had a chance at gaining his freedom, not by manumission, like his sons, but by escaping. The Ur III documents include other examples of runaway slaves;[77] Lu-Nanna might have heard stories about them. He apparently knew he had to get out of Umma and to flee as far away as possible to avoid being captured and brought back. He was local to the area and would have had a good sense of the countryside around his city;[78] here was his opportunity.

In the terse language typical of court proceedings, the scribe wrote about Lu-Nanna that "The slave [was thought to have] died in Anshan where he fled."[79] Lu-Nanna almost managed to gain his freedom. He had walked more than 850 kilometers (more than 525 miles), probably traveling south along the river to the Lower Sea (the Persian Gulf) then turning inland to the southeast, making his way through high mountain passes, until he reached Anshan. If he managed to travel 24 kilometers (15 miles) a day (which was considered normal), it would have taken him thirty-five days to get there. He was in danger the whole time, not just from cold and hunger but from men who were sent out specifically in pursuit of fugitive slaves. Lu-Nanna no doubt avoided main roads wherever he could (though mountain passes would not have allowed him to stray far from the road), and he probably traveled at night and hid from passing caravans. Some of the men searching for him and other fugitive slaves were well organized and supported by the king. One such official, a man named Shugatum, received rations of stew, fish, beer, and bread from the Ur government when he was "traveling to capture runaway workers, slaves of (the goddess) Ninhursag," which he did regularly.[80] Shugatum's main priority was to find institutional slaves who had run away from the temples or palaces, but he would have been on the lookout for privately owned slaves as well.

Everyone knew that owners paid rewards for captured fugitives. One such reward was even enshrined in Ur-Namma's laws: "If . . . a female slave escapes and crosses the township limits, and someone brings her back, the owner of the slave will pay two shekels of silver to the man who brought her back."[81] (If an equivalent law existed for a male slave like Lu-Nanna, it is lost, but a similar reward would have been expected.)

Once he made it to Anshan, Lu-Nanna seems to have come up with an ingenious idea. He contrived to send back word to people in Umma that he had died. Now perhaps the authorities would stop looking for him. But this tale does not have a happy ending; Lu-Nanna's luck ran out. In Anshan, a man named Gudea, son of Gududu, recognized him. (This was not, of course, the king of Lagash named Gudea, though his name may have paid tribute to the earlier king.) Somehow Gudea captured Lu-Nanna and brought him all the way back to Umma. Unfortunately, the court record gives us no clue as to how he did so, but it would have entailed another thirty-five-day journey.

Lu-Nanna might well have been imprisoned when he got back to Umma. Prisons didn't comprise a major part of the judicial system but were used as a way to house criminals before trial,[82] or before punishment, and to keep runaways under watch before returning them to work.[83] Ur-Namma's laws include just one reference to imprisonment, but for a different reason: "If a man keeps someone captive, this man will go to jail (and) pay fifteen shekels of silver."[84] This was an eye-for-an-eye (lex talionis) law, making the offender suffer the same misery as his victim, in addition to paying a heavy fine.

In spite of the fact that fines were much more common than prison sentences, prisoners did have a patron goddess, Nungal, who watched over prisons and punishments.[85] Lu-Nanna might well have prayed to her as he awaited trial.

Copying a Sumerian hymn written in praise of this goddess was a popular written assignment for students in schools in the city of Nippur about three centuries later, in the eighteenth century BCE. Forty-three whole and partial copies of the hymn have been found there on clay tablets and fragments.[86] It's unclear when the hymn was originally written, but it might already have been known in the Ur III period. As so often is the case—as with Sargon's royal inscriptions and Enheduana's hymns—these later scribes kept alive documents that would otherwise be lost to us.

The Hymn to Nungal may actually have been written by a prisoner during his incarceration. The original author seems to have been a scribe praying to Nungal to protect him from the death penalty.[87] As an eyewitness to prison life, the scribe provides a description of the prison. It was a bleak place, the "house of sorrow," to which men were led in blindfolds.[88] The men imprisoned there longed to get out, counting the days, but losing track of time:"Brother counts for brother the days of misfortune, (but) their calculations get utterly confused."[89] If Lu-Nanna was locked up in such a place he might perhaps have cried out for help:"The interior of the House gives rise to weeping, laments, and cries."[90] The sense of being trapped was palpable—the men longed for the door of the prison to open for them: "The men in there, like sparrows held by the talons of the big owl, look towards the opening like to the rising sun."[91]

The authorities seem to have seen the prison as more than a form of punishment, however. The scribe wrote that "Its brick walls crush the evil ones, but give birth to honest men."[92] This was not the only time that the author mentioned this idea—that imprisonment could also work to rehabilitate criminals and help bring them back into society. Using what were purported to be Nungal's own words, the scribe wrote at the end that the goddess had "built it (the prison) with compassion. I soothe this man's heart, I cool him down."[93] She likened the process to burnishing precious metal, making the prisoner "shine from among the dust."[94] She did this, she said, for the benefit of the prisoner's personal god, to make the prisoner a good person so that he could be returned "to the good hands of his god, so that this man's god be praised forever, so that this man may praise me (and) tell about my greatness."[95] Lu-Nanna, like everyone else, would have believed he had a personal god and goddess, who watched over him. The hymn suggests that a man's behavior reflected on his god, and his rehabilitation into society after a crime was also a source of praise for the god, and for the goddess Nungal.

Lu-Nanna's court appointment arrived, and he was taken to the judge, meeting his captor Gudea there. Also present was Uda's son, who had inherited his father's slaves, including Lu-Nanna, after his father's death. The judge instructed Gudea to swear an oath that he was telling the truth. Gudea was happy to do so, knowing that a reward awaited him. Gudea received much more than the two shekels Ur-Namma had specified for the return of an enslaved woman; Uda's son was to pay him ten shekels for his efforts. This was as much as the value of an adult male slave;[96] clearly Lu-Nanna's return was appreciated. In the end, the unfortunate Lu-Nanna wound up right where he started: Uda's son "appointed (Lu-Nanna) to his bowman service."[97]

As in the case of Geme-Suen's silver loan, Ur-Namma's laws were somewhat relevant to this trial, but none of them matched the situation exactly. The large reward given to Gudea, son of Gududu, was determined by the judge, who perhaps took into consideration the great distance Gudea had traveled to bring Lu-Nanna back.

As you will have gathered, slavery was widespread in the Ur III period, but in some cases it is oddly hard to define who was and who was not considered to be enslaved. Slaves who worked in domestic situations had different experiences from slaves who worked for the palace or temples. Slaves were treated in very different ways depending on their situations. Some people who were described with the term for "slave" in the Ur III period seem to have been something more like servants, with considerable freedoms and even authority over others.[98] Slaves whose status was caused by debt were formerly free people who would be freed when the debt was considered to be paid, but slaves who had been purchased had no legal way out. The steady stream of fugitives testifies to that.

Even the Sumerian terms that we translate as "slave" could be vague in meaning. The word for a male slave was "*arad*" and the word for a female slave was "*geme*," but a whole group of women who weren't necessarily slaves were also called "*geme*": women who worked as laborers for the great households of the temples and palaces.[99] Some of them were enslaved, some were not. On the other hand, the hunters of fugitive slaves went looking for low-ranking institutional workers as well as slaves, not just *geme* women but also their supposedly free male equivalents, known as "*gurush*."[100] These low-ranking, unskilled workers couldn't be bought and sold, but they had no choice about where they worked and they were punished if they fled. Their status may have been a step above slavery, but not by much.[101]

One group of such institutional workers weren't even adults. The term used to describe these children translates as "left to themselves."[102] They had no families to support and nurture them, just the great households for which they worked. It's not that they were all orphans (though some were). Most were described by the name of either a father or mother, but their parents hadn't brought them up, hadn't put them up for adoption, and hadn't left them with a relative. Instead, the children had been placed in the palace or temple, "left to themselves," to work under armed guard, almost as though they were slaves.[103]

As we have seen, household and family were important in a great many ways in the ancient Near East, and one has to imagine that these children, lacking the safety net of a family, were vulnerable and very much alone. The term used for them is sometimes translated as "waifs."[104] One waif even seems to have been thrown into a well soon after birth and presumably left for dead. Fortunately, he didn't die, but had been rescued from the well and brought up through babyhood (though we don't know by whom), before starting service to the temple when he was a young boy. His name revealed his difficult start in life: he was Putapada, which meant "Found-(and-pulled)-from-a-well."[105]

The waifs all were provided with barley to live on: the younger ones were given 20 liters of barley per month, and the older adolescent ones were given 40 liters, which was enough to live on. Most people who worked for the palace had families to go home to (even enslaved people weren't separated from their families), but the waifs seem to have had no one.

Many of the waifs were listed as being the children of prostitutes.[106] Perhaps their mothers could not take care of them while continuing to work, perhaps some of the mothers had died, or perhaps the children had been removed from their mothers. Curiously, although prostitution is sometimes referred to as "the world's oldest profession," there is little evidence for it in documents from the ancient Near East. Presumably some women were paid for sex in many eras, but we can't be sure. Only occasionally, as here, when a child had been separated from his mother, and her profession was listed, do we get a glimpse of a world beyond the normal realm of scribes and administration. In this case, the records hint at an intimate, profound tragedy for the mother and child.

The armed guards who watched the waifs were presumably there to prevent them from running away. One census list of people working under armed guard in the town of Girsu included not just 250 waifs but also many other people at the margins of society.[107] They had recently been moved from one public organization to another and were being registered and counted. It was a mixed group of poor people: the waifs, men in "gangs" (and sons of men in gangs), wives of men who had escaped, a few weavers, slaves, and fullers. Another document listed the barley that these new arrivals had received. It must have been a harsh life for all of the people on these lists, but especially for the unwanted children among them.

Shulgi of Ur: A Divine King and Administrative Reformer

King Ur-Namma's death came suddenly. According to a line in a literary account that may have been commissioned by his widow Watartum, he might have died in battle, but he might also have died naturally.[108] Whatever the cause, his death seems to have brought great sadness to the land, according to the author: "Because [the evil] made the faithful shepherd leave. They weep bitter tears in their broad squares where merriment had reigned. . . . They spend (their) days in lamenting the faithful shepherd who has been snatched away."[109] Throughout the lament, the king is referred to as "Shepherd Ur-Namma." The king as shepherd was a compelling and lasting image; many later Near Eastern kings endeavored to be seen the same way.

The kings of the Third Dynasty of Ur managed to hold much of Mesopotamia together for about a century. Ur-Namma's son, Shulgi (see Fig. 7.5), ruled over the kingdom for almost half this time, a remarkable forty-eight years (2094–2046 BCE). During the first twenty years of his reign he continued traditional practices and maintained his father's priorities. Shulgi finished Ur-Namma's building projects—the ziggurats, the E-hursag palace at Ur, the wall around the sacred temenos. His father had married one of his sons to a princess from the Syrian city of Mari; Shulgi, in turn, arranged a marriage for his daughter with the king of Anshan, in what is now Iran.[110] And he followed the lead of Sargon and Naram-Sin in appointing his daughter to be the *en*-priestess of Nanna at Ur.

Then, around the middle of his reign, Shulgi began to shake things up. He decided, following the audacious lead of King Naram-Sin of Akkad a

Fig. 7.5 Bronze statuette of King Shulgi of Ur from a foundation deposit, Ur III period, early twenty-first century BCE. (Metropolitan Museum of Art)

century and a half before him, that he was, in fact, not just a king but a god; accordingly, he had hymns composed in his own honor. Scribal students copied these hymns for centuries as literary classics, which ensured Shulgi's fame through subsequent generations. He even insisted on being worshiped, with his E-hursag palace serving as his temple.[111] This went beyond even what Naram-Sin had commanded.

Shulgi also reorganized the cities of the empire and set up a new system for collecting taxes, called the "*bala*" system. A governor, installed in one of about twenty provinces in Sumer and Akkad, took control of the economy there, particularly of the temple estates and the irrigation systems that watered them. The provinces then paid taxes to the king. The payments were made in animals, grains, and other staples, and people were required to fulfill work obligations; together, these were called "*bala*." Each province owed the *bala* during a different month, to keep goods coming in throughout the year. It was not only a one-way arrangement, however. Goods were also redistributed back to the provinces as needed. Provinces were also home to military governors, appointed by the king. These men oversaw state fields that were allocated to soldiers and to some other government officers as their compensation.

The whole project of administering this system depended on an army of scribes keeping records of every sheep, goat, ox, and bushel of grain that came into and went out of the royal warehouses. Much of the processing of goods took place at a specially constructed redistribution center that Shulgi founded near Nippur. It was called Puzrish-Dagan and was the origin of many of the Ur III records.

Shulgi's administrative reforms affect us now, as we look at the sweep of ancient Near Eastern history, because the scribes who ran this system created a veritable flood of cuneiform records (see Fig. 7.6). About 100,000 tablets written in the Ur III period have been found so far, and hundreds

Fig. 7.6 Sealed cuneiform tablet recording workers needed for irrigation work, from Umma, c. 2042 BCE. (Metropolitan Museum of Art)

of thousands more must remain in the ground. It's estimated that about 500,000 cuneiform documents are housed in museums and private collections around the world from all eras of ancient history,[112] so about a fifth of them were written during the Third Dynasty of Ur, most of those from Shulgi's reign and those of his successors. They represent just a few decades out of the more than 3,000 years that cuneiform was in use. It's not clear whether this is because many more administrative records were kept during the Ur III period than at any other time, or whether this is an accident of excavation. But the ubiquity of these documents means that the Ur III period looms large in Mesopotamian studies. Thousands of the tablets can be found on a website called the Cuneiform Digital Library Initiative (CDLI).[113] CDLI houses images, transliterations,[114] and some translations of more than 320,000 cuneiform tablets, a number that is constantly growing.[115]

The Ur III tablets provide a vast wellspring of information for studies of many aspects of life—agriculture, dairy farming, shipping, trade, forestry, pottery manufacture, religious festivals, and on and on. Countless names appear on these tablets. Each of them was a living, breathing person whose life consisted of much more than being a line item on an administrative record kept by the local governor or temple. I've chosen to highlight the legal system, slavery, and waifs in this chapter, but I could have taken you to many other workplaces and institutions to meet many other people.[116]

Curiously, even though the Ur III period is so extraordinarily well documented, a fundamental question about the era remains unresolved: Did the king control the entire economy? Some scholars have seen this period as one marked by a tyrannical desire for control on the part of the kings, who owned all the land and all the workshops, with their subjects being paid in barley and functioning as little more than slaves to a vast bureaucracy.[117] Others believe this to be an illusion created by the documents that survive. Since only the great institutions—the temples, palace, and governors' households—had access to literacy, we only have records of the activities that they oversaw.[118] These certainly involved much of the population, but might there not have been space for a little private enterprise? A study of the use of silver in this era indicates that some local trading took place, in addition to that done by the great institutions.[119] People seem to have had access to some wealth beyond their subsistence fields or monthly pay, perhaps by selling vegetables from their gardens, or cloth or pottery that they created. And some individuals, like Geme-Suen who was in a position to lend two minas of silver to another woman, apparently controlled considerable wealth. Perhaps not every corner of the economy and society was controlled from above. Other scholars argue that even the written records from the great institutions can be interpreted differently. The Ur III administrative organization may not have been radically different from those that had come before. It may not, strictly speaking, even have been a bureaucracy.[120] Unlike a classic bureaucracy, the administration still had a concern for individuals, it allowed families to hold on to offices across generations, and it depended on local institutional households, such as the temples that had dominated Mesopotamian society and economy ever since the Uruk period.[121] It's true that people in the Ur III empire were subject to patriarchal households, including the great households of the temples and palaces, which continued to form the basic social and economic building blocks of Mesopotamian society. But for most people, their contact with these institutions did not go beyond the level of their city or region. The governors sent a portion of the yields of their estates and the manufactures of their subjects as *bala* payments to the king, but the average person in the empire had little direct contact with, or perhaps even awareness of, the supposedly tyrannical kings in Ur.

PART IV

The Early Second Millennium,

2000–1750 BCE

Chapter 8

Sparring Kings and Their Military Commanders

The journey from Ur to Nippur followed the course of the river the whole way. It was always a slow journey upstream because going by boat was no faster than walking—both the current and the wind were against you. Boats could be towed upriver, but not sailed, so there was no advantage to northbound river travel in terms of speed. From the levee next to the river, a traveler passed a continuous succession of green fields and date palms that flanked the dirt road, with villages and towns scattered along the way. The trees and buildings sometimes hugged the road, allowing no view beyond; but sometimes the view spread out to encompass land that lay completely flat as far as the eye could see to the east and west, the wide river valley barely changing in elevation for hundreds of miles. The biggest cities stood out on the horizon, on top of high tells, surrounded by city walls; smaller communities barely rose above the fields.

The divine King Shulgi of Ur had claimed, in a self-congratulatory hymn, to have run this route, from Ur to Nippur (and back, in a raging storm, no less), in a single day,[1] but a normal human being could never have done this. The two great cities were about 195 kilometers (120 miles) apart, so the one-way journey alone would have taken about eight days at the usual pace of 24 kilometers (15 miles) a day.

The Town of Kisurra

About five days after leaving Ur, anyone traveling north on this route reached a town named Kisurra. It was a good place to stop and rest for the night. Kisurra had been founded in the Early Dynastic period, and its citizens had been quietly getting along with life ever since. It had the basic features one would expect of a Sumerian city—it was built on a tell and boasted a temple to the local god, along with smaller temples and shrines to other gods, a city wall, and a palace for the local ruler. But it wasn't a particularly important place. It had been overshadowed for centuries by more powerful Sumerian cities: Nippur, home to the temple of Enlil, king of the gods; Uruk, which was still an impressive place, even 1,800 years after it first grew to be a city; Girsu, capital of the kingdom of Lagash; and, of course, Ur, which had been home to the great Third Dynasty and the temple to Nanna where Enheduana and so many subsequent *en*-priestesses had lived and worked.

Kisurra was much smaller than these metropolises, extending over only about 20 hectares (50 acres)—about the size of the terminal at Grand Central Station in New York City. A man who visited the site during the excavations in 1904 provides one of the few published descriptions of the place. He noted that it was "a small, low, and rather insignificant ruin."[2] Kisurra, in spite of its ordinariness, had a fairly tumultuous history, thanks to the dubious honor of being located pretty much directly on the border of two kingdoms that dominated southern Mesopotamia throughout the twentieth and nineteenth centuries BCE: Isin and Larsa.

Ishbi-Erra of Isin: Usurper

By 2000 BCE, Ur-Namma's dynasty in Ur had lost its grip on Sumer. A number of factors led to its decline. Scribes later blamed this loss on the arrival of a new group of people, the Amorites, who supposedly disrupted the peace, but scholars have discounted this.

Amorite was a Semitic language that began to spread throughout Mesopotamia around this time; it was the native tongue of a group of people who may originally have come from the west. But they had lived in Mesopotamia long before the end of the Ur III period and had not invaded or suddenly arrived. A king of Ur went to the trouble of building a long wall between the Tigris and the Euphrates Rivers to try to keep the Amorites out, but it didn't work. They were already too integrated into Mesopotamian society for a wall to have made any difference at all. Over the next few centuries, kings with Amorite names and Amorite ancestry

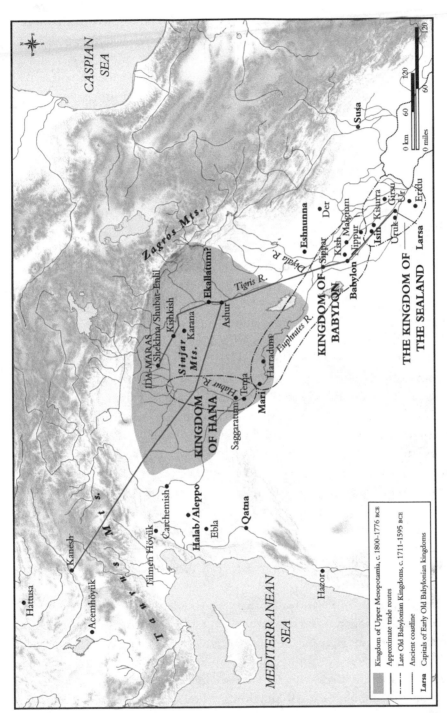

Map 2 Map of the Near East from 2000 to 1500 BCE

led many Mesopotamian kingdoms, notably in Babylon, where the most prominent Amorite king was named Hammurabi. We will return to him later. The Ur III kingdom collapsed for more prosaic reasons, one of them being that it continued to be nearly impossible to hold together, for any length of time, large groups of people who were spread over a wide area. Successful long-lasting empires were still a long way off in the future.

For now, the ruler of another city, a close neighbor to Kisurra, was claiming to be the successor to the Ur III kings. This city was Isin and its new ruler was named Ishbi-Erra (2017–1985 BCE). Ishbi-Erra was not a member of any royal family. He had been an official working for a king of Ur, Ibbi-Sin (2028–2004 BCE), who—thanks in part to the treachery of Ishbi-Erra, but also to the breakdown of the central government—proved to be the last king of Ur's Third Dynasty. Ishbi-Erra claimed the throne for himself and moved his capital city upstream to Isin.[3]

His reign was long, lasting thirty-three years, which gave him plenty of time to establish his right to be king and to strengthen his grip on his realm. If we can believe his year-names, Ishbi-Erra followed the lead of the Ur III kings: he destroyed cities and conquered armies, created furniture for temples, founded irrigation projects, built a new city wall, and, going all out in the priestess department, dedicated eight women as priestesses to gods in cities around his kingdom.[4] Ishbi-Erra emulated kings going all the way back to Sargon when he appointed these holy women. One of them, Enbarazi, was identified as being his daughter.[5] (Only one of Ishbi-Erra's years was named for the appointment of a priest; it was generally the case that priests' appointments were less likely than those of priestesses to be commemorated this way, or perhaps they were simply less common.)

Ishbi-Erra and the kings who were his descendants are known as the First Dynasty of Isin; they dominated much of Sumer during the 1900s BCE. They did their best to make it seem as though the Ur dynasty had not ended. In fact, they continued to call themselves "Kings of Ur" for seventy years.

But their kingdom was smaller than the kingdom of Ur had been. As we have seen, Mesopotamia was rarely successfully unified, and the collapse of the Ur dynasty allowed the land to return to its more usual condition, with several states coexisting and periodically battling and negotiating with one another. Each kingdom was centered in a capital city, and each contained a number of vassal kingdoms, whose leaders were considered to be "sons" of their overlord, and who often were married to his daughters. These kingdoms extended not just throughout Mesopotamia and Syria, but apparently even into the Levant. Some cuneiform documents found at the Canaanite site of ancient Hazor, in what was (much later) the biblical land of Israel, were written in a language and script typical of this period throughout the region.[6]

Of the regions that had been within the kingdom of Ur, some northern lands became independent of Isin,[7] as did the southern regions of Uruk and Larsa.[8] Nevertheless, the people living in much of Sumer would have found their lives more or less unchanged, and many of them might even have been unaware that the capital city had moved north from Ur to Isin, or that the new kings were unrelated to the old ones. Administrative texts found in temple archives show that the new administration was just as concerned with every detail of goods received and manufactured as the old one had been; there wasn't even a discernable break in record-keeping.

The language of government and religion continued to be Sumerian, even though the kings of Isin spoke Akkadian as their native language. Just as the Ur III kings had commissioned hymns in their own honor, so did the kings of Isin, even copying the patterns of the older hymns. A king of Isin who put out a collection of laws in the 1930s BCE emulated Ur-Namma by composing them in Sumerian.[9] Kings of Isin married their daughters off to kings of Anshan, just like Shulgi and other Ur III kings before them. For a whole century there seems to have been no desire on the part of the Isin kings to boast of a new era, or even to claim preeminence for their city.

The Kingdom of Larsa

By the time of Ur's conquest, the kingdom centered at Larsa, south of Isin and just to the east of Uruk, had become Isin's main competitor for power in Mesopotamia. It's difficult to imagine what this era was like for the people living through it, as Larsa began to stretch its muscles, calling up troops, setting its sights on cities that had long been paying taxes first to Ur then to Isin. Were the people of Larsa proud when their king Gungunum (1932–1906 BCE) captured Ur in 1926 BCE and ended the Isin kings' pretentions to be a continuation of the Ur III dynasty? It was only then that the Isin kings gave up calling themselves "king of Ur" and switched to regular use of the title "king of Isin."[10] What was the people's reaction when, a few years later, the next king of Larsa, Abi-sare (1905–1895 BCE), claimed that he "smote with his weapons the army of Isin"?[11] Isin was not defeated, but it was struggling. The next king of Larsa, Sumu-El (1894–1866 BCE), pushed the border of his kingdom north into lands that had long belonged to Isin, including little Kisurra.[12]

The era from around 2000 to 1800 BCE has been dubbed the "Isin-Larsa period." The rulers of Isin tried to maintain old traditions but eventually were unable to continue the relatively calm and orderly administration that had characterized the Third Dynasty of Ur, nor could they hold onto Ur's empire. Larsa gradually chipped away at Isin's domination, eventually becoming the greater power, though Isin continued to control a gradually shrinking area in the center of the region.

In some cities near the border between Isin and Larsa, residents might have been hard-pressed to keep track of which kingdom they were living in at any given time. Kisurra, located only about 19 kilometers (12 miles) from Isin,[13] was in exactly this situation. The documents written there show that people leased fields, herded cattle, lent one another silver and barley, got married, adopted children, farmed, and paid taxes, and they show that generations of parents and children succeeded one another in an orderly fashion, with no apparent major crises or massacres interrupting daily life.[14] But for decades, the city bounced back and forth from the control of one kingdom to another.

The evidence for the topsy-turvy nature of the kingdom of Kisurra is reflected well in the dates on the documents that were written there. Each king who controlled the city demanded that contracts and government records be dated by the year-names of his own reign. And so, in the early 1920s BCE, we see kings of Isin being replaced by King Gungunum of Larsa, who took over Kisurra and who imposed his year-names. But, late in the decade, by 1921 BCE, the city was back in the kingdom of Isin, with that king's year-names replacing those of the king of Larsa. For a brief time Kisurra claimed independence—four kings of a local dynasty controlled the land (and the year-names),[15] but then the king of Larsa was back again in 1910 BCE. Twelve more years passed and the city was again in Isin's kingdom. Nine more years and it was in Larsa again. And so it went, on and on for decades, in dizzying succession, until 1802 BCE.[16] During the periods when Kisurra was independent, its kings issued year-names to be used throughout its small territory, and people proudly swore oaths in the name of the local god, Ninurta.[17] But then the city would be swept back into the orbit of either Isin or Larsa and the Kisurran people would pay their taxes to other lands and swear their oaths to the gods of other cities.

Here's the strange thing, though. You would expect this to have been a time of constant warfare and bloodshed with never-ending battles, desperate sieges, and Homeric heroics on the battlefield. But the evidence doesn't back that up. Although military skirmishes do seem to have been common, the cities near the border of the two kingdoms, and even some cities far from the border, generally seem to have transferred their allegiance from Isin to Larsa, or vice versa, without much of a fuss.

Sumu-El of Larsa and Erra-imitti of Isin: Border Wars

In 1888 BCE, Kisurra was under the control of Larsa. We know this not because of a destruction layer bearing witness to a war for control of the city, or because the king of Larsa bragged about it, but simply because of those documents that start to be dated to the reign of King Sumu-El of Larsa.[18] Sumu-El was a king who didn't shrink from touting his military achievements—he named more than half his years after victories against enemies—so it's odd that he didn't ever mention Kisurra in his year-names or his surviving royal inscriptions. But Sumu-El struggled to hold onto Kisurra nonetheless. Around 1868 BCE, twenty years after Sumu-El took control there, an aggressive new king of Isin, Erra-imitti (1868–1861 BCE), sent troops into the area to fight against Sumu-El's army from Larsa, with the conflict centering on the region around Kisurra.

For once, it's possible to view this struggle from something other than the bird's-eye view that we normally get—the flattened landscape of words in year-names that simply name the cities and whether they had been "destroyed," "smitten," "defeated," or "seized" by the conquering king. Instead, letters have survived that King Sumu-El sent to his officers in the midst of the hostilities, between around 1870 and 1865 BCE, when the outcome of the skirmish was far from certain.[19] Perhaps the king was writing from his palace at Larsa, but it's more likely that he was positioned somewhere near the border of his kingdom, leading some of the forces himself. He received regular messages from his officials, and it seems likely that he was relatively close to the front lines when he read them and replied (see Fig. 8.1).

The situation on the ground at the time is a little hard to reconstruct from the letters. There's no timeline or map of operations, and Sumu-El didn't date his correspondence (it just wasn't Mesopotamian practice to do so), so we can't even be sure of the chronological sequence in which to read them. But we can still learn a lot about how the conflict played out.

"Important!" the king wrote in one letter to the heads of his security forces. "Your watches must be strict!" This abrupt language was often the way he began a letter. He continued, "Why do you keep releasing troops from service so acquiescently?"[20] It's hard to imagine why the commanders would be releasing their forces; it certainly didn't please Sumu-El. He had

Fig. 8.1 Letter from Larsa concerning the detention of some soldiers, Isin–Larsa period. (Yale University, Peabody Museum)

received some important intelligence suggesting that his enemy, the king of Isin, was waiting for just such a moment of weakness to attack.

Sumu-El continued, "Just now, [King] Erra-imitti (of Isin) is giving orders to march on (the town of) Shayana. Make no mistake, as soon as your numbers have decreased, he will reach out against me and do some damage." You can imagine Sumu-El pacing back and forth, dictating his letter, trying to figure out how to impress upon his heads of security just how dire the situation could become, but only having a tablet carried by a messenger with which to inform them. He closed the letter with another abrupt command: "Important! Do not release troops from service!"[21]

Shayana was not a major place, but it was Sumu-El's obsession right now. He wrote three more letters to the heads of security about it.[22] In one, it's clear that the town of Shayana had stayed in his hands. Erra-imitti must have been unsuccessful in his attack. After Sumu-El's usual command to make sure that "The watches must be strict!" he made three requests about Shayana. First, his troops should not touch the barley located there; second, "the city wall must be in good repair,"[23] perhaps in preparation for a threatened attack; and, third, the officials should "take an oracle for Shayana and its troops, for the whole month, and [have it brought] to me." He asked for this again in another letter. He really needed the monthly oracle for Shayana to be taken.[24] Oracles were crucial in wartime; they revealed what the gods had in mind for the armies. Would he be able to hold on to Shayana? Or would Erra-imitti prevail? Later we hear that apparently Shayana did withstand an attack by Isin's forces, but the city wall sustained damage because of a fire. The heads of security were now required to send builders to repair the wall.[25]

Strikingly, there are no mentions in the surviving letters of casualties on either side. This hardly sounds like a fight to the death on the part of Erra-imitti, or even a concerted effort to recapture territory. There's something rather lackadaisical about it all. One letter even describes the movement of the enemy troops of Isin as "dragging" on to the next city after provisioning themselves.[26]

Perhaps because of the slow pace of military action, King Sumu-El seems to have worried that his generals were not 100 percent focused on keeping the enemy at bay. That phrase, "Important! Your watches must be strict!" or sometimes "Important! Don't fail in your duties!," conjures up an image of a man keen to have his orders followed, but unconvinced that they would be. He really did want his military chiefs to pay attention to what he had to say, after all, so he threw in that first word, *apputtum*, which can be translated as either "Important!" or "It is urgent!"—to wake them up when the letter was read aloud to them.

Almost all the letters focused on whatever command Sumu-El wanted his subordinates to carry out at that time. In some cases, he had heard rumors of behavior by his security agents that he couldn't understand: Why were they distributing grain in the countryside when it would be needed in town for a siege that seemed inevitable? Why were they quarreling among themselves? He doesn't seem to have necessarily cared about the answers to these questions; he just wanted all this negligence to stop.

In other letters, though, he did ask for answers, and even for formal written reports: How many forces did two particular generals command and why had they not been deployed? What battle gear did another two men have? No doubt, letters flowed in the other direction as well when the officials wrote back, but the archive from which the letters came didn't include the replies.

Sumu-El was a practical man, who sometimes had to rein in the ambitions of his generals. At one point, several high-ranking men were leading an effort to quickly build a fort to defend Larsa's territory, somewhere along its border. They had grand ambitions for an eighteen-acre edifice. Sumu-El wrote to them at least twice to try to convince them to bring their plans down to earth: "The four acres that I told you, that will be enough. Build that,"[27] he wrote. He said that the walls could be complete in ten days, rising by four cubits per day. He admitted that the fort might grow larger thereafter: "later let us enlarge it proportionately." But that eighteen-acre dream? "Should we make it eighteen acres, that would be too much."[28]

In the meantime, he was trying to make decisions about where to send troops and where to send silver to pay for hired men, and it drove him a little crazy when the information he needed was not forthcoming. In one letter he described a vast quantity of silver that he had sent out, and he wondered aloud what on earth had happened to it all: "First I had twenty minas (pounds) of silver delivered to you. A second time I had forty minas of silver [delivered] to you. A third time one talent (60 minas)!"[29] These 120 minas represented about 54 kilograms (120 pounds) of silver—a vast sum in a land with no mineral ores of its own—enough to have paid hundreds of workers for years. The king demanded, "Report to me in writing all the silver that there is! Have a checklist brought to me!"

The messages were sometimes transported by a man named Puzur-Numushda.[30] Typically, the king ordered, "Send Puzur-Numushda to me!"[31] But Puzur-Numushda was more than a messenger. He also received letters from Sumu-El, addressed to him along with a powerful commander named Beli-ay-annadi, that show that he was one of the men directly in charge of running the campaign, receiving direct commands from the king. But the fact that Puzur-Numushda could travel to wherever the king was stationed, and that letters regularly passed between the king and the vulnerable cities on the border, suggests that the warfare between the kingdoms was localized and limited. In fact, engagements seem largely to have consisted of sieges, city walls set on fire, and then repairs to the damage. Perhaps the troops from both kingdoms also looted the towns they captured, but, oddly, this is not mentioned by Sumu-El, at least not in the letters that we have. And, again to judge from the letters, the damage done in these wars seems to have been more to property than to people.

Pihatni-ipiq: A High Official of Sumu-El

One high-ranking official whom Sumu-El seems to have trusted was named Pihatni-ipiq. We don't know his title but, to judge from his responsibilities, he might have been a provincial governor.[32] At one point, during the ongoing campaigns near the border, the Heads of Security (those anonymous commanders to whom Sumu-El often wrote) had sent word that they needed a lot more troops, so the king sent their request on to Pihatni-ipiq. King Sumu-El had no doubt that he would follow through; he assured the Heads of Security that Pihatni-ipiq "will dispatch one thousand troops to you."[33] We can only guess what this must have involved. Did Pihatni-ipiq have to redeploy troops from one region to another? Or did he have to call up men who were off duty and busy with farming? How did he choose who would be sent? Who wrote the directive? Where did they gather? How far did the troops travel? How long did it take to organize this? All those details are omitted from the king's terse note. We know only that the king asked and Pihatni-ipiq came through for him.

Just one letter survives from Pihatni-ipiq to King Sumu-El, and it reveals more about their relationship. Pihatni-ipiq was surprisingly forthright. First, he reassured the king that "The town is well and the guards are well."[34] We don't know where he lived, but the king would have known which town he meant. He was reassuring the king here, answering the constant demand that "your guards must be strong!"[35]

This letter actually has nothing to do with the troop movements or the threat from King Erra-imitti of Isin. Instead, Pihatni-ipiq wrote about making the best use of agricultural workers who were available for harvest time so that crops would not be lost. The harvest took place in April and May, just when the river reached its highest level and threatened to flood. It was always a challenge for administrators to make the best use of the available corvée laborers and paid workers—assigning some to harvesting and others to flood control.[36] It's striking that Pihatni-ipiq wrote to the king as "you." Most officials, not just in Larsa but in other kingdoms as well, referred to the king as "my lord" in their letters and avoided using the second person.[37] The king seems not to have minded; Pihatni-ipiq was close enough to him that this familiarity didn't cause offense.

The commander named Beli-ay-annadi had been on the receiving end of many of Sumu-El's slightly panicky letters urging him that "The watches must be strict!" but he also was sent a letter by his colleague Pihatni-ipiq about a much more prosaic topic, namely a quantity of barley to be used for feeding animals. Cattle and sheep had to be fattened up for the forthcoming Great Festival. Soldiers were mentioned in this instance, but only in the context of a civilian purpose: they were to be assigned to "escort the fatteners" of the cows and sheep when they were sent off to Pihatni-ipiq.[38] The letter shows that, even during times of warfare, not every day was taken up with fort building and troop mustering and oracle reading to prepare for attacks from Isin. The religious festivals that marked the passing of the year continued to be celebrated in the kingdom of Larsa, and Pihatni-ipiq was involved in those as well.

Over the course of his reign, Sumu-El seems to have managed to take control of the town of Kisurra and then lose it, and then gain it back, and then lose it again, several times. Once, he lost Kisurra not to Isin but to the king of Babylon, to whom we will return. At another point, after a local man of Kisurra named Manna-balti-El had claimed the throne and issued his own year-names, Sumu-El brought Kisurra back under the rule of Larsa and Manna-balti-El became his vassal. These two kings cemented their relationship with the marriage of Sumu-El's daughter, Shat-Sin, to the crown prince of Kisurra. Princess Shat-Sin had a cylinder seal carved to reflect her new status. Its inscription reveals her complicated ties: she was "Shat-Sin, daughter of Sumu-El (king of Larsa), daughter-in-law of Manna-balti-El (vassal of Sumu-El and king of Kisurra), wife of Ibni-Shadu (crown prince of Kisurra)."[39] After she moved to the palace at Kisurra, Princess Shat-Sin no doubt kept up a regular correspondence with her father, letting him know about the politics of the court of her father-in-law, and later of her husband when he became king. A letter written by her was found during the brief excavations at Kisurra. The letter isn't to her father; she wrote to one of the high officials in the city telling him to bring an ox to a particular place when her father, Sumu-El, was ill. Shat-Sin was a chip off the old block. Her tone in this letter was just as authoritative as her father's in his correspondence (though she refrained from telling the official that his watches must be strict).[40]

The end result of the battles with Erra-imitti was not good news for Sumu-El. Larsa lost control of Kisurra, and of the much more important city of Nippur.[41] At that point it seemed that Isin was gaining strength; its apparent decline was not a given.

Sumu-El's Reign

Quite a lot more is known about Sumu-El, beyond his letters from the battlefield. He had come to power in 1894 BCE, as the seventh king of Larsa. It had been thirty-two years since his predecessor King Gungunum had taken control of Ur and ended the era in which Isin could claim to be home to the "kings of Ur." Larsa, rather than Isin, now saw itself as Ur's rightful heir.[42]

Many of the kings of Isin and Larsa left little behind. For some, not a single royal inscription remains, not even something as simple as a cylinder seal belonging to a servant of the king. That is true of the first three kings of Larsa.[43] We don't know their year-names; they may not have issued any. For the first two, it's not even clear that they were "kings of Larsa" at all—they might have been subject to Ur or Isin.[44] Their names appear on lists of kings in modern books looking just as robust as anyone else, but a little searching reveals that there's almost nothing behind those names. They were real people, of course, with officials and families, enemies and intrigue, diplomatic crises and proud achievements, but we know nothing of them.

Sumu-El is different. In addition to his vivid letters, he was the author of two known royal inscriptions, seven inscriptions that mention him on cylinder seals and other objects belonging to servants,[45] thirty-one year-names,[46] and many administrative documents written during his reign (though, unfortunately, no images of him survive). They all attest to his aggressive efforts to expand Larsa's kingdom and to undermine the power of Isin.

As we have seen, Sumu-El was proud of his military victories and keen to let everyone know about them in his year-names and inscriptions. Curiously, though, none of the details from his letters were mentioned in his year-names for the period toward the end of his reign when he was locked in the ongoing struggle over the border with Isin. He didn't boast of capturing Kisurra in 1875 BCE, or of thwarting Erra-imitti's attempts to besiege his cities, or of arranging for his daughter to marry the crown prince of Kisurra. Instead, throughout the period covered by the letters, he just kept repeating more or less the same year-name over and over. His twenty-fifth year in power, 1872 BCE (which was two years before Erra-imitti came to the throne in Isin), was called "The year: Enshakiag-Nanna, the *en*-priestess of (the god) Nanna, was installed."[47] With a surprising lack of bombast, 1871 became "The year after the *en*-priestess of Nanna was installed." In 1870, Erra-imitti took the throne in Isin, presumably beginning his threats on Larsa, but Sumu-El maintained his silence on such matters in his kingdom. It was "The second year after the *en*-priestess of Nanna was installed." This continued right to the end of his reign, all the way through "The sixth year after the *en*-priestess of Nanna was installed." Perhaps he was particularly proud of his appointment of the priestess Enshakiag-Nanna. She was, after all, a successor to Enheduana, with the same position at Ur (though more than 400 years later), and Enshakiag-Nanna's presence there cemented Sumu-El's claim to be the king of Ur, the successor to the divine kings of the Third Dynasty. On the other hand, he might have repeated variations on the same year-name over and over because matters in his kingdom were not as good as they might have been and he could come up with nothing better to commemorate. Erra-imitti was, after all, able to reclaim the border lands for Isin during those years.

We don't have the letters of Erra-imitti of Isin to tell us his side of the story of the conflict with the king of Larsa, but he probably saw Sumu-El as the instigator of hostilities, rather than the other way around. We do have his year-names, however, and in 1865, two years before the death of Sumu-El in Larsa, he proudly boasted, that it was "The Year: Erra-imitti, the king, seized Kisurra." Another version of the year-name said that he "destroyed Kisurra."[48] This wasn't an empty boast; sure enough, the year-names on the tablets from Kisurra changed again after the twenty-eighth year of Sumu-El. They were, once again, dated to the years of the king of Isin. Poor Kisurra, if Erra-imitti really did "destroy" the city, or even part of it, the people there must have been getting very tired of being pulled like the rope in a tug-of-war between two ambitious kingdoms.

Sumu-la-El of Babylon: The Beginning of a Dynasty

Throughout the twentieth century BCE, the central part of Mesopotamia had been divided into city-states that, like Kisurra, were sometimes independent and at other times subject to greater powers. One of the relatively obscure cities was called Babylon. It's unclear whether Babylon was independent or subject to Isin through most of the Isin-Larsa period; there are no documents from there at all from the first century of that era.[49] The nearby city of Kish was briefly independent and its kings issued royal inscriptions, so Babylon, too, might have been independent, at least for a while.

The shifting political situation in central Mesopotamia began to change during the same decade that Sumu-El of Larsa was writing his letters and strategizing about how to limit the damage inflicted by Erra-imitti of Isin. A new king had taken the throne of Babylon and was beginning to make his presence known. This man had a confusingly similar name to that of his contemporary in Larsa: he was Sumu-la-El (1880–1845 BCE). He founded an Amorite dynasty, one that lasted for almost 300 years and put Babylon firmly on the map as a center of power and influence. (Its most famous king, Hammurabi, ruled a century after Sumu-la-El.)

In fact, it had been Sumu-la-El of Babylon, not the king of Isin, who in just his third year on the throne (1878 BCE) seized control of the city-state of Kisurra. The king of Larsa grabbed it back within just three years (only to lose it to local rule and later to Erra-imitti of Isin), but this was a foretaste of things to come. Babylon was becoming a significant presence in the region.

Sumu-la-El's name shows up on documents from Sippar quite early in his reign. Sippar was two days' travel to the north of Babylon and had been home to an independent local dynasty. We know about the local kings mostly from their names appearing in oaths on contracts—people who needed to swear an oath usually did it in the name of the local god and king. Babylon's involvement in Sippar's affairs shows up when people started swearing in the name of Sumu-la-El as well as the local king of Sippar. This local king had presumably become a vassal of Babylon. By the thirteenth year of his reign, Sumu-la-El's name appeared alone.[50] Babylon had taken direct control of Sippar; the vassal was gone. By his nineteenth year, Sumu-la-El of Babylon had conquered the nearby city of Kish, followed the next year by Kizallu, which was probably to the south (its location hasn't been found).

Like his contemporary, Sumu-El of Larsa, many of Sumu-la-El's year-names are full of military bombast, boasting of the cities he conquered. But the name of his twenty-second year on the throne is strikingly different. It was "the year in which he made for Marduk a magnificent throne dais adorned with silver and gold."[51] You will be hearing a lot about the god Marduk, city god of Babylon, in later chapters of this book, as he eventually became one of the greatest and most powerful of Mesopotamian gods. This seems to be the first reference to him by a Babylonian king.

Enlil-bani of Isin: A Gardener Becomes King

By 1863 BCE, King Sumu-El of Larsa had been dead for three years. Larsa was rising in power and importance under his successor. King Sumu-la-El of Babylon was in his seventeenth year and busily expanding the borders of his own kingdom. Meanwhile, previously dominant Isin faced one defeat after another. And then something remarkable happened there. Or rather, it *may* have happened. We only know about this episode from a much later chronicle, but the names are right, so perhaps it really took place.

It seems that an eclipse of the moon occurred, terrifying everyone who witnessed it. The Mesopotamians had no way to know that the eclipse happened because the Earth passed between the moon and the sun and cast its shadow across the moon. To Mesopotamian eyes, the bright, reassuring face of the moon gradually seemed to be swallowed up by darkness and was replaced by a round red shadow in the sky. Diviners believed that it signaled the death of the king.

Erra-imitti acted in his own self-interest, and he may have been the first king to come up with a solution to the threat of his imminent death. At any rate, he's the first one that we know of to do this (there were others who followed his lead in later centuries). According to the later chronicle, "Erra-imitti, the king, installed Enlil-bani, the gardener, as a substitute king on his throne. He placed the royal diadem on his head."[52] The plan was that this gardener, Enlil-bani, would serve as king in place of Erra-imitti—living in the court, being served by attendants—and that the gods could go right ahead and carry out their threat to kill the king, but they would choose the gardener-king instead of the real king, Erra-imitti. Just in case the gods failed to follow their cue, the real king would have the substitute king killed, after which Erra-imitti would retake the throne, the prophecy having been properly fulfilled. This, at least, is what happened in later centuries when a substitute king was installed in order to fulfill, and outwit, a prophecy of death to the king.

But the gods seem to have been wiser than Erra-imitti anticipated. Instead, "Erra-imitti [died] in his palace when he sipped a hot broth. Enlil-bani, who occupied the throne, did not give it up (and) so was sovereign."[53] Fact or fable? It seems like a fairy tale, and yet it may well have happened. There is no record from the time of this remarkable occurrence, only ones that were written much later. But then, not many royal records survive from this period; it might simply be lost. Enlil-bani is unlikely to have bragged in a royal inscription about this odd way of coming to power. Being a gardener was not a normal preparation for the throne, after all.

So perhaps the real king did die, as the gods had foretold with the lunar eclipse. One can imagine Erra-imitti sipping his hot broth and then suddenly falling to the ground. Did he choke to death, or have a heart attack, or was he perhaps even poisoned? At this point the gardener, Enlil-bani, who had been placed on the throne simply as a convenience in order to spare the king, could have justifiably argued that the gods had wanted him to rule. What were the chances? There he was, ready to give up his life for the gods and the kingdom, and suddenly it was clear that he was the gods' choice, after all. They had seen through Erra-imitti's ruse and killed him anyway.

In the end, Enlil-bani (1860–1837 BCE) left far more evidence of his reign than did the ill-fated Erra-imitti. He commissioned an inscription to be impressed onto the bricks of a building that he constructed in Isin. It began, "Enlil-bani, shepherd who makes everything abundant for Nippur, farmer (who grows) tall grain for Ur,"[54] which sounds like a slight nod to his humble agricultural beginnings. But he also claimed religious powers. He "purifies the mes (cosmic truths) of (the city of) Eridu," and was the "favorite en-priest of Uruk." At this point he came to his titles: "king of Isin, king of the land of Sumer and Akkad," the latter being the title given to the kings who claimed to control all of Mesopotamia. He was their rightful successor. Note that, unlike most kings, he didn't name his father. Why would he? His father had not been royal. Instead he emphasized that he was the "spouse chosen by the heart of the goddess Inana." And, like Erra-imitti and the other kings of Isin before him, Enlil-bani added the divine symbol in front of his name. Notwithstanding his humble start in life, he asserted that he was himself a god, an appropriate husband for the goddess Inana.

His contemporaries might have been dubious to start with, but Enlil-bani actually seems to have been a successful king. Early on, he released his subjects in Isin from paying taxes and serving as laborers.[55] This was a smart move. The previous king, Erra-imitti, probably had sons who normally would have had a stronger claim to rule than Enlil-bani did. In the face of this, Enlil-bani needed popular support. What better way to get it than to cancel taxes and corvée labor duties? But this doesn't seem to have been an entirely cynical choice. Year after year, the accidental king attempted to endear himself to his people, for example by having canals dug that would expand the agricultural land of the kingdom.[56] He also lavished attention and wealth on the gods, providing them with thrones, daises, gold and copper statues, new temples, and priests and priestesses to serve them.

Unlike his predecessors and contemporaries in other states, Enlil-bani's twelve surviving royal inscriptions and twenty-four surviving year-names made no mention of attacking other cities. Even in a poem written in praise of him, the author emphasized the king's goodness and kindness rather than his prowess or fearsomeness. Yes, "your troops triumph over hostile troops" (though no specific victories are mentioned), but the foreign leaders didn't quake in fear; instead "all sovereigns become allies with you and you soothe their quarrels."[57] The generous ex-gardener did not "kill transgressors" and his "governors suffer[ed] no injuries."

Besides building temples, Enlil-bani had his laborers and engineers rebuild the city wall around Isin and construct a palace.[58] He made a special gift to the goddess Ninlil by installing two copper statues in her temple, 117 years after they had first been fabricated by an earlier king. It's unclear where they had been languishing in the meantime, but Ninlil finally benefited from their presence. In exchange, the king's inscription records that Ninlil "had the god Enlil (her husband) lengthen the lifespan of Enlil-bani."[59]

Enlil-bani's fame in subsequent generations came the same way as Shulgi's. The hymn written in his praise became a standard part of the school curriculum. Scribes copied it for generations as they learned to write and as they learned Sumerian—not a bad outcome for a man who was slated to be executed in place of the real king. Ultimately, he *was* the real king.

It would be fitting to conclude this section with a fable-style ending, to tell you that the lowly gardener king was able to turn around the fate of his kingdom, and that Isin was renewed under his wise rule. But it was not to be. By 1837 BCE, when Enlil-bani died, Isin was little more than a city-state, eclipsed by the dominant presence of Larsa.

Throughout the kingdom's decline, though, Isin's kings maintained a sense of grandeur. They continued to present themselves as gods, something claimed by only two of the kings of Larsa.[60] At the end of the reign of the second-to-last king of Isin, Sin-magir (1827–1817 BCE), someone in the royal court decided to add the names of the kings of Isin to the Sumerian King List that had been in circulation at least since the reign of King Shulgi of Ur, more than 200 years before.[61] By adding his dynasty to the end of this list, Sin-magir was claiming to be the divinely ordained successor to all the great kings and dynasties of the past, including Sargon and the subsequent kings of Akkad, Ur-Namma and his successor kings of Ur. There was, unsurprisingly, no mention of Larsa.

But five years before Sin-magir's death, a young rival named Rim-Sin had taken the throne in Larsa, and twenty-eight years after that, Rim-Sin finally conquered Isin, bringing the dynasty to an end. But the future in Mesopotamia did not belong to Larsa. A younger contemporary of Rim-Sin, Hammurabi of Babylon, was about to put his city on the map, where it stayed forever.

Chapter 9
Merchants and Families

At some point during the Isin-Larsa period, a scribe wrote down an itinerary, carefully listing on a clay tablet all the stops on a land route that stretched north and west from Larsa to Syria.[1] The tablet includes seventy place-names, each representing the endpoint of a day's journey of about 24 to 29 kilometers (15 to 18 miles). Many of the places are not known from any source outside of this list—these must have been the names of small villages or even inns along the way—but others were major cities. This tablet gives us a window into travel during this time, and we know that people did travel—a lot—many of them probably using this exact route.

The itinerary makes mention of an army and it seems to be the record of, or maybe a plan for, the movement of a group of soldiers right across Mesopotamia and Syria. It's unclear why they were traveling so far; perhaps they were going as reinforcements to support an ally in warfare, or perhaps they were functioning as an armed guard, accompanying luxury gifts sent by one king to another.

Soldiers were not the only ones to use the route, however; far from it. Even if they didn't travel the whole way, any number of people would have needed to take this road, including messengers, merchants, traveling artisans, people visiting distant relatives, and government officials.

A Journey North from Larsa

A group of travelers following the itinerary would have traveled north from Larsa, hugging the route of the Euphrates (see Map 2). They passed the familiar repeating sights of palm trees, long rectangular fields flanked by canals, and villages of mudbrick houses.

The travelers arrived in Babylon after being on the road for seven days. Even at times when the kings of Larsa and Babylon were hostile to one another, people probably had little difficulty entering the enemy city. Babylon had a city wall and a palace, and it would not have struck visitors as all that different from the other cities they had passed along the way.

An envoy transporting a letter from King Sumu-El of Larsa to King Sumu-la-El of Babylon would have ended his journey here. The rest of the itinerary off toward Syria would have been irrelevant to him. He delivered his letter to the king and could have returned to Larsa with an answer for his own king, possibly inside two weeks, especially if he took a boat downstream, which could have sped up the return journey.

We read that the soldiers about whom the itinerary was written stayed in Babylon for eleven days and then continued on.[2] They were not alone; many travelers needed to go farther. Notable among them were textile weavers and traders. The best fabrics were made in the south—that was common knowledge—and southern cloth became ever more valuable the farther from home it was sold. Weavers from Larsa could get a good price if they sold their goods to trading caravans that kept going beyond Babylon and headed for the city of Ashur. Caravans from the south regularly brought textiles to Ashur, and their arrival was anxiously anticipated there.[3]

The traders from the south would, therefore, have continued on from Babylon to Sippar, where they arrived two days later. So many people took this road that inns were provided along the way where one could find a bed and food. In other regions, and probably in Sippar as well, these inns even provided places to store valuables. Sippar was a big city, home to the sun god Shamash, and it probably provided several types of accommodations. As in Babylon, the soldiers following the itinerary stayed in Sippar for longer than one might expect—ten days this time. We are not told what they were doing there, but they were clearly in no hurry to get to their final destination.

The next stretch of the itinerary left the banks of the Euphrates behind and took the soldiers (and our trading caravan carrying southern textiles) north along the route of a wide canal that flowed from the Tigris to the Euphrates, and then north again along the Tigris River toward the city of Ashur. The soldiers from Larsa paused again for another ten days not far from Sippar at a place called Apil-Sin where they "girded themselves," perhaps before moving on into hostile territory. Had they not stopped, the journey from Sippar to Ashur would have taken eleven days; travelers following the itinerary apparently continued to keep up the grueling pace of about 24–29 kilometers per day.

The City of Ashur

Visitors approaching on the road from the south might not have noticed the rise in elevation that marked the approach to Ashur, but they would have seen the curved city wall from quite a distance. When Ashur was founded, around 2500 BCE, its early inhabitants no doubt realized that the triangular site would be relatively easy to defend. It needed just one stretch of city wall, because two branches of the Tigris River came together here and had cut high escarpments out of the rock. The city towered 40 meters (about 130 feet) above the river, with the rivers providing a natural moat and steep cliffs on two of its three sides.

By this time, the early second millennium BCE, Ashur extended over about 40 hectares (about 100 acres) and had a population of just 5,000–8,000 people. A thousand years later, it would become a great city, the religious heart of the immense Neo-Assyrian Empire, but no one would have guessed of its future glory at the time when our textile caravan from Larsa arrived there. A Larsan trader visiting Ashur for the first time would not have been impressed by its size, but he might have noted some striking differences from the southern cities he knew. First, there was the local dialect. Although someone speaking the southern Mesopotamian version of Akkadian could understand the dialect of Ashur, the two were distinct, even when written down. The Assyrians (as the residents of Ashur are traditionally called) also used different month names for their calendar from those of their southern neighbors, and their artists created distinct cylinder seals.

Even the city itself would have felt a little foreign to someone from Larsa. For one thing, the citadel on which it was built was natural and rocky, rather than being the result only of the accumulation of human debris, as was the case for southern tells. Its people had an unusual city god as well. Ashur (who shared his name with his city, also an uncommon phenomenon) wasn't a cosmic god, but seems to have been in some way embodied in the rockface below the temple.[4] At the highest point of the city, overlooking the river, stood the imposing temple to the god Ashur. It would have been inconceivable to the Assyrians to build a temple to Ashur in any location other than this—this was where Ashur was physically present. The temple was large, measuring 108 meters (354 feet) by 54 meters (177 feet), with a central courtyard, and although it was frequently rebuilt and restored, its physical plan remained almost unchanged until the seventh century BCE.[5]

The government in Ashur was very different from those of its southern neighbors. Even though the city-state had a hereditary ruler, these men didn't use the title "king." Each one was a "governor" (*ensi*) who served the god Ashur (though we refer to them as kings anyway). In the eyes of the Assyrians, the god himself was in charge. In practice, though, much of the power in Ashur was held by a City Assembly. It was this assembly, rather than the king, that made decisions and it could also serve as a court of law.[6]

Even though the fields around Ashur were not particularly productive, the city flourished. It had a singular advantage: Ashur was located at a crossing of several traditional roadways. You might think that this would have inspired the kings there to impose high taxes on any traders passing through town, and thereby to increase the fortune of their city. But an early king made a very different decision. Erishum I of Ashur, who ruled from 1974 to 1935 BCE (a whole century before Sumu-El ruled in Larsa), proclaimed that no taxes at all would be imposed in Ashur on traded goods, including metals like gold, silver, copper, and tin, and even on staples like barley and wool.[7] Trade there was to be free. Did Erishum proclaim this decision because he foresaw that it would be a boon to his state? Or did he do it for more pragmatic reasons that resolved some issue of the time about which we know nothing? Either way, it turned out to be a wise choice.

What happened was that merchants interested in buying or selling metals and textiles from across the region seem to have gravitated to Ashur, where they would not owe taxes on the transactions. Assyrian entrepreneurs then purchased these goods—especially tin and lapis lazuli from the east, and textiles from the south (and from weaving enterprises in Ashur itself)—and found ways to sell them in distant markets that needed or wanted them. The market that proved the most profitable for Ashur was far to the west, in Anatolia.

Our textile caravan from Larsa might have received not just one offer for their cloth there, but competitive offers from a number of trading firms.

Of course, woolen cloth was woven in Ashur as well, but local textiles were considered less valuable than those from the south.

The movers and shakers in Ashur, including the members of the City Assembly and various high officials, were almost all merchants. For 200 years, from around 1970 to 1770 BCE, Ashur's heart and soul, its economy, its very raison d'être, lay in its merchants and their far-flung trading activities. It's no wonder, perhaps, that the merchants commanded so much power, and that the Assyrian kings were relatively weak.

Every year, one of the merchants living in Ashur (though many of them did not live there, as you will see) was chosen to be the principal official for the city for that year, the limmum. The choice of who would take this role seems not have been on the basis of his wisdom or skill or even interest in the job; instead, the limmum was selected by lot.[8] This man became responsible for collecting taxes, making loans, and convincing people to repay their debts. He lived in a public building for the year, assisted by a number of other officials.

It is emblematic of the difference between Ashur and the contemporary southern kingdoms that the kings in Ashur did not name the years after their great achievements, as kings did in the south. Instead, each of the years was named for the limmum officer who served that year. Each man may have been chosen by chance, but he gained a kind of immortality from his service—his name continued to be used for decades afterward to refer to events in the year of his limmum-ship. (Although women participated in trading activities and worked for merchant firms, the limmums were all men.) And now, all these thousands of years later, historians continue to use these names to understand the sequence of events of the era, even if the lives and achievements of the individual men are largely lost to us.

A master list of 145 of the limmum names, inscribed on a cuneiform tablet, was found in 2001, and other lists that have been found can be compiled to provide a sequence of the names of limmum years from 1972 to 1718 BCE. In ancient times these lists helped scribes keep track of the sequence of years and to calculate how much time had elapsed between, say, the year Iphurum, son of Ili-elliti, and the year Shu-Ishtar, son of Ikunum (not to be confused with Shu-Ishtar, son of Shukutum, who had served as limmum two years earlier!). Now historians find the lists to be crucial for the reconstruction of the chronology of what is called the Old Assyrian period, which was contemporary with the Isin-Larsa period in the south.

We know a great deal about Ashur in this era; it is one of the best-documented eras in all of Mesopotamian history. Oddly enough, though, this is not because of findings in the city of Ashur itself. There, a paltry number of royal inscriptions and only twenty-four clay tablets have been found.[9] If all we had as evidence for the state of Ashur in the early second millennium were the documents that came out of the ground in the capital city, we might think that Ashur was not unlike the kingdoms of the south. In particular, we would know nothing of its remarkable trading activities. Its kings made many of the usual boasts in their inscriptions. They were especially concerned with noting their piety in building and reconstructing temples for the gods.

One early king of Ashur seems to have claimed to have conquered lands in the south. This was King Ilu-shuma, who ruled in the early twentieth century BCE, and boasted that he "established the freedom of the Akkadians (southern Mesopotamians) and their children. I purified their copper. I established their freedom, from the marshes and Ur and Nippur, Awal, and Kismar, Der of the god Ishtaran, as far as the city (Ashur)."[10] It's an odd way to describe a conquest, though, and most of the named cities clearly didn't fall under the actual rule of Ashur. It may be instead that Ashur was successful in a bid for trading privileges with these regions, even before Ilu-shuma's son Erishum I abolished taxes on traded items.

The City of Kanesh: Trading Center in Anatolia

The reason we know so much about Ashur, even in the absence of much written evidence from the city itself, is that as many as 22,460 documents written by merchants from Ashur have been excavated hundreds of miles from the city, at a place called Kanesh, now called Kültepe, all the way off in central Anatolia not far from the modern Turkish city of Kayseri.[11] The city of Kanesh, it turns out, was the focus of the trading activities of the merchants of Ashur, the place where the merchants (who ran the City Assembly and served as *limmums*) created their wealth, and a place where many men from Ashur lived and worked. Excavations there have shown that Kanesh was inhabited by local Anatolians, for the most part, while the Assyrians lived in a community, often referred to as a colony, on the outskirts of the town.

The documents from Kanesh are astounding. They provide details about all manner of complex and ingenious details of trade in the twentieth and nineteenth centuries BCE. They even tell us how Ashur was ruled—it is from the Kanesh texts, not from anything in Ashur itself, that we know about the City Assembly, the annual appointment of the *limmum*, and the roles of other officials. And most of all, the tablets tell us about the people who lived in Ashur and Kanesh—about their interests and concerns.

The whole trading enterprise was based on the fact that the people in Kanesh wanted to acquire tin and textiles, and that the people in Ashur wanted silver and gold. The Assyrians therefore met this need by bringing tin and textiles to Anatolia, and selling them (at a hefty markup) in exchange for silver and gold, which they then carried back to Ashur.

How did the Assyrians discover an untapped market hundreds of miles from home? We don't know; by the time the texts that survive were being written, the trading system was thoroughly established. But we do know that the Assyrians weren't alone; Syria was home to a competing network of merchants who also traded with Anatolia. According to a letter found in Kanesh, merchants from the Syrian city of Ebla showed up there at one point, interested in trading copper. Also, seal impressions of Syrian kings and a Syrian princess have been found in an Anatolian palace at a place called Acemhöyük. Even the Babylonians seem to have been involved in long-distance trade. A Babylonian official named Lagamal-gamil used his personal seal on a door sealing at the Anatolian site of Tilmen Höyük. He was probably there to trade for timber, silver, or wine.[12] Unlike at Kanesh, we don't have thousands of documents recording these other trade networks, but this doesn't mean that such documents don't exist in the ground somewhere. The fact that so much research has been done on Assyrian trade gives the impression that the Assyrians somehow monopolized long-distance trade in this era, but it's almost certainly not true. The Assyrian merchants provide a case study of a phenomenon that may have been widespread. Trade was no longer monopolized by the great temples and palaces in this era, and private merchant enterprises took full advantage of this.

Textiles and tin in one direction, silver and gold in the other—that was the core of the Assyrian operation, and these commodities maintained an enterprise upon which families could get very rich. But here's a strange thing—the Anatolians who snapped up Mesopotamian cloth weren't short of wool; they could and did make their own fabric on local looms.[13] They simply seem to have particularly treasured the Mesopotamian textiles (and especially those not from Ashur but from southern cities like Larsa). It seems that, in the eyes of the people of Kanesh, the Mesopotamians made better cloth than they did. Perhaps it was finer, or warmer (good for Anatolian winters), or in brighter colors, or it had more patterns or embroidery than local wares. We have no way to know, because not a shred of it survives. All we have instead are the Akkadian words for different types of textile wares, which bring to mind no images at all.

As for tin? Everyone needed tin. Ever since the invention of bronze, tin was a necessity, not a luxury. But it didn't originate in Ashur. The tin used throughout the Near East at this time seems to have been mined in what is now Uzbekistan, at a staggering distance of about 2,700 kilometers (1,680 miles) from Ashur.[14] We know almost nothing about the journey that brought it to Ashur—who mined it, who refined it, who carried it across Iran and into Mesopotamia (though we do know that, just as was true of the southern textiles, it wasn't the Assyrians who did this—foreign merchants brought the goods). No doubt, their trading mechanisms were just as complex as those we do know about, of the Assyrians who bought the tin from them and moved it on farther west. Each time it changed hands, the tin became more and more expensive. In Ashur one shekel of silver bought fourteen shekels of tin. By the time it reached Anatolia the price had doubled; a shekel of silver bought only seven shekels of tin.[15]

When the Assyrians came home with silver from Anatolia, they were, in a way, bringing home not a commodity, but hard cash. Silver provided the foundation of the Mesopotamian economy by this time, even though every shekel of it had to be imported. People were sometimes paid for their work in silver, loans were made in silver, houses were bought in silver. The Assyrians who brought it back with them from Anatolia could immediately invest it right back into their businesses, buying more tin and textiles for the next trip.

Gold, curiously enough, was not a medium of exchange like silver. In fact, gold was categorically not to be sold to anyone outside their community; the City Assembly had created a legal prohibition against it: "Assyrians can sell gold among each other but, in accordance with the words of the stela, no Assyrian whosoever shall give gold to an Akkadian, Amorite or Subarean. Who does so will not stay alive!"[16] It was, though, prized for jewelry and was even more valuable and rare than silver.

Kanesh has been excavated in a systematic way since 1948. It is a truly huge site, one of the largest occupation mounds in Turkey. Not only is the tell itself 550 meters (1,800 feet) across and 20 meters (65 feet) high, but suburbs extended around the town as well.[17] Sometimes an ancient city takes on more importance now than it really had in ancient times just because it has been excavated (and especially if documents were found there), but this isn't the situation with regard to Kanesh. It would have been well known and important in ancient times because it was located in a strategic spot on the Anatolian plateau; like Ashur, it benefited from being at a crossroads of routes that had been traveled for centuries. One was a north-south road, coming up from the Mediterranean in Cilicia, one was an east-west road, and the last was a southeast-west road.[18] The people of Kanesh suffered through cold, snowy winters and hot summers. But the region's average of sixteen inches of rainfall, spread across the year, allowed farmers to grow their crops without the need for irrigation canals, and they seem to have had no shortage of food.

Kanesh, like other Anatolian city-states of the time, was ruled by a royal couple, the king and queen holding power together, though the king generally took the lead, and men dominated the official positions that supported the administration.[19] Their palace on the tell commanded the heart of their city. In the twentieth century BCE, the palace seems to have been circular, which is odd, because rectangular buildings had long been the norm in Anatolia.[20] The city also housed temples to the local gods, and large residential districts. The people of Kanesh would not have thought of themselves as living in a backwater, or in somewhere peripheral to their neighbors in Mesopotamia. Although the Assyrians played a big role in trade in their region, the more important connections for the people of Kanesh were with neighboring states, each with a capital at a major city.[21] Like almost all ancient peoples, they probably believed themselves to be living in the center of the universe. Theirs was an urban, sophisticated culture, and (as in other parts of the Near East) the Anatolian city-states seem to have frequently gone into battle against one another.[22] The Assyrians were in Kanesh to trade not by some happy accident but because, if you wanted to get hold of silver, it was the place to be. When necessary, the merchants coped with the disruptions caused by local wars or coups, writing letters to warn one another of potential difficulties.

One curious thing about the culture of Anatolia in this period is that all of their administration, all of their building, all of their communication, everything they did, appears to have been achieved without the use of a writing system. Until the Assyrians showed up, scribbling away in cuneiform and littering the town with thousands of clay tablets, the ancient Anatolian sites are silent, devoid of texts. However, it's possible that the Anatolians did have their own script, a system of hieroglyphs (which is well known in Anatolia for later eras), but that they wrote only on organic materials at this period.[23] These documents would have disintegrated. Although the evidence is limited, this would help explain how Anatolian officials could manage the administrative complexities faced by the governments there.

The cuneiform tablets of the Assyrians weren't found in the palace at Kanesh, or in other public buildings, or on the tell at all, for that matter. They were found in private houses in the suburbs to the northwest of the main city. This is where the Assyrians had settled, living among local Anatolians in an area of dense housing, with no parks or open spaces. They called this area the "karum" or trading center. The main roads in the karum ran parallel to one another, and were wide and paved, with drains built under the paving to prevent flooding. Smaller dirt roads led from the main streets to blocks of houses or to individual front doors. The town would have been crowded and noisy, like Mesopotamian towns of the same era, though the streets looked different, with houses built of stone and wood rather than mudbrick.

Archaeologists found at least seventy archives in the houses of the karum, each of them representing the business activities of a family of Assyrian merchants between around 1970 and 1835 BCE. The documents tended to be found in a storeroom in a house, where they were kept in boxes, jars, or baskets, or on shelves. The merchants kept their clay tablet records for a surprisingly long time—and not just contracts, business reports, and judicial records that might need to be referenced later, but letters between family members as well. Some families archived just a few documents, others kept hundreds. From these, we know the names of the merchants and the names of their relatives and employees, and we know about their trading ventures, their troubles, their profits and losses, their family tensions, and their joys. Unfortunately, for most of the merchants, we don't know exactly which archive came from which house. Oddly enough, when archives can be linked to particular houses, they don't necessarily correlate with one family. A single house could contain the records of several merchants. This seems to be because merchants didn't like to leave their archives or other valuables in their own homes when they were away—the records could instead be entrusted to someone else in their absence, and that is where they were found, all these centuries later.[24]

Ashur-idi, Ashur-nada, and Their Relatives: A Trading Family

One of the houses was home to a man named Ashur-nada, son of Ashur-idi. One hundred seventy-six documents relating to him and his family have been published, so we know a great deal about them.[25] None of their records were discovered during formal excavations, unfortunately; they were sold on the antiquities market in the early twentieth century, before excavations began, and are scattered in museums around the world. Ashur-nada is one of the few ancient Near Eastern individuals (other than kings) for whom enough evidence survives that an entire book has been written about him and his world; it was authored by historian Mogens Trolle Larsen.[26]

Ashur-nada might have lived in almost any of the known houses in the *karum*. We can, though, guess what his home might have looked like; many of the houses were similar in structure (see Fig. 9.1).[27]

It would have been entered from the street by walking down a few steps. This was because the street level rose over time (as a result of mud and refuse that accumulated there), whereas the floor of the house was swept regularly and its level remained unchanged. A small hallway area led into a large main living room, which also often served as a kitchen. It had an oven, a hearth, and storage bins for grain, along with grinding stones and pestles. In winter, the heat from the oven would have been welcomed by the family that gathered there. Houses in the *karum* were built right up against one another, often sharing walls, which would also have insulated the rooms from cold in winter and heat in summer. A second downstairs room provided space for storage. Some such rooms were heavily built and secured, probably so that the merchants could store the textiles and tin that they planned to sell, or the silver and gold they were shipping home, and this is where Ashur-nada's archives would have been kept as well. Some houses had a third downstairs

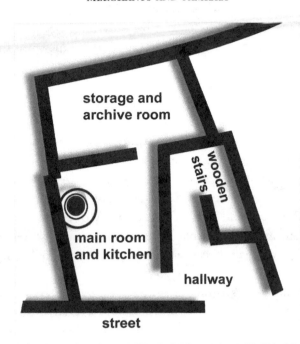

Fig. 9.1 Simplified plan of a house used by an Assyrian merchant in the *karum* at Kanesh, twentieth–nineteenth century BCE (based on Hertel 2014, 38, Fig. 9).

room, and many had a well-built stairway of wooden steps, presumably leading to a second story. Some of the households had as many as nine or ten people living together, so they probably slept in several different rooms on both floors.

Ashur-nada was the Anatolian representative of his family's firm, which was headed by his father, Ashur-idi, who lived back in Ashur. Ashur-idi wrote regular letters to his eldest son Ashur-nada, and to his two other sons.[28] All three of the brothers were involved in the business and all of them lived most of the time in Anatolia, far away from their homeland.

The family patriarch Ashur-idi was not a calm man. He had a lot on his plate. The success of the family business ultimately came down to him. A lot of people, not just his sons and their families, depended on him to keep everything running smoothly. It's a curious fact that, even though Ashur-idi must have thought about the activities of the family firm in Anatolia every day of his adult life, there's no evidence that he ever actually traveled there.[29] Perhaps this contributed to his nervousness; the only way he could contact his sons in Kanesh was by letter, and his only means of persuading them to do what he requested for their shared trading business was through the vehemence of his language.

I should note here that, unfortunately for historians, the merchants of Ashur tended to use the same personal names over and over when naming their children. There were, for example, at least twenty-five different men named Ashur-idi (each of them listing a different man as his father) among the Assyrian merchant community, and twenty-two men named Ashur-nada.[30] That means that a random reference to Ashur-nada that doesn't identify him by his father's name could be to the merchant we are interested in, or could be a reference to any one of twenty-one other men; it is often almost impossible to know which man is intended.[31] Only when his father was named can we be certain that we're dealing with the right man.

As far as Ashur-nada's family in Ashur goes, the name of his mother is unknown. Ashur-idi remained married to this woman, the mother of his three sons, but they only ever referred to her in letters as "our mother." Although no such images survive from Ashur or Kanesh, a Mesopotamian terracotta plaque of a man and woman provides a clue about the ideal of married life. The couple have their arms around one another and seem affectionate (see Fig. 9.2). Even in an arranged marriage, the Mesopotamians hoped that the husband and wife would become fond of one another. That said, one imagines that Ashur-idi's wife must have needed reserves of patience to cope with the ever-roiling emotions of her husband.

Most wives of Assyrian merchants were involved in the family business, and this was probably true of Ashur-idi's wife as well. Such women lived in Assyria, never traveling to Anatolia with their husbands (if their husbands traveled), but corresponding with them regularly. Women were responsible for weaving cloth not just for the household, but also for sale in the long-distance trade. They received pay for the textiles they made, money that was theirs to keep. Sometimes, though, they were unable to keep up with the demands of the men in the family for cloth to sell. One woman wrote to her husband: "As to the textiles about which you wrote to me in the following terms: 'they are (too) small, they are not good'; was it not on your own request that I reduced the size? And now you write (again), saying: 'process half a mina (of wool) more in your textiles.' Well, I have done it."[32] One can sense this woman's exasperation with the changing requests.

Fig. 9.2 Molded terracotta plaque of a couple, c. 2000–1700 BCE. (Metropolitan Museum of Art)

Having brought up her three sons to adulthood (along with daughters, possibly, though they are not mentioned), Ashur-idi's wife then committed to bringing up three or more of their grandchildren, namely Ashur-nada's son and daughters who lived in Ashur. The grandparents took them in presumably after the death of their mother.[33] Perhaps Ashur-nada wanted them to learn about the family business, or perhaps he simply couldn't bring them to Kanesh to be with him until they were older.

The children do not seem to have been happy in Ashur, though. Something drove them over the edge and they ended up renouncing their grandparents in Ashur and setting off for Anatolia to be with their father. Ashur-idi wrote to his son Ashur-nada about this, at the end of a fairly routine letter about tin and textiles. He wrote, "I have raised your son, but he said to me: 'You are not my father.' He got up and left. Also your daughters have I raised, but they said: 'You are not our father.' Three days later they got up and left to go to you." It's curious that the usually volatile Ashur-idi described this so calmly, belying what must have been a major family crisis. He even ended the letter with the non-committal "so let me know what you think."[34]

This terse passage leaves so many questions unanswered. The children must have been at least teenagers at this point. What triggered their departure? How did they get to Anatolia? What did Ashur-nada do when he found out about this? Was he angry? Was he sympathetic? We don't know, but we do know that the children needed a loan in order to cover their expenses after they left their grandparents' house, and also probably to pay for their journey to Anatolia.

Luckily, Ashur-nada had a friend in Ashur who decided to help the children find a loan to support themselves. But he wasn't about to pay for the cost himself; that was their father's responsibility. This friend wrote to Ashur-nada, before the children made it to Kanesh. The friend wrote that he and another man "have borrowed 30 minas of copper in a merchant-firm, at the (interest) rate 10 shekels per mina (monthly), and your son and daughters have spent it. . . . Please take care to send the silver and the accrued interest so we may pay in full to the merchant." This was a lot of copper. A mina was about equivalent to a pound, or 450 grams, so the friends had borrowed (and the children had spent) about 13.5 kilograms of copper. The children needed more, though: "Also, send silver so that your children do not starve."[35]

In any event—family dramas aside—like the heads of all the Assyrian merchant families, Ashur-idi devoted a lot of his time to accumulating textiles and tin to be shipped to Kanesh. In order to buy the goods, he was in constant need of silver generated from the goods that had already been sold, and he needed it to be sent back to Ashur as quickly as possible and not hoarded by family members in Anatolia.

The Ashur-idi merchant firm wasn't a particularly large or wealthy one. They did fine much of the time, but there's a note of panic in many of Ashur-idi's letters, as though the whole enterprise might collapse at any moment. At one point, things got so bad that he told Ashur-nada and one of his brothers that they must take the drastic step of selling off most of their assets in Kanesh: "Please," he wrote, "the very day you hear this letter, you must offer for sale the houses, both of your slave-girls and both of your grinding-girls, and send me the silver!" This wasn't just Ashur-idi being dramatic (though he could certainly be guilty of this); he realized that this abrupt sale would leave his sons with nowhere to live. He continued, "Then you must rent a house and settle there." But he wasn't done with his appeal. He repeated himself: "Please, please, pay heed to the words of the letter! Sell everything!" It was worth pointing out that the gods would punish the men if they disobeyed: "If you have not sold (everything)—as the words of the gods are urgent—you will perish!"[36] Ashur-idi had creditors and investors he needed to pay, and every moment wasted brought him closer to bankruptcy.

Of course, his letter would have taken weeks to get to Kanesh, and even if Ashur-nada and his brother did as their father requested and sold their houses and slaves the very day they got the message, the silver this generated wouldn't have reached Ashur for months after Ashur-idi sent the letter. One has the sense that the sons probably didn't obey the command, and that Ashur-idi, despite his protestations, did in fact survive financially and continue to trade. There's even an Ashur-idi, described as the son of Shuli, who served as *limmum* at a time when our Ashur-idi would have been quite elderly. We can't be certain that these two were the same man, but there are several indications that they might have been. It's rather heart-warming to think of him administering the city of Ashur for a year in his old age, an eminent figure in the community, though perhaps the people he worked with might have been less than happy with the situation, if his temperament was unchanged.

The logistics of the trade between Ashur and Kanesh are well understood. Once a merchant such as Ashur-idi had gathered together a shipment of the right size, he had to join, or create, a caravan to transport it. For this, trained donkeys were essential. Donkeys were really the fifth major item of trade. They were purchased in Ashur and often sold, along with the tin and textiles, once the caravan reached Kanesh. A donkey cost around 16 or 17 shekels of silver and then also had to be furnished with trappings for the trip, such as packsaddles and blankets, which cost another 2 or 3 shekels, so the donkeys were big investments. Fortunately, if they made it to Anatolia (and not all of them did), they were worth more there and could be sold for a profit. Some were simply kept on hand by the merchants for further trading missions within Anatolia.

Each male donkey could transport approximately 75 kilograms (165 pounds) of merchandise.[37] Males were preferred because they were stronger than females, and the merchants needed to hire men to drive the donkeys, with no more than two donkeys assigned to each driver. As the caravan grew in size, with more merchants signing up to join in, there must have been a lot of activity on the streets of Ashur. Tin was packed into saddlebags, which were slung over a blanket and packing saddle so as to rest on each side of the donkey. Textiles were rolled up and placed on the donkeys' backs. As many as 300 donkeys could be involved in a single caravan, with as many men accompanying them.[38] Letters in clay envelopes were entrusted to men making the journey, with clear instructions about whom they were to be delivered to. Presumably some other people, like the children of Ashur-nada, joined the caravan simply because they needed to get to Anatolia. Everyone going traveled on foot—the donkeys were too valuable as pack animals to take riders.

Ashur-idi rarely contributed more than two donkeys to a caravan. His letters often refer to a shipment of two talents and ten minas of tin, along with from 4 to 75 textiles.[39] When no tin was sent, Ashur-idi's contribution to the caravan usually varied from 11 to 72 textiles—a single donkey could carry between 20 and 30 of them. On one occasion he managed to put together 144 textiles, but that was a remarkable amount for him.

Once the caravan was assembled, the merchants and donkeys left the city in a long procession, and could travel west on one of a number of roads, all of which seem to have avoided passing through the rival trading territory of the western Syrian kingdoms. A lot of research has been done to identify the exact routes taken, but we can't be completely sure how they went. The merchants visited karums in towns along the route in northwest Syria, and then the whole caravan ventured up into the Taurus mountains, making its way through well-traveled passes. Inns along the road provided fodder for the donkeys, but the general sense one gets is that the merchants didn't spend a lot of time worrying about donkey welfare and that the donkeys weren't especially well taken care of. When one died or ran away it was possible to buy a new one in the next town, or to rent one for a stretch of the journey. This was not a situation in which the arrival of merchants in a town was ever a surprise—along the whole route, the local people expected the regular visits of caravans and must have found many ways to take advantage of the merchants' needs. Donkeys were probably readily available.

It's intriguing to wonder about what languages the Assyrians used once they were out of the Akkadian-speaking regions of northern Mesopotamia. In Kanesh, several local languages were spoken, notably the Indo-European language of Hittite (to which we will return later),[40] but also some other Indo-European tongues and a local language known as Hattic. Almost certainly the merchants who regularly lived and traded in Kanesh were at least bilingual and were comfortable speaking Hittite when they were there, but did they also speak Hurrian, for use when traveling through northern Syria? Did they hire translators? Did the local people along the route learn to understand and speak Akkadian so as to be able to work with the caravans? Probably it was a mix, depending on the individuals. In whatever way they did it, they managed to communicate just fine.

There's evidence that during the summer the caravans may have traveled in the early morning and late evening, and perhaps even at night, so as to avoid the heat of the day. In the wintertime, the passes through the mountains were often covered in snow, making travel impossible. Timing a caravan trip right was important. If everything worked well, the journey from Ashur took six weeks. One imagines that some of the travelers became close friends in the process (if they were not friendly already, given that these journeys took place regularly) but that tensions erupted from time to time as well.

Once the donkeys and merchants finally reached Kanesh, they had to stop first at the palace of the local king and queen, pulling up in the big circular courtyard. There, the king of Kanesh got to choose what he would take as his taxes on each load (he took a 10 percent tax—one out of every ten textiles) and he could also purchase additional goods from the merchants at the going rate if he chose to. This was all governed by a detailed treaty between the king and the merchants to which they had all sworn an oath.[41] In exchange for the taxes that he received from the merchants, the king agreed to protect them while they were in his realm, even to the point of paying them for any textiles that were stolen from them there. The king of Kanesh also agreed not to use his position of power to intimidate the merchants. He could not "take [a textile] away by force," nor could he "purchase it at a low price."[42] He had to be fair to the Assyrian merchants so that the trading relationship they enjoyed continued to be productive for all parties.

The traveling merchants were then allowed to leave the main city through the gate and arrive, finally, at the homes of their Kanesh-based family members in the *karum*. Ashur-nada would have greeted his children when they arrived (happily, one hopes, in spite of the money they had cost him by leaving their grandparents) and checked all the goods from Ashur against the letter that listed what had been sent. The men who worked for the firm no doubt sat down together soon afterward and decided which items in the shipment should be sold there in Kanesh and what should be sent on to one of the forty other towns and cities in Anatolia where Assyrian merchants did business. They had to decide which of the brothers would take the goods and when would be a good time to do so. Everyone also certainly asked questions, shared gossip from home, and caught up on what had been happening in Kanesh. There must have been news of babies and marriages, illnesses and deaths in both communities. Ashur-nada's children were presumably anxious to explain their defection from their grandparents' care, and full of excuses for why and how they used up the 30 minas of copper that their family friend had borrowed for them.

After they arrived in Kanesh, Ashur-nada's children would have initially joined his household there. Their father had an Anatolian wife and a second family, as did many of the merchants. This was true even of merchants who, unlike Ashur-nada, still had a wife alive in Ashur, even though marriage was supposed to be monogamous in Ashur.[43] Marrying a second (Anatolian) wife was not a secret nor was it frowned on. As long as each wife stayed in her separate region, the arrangement was considered respectable.[44] Ashur-nada's children from Ashur probably met their stepmother (who gloried in the name Shishahshushar) and their half-siblings for the first time when they arrived. For that matter, the children were probably not particularly familiar with their father, as he seems to have resisted traveling to Ashur and generally stayed in Anatolia as much as he could. (It's tempting to speculate that he could cope with his temperamental father better at a distance of several hundred miles than when in the same room!)

Ashur-nada's letters are much less emotional than those of his father. He seems to have been uncomplicated and businesslike, though he did lose his patience a little with his father sometimes. Once, when Ashur-idi accused him of not repaying him some silver, Ashur-nada wrote back, "instead of sending me these angry messages, let [the gods] Ashur and Ilabrat be my witnesses that I have scraped together what I had in my possession, and that I did pay . . . my balance payment."[45]

Ashur-nada may not have seen his children all that much even after they moved to Kanesh to be with him, because he was often away traveling around Anatolia. His archive includes plenty of letters written home from these trips. His work beyond Kanesh was not just in selling goods that had arrived from Ashur; he also bought and sold local copper and wool in the course of his travels, profiting in the end by obtaining more silver.

The name of Ashur-nada's son, who had left his grandfather so dramatically, was Iddin-Ishtar, and it's clear that his relationship with his grandfather remained rocky long after he and his sisters had moved to Anatolia. Iddin-Ishtar began working with his father Ashur-nada for the family firm and eventually, after his father's death, he took over control of the Anatolian branch. So presumably he grew up to be an upstanding member of the community. But his mercurial grandfather didn't trust him. On one occasion Iddin-Ishtar was back in Ashur, presumably for business reasons, and he succeeded in angering his grandfather again. Ashur-idi wrote, "As to Iddin-Ishtar—not only has he continually robbed me, he took me to the office of the firm, and then he broke into the house and absconded!"[46] Ashur-idi didn't just want to be repaid for the amount that he maintained had been stolen from him by his grandson, he wanted personal vengeance. He told Ashur-nada to "seize Iddin-Ishtar and have him pay 3 minas of silver out of his own silver, and send him to me so I can release my anger on him!"

There's less information in the letters about the silver that was sent home than about the goods that were shipped to Anatolia in the first place, but what was sent back to Ashur was never heavy enough to warrant using a donkey. The average that the Ashur-idi firm sent back at any one time was about 7.5 minas of silver.[47] A mina was approximately a pound, so a man could carry the silver back easily. Fortunately, a mina of silver in Ashur could be exchanged for 14 minas of tin, or a great many textiles, so the whole system was profitable, even for a relatively small trader like Ashur-idi.

Trade continued between Ashur and Anatolia for more than a century, but life and government in Ashur were upended in the early eighteenth century BCE when an imperialistic king named Shamshi-Adad expanded his control over all of Upper Mesopotamia. His empire and its successors provide the historical context of the next chapter.

Chapter 10
Princesses and Musicians

We began the previous chapter following the Old Babylonian itinerary that took a group of soldiers north from the city of Larsa to Ashur. There we left them, in order to pursue a different path, venturing off with the caravans of traders who traveled to Kanesh in Anatolia. But we will now return to the original itinerary. According to the text, someone moving on north from Ashur on the ancient road arrived, a day later, at a city called Ekallatum.[1] Unfortunately, the location of Ekallatum remains unknown and the site has never been excavated, but it was an important place. Although the itinerary was probably written in the mid-eighteenth century BCE,[2] the same roads were in use before then, so let us say that a visitor was making the journey in the late nineteenth century BCE, when the trade between Ashur and Anatolia was winding down. If so, he might have arrived in Ekallatum at a moment of crisis.

King Shamshi-Adad I of Upper Mesopotamia: An Empire Builder

Ekallatum had previously been subject to its neighboring kingdom, Ashur, but it had recently been attacked and conquered by forces led by a man named Shamshi-Adad (1807–1776 BCE).[3] Shamshi-Adad was a larger-than-life figure, a conqueror who came from an obscure background but eventually forged an empire that stretched across northern Mesopotamia, overshadowing every other Near Eastern leader of his time.

He was only about eighteen years old when he had succeeded his father to the throne of Ashur around 1836 BCE; his father having seized that throne rather than inheriting it.[4] But the early years of Shamshi-Adad's reign seem to have been unremarkable; even after eighteen years of rule he was not a match yet for a king of neighboring Eshnunna who attacked Ashur. Shamshi-Adad promptly fled for safety to Babylon.[5] He seems to have found a new determination there; he would reclaim his kingdom.

We have no idea how he gathered soldiers to support him as he marched north to conquer Ekallatum, but he did so (his troops probably following that same road laid out in the itinerary), and he succeeded in his conquest. He declared that Ekallatum was now his capital city.[6]

When our traveler arrived in Ekallatum on his journey north, perhaps Shamshi-Adad was already recruiting troops, collecting supplies, and having weapons manufactured, ready for an attack on Ashur, his original capital. He captured it three years after taking over Ekallatum. It was only at this point, around 1807 BCE, that the later king lists considered Shamshi-Adad's reign to have truly begun. He must have been around forty-three years old. Now he set about expanding far beyond Ashur's traditional borders, building a new empire, a northern one, extending all the way across northern Iraq and throughout what is now northern Syria.

This goal presented challenges that might have seemed insurmountable. For one thing, two powerful kingdoms already dominated the region: Mari to the west, with its capital on the Euphrates, and Eshnunna to the east, with its capital on the Diyala River, east of the Tigris. The kings of these regions had got wind of Shamshi-Adad's growing power and bigger ambitions. He was enough of a worry to them that the kings of Mari and Eshnunna joined together in an alliance with one another, and Mari allied with a third great Syrian power, Yamhad, which was centered northwest of Mari in Aleppo.[7] These alliances represented more than treaties. The royal families intermarried, as the kings married princesses from one another's realms. They seemed to represent a formidable united front against the newly imperialistic Shamshi-Adad.

But it was tough for the peoples of Northern Mesopotamian ever to be truly united. The region was home to a number of Amorite-speaking peoples who were loosely organized into big communities that recognized a common identity, and those big communities often distrusted one another. They're often referred to as "tribes," but that term comes with a lot of cultural baggage. They're also often referred to as "nomads," but many of them were not particularly nomadic.

Families, as we have seen, formed the core building block of society throughout the Near East. This was even more true among the Amorites. One was born into a family—parents, children, grandchildren—just the way people are everywhere. That family was part of a bigger family. For nomadic herding communities this might be the group with whom they migrated regularly, all of whom might be distantly related to one another. In a town, the community might be a neighborhood dominated by cousins, second cousins, in-laws, and so on. All this would have been true of anyone across the Near East. But for the northern Amorites, that wider extended family identified as part of an even bigger family, which comprised—for lack of a better word—their tribe. In Syria in the early second millennium BCE, Amorite-speaking people grew up knowing if they belonged to the Banu-Yamina ("sons of the right," or "sons of the south") or the Banu-Sim'al ("sons of the left," or "sons of the north"). These Yaminites and Sim'alites nursed a long-standing antipathy toward one another.

Someone who lived in a city might also have identified as being a citizen of that place, and perhaps also recognized that he or she was subject to a kingdom, but wider family and tribal identities seem to have been particularly important. It was the king who imposed taxes and called up troops, but one's local tribal "*sugagum*" leader inspired particular loyalty as well. Northern kings acknowledged the influence of the tribal leaders and worked with them.

This meant that politics, alliances, and rivalries in the north were a little different from those of the south. Although northern kingdoms had capital cities, just as in the south, and their kings were supported by vassals, and their provinces were overseen by governors, a good percentage of the population was nomadic. The royal administrations needed the nomads for military service and to help with harvests and construction projects, so their seasonal arrival in the cities was eagerly anticipated by the kings and their officials. More hands were welcome.[8] But organizing the nomadic workers tended to present a challenge, and wars in which they served had to be fought when they were available (and when the farmers, who were also drafted, could be spared). That meant that most fighting took place in the summer. Besides, one always had to take tribal affiliations and antagonisms into consideration when forming coalitions.

Returning to the itinerary, as our traveler left Ekallatum, the road headed north and west into territory dominated by these nomadic groups, an area that was eventually to become the heart of Shamshi-Adad's empire. At the end of each day's journey, the list gives the name of a place where a traveler could rest, but, as we have seen, many of these may have been just small villages. No advice is provided for the traveler, unfortunately, about places to stay or interesting sights in the area. That was not the purpose of this text. We do know, though, that the road left the Tigris and headed northwest around a town known as Kishkish, toward the eastern end of the Sinjar mountains, which rose up abruptly from the plain to the left side of the road.[9] Seen from above, the mountain range is shaped like a long thin cigar jutting up through the mostly flat landscape, and people avoided passing over it. Beyond it, though, eight days' journey from Ekallatum, our traveler would have arrived in a rich area of farmland, threaded through with small rivers and wadis that all flowed south toward the Habur River. This entire region, commonly known as the Habur triangle, had suffered a loss of population toward the end of the Akkadian Empire around 2200 BCE, probably because of the severe drought of that era, and its cities had only begun to be repopulated around 1900 BCE, about a century before Shamshi-Adad's time.[10] Now, though, rainfall and the region's many natural springs made the land fertile again.

In order to gain control of this Habur triangle region, Shamshi-Adad had to fight the forces of a man named Yahdun-Lim, the powerful king of Mari. The contested region was distant from both their capital cities—farther, in fact, from Mari than it was from Shamshi-Adad's capital of Ekallatum. Neither king had a strong claim on the loyalty of the people in the Habur triangle, but Shamshi-Adad ended up being victorious. His surviving inscriptions never tell us exactly how he did this.

In the eastern section of the conquered region, on one of the rivers that fed into the Habur, was a big tell, which had previously been the site of an ancient city named Shekhna. Shamshi-Adad decided to rebuild the abandoned city, to make it his new capital, and to give it a new name: Shubat-Enlil, the "dwelling place of Enlil."[11] Of course, the god Enlil already had a home, his ancient and venerable city of Nippur, but it was in keeping with Shamshi-Adad's hubris that he would want the king of the gods to take up residence at the center of his new empire.

The king met with architects, called up workers, and began construction on the monumental public buildings of Shubat-Enlil. Excavations there in the 1980s revealed that Shamshi-Adad's city was 90 hectares (222 acres) in extent.[12] It featured a palace and a thick-walled temple with remarkable engaged columns. Some had fat spirals all the way up, like giant rope spools, and others were made to look like palm tree trunks.[13] (Shubat-Enlil, at its height, was another stop on the itinerary, and it would have been an impressive place to visit.)

Even as construction began at Shubat-Enlil, Shamshi-Adad was still expanding his empire to the southwest, pursuing the king of Mari and his army into the heartland of their kingdom, so that eventually Shamshi-Adad's empire extended over all the lands that had previously been ruled by the kings of both Ashur and Mari. He doesn't seem to have written about his campaigns, but he did thank the local god of Mari for his victory, by providing the god with a "great throne of ebony which was methodically made with everything pertaining to the goldsmith's art."[14]

Shamshi-Adad decided on an innovative way of ruling such a big, unwieldy domain. Rather than trying to control everything himself, he created a triumvirate of kings, with his sons Yasmah-Addu and Ishme-Dagan ruling alongside him. Each man had his own capital: Shamshi-Adad at the city of Shubat-Enlil in the north, Ishme-Dagan at the original capital of Ekallatum in the east, and Yasmah-Addu at the newly conquered Mari, to the south of Shubat-Enlil. But the three men were not equals. The sons answered to their father, and this caused tensions, especially between Shamshi-Adad and his younger son, Yasmah-Addu.

We know about this because Yasmah-Addu's capital city and palace at Mari have been extensively excavated since 1933, by successive teams of French archaeologists, and because Mari (like Girsu, Ebla, and Kanesh) has proved to be one of the greatest Near Eastern sites in terms of its preserved archives: more than 20,000 cuneiform tablets have been found there. Some of them are the original letters sent by Shamshi-Adad to Yasmah-Addu, and many of them reveal his micromanagement of his son's realm.[15]

Beltum of Qatna and Yasmah-Addu of Mari: A Diplomatic Marriage

Soon after Yasmah-Addu took up residence in Mari, his father Shamshi-Adad decided that he needed closer ties with a kingdom directly to the west: Qatna, which extended from the desert oasis town of Palmyra to the

Mediterranean coast. The king of Qatna was named Ishhi-Addu and, in the giant international hierarchy in which everyone had a place, Ishhi-Addu was considered to be the equal of Yasmah-Addu. The treaty that Shamshi-Adad negotiated with the king of Qatna concluded, as was usually the case, with a diplomatic marriage between their two royal families. A princess of Qatna, named Beltum, was to marry Shamshi-Adad's son and co-ruler, Yasmah-Addu. In this instance, unlike in the previous royal marriages that we've encountered, letters survive that reflect the stages of the negotiations, along with details of Beltum's subsequent life in Mari.

A lot of wealth changed hands before the bride and groom even met. Shamshi-Adad wrote to Yasmah-Addu to tell him that "to give a small *terhatum* (gift to the bride's father) would be embarrassing," so he would be sending the king of Qatna "1 talent 10 minas (32 kilograms or 70 pounds) of silver, 12 minas (5.5 kilograms or 12 pounds) of gold, [x] thousand sheep— (worth) 1 talent of silver (27 kilograms or 60 pounds), [x] hundred cattle— (worth) 1 talent of silver."[16] In another letter he wisely reminded his son to "set a protective guard over this silver."[17] Beltum, the bride, would, in turn, bring a significant dowry from her father, worth "10 talents of silver plus garments worth 5 talents of silver"[18] for a total value of 15 talents (c. 408 kilograms or 900 pounds) of silver. This was a pretty staggering amount of wealth; it would probably have been made up of furniture, jewelry, utensils, sheep, cattle, and servants in addition to the clothing and silver.

Negotiations complete, King Ishhi-Addu of Qatna was happy with the arrangements, and he assured Yasmah-Addu that, with the marriage, "this house has now become yours and the House of Mari has now become mine. Whatever you desire, just write me and I will give it to you."[19] The border between their two lands would be open: "Your sheep and nomads should cross over this way, so that my sheep and yours could graze together."[20] This was the ideal outcome of a peace treaty. It was voiced so often in similar circumstances that it cannot have simply been rhetorical. As a result of the marriage, the two kings really had joined their families together; they had become, to their minds, one household.

Princess Beltum began the journey to her new home, which probably included an uncomfortable twelve-day donkey ride across the Syrian desert (since camels were not domesticated for another 800 years or so),[21] stopping at the oasis of Palmyra on the way, before reaching the green valley of the Euphrates and heading south to Mari.[22] Meanwhile Shamshi-Adad was sending slightly panicky letters to his son Yasmah-Addu, to make sure that he was preparing suitable rooms in the palace for his new bride; "There are many chambers in the Palm Palace. A chamber should be prepared for her and house her there. Do not house her externally," he wrote.[23]

Beltum might have been quite young, though she was certainly at least adolescent. One of her attendants was a woman described as her "*ummum*."[24] This literally meant "mother" but it was probably her childhood nanny. The nanny's company must have been comforting to Beltum in her new home as she faced the pressures of becoming the queen of this foreign land of Mari. The nanny was not particularly welcome, however, among the staff at Mari. One high official wrote to the king that "had only this woman, who raised Beltum since her youth and knew her ways, been kept away from her when Beltum was leaving Qatna!"[25] The official complained that the nanny was nothing but trouble, breaking unspoken palace rules right and left. The nanny even allowed Beltum to be out in the courtyard with her female singers during the hot hours of the siesta, and "Beltum suffered a sunstroke when in the Multicolor Court and has been ill ever since."[26] One theory about this episode is that Beltum may have been so miserable in Mari that she was attempting suicide by spending time in the sunshine at midday, which was known to be dangerous.[27] But this seems unlikely; it's more probable that Beltum was young, impetuous, and willing to ignore the court's rules of decorum. Eventually, she recovered from her illness.

The tie between a young elite woman and her nanny could be strong. A few decades later, a young singer named Shewirum-parat was transferred away from the palace at Mari, where she had lived, to another city within the kingdom, and her nanny went along with her. Once there, her nanny was taken away from her and placed in the household of a high official. Young Shewirum-parat was so distraught that she wrote directly to the king of Mari to ask him to intervene for her: "You must wipe away my tears.... Give me my nanny and I shall bless you before (the gods) Addu and Hebat. May my lord not keep this woman from me."[28] No letter survives to tell us whether the king chose to help her.

The Palace at Mari

The palace in Mari, where Beltum took up residence in her new royal apartments, and from whence Shewirum-parat was later so abruptly moved, was extraordinary. It happens to be one of the few Old Babylonian palaces ever recovered, but it wasn't typical. Even in its time this was well known. Other kings gushed over the features of the palace in their letters and made special visits just to see it. The building extended over 2.5 hectares (6 acres), and, even if security had permitted it, a visitor could scarcely have hoped to visit the 300 or so rooms on the ground floor (its second story might have held almost as many again).[29] It's unlikely that even the king himself was well acquainted with all of the rooms.

When the building was excavated, some of its walls still stood 5 meters (16 feet) high, and its sophisticated drainage system was largely intact. The perfectly engineered drains, incredibly, still worked to rid the palace ruins of rainfall after being excavated and were typical of the fine design of the whole palace.[30] I should note, though, that this was not Yasmah-Addu's doing. He acquired the palace as a result of his father's conquests. It had been built up and elaborated by generations of local kings of Mari, ever since the Early Dynastic period, when Mari and its rulers had been the chief rivals of Ebla, when that city was ruled by such royal couples as Ishar-damu and Tabur-damu.

In Yasmah-Addu's time, the Mari palace was divided into several extensive suites of rooms, used for a variety of purposes and laid out around two huge courtyards (marked as 3 and 10 in Fig. 10.1). The grand front entrance, on the north side (1), led to a wide reception room (2), from which visitors would have been ushered into the sunny glare of the main courtyard (3), which was about 1,600 square meters (17,000 square feet) in extent, or about the size of four basketball courts. Nine doorways led from this relatively public space to more private parts of the palace.[31] Incredibly, the walls still stood so high when excavations were taking place that some of the tops of the doorways were intact.

As one arrived in the main courtyard from the entrance rooms, the kitchens (4) lay through the first door immediately to the left. Behind the left-hand wall of the court were rooms where goods brought to the palace had to be registered (5). Someone bringing jugs of wine or pots of oil, for example, would have dropped them off there.

A door facing you on the left-hand side of the opposite wall led to more administrative rooms and, beyond them, a temple (6). Another door on the same wall, but to the right, led through narrow corridors to a long magazine of storerooms and a maze of craft workshops (7). One of these workshops might well have been a room for the millers, similar to one

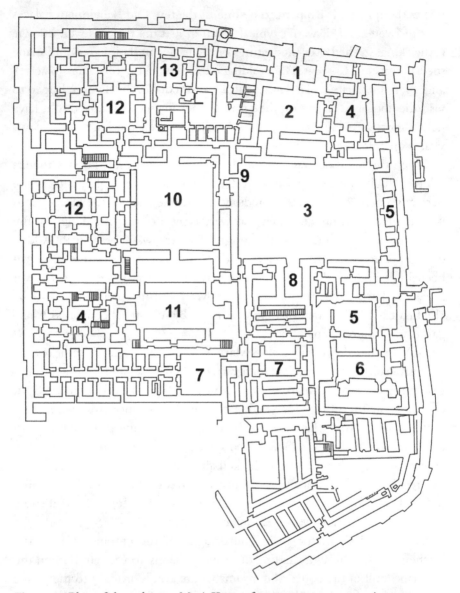

Fig. 10.1 Plan of the palace at Mari. Key: 1: front entrance, 2: reception room, 3: main courtyard, 4: kitchens, 5: administrative suite, 6: temple, 7: storerooms and workshops, 8: audience hall, 9: entry door to private quarters, 10: palm court, 11: throne room: 12: domestic quarters, including the *tubqum* for palace women, 13: bathroom (based on Kohlmeyer 1985, 196).

excavated at the contemporary palace of Ebla. There, grinding stones had been set up on low benches along the walls so that as many as sixteen women (and probably more) could crouch together for long hours to grind wheat and barley into flour for the palace. This took none of the creativity or expertise required of weavers; it was backbreaking work and may have been delegated to captives.[32]

Between the two doors—the ones to the guest quarters and to the workshops—and directly facing the main gate into the court, stood the wide entrance to an audience hall (8), open to the courtyard and approached by a semi-circular stairway. Perhaps the king periodically made appearances here to greet the throngs crowding the main court.

Finally, in the wall to your right stood a door (9) that no doubt was heavily guarded. It provided access to the quarters inhabited by the king and the royal household. A messenger with a letter for King Yasmah-Addu from his father Shamshi-Adad would have been allowed through this door, plunging into a long, dimly lit L-shaped hallway. The messenger's eyes would have taken a moment to adjust to the dramatic change in light. The rooms of the palace seem to have had no windows at all—the archaeologists found none, even in walls that still stood to the full height of the first floor.[33] All the natural light came through doorways from the courtyards, though admittedly those doorways could stand as much as 5 meters (16 feet) high. Walking through the palace, one would therefore have experienced a constant contrast between the brilliant sunshine of the courtyards, the comfortable shade of rooms adjoining them, and the deep gloom of windowless rooms at any distance from an exterior door.

The corridor leading to the royal apartments was 20 meters (65 feet) long, but at the end of it the visitor could see, on his left, brilliant light from a door into a second large courtyard (10), the king's own open space at the center of the palace complex. This court, which was about 900 square meters (close to 10,000 square feet) in extent, was planted with palm trees for shade, its plastered walls decorated with brightly colored frescoes. Some of these paintings, remarkably, had survived in the ground through all the millennia until the court was excavated. This was probably the "Multicolor Court" where Beltum had spent her ill-advised jaunt in the midday sunshine. One dramatic painting centered on an image of a king and the goddess Ishtar, who was dressed as a warrior (see reconstruction in Fig. 10.2).[34]

Fig. 10.2 Investiture painting from the wall of the palm court at Mari, mid-eighteenth century BCE. (© RMN-Grand Palais/Art Resource, NY/Art Resource)

Like King Ur-Namma on his relief stela, the unnamed king of Mari in this painting stands facing the deity, and the deity hands him a rod and a circular object. This was a loop of rope in the earlier Ur III image, but now the circular object seems to be a ring. The rod and the ring had, by now, come to represent not building tools but a king's general authority to rule. Anyone waiting in the courtyard before meeting the king would have been reminded of the close connection between the king and Ishtar, and of her divine support for his rule. Around the central image, the artist had painted a landscape of stylized trees, fantastic animals, and attending goddesses in brilliant colors. The walls of other palaces had probably often been painted with such scenes, but they almost never survive.

A regular splash of running water came from two almost-lifesize fountains shaped like goddesses, with water coursing from the pitchers in their hands, echoing exactly two goddesses painted in the fresco. Beyond them was a further large antechamber, and finally, beyond that, the throne room itself (marked as 11 in Fig. 10.1).

The messenger visiting Yasmah-Addu must have been appropriately awed by this dark, yawning space. The throne room was the biggest room in the palace, with a raised platform supporting several antique statues of past kings of Mari at one end. Such statues never seem to have served the role of family portraits—the kings represented by these ones actually ruled hundreds of years earlier and were not even related to the later kings of Mari. Just as in the temple ceremonies of the Early Dynastic period at Ebla and Lagash, the statues of dead rulers still had power and still required rituals in their honor. The current king seems to have depended upon their support. The king's own raised throne stood at the opposite end of the room from the statues and would itself have been a fine work of art. Thrones, both for kings and for gods, were often mentioned in year-names and inscriptions. They don't survive, but they must have been grand. The king, at the center of this tableau, at the end point of the journey through the palace, must have hardly seemed mortal.

Yasmah-Addu's correspondence, though, shows that he was entirely mortal, and often in trouble with his father. A scolding message from Shamshi-Adad (of which there were many), read aloud by a messenger in this grand setting, must have seemed incongruous.

To the west of these ceremonial rooms lay the rabbit warren of domestic quarters built around small courtyards (12), where the king's family and royal household lived, including the chambers of the new queen Beltum. The palace even featured a bathroom (13), with a fireplace for warmth in winter and boasting the most up-to-date fixtures—here, again, the plumbing of Mari was state of the art. The king enjoyed his bath in one of two terracotta tubs and had the luxury of an indoor toilet flushed by a drainage channel.[35]

The Mari palace provided an opulent stage-set for the events and dramas that played out there. For example, one banquet hosted by Yasmah-Addu was enjoyed by hundreds of people. These were not just high officials but included "21 couriers, 25 palanquin-carriers, 24 builders, 22 spear-carriers, 26 bath-workers (barbers) ... 10 drink-servers, 10 irrigators."[36] The amount of food that must have been cooked and served by the palace kitchens for such events is astonishing. The king certainly enjoyed banquets, with their convivial conversation and music. Yasmah-Addu didn't mind the fine food and wine either. He had found a reliable supplier of wine in the person of his ally the king of Carchemish, who on one occasion sent him, as he put it, "fifty jars of wine, of the sort that I drink."[37] The palace also became a center for artisans and musicians. Yasmah-Addu seems to have genuinely delighted in music, and he welcomed musicians from all over the kingdom to his palace. His father Shamshi-Adad was unconvinced that this was a good thing; he suspected that they went to Mari to gamble and drink.[38] But Rishiya, the king's chief musician, maintained a conservatory of talented singers and musicians. Mari in Yasmah-Addu's time was not without its scandals, but it seems to have been a lively place.

Zimri-Lim of Mari: Change of Regime

Early in his reign, Shamshi-Adad used the title "King of Ekallatum," but as he spread his control over a wider and wider area he stopped giving a name to his kingdom. He was simply, according to his inscriptions, "king of the universe."[39] As he grew old, however, Shamshi-Adad faced more challenges from younger kings of neighboring lands. In the end, his empire barely outlived him. After his death in 1776 BCE, rebellions broke out and local forces in the region of Mari unceremoniously deposed Shamshi-Adad's son Yasmah-Addu, who disappeared from history. We don't know what happened to his wife Beltum, but it seems likely that she was spirited away, back to her father's kingdom of Qatna.

Yahdun-Lim, who had been the last local king of Mari before Yasmah-Addu took over that land, was survived by an heir who was ready to retake the throne there: this was his nephew, a man named Zimri-Lim. He had been living in exile in Aleppo throughout Yasmah-Addu's tenure in Mari and quickly claimed his dynastic throne once Yasmah-Addu was gone.[40] Meanwhile, Shamshi-Adad's other son and successor, Ishme-Dagan (1775–1735 BCE), was unable to maintain much of his father's empire; he was eventually reduced to being a relatively minor king of the land of Ashur.

Zimri-Lim (1774–1762 BCE) only ruled Mari for thirteen years, but they were some of the best-documented years in all of Mesopotamian history, thanks to the thousands of tablets found in the palace. Just as the abundant Ur III tablets have given rise to a vast bibliography of studies of every imaginable detail of that era, so too have the Mari tablets. Scholars in this field enjoy the added pleasure of working on the sometimes politically charged, gossipy, and impassioned letters that passed between members of the court and the royal family. Some of the correspondents come across in them as vivid personalities.

Once Zimri-Lim moved back into his uncle's palace at Mari, life there continued much as before, but with a mostly new cast of characters. Some of Yasmah-Addu's officials and servants were allowed to stay on into the new court, however. They included the chief musician, Rishiya. Zimri-Lim must have heard about Rishiya's reputation for being disorganized and irresponsible in his private life—in King Yasmah-Addu's time Rishiya hadn't maintained the farmland he had been allocated and it had been taken away from him[41]—but he played a valuable role at court and, notwithstanding his faults, Zimri-Lim had decided to keep him.

A couple of years after Zimri-Lim took the throne of Mari, he married a princess from Aleppo named Shibtu, daughter of the king in whose palace he had spent his exile. Zimri-Lim trusted Rishiya enough to ask him to undertake the journey to Aleppo to make the arrangements for his royal marriage.[42] This assignment probably had little to do with Rishiya's musical talents and more to do with his comfort and dependability around women. At this point Zimri-Lim was already married to his chief wife[43] and had a number of grown daughters, some of them perhaps by other wives. He set about arranging diplomatic marriages of some of these princesses to various vassal kings, even as he was negotiating his own marriage to Shibtu. Zimri-Lim ended up with at least twelve wives (of whom Shibtu was his closest advisor and second-in-command) and a great many daughters, but apparently only three sons.

The world of the women of Mari can be examined through the letters of high-ranking women. Historian Nele Ziegler has done extensive research, especially on administrative texts found in the palace, that reveals a lot about women who were not as prominent, such as musicians.[44]

Bazatum and Rishiya: Musicians

A girl named Bazatum is listed as one of the musicians at Mari from the beginning of Zimri-Lim's reign. We don't know where she was born or who her parents were, but she was apparently from an elite family.[45] As a girl, she lived in the king's palace at Mari, along with many other women, about half of whom were musicians. The palace women also included royal family members, teachers, scribes, servants, cooks, and nannies. They were sometimes listed all together on the palace records, probably because many of them lived in a suite of more than sixty rooms grouped around courtyards in the area of the royal quarters, just beyond the palm tree court and the king's throne room.[46] The people listed in this group weren't exclusively female—the three young royal princes were included (presumably because they lived with their mothers), as were male doorkeepers. The women's quarters were called the "*tubqum*."[47] The women weren't confined there; they seem to have been free to move around, and some of them had jobs in various parts of the palace, though the doors to their quarters were bolted at night and during the afternoon siesta. It does make sense that a large group of mostly unmarried women would have had their sleeping quarters separate from those of the men who lived in the palace, and that doorkeepers (both male and female) were employed for their protection. The *tubqum* was a complex where the palace women could live safely together in a protected area within a large household dominated by men, while spending their days surrounded by and working with both men and women.

Bazatum therefore lived in the *tubqum* and spent her days working with a small group of fourteen girls, all of them musicians.[48] The girls of her group were known as the "small musicians"; they were not yet grown women but most of them would eventually join the older group. The small musicians seem to already have been thoroughly proficient at their art, though. They received pay and were distinct from lower-ranked musicians who were considered to be apprentices.

A lot of musicians, more than a hundred in fact, found employment in and around the palace at Mari in Zimri-Lim's time. Most of them were women, and many other women learned to play music, as non-professionals.[49] Bazatum's ensemble was one of the more prestigious groups to belong to, to judge from their level of pay. Lower in rank were the "women of the House of the *Tigum*-instrument," who were paid less and didn't live in the palace. The physical House of the *Tigum* was apparently also the conservatory where they studied and maybe lived.[50] There, too, the women were divided by age into "musicians" and "very small musicians,"[51] who were probably young girls.

The reason we know about all these ensembles was that they received their pay in the form of oil or wool, and the scribes recording these payments always listed the names of the musicians in each group in the same order—the order of their importance. This was true even though the women in most groups all received the same pay. In Bazatum's ensemble, the list always began with a girl named Tahsin-Admu;[52] Bazatum was listed fourth. Perhaps Tahsin-Admu was their leader, or perhaps she just had the most influential father. The girl listed before Bazatum was named Beltani; she was slightly higher in status than Bazatum. We know that Beltani had been born into a royal family, possibly even the family of the former king Yasmah-Addu,[53] so Bazatum might have had a royal background as well. The two girls seem to have been close friends, and both had interesting lives ahead of them.

The scribes who recorded their pay unfortunately didn't care what instruments the girls and women played—they never listed them. Bazatum and Beltani may well have played the lyre, which was considered a woman's instrument, whereas men were more likely to play the harp (see Fig. 10.3).[54] (The girls may also have been singers, but that wasn't their primary area

Fig. 10.3 Molded terracotta plaque showing a harpist, c. 1800 BCE. (Renée Lessing-Kronfuss/Art Resource)

of expertise.) The lute was also a popular instrument, but it seems to have been played more by the common people than by the palace musicians.[55] None of the musical instruments from Mari survive, but some images of instruments can be seen on terracotta plaques from the time.

Rishiya, the chief musician, was in charge of everything pertaining to music in the palace: the manufacture and repair of the instruments, the choice and training of the musicians, the appointment of musicians to particular positions, and the plans for rehearsals and performances.[56] Rishiya's house in Mari (which was separate from the palace) served as the conservatory for all the many musicians whom he mentored.[57] It has never been excavated, but it must have been large, and it must have been loud, full of music and singing. (Perhaps Rishiya's neighbors sometimes wished that the percussionists could rehearse in the temple or the palace rather than next door.) Women must have passed one another as they entered and left through the front door, greeting each other as they carried their instruments in for classes or rehearsals. Beltani and Bazatum were immersed in this community.

On one occasion, Zimri-Lim wrote to his wife Shibtu about some female captives who were being selected as prospective musicians, to remind her to "be careful with their food-rations so that their looks will not change."[58] This implies that, for some captives, life in the Mari palace could be harsh, that they might receive inadequate provisions and grow thin.[59]

Zimri-Lim was certainly aware that good food distributed in adequate amounts helped strengthen his community against a threat they all shared: illness. Diseases could spread easily through the palace population, many of whom lived in close quarters with one another. In their world, before vaccinations or antibiotics, once someone became ill they could only wait and hope that it passed and the victim recovered.

Although this was millennia before scientists discovered viruses and bacteria, the people of Mari were already aware of some strategies to try to limit the spread of disease. On one occasion, a maid named Nanna had become ill. People around her must have noticed her fever and weakness; they were worried for her health and for their own as well. Nanna's condition had reached the attention of the king, who was concerned because, as he wrote in a letter to Shibtu, "since she is often at the palace, it will infect the many women who are with her."[60] Interestingly, he suggested some practical guidelines: "No one is to drink from the cup she uses; no one is to sit on the seat she takes; no one is to lie in the bed she uses, lest it infect the many women who are with her." You can imagine how difficult these guidelines might have been to implement, but the people of Mari had figured out that sharing rooms and cups with someone who was sick made one more likely to catch their illness, so they probably tried hard to isolate Nanna.

The king suggested even more radical measures when Shibtu wrote to tell him that a different woman had fallen ill. This woman, he said, should not even be allowed in the same building with others: "This woman must remain in a separate house. No one must enter into her presence."[61] He knew this would not be easy. He mused: "Now I fear that a separate house may not be available." In her case, the king instructed that omens should be taken—did the gods intend that the woman would live or die? But he still seemed uncertain of what to do, even if the oracles looked bad: "(How should) this woman be treated? Whether she dies or lives, many women in either case will become ill because of this woman." He felt powerless in the face of her illness and the toll it would take among his dependents.

Diseases affected the powerful just as much as they affected maidservants like Nanna. At one point during Yasmah-Addu's reign, even Rishiya, the chief musician, had developed a severe illness. Apparently as soon as Rishiya began ailing, King Yasmah-Addu had written to his father King Shamshi-Adad, in Shubat-Enlil, to ask him to send his best physician, Meranum, to Mari to care for Rishiya. But now Rishiya was bedridden, and Yasmah-Addu wrote more urgently. "Rishiya is now in bed for his life. He is very ill. If it pleases Papa, Meranum must arrive here quickly if he is to restore Rishiya's life. He must not die."[62] Evidently Meranum's ministrations, or Rishiya's immune system, or both, prevailed. As we have seen, the chief musician outlasted King Yasmah-Addu at Mari and continued training and organizing the program of music at the palace.

The musical training that musicians received was rigorous, and they were expected to work hard at it. One dialogue from a different period seems to record banter between two apprentice musicians—men in this instance. One of them gossiped nastily about another:

Even if he took up the *zami* instrument, he would not know the craft of music
    making,
He is the most backward among his colleagues,
With an unpleasant sound and voice;
Too thick for Sumerian, his tongue cannot get it right,
He is not up to singing a song, never even opens his mouth.[63]

Clearly, it was important to excel and, although this dialogue was probably a satire, some students may have been similarly unkind to others who were less skilled.

The girls Bazatum and Beltani may have specialized in more than one instrument. A contract in which a boy was apprenticed to learn music from a mentor listed four different instruments that he was expected to master—quite a feat.[64] Unfortunately, even though the names of instruments were listed, we can't be sure exactly what each term meant.

The lyre was a favorite at the palace. Like a harp, it was played by plucking the strings, but, unlike a harp, a lyre had a bridge. Lyres had a long history already; beautiful, elaborately decorated ones, with inlaid designs and decorative three-dimensional bulls' heads in precious metals, had been buried with the royal attendants in the tombs of Ur centuries before. The ones that Bazatum and Beltani learned to play didn't have the bulls' heads, though—those had been out of fashion for quite a while.[65]

The women's main role was probably to play music at banquets. Like Yasmah-Addu before him, Zimri-Lim hosted these frequently in the palace, sometimes with dozens of people in attendance. The seating chart was as hierarchical as the ration lists, and guests squabbled over who would get to sit closest to the king. Etiquette and decorum were clearly valued; everyone noticed when someone behaved badly. On the other hand, the mood seems to have been festive. Feasting well meant eating good food, and drinking beer or wine. Zimri-Lim could even offer his guests iced drinks, which must have been very welcome on hot Syrian summer days when the temperature could reach 45 degrees C (113 degrees F). One of the few royal inscriptions that survives from his reign commemorates his construction of an "ice house" upstream in the city of Terqa, which, he boasted, "no king since time immemorial had built on the bank of the Euphrates."[66] (Terqa was the capital of the province in the Mari kingdom that was closest to the city of Mari.) Musicians contributed to the atmosphere at the king's feasts. Ever since the Early Dynastic period, images of banquets had included lyre players. You can see one at the top right of the peace side of the Standard of Ur (in Fig. 3.7)—a man in that case, with a female singer behind him. Musicians at banquets are mentioned in the Mari letters and administrative documents as well.[67]

Music played for the gods was a different matter and seems to have been more somber. Certain tunes were prescribed for particular rituals and ceremonies, which were organized and largely performed by lamentation priests, the *gulas* we have encountered before. These men assisted with funerals as well, but were not involved in music for the king's banquets.

Drums and percussion instruments seem to have appealed to the gods, and many kinds of them existed. On the back of the stela of Ur-Namma, created a few centuries earlier, two men were depicted playing a huge drum, which, standing upright on its round rim, was almost as tall as they were.[68] This was probably what was known as an "*alum*." *Alum* drums were so large and impressive that the creation and dedication of one in a temple was considered worthy of commemoration in a year-name.[69] *Alum* drums received their own oil offerings, the oil being necessary to treat the leather drumheads.[70]

A bronze kettledrum could also be dedicated to a god, and these too were mentioned in year-names.[71] The resonant sound of the drums must have throbbed through the very walls of the temples; they were described as rumbling or roaring like a storm.

Music was considered essential for calming the hearts of the gods. This was one of the reasons musicians played such a central role in the culture, because the gods and goddesses loved music. Hearing music made them less likely to punish humans; it soothed their anger.

It's unclear whether palace musicians played for many temple ceremonies or whether the temples generally used their own ensembles. A shrine for the goddess Ishtar was located inside the Mari palace, though, so Bazatum's ensemble might have played music in a ritual for Ishtar that was recorded on a tablet found in the palace.[72] At the heart of this ritual was a lyre.[73] This lyre was deified and was worshiped as the goddess Ninigizibara. Her cult was practiced not only in Mari but in other Old Babylonian cities as well.[74] The instrument itself was the subject of worship, as though it were a cult statue.

The ceremony started in Ishtar's temple early in the morning with a purifying ritual. The two goddesses, Ishtar (in the human form of her statue) and Ninigizibara (in the form of the sacred lyre), faced one another in the sanctuary. They weren't alone; the place was packed with divine statues. The author of the text detailing the ritual notes that "to the left of Ishtar sit (the warrior god) Latarak and the Dingirgubbu deities,"[75] and he later refers to the presence of the (statue of) the great sun god Shamash as well. Then, "the emblems of the goddesses"—their holy symbols—were "brought out from their shrines and are placed in the temple of Ishtar, to the right and the left."

After the purification, a group of musicians entered the temple and arrayed themselves around the sacred lyre goddess, with lamentation priests to her left and female singers to her right. More women singers stood behind them. Oddly, a group of skilled craftsmen, "their tools at the ready," were also present—a brewer, a carpenter, a leather-worker, a cord-maker, and a fuller— along with some barbers, "blades (ready)." The ritual text never tells us what they were there for or why it was important that they be equipped for work.

It was now time for the king to enter. He wore a special robe that had been woven of a rare type of wool just for this event,[76] and he seated himself on a throne traditionally known (for whatever reason) as the "sailor's seat." But he wasn't the center of attention. His seat was behind the group of lamentation priests. "A king's courtier" we are told, sat "on a lower chair by the king's side" and domestic servants stood to his right and left.

Once the king was seated, the music began. The author of the ritual text named each piece and noted the actions that accompanied it. First came the lamentation priests singing a lament called "*Uru.amma.daru.bi.*" You may remember the lamentation priests, or "*galas,*" from the funeral of the Early Dynastic queen Baranamtara. Here we are, about 600 years later, and the *gala* priests were still singing in the Emesal dialect of Sumerian, the dialect associated with women, and in a falsetto range.[77] They were still listed as men, but, as we have seen, their gender was not rigidly defined. *Galas* could have children, so they seem not to have been eunuchs. The *galas* were evidently brilliant musicians and singers, and were essential to the cult; they were the ones who could assuage the tempers of the gods most successfully.

As the ceremony progressed, the assembled gods witnessed processions and performances by people who seem to have been fire-eaters, wrestlers, dancers, and acrobats. These took place during a chant called "*Annuwashe,*" throughout which the king was required to stand up. Perhaps the deep rumblings of the drums could be heard behind the melodies that were sung, or the women musicians produced harmonies on their lyres. These actions and songs must have had meaning for the people involved—as did a later segment of the ceremony when a priest sprinkled water on the deities Ishtar and Shamash, on the musicians, and on the king—but those meanings are indecipherable to us. What was important was that these actions and this music, done just so, made the gods happy. The very predictability of the whole event was probably reassuring to everyone involved. The ancient melodies echoing through the temple of Ishtar didn't just soothe the hearts of the gods, they no doubt raised the spirits of the participants as well. The ceremony doesn't seem to have been a public event, however. There's no mention of an audience. It was all done for the gods.

To return to the ensemble of small musicians, life changed for Bazatum and Beltani after the first few years of Zimri-Lim's reign: both of them got married. Beltani was first, and she married the most powerful man in the land: King Zimri-Lim himself. She wasn't one of his concubines, but she wasn't a particularly highly ranked wife either. Her name appears third from the end of the list of his twelve wives.[78]

Bazatum, unlike Beltani, left the city of Mari when she got married, to live about 45 kilometers (28 miles) upstream near the city of Terqa. Her husband was one of the highest officials in the land, a former governor of Terqa named Sammetar, whom Zimri-Lim often depended upon.[79] He was so favored by the king that he traveled in an expensive palanquin carried by attendants, rather than in a chariot. Although impressive, this caused Sammetar some embarrassment, because most of Zimri-Lim's vassals—who were, of course, kings themselves—traveled in chariots, which were considered less prestigious. Sammetar, aware of the fact that his palanquin might be seen as too ostentatious for an official, wrote to Zimri-Lim at one point for advice. Should he avoid using it? He was willing to give it up if necessary.[80] Clearly, though, he enjoyed the impression it made. He wrote, a little smugly, that, by sending the palanquin, the king "has certainly granted me great prestige; the whole land has heard (about it)."[81]

Sammetar's father had been an eminent figure in the city of Terqa during the reign of Yasmah-Addu, so his was a well-established family.[82] Bazatum's engagement to Sammetar must have seemed to be a good match. No doubt her father (if he was still alive) was pleased to have gained a powerful son-in-law. But it's highly unlikely that Bazatum had any say in whom she married, and her new life may not have been easy. She was much younger than Sammetar, and she was his second wife. Sammetar's first wife was a woman named Karanatum, who lived in Mari.[83]

Bazatum moved to her husband's country estate near Terqa, and she took on the oversight of a weaving workshop run by four male textile supervisors.[84] These men were described as working "in the house of Bazatum"[85] (which was probably a wing of Sammetar's house).

The estate was located on the opposite bank of the Euphrates from her husband's home city of Terqa, and from Mari as well.[86] Getting there would have required taking a boat, so it might have seemed a little remote. The countryside in the region would have been lovely, with shady orchards and quiet lanes, as has still been the case recently. But living there must have been quite a shift for Bazatum after her sociable childhood in the Mari palace. The textile work was familiar, since almost all women knew how to spin and weave, but it was rare for a woman to have authority over male overseers. Did this cause any difficulties for her? Did she miss the city and the members of her music ensemble? Did she still find any occasions to play music? Unfortunately, we have no answers to these questions.

Being a second wife also had its complications. It was unusual for any man but the king to have more than one wife (and a woman never had more than one husband); monogamy was the norm for almost all Mesopotamians. Only a very few officials, at least at Mari, married more than one woman,[87] so Bazatum would have had few role models for how to behave as the second wife of a magnate. Also, she seems—and this was surprising—to have been higher in rank than Sammetar's first wife, Karanatum. A fragment of a tablet records jewelry allotted to them both, and it reads, in part, "1 shekel of gold, 1 ring of silver, weighing 4 [shekels] to Bazatum; 1 shekel of gold, 1 ring of silver, weighing 4 [shekels] to Karanatum."[88] Bazatum's name coming before that of Karanatum is jarring, because it suggested that she was more important. As a second wife, Bazatum's rank should have been lower, unless, like her friend Beltani, she had been born into a royal family.[89] This ambiguous hierarchy between Bazatum and her fellow wife cannot have made her married life any easier.

Bazatum's friendship with her fellow musician Beltani seems to have continued after they were both married. Although no letters survive to attest to their friendship,[90] a text records that when Beltani needed someone to take care of her jewelry box, she chose Bazatum.[91] Perhaps they occasionally were able to meet up in Mari when Bazatum traveled there, and they remained close.

Bazatum's marriage turned out to be short-lived. Her husband Sammetar became ill soon after Bazatum moved to his estate. He wrote to King Zimri-Lim apologizing for having to miss an important festival—he was too sick, he said, to make the journey.[92] Not long after this, a priestess who was close to Sammetar and his family wrote to Zimri-Lim to tell him, laconically, "A young officer informed me that Sammetar has died. My Star (the king) should know that."[93]

The usual practice, after the death of a high official, was for royal inspectors to descend on his estate to determine if there were items there that belonged to the palace and might need to be reclaimed. Sure enough, Zimri-Lim soon sent officials to Sammetar's country estate to inspect and record his property. These men were thorough, making their way through the dead man's estate, counting and recording details of everything from plow teams, to goats (314 of them), textiles, bronze household utensils, animals in the courtyard, barley, jugs of wine, and workers. They then moved on, across the river, to Sammetar's other home in Terqa and made notes that were just as exhaustive of his goods there.[94] Many items, especially those made of metal,[95] were seized and taken back to Mari, perhaps because they were the property of the king and had been used by Sammetar during his lifetime, or perhaps to repay debts that he still owed to the palace.

While they were at Sammetar's houses, the inspectors registered Bazatum's personal property as well—she owned vessels, barley, oxen, jewelry, and some personnel in the country house, along with a herd of eighty-four sheep and goats that grazed on land near Terqa—though none of these were taken away from her.[96] Her possessions must have been included in her dowry and bridal gifts, which would have been kept distinct from the property of her husband Sammetar.[97]

Sammetar had also maintained two households in Mari itself, to which the inspectors turned next. There he had maintained a huge staff of servants, cooks, textile workers, singers, butlers, barbers, and even a female physician.[98] He had been a rich and powerful man.

As his widow, Bazatum initially seems to have continued to live in her wing of his country home near Terqa, but we know nothing of what happened to her after that. It would have been fortunate for her if she did continue to live in the region of Terqa, because in just a few years the city of Mari was embroiled in turmoil.

In the fifth month of what turned out to be the last year of his reign, Zimri-Lim had been traveling in the northern Habur triangle region, leaving Queen Shibtu in charge of the palace at Mari. This was not unusual. Even when Zimri-Lim went to visit his wife's parents, the king and queen of Aleppo, their daughter Shibtu stayed in Mari to take care of everything for him and to keep him informed, by letter, of any major concerns.[99] He was now about to start on his way home with his entourage, traveling downstream along the Habur River toward the Euphrates. He dictated a letter to Queen Shibtu and sent it via a fast messenger: "I am just now heading (to Mari), making the trip," he wrote to his wife, "Reach Saggaratum ahead of me." Saggaratum was a provincial capital at the confluence of the Habur and Euphrates Rivers, north of Mari, and south of the Habur region that Zimri-Lim was leaving. "As you head out, bring with you to Saggaratum a seven-woman (musical) ensemble, [the songstress] Ahatum who is now by you, and the musical instruments made with gold."[100] It's unclear why Zimri-Lim was in particular need of the seven-woman musical ensemble when he got to the town of Saggaratum, but it wasn't the only time that he had asked this group to travel. On another occasion when he was away from Mari he wrote for them to be sent to him, along with their instruments, and some singers.[101] Music had continued to play a big part in the life of the palace at Mari throughout Zimri-Lim's reign, and perhaps on this occasion the king wanted to impress the court of his governor in Saggaratum with the talents of his court musicians. Zimri-Lim, who had a taste for the opulent, often mentioned his desire for instruments made of gold, as he did here.

At this point, nothing seemed to be amiss for Mari and its king. The records show that, over the next few months, Zimri-Lim gave and received gifts from other kings, traveled to Terqa, celebrated a festival for Ishtar (no doubt with the usual musical contributions from the *gala* priests), and held banquets, just as before. And then, suddenly, no more tablets were written.

Two years later, the palace of Zimri-Lim—that sprawling, glorious complex—burned to the ground and was never rebuilt. It must have burned for hours, perhaps for days. The people of the city experienced the strange horror of witnessing the destruction of a monument that must have seemed eternal and that had for centuries represented continuity, even when dynasties had changed. Fortunately, by the time of the fire, palace residents had long since moved out; the contents of the palace had been sorted through and the finest treasures removed beforehand. Now fire poured out of the rooftops and the doorways. Ceiling beams holding up the second floor burst into flames, and upper floors collapsed. The fire was so hot that it baked hard the bricks in the walls and the clay tablets in the archives, serendipitously preserving them for us, their unimagined readers, far in the future. After the fire burned out, some of the walls that still stood were torn down and objects left in the rubble were never recovered. The fire bore all the markings of a hostile act.

What happened to Zimri-Lim and how the palace came to be destroyed remain a puzzle, but the Babylonians were definitely involved. The king of Babylon, Hammurabi, even boasted about taking control of Mari in two of his year-names, though he had previously been a close ally of Zimri-Lim's. In the next chapter we will look into Hammurabi's career, and will come back to Mari, to try to understand this catastrophe.

PART V

The Old Babylonian Period,

1792–1550 BCE

Chapter 11

A Lawgiver, Land Overseers, and Soldiers

I don't think there's a world history survey in existence that fails to mention Hammurabi of Babylon (1792–1750 BCE). Even if only two or three pages are devoted to all of Mesopotamian history—all 3,500 years of it—Hammurabi still makes it in there. The reason for his presence, always, is his "law code." Most of the histories even quote some of the laws, often favoring the "eye-for-an-eye" ones. These laws aren't particularly typical (strictly speaking, there are just three of them in a collection of almost 300 laws),[1] but they sound biblical, which makes for an interesting connection. Somehow, Hammurabi is the most familiar name in all of Mesopotamian history.

This might have surprised him. Like just about every Mesopotamian king, Hammurabi thought pretty highly of himself, but would he have believed that he was the most important king of all? For most of his reign, definitely not. He was far from being the first king to promulgate laws (we have already met Ur-Namma, who holds that distinction, at least as far as we know), and he didn't assemble his law collection until the last years of his life; he didn't start building an empire until he'd been on the throne for thirty years; he never used the divine symbol in front of his name to suggest that he was a god. So why do we have a disproportionate sense of his importance?

Hammurabi: Pious King and Lawgiver

Hammurabi's laws were first discovered in 1902 at a time when most of the interest in the ancient Near East came from its association with the Bible.[2]

It didn't hurt his immediate rise to fame that the laws were recovered on an impressive stone stela with a beautifully carved relief sculpture atop columns of cuneiform inscribed in a fine, archaizing script that is lovely to look at, even for those who can't read it (see Fig. 11.1). And once the inscription was read (which was almost immediately), the contents were declared to be the world's first laws, and scholars immediately drew comparisons with biblical law. Hammurabi was heralded as a predecessor of Moses, receiving the laws from his god, Shamash. Even the subsequent discovery of earlier laws, which quickly knocked Hammurabi from his pedestal as "first lawgiver," did nothing to eclipse his fame. He was in the history books from day one of his rediscovery and he has remained there.

Obviously, we will get to his laws, but I'd like to look first at Hammurabi in his early years on the throne. At that point he wasn't very different, in his achievements and challenges, from Sumu-El of Larsa, Enlil-bani of Isin, or Zimri-Lim of Mari, or, for that matter, from most of the other kings

Fig. 11.1 Diorite law stela of King Hammurabi of Babylon, found in Susa, mid-eighteenth century BCE. (© RMN-Grand Palais/Art Resource, NY/Art Resource)

who ruled in the early centuries of the second millennium BCE. Initially Hammurabi's Babylonian kingdom existed in the shadow of three much more powerful states: Upper Mesopotamia to the north, Larsa to the south, and Elam to the east. When Hammurabi ascended to the throne in 1792 BCE at the death of his father, he was a young man. The now middle-aged Shamshi-Adad was still ruling the wide reaches of Upper Mesopotamia. Larsa, which continued to dominate Sumer, as it had for a century ever since the time of Sumu-El, was now ruled by king Rim-Sin (1822–1763 BCE). He, like Shamshi-Adad, was at least a generation older than Hammurabi; he had already been in power for thirty years and, during that time, had dramatically increased the size of his kingdom. He had even finally conquered Larsa's longtime rival, Isin.[3] Unlike almost all the earlier kings of Larsa, or of anywhere else in the 1790s BCE, Rim-Sin considered himself to be a god. The third power, Elam, is less well known to us, but was apparently the most powerful of them all. Siruk-tuh (early eighteenth century BCE) was its leader when Hammurabi first ruled.[4] He and later kings of the Elamite dynasty were referred to as "great king" and "father" by kings in Syria and Mesopotamia and were the only kings that the Mesopotamian kings considered to be higher in status than themselves.[5] The Elamite rulers had become increasingly involved in Mesopotamian politics; in fact, Rim-Sin of Larsa himself was of Elamite descent, notwithstanding his Akkadian name.

Hammurabi's life is, however, considerably better known than those of his contemporaries; he even is the subject of two book-length biographies.[6] Hammurabi seems initially to have had no delusions of grandeur. His year-names show that he busied himself with the usual concerns of the leader of a smallish kingdom—appeasing the gods, digging canals, restoring city walls, and so on. He married and had children. He wrote letters and sent his diplomats to negotiate with allies. He forged treaties with his vassals in which they pledged their allegiance to him, and treaties with his allies in which they pledged to support one another in times of war and to extradite fugitives. He fought small local wars. After the death of Shamshi-Adad and the independence of the kingdom of Mari, Hammurabi became friendly with Zimri-Lim. They corresponded and sent envoys to one another's courts. Hammurabi sent his sons to visit Mari,[7] and one of them may even have taken up residence in a house in Mari's provincial capital of Terqa.[8]

In 1765 BCE, troops from Elam, the powerful kingdom to the east, began an aggressive campaign in Mesopotamia, attacking the northern kingdom of Eshnunna. Recognizing that Elam was about to become a threat to both Babylon and Larsa, Hammurabi agreed to join forces with king Rim-Sin of Larsa—they might stand a better chance together than apart.[9] But their alliance didn't last; Rim-Sin delayed sending troops to help Hammurabi, and then Hammurabi claimed that his own lands had been raided, not by Elamites but by soldiers from his supposed ally Larsa. A big shuffle in alliances took place, messengers stopped traveling between the courts of Babylon and Larsa, and, in 1763 BCE, Hammurabi, with assistance from Zimri-Lim of Mari, launched an attack on Larsa.

Babylon's Conquest of Larsa

Hammurabi's victory, in his thirtieth year on the throne, over Rim-Sin of Larsa marked a dramatic moment. It came at the culmination of a six-month siege of the capital city and was commemorated in his thirty-first year-name, in which he boasted:

> Year: Hammurabi the king, trusting [the gods] An and Enlil, who marches in front of his army, and with the supreme power which the great gods have given to him, destroyed the troops of Emutbal, and subjugated its king Rim-Sin, and brought Sumer and Akkad to dwell under his authority.[10]

Emutbal was another name for Larsa; its now very elderly king, Rim-Sin, had been on the throne for an unprecedented sixty years. He would probably be better known to us today for his own achievements were it not for his bad luck in being a contemporary of Hammurabi, and his even worse luck in having been conquered by him. In all of Hammurabi's forty-three year-names and among the twenty lands he boasted of conquering,[11] Rim-Sin was the only enemy king he referred to by name. Rim-Sin was a legend among kings, and he had been defeated. He and his son were taken prisoner, an ignominious end to an extraordinarily long and mostly successful reign.

Hammurabi seems to have found a new passion for empire building after this. He didn't rest on his laurels: he was off again on campaign the very next year, defeating the armies of three additional lands and conquering another, and commemorating that fact in the name of his thirty-second year. In the thirteen years from his thirtieth to his forty-third (and last) year on the throne, Hammurabi claimed the remarkable feat of having defeated seventeen lands and regions, returning to several of them over and over again.

This brings us back to the mysterious destruction of Mari that we discussed in the last chapter. In naming his thirty-third year, Hammurabi boasted that he "overthrew in battle the armies of Mari and Malgium," and two years later, in his thirty-fifth year, he, "by the orders of An and Enlil, destroyed the city walls of Mari and Malgium." But this just doesn't make sense. Hammurabi's own son was in residence in Mari just the year before the first supposed attack, and Hammurabi had given no indications of suddenly turning against Zimri-Lim.

A theory put forward by Jack M. Sasson might solve this question. Sasson has been researching and writing about Mari throughout his career and pondering the city's strange fate. He proposes that Zimri-Lim died suddenly, and probably naturally, leaving no obvious heir. His surviving sons were both children and neither was old enough to take the throne.[12] Hammurabi initially may have been invited to Mari to help, either to assist the officials and queens of Mari in finding a new king, or simply to provide troops to protect Mari during the difficult time when there was no obvious heir to the throne. Hammurabi was, after all, an old ally of Zimri-Lim's. This helps to explain the last part of his thirty-third year-name in which he wrote that he caused "Mari and its territory . . . to dwell under his authority in friendship."[13] "Friendship" doesn't sound like forced submission. That said, Hammurabi was in an empire-building mood, and Sasson suggests that the attraction of bringing Mari into his realm might have been too great to resist.

Hammurabi and his scribes scoured through the Mari palace archives, reading each letter, and choosing the most important ones to be taken back to Babylon. The tablets haven't been found there, but inscribed clay tags survive in the ruins of the Mari palace providing evidence that this process took place. The Babylonians also chose some fine statues to remove (these statues from Mari were found in Babylon), along with other treasures from the palace that were made of metals or fabric that would not have survived to be found today.

Hammurabi claimed that the gods Anu and Enlil told him to destroy the city walls of Mari, and Sasson takes him at his word.[14] If, through signs or omens, Hammurabi really believed that the gods had told him to carry out this destruction, who was he to argue? He seems to have made sure, at least, that no one would get hurt when the palace was burned down.

Mari now marked the northern boundary of Hammurabi's empire. The city of Terqa, just a few miles upstream, continued to be occupied and soon had its own dynasty of local kings. Mari had been known as "the kingdom of Mari and the land of Hana." The new kings, no longer in control of Mari, probably called their realm simply "the land of Hana."[15]

Administration of Hammurabi's Empire

While Hammurabi's troops (and perhaps the king himself) were off on these almost annual campaigns all over the Euphrates and Tigris river valleys and up into the mountains, something had to be done about administering the newly conquered lands. Hammurabi seems to have decided not to try to enforce a brand-new system of government on his new subjects, but he certainly wanted to benefit economically from them.[16] His subjects in the region of Larsa (now called the province of Yamutbalum) would still, of course, pay taxes, but they would continue to pay them to their local cities (the capitals of their former kingdoms), and the administrators there would send them on to Babylon. In governing, Hammurabi employed many of the existing officials and civil servants and made good use of institutions that were already in place. Some public officials who had previously worked for the palace of Larsa, or Mari, or Eshnunna, or anywhere else, now worked for the palace of Babylon, but Hammurabi also introduced high officials from Babylon to oversee everything. On the other hand, he left the local structures of towns almost completely alone; the mayors, assemblies, and councils of elders continued to function just as before. Local matters didn't concern Hammurabi's officials; these were dealt with entirely by the officials in that particular town or district.[17] But the taxes from the new regions would be useful to him. In order to ascertain more about this potentially rich source of funds, Hammurabi imposed a census on Larsa. He probably did the same in other parts of the empire as well.

Sin-idinnam and Shamash-hazir: Governor General of Larsa and Land Overseer

That's the big picture, but what did this mean on a day-to-day basis for people living in Larsa and adjusting to life under Babylonian rule? Fortunately, we have a view from the ground showing just how this worked (and sometimes didn't work), in the careers of two men who worked directly for Hammurabi in Larsa: Sin-idinnam and Shamash-hazir. Both were Babylonians who were appointed by Hammurabi, and both wrote to the king and received replies from him on a regular basis. Luckily, many of these letters survive.[18]

Sin-idinnam was the more powerful of the two men, administering the province of Larsa, overseeing its governors, and reporting directly to Hammurabi.[19] His title isn't known, but it's likely that he was the governor general for the province.[20] Hammurabi wrote to him frequently, apparently micromanaging Sin-idinnam's work, which may have meant that he didn't have a lot of autonomy. On the other hand, he did have authority over the governors in his region and Hammurabi tended to write to Sin-idinnam, rather than directly to the governors, when he needed something from them.

Sin-idinnam was responsible, among other things, for making sure people paid their taxes and that the taxes subsequently arrived in Babylon. This wasn't an enviable aspect of his job; people generally weren't keen to pay taxes, and the king wasn't patient in waiting for them. The Babylonian king wrote to Sin-idinnam on one occasion, demanding that livestock be sent quickly: "As soon as you have read this letter of mine, issue a written order to all the governors of the lower district who are under your authority, that they should bring up to Babylon oxen and sheep from the stores which are at their disposal (being) the contribution in accordance with the share (that is due)."[21]

It's interesting to see from this that Sin-idinnam was clearly literate. Hammurabi said that Sin-idinnam would have "read" rather than "heard" the letter. And he was instructed to do some writing of his own—to "issue a written order" to the governors over whom he had jurisdiction, telling them that they were to bring their contributions of oxen and sheep directly to Babylon. Bringing the animals directly to Babylon was actually rather unusual, and must have been quite a challenge. The only way to get the oxen and sheep there was alive and on foot. So they must have been herded along the long route from Larsa to Babylon, a distance of 130 kilometers (81 miles).[22]

The king normally was more practical and wanted taxes to be paid only in barley and silver.[23] But many taxpayers didn't have barley or silver to contribute. They had the products of their gardens and orchards—garlic, onions, dates, and so on—or the products of their herds—wool, or living animals. These were brought in to the warehouses at Larsa and had somehow to be converted into barley and silver. This is where a man named Shep-Sin, the overseer of the merchants of Larsa, came in.[24] He was a powerful man whose role intersected the worlds of the palace and the private sector. The taxes were paid to him and he found private distributors of grain and silver who were willing to buy the tax goods from him and to pay for them in the commodities he needed. He then owed a set amount of grain and silver that had been determined by the king and which he sent on to the palace.[25] Anything extra that he took in was a bonus that he, and the officials he worked with, could keep.[26]

By the time of Hammurabi, much of the agricultural land in the expanding kingdom of Babylon was owned by the palace, but a lot (at least in the northern part of the kingdom)[27] was now also privately owned and could be bought and sold. This resulted in a distinctive feature of this era— many city-dwelling people kept archives in their houses to keep track of their property, and many of those archives have been found. People bought and sold houses, fields, and orchards, or leased them out. They borrowed silver and negotiated terms to pay it back. They hired laborers to work their land and laid out the terms of their employment, even including holidays and bonuses after the harvest. Wisely, they kept records of all these transactions for future reference. Although scribes wrote the documents, many land-owning people were probably literate, at least in being able to read the contracts that pertained to them.

In the newly acquired southern part of Hammurabi's empire, fields were not often bought and sold, though people did regularly sell houses and orchards.[28] But the land that had previously belonged to the state of Larsa now was the responsibility of Hammurabi and it was his to allocate and manage.

Keeping track of land in the region of Larsa was the responsibility of our second official, Shamash-hazir, who had the title "*shassukkum*."[29] He had a complicated job. Around Larsa lay hundreds of square miles of land, broken up into fields and orchards, some of it in private hands, some of it belonging to the state, some belonging to temples. Once Hammurabi had defeated Rim-Sin and taken control of Larsa, he didn't claim to own all the land in the kingdom; he recognized and respected the rights of landowners.[30] But he was very keen to find out which properties were now his (that is, which lands had previously belonged to the palace of Rim-Sin), because he had a use for them. Rather than paying state employees in barley, Hammurabi granted the use of land to some of his soldiers, workers, and other servants for them to cultivate in order to support their families. When soldiers were paid this way it was called the "*ilkum*" system—the land allotted to a soldier or other worker was his *ilkum*, and the work associated with farming it, along with his military service, corvée labor, and the taxes he paid, were also considered to be his *ilkum*.[31]

This was, in many ways, an easier system than monthly salaries paid in barley and other staples. It did not require the redistribution of vast amounts of grain, wool, and oil, or the conversion of goods into silver. It did not require multiple documents to be written and preserved in order to record the goods a man had received and when he had received them. A man simply was allocated a plot of land, he took control of it, . . . and that was it. The food he produced from it constituted his salary, though he also had to pay a proportion to the government. It was palace land, after all. There were restrictions, of course: he couldn't sell the land, and he may have lived in fear of its being taken away from him by the king, but it provided stability for his family.

Other palace land was awarded to high officials in much the same way, though in larger amounts, and this was not called an *ilkum*.[32] The work on the land of high officials seems to have been allocated to entrepreneurs who paid a set rent in produce and silver. The state provided them with the necessities for farming, such as plows, draft oxen, and irrigation water.[33] These men could potentially make a profit if they were able to produce more from the fields and orchards than the king anticipated, and in turn the king didn't have to worry about finding a seasonal workforce for his fields; the entrepreneurs did that themselves. Entrepreneurs like this didn't just work for the palace—they also farmed land for temples and wealthy landowners as well.[34]

The landscape around Larsa might have looked bucolic and uncomplicated—field beyond rectangular field stretching along the river to the horizon, interwoven with gently trickling irrigation canals—but each field had an individual story. It could be privately owned and farmed by its owner and his or her family, or owned by a private individual but farmed by a tenant or by hired laborers. It could be owned by the state and farmed by an entrepreneur, or owned by the state and awarded to a worker as an *ilkum*. It could be owned by a temple and farmed by temple employees, tenants, or hired laborers, or it could be owned by a temple and in the hands of an entrepreneur. Rich families who owned vast private land holdings could also function much like temples in the ways in which they managed their land.

Into this byzantine situation came Shamash-hazir, valiantly trying to track down information about who farmed, and who owned, every field in his region and sending regular reports to the king. He must have gone out regularly into the countryside, to talk to people as they plowed or weeded their fields and maintained their irrigation ditches. His first goal was to identify who was a tenant and who was an owner, and to find out which tenants worked for private owners and which worked for the state of Larsa. Owners would need to prove their right to the land by showing him contracts or providing witnesses. Shamash-hazir's ultimate goal was to identify lands that Hammurabi could use for land grants and *ilkum* allocations. Lands that had belonged to the state of Larsa were sometimes seized from the person who had been farming them and reassigned to one of Hammurabi's workers or members of the military.

When a soldier or worker was awarded an *ilkum*, giving him the right to cultivate some public land, he received a tablet from his supervisor, which he took to Shamash-hazir. The harried official then had to figure out which field to allocate to him. He headed out for the relevant plot of land, taking a surveyor with him, along with the man who would farm the land. Presumably this journey could take hours or even days. Larsa was a large province and Shamash-hazir seems to have overseen most of the state's agricultural land. When they reached the place, the surveyor measured the sides of the field and Shamash-hazir then symbolically hammered a stake into the center, an action that was witnessed by its new recipient.[35] What a relief it must have been for this man—he now had a means to support himself and his family. If he lived near the field (which was presumably the ideal situation) he could farm it himself, unless his work for the palace took him away from home. In that case, he could set his sons to work (if they were old enough), or hire a local workman. Sometimes, though, the field was simply too far from where the man lived for anyone in his family to farm it. He then had no choice but to hire a tenant from the region, to charge him rent, and to hope that the rent was paid.

This might seem to be the end of Shamash-hazir's involvement in that particular field, but sometimes, regrettably, he made mistakes. Sometimes someone else showed up on that precious plot of public land and claimed that it was his property and that the new man had no right to it. As you might imagine, the original owner in such a situation was outraged and lost no time in hiring a scribe to write to complain—often directly to the king himself. One letter written by Hammurabi to Shamash-hazir noted that the king had received a complaint: "Sin-ishmeani, the . . . date gardener . . . brought this to my attention," he wrote, and he quoted the date gardener: "Shamash-hazir has appropriated land of my family's estate and has given it to a soldier." Hammurabi was unhappy about this and reprimanded Shamash-hazir (see Fig. 11.2). The king wrote, "Is perpetual land ever to be taken away? . . . Return the field to him."[36]

In this case, it turned out that the land wasn't actually the king's to have awarded in the first place. But even public land that had been given out in the form of subsistence fields was seen as being "owned," in a manner of speaking, by the person who had farmed it for a long time. The king

Fig. 11.2 Letter from King Hammurabi of Babylon to his official Shamash-hazir concerning a field, mid–eighteenth century BCE. (Yale University, Peabody Museum)

couldn't just take it away arbitrarily, unless the man no longer worked for the palace. Again Shamash-hazir would find himself in the middle of a dispute. One official wrote to him complaining that a particular man had enjoyed control of a field for forty years. Shamash-hazir had proposed that it be given to someone else. But, as the letter writer noted, this new man had "showed up for service (only) this year."[37] This wasn't appropriate. The land should have stayed in the control of its longtime cultivator. Shamash-hazir would have to find a different field for the man who was new to the king's service.[38] By helping his subjects in this way, Hammurabi was able to be more than a distant overlord; he created a bond with them and seemed to be on their side.[39] They, in turn, seem to have viewed the king favorably; the region didn't rebel against Babylonian rule during his reign.

It was not just existing agricultural land that Shamash-hazir was responsible for allocating. Hammurabi also commanded the labor-intensive work of opening up new canals (some of them initially planned by Rim-Sin), creating new agricultural land that could be awarded to soldiers and civil servants for farming. A generation later, such new land was often given to soldiers from other lands, such as Elamites and Kassites, who were, by then, fighting in Babylon's armies.[40]

The irrigation system that watered all these fields also had to be maintained. This involved periodic dredging of the canals, maintenance of water control mechanisms such as flow dividers and gates,[41] and regulation of the users of the water to ensure that no one took more than their fair share. On one occasion Sin-idinnam was responsible for making sure that a main canal in the Larsa region was cleared so that neighboring Uruk got enough water—Hammurabi told him that he had just three days to get the work done; Uruk was suffering.[42] Likewise, Shamash-hazir was responsible for organizing the local irrigation work and the laborers who could execute it. Among other things, he had to calculate the number of men and the number of days that would be needed. Hammurabi wrote once to instruct him to "determine the (amount of) earth that it is right to remove from the canal" and to send reports.[43]

Sometimes the water in the rivers and canals was too low, as in the case of the blocked canal that was causing the people of Uruk to suffer. At other times it could rise dangerously high, especially during flood season (which was also, diabolically, the harvest season). In this case more laborers were needed to dig diversion canals to deflect floodwaters to areas where they would do less damage. Again Shamash-hazir was called on to take care of all the details and to find enough local workmen.[44]

In one letter, Shamash-hazir wrote to tell Hammurabi that an opening on a river had been dammed and "all the water has been poured into the canal of Edinna."[45] He asked the king to have two other officials take over responsibility for this. The king wrote back, noting that he had done just as Shamash-hazir requested; he had commanded these officers to "assign the proportion to their troops, strengthen the (dammed) opening . . . , and make them cultivate the land of the state that they are managing."[46]

In these letters to and from Shamash-hazir and Sin-idinnam we can observe the mechanisms they used for keeping the rivers and canals under control and in good order, but this was not just a phenomenon of their era. Systems like this existed throughout Mesopotamian history. Irrigation and flood control could never be neglected; the entire population of the region depended on them. Every person subject to the corvée labor draft (that is, most of the male population) must have spent some of his adult life in the backbreaking work of dredging canals, digging new channels, rebuilding flow dividers, and building up levees. The organization of this work fell to local administrators like Shamash-hazir.

In many of the letters to Shamash-hazir, Hammurabi reminded him to hold on to, or to consult, existing records—there is a lot of mention of "tablets" and "reports." Shamash-hazir's physical office hasn't been excavated, but it must have included rooms full of documents that he could consult if disputes arose. The tablets may have been organized by date, with inscribed clay labels identifying the contents of shelves or boxes to help the administrator find the documents he needed. Such labels have been found at a number of sites.

For many people complaining about field allocations, Shamash-hazir also had the job of deciding who was in the right. He had to "investigate their cases and render them a final verdict."[47] This involved consulting records and talking with witnesses and landowners. At least once, Hammurabi summoned Shamash-hazir to come to see him and told him to bring tablets with him so as to account for his activities.[48] One wonders how the tablets were transported safely so that they were easily accessed and didn't break. Perhaps they were placed in boxes or baskets, each devoted to a particular case or period of time, and probably they were wrapped so that they didn't bump up against one another. Land allocations and disputes were probably managed in a similar way in other Old Babylonian kingdoms, by men with similar positions to that of Shamash-hazir, but his is the most extensive archive that survives.[49]

As though Shamash-hazir didn't have enough to do, he was also responsible for overseeing the shearing of sheep owned by the palace in Larsa. This was no small affair. It took place in the month that corresponds to our late December and early January, and must have involved tens of thousands of sheep. Shamash-hazir's superior, Sin-idinnam, hired 1,000 workers for the job on one occasion. "Shearing" is actually a misnomer. The Akkadian term was "plucking." Before the end of the Bronze Age, domestic sheep did not continuously grow wool, and the wool could be combed or plucked when their coats shed in the spring.[50] The vast piles of plucked wool were stored in a dedicated building, known as the "plucking house," ready to be transformed into thread and then cloth.

Even though we've repeatedly come back to the importance of textiles to the Mesopotamian economy, it's a little hard to imagine the actual logistics of managing the herds of sheep and goats. Maintaining the health of the animals was just as important, to Mesopotamians, as farming their fields. The growing of wheat, barley, and dates is easier to follow in the records, with all its attendant worries about the seasonal agricultural cycle, irrigation canals, crop yields, orchard management, and so on, but the enormous numbers of sheep and goats would have been a very visible feature of the ancient landscape, as they grazed in the steppe lands just beyond the fields and regularly were herded together for plucking. Those textiles that the Assyrian merchants profited from in Anatolia remained central to the Mesopotamian economy throughout ancient times. In a way, sheep and goats were the ideal commodity. They ate grasses in areas that were too dry for cultivation, sheep provided vast amounts of wool and goats provided milk, and they reproduced themselves with minimal intervention.

Herds of goats and sheep made up a significant amount of the wealth of just about every temple and palace, and a "shepherd" of the royal herd was not the rustic, simple figure that might come to mind. Chief shepherds were required to keep accounts of their own activities and of the animals, to keep track of all the products that derived from the herds (such as milk, wool, skins, and lambs), and even to compensate the king if the expected quantities of goods were not forthcoming.[51] When an animal died, a knacker was brought in to make sure that the carcass didn't go to waste—the skin, wool, and even the tendons were removed and sold.[52] The shepherd had to account for this to the king as well.

In return, the king was attentive to the needs of the shepherds. In one letter to Shamash-hazir and some others, Hammurabi wrote, "(As for) the herdsmen of the cattle and the sheep and goats . . . two-thirds of those herdsmen have been holding a field for a long time; one third of them do not hold a field." The herdsmen who "held a field" had already been given land with which to support their families, by the palace. The others had not. Given that herdsmen needed to be with their flocks, they presumably hired tenant farmers to cultivate the land for them. This was common. Hammurabi continued his letter, reminding Shamash-hazir that he had written to him about this before and giving him additional guidelines:

> When I instructed you, I told you to give fields to the herdsmen who do not hold fields. As I have instructed you, you shall not oust the herdsmen who have held fields for a long time from their fields; give fields to the herdsmen who do not hold fields, according to the proportion that has been told you. There shall be no one among the herdsmen of the cattle and the sheep and goats to inform me that no field has been given to him.[53]

Hammurabi didn't want to hear any complaints about this; Shamash-hazir had to find land to support all the herdsmen.

Curiously, after the plucking of the king's sheep had taken place, Hammurabi wasn't interested in using all the wool that the sheep produced. Some of it was certainly transferred to palace textile workshops, perhaps in Babylon, but also perhaps in Larsa, to be transformed by palace spinners, dyers, and weavers into textiles for the king and his court. But the sheep produced much more wool than the palace needed. Now that many state employees were paid in land, rather than in food and wool, the rest of the wool from the palace herds could be sold, with the proceeds sent on to Babylon. Shep-Sin, the overseer of the merchants, got involved here as well, just as he did in the conversion of taxes from commodities to barley and silver. He sold much of the wool from the palace sheep to private individuals who processed it themselves, and some of whom were no doubt involved in the kind of long-distance trade that took the Assyrian merchants to Anatolia. Shep-Sin had to send a fixed amount of silver to the palace from the sale of the wool, but again he could profit nicely from this, keeping the amount that he received that was above what was due to the palace.[54]

Hammurabi seems to have been involved in every detail of the work of Sin-idinnam and Shamash-hazir. His letters to his officials in Larsa were well-informed and thoughtful. He seems to have cared a great deal about the welfare of his subjects and, in many instances, he protected them against the loss of their land or livelihood. He constantly asked for reports and had his officials send people to him in Babylon if his direct intervention was needed. Only a tiny fraction of his correspondence survives. Presumably he also wrote to officials in other provinces right across the empire, and one suspects that he cared about what happened in all of them. He seems to have been deeply involved in matters throughout his empire, not just with regard to year-name-worthy achievements like building city walls and defeating enemies, but even with regard to intricate details of the allocation of individual fields and the care of the palace herds. In return, he received vast amounts of wealth in taxes and rents on palace-owned land and his empire thrived.

Hammurabi's Laws

Toward the end of his long life, Hammurabi decided to put out a proclamation that would be posted in public, on big stone stelas. One of them has survived intact and is now in the Louvre Museum in Paris. It's the one I described at the start of this chapter: seven feet tall, a polished block of basalt, with a relief sculpture of Hammurabi at the top, receiving his right to rule from the sun god Shamash (Fig. 11.1).[55] We know this stela best for the hundreds of laws that are preserved on it—this is the so-called "Code of Hammurabi"—though the laws do not make up the whole text.[56]

The inscription was written in a very archaic script, as though someone today were to use the font from the Guttenberg Bible, and the text runs in columns that were read from top to bottom, not in lines read from left to right as was normal in his time. Perhaps this lent a certain gravitas to the monument. The first five of the fifty-one columns of text laid out Hammurabi's right to rule and his achievements. This section is known to us as the Prologue (comparable to the prologue to Ur-Namma's earlier laws) and it translates into English as three very long sentences. In the longest, exhausting, middle sentence, Hammurabi emphasized his generosity and piety, and he did so over and over again. He named many of the cities he now ruled and noted how he had helped each one. He was one who "heaps abundance and plenty" for Nippur, the "enricher of the city of Ur," who "shows mercy to the city of Larsa,"[57] and so on. He reminded readers of his military victories, proclaiming himself to be a "peerless warrior," and, more floridly, "the enemy-ensnaring throw-net" and "the fierce wild bull who gores the enemy." But mostly Hammurabi presented himself as an all-around good guy, a "shepherd of the people," "the protecting canopy of the land," "the judicious one," and "the pious one."[58] He ended the Prologue with the raison d'être for the laws (which comprises by far the shortest of the three sentences): "When the god Marduk commanded me to provide just ways for the people of the land (in order to attain) appropriate behavior, I established truth and justice as the declaration of the land, I enhanced the well-being of the people."[59] It was all, he said, for the people, it was all about being appropriate and truthful, and it was all done at the command of Marduk, the great god of Babylon. And then Hammurabi launched into almost 300 laws that covered many obscure circumstances of everyday life but, it must be said, failed to address some huge issues, such as what the penalty should be for murder.

The laws paint little pictures—you can imagine the court cases that generated them, hiding behind the words. Look at law 266, for example: "If, in the enclosure, an epidemic should break out or a lion make a kill, the shepherd shall clear himself before the god, and the owner of the enclosure shall accept responsibility for him for the loss sustained in the enclosure."[60] This must have happened, perhaps not often, but enough to warrant the law's inclusion in the list. A shepherd woke up and found a sheep or goat dead in the enclosure where the herd was being kept, killed by a disease. Or perhaps several animals were dead. Or perhaps it was not a disease, and the shepherd was awake when the animal died but powerless in the face of a lion who might just as easily kill the shepherd himself. He was alone, without witnesses. You remember how the shepherds who answered to Shamash-hazir had to keep track of every animal in their care and even to detail the use of every part of an animal carcass. Was this shepherd responsible for the loss? These were not his own animals and he had not been negligent. It would have been a scary moment. How could he prove his innocence? Would he have to pay for the loss? That could have been financially devastating. But the gods knew the truth. So the shepherd went to the temple and swore an oath before a god's symbol about what had happened, and that was enough. He, like everyone else, would never have sworn a false oath. The owner of the enclosure had to absorb the loss.

You can read almost any of the laws this way, envisioning, with little effort, the scenario behind it. As in the time of Ur-Namma, there is little evidence, in records of court cases, for the laws actually being consulted by judges or of the harsher punishments ever being imposed. We don't even know how the basic death penalty was carried out in Mesopotamia at this time. When a law pronounced the verdict that "he shall be killed," what did that mean? Was the guilty person hanged? Bashed in the head with a mace? The laws only elaborate if the death penalty was specifically designed to match the crime, but the normal death penalty was never specified. The laws were still probably drawn up from legal precedents; judges were under no obligation to follow them, and they seem to have avoided imposing the death penalty except in the case of truly egregious crimes. The judicial system worked in the same way that it had during the Ur III period, largely independent of the written law. But the laws do reveal wonderful details about daily life because they reflect the concerns that led people to go to court.

A whole group of the laws concerns the type of men for whom Shamash-hazir found land—soldiers called up for military service and rewarded with *ilkum* property. Since just about every able-bodied man in the land was subject to military service or corvée labor service, or both, the rules about the *ilkum* were important to a great many families.[61]

Mashum: Soldier

In order to look at how the laws reflected real dilemmas, let's take as an example a soldier who was mentioned in two of Hammurabi's letters to Shamash-hazir: Mashum. He was one of three soldiers who received an allocation of a field of 2 *bur* from the king, a field that had been part of a much larger estate belonging to another man.[62] His allocation was equivalent to about 32 acres.[63] A sergeant named in the same letter received twice as much, and a captain four times as much. Frankly, we know nothing else that was specific to Mashum; his name only appears in the two letters to Shamash-hazir, both discussing the same land provision.[64]

Like all soldiers, Mashum had an obligation to fight for the king in exchange for the land that he and his family were allowed to work.

Hammurabi's laws were strict about this *ilkum* obligation: Mashum couldn't back out of it, nor could he hire someone to go in his place. The law was categorical; it proclaimed that if he hired a replacement, he "shall be killed; the one who informs against him shall take full legal possession of his estate."[65] Mashum also couldn't sell the field; after all, it wasn't his to sell.[66]

He was, though, protected from being abused by his superiors, or at least that was the ideal (if the laws were followed). One law specified that captains and sergeants were not allowed, on pain of death, no less, to "take a soldier's household furnishings, oppress a soldier, hire out a soldier, deliver a soldier into the power of an influential person in a law case, or take a gift that the king gave to a soldier."[67] Hammurabi might have been tough in his demands of his troops, but he was on their side when it came to possible abuses by their commanding officers (though, admittedly, I know of no actual court cases in which a penalty like this was imposed).

For most of the year Mashum would have been at the farm that Shamash-hazir had allotted to him, working the land with his family, maintaining the small canals that provided water, feeding themselves from the barley grown in the fields, the dates from the orchard, and the vegetables from the garden, and paying taxes on what they produced. But for some specified number of months of the year, Mashum had to go off on campaign for the king. This was, of course, a dangerous undertaking and he was at risk; he could die, or he could be taken prisoner. Oddly, Hammurabi doesn't specify in the laws who would take over the use of the land if a soldier like Mashum died on campaign. Would his wife and children be evicted? Where would they go? We don't know. It's one of the countless situations about which the king had nothing to say in the laws. But Hammurabi did make an allowance for a soldier being caught and imprisoned by the enemy: in this case, the soldier's son could take over his *ilkum* land, but only if the son were old enough. (If so, Mashum's son would have to fulfill his father's military obligation as well.)[68]

Suppose, though, that Mashum was a relatively young man when he was captured and that his son was still a child. Mashum's wife would have been in a terrible situation. She was living on a farm that was only hers to work because of her husband's *ilkum*, but her husband was now a prisoner in some distant place, and she had young children to support. Hammurabi had thought of this: "If his son is too young and is unable to perform his father's *ilkum*, one third of the field and orchard shall be given to his mother, and his mother shall raise him."[69] One third of the original field wasn't much, but it was enough to keep the family fed. The woman would have worked the land and tended the orchard herself, perhaps with help from relatives and hired laborers, as she waited anxiously for word of her husband, their young son anticipating having to take over his father's responsibilities as soon as he was old enough.

And what of Mashum, imprisoned, as we have imagined him, in a land that was an enemy of Babylon? Surprisingly, this was a common enough occurrence that a mechanism existed for his return. He would be ransomed. This seems to have been a given, to such an extent that it might have been more lucrative to the enemy to capture soldiers on the battlefield than to kill them. Hammurabi describes the process: "a merchant redeems him and helps him to get back to his city."[70] That was the first step. Merchants, in this era, were pretty much everywhere. They had the money to pay a ransom, spoke the local languages, and knew the local customs. But, of course, they wouldn't have paid the ransom as a charitable gesture. Someone had to pay them back. According to the laws, a wealthy soldier had to pay the merchant back for the ransom with his own funds. But there was a kind of insurance for the poorer soldiers. "If there are not sufficient means in his estate to redeem him, he shall be redeemed by his city's temple."[71]

Temples were rich institutions, and most could afford this expense on behalf of their local soldiers. But apparently this was not true of all. "If there are not sufficient means in his city's temple to redeem him, the palace shall redeem him."[72] One wonders if there were times when the priests or priestesses thought that the king should pay the ransoms, even if their temple had enough money on hand; it wasn't the temple that had led the troops off on campaign, after all. But one way or another, a captured soldier like Mashum would get home and his ransom would be paid. There was just one proviso at the end of this law about ransoms: "his field, orchard, or house will not be given for his redemption."[73] Those still belonged to the king and they couldn't be sold or traded or given away by the *ilkum* holder to anyone else, ever.

These insights into the lives of Mashum and soldiers like him come from just a handful of laws. It doesn't really matter whether or not the laws were actually enforced to the letter. For example, it appears that the death penalty for hiring a substitute was a fiction, entirely an attempt at a deterrent; soldiers recruited substitutes to serve in their place all the time and could get permission to do so.[74] Instead, the laws show us some of the basic features of their lives and the ways in which Hammurabi wished to make the system run smoothly. The laws do the same for innumerable other aspects of ancient life, providing us with a vivid sense of what people cared about, what regularly went wrong, and how the judicial system was designed to help.

They even show that poor people were treated differently from rich people, but generally not in the cruel way that many people assume.[75] The poor were not necessarily treated more harshly than the rich. For example, the actual *lex talionis* laws are as follows:

If an *awilum* should blind the eye of another *awilum*, they shall blind his eye.
If he should break the bone of another *awilum*, they shall break his bone.
If he should blind the eye of a commoner or break the bone of a commoner, he shall weigh and deliver 60 shekels of silver.[76]

The term "*awilum*" meant a "gentleman" in the sense of a person of some means (though not necessarily a rich man). The only laws about these particular types of injury concern situations where the perpetrator was an *awilum*. So, clearly, the upper classes were not above the law. And the "eye-for-an-eye" rule here, had it been applied equally, would hardly be kind to a poor person. In that case, a poor man who had been blinded in one eye by a richer man would get nothing from the courts but the satisfaction that his attacker had suffered the same fate. The laws, instead, fined his attacker 60 shekels of silver. This was equivalent to 10,800 barleycorns of silver. According to the law 274, a textile worker earned 5 barleycorns of silver a day.[77] Sixty shekels of silver therefore represented 2,160 days' pay for a textile worker—almost six years. So no doubt the poor man would much prefer to receive six years' salary than to know that the man who attacked him was now blind in one eye.

In a similar spirit, Hammurabi ruled that physicians should charge their patients for treatment on a sliding scale depending on wealth. An *awilum* was charged 5 shekels to have a broken bone fixed, whereas a commoner had to pay only 3 shekels for exactly the same procedure.[78] This is hardly a system that was baldly weighted in favor of the wealthy. It was, however, weighted against enslaved men and women, who were valued less than commoners and *awilum*s. But even they had some protections, including in situations in which a slave man married an *awilum*-class woman.[79] Classes were not set in stone; people could marry outside their social class. They could even slip from *awilum* to commoner or from *awilum* to slave if life was tough—especially if they got into serious debt.

These kinds of details are what really make Hammurabi's laws so valuable to us. It's not that they were written particularly early, or that they were particularly brutal (for the time, they weren't at all), or that they reflect some sort of rigid class structure, or that they were an important part of the legal system. They don't even constitute a code of law, strictly speaking. There are way too many holes, way too many crimes and legal dilemmas that are simply not addressed. Like Ur-Namma before him, Hammurabi did not aim for the list to be comprehensive.

Hammurabi's laws are just really well preserved, there are a lot of them, and they tell us a great deal about how society and the legal system worked. Like us, later Mesopotamian scribes thought the laws were useful to study. Sections of Hammurabi's laws have been found among school texts from subsequent centuries, though, for once, we can also see the original stela— we are not dependent on those later copies made by scribal students. More than a thousand years after they were first written, a copy of the laws was kept by an Assyrian king named Ashurbanipal in his palace library. We will return to him later.

After forty-two columns of laws about marriage and divorce, inheritance, adoption, trade, land usage, irrigation, professional responsibilities, the hire of men and animals, and an attempt at price and wage controls, along with a relatively small number of laws about premeditated crimes such as theft, rape, and perjury, Hammurabi added an epilogue. In it, he claimed that "I enhanced the well-being of the land. I made the people of all settlements lie in safe pastures. I did not tolerate anyone intimidating them. . . . I held the people of the lands of Sumer and Akkad safely on my lap. They prospered under my protective spirit." He wrote also that he promulgated his laws "in order that the mighty not wrong the weak, to provide just ways for the waif and the widow."[80] The letters he wrote to men like Shamash-hazir show that this wasn't just propaganda. Hammurabi lived up to his promise, watching out for people who might otherwise have fallen victim to the system because they were not important or powerful.

Chapter 12
*Naditum*s and Scribal Students

It's a curious fact that many private houses in the Old Babylonian period, even ones that weren't functioning as small schools, included the archives of the families who lived in them.[1] During the Ur III period and earlier, cuneiform tablets were almost always found in institutional buildings, where they had been written and stored by scribes who worked for the relevant palace or temple. The average person in those earlier eras had little contact with, or even need for, the written word—cuneiform was used almost exclusively by the religious and political administrations.[2] But, starting in the Isin-Larsa period, something very different was happening. Writing began to be useful, and to be used, by people throughout many levels of the society.[3] This was part of the larger phenomenon that we have already seen for this era—the privatization of much of the economy and the loss of centralized control over some people's lives on the part of the palace. Families of merchants from Ashur could trade in Anatolia without their activities being commissioned, or even overseen, by the king. Individuals (at least in some parts of Mesopotamia) could buy and sell land and houses. People could take one another to court. All these actions required some sort of record-keeping, so it became valuable to be able to read and write. And with all of this activity, people traveled more, and found more of a need to keep in touch with one another over long distances. For this, a written letter was much more reliable than an oral message. Again, writing filled a need that hadn't really existed before for many people. The personal archives found in private homes often included letters and contracts relating to the family's activities, and sometimes they also included scribal exercises— evidence that some member of the family went to school. As a result, many aspects of daily life are well understood in this era, particularly in the cities of Sippar and Nippur.

The City of Sippar

During the reign of Hammurabi, Sippar played an integral role in the kingdom. It was actually made up of two cities—Sippar-Yahrurum (the main city) and Sippar-Amnanum (the suburb)—6 kilometers (3.7 miles) apart from one another and just 60 kilometers (37 miles) north of Babylon.[4] The main city (which I will refer to as just Sippar) was home to the god of wisdom, Shamash, the sun god himself. Shamash's temple, the Ebabbar (meaning the White Temple), would have been one of the biggest buildings in Mesopotamia, dominating the southwestern side of the rectangular city. The sacred temenos area around the temple of Shamash was immense—8.3 hectares (20.5 acres) in extent. It occupied about a tenth of the city.[5] Sippar was surrounded by a high wall with a canal beyond it.

Sippar, like Ashur at around the same time, had a special trading relationship with a distant land. In their case it was with the city of Susa, to the east of Mesopotamia. The evidence for this trade isn't anything like as vast or detailed as we saw with the Assyrian colony at Kanesh, but that is perhaps because the trading quarter at Susa hasn't been found, or because it didn't burn down and thereby preserve the documentation. Tablets found at Sippar mention traders who traveled directly to Susa, such as a man named Iddin-Amurru, who went to Susa for repayment of a loan that he'd obtained there.[6] And, in turn, one group of tablets found in Susa is full of the Akkadian names of expatriate Sipparians, but they mention almost no local people with Elamite names.[7] The oaths on these contracts are made in the names of Shamash, the god of their Akkadian home city, and Inshushinak, the local god of Susa. Clearly Susa was under local rule, but was home to a community of men and women from Sippar, who had probably settled there to benefit from trade. The Sipparians, not the people of Susa, seem to have been in control of this trade.

Hammurabi himself devoted plenty of attention to embellishing Sippar and glorifying Shamash. In his fifteenth year, according to the name of that year, Hammurabi "made seven statues in copper for Shamash in the temple Ebabbar."[8] In his twenty-third year he laid the foundations of the city wall of Sippar. Construction on the city wall must have gone on for two years, ending in his twenty-fifth year when he boasted that it was done; Hammurabi had "rebuilt the destroyed great city wall of Sippar for (the gods) Shamash and Sherida." The very next year, Shamash received a great throne in reddish gold from Hammurabi (as did the gods Adad and Sherida). After eighteen year-names that mostly commemorated military victories, Hammurabi was back in Sippar late in his reign, in his forty-third year, working again on the city wall. He "made the wall of Sippar, the eternal city of Shamash, out of great masses of earth." This preoccupation with the city wall of Sippar is even seen in one of his royal inscriptions: "At that time, in order to increase (the amount of) food, I piled up a dike in the irrigation districts, built the wall of the *gagum* upon it, dug there the canal Aya-ḥegal and poured abundant water in it."[9]

Naditums in Sippar

In this last inscription he wasn't writing about the entire city wall; he was focused on one part it, "the wall of the *gagum*." The *gagum* is a fascinating phenomenon, something unique to the Old Babylonian period. It was an integral part of the city of Sippar, a sector of the city near the Ebabbar temple. There were *gagum*s in several cities in the kingdom of Babylon at the time, almost like the slightly earlier *karum*s (trading quarters) of Assyrian merchants in Anatolia. Like the *karum*s, they were places of great economic activity, with their own officials. The "house of the *gagum*" stood somewhere in this quarter of the city, housing its administration. We know from private documents that the people living and working in this sector, known as *naditum*s, bought fields, orchards, and houses, leased land to tenants, and lent silver at interest. Their activity was essential to the economic prosperity of Sippar as a whole. The *naditum*s were formally devoted to the god Shamash, but the wealth that they accumulated did not become the property of the temple; the *naditum*s owned their own wealth, which they were able to pass down to their successors or transfer to their families. One might expect these *naditum*s to have been powerful men, not unlike the merchants in the Old Assyrian trade network. But the *naditum*s were all women.

Plenty of cuneiform tablets survive that attest to their activities, especially letters, contracts, and administrative texts. They show that the *naditum*s had been born into rich and powerful families and they were not allowed to marry or to bring up biological children (though they could adopt). These women were sent to the *gagum* at a young age by their fathers or guardians to serve a religious purpose, namely, to pray to Shamash for the welfare of their families. In their correspondence with family members and others the women made pious statements and included prayers, reflecting their religious devotion to Shamash and his divine wife Aya. (Erishti-Aya, a *naditum* and princess of Mari, wrote in a letter to Zimri-Lim that she saw herself as "the praying emblem who prays constantly for her father's life.")[10] The women spent their whole lives as members of the *gagum*, supported by wealth provided by their fathers and brothers. But they were not just pious religious functionaries. The *naditum*s were also expert businesswomen who worked for the temple, for themselves, and for their families.

Unfortunately, the first excavations at Sippar, when most of the *naditum* documents were recovered, took place early in the history of archaeology, starting in the 1880s. They were led by Hormuzd Rassam, an Iraqi archaeologist working for the British Museum.[11] This was the time of large scale, fast digging, when little attention was paid to the details in the ground; when a team of hundreds of local workmen "attacked all the points of the city," in the words of an archaeologist at Sippar, and few records were kept of where they dug or what was found.[12] It's not surprising therefore that, although between 70,000 and 80,000 cuneiform tablets were recovered from the site,[13] we have almost no idea where they were found. Many of them, in fact, were purchased at the time from local people who had dug them up, so even the archaeologists may not have known where they came from.

This means that we can learn much less about the workings of the *gagum* than would have been true if the tablets' archaeological context had been recorded. Had those tablets been excavated today, it would be possible to know whether individual *naditum*s kept their own records in their houses, or whether a collective archive was kept in the administrative building, and how that archive was organized. Fortunately, more recent excavations at Sippar, organized by the University of Baghdad since 1978, have recovered around 200 tablets and fragments from this same period, and many of them mention women, some of whom were clearly *naditum*s and other religious functionaries (and others may well have been, even though they lack the title). These were all found in private houses, which shows that the *naditum*s could store their records in their homes.[14] A temple or administration building archive is still, of course, a possibility as a source of the earlier documents— no temple or public building was excavated in the recent campaigns.

We know from the ancient contracts that the houses owned by the naditums were mostly tiny—42 percent of them were smaller than 1 SAR, which was 36 square meters (387 square feet), and an additional 17.7 percent of them were smaller than 2 SAR or 72 square meters (774 square feet).[15] A woman who inherited a "house" of one-third of a SAR, or 12 square meters (129 square feet)—and this was not an uncommon bequest— was presumably inheriting just a room of about 3 by 4 meters in a larger building. It would be fascinating to see how these houses were structured.

Previous generations of historians often thought of the naditums as ancient nuns and (based in part on the tiny houses they owned) envisioned them living in cells in a cloister, isolated from the rest of the city. But in some of the contracts, the naditums' houses were described as being located on streets, next to neighboring houses owned by other people who were not naditums. Besides which, the naditums were homeowners, not tenants.

Some of houses owned by naditums even adjoined taverns, which in turn were also owned by naditums. This fact clashes with one of Hammurabi's laws, which has often been cited to suggest that the naditums had to live such moral lives that they couldn't even enter a bar (let alone own one) without being put to death. The law states: "If a naditum or an ugbabtum (another type of religious woman) who does not reside within the gagum should open (the door to?) a tavern or enter a tavern for some beer, they shall burn that woman."[16]

As it turns out, naditums owned many taverns mentioned in the Sippar texts.[17] The thing is that these owners were all naditums who lived in the gagum and were part of its administrative structure. Remember that Hammurabi's law specifies that it was only naditums who did not live in the gagum who would be punished for opening or entering a tavern. Perhaps the law had nothing to do with imposing moral purity on naditums, but instead was designed to protect the naditums who were business owners and perhaps to maintain the gagum's possible monopoly on tavern ownership.[18]

The Iraqi excavations at Sippar in the 1980s revealed a collection of houses that look as though they might be part of the gagum.[19] They were northwest of the Shamash temple, lined up along narrow streets (see Fig. 12.1). The neighborhood dates to the same period as the naditum documents—the early to mid-second millennium BCE—and seems to have been planned, with streets that were carefully laid out and that ran parallel to one another. Along each street, completely filling the space between them, stood dense

Fig. 12.1 Plan of an excavated neighborhood in Sippar, area V 108, showing a street with a row of very small two-room houses that might have belonged to *naditum*s, mid-eighteenth century BCE (based on Al-Rawi and Dalley 2000, iv, Fig. 4).

blocks of small houses, most of them with just two rooms, packed together, and often sharing thick walls. Many of the houses are of exactly the same plan. A door in the front wall of the house opened into the left-hand side of the tiny main room, which measured just three by two meters. A door on the right-hand side of the facing wall in this room led to an even smaller room at the back of the house, also three meters wide, but just about one meter deep. Given that the latter room always shared a back wall with a house on the next street, the back rooms probably had no windows. These structures are closer to the scale of cells than houses, much too small for a family, and yet they seem to have been lived in.[20] Nothing like these houses is known from elsewhere in Mesopotamia—not only are they so small and regular, they do not even have burials under their floors.[21]

All this makes sense if they were *gagum* homes. A single *naditum*, living alone, might have found such a small house perhaps cramped, but not unlivable. The neighborhood would have been full of women, all of them devoted to the sun god. We know that many of the *naditum*s also owned houses in Sippar in other neighborhoods outside the *gagum*; perhaps they didn't live in their *gagum* rooms all the time and often enjoyed the more spacious quarters of their second homes. The *naditum*s were buried in a cemetery, which also explains the lack of burials under the houses.

About fourteen tablets from the excavations in the 1980s clearly seem to have come from this neighborhood of tiny houses.[22] Eight of them pertained to the activities of women, including three letters apparently written by or to women,[23] a silver payment by a woman,[24] a loan payment by a woman,[25] two loans taken by women,[26] and a note recording dates delivered to a woman.[27] The contracts among these documents were witnessed almost entirely by women, and many of the female names were the ones typical of *naditum*s. So, it's tempting to see this neighborhood as part of the *gagum*.

And yet . . . six of the documents in this group of excavation numbers have nothing at all to do with women, including two that were categorically found there.[28] One of these was found in the front room of one of the two-room houses that just cry out to be identified as the quarters of *naditum*s.[29] It records two men taking a loan of barley from another man, and every witness was a man. Not a *naditum* in sight. If this area was the *gagum*, and these small houses were home to *naditum*s, why would they be keeping records like this?

Curiously, other documents found during the excavations in the 1980s and pertaining to *naditum*s were found in another neighborhood altogether, one marked by spacious houses and much less urban planning.[30] Here too, the *naditum*s do not seem to have been separated from other people; they lived and worked with their brothers and other family members, their archives intermingled.[31] It seems that both neighborhoods were within the *gagum* and that it was far from being a monastic institution of secluded women. *Naditum*s lived among people (men and women) who were not *naditum*s.[32]

Another recent realization is that the physical *gagum*—the houses and other properties belonging to the *naditum*s—was overseen by an institution that was also known as the *gagum*. Just as the physical market or "*karum*" in Kanesh also had an administrative structure with the same name, so too did the *gagum*. The highest position in its administration was the "overseer of the *naditum*s." This official, in the time of the kings before Hammurabi, was generally a woman.[33] Later, men took over the position. Men also, at all times, held all the other administrative positions in the *gagum*: the keeper of the gate of the *gagum*, the scribe of the *naditum*s, the judge of the *naditum*s of the *gagum*, the chief of the workforce of the *gagum*, the messenger of the *gagum*, and so on.[34]

The women living there were not independent of men, clearly. But they had more autonomy than most women in the society, and there is no indication that anyone, male or female, believed them to be incapable of assuming responsibilities and taking initiatives that were generally limited to men, nor that they would be incapable of doing them well. After being initiated as a *naditum*, a woman could and did assume various economic, religious, and legal responsibilities, just as unmarried priestesses had been doing for centuries in Mesopotamia. What was different in the Old Babylonian period was that entire communities of unmarried women lived together and filled these roles. A number of Mesopotamian cities at the time housed a community of *naditum*s, many of them dedicated to the god Marduk, rather than Shamash, but the *gagum* at Sippar is the best known because of the many tablets found there.

At the height of Sippar's prosperity, during the reign of Hammurabi, the *naditum*s were responsible for at least a third of the buying, selling, and leasing of fields and houses in the city. Far from being secluded in a cloister, they interacted with the wider world, made loans, and got rich (that is to say, even richer than they already were, given that they started out with wealth). Having no biological children, they were not tied to the usual premodern woman's cycle of pregnancy, birth, nursing, weaning, and then pregnancy again, and the accompanying demands of taking care of many small children. They come across in the records as women who took advantage of this freedom with a vengeance.[35] The *gagum* may even have been involved in the long-distance trade with Susa, helping to fund and organize this lucrative business.[36] *Naditum*s appear in legal texts—contracts and court cases. They were quite prepared to take people to court if they had been wronged, and to assemble witnesses in support of their claims.

The life of a *naditum* was, however, constrained in many ways, in spite of her relative autonomy. Most importantly, a woman did not have a choice whether or not to become a *naditum*. That decision was made by her father before she even reached adolescence.

It's a bit of a puzzle how the institution got started in the first place. Why would a rich father (*naditum*s were almost all from wealthy and powerful families) choose one of his young daughters and send her off to a *gagum* to live there for the rest of her life? It wasn't a cheap option; he had to provide her with a considerable dowry, equivalent to the inheritance he would provide for one of his sons. And, unlike an inheritance, the father had to provide it to her before he died. One *naditum* named Shat-Aya was given a vast amount of wealth as her dowry when she became a *naditum*. It included real estate (five fields, an orchard with a tower, a large house, a tavern, and several shops on the main street of Sippar), along with metals (4.5 kilograms or 10 pounds of silver and 9 kilograms or 20 pounds of copper), animals (oxen, cows, and sheep), household items, and twenty slaves.[37] The reason for the decision to dedicate her to a life in the *gagum* must have been partly what the Mesopotamians of the time said it was—to have a family representative cultivate a close relationship with the sun god who would then watch out for them all. We should never underestimate how deeply the Mesopotamians believed in the power of their gods and how much they longed for ways to influence them. The *naditum* was a living, breathing version of the Early Dynastic statues set up in temples to pray for the life and health of the family of the man or woman they represented.

But a father's decision to place his daughter in a *gagum* may have been pragmatic as well as pious. Elite women faced few options in terms of their marriage prospects. They rarely married beneath their rank or outside their perceived group. If an appropriate husband could not be found, a daughter could be devoted to a god and the family would not only have saved face; they would have benefited.[38]

Many *naditum*s had a reputation for successfully managing and increasing their families' wealth. After the death of a *naditum*, her dowry (along with any additional wealth she had managed to accrue through leasing fields, lending silver, or hiring out slaves) could revert to her brothers. This seemed to have been a good investment strategy. The dowry given to a non-*naditum* woman when she married, in contrast, left her father's family and was controlled by her husband. She was still the owner of her dowry and it was passed on to her children, but it no longer contributed to the wealth of her father or brothers. The fact that many *naditum*s came from families that sent several girls to the *gagum*, generation after generation, suggests that it was considered a wise decision, whether economically or religiously, or both.

Awat-Aya: Initiate *Naditum*

In any event, whatever the reason a girl was chosen, her dowry was put together and the day came for her to enter the *gagum*. This took place during a three-day festival, the "*sebut shattim*," which was celebrated in honor of Shamash every December or January. As many as 300 women are known to have lived in the *gagum* at Sippar during the reign of Hammurabi,[39] so perhaps quite a few girls participated in the initiation each year.

One girl who went through this was named Awat-Aya.[40] The *gagum* kept an account of the expenses involved in her induction, and that record survives and gives us a sense of what the experience might have been like.[41]

The participants seem to have thought of the initiation as a type of wedding, but one in which a girl such as Awat-Aya was to spiritually marry the sun god. After all, she brought a dowry with her, and there was no human groom involved, just Shamash.

As in a normal wedding, the wealth didn't flow just one way; the administrator of the *gagum* also provided a present for the girl's father. In Awat-Aya's case, her father had died before her induction as a *naditum*, so the gift was made from the *gagum* to her eldest brother, Mar-ersetim. The tablet lists what he was given: "3 . . . vessels, 2 fish, 1 . . . bowl of 1 sila capacity," with their value helpfully added: they were equivalent to half a shekel of silver. This was all, says the text, "when the young girl entered the *gagum*." Her brother also received "1 shekel of silver [and] a belt."[42] The administrator of the *gagum* provided a gift to the initiate Awat-Aya herself at this time, "a shekel of silver for two rings." The list went on and concluded with a statement that the whole gift was worth "altogether 4 3/5 shekels, 25 grains of silver." Tellingly, this gift is called a "*biblum*," which was the term for a betrothal gift. Awat-Aya was engaged, but not to a human man.

Even the Sumerian equivalent of the Akkadian term "*naditum*" confirms this analogy. In Sumerian, she was called a "*lukur*" of Shamash, which was also the term for a man's second wife. The god's first wife was the goddess Aya. The initiate became, in a way, one of Shamash's second wives. There was no vow of chastity involved; *naditum*s couldn't marry human men or raise biological children, but nothing has been found in writing that insists on their chastity. On the other hand, nothing has also been found to suggest that they engaged in prostitution, or in any kind of "sacred marriage" ritual with a man representing the god.

The three-day initiation event seems to have been a happy celebration, one that was enjoyed and remembered fondly by the girls who were being inducted. The "thread of Shamash" was placed on a girl's arm; this distinguished her from her friends and relatives—it was clearly an honor to receive it.[43] More remarkable yet, the inductees were brought into the presence of the gods themselves, probably at the very heart of the Ebabbar temple. No civilian would be allowed this privilege. The statues of Shamash and Aya were probably made of precious metals, wearing exquisite clothes, each placed high on a dais and seated on a throne. They must have shone in the lamp light in the holy sanctuary, which would have had little in the way of windows. One *naditum* remembered this moment fondly. She wrote to a friend that "When I saw you, I was delighted by your arrival . . . just as I was when I entered the *gagum* and got to see the face of my mistress (the goddess)."[44]

Some of the girls took on a new name at this point, one that was appropriate to their role as devotees of the sun god. Amat-Aya's name was a popular one. It meant "servant girl of (the goddess) Aya." More than a hundred *naditum*s at Sippar, for example, are known to have been named Amat-Shamash ("servant girl of Shamash"). Erishti-Shamash was another popular choice ("request from Shamash"), and many other names honored Aya, the divine wife of Shamash.[45]

Over the course of the three days of the *sebut shattim* celebration, food was allocated and carefully listed on the tablet concerning Awat-Aya's initiation. The meals included meat (such as from the "neck tendons of an ox" and "a shoulder of a sheep"), fish, and flour, and the lists include various vessels that must have held oil. On the third and last day there was "1/3 shekel for beer which the young girls drank." Each time, the meticulous *gagum* scribe noted not only what food had been distributed but exactly how much it was all worth in silver.

On the second day, the initiates participated in the "memorial day of the *naditum*s" when they seem to have gone to the cemetery to perform rites for the women who had come before them. Normally, family members performed such ancestral rites; for the new *naditum*s, this memorial day provided them with the assurance that, even though they would never have biological children, their new family of religious women would be there for them throughout their lives and even after death.⁴⁶

It's unclear how the initiates spent their first years. Strikingly absent from the dowry we know about, that of Shat-Aya, was a house in the *gagum* itself, though she must have had a place to live there. No doubt most of the girls were, in a way, joining a branch of their family that was already established in the *gagum*. Many of them probably had an aunt who was already a *naditum* and with whom they could live until they acquired their own rooms or houses.

The girls apprenticed with the older *naditum*s, who presumably helped them manage their dowry properties. Many, if not most, of the girls learned to read and write. Quite a few of their records don't list a scribe because they were clearly written by a *naditum* herself and she didn't need to hire a scribe. Indeed, some legal texts specifically mention a *naditum* who could write tablets. Other records do credit a scribe and that scribe was sometimes a woman.⁴⁷

A woman named Humta-Adad, who lived in a house in Sippar that was excavated during the 1980s, may have been a teacher of female scribes. She wasn't a *naditum*, but she was a priestess, called a *qadishtum*, devoted to the storm god Adad.⁴⁸ Her house was on a corner, with the front door opening onto a broad street. The house was long and narrow, with three rooms in a row, one behind the next.⁴⁹ The back room contained a jar full of cuneiform tablets, including many contracts relating to Humta-Adad's business dealings and those of her brother. Her archive wasn't restricted to contracts, however. Humta-Adad also had kept incantations, a hymn, and— tellingly—school exercise tablets.⁵⁰ She may have taken on female pupils who came to her house to study.

Amat-Shamash: A *Naditum* in Need of Help

The *naditum*s couldn't obtain everything they needed in the *gagum*, and sometimes they had to appeal to their siblings and other family members for support and sometimes for food, in exchange for the prayers that they offered to the gods. A good example is seen in a letter that was found at the site of Tell al-Rimah sent by one of the many women named Amat-Shamash.

This Amat-Shamash, who lived in Sippar, was the sister of Iltani, the queen of a kingdom called Karana, to whom she was writing. She started the letter with a classic blessing used by *naditum*s in their correspondence: "May my Lord (the sun god Shamash) and my Mistress (the goddess Aya) grant you eternal life for my sake!"[51] She continued the letter with a story: Iltani's husband, King Aqba-hammu, had visited Amat-Shamash in Sippar where she "esteemed him highly, as was fitting for my status as a *naditum*, and he too esteemed me especially highly." The king, her brother-in-law, promised to have, in his own words, "anything you need sent to you in a fully laden ship." In exchange he asked her to "Pray for me to your Lord." This was what *naditum*s did, after all—intercede with the sun god Shamash on behalf of their family members. A ship full of supplies was surely a reasonable exchange for that. So she had followed up and had written to king Aqba-hammu, upon which he sent her two servants—not exactly a boat full of supplies, but apparently a good substitute.[52]

To judge from this and other letters, from and to *naditum*s, the prayers that they offered to the gods represented an important part of their duties. They prayed to Shamash for protection of the men in their families, and to Aya, his wife, for protection of the women. There seem to have been sacrifices in the morning and evening at which the *naditum*s prayed; perhaps they were in attendance at the temple regularly for this purpose. Sometimes they even provided lambs for sacrifice.[53]

Ideally, their family members, like Aqba-hammu, appreciated these interventions with the gods and, in a way, paid the *naditum*s for their services by providing them with gifts and food. But some family members were less forthcoming, and this could annoy a *naditum*. In Amat-Shamash's letter, her tone changed as she turned to what she clearly saw as neglect by her sister. Amat-Shamash wanted Iltani to behave more like her husband Aqba-hammu. It turns out that Iltani had never asked Amat-Shamash to offer prayers for her, and (perhaps as a result) had sent Amat-Shamash no gifts. "You never have a jar of good oil sent to me," Amat-Shamash complained, "anything at all."

But be that as it may, she had a more pressing concern and she needed her sister's help. She continued, "the slaves that my father gave me have grown old." Her father had provided these slaves as part of her dowry, but that was now some time ago. She wrote that she had sent a half mina of silver to the king and she wanted him to send her "slaves who have recently been captured and are tough." Iltani would need to intercede with the king on Amat-Shamash's behalf in order to make this request. But Amat-Shamash wasn't asking her sister to do this for nothing; she included with her letter some "first quality white wool for a wig and a basket of shrimps."[54]

There were some things that the *naditum*s could acquire easily; others were only possible with the help of family members. For Amat-Shamash, slaves seem to have fallen into the latter category. Her letter is not unlike any number of Old Babylonian letters written from one sibling to another; a woman needed something that was available in her sibling's city, so she requested it and sent in exchange items that presumably her sibling needed. The difference lies in the fact that one thing a *naditum* could offer in exchange for goods was direct access to the sun god and his divine wife.

*Naditum*s in Old Age

As they grew older, *naditum*s increasingly depended on their nieces who were also *naditum*s, and many chose to adopt a niece as a daughter—or even to adopt more than one niece. These younger women took care of their adopted mothers and helped manage their properties. The *gagum* itself was not an organization concerned with the welfare of its members in their old age (in this, again, they were not like convents); the *naditum*s had to watch out for themselves.

This new relationship of niece as adopted daughter worked nicely for the women involved, but it complicated the whole inheritance situation. An older *naditum*'s brothers and male relatives generally seem to have assumed that her wealth would return to them. But she had the final say in where her inheritance went, and many *naditum*s wrote up wills in which their property would go to their adopted daughter or daughters. (*Naditum*s tended to have longer lives than other members of their family and often outlived their brothers. They seem to have been even less inclined, in their wills, to bequeath their wealth to their nephews.) Quite a few of the *naditum*s' daughters ended up in court, fighting against their adoptive mothers' brothers (one of whom might, of course, be the woman's own biological father) for the right to their property.

A woman without a niece in the *gagum* had another option—she could adopt one of her slaves to take care of her in old age.[55] These were, surprisingly, not just women. Male slaves were also sometimes adopted. They retained their enslaved status, even while becoming the son or daughter of the *naditum*. Unlike the nieces, they didn't inherit much on her death. They did, however, gain their freedom.

Elletum: A Scribal Student in Nippur

Sippar was one of many cities housing *naditum*s during the reign of Hammurabi; another important center for them was in Nippur, home to Enlil, the great god of the whole Mesopotamian region. Nippur was north of Isin and south of Babylon, and by the reign of Hammurabi it had been a major city for hundreds of years. In Nippur, the right of women to become *naditum*s had been held strictly within certain families that had lived within the city for a long period of time.[56] As in Sippar, *naditum*s could own houses that adjoined those of people who were not affiliated with their religious community.[57] One of the neighborhoods in Nippur that was home to a *naditum* is of interest to us for another reason. It was also the location of a house that is worth a special visit.

As in almost all Mesopotamian cities, the houses in this neighborhood of Nippur (dubbed area TA by the excavators) were densely packed together along streets that zigzagged and collided with one another in unlikely places. A wide boulevard could reach a crossroads only to continue beyond it as nothing more than a narrow alley; corners jutted out into streets; streets dead-ended into front doors. Within the buildings, a wall could have been added across a room or courtyard to divide what had been a large house into two smaller ones. This was not a planned community. Builders over time had respected the need for certain roads to remain wide enough for the passage of carts and pedestrians, but the abrupt corners must have resulted in traffic jams and plenty of shouting from time to time.

Near just such a right-angle turn in a major road was a house that archaeologists referred to as House F (see Fig. 12.2). It was 250 meters (820 feet) south of Enlil's great temple,[58] and was excavated by teams from the University of Chicago and the University of Pennsylvania in 1951 and 1952. It showed itself right away to be an unusual place. More than 1,400 tablets were found there—a phenomenal number for what seemed at first to be an ordinary house in an ordinary neighborhood.

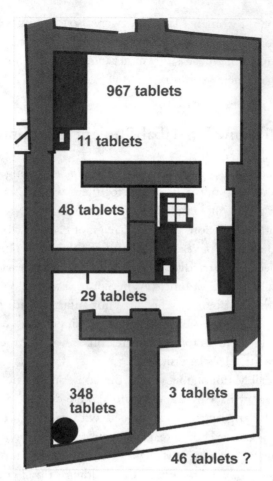

967 tablets

11 tablets

48 tablets

29 tablets

348 tablets

3 tablets

46 tablets ?

Fig. 12.2 Plan of House F in Nippur, mid-eighteenth century BCE (based on Robson 2001, 41, Fig. 3).

Cuneiform tablets were so abundant in the house that, at one point when it came to be remodeled, tablets had been reused as building material.[59] Why had so much writing taken place here? It wasn't a big place; it boasted only about 45 square meters (484 square feet) of living space. There were two courtyards, one surrounded by three small rooms, and a larger one in the back of the house.[60] The excavators found an oven for cooking, broken pots, even a fragment of a clay version of a board game also known from the royal tombs of Ur. Someone had lived there, cooked, passed the time playing games with friends, slept on the roof.[61] But that same someone had also taught there, and that is what makes House F such an arresting place to visit. Finally, after being so grateful for the literary works that the scribal students kept alive through their studies, we can visit one of their schools.[62]

Visiting House F, a guest would be struck by curious installations in three places in the rooms. These were rectangular waterproof clay bins built into the floors. Students used them to recycle their tablets. Once a written exercise was done, the valuable clay could be turned back into a pristine tablet for the next exercise. Or, as in the case of many rectangular tablets in House F, the abandoned and unwanted tablets could be piled up to build benches, or even stacked and plastered over to create new bins for recycling other tablets.[63]

With the growth of literacy in the Old Babylonian period, one might expect to find the inauguration of a big corresponding new institution, the school, where more people could learn this important skill of writing. Oddly enough, the opposite seems to be true. In the earlier Ur III period, big schools probably existed, run by the great households of the palace and temples, in part to prepare civil servants to keep all those thousands of records of sheep, barley, beer, wool, and so on. The Ur III kings also had a more personal reason for promoting scribal schools—their own immortality. King Shulgi had expressed this hope in a hymn to himself: "May my hymns be in everyone's mouth; let the songs about me not pass from memory. So that the fame of my praise . . . shall never be forgotten, I have had them written down line by line in the House of the Wisdom of Nisaba in holy heavenly writing, as great works of scholarship. No one shall ever let any of it pass from memory."[64] The "House of the Wisdom of Nisaba" might have been a scribal school associated with the temple of Nisaba.[65] The scribes were trained there to run the king's administration while also memorizing and copying royal propaganda.

The Ur III schools may have educated dozens or even hundreds of students at a time.[66] But in the Old Babylonian period, schooling became more privatized, just like the economy. If you wanted your son to be literate, you sent him to the house of a scribe to learn from a master, just as the *naditum* women did with the girls who learned to read and write in Sippar. Evidence for these types of small scribal schools in houses can be found at many sites across the Near East.

The master scribe who lived in House F (whose name we unfortunately don't know) took on students who were intellectually ambitious. They were training to become not just scribes but scholars. They would keep alive great works in Sumerian, and they devoted years of their lives to this pursuit. It's unclear how many students studied there, or how long they pursued their studies, but the house could have held only a few students at once.[67] Only one scribe signed his name to any of the hundreds of school tablets found in the house. This was a young man named Elletum.[68] The tablets found in House F allow us to follow a young scribe like Elletum through the different stages in his training.

As a young boy, Elletum certainly still lived at home with his parents and walked to House F, the nearby school he attended during the day. Almost all the houses in the neighborhood contained at least a few school exercise tablets when excavated, so it seems likely that most of the families there sent at least one of their sons to one of the local master teachers who taught in their houses.[69] Elletum may have been as young as five or six when he started attending school. One scribal exercise from the Ur III period describes a boy's day. It was written by a man looking back on his childhood. "When I arose early in the morning," wrote the author, "I faced my mother and said to her: 'Give me my lunch, I want to go to school!' My mother gave me two rolls, and I set out."[70] Elletum would have arrived at the door of House F at a set time of day, perhaps fearing the wrath of "the fellow in charge of punctuality" who berated students if they arrived late. He turned to the right from the entrance hall of the house and passed into a courtyard, with benches and tablet recycling bins. This was where the boys had their lessons.[71] Beyond it was a room where tablets were stored, and where almost 1,000 of the school tablets were excavated.[72] As the Ur III author put it, "I entered before my teacher and made a respectful curtsy"[73] then he took his seat on a bench, next to a handful of other students, and began his schoolwork.

The curriculum pursued by beginning students started with the mechanical process of simply getting a stylus to do what they wanted it to, when pressed into clay.[74] This is harder than you might imagine. The stylus was made of reed or bone with a fine tip that created a slight wedge shape when impressed in the clay at an angle. The scribal students practiced the vertical lines, horizontal lines, and angular wedges that made up all the more complex signs they would later need to compose, and they did this over and over again. Each tablet was surveyed by the master then scraped clean or sent to the recycling bin. Next, the students moved on to simple signs that took more than one stroke of the stylus, and from there, in turn, they progressed to what are called tu-ta-ti exercises—copying signs that were related by sound, having the same first consonant and different vowel sounds.[75]

Early attempts at writing were often done on round tablets, which were only ever used in school (see Fig. 12.3). Children's handwriting on these school tablets is big and often charmingly clumsy in comparison with the teacher's neat example. One can imagine Elletum sitting on his bench in

Fig. 12.3 Round school exercise tablet, on which a beginning student practiced writing the name of the god Urash, Old Babylonian period. (Metropolitan Museum of Art)

the shade, hunched over his tablet, struggling to get his stylus to produce the right lines and angles.

This part of the process was probably not unlike many apprenticeships in other types of trades. If you were going to learn to make pots, for example, you probably spent months just coiling clay, or copying patterns onto pieces of broken pottery to get them right, or turning the pottery wheel for your master. No one would have trusted you with making or decorating a pot right away. Similarly, an apprentice scribe probably toiled away for ages before being given any real words to write.

When his handwriting was finally neat enough to move on—when his cuneiform signs were small enough and controlled enough—Elletum would have been allowed to start to copy lists of Sumerian and Akkadian personal names. This might seem rather arbitrary as a choice of what to write but, as we've seen, everyone's name had a meaning as a short phrase or sentence. These usually had to do with devotion to a particular god, such as the name Sin-idinnam, which meant "the god Sin gave me [a son]," so the purpose of learning them was twofold. Obviously, a scribe would need to know how to write names in the course of his career, but he also got practice with the names of gods and simple verbs this way as well.

And on it went, as Elletum continued to attend school year after year, gradually moving on to copying more complicated words and later memorizing the spellings of hundreds, or even thousands, of nouns.[76] The curriculum varied a little, depending on the choices made by the master scribe who was doing the teaching. For whatever reason, the teacher in House F dispensed with the tu-ta-ti lists, for example.[77] But the lists the students did learn were remarkably standardized, passed down by one generation of scribes to another over centuries, and shared from Syria to Mesopotamia to Elam.[78] Over the course of his elementary education a scribe studied a standard set of twenty-four large tablets that held a total of 3,300 lines, just listing nouns. These weren't dictionaries or encyclopedias, just lists. The master must have provided an oral translation from Sumerian into the scribes' own language of Akkadian.[79] When they got to lists of professions, the young scribes were learning from a volume so ancient that many of the words were probably never used outside the classroom.[80] It was, in fact, a list of professions, copied by Elletum and eventually abandoned in the house, that provides us with his name.[81]

By now Elletum and his classmates were sometimes given a different type of tablet to write on. The master scribe wrote out the relevant lines that the student was to learn on the left-hand side of a rectangular tablet. The student dutifully copied the lines on the right-hand side. After his master had seen (and presumably critiqued) the student's work, he didn't recycle the tablet—that would be a waste of the master's beautiful exemplar on the left. Instead the scribe wiped his own work clean with a stone eraser, or just with his fingers (you can often see the scribe's fingerprints when he did this) and tried it again.[82] Or perhaps he passed the exercise tablet on to a fellow student and began work on a new list of nouns.

If this sounds dull, it almost certainly was. In fact, if a scribe, like many of the students in House F, continued his training past the elementary stages, he got the chance to copy essays that reminded him just how dull and rigid the education system was, like the one quoted above. It satirized the experience of a boy educated in one of the large schools that had existed in the Ur III period when it was written. Scribal masters were still using this essay as part of the curriculum in the Old Babylonian period. Another passage gives us a sense of the rules a student had to follow:

> The door monitor (said), "Why did you go out without my say-so?" He beat me.
> The jug monitor, "Why did you take [water or beer] without my say-so?" He beat me.
> The Sumerian monitor, "You spoke in Akkadian!" He beat me.
> My teacher, "Your handwriting is not at all good!" He beat me.[83]

An Old Babylonian scribal master who taught in his home, like the one who owned House F, would not have had space for any of the monitors who are mentioned in this school assignment. But the basic curriculum hadn't changed much since the Ur III period, and perhaps the corporal punishment hadn't changed either. Our scribe might well have lived in fear of beatings from his teacher.

Before Elletum got to the point of copying these stories about school, though—before he started the advanced curriculum—he encountered a new subject of study: mathematics. Around the same time that the students were learning to write the names of professions and titles, they began memorizing multiplication and reciprocal tables, learning the systems used for weights and measures and copying the relevant signs.[84]

We know that the scribal master in House F taught elementary mathematics to his students because 9 percent of the 1,425 tablets found there were mathematical,[85] mostly comprising lists and tables that the students needed to memorize (see Fig. 12.4).[86] These included multiplication, reciprocals, square roots, and cube roots. But some other scribal schools in Nippur and elsewhere were run by mathematicians. In addition to the elementary curriculum, their students mastered arithmetic and discussed complex word problems. The mathematicians who ran these schools also came up with creative mathematical problems to share with other mathematicians. Some mathematical documents among their records were not for teaching at all, but just for communicating ideas with colleagues.[87]

Mesopotamian mathematics reached its height in the Old Babylonian period; more evidence of mathematical learning and inquiry survives from this era than from any other in the ancient history of the region.[88] The sexagesimal system that we encountered in the first tablets from Uruk[89] was still in use—it was never supplanted in the ancient Near East. Having 60 as the base number seems to have worked very well in all their practical uses of mathematics, which mostly revolved around measuring and dividing land, and organizing and providing for workmen. By the beginning of this period, scribes had invented a place value system to aid in calculations and as a way of transferring from one system of weights and measures to another. The largest units were on the left, followed by progressively smaller units.

Fig. 12.4 A cuneiform tablet with a multiplication table, Old Babylonian period. (Metropolitan Museum of Art)

Hence, a number written with the cuneiform signs that we would read as 17 24 was understood to indicate (17 × 60) + 24 = 1,020 + 24 = 1,044, whereas a number written 24 17 equaled (24 × 60) + 17 = 1,440 + 17 = 1,457.[90] For the first time, the place values of the numbers had meaning.

Historian Eleanor Robson has done extensive research on both the structure and the social setting of Mesopotamian mathematics. She argues that one reason for the increased emphasis on mathematics in this era may lie in the kings' own priorities. Many of the Old Babylonian kings put an emphasis not just on promoting justice in terms of seeking evidence and making fair decisions, but on the kind of justice that demanded accuracy in measurement.[91] They wanted to make sure that those fields allocated by men like Shamash-hazir were just the size recorded, that an inherited orchard was divided equally between brothers, that the temples the kings commissioned were well designed and engineered, and that workers received fair pay appropriate to the number of days they had worked. The literate men (and a few women) who took responsibility for all these aspects of the administration needed to understand numbers, weights, measures, and geometry. They had to learn it all in school. But they learned it in ways that don't look much like mathematical thinking today, and not just because of their base-60 system. The scribes produced very few diagrams (even when geometric principles were discussed) and thought about numbers without using equations. They came up with accurate answers to their real-world (and imagined) mathematical problems, but they did so in sentences full of verbs such as "append," "turn around," "accumulate," "break," and "tear out," rather than the abstract symbols used today such as $+$, $-$, $\times$, $\div$, and $\sqrt{}$.[92]

Although mathematics has continued to be practiced in Iraq ever since the time of these early mathematicians, much of the Old Babylonian mathematical knowledge was lost with the collapse of this era, and it turns out that even the later forms of Mesopotamian mathematics probably didn't have a discernable influence on Greek thinkers.[93] The Greeks seem to have rediscovered and invented new ways to approach mathematical problems that had been solved more than a thousand years before.

To return to House F, the elementary curriculum pursued by Elletum ended with the study of contracts and proverbs. Scribes copied samples of realistic legal documents that they could emulate later when out working in the real world.[94] The proverbs seem at first glance to be wise sayings that perhaps reflected folk tradition. They were terse, sometimes funny, and may have rung true to the scribes in ways we often can't understand. But some scholars have suggested that we may have misunderstood these proverbs. Perhaps they weren't well-known phrases after all; perhaps they were written just for the curriculum, specifically to teach grammar. This would explain why some of them make no sense at all.[95]

This seems to have been the point in the curriculum when many young men ended their scribal training. They had rudimentary mathematical skills and took their multiplication tables and other useful tablets with them to consult in the future.[96] They had learned how to write; they had mastered the nouns and verbs they needed. They could read and write letters and contracts. But some of these former students may have done little writing in their lives after this. For many people it would have been enough to be able to read the contracts, letters, and lists that came their way in everyday life. They could always hire a more advanced scribe if they needed to have a document written.

In House F, though, most of the scribal students seem to have stayed on for the advanced training in Sumerian that was the real expertise of their master. These young men were not just learning a craft that they could use for a job; they were becoming scholars who would belong to an elite intellectual community, one that was conversant in Sumerian and its literature.[97] Sumerian wasn't a spoken language by this time.[98] The intense focus on it was, in a way, an attempt to hold on to what they thought of as a golden age in the past, and even to define a Sumerian culture that brought order and authority to what was for them the modern world.[99] When you think about it, the in-depth study of old stories and hymns in a dead language wasn't a particularly practical thing to do. The fact that this literary world existed shows that their culture allowed space for reflection and intellectual pursuits quite separate from the needs of the palace and the gods. Elletum may well have been among the students who stayed on. Later, after he had finished his schooling, his name appears as a witness to three contracts found in this same part of town;[100] he seems to have become a member of a community of literate and powerful men.

The advanced training curriculum was all designed to expose the scribes to Sumerian literature. Since they didn't speak Sumerian natively, the curriculum gradually brought in more complicated grammar over time. Around 600 of the tablets from House F featured excerpts from Sumerian literary works—this was obviously a crucial part of the curriculum.[101]

Assuming he did, in fact, continue in school, Elletum would have begun his advanced studies with four literary works that just about every scribe copied at the beginning of his study of literature. They were not epic poems or stories; they were all hymns. Their appearance in scribal training programs is so uniform and ubiquitous that they have been dubbed the Tetrad.[102] Three of the hymns were dedicated to dead kings, all of them rulers of Isin, which suggests that this part of the curriculum had its roots at the height of Isin's power, before Hammurabi brought that region under Babylonian control. The fourth hymn in the Tetrad was to the goddess Nisaba, who watched over scribes. These hymns were wisely chosen for their simple Sumerian and for the way in which the verb forms became gradually more complex.[103]

Scribal students then moved on to other, more complicated, Sumerian texts. Ten more literary works with more difficult grammar (now referred to as the Decad) were found in multiple copies in House F.[104] A further fourteen literary works seem to have been favorites of the teacher. He had the students write out many hymns, stories about gods and heroes, and tales of scribal school. These, and other literary works, were used so routinely that they were actually listed in catalogs on clay tablets, the way one might list assigned readings on a syllabus. The sequence of works might seem odd to us. Students didn't study myths, then incantations, then hymns, then lamentations, for example. The genres were all mixed up together. They don't seem to have served as religious instruction, or even, by this time, as propaganda for kings (the ones honored were long dead), though some of them did raise some philosophically interesting questions.

In the course of his advanced studies, Elletum almost certainly copied and memorized stories pertaining to an ancient hero and king of Uruk known as Gilgamesh. He's another of the big names of ancient Near Eastern history, like Sargon and Hammurabi, but the familiar epic about his search for immortality had not yet been written in Elletum's time. Until the Old Babylonian period, Gilgamesh had been known as Bilgames, and he featured as the hero of a number of Sumerian poems that had been passed down orally over generations. At some point during the Ur III period, scribes began writing these tales down and using them as school exercises. Hundreds of years later, around the thirteenth century BCE, these poems and other works about the hero eventually inspired an author named

Sin-leqi-unnini to write the version of the Epic of Gilgamesh that is well known today, but that was still far off in the future when Elletum was in school.

In House F, three of the old Ur III Sumerian poems about the adventures of Bilgames and his servant Enkidu were still being studied.[105] These stories shared a theme: just as in the later epic, Bilgames didn't want to be forgotten; he was seeking some kind of immortality. One story quotes Bilgames saying in despair, "my gaze fell on a corpse drifting down the river, afloat on the water: I too shall become like that, just so shall I be."[106] To avoid this ignominious end, Bilgames set out to become famous by negotiating with, and tricking, a giant monster named Huwawa who lived in a distant cedar forest (though Enkidu ended up killing Huwawa, against Bilgames's wishes). In another story that Ellatum would have copied, Bilgames and Enkidu, perhaps again seeking notoriety, killed a sacred bull, the Bull of Heaven, which had been sent to Earth by the goddess Inana.[107] The third Sumerian story was about Bilgames, Enkidu, and the Netherworld.

But one of the works copied by a scribal student was different in many ways—it was relatively new at the time, and more ambitious than the earlier tales. Bilgames's name had been changed to Gilgamesh, and the tale was written in the contemporary Akkadian language (though the text was bilingual, also including a translation into ancient Sumerian).[108] A fragment of this new work about Gilgamesh was found by the archaeologists in House F, and it can be combined with other fragments from elsewhere to get a sense of what its author had achieved. It was apparently the first iteration of the Epic of Gilgamesh, perhaps the earliest epic poem ever written, and it dealt with themes of friendship, fame, kingship, and fear of death, in ways that are still compelling today. This early epic contained many of the events repeated by Sin-leqi-unnini in his later version, which the Mesopotamians called "He Who Saw Everything," from its first line. The title of every literary work was its first line.

The name of the author of the earlier Old Babylonian epic is unknown, and much of the story is missing from the fragments that have been found, but it was clearly a masterwork that integrated ideas from many earlier Sumerian stories. It was called (again after its first line) "Surpassing All Other Kings."[109] Elletum might well have been familiar with the whole epic, even though just a small part of it was retrieved from the school where he studied.

The author of "Surpassing All Other Kings" promoted the character of Enkidu to a higher position than before—he was now Gilgamesh's friend and equal, not his servant. The friends still fought Huwawa, and they still did it for fame, in order that "[A name that] is eternal I will establish forever," as Gilgamesh put it,[110] but now there was no negotiating with the giant; they intended all along to kill him.[111]

In a missing segment of the epic, Enkidu died, leaving Gilgamesh devastated at the loss of his friend. The author captured the king's anguish and refusal to believe that Enkidu could be gone:

> "Enkidu whom I loved so deeply,
> who with me went through every danger:
> he went to the doom of mortal men.
> Weeping over him day and night,
> I did not surrender his body for burial—
> 'Maybe my friend will arise at my cry!'—
> for seven days and seven nights,
> until a maggot dropped from his nostril."

After this shock and the deep sadness it engendered, Gilgamesh decided that no longer was it enough for him to achieve lasting fame. He wanted to live forever. He feared death as never before.

In the course of his wanderings after Enkidu died, Gilgamesh came upon a woman who owned a tavern. Her advice to him is extraordinary. Consider, Gilgamesh was a powerful king in this tale, one who had many heroic adventures, who led warriors, who was even in regular conversation with the gods. She said to him:

> "O Gilgamesh, where are you wandering?
> The life that you seek you never will find:
> when the gods created mankind,
> death they dispensed to mankind,
> life they kept for themselves.
> But you, Gilgamesh, let your belly be full,
> enjoy yourself always by day and by night!
> Make merry each day,
> dance and play day and night!
> Let your clothes be clean,
> let your head be washed, may you bathe in water!
> Gaze on the child who holds your hand,
> let your wife enjoy your repeated embrace!
> For such is the destiny [of mortal men]"[112]

The tavern keeper didn't tell Gilgamesh to be a hero, to fight, to make a name for himself. She told him to go home, to be a devoted husband and father, to take care of his body and clothes, and to be happy. He should enjoy the life he had, not continue in pursuit of eternal life. And, she said, the most important aspects of the life to enjoy were those that he shared with almost all his subjects: food, dance, cleanliness, home, and family.

Gilgamesh didn't pay much attention to the tavern keeper's message; he continued his quest, going in pursuit of the one man known to have defeated death, a hero named (in this version) Uta-naishtim. We don't have the end of the Old Babylonian version of the epic, but it might have matched the later version. If so, Gilgamesh eventually reached Uta-naishtim and asked him for the secret to eternal life. That secret was, however, beyond Gilgamesh's reach. Uta-naishtim had only received this gift from the gods because he had managed to survive a worldwide flood by building a boat and riding out the storm with his family and many animals. This earlier version of the biblical Noah assumed several different names in Mesopotamian literature, but his character was always the same, as were the basic outlines of the story. After landing his boat on a mountaintop and giving thanks to the gods for his survival, the gods in turn gave him eternal life.

In the later version of the Epic of Gilgamesh, the flood survivor (there called Ut-napishtim) took pity on Gilgamesh after telling his tale, and told him how to obtain a plant that would make him young again. But he failed to hold onto the plant, leaving it to be found by a snake. Eventually Gilgamesh made it back to his home city of Uruk, apparently reconciled at last to his own mortality, and proud of the city he ruled.

How much of this might have been in the Old Babylonian version is impossible to say, but Gilgamesh almost certainly encountered Uta-naishtim and probably heard his story about how he gained immortality. Perhaps Elletum, as he copied the story, was moved by the tavern keeper's speech, or provoked by the ideas of death and immortality. The story of Gilgamesh lived on for centuries. In our own time, translations and retellings of the later epic still inspire readers.

We have no way of knowing what the master teacher taught his students about Gilgamesh (or any other literary works). A great deal of the instruction must have been oral—perhaps the teacher engaged his students in thinking about the meanings and ramifications of the literature they read.

When they had learned all they could from their master, the scribes would have been employed in any number of ways—by the palace perhaps, or a temple, or as physicians, diviners, judges, or surveyors, or to record court cases and contracts. Their literacy was valuable. They also seem to have participated in scholarly discussions with others and sometimes to have collected and copied important works. They were interested in old ways of writing signs, archaic meanings of words, and, generally, the history and structure of their writing system.[113] Some of them almost certainly started taking on students of their own, continuing the cycle.

Not everyone who was literate shared this experience, though. People like the merchants who traded in Anatolia probably had a much more rudimentary education than the scribes of House F. The merchants would have apprenticed to a scribe (probably in someone's home) for long enough to learn the signs necessary to write a letter in Akkadian or to keep a record of a sale or a debt, and then they stopped. They didn't need to master the old literary language of Sumerian. The letters they wrote to one another included very few logograms, which were Sumerian signs that stood in for whole words. Logograms were used as quick abbreviations of their Akkadian equivalents and were employed by scribes with an advanced education. Some of the Assyrian merchants used only a few dozen cuneiform signs regularly—a relatively easy number to learn.[114] Although some of their letters were meticulously written in a fine script, on other occasions the handwriting in the letters could be sloppy, leaving out wedges here and there. In these cases, writing was completely utilitarian. It got the job done. If an Assyrian merchant had encountered an epic poem or a Sumerian hymn, he might not have been able to make head or tail of it.

As literacy became more widespread in the Old Babylonian period, the style of handwriting became more efficient. This was not just true of the Assyrian merchants. Across Mesopotamia, a cursive style that varied region by region replaced the formal calligraphy of the Ur III scribes.[115] Scribes now needed to be able to take dictation, so they had to be able to write fast. Unnecessary curlicues (or their wedge-shaped equivalents) fell away. If someone else could make sense of what you wrote, that was enough.

The *naditum* women of Sippar and the scribes in Nippur were among hundreds of thousands of people who must have benefited from the relative stability of Mesopotamia in Hammurabi's time. In these chapters about the early second millennium, we have knocked on just a few doors, so to speak, peering for a moment into Ashur-idi's textile business, into Shamash-hazir's struggles to confirm the land claims of shepherds and soldiers, into Awat-Aya's feast-filled initiation ceremony, and into Elletum's classroom, while passing by the records of countless other moments and other lives. This phase of the mid-second millennium BCE provides us with so many options of doors to knock on because literacy was no longer confined to the great institutions. Writing had at last been put to use by private individuals, and their letters, contracts, and lists, often found in their own houses, shine a much brighter light than before on people who did not necessarily work for the palace or for a temple.

Chapter 13

Barbers, Mercenaries, and Exiles

T he young scribes continued to study to become scholars in House F at Nippur throughout the reign of Hammurabi, but soon after his death, the world around them faced growing turmoil. The warm relationship that Hammurabi seems to have achieved with his subjects, and the loyalty he inspired, did not continue into the reign of his son, Samsu-iluna (1749–1712 BCE). In the eighth and ninth years of the reign of Samsu-iluna, people in the southern reaches of his empire began to rebel, declaring their independence and placing local rulers on the thrones of their new, small kingdoms. In 1739 BCE, House F was abandoned, along with much of its neighborhood in Nippur, and the scribal school was never re-established. In Larsa, a man who became king took the name Rim-Sin (1741–1736 BCE), perhaps hoping to capture the magic (and legitimacy) associated with the great Rim-Sin I, the last king to have ruled an independent Larsa; he took control of Nippur. Samsu-iluna had his hands full fighting these rebels, and he mentioned them frequently in his year-names. Within four years, from year 9 to year 13, he had fought a people called the Kassites, along with the lands of Ida-Maras and Eshnunna in the north, and Uruk, Ur, Larsa, Isin, Kisurra, and other lands to the south.[1] The king of newly independent Uruk was also fighting in the same regions, against many of the same enemies, including Eshnunna and Isin,[2] though he was not on the side of Samsu-iluna of Babylon. It was a tumultuous time.

Samsu-iluna himself wrote about this era of warfare in an inscription, though he presented it as a glorious victory: "at that time I defeated with weapons, eight times in the course of one year, the totality of the land of Sumer and Akkad which had become hostile against me. I turned the cities of my enemies into rubble heaps and ruins. I tore out the roots of the enemies and evil ones from the land. I made the entirety of the nation dwell according to my decree."[3] How much of this was true?

He does seem to have been successful in battle against Larsa, about which he boasted, that "The year was not half over when he (Samsu-iluna) killed Rim-Sin (II) who had caused Emutbala to rebel, (and) who had been elevated to the kingship of Larsa. In the land of Kish he heaped up a burial mound over him." But the rest of Samsu-iluna's boasts ring hollow: "Twenty-six rebel kings, his foes, he killed; he destroyed all of them. He defeated Iluni, the king of Eshnunna, one who had not heeded his decrees, led him off in a neck-stock, and had his throat cut. He made the totality of Sumer and Akkad be at peace, made the four quarters abide by his decree."[4] If that had all been true, why did Samsu-iluna stop commemorating southern campaigns in year-names after his thirteenth year? He seems instead to have given up on trying to control those lands. The "totality of Sumer and Akkad" was actually not at peace, not at all, and Isin, just to the south of Babylon, was probably by now the southern border of his empire.[5] By the time of Samsu-iluna's twenty-eighth year, even local Isin, so close to Babylon, was out of his reach—no tablets dating to his year-names have been found there after his twenty-seventh year.[6]

The south was suffering not just from local wars but also from a drought that affected much of the Near East.[7] There was never much rain in southern Mesopotamia, of course, but the rains had diminished in Anatolia at this time as well, meaning that the great Tigris and Euphrates Rivers were lower in their riverbeds, and river water was essential for all life in the south. Without enough of it, people couldn't farm, they couldn't transport goods on the river, they might starve.

Archaeologists went looking for occupation levels dating to this era at the great cities that had dominated Mesopotamian history for so many centuries, but they found nothing. Southern cities like Ur, Uruk, Isin, Girsu, Larsa, and Eridu—all of which had been home to the brilliant culture of the Sumerian city-states, and had continued to thrive under the Akkadian kings and during the Third Dynasty of Ur—they all were at least partially abandoned during the reign of Samsu-iluna.[8]

Right when we would like to know more about this, the scribes fail us. Few documents were left lying around houses or public buildings in these newly empty cities, so it's not clear just how much of the crisis was caused by the drought. Probably the people suffered famine or disease as well. Even Nippur—home to all those eager young scribes who had been learning their esoteric Sumerian literature from the master teacher in House F— even there, the texts fell silent for a while.[9] Some of the residents hung on, hoping for a better future. Some moved away. Many no doubt died.

A new kingdom, calling itself the Sealand, materialized to rule over the apparently depopulated southern region. It must have been centered on the marshlands south of Ur. Its kings were able to muster troops to fight against Samsu-iluna and to take control of Nippur in Samsu-iluna's twenty-ninth year. The Sealand was to continue to be a thorn in the side of the Babylonian kings for more than a century.

Samsu-iluna's Northern Campaigns

Babylon could have returned to being one of the smaller states in the region, its once impressive empire having lasted just a few decades. But Samsu-iluna compensated for the losses in the south by trying to expand his empire to the north, beyond even the regions that his father Hammurabi had been able to conquer. He bragged, in the name of his twenty-sixth year, that he had supervised the quarrying of stone in faraway Amurru, to the northwest, and we know from archaeological discoveries in Syria that this claim wasn't just hot air. A garrison town on the Euphrates called Harradum was controlled by Samsu-iluna—the documents from there date to his reign, starting in his twenty-sixth year. Two years later, in his twenty-eighth year, he attacked two kings named Yadih-abum and Muti-hurshan and "crushed [them] like a mountain with his terrifying . . . weapon and his mace."[10] He was so proud of this victory that he named the three subsequent years after the same event.

Gimil-Ninkarrak: A Chief Barber and His Neighbors

Unfortunately, we have no idea who Muti-hurshan was or where he ruled, but we do know something about Samsu-iluna's other enemy, Yadih-Abum. This king, who was more commonly known as Yadih-Abu,[11] ruled a land that lay just beyond the northern limit of Hammurabi's conquests, on the Euphrates River in Syria. This was the kingdom centered at Terqa that carried on under local kings after the destruction of neighboring Mari. The land was probably called Hana—at least that was true later in its existence— but at this point we don't know its name because none of the known texts mentions it. Hana is not a well-known kingdom but it was remarkably resilient over those centuries. Its independent history was just beginning during Samsu-iluna's reign.

As is so often the case in Mesopotamian history and archaeology, the fire and fury of the king's rhetoric in his year-name are reflected on the ground by . . . nothing at all. Samsu-iluna claimed to have "crushed" Yadih-abu, but that king's capital city of Terqa seems to have hummed along just fine throughout Yadih-abu's reign and into the reign of his successor, King Kashtiliashu, and beyond. The excavations there show no sign of Babylonian troops or any Babylonian presence at all at this time. Archaeologists haven't even found any texts dating to Samsu-iluna's reign. But it's not impossible that the city of Terqa did come briefly under direct rule from Babylon and that we just don't yet have documents to prove it.

In his thirty-third year, Samsu-iluna boasted in his year-name that he "restored completely all the brickwork of the city of Saggaratu."[12] Saggaratu was to the north of Terqa; it was, in fact, where Zimri-Lim of Mari had arranged to meet his wife Shibtu with an ensemble of seven musicians only a few decades before. It's highly unlikely that the Babylonian king could claim credit for this construction project unless it was at least underway (though "*all* the brickwork" has a certain hyperbolic ring to it). So Samsu-iluna probably did have a presence in the region around Terqa.

At Terqa, only a small part of the city has been excavated from this period, and it's probably not the neighborhood that Yadih-Abu would have chosen for future generations to visit. It's not his palace, or the great temple to Dagan, or the city wall. Those grand buildings suffered one of two possible fates. Either they are still there, but hidden underneath the modern village, called Ashara, that still sits on top of the tell, or they have long since fallen into the Euphrates. The river sliced off most of the tell at some point in its history, leaving just a semicircular section standing, like a half-eaten cake. What was found at Terqa, though, was a collection of houses and a small neighborhood shrine from this era, clustered along a narrow alleyway right at what is now the edge of the tell (see Fig. 13.1). One of the houses was

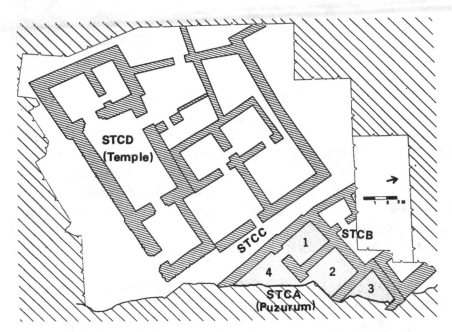

Fig. 13.1 Plan of Area C at Terqa, late eighteenth century BCE. Gimil-Ninkarrak seems to have lived in the building adjoining the temple, his neighbor Puzurum lived across the road in building STCA (Undena Publications, Rouault 1984, ix, Fig. 1).

chopped off by erosion from the river centuries ago, so that one half of its pantry was found full of pots and the other half was completely missing, the sheer side of the cliff face of the tell in its place.[13]

Among the inhabitants of the neighborhood that the excavators discovered, the most influential man was named Gimil-Ninkarrak (he was active c. 1710–1680 BCE).[14] Twelve documents name him, and a number of these were found in a house where he probably lived, next door to the shrine.[15] One of them reveals that he served as the chief barber.[16] This was an exalted position. A chief barber did much more than shave and cut hair; with his sharp blade regularly near the throats of many powerful men in the court, Gimil-Ninkarrak would understandably have been one of the local king's most trusted advisors. This was true of barbers throughout Mesopotamian history.

Gimil-Ninkarrak, as chief barber, would have overseen the work of barbers throughout Terqa. Barbers were professionals who shaved hair for all classes of men.[17] Ur III texts show that, rather than setting up in a permanent workplace, the barbers seem to have traveled to their clients, carrying willow wood for heating water, and stools for their clients to sit on.[18] But there were "bathing places" as well, where it seems that some clients regularly went for a shave.

And who needed shaving? Earlier, in Early Dynastic times and right on through the Ur III period, some men were shown in sculptures with their heads and beards completely shaven. Gudea never wore a beard in any of his many statues. Barbers would have been regularly employed to keep such men clean-shaven. They used a copper razor called a *naglabu* that was also used by surgeons,[19] and there was definitely a connection between barbers and surgery, perhaps not surprisingly, since barbers were trusted to use sharp knives with great care.

Men grew their beards long by Gimil-Ninkarrak's time, the Old Babylonian period, but there was still work for barbers. Artworks show that the beards of high-ranking men were perfectly coiffed, sometimes into long ringlets. Beards and hair would also need to have been cut and shaped, and unwanted facial hair shaved. According to Hammurabi's laws, barbers also were tasked with shaving the heads of enslaved men and women in a way that set them apart from the rest of the population. This was a serious responsibility because a barber could also provide the key for an escaped slave to avoid notice. If an enslaved person could convince a barber to shave off his or her "slave-hairlock," it would be possible to blend into society. The laws stipulated a severe punishment if a barber did this knowingly, but if he had been tricked into it, he wouldn't be punished.[20]

You would think that a bald runaway slave would still stand out in a community full of men with long hair and beards, but it seems that men who worked in temples still shaved for reasons of ritual purity. Barbers could be employed by temples for this reason.[21] But barbers had many other responsibilities, besides shaving. They were more often mentioned as administrators than as people involved in cutting or shaving hair.[22] They often took on important responsibilities, and several of them received cylinder seals from their king—a sure sign of royal esteem.[23]

This was true of Gimil-Ninkarrak as well. He was the proud owner of a beautiful cylinder seal that had been a gift from King Kashtiliashu (the successor to Yadih-Abu, the king who had fought Samsu-iluna of Babylon). It was engraved with an image of a goddess, along with Gimil-Ninkarrak's name and the name of his father. The inscription also noted that Gimil-Ninkarrak was the "servant of Kashtiliashu." The seal had gold caps at the top and bottom, each of them intricately decorated with minute granulated gold beads set in triangular shapes. The seal itself doesn't survive, but he rolled it on some of his documents, so we have its impression.[24]

In documents from Gimil-Ninkarrak's house, from those of his neighbors, and from the shrine to the goddess Ninkarrak, a whole community emerges. The people there didn't mean for these records to survive—no one had curated them or placed them carefully in jars for safekeeping. They were strewn around as textual garbage, no longer needed, ground into dirt floors or left in place when a room burned down, not important enough to retrieve. They comprise the usual culprits, the types of documents often found in Old Babylonian homes—contracts for the purchase of fields and houses and for the hire of laborers, loan agreements, lists of people receiving rations, letters, a few school exercise tablets. Although dozens of people are mentioned in them, five families predominate. They knew one another over at least four generations. They were one another's neighbors and they owned adjoining fields. They witnessed one another's contracts. Some of them were, clearly, friends. The names of many members of the families appear in a list of offerings to Ninkarrak that seems to have been displayed in her shrine, so the families were united in their devotion to their neighborhood goddess as well. In keeping with his importance to the local community, Gimil-Ninkarrak's name is near the top of the list, behind only the king and a dignitary.[25]

His duties as chief barber may have taken him to the king's court from time to time, but most of the time, Gimil-Ninkarrak's life seems to have been very similar to those of his neighbors. Like them, he owned fields and hired laborers to help him farm. He was available when his friends and relatives needed witnesses for their contracts, and they, in turn, showed up when he needed them to witness the formulation of his own contracts. He hired a younger man, a scribe named Pagirum, to write up one of these documents. Pagirum and Gimil-Ninkarrak seem to have known one another well; in fact, Pagirum probably also worked for the king in some capacity, because he later received a royal grant of land. And here's one of those clues that leave us wondering: each man had one son that we know of, and each named his son Iddin-Addu.[26] Gimil-Ninkarrak and Pagirum both could have explained this apparent coincidence to anyone who asked. Perhaps they shared a friend or relative whose name was Iddin-Addu and they named their sons for him. Perhaps both of their sons were named in honor of an omen from the god Addu. Or perhaps it really was just a coincidence. Whatever the case, any later person who is described as "the son of Iddin-Addu" could have been the grandson of Gimil-Ninkarrak or the grandson of his friend Pagirum. We can't know. The fact that certain names were popular and used frequently within a community makes it singularly difficult to reconstruct family trees from our distance of more than 3,700 years.

Abi-eshuh of Babylon: A King and His Dam

After Samsu-iluna's death in 1712 BCE, his son Abi-eshuh (1711–1684 BCE) took the throne in Babylon. He seems to have been obsessed with tackling the crisis in the south and bringing an end to the power of the Sealand. After what must have been extensive consultation with engineers and advisors, he came up with a novel and, frankly, cruel idea for how to do this, one that seems not to have been tried before but was emulated many times in later history. If the marshes of the south could be made to dry out, the Sealand kings would be crippled and their people would die. Nature was doing a pretty good job of depriving southern Mesopotamia of water already; no doubt the king knew this. But what if he could speed this process along? And what if the same scheme could provide more water to cities that he hoped to repossess and bring back under Babylonian control?

Abi-eshuh's Machiavellian idea was to build a dam across the Tigris and to channel the Tigris water west into the Euphrates. The cities downstream on the Tigris would be devastated by the loss of the water, while the cities downstream on the Euphrates would get a new infusion of water and hope.[27] As it happened, Abi-eshuh's grandfather Hammurabi had already provided one of the keys to making this possible. Back in year 33 of Hammurabi's reign he had commemorated the construction of a canal, which he had modestly called "Hammurabi is the abundance of the people."[28] It flowed from the Tigris to the Euphrates at a point where they run relatively close together and continued south from there. Hammurabi had said that the canal would "establish the everlasting waters of plentifulness for Nippur, Eridu, Ur, Larsa, Uruk, and Isin."[29] In Hammurabi's time, plenty of water had still flowed in the Tigris beyond the canal to supply the ancient cities of Umma, Girsu, and Lagash that lay along its banks. As far as Abi-eshuh seems to have been concerned, though, those Tigris cities weren't worth saving, not if it meant that he could get rid of the kings of the Sealand and devastate the marsh areas in which they and their subjects lived.

This was not a project that could be done without the gods' support, so Abi-eshuh dutifully consulted them through oracles. One of these oracles was recorded and it became a historic document, copied by scribes again and again, so that the version we have of it was written down centuries after Abi-eshuh's reign.[30] It notes that after all the planning was complete, a lamb was sacrificed and the diviner extracted its liver so as to examine its parts, "read" them, and come up with an answer to the following question:

> Within the month Abu, up to its thirtieth day, (on) the day that he (Abi-eshuh) identified, thought about and planned, the day he intends and desires, should they (the troops) open a coffer dam on the east bank of the Tigris, should they place breadth facing length, should they heap in reeds and earth and so make a barrage?[31]

The diviner was asking not just whether the gods thought the dam was a good idea, but also whether they approved of the date the king had chosen to begin the work. It's curious to see how Abi-eshuh's enthusiasm for the project even comes through in the question—he had "thought about and planned" the project; he "intends and desires" a particular date. Was he trying to influence the gods to say yes?

The oracle question continued with more details about the dam. The answer from the gods? Yes. He should do it.[32] Work began at once.

Consulting with the internal organs of sacrificed animals, known as extispicy, was a routine way to receive communications from the gods. It involved a kind of scientific thinking, in that the diviners believed in making observations, writing reports, and consulting those reports later in the hope of anticipating future events. (Though, of course, we would not find a scientific connection between the shape of a liver and the success of a military or building project.) The diviners who trained in reading oracles kept records; these types of priests were always literate. We'll look into their work more later.[33]

Nothing remains of his dam now, but Abi-eshuh was deeply proud of it. He named the year in which it was built "the year King Abi-eshuh, by the exalted might of Marduk, placed a dam on the Tigris."[34] And then he quickly realized that his fabulous dam needed to be protected and maintained. No doubt the people who still lived downstream were furious and terrified. Where was the water they needed to grow their crops? How could they navigate boats on a river that had slowed to a trickle? A dam made of earth and reeds was vulnerable not just to the pressure of the water that now swept away to the west, down Hammurabi's canal and into the Euphrates, but also to attacks by people suffering from its effects and no doubt determined to tear it down. The king set about building a fort right by the dam, which he would man with troops. He named it Fort-Abi-eshuh, or Dur-Abi-eshuh in Akkadian. This fort also was the subject of a year-name: "The year King Abi-eshuh built Dur-Abi-eshuh above the barrage of the Tigris."[35] It actually wasn't the first fort that he'd named after himself. There was already another one on the Euphrates where Hammurabi's old canal joined it.[36]

Now that he was in fort-building mode, Abi-eshuh constructed and manned forts in seven locations right along the Euphrates, including at Nippur (which was back under Babylonian control)[37] and Uruk.[38] Abi-eshuh and the kings of Babylon who succeeded him relied strongly on armed forts in order to rule their land; at least twenty-eight forts were in operation across the country, though by this time the kingdom of Babylon boasted only four actual cities: Babylon, Sippar, Dilbat, and Kish.[39]

We know about the world of Dur-Abi-eshuh because hundreds of tablets were written there and have been published.[40] These records show that, although the south was suffering from drought, it wasn't completely empty of people—at least not along the Euphrates. The towns on the Tigris, in contrast, suffered just as Abi-eshuh must have planned. Archaeologists working there found nothing but ghost towns during this era.[41]

Marduk-lamassashu and Ibni-Sin: A Vizier and a Commander in Dur-Abi-eshuh

Throughout the reign of Abi-eshuh, troops traveled easily up and down the Euphrates in boats. They also sailed from the Euphrates to the Tigris and back, along Hammurabi's canal, which was wide and deep enough for boat traffic. One of the administrative documents recorded rations of beer for a trip made by twelve charioteers between the two identically named forts:

6 beer vats . . . as travel provisions for 12 charioteers who went by boat from
Dur-Abi-eshuh at the Tigris-dam to Dur-Abi-eshuh at the outlet of the
Hammurabi-is-the-abundance-of-the-people canal and have returned.
(The beer vats) were given to them when troops stayed in Dur-Abi-eshuh at
the outlet of the Hammurabi-is-the-abundance-of-the-people canal.[42]

The forts were manned not just with Babylonian men, but with mercenaries
from neighboring lands as well, including ones that recently had been
enemies of Babylon.[43] Some soldiers and commanding officers were
identified by their nationality—including Kassites, Suteans, and Elamites—
and some by their home cities. The men came from as far afield as Aleppo
in Syria (ancient Halab) and Arrapha in the far north of Mesopotamia.[44]
This was a widespread phenomenon in this era; the Babylonian army was
manned by thousands of foreign mercenaries.[45] They no doubt spoke many
different languages, but they shared a common employer, and all were
provided with monthly pay. The scribes kept track of all of it.

A number of men show up over and over again in the records—men
like the cupbearer with the patriotic name Hammurabi-lu-dari who, in the
twentieth year of Abi-eshuh's reign, was often given the responsibility of
receiving barley that would be allocated to troops and workers.[46] He had an
inscribed seal, which he sometimes used to seal the relevant receipt tablet.

Another impressive figure who must have been a familiar sight in Dur-
Abi-eshuh was the vizier Marduk-lamassashu. In years 19 to 21 of Abi-
eshuh's reign, he often worked with a commander named Ibni-Sin (and
sometimes, in year 21, with *two* commanders both named Ibni-Sin, which
must have been the cause of some confusion). The standard phrase in which
their names appeared was: "(The barley) was given to them (the craftsmen,
or troops, or particular groups of soldiers, listed above this section), when
the troops stayed in Dur-Abi-eshuh at the outlet of the Hammurabi-is-
the-abundance-of-the-people Canal" and then came the names of the men
overseeing the troops on that occasion: "with Balassu-lirik, the overseer of
the barbers, Marduk-lamassashu, the vizier, Sumu-hammu, the commander,
Ibni-Sin, the commander, and Ibni-Sin, the commander."[47]

One can't help wondering what these men were like. Balassu-lirik,
the overseer of the barbers, might have been the most powerful man on
this team—as we saw with Gimil-Ninkarrak in Terqa, this was a position
invested with more influence than one might think. Marduk-lamassashu, as
vizier, would also have had the king's ear. He presumably traveled with the

troops and their commanders regularly between Babylon and Dur-Abi-eshuh. Was he distant and remote, or did he chat sometimes with Ibni-Sin as they supervised the troops together? There's no way to know. Marduk-lamassashu lived on into the reign of the next king, Ammi-ditana, and still held his powerful position.[48] Most of these individuals were completely lost to history until the recent publication of these records brought a small window into their world back to us, glimpsed (as so often is the case) through the prosaic records of barley and beer distributions.

So—was Abi-eshuh's diabolical plan successful? Did he defeat King Ili-ma-ilu of the Sealand by depriving his country of water? Not at all. A later chronicle recalled this moment: "Abi-eshuh, son of Samsu-iluna, tried to defeat Ili-ma-ilu so decided to dam the Tigris, but though he dammed the Tigris he did not defeat Ili-ma-ilu."[49]

Nevertheless, the forts named for Abi-eshuh continued to be occupied and manned for another century, through the reigns of the subsequent kings of Babylon: Ammi-ditana (1683–1647 BCE), Ammi-saduqa (1646–1626 BCE), and Samsu-ditana (1625–1595 BCE). And the kings of the Sealand, whose homeland had *not* in fact been devastated as a result of Abi-eshuh's canal, continued to cause them frequent difficulties. Although the Babylonian kings maintained a fort all the way to the south in Uruk, it was a lonely outpost; Babylonian control didn't really extend beyond Nippur (which was just south of the Dur-Abi-eshuh on the Euphrates). Even at Nippur, life was dramatically different from the comfortable times of the scribes in House F. That earlier era must have seemed like a different world.

Abandonment of the City of Nippur

The city of Nippur had been largely abandoned after the thirtieth year of Samsu-iluna's reign.[50] But its vast and imposing temple, called the Ekur, was still there. It could not be shut down—it was, after all, home to Enlil, the greatest of the Sumerian gods, and had been the holiest place in southern Mesopotamia at least since writing began in the Early Dynastic period, almost a thousand years before. A group of priests and officials were still living and working there throughout the reign of Abi-eshuh and into the reign of Ammi-ditana. But their peace was broken in Ammi-ditana's eleventh year (1672 BCE), when the city of Nippur was violently attacked by troops from the Sealand.

People who had still been living in Nippur were forced to flee north to Dur-Abi-eshuh, where they would be safe behind the walls of the fort. Some officials in Dur-Abi-eshuh wrote to tell the king about their arrival from Nippur, keeping a copy of the letter for the fort's own archives:

> To our Lord (Ammi-ditana) speak. Thus report your servants:
> Our Lord's city (Dur-Abi-eshuh) and troops are well.
> In the eleventh month on the twenty-eighth day, the citizens of Nippur who fled from Nippur to Zibbat-Narim (probably another name for Dur-Abi-eshuh), spoke to us as follows: "In the eleventh month on the nineteenth day five hundred enemies with equids and conscripts arrived at Nippur. They entered the Ekur-temple."[51]

This was a catastrophe. The enemy troops had not only breached the city walls, they had entered the holy shrine of Enlil, and now were inside and damaging its sacred spaces. The next few lines of the letter are, unfortunately, broken, but it's clear that the enemies went on a rampage of destruction and looting: "The walls of the temple were pierced (?) . . . They robbed . . ." But then somehow the people of Nippur were able to defend themselves. The tide turned. "They became afraid. The horsemen (?) took cover and took off."[52]

The Sealand forces were not finished with Nippur, however. Just six days later, they were back: "In the eleventh month on the twenty-fifth day three hundred enemies with equids entered the Ekur again." Once again, the text is broken at a crucial point, but again the forces defending Nippur were, perhaps surprisingly, victorious. After the break we read that "the enemy has been defeated." Sort of. The writer, continuing to quote the people who had fled Nippur, added, "However, the enemy is still arriving at Nippur daily."[53] The letter was sent to King Ammi-ditana by two men described as "express messengers."

Nippur continued to suffer—it was mentioned in the documents from Dur-Abi-eshuh for the last time during the reign of King Ammi-saduqa. But by then, with the original Ekur in ruins and in enemy hands, a new version of the Ekur temple had been built in the safer quarters of Dur-Abi-eshuh, the one on the Tigris.[54] People still hoped, though, that someday the original temple would be restored so that Enlil could move back to his ancient home. One man's seal inscription reads, plaintively, "May [the scribe]

Nanna-mesha, who reveres the god Marduk, (live to) see the restoration of the Ekur temple and of Nippur."[55]

Enlil-mansum: Temple Official

Meanwhile, the exiled officials of the Ekur temple continued to work in support of Enlil from their new quarters at Dur-Abi-eshuh. An official named Enlil-mansum had the title of "*neshakkum* of Enlil." There were several men with this title, but it's unclear exactly what they did.[56] Enlil-mansum probably had a religious role, but the tablets that survive from his professional career pertain to his commercial activities.[57]

Enlil-mansum had close ties with an important man in Sippar—Marduk-mushallim, who managed the palace finances.[58] Marduk-mushallim was a special confidant of King Ammi-saduqa, in fact. In a particularly difficult year, the king wrote to him to warn him of potential attacks on Sippar, and Marduk-mushallim was thoroughly loyal to the king in return.[59] On one occasion he even alerted a superior (it's not clear who this was) that one of his fellow officials at Sippar was not following the king's orders. When Marduk-mushallim objected to the behavior, this man had told him: "Do not accept his (the king's) order."[60] Marduk-mushallim was having nothing to do with such insubordination. He rushed off his letter, assuring his boss that he would continue to follow orders, while revealing his fellow official's treachery.

Marduk-mushallim sometimes financed Enlil-mansum's business ventures. The contracts they drew up mention a number of men who worked as couriers or traders for Enlil-mansum or witnessed his contracts. These tablets give us a sense of the close ties between people who were living and working in Dur-Abi-eshuh at this time.

Nanna-mesha (he of the wistful seal inscription) was a member of this community. He was not just a scribe. Like Enlil-mansum, he was a *neshakkum* of the Enlil temple. It's no wonder that his seal inscription bemoaned the loss of the temple. The two men worked together, and Nanna-mesha turned up as a witness to one of Enlil-mansum's contracts that helps reveal what his traders were buying for him on their business trips.

This contract was for the purchase of an enslaved woman "from the city of Awil-ili."[61] Enlil-mansum paid 12 shekels of silver for her. She was presumably destined for the temple, rather than for his own household. The clauses end by noting that there would be "three days for investigation, one month for epilepsy," and that "he (Enlil-mansum) will be responsible for claims on her in accordance with the royal regulation."[62] Almost all the slave sales ended this way. Epilepsy was a particular worry, as it was believed to be caused by the gods.[63]

All the sale documents that mention Enlil-mansum were for the purchase of slaves—mostly women but some men. Many of the enslaved people came from distant cities in Elam, Gutium, Subartu, and Andarig.[64] There seem to have been no "markets" where slaves could be bought within Babylonia during this era; perhaps there never had been. People generally lost their freedom as a result of falling into debt; this happened in all areas. So when the temple of Enlil wanted to purchase slaves, it seems it could not do so locally. Enlil-mansum sent his traders to distant regions for this purpose; he could trust that, for the enslaved people there, unlike those with local roots, their status would not change. No matter the reason why they were enslaved originally, they would not be freed in Dur-Abi-eshuh as a result of, say, resolving a contract or paying off a debt.[65] They would be trapped in slavery for life, far from their homelands. Enlil-mansum's impassive contracts tell us nothing of the heartbreak this must have occasioned. The temple of Enlil seems to have had an ongoing demand for enslaved men and women.

Ahunatum, a son of Enlil-mansum, got himself into serious trouble, perhaps during a trading mission either for his family or for the temple of Enlil. He was captured sometime during the second year of King Samsu-ditana (1625–1595 BCE) and held hostage. Someone must have sent a ransom request to his father, Enlil-mansum, and it was for a huge amount of silver: a whole mina.[66] This was toward the end of Enlil-mansum's career; he was probably getting on in years and would not have been able to make the trading journey himself.

Was this kidnapping a scare? Or perhaps Enlil-mansum wasn't too surprised to get the ransom request—in this era, kidnappings of river traders seem to have become fairly common.[67] In any event, Enlil-mansum determined to pay the ransom, and somehow got the silver together. He entrusted the payment to a merchant who was going to the region where Ahunatum was being held and would get the kidnappers to release his son.[68] He also gave the merchant some oil with which to obtain a donkey "for safe transport," and put it all into a contract.

We don't know how this story ended; no record survives of Ahunatum's return, nor do we know when or how Enlil-mansum died. He was still alive two years after the kidnapping, lending silver to another man, not for a long-distance trip to buy slaves but to buy barley locally.[69]

Nine years later, Enlil-mansum's brother seems to have taken over his business. He too was a *neshakkum*, living in Dur-Abi-eshuh, and he lent silver on one occasion to a cook and his wife, to be paid back in barley.[70] The penalty for not paying back the barley was stiff—half a shekel of silver extra per shekel borrowed! The family's unsavory business dealings continued, for a while at least, until the records come to an abrupt end, at a time when all of Babylonia was thrown into turmoil.

Hattusili I: Expanding the Hittite Empire

In the mid-seventeenth century BCE, during the same time that Enlil-mansum was engaging in his trading expeditions, and the kings Ammi-saduqa and, later, Samsu-ditana of Babylon were struggling to hold on to the vestiges of the empire that their predecessor Hammurabi had created a century before, a kingdom in Anatolia was changing in ways that had a lasting impact on the whole Near East.

The people living on the Anatolian plateau were descendants of the population who had lived there during the time of the Old Assyrian colonies at Kanesh, still speaking the same language, which they called Neshite, but we call Hittite. Hittite was an Indo-European language, the very earliest one to be written down. Indo-European languages had existed long before this and had already diverged dramatically from Proto-Indo-European, which was the shared ancestor to ancient Hittite, Celtic, Latin, Greek, Germanic, Old Persian, Sanskrit, and all their Indo-European descendants, including modern Persian and Hindi, and most modern European languages, such as English, German, Spanish, French, Czech, Polish, and all the other Germanic, Romance, and Slavic languages.

Around 1750 BCE, a new capital city was established high on the Anatolian plateau at a site now called Boğazköy, 200 kilometers (124 miles) east of modern Ankara. A town had existed there since before the time of the Assyrian colonies, though it had been abandoned. But it was an ideal spot for a well-defended capital,[71] with steep escarpments on two sides, carved by rivers flowing through the rocky landscape. The town was called Hattusa and, over subsequent years, it became home to many palaces, temples, and formidable fortifications, along with extensive residential districts. Thousands of cuneiform tablets were found there during excavations, supplying much of our knowledge of Hittite history.

The king who chose Hattusa as his capital may have originally ruled from Kanesh (also called Nesha),[72] and he took the name Hattusili, "man of Hattusa," probably in honor of his new capital. Since several later kings adopted the same name, to us he is Hattusili I (1650–1620 BCE). Hattusili didn't invent the idea of an Anatolian empire; his predecessor Labarna had made plenty of progress in that, conquering many smaller kingdoms. But Hattusili wrote about his conquests in cuneiform, so we know much more about him, and his conquests were more extensive.

In his annals he described little but battles and raids, often boasting that, after destroying a city he "took possession of its property and carried it off to Hattusa."[73] It became important for a Hittite king to prove his prowess on the battlefield and to outdo his predecessors in his conquests.[74] Hattusili I may have initiated this model of kingship. Like Mesopotamian kings, Hattusili believed that the gods had chosen him to rule. He wrote, "To me, the king, the Sun God and the Storm God have entrusted my country and my house (the palace) and I, the king, will protect my country and my house."[75]

Hattusili I even took his army on campaign beyond Anatolia; on at least two occasions they crossed the Taurus Mountains and moved south into Syria, where the king continued his habit of destruction and looting, this time in the long-established and prosperous kingdom of Yamhad (the former ally of Mari). But the Hittite troops could not stay too long in Syria when they were fighting there. By late autumn they had to be home. The snows on the Anatolian plateau made travel impossible through the winter months.

Hattusili did not destroy Yamhad's capital city of Aleppo, however. That particular act of violence was committed by his grandson and successor, Mursili I (1620–1590 BCE), once again bragging that he had outdone the achievements of the kings who came before him.

One benefit of these Syrian campaigns was that the Hittites decided to adopt the cuneiform writing system that they encountered there.[76] Hittite scribes probably learned to write Akkadian and Sumerian in cuneiform from Syrian teachers who set up schools in Hatti, at least to start with. Later, the scribes adapted cuneiform to be able to record their own language of Hittite. Early documents like Hattusili I's annals only survive because scribes copied and recopied them.

Although the Hittite kings were responsible for their brutal campaigns of conquest at this time, and made no apologies for this, daily life in the Hittite heartland was no more violent than elsewhere in the Near East. Yes, men were regularly called up on campaign and must have witnessed and participated in terrible bloodshed and destruction,[77] but at home they and their families farmed, traded, went to court, married, and worshiped the gods much like their Syrian and Mesopotamian neighbors. The many cuneiform tablets found at Hattusa attest to this.

Samsu-ditana of Babylon: The End of the Dynasty of Hammurabi

King Samsu-ditana proved to be the last king of Babylon in this era. Some enemy force destroyed and looted Babylon in 1595 BCE, but we don't know how this happened or what led up to it. Like a good detective story, tantalizing clues remain, but we can't be sure what they mean.

The clues appear in documents, most of which were written considerably later, and by peoples who had by then become powerful in the region.[78] One of the documents was a later Hittite inscription, and the Hittites have often been assumed to have been the sole aggressor against Babylon. The end of Babylon is mentioned in just two cryptic sentences of the inscription: "Now later he (Mursili I) went to Babylon. He destroyed Babylon and fought the Hurrian [troops]. Babylon's deportees [and] its goods he kept in Hattusa (his capital city)."[79] According to this, it was the Hittites who attacked and sacked Babylon, taking captives and loot back home with them (as they had done in Syria). But why did the Hittites find themselves fighting Hurrians apparently in Babylon? Hurrians lived far away from Babylon in northern Syria. More peoples were involved than just Hittites and Babylonians.

Another textual clue is found in a document from Babylon. Surprisingly, it says nothing about the Hittites, though it does describe a chaotic time in the reign of King Samsu-ditana: "When at the time of Samsu-ditana the borders of Sumer and Akkad were altered by the belligerence of the Amorites, the uprising of the Hanaeans, and the army of the Kassites, the design of the land had been obliterated and its borders unmade."[80] This writer would have us believe that three non-Hittite groups of people were responsible for the chaotic "unmaking" of the borders of the Babylonian kingdom: the Amorites, Hanaeans, and Kassites. The Amorites we have already met; even Hammurabi was an Amorite. By now, they lived pretty much everywhere in Syria and Mesopotamia. The Hanaeans were the people who lived north of Hammurabi's Babylonian empire in what was now probably called the kingdom of Hana, the area where the barber Gimil-Ninkarrak had lived in the reign of Kashtiliashu. The Kassites were relatively new to Mesopotamia, but had been mentioned as troublemakers since soon after Hammurabi's death. They spoke a language that was completely unrelated to Akkadian and Amorite and they may have originated in regions to the north of Babylonia. So it seems that attacks on Babylon may have come from all directions.

Another theory, proposed by historian Seth Richardson, is that before the kingdom was attacked from outside it had already been disintegrating from within.[81] Fortresses, like the two Dur-Abi-Eshuhs, were spread throughout the countryside in this era and, as we have seen, they were staffed by mercenary soldiers from many different lands. These soldiers may have been paid to fight Babylon's enemies, but their loyalty to the Babylonian king was minimal. The mercenaries could have been inspired by warlords to rebel and could have been responsible for the demise of Hammurabi's dynasty.[82]

Archaeological evidence has been found that supports the idea of a violent period within Babylonia decades before the end of the dynasty. For example, a house in Sippar-Amnanum had been home to a lamentation priest named Ur-Utu whose life was turned upside down perhaps by just such a rebellion. It took place in the eighteenth year of King Ammi-saduqa (the penultimate king of the Babylonian dynasty).[83] Ur-Utu lived in a comfortable house in Sippar-Amnanum where he had grown up, and he kept an archive of more than 2,000 tablets there.[84] He had just begun a renovation of the house when he suddenly needed to evacuate. Hostile forces must have already been in the streets when Ur-Utu was sorting through his cuneiform tablets, madly trying to find the ones that were most important to him. He couldn't leave without a group of contracts pertaining to real estate (these went back hundreds of years), which proved that he had the rights to his extensive fields, and he also needed to take some contracts for loans that were still outstanding; a number of people owed him silver and barley.

He had the tablets in a box and was rushing through his house. He must have heard the soldiers outside the door and the shouts of his neighbors. Then, suddenly, his house was on fire, the wooden ceiling burning fiercely, and he just had to run. He tripped and dropped the box of tablets. It was too late to salvage them; the fire was out of control. Ur-Utu fled for his life.

If Ur-Utu survived the attack, either he decided that he did not need his archive (not even the tablets that he had been trying to take with him) or he was not allowed access to his house after the fire was put out. He never returned to clean up the mess made by the fire, or to reclaim his possessions, and neither did anyone else.[85] His ancestral home was abandoned, and soon that was true of the whole city of Sippar-Amnanum around it.[86] Ur-Utu's tablets stayed exactly where they were for more than 3,500 years until discovered by archaeologists, who were able to reconstruct the last minutes of his escape by the odd groupings of tablets in the rooms and on the floor.[87] If an internal Babylonian rebellion brought devastation to Sippar-Amnanum, it was followed by an invasion from beyond the Babylonian borders.

Samsu-ditana has always been considered the unlucky final descendant of Hammurabi, the king who witnessed this invasion of the great city of Babylon and perhaps died as a result. But no inscription from Samsu-ditana's own time identifies him as being related to the previous kings. Perhaps he was one of the warlords himself, leading the destruction of cities and houses, like that of Ur-Utu, before usurping the throne.[88]

No matter who he was, Samsu-ditana gradually lost control of the remaining cities within the Babylonian kingdom over the course of his reign. Hanaeans, Amorites, and Kassites played a part in this, to say nothing of Hurrians, Elamites, and people from the Sealand, who seem also to have been involved.[89] It must have been an unstable and dangerous time.[90] The Hittite raid on Babylon, led by King Mursili I, could have been the final nail in the coffin of a kingdom that had been collapsing for decades. It's no wonder that almost no documents were written for a very long time afterward.

The gap in the records that follows this period is really striking. The sixteenth century BCE is a real "Dark Age," not in an old-fashioned, pejorative sense, but as a time that we know almost nothing about, as though the lights had been turned out. Scribes across Mesopotamia and other parts of the Near East seem not to have been needed and to have stopped taking students. Even some mathematical knowledge was lost for good as scribal schools closed their doors.

Only two Mesopotamian kingdoms in the sixteenth century BCE are known to have kept on producing documents. One was the Sealand in the south,[91] and the other was Hana in the north,[92] but neither is understood well. Perhaps in the future they will help fill in our understanding of this era. The Hittites, too, continued to produce some documents during this time, though Hatti descended into crisis after its attack on Babylon.

One text written during the Dark Age (but only preserved in a later copy) provides us with a glimpse of an improvement in relations between the Hittites and their Babylonian neighbors.[93] It shows that the Hittite kings began to take tentative steps to join the international diplomatic community. The document is called the Agum-Kakrime inscription and it reveals a surprising, though still only vaguely discernable, new world after the end of Hammurabi's dynasty, in which a Kassite dynasty had taken control of Babylonia. The Kassites, you may recall, were one of the groups who provided mercenary soldiers to the previous Babylonian kings and who had been among the groups threatening Babylonia. Now they were in charge in Mesopotamia and remained so for centuries.

A Kassite king of Babylonia named Agum had succeeded in convincing the Hittites to return the state gods Marduk and Sarpanitum to Babylon. The statues of the gods had been taken during the Hittite attack, and seem to have been held hostage for twenty-four years. The Babylonians, of course, were desperate to get them back. Agum's mission must have entailed diplomatic negotiations, presumably with letters and messengers passing back and forth between Babylon and the Hittite capital. Eventually, though, when the gods returned home, Agum notes that they were sent from Hana, halfway between Hatti and Babylon. This peaceful transfer of the gods back to their homeland gives us a preview of the next era, one that eventually became a model of diplomacy and international cooperation.

PART VI

The Late Bronze Age, 1550–1000 BCE

Chapter 14
Businessmen, Charioteers, and Translators

During the 1420s BCE, Ilim-ilimma was a man to be reckoned with in the town of Alalakh, which was located in the northern Levant.[1] He had been born into a family who did well for themselves—his father, Tuttu, was a businessman—and Ilim-ilimma had a seat among the power brokers of the town. To judge from the few documents that survive from his archive, he spent time with the local royal family and with army generals, but was not averse to making himself richer from the misfortunes of others. But we only know about him from contracts and lists; it would be good to think that he was a kinder man than one might conclude from what he left behind though, honestly, it seems unlikely.

The documents that tell us about Ilim-ilimma, and many other citizens of Alalakh, were excavated by Leonard Woolley when he led an archaeological expedition there in the 1930s and 1940s. This was the same British excavator who had found the royal tombs of Ur a decade before, and he had been knighted in 1935 for his archaeological discoveries—he was now Sir Leonard. He uncovered hundreds of tablets in Alalakh's finely built stone palace, in what he dubbed Level IV of the city's existence, dating approximately to the fifteenth century BCE. Nine of these documents pertain to Ilim-ilimma, son of Tuttu, just enough to glimpse his life and to wish we knew more.[2]

Ilim-ilimma had an unusual name. It had been the name of an early king of Alalakh, and he also shared it with the son of the current local king. He was important enough that his personal archive was kept (and ultimately found) in that king's palace, so he seems to have been close to the royal family; he might even have been named in honor of the earlier king.[3] One wonders if having the same name as the crown prince was a source of annoyance to Ilim-ilimma, or whether it was perhaps an advantage. In any event, we know for certain that he and the crown prince were not the same man, though they did know one another.[4] Both of their names were included on a document drawn up by a palace scribe, a list of horses that had been allocated to important individuals. Ilim-ilimma the prince and Ilim-ilimma son of Tuttu each received a pair of female horses.[5] Both men, almost certainly, used these mares to pull their chariots in battle. By their time, chariot warfare had become a crucial part of any military engagement.

One reason for this transformation of military strategy was that the technology of manufacturing chariots had improved enormously. They bore almost no resemblance to their clunky predecessors. Being a charioteer in warfare may have been dangerous in their time, but it was also prestigious. Gone were the wooden boxes with solid wooden wheels, pulled along by donkeys, which had been used since the Early Dynastic period. In their place were horse-drawn lightweight vehicles with two spoked wheels that were capable of high speeds and could be maneuvered easily. They were used not only in Alalakh but in many regions of the Near East, including in Egypt (see Fig. 14.1).

Two men rode in each chariot—a bowman, like Ilim-ilimma, and a driver who also held a shield to protect them both. Horses had been domesticated for some time and now they were being trained to pull these chariots. Horses were faster and larger than donkeys, which had been so valued in the past, and kings now were looking to buy and raise the best horses

Fig. 14.1 Relief sculpture showing a spoked-wheel chariot, from Amarna in Egypt, 1352–1336 BCE. (Metropolitan Museum of Art)

available and were hiring horse trainers. Chariot forces were expensive to maintain and to train, but the investment was worthwhile, even necessary, for a major power.[6]

Scholars used to propose theories about where this new form of chariot was invented and further theories about how the kingdom responsible for the development might have gained an important advantage over its neighbors in warfare. But there is really no way to know where the new design of chariot came from, because every Near Eastern kingdom of the age adopted it at pretty much the same time. The same basic chariot design even made it all the way to China, which was ruled at the time by the Shang dynasty; it seems that once any leader had seen this technological wonder, he set his engineers to the task of trying to build some chariots of his own.

Alalakh before the Late Bronze Age: A Town on the Border

It would have been important for forces in Alalakh to master chariot warfare, because the city was located in a spot not unlike that of Kisurra during the earlier Isin-Larsa period (though hundreds of kilometers distant): it was right at the border between two powerful kingdoms, Hatti in Anatolia and a new state called Mittani in Syria. Before we find out more about Ilim-ilimma and his world, we need to understand a little about the history of his city, Alalakh, and of the empire of Mittani. The imperialistic stirrings of Hatti and Mittani had already buffeted Alalakh before Ilim-ilimma's time.

The setting of Alalakh, in the Amuq valley in the northern Levant, was deceptively bucolic. The valley was green with vegetation from ample rainfall, and cozily surrounded in most directions by low hills. To the west, the Amanus Mountains stood much higher on the horizon, their slopes cloaked in forests of cedar trees.[7] Alalakh lay close to the Orontes River, which winds through the valley. Although it was not navigable, the river had carved a pass through the Amanus Mountains, providing a relatively easy road to the Mediterranean.[8] Other ancient routes passed through the valley, leading from Egypt in the south to Anatolia to the north, and from the Mediterranean coast to Babylonia and Assyria to the east. The cedar forests in the Amanus range had long provided wood for Babylonian building projects; Alalakh was ideally situated to take advantage of the trade. Plus, it

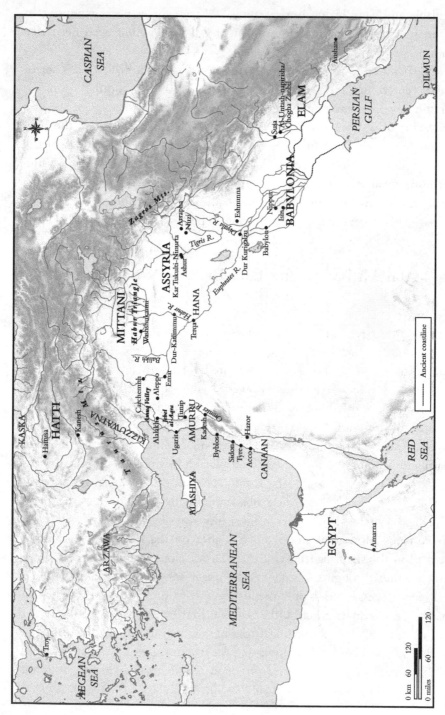

Map 3 The Near East from 1500 to 1000 BCE

enjoyed a relatively mild climate, so that even in summer the cool winds from the Taurus Mountains kept the weather from becoming unbearably hot. Crops flourished. Stone was readily available for construction. The Amuq valley was an ideal place to settle and, unsurprisingly, people had been living there for thousands of years.

Unfortunately, though, those same advantages made Alalakh and its region something of a target for greater powers. It was not a big city, just 22 hectares (54 acres) in extent, with a relatively small but well-built palace, temples to the local gods, and a flourishing economy. It was almost always subject to a stronger kingdom in the region. During the Old Babylonian period this had been Yamhad, with its capital at Aleppo. At one point, Zimri-Lim of Mari had decided that he wanted control of Alalakh, so he had actually offered to purchase the whole town from his ally, the king of Yamhad.[9] You will not be surprised to hear that he failed. The king of Yamhad held onto this treasure of a town.

In the late Old Babylonian period, Alalakh's fate changed. It was one of the first northern Syrian cities to be attacked and destroyed by the Hittites when they began hostilities against Yamhad in 1600 BCE. Alalakh probably suffered further ravages when the Hittite king Mursili I moved troops beyond Syria to Babylon in 1595. But afterward, the people of Alalakh duly rebuilt and reoccupied their town.

The Hittites did not forget their interest in this area; they returned several times. By 1500 BCE, Mittani and Egypt shared the Hittites' desire to control the Amuq valley and the Mediterranean coast.

The Puzzling Beginnings of Mittani: A Little-Known Empire

A new era, which began around 1550 BCE and lasted for more than 300 years, is known as the Late Bronze Age, and it was in many ways strikingly different from anything that had come before it. Although the period started out in a blaze of antagonism and warfare, eventually (after Ilim-ilimma's lifetime) the Late Bronze Age proved to be among the most peaceful eras in ancient Near Eastern history, with the great powers of Egypt, Hatti, Mittani, Babylonia, and (later) Assyria mostly choosing to interact and cooperate together rather than to fight one another. It marked an international age of alliance or "brotherhood" among great kings.

Once this brotherhood was established, an army of messengers, diplomats, and translators worked incessantly to maintain it. They were almost always on the move, traveling from one country to another on the well-worn roads we have encountered before, including through the Amuq Valley and its provincial capital of Alalakh, and on newer routes to lands that had previously been outside the orbit of the Near Eastern states.

Peace in the Late Bronze Age was to be hard-won, however, taking almost a century to establish. Early kings of the new state of Mittani seem to have had little interest in keeping to themselves in the Habur region in northern Syria where they had their capital city of Washshukanni. This was the same area from which Shamshi-Adad had ruled his empire of Upper Mesopotamia 300 years earlier. Over the course of the fifteenth century BCE, Mittani aggressively expanded its borders west to the Mediterranean and east to Assyria, ultimately ruling over an even larger empire than the one Shamshi-Adad had controlled. Quite early in this expansion, the city of Alalakh once more became subject to the greater forces that surrounded it and was subsumed into the kingdom of Mittani.

The story of how Alalakh joined Mittani was remembered and recorded. At the beginning of the fifteenth century BCE a local king of Alalakh named Idrimi gathered allies who tried to fight the newly imperialistic Mittanian army, but ultimately he gave up and joined the kingdom, swearing his allegiance to its king and becoming his vassal.[10] His life story was written as an autobiography carved in cuneiform onto a rather forlorn looking statue of him, which was excavated by Woolley and is now in the British Museum (see Fig. 14.2). Mittani was swallowing up areas to the west of its heartland, and no doubt many other local princes experienced the same fate as Idrimi.

You might expect such a dominant kingdom as Mittani to have left a great hoard of documents, ones like Idrimi's autobiography and other royal inscriptions, from which we could reconstruct the details of its political, social, and economic history. But in fact Idrimi's account is unique and Mittani is probably the least known of any great power in any era of Mesopotamian history. No royal inscriptions survive beyond short lines of text on cylinder seals. We have no images of the Mittanian kings. Only a few dozen extant documents even name the kings. The problem is that, although thousands of documents must have been written in the palaces and temples of Mittani, they have not been found. Even tablets excavated from provincial towns that were ruled by the kings of Mittani—like Alalakh,

Fig. 14.2 Stone statue of King Idrimi of Alalakh, inscribed with his autobiography, from Alalakh, early fifteenth century BCE. (© The Trustees of the British Museum)

and like a town called Nuzi in northern Iraq—rarely mention the great kings who controlled them.

This means that there are a great many things we don't know about Mittani. We don't know, for example, the exact location of its capital city in the Habur region, or the sequence of its kings, or the lengths of their reigns, or the structure of the government. Even the name of the kingdom itself is uncertain. The name Mittani was spelled in several different ways by its kings, on their cylinder seals and letters,[11] and scribes in other lands spelled the same word in two more ways.[12] But the land also had a number of completely different names, depending on who was writing about it.

To the Egyptians, Mittani was called Naharina; the Hittites referred to it as the Hurri-land (for its Hurrian inhabitants); and the Babylonians (and Mittanians themselves, for that matter) often called it Hanigalbat. The terms all seem to have referred to the same place.

Presumably when Mittani's capital city of Washshukanni is identified and excavated,[13] more tablets will be found and a whole new field of cuneiform studies will open up. But for now, we just have clues and fragments, and a clear sense that we are missing a big chunk of ancient Near Eastern history.

Particularly puzzling are the names of the kings. Although the heart of Mittani was home to speakers of the Hurrian language, its rulers had throne names that did not make sense in Hurrian. Instead, their names consisted of phrases in Indo-Aryan, a language later spoken in northern India. No obvious explanation exists for this, especially when one considers that there is no evidence that anyone at all in Mittani—even the kings—spoke an Indo-Aryan language.[14] The kings, like their subjects, were native speakers of Hurrian and had Hurrian personal names before assuming Indo-Aryan throne names. It's true that a few Indo-Aryan terms show up in Mittanian texts—a very few—but as far as we can tell, almost no one knew what they meant. This was certainly not a situation (as it has often been described) of an Indo-Aryan elite ruling a Hurrian population. Mittani was a Hurrian-speaking state with a Hurrian royal family, who must have had some sort of contact with an Indo-Aryan-speaking population, from whom they got their official names.[15] How that happened is anyone's guess.

Other powers also began flexing their muscles in the early fifteenth century BCE and attempting to assert dominance over their neighbors. To the north and west of Mittani lay the land of Hatti, which grew stronger than before. As was true in Mittani, Hatti's leaders were keen to take control of the coast of northern Syria, along with the coastal valley of Kizzuwatna, at the northeast corner of the Mediterranean coast.

Egypt, under its Eighteenth Dynasty pharaoh Thutmose I (c. 1506–1493), was in the same expansionist mood, sending troops farther north than ever before. Thutmose I may have assumed that he could easily take control of the entire eastern coastline of the Mediterranean, but in northern Syria he encountered Mittanian forces, which put the brakes for now on any Egyptian thoughts of extending its empire beyond Canaan.

The shared interest of the rulers of Hatti, Mittani, and Egypt in taking control of this one section of the northern Levant may have had something to do with the cedar forests that grew there, the trade routes that passed through, and the access to seaborne trade. This was the same period that saw the growth of a kingdom on the nearby Mediterranean island of Cyprus, known as Alashiya, which was only 71 kilometers (44 miles) south of the coast of Hatti, and 105 kilometers (65 miles) west of the coast of Mittani. Alashiya was rich from the vast supplies of copper ore in its mountains. Meanwhile, farther to the west in Greece, the Mycenaean culture was beginning to flourish. It, too, depended deeply on trade.

Away from the coast, and south of Mittani, Babylonia continued to be ruled by a dynasty of kings with Kassite names. They looked in a different direction for their expansion; they were not interested in fighting the other land-hungry kings in the northern Levant. Instead they turned southward to expand, taking over the region that had been known as the Sealand by 1475 BCE and continuing all the way south in the Persian Gulf to take control of the land of Dilmun (Bahrain).[16]

Later, a Mittanian king named Saushtatar, who lived in the last decades of the fifteenth century BCE, expanded the Mittanian Empire to its greatest extent. He seems to have been remembered in subsequent generations as the great hero of the empire. It was his cylinder seal that later kings of his dynasty continued to use when they sealed clay tablets. And it was during his reign that Ilim-ilimma, son of Tuttu, was alive.

Ilim-ilimma: A Charioteer and Lender at Alalakh

The fifteenth century BCE was therefore a time of change, and a time when wars frequently disrupted the lives of ancient Near Eastern peoples, especially in the Levant. Each of the kingdoms developed new strategies to employ in their battles against their neighbors. For the kings of Mittani, one approach was to assign their citizens to well-defined social classes and to demand different kinds of state service from the members of each class. This was not an old tradition in the region of Alalakh. There is no sign of it before the kings of Mittani took over there. But soon after Alalakh had been captured and brought into the kingdom of Mittani, the government set about organizing its population into classes.[17]

This brings us back to Ilim-ilimma. The classes at Alalakh had been established before his lifetime, and we know that he was a member of a social class called the *maryanni*. This meant that, in times of war, he would have served as a chariot warrior.

Ilim-ilimma's name appeared on a list of thirty-four *maryanni* men, who represented the city's elite.[18] The list was one of many census records preserved in the palace at Alalakh that recorded people's names along with their social classes. Although this preoccupation with social class was a new phenomenon, it was one that seems to have spread right across Mittani. Administrations in earlier Near Eastern kingdoms had little interest in defining people by social class. Although in his laws Hammurabi had made some distinctions among free individuals between a higher class (the *awilum*s) and a lower class of commoners, in other contexts these terms were rarely used in association with actual named people. It's not even clear how, or on what occasions, the two classes were distinguished in Old Babylonian times. In Mittani, though, one's social class was an important part of one's identity.

The four classes listed on the census records in Alalakh, and in another Mittanian town called Nuzi far to the east, were as follows. The *maryanni*—men like Ilim-ilimma—comprised the elite in society. The other classes were known as the "released ones"; "doers of *ilku* service" or "peasants"; and "tenants" or "poor."

According to historian Eva von Dassow, the *maryanni* were distinguished from the rest of the society by their right to fight in chariots and their exemption from corvée labor duties, such as work on state building projects.[19] The term *maryanni* comes from a borrowed Indo-Aryan word, *márya*, which meant "(young) man." (The *-nni* at the end was a Hurrian word ending.) But to the east in Nuzi, the census takers did not use this word. They called men of this class "chariot riders," using an Akkadian term,[20] which confirms that chariot fighting was a distinguishing feature of men in this class in both cities. Presumably the same was true across Mittani.

The "released" individuals were artisans along with specialists in such fields as horse training. They worked for the great institutions and for the *maryanni*. These people merited the designation "released," not because they had been freed from slavery, apparently, but because, like the elites, they were released from performing corvée labor.

Next were the peasants, who constituted the mass of the population. They worked hard, farming their allocated *ilku* fields and orchards to support their families,[21] like their counterparts during the Old Babylonian period. They also had to show up when summoned for corvée labor duties and for obligatory military service.[22] These men had no chariots; they served in the infantry.

At the lowest rung of society were the tenants who, unlike those in the other three classes, had lost their rights to land. These men farmed for others and paid rent, but they were still subject to military and corvée service.[23]

You may have noticed that, in this class system, no men were exempt from the military. No matter what class they belonged to, men fought for the king of Mittani when he needed them. If he was in the mood to expand his empire, or if he needed to defend the land against the Egyptians or the Hittites, they were called up. The troops of Alalakh even fought from time to time against kingdoms that should have been their allies—other kingdoms that lay within the Mittanian Empire. This happened at least once during Ilim-ilimma's lifetime. A treaty found in the palace at Alalakh was negotiated after a war between the king of Alalakh and the king of a neighboring land called Tunip,[24] both of them vassals of the king of Mittani.

Although Ilim-ilimma son of Tuttu almost certainly fought in this battle against Tunip, and perhaps at other times as well, the records that survive from Alalakh tell us nothing about his exploits on the battlefield. They shine a light, instead, on his private transactions and his clear desire to increase his personal wealth.

He was a shrewd businessman. On at least three occasions he lent silver to fellow citizens. Two of those loans stipulated that the borrowers (and, in one case, the borrower's wife as well) would work in his house as indentured servants until they had paid off their debts.[25] This type of loan seems to have been uncommon and it would have been challenging for the debtors, who had to physically serve their creditor while accumulating the money they needed to pay back the loan with interest. Ilim-ilimma had contracts drawn up that laid out all the details of the agreements, which he kept in his archive.

Ilim-ilimma also purchased two women, presumably as slaves, one of them for a prohibitively high price of 1,000 shekels.[26] The normal price for an enslaved woman was about 50 shekels, which was, indeed, the price of the second woman that he bought.[27] Why was the first woman worth twenty times as much? It was not a scribal error—the number 1,000 was written out clearly as a word, and Ilim-ilimma paid seven sellers (six men and one woman) for the enslaved woman—this was a much larger number of sellers than usual. We simply don't know why he paid so much. Perhaps she was a talented musician or artisan.[28] But nothing more is known about her. The contract doesn't even provide her name.

In one legally convoluted transaction, Ilim-ilimma had himself adopted by another man.[29] The "adoption" was designed so that Ilim-ilimma could legally inherit the wealth of his "father" after that man's death. The older man had no way out; clauses in the contract required that, if he did not respect the contract, he would lose all his property, and he would lose it to Ilim-ilimma, of course. Ilim-ilimma's own property was protected. If he reneged on the contract, all he would lose would be the right to inherit the wealth of the man who had supposedly adopted him.[30] Clearly, this was not a real adoption. It was not even created because Ilim-ilimma felt the need for a father; he was already an adult at this time and, in any case, Tuttu had played that role in his life (though Tuttu was probably dead by now). It was, instead, a way for Ilim-ilimma to gain control of the estate of a man who must have been, in some way, beholden to him—a man whose actual relatives lost their inheritance as a result.

The contracts that record these transactions all start with the same phrase. The scribe wrote, each time, that the events described took place "in the presence of" the king of Alalakh. The king also sealed each tablet at the top of the front side.

This was not just true of Ilim-ilimma's contracts, it was true of all the contracts found in occupation Level IV of the city. The king was deeply involved in the business activities of the people in his close circle and made a point to be present whenever they undertook important transactions. The witnesses to these contracts were also often high-ranking members of the court and the society, some of whom had been listed on the tablet of *maryanni* men in Alalakh.[31] But all the tablets from Woolley's excavations were found in the king's own palace. Perhaps contracts stored in private houses might be different, with less involvement of the local king.

When the king of Alalakh himself was the subject of important transactions or litigation, it was the great king of Mittani in whose presence the contract had to be drawn up. This was true of two contracts found in Alalakh. For both, King Saushtatar seems to have traveled all the way from his capital city to decide the cases.[32] It is striking that these contracts, unlike almost any written before this time, listed no witnesses at all. It seems that the great king's presence and his seal on the tablet eliminated the usual need for other witnesses; the tablet itself was apparently evidence enough.

This was not just true in Alalakh; contracts drawn up in the presence of the great king of Mittani have been found at other cities as well. It was also true of many contracts written in Hittite lands. And each time that the great king was present, his royal seal was impressed on the tablet. Throughout Syria and Anatolia, great kings seem to have been more willing to travel around their kingdoms to serve as judges and witnesses for important court cases and contracts than in previous eras. And yet, when you look at the majority of tablets from the great kingdoms of Mittani and Hatti, it was the local kings—the vassals of the great kings—who were more directly involved in, and who had the greater impact on, people's lives.

Ilim-ilimma's career spanned two generations of kings of Alalakh. In time, the crown prince who shared his name became king, and he, in turn, was present as king when Ilim-ilimma needed to have contracts drawn up. On one such occasion a whole Canaanite family—father, mother, and son—needed to borrow 24 shekels of silver from Ilim-ilimma.[33] He agreed. The man was named Ba'laya, and his profession was listed as "hunter." Surprisingly, given Ilim-ilimma's evident love of silver, he was willing to accept the interest on the loan in the form of 200 turtledoves. Presumably the hunter would capture these birds, and they must have been worth at least the value of the interest payment. Were the birds to be delivered alive or dead? The contract doesn't specify. If he delivered them dead, they would not have been useful as food for long, because of the lack of refrigeration. If Ba'laya delivered them alive, did Ilim-ilimma own a dovecote in which he could house them all? Either way, there was to be no negotiation about this interest payment. If the 200 turtledoves did not appear at the first of the year, Ba'laya was to be imprisoned, and "if Ba'laya runs away, disappears, or dies, his wife, his children, his property serve as deposit for . . . (the loan)."[34]

We do not know the fate of Ba'laya, his wife and son, or the turtledoves. Nor, for that matter, do we know the fate of Ilim-ilimma son of Tuttu. His namesake, the local king Ilim-ilimma was the last king to live in the Level IV Alalakh palace. Perhaps the king moved the capital to another city in the region.[35] If so, perhaps Ilim-ilimma, son of Tuttu, moved there as well, though he left his written contracts behind.

Diplomatic Overtures and the Attainment of International Peace

Alalakh ended up being destroyed again in the course of yet another battle for the region. The sacking was again probably the work of Hittite troops, but they may have been fighting in collaboration with the neighboring kingdom of Tunip. Alalakh and Tunip had been bound together by a peace treaty, but one side or the other seems to have broken it.[36]

The fighting in Alalakh—between Mittani and Hatti, and with neighboring lands—must have seemed interminable and was only made worse when Egypt again got involved. During the same reign of Saushtatar of Mittani (and therefore probably during Ilim-ilimma's lifetime), the pharaoh Thutmose III (c. 1479–1425 BCE) gathered a great force of soldiers and marched on Mittani from the south. The clashing of great powers in the northern Levant probably took many lives and destroyed property over a wide area. Thutmose claimed to have removed a great deal of Mittanian wealth which he transferred to Egypt when he returned (though Mittani remained undefeated, in spite of Thutmose III's claims of victory).

Perhaps it was a shock to each of these imperialistic rulers—the kings of Mittani, Egypt, and Hatti—to find that victory was not a given when they went to war against one another. They each had little trouble taking over lesser powers: Egypt had conquered neighboring Canaan to the north and Nubia to the south; Hatti had conquered many lands across Anatolia; Mittani had conquered Assyria and most of Syria. But faced with fighting one another, none of them seems to have made much headway. The coastal valley of Kizzuwatna, for example, passed back and forth between Hatti and Mittani as they repeatedly fought for control of it. Kings died and were succeeded by their sons and still the battles continued. But at some point, the kings of the three lands seem to have reached the conclusion that each was incapable of conquering the others.[37]

The next step in their relationship was remarkable. The previously belligerent pharaoh Amenhotep II (1427–1400 BCE), who with his troops had campaigned ferociously against Mittani at the start of his reign, suddenly ceased his military activities in his ninth year. Instead, he boasted of riches flowing into Egypt from the kings of Hatti, Babylonia, and Mittani. "Each one," he wrote, "tried to outdo his counterpart with gifts of every foreign land."[38]

No matter what Amenhotep II wanted his subjects to believe, however, these gifts did not represent tribute being sent to Egypt by the other kings. Almost certainly, the four great powers had come to a shared agreement. Instead of fighting one another and looting one another's lands, they realized they could obtain the same benefit by willingly and formally exchanging luxury goods, just as Mesopotamian kings had done for at least a thousand years, since the time of the kings of Ebla. Amenhotep II simply did not mention to his subjects the gold that he sent abroad in exchange for the "gifts" sent by his new allies. A new era of peace had begun.

We know that, a generation later (and perhaps already in the time of Amenhotep II), these four great powers had negotiated peace treaties, were engaged in formal diplomatic relations, and had even become members of one another's families through dynastic marriages. Remarkably, they all accepted the Mesopotamian diplomatic system wholesale, even to the point of writing to one another only in cuneiform on clay tablets and almost always in Akkadian, which was the native language only of the Babylonians.

Their envoys all adopted the same set of conventions, most of which already had a millennium-long history. These rules were so carefully observed that they must have been learned by the envoys rather than acquired through observation. Although individual kings occasionally tried to push the limits, they could expect their allies to push right back when they did; adherence to the system was part of being a member of the brotherhood.

The following were the (probably unwritten) rules:

First, with regard to titles, each king was to be regarded as the equal, the "brother," of his ally. Each considered himself and his allies to be "great kings," and these titles—brother and great king—could not be used by kings outside the brotherhood without permission.

Second, each king chose experienced diplomats to represent him in the courts of his allies, and the envoys were expected to visit the ally's court at least once a year. They traveled in pairs, one from each of the two courts that constituted that particular alliance. Under certain circumstances, an envoy could be detained in the ally's palace, but this detention had to be explained in a letter transported by a separate messenger. Envoys were the eyes and ears of their royal employers and were to be treated well, receiving banquets and personal gifts on arrival in the foreign court. Even detained diplomats lived comfortably.

Third, they wrote regular letters to one another. When an envoy traveled to another court, he carried a letter from his king, written in the lingua franca of Akkadian on a single clay tablet. Each of these letters began with a formulaic greeting in which the king sent wishes for the well-being of his "brother," and in which he assured him that all was well with him too. In their letters, the kings were careful never to show weakness or to suggest even a hint of a difference in status or wealth between them. They were equals, period. As a Babylonian king wrote to the Egyptian pharaoh: "Furthermore, as I am told, in my brother's country everything is available and my brother needs absolutely nothing. Furthermore, in my country everything too is available and I for my part nee[d] absolutely nothing."[39] This was patently untrue since one of the main reasons for their alliance was to obtain goods from one another, but to admit that would have been a sign of weakness. It also seems to have been taboo in the letters to engage in any saber-rattling. The kings never threatened one another, no matter how annoyed they got (and they certainly did get annoyed).

Fourth, the envoys almost always transported valuable "greeting gifts" from one king to the other. These had to be of approximately equal value and represented luxury goods to which the sending king had access—gold, silver, horses, chariots, lapis lazuli, perfume, and so on. A king could request a particular gift from his ally but he had to depend on the ally's goodwill to send it; no enforcement mechanisms existed. These were not trade relationships with invoices and receipts; they were based on trust. The exchange of luxury gifts was the carrot that kept the kings engaged with one another, and it was also often the main sore point between them. Almost none of the other kings ever thought the pharaoh had sent them enough gold.

Fifth, the kings married one another's daughters. Well, this was true of all the lands except for Egypt. The Egyptian kings agreed to maintain all the practices the Mesopotamians had been insisting upon in their diplomatic system for centuries . . . until it came to marriages. They were happy to accept royal brides from other lands, but as one pharaoh put it, "From time immemorial no daughter of the king of Egy[pt] is given to anyone."[40] This was non-negotiable. Egyptian princesses would not be arriving at foreign courts with dowries and entourages of servants. They would, instead, be staying in Egypt. But the other kings seem not to have been too upset. Marriages could go either way between equals; it didn't really matter which king sent a princess and which king received one as a bride. Given that Mesopotamian kings seem never to have married the daughters of their vassals, the slight advantage, in their minds, lay in being the father-in-law rather than the son-in-law. The pharaoh, on the other hand, collected foreign brides as though they represented tribute.

And, finally, all the kings negotiated and abided by peace treaties. Unfortunately, none of the peace treaties between the great kings of this era survives, but they were mentioned in the letters and we know that they were sworn in the names of the gods of both lands.

This was just a remarkable historical moment. These powerful kings who had never met one another (as they occasionally admitted), and whose lands had recently been enemies, decided to put aside their pride and their pompous assertions of world domination, and to collaborate. The goal was selfish enough—the acquisition of more wealth—but they seem also to have relished the peace that came with it.

We know about all this because the Egyptian pharaohs kept their international correspondence in a special archive room of the palace and, incredibly, the letters survived there in the ground for thousands of years before being discovered in the late nineteenth century of our own era. The site has the modern name of Amarna, which has given its name to the tablets themselves—the Amarna letters—and to the whole "Amarna period" that they document. The contrast with the chaos of the fifteenth century is stark and must have come as a relief to people all across the empires, but especially in those regions that had been fought over for so long.

Our attention will turn therefore from charioteers to diplomats, and especially to translators, because the whole system depended on them. As is still true today, a translator was responsible for communicating ideas that had been formulated in one language by relaying them in another, without changing the meaning. During this particular era, the continued relationship between great powers could rest on a translator's ability to get the message right.

Being a translator was a very ancient profession. Even before the first cities were built, speakers of Sumerian and Akkadian shared the Euphrates and Tigris river valleys and must have been able to communicate with one another. As we've seen, soon after cuneiform writing was invented, scribes figured out how to use the script to write in languages other than Sumerian; by the Early Dynastic period it had been adapted to record Akkadian and Eblaite. A glossary found at Ebla that lists Sumerian words and their Eblaite equivalents is the earliest known example of a systematic attempt to correlate words in one language to another. From this we know that people were aware that it was possible to express the same ideas using completely different and unrelated languages in order to do so. But this realization almost certainly predated the period covered by this book; it took place before the development of cities. People had been trading over long distances for thousands of years before this, and languages that were just as sophisticated as any used today had been spoken for at least tens of thousands of years. As far back as 400,000 years ago *Homo erectus* was capable of speech,[41] and *Homo sapiens* hunters and gatherers communicated with one another without difficulty. Language made it possible for humans to settle across the globe. Unimaginably long before anyone conceived of writing languages down and listing their vocabularies, humans from distant places had been coming in contact with one another and finding ways to communicate.

Hane of Egypt: A Translator

Most of the translators of the Amarna period remain anonymous, not even mentioned by the scribes, envoys, kings, or queens who depended upon them, but we do know the names of a couple of them. One was a man named Hane who lived in the mid-fourteenth century BCE. He must have grown up in Egypt—his name seems to be Egyptian—but he spoke fluent Akkadian and probably Hurrian as well.

Hane gets just one brief mention, in a letter written by a very verbose king of Mittani named Tushratta (mid-fourteenth century BCE).[42] The king was writing to his ally, Amenhotep III of Egypt (1386–1349 BCE), about a marriage that was taking place between their families; the pharaoh was about to marry Tushratta's daughter. By Tushratta's normal standards, this was a short letter—just forty-one lines long—and it reads like a sigh of relief.

Tushratta's daughter Tadu-Hepa had recently left for Egypt, traveling with her dowry (which included more than 1,500 items, many of them immensely valuable), a separate enormous hoard of gifts for King Amenhotep III, and 300 attendants. They were accompanied by innumerable Egyptian guards.[43] In his letter, her father wrote that "I have given my daughter to be the wife of my brother, whom I love."[44] Months of planning and negotiation had finally come to an end, and now the king could only hope and pray the princess and her fabulous gifts would all arrive safely in Egypt and that Amenhotep III would approve of this new bride, whom he had not yet met.

Tushratta then launched into what almost sounds like a prayer: "May (the Hurrian gods) Shimigi and Shaushka go before her. May they make her the image of my brother's heart. And may my brother rejoice on t[hat] day. May Shimigi and Shau[shka] give [to] my brother a gre[at] blessing and wonder[ful] joy. May [they bless him], and may my brother, li[ve] forever."[45] One can feel in his words his fervent desire for the marriage to be a success.

At this point, he switched gears, moving on to praise the two Egyptian officials who had done the most to bring the marriage plans to a successful conclusion: Mane, the envoy, and Hane, the translator. This passage is one of the warmest and the most complimentary in all the Amarna international correspondence between great kings. Tushratta wrote of the Egyptian men that "their report was excellent" and that "in everything about them, I have never seen men with such an appearance."[46] Accordingly, Tushratta said he had "ex[alted]" the two men "like gods" and had "given [them] many presents and treated them very kindly." He prayed for them as well: "May my gods and the gods of my brother protect them."[47]

Most great kings in this era were much cagier than this when writing to one another, and some, Amenhotep III included, didn't hesitate to blame envoys for making mistakes or jeopardizing the good relationships between themselves and their allies.[48] Tushratta didn't play these games; he admired the Egyptian envoy Mane and was happy to let the pharaoh know it. He even specifically asked for Mane to be sent to Mittani on occasion; Mane was the Mittanian king's clear favorite among the envoys from the Egyptian court. Hane's contributions in interpreting during the marriage negotiations must also have been exemplary to have warranted this rare praise, though in all the other letters from Tushratta, a translator's presence is assumed but not acknowledged.

By the time that Tushratta was dictating this letter, Mane and Hane were probably already well on their way to Egypt, accompanying princess Tadu-Hepa and her extensive bridal party. Tushratta's own scribe wrote down his words, and he notes in the letter that a Mittanian envoy named Nahramashshi would be carrying the letter to Egypt. The letter was in Akkadian, but that was not how Tushratta had composed it. He would have dictated the letter in his native Hurrian and one of his own translators had rendered it in Akkadian.

Tushratta then approved the letter (probably by having a scribe read it back to him) and gave it to Nahramashshi. He also entrusted him with extravagant gifts for the pharaoh: "one polished *nahra* for making mirrors" and "one *maninnu*-necklace of pure lapis lazuli, pure lapis lazuli and of gold."[49] He emphasized the prized lapis lazuli by repeating it twice.[50] Tushratta hoped that the necklace might symbolize a lasting alliance between the two lands; he wrote, "may it rest on the neck of my brother for one hundred thousand years!"[51]

The Mittanian envoy Nahramashshi was no doubt accompanied on his journey to Egypt by an armed guard to protect the valuable gifts, and probably also by an Egyptian envoy who was returning to his own country. Nahramashshi and his small group probably caught up with the princess's entourage en route; they could travel much faster than her unwieldy procession.

As soon as this group reached the Egyptian border, Hane would have been needed regularly to serve as the voice of the expedition: making arrangements, greeting officials, and translating for the Mittanian team. No doubt several people in the group were bilingual, but Hane had particular authority as the pharaoh's official translator.

Once the group reached Amenhotep III's court and the envoys and translators had been granted an audience, Nahramashshi greeted the pharaoh on behalf of Tushratta and gave an overview of what was in the Mittanian king's letter.[52] When he was done, it would have been the pharaoh's own scribe who read Tushratta's letter aloud in Akkadian to Amenhotep III, and Hane who translated it into Egyptian.[53] Each king trusted his own translators under these circumstances more than those of his allies.[54]

By the time Amenhotep III heard the message in the letter, it had already been translated twice. Tushratta's Hurrian words had become—through the work of one of Tushratta's own scribes—the Akkadian letter, which in turn had been transformed orally into a message in Egyptian by Hane. Akkadian made for a useful lingua franca, but there was plenty of room here for mistakes or misunderstandings to creep in. The correspondents were aware of this and sometimes a king added words to assure his ally of his good intentions. In a later letter to Amenhotep III, Tushratta declared that, no matter how his words might turn out when translated, "The word that Mane will communicate to my brother is gracious and true. . . . It is not evil (and) not hostile towards my brother."[55] It might have been particularly important to include this disclaimer on this particular letter because (unlike any other) it had been written down in Tushratta's native Hurrian, not Akkadian. Presumably no one at the Egyptian court would have been trained to read Hurrian, so getting the letter translated into Egyptian for the king to hear might have been a challenge. Amenhotep III could have depended on a Mittanian scribe for the translation, but that man's Egyptian might have been less adept than the pharaoh wished. The fact that the letter was a whopping 493 lines long did not make things easier.[56]

Supporting the multilingual communication between kings was an education system in which scribes and translators across the Near East were taught to read and write in a standard style of Akkadian.[57] Hane certainly had gone to school in Egypt. He would have learned to write his native Egyptian language in both hieroglyphs and the cursive hieratic script but, unlike most Egyptian scribes, he also mastered the Akkadian language and the cuneiform script. It could be that Hane had grown up hearing and speaking Akkadian as well as Egyptian. Plenty of women in the Egyptian court spoke Akkadian as their native language—princesses from Babylonia who were married to the king, for example, along with their hundreds of attendants. If Hane had been the son of a Babylonian lady-in-waiting or musician, he might have been encouraged by his mother to speak her language and have been bilingual from birth. On the other hand, he might have been the son of a court translator, since professions tended to run in families. If so, his father probably spoke to him in Akkadian as a boy, to prepare him for his future career.

We get a glimpse of Hane's education from twenty-nine scribal exercise tablets that were written by the students at the Egyptian court school, which was located near the records office at Amarna.[58] They show that, just like a Mesopotamian scribe learning to write his own language, Hane started his cuneiform training by learning to write signs on clay (the tu-ta-ti exercises),[59] after which he moved on to lexical lists and names. Eventually he was required to copy literary works and myths.[60]

The school tablets from Amarna were written by a later generation of students who studied at the successor to the court school that Hane had attended. The tablets from Amarna show that, soon after joining the alliance of great kings, a pharaoh (perhaps Amenhotep II) must have invited a Mesopotamian scholar to create the school so that the Egyptian scribes and translators were prepared to help their kings participate in international diplomatic exchanges. It's even possible to identify the origin of the founder of this school; the curriculum he chose is the same one found at a city called Emar on the Euphrates in Syria.[61] Emar would have been ruled by Mittani at that time, so the Egyptian school had a Mittanian founder. (We will return to Emar in Chapter 16.)

One tablet found in Amarna even included a list of a few Egyptian words and their Akkadian equivalents, but this wasn't a regular school text, and it wasn't in the type of handwriting that Egyptian scribes used for cuneiform.[62] It seems, instead, to have been written by someone who grew up speaking Akkadian, someone who wrote in an assured Mesopotamian cuneiform hand and was learning to speak Egyptian.[63] The Egyptian words were written phonetically in cuneiform in a column on the left, with their Akkadian equivalents on the right. The words include such useful terms as house, door, bolt, door-socket, chair, bed, and table, along with terms for numbers (written in numerals on the Akkadian side, but phonetically in Egyptian).[64] The scribe who wrote it even inadvertently added an Akkadian case ending to an Egyptian word, which is not something an Egyptian would have done.[65] We tend to think of Egyptian as an ancient language that was written only in the hieroglyphic and hieratic scripts, but this list shows that even Egyptian could be written in cuneiform. Hypothetically, the reverse was also true and Akkadian could have been written in hieroglyphs, but hieroglyphs were not generally used to record other languages. Scripts are not the same as languages. Just as any language can be written phonetically using our Latin alphabet—some with more difficulty than others—so any language could hypothetically be written phonetically in cuneiform. More difficulties arose in some languages, especially because cuneiform signs comprised syllables, not individual consonants and vowels, but this did not stop scribes from trying.

Once he had mastered both languages and scripts, Hane began his career in the Egyptian civil service, eventually gaining the pharaoh's trust to such an extent that he was appointed as Egyptian translator to the court of

Mittani. In this capacity he always worked with other men such as fellow Egyptian scribes who wrote and read the letters, the Egyptian envoys (like his colleague Mane) who transported them and negotiated for their king, and their counterparts in the court of Mittani.

These men shared experiences that few of their contemporaries could imagine. They had access to some of the most exclusive areas in the royal palaces, not just in their homeland but in another land as well; they spoke in person to the great kings of both lands. Unlike even the kings themselves, they understood the etiquette in the allied king's court—when to wash their hands, when to bow, when to speak, what was implied by the seating arrangement at banquets. They saw for themselves how much gold decorated the furniture and the walls, and how the servants were treated. They heard the court musicians play and they ate the best food.

The men also shared the experience of the exhausting travel involved in getting from one court to the other. From the capital city of Mittani to the capital city of Egypt was a one-way journey of about 2,400 kilometers (1,500 miles). Traveling at the normal pace of 24 kilometers (15 miles) per day, the trip would have taken more than three months. Fortunately, the lands they passed through were at peace with one another, mostly being subject either to Mittani or to Egypt, though bandits always presented a threat. As they traveled, the men must have talked together, which raises the question—in which language? All of them must have been at least bilingual, and probably multilingual, able to converse with one another in their own languages of Egyptian and Hurrian, as well as in the lingua franca of Akkadian. They probably even understood the related Semitic languages that were spoken in the Mediterranean lands they passed through. But probably only official translators like Hane had been trained to write confidently in more than one language.

Sometimes, though, even a translator could struggle. Concepts that were clear in one language did not always have an obvious equivalent in another. Even terms that translated directly might have had different nuances. This is, of course, still true of all translation today. Particularly tricky for Hane must have been the idea of "love," which in Akkadian was the verb *ramu*. You may have noticed, in the letter that began this section, that King Tushratta of Mittani called Amenhotep III "my brother, whom I love."[66] He wrote about his love for the pharaoh a lot, much more than any other of the great kings. He added it to the greeting formula almost every time, and, in the body of his letters, a version of the word "love" appeared, on average, once every thirteen lines.[67] In Tushratta's very first letter to Amenhotep III, in which he proposed re-establishing an old alliance between their two lands, he justified this overture in terms of the love between their ancestors: "My father loved you and you, moreover, as for my father, you loved him and my father, because of (that) love, [g]ave to you my sister (as a wife)."[68] In Tushratta's mind, the whole brotherhood, including the diplomatic marriages, was built on the love that the kings had for one another, notwithstanding that they had never met.

The strange thing is, Tushratta was alone in this. None of the other great kings ever mentioned loving one another in their letters. They did refer to feelings of friendship and brotherhood toward their allies, but not love. Was Tushratta just much more affectionate than his fellow kings? Possibly. There are some indications that Mittanians did talk more about love, at least within their diplomatic relationships, than people did in other lands.[69] But Tushratta's message might have been interpreted differently by the pharaoh. Whether he intended it or not, his letters to the Egyptian king expressed a subtle message of subservience.

You see, for centuries, when someone wrote about love in an Akkadian letter it tended to be as a statement of loyalty, which was another meaning of the verb "ramu."[70] Someone who began a letter with the greeting "To so-and-so, speak! This is what so-and-so, who loves you, says,"[71] the writer tended to be of lower status than the recipient. Equals rarely if ever wrote this way in Akkadian but, as a native Hurrian speaker, Tushratta might not have known this.

Love did come up in other contexts in letters, but it wasn't often there as a way to indicate affection. For example, a writer could use it as a kind of emotional blackmail. The king of Babylon did this in the only Amarna letter written by a great king (other than Tushratta) that mentioned love. He wrote to the pharaoh, "If you love me, they (some Assyrian leaders) will conduct no business whatsoever."[72] That "if" was a way of needling the pharaoh, with an understood subtext that, if he did not do what was requested, he was not a true ally.

So "love" was a complicated verb, and when Tushratta spoke in Hurrian of loving the pharaoh, he might have meant something very different from the overtones that the phrase acquired in Akkadian, and, for all we know, Amenhotep III may have understood something else again when he heard it in Egyptian. The great kings were constantly jockeying for status. Although they were equals, they were also masters of subtle attempts to raise themselves above the rest. Tushratta seems to have erred in the wrong direction. In his desire to emphasize how close he felt to Amenhotep III, he made himself seem to be a less important king.

Was the Mittanian translator aware of this nuance? Was Hane, as the Egyptian translator? Possibly not, unless they had grown up completely immersed in Akkadian. Native speakers understand subtleties that go beyond translation.

In another way, Tushratta could have been seen as groveling a little to the pharaoh, whether consciously or not. He had a curious habit when he wrote to the Egyptian king: he avoided calling him "you." Instead, he repeatedly wrote in the third person about "my brother." This may have been intended as a reminder of their alliance and equality, of course, but the third person was almost always used by vassals and servants when they wrote to kings. The other great kings were happy to refer to one another as "you."[73] Tushratta had less and less success in getting the pharaoh to respond to his letters. His subservient tone might not have helped.

On another occasion that depended on translators, Amenhotep III wanted to develop an alliance with a king in the western Anatolian land of Arzawa, and again we see language problems creep into diplomatic relations. Arzawa's neighbor, the Hittite Empire, was suffering through a period of decline, so it behooved the Egyptian king to create an alliance with the newly powerful land of Arzawa, and of course to marry an Arzawan princess. Amenhotep III seems to have sent an envoy all the way across the Mediterranean with an oral message expressing this interest, but apparently he did not send a corresponding letter. Perhaps he thought that no one in the Arzawan court was likely to be able to read Akkadian. If so, he was right; Tarhundaradu, the king of Arzawa, wanted to respond to the pharaoh's message in writing, but he was not a member of the international diplomatic network and he had no scribes on his staff who were trained in Akkadian who could draft a reply. (He would have had no scribes who could write in Egyptian, either; it seems that almost no one did, outside of Egypt.)

So Tarhundaradu replied in Hittite in a letter that extended over two tablets (which was highly unusual, especially for a relatively short letter), only one of which survives—the second half of the letter. It's unlike any other international letter. Tarhundaradu was clearly annoyed at the way he had been contacted by the pharaoh. He said that he didn't trust the Egyptian messenger, Kalbaya, and that "he conveyed [the message] orally, but it was not written on the tablet."[74] He demanded to be treated properly: "So send Kalbaya back to me quickly together with my messenger, and write back to me on a tablet concerning this matter."

Touchingly, the Arzawan scribe who wrote the letter included a private postscript to his counterpart in Egypt. After finishing the king's message, he added an elaborate blessing to "the scribe who reads aloud this tablet," perhaps hoping that the gods would help the Egyptian scribe understand what he had written, and then asked him to add a postscript to his own return letter: "You, scribe, kindly write to me and put your name at the end."[75] He also pleaded for future letters to be written in Hittite: "Always write in Hittite the tablets that they bring here."

Again, one can imagine the difficulty that was now faced by the Egyptian scribes when the Arzawan messenger arrived with this letter in Hittite. The court was presumably combed for any scribe who could read and write in Hittite who could translate the letter from Arzawa and then translate and record the pharaoh's reply. It seems that one of Amenhotep III's wives was from Kaska,[76] a land to the north of Hatti; perhaps one of her literate attendants helped out.

A letter was duly written in return, in which Amenhotep III pointedly did not refer to Tarhundaradu as a "brother" or a "great king," though he continued plans for an alliance and diplomatic marriage.[77] The letter was indeed in Hittite, but, as its modern editor noted, the Egyptian scribe "writes in a very clumsy and faulty Hittite, showing that he was not a very good translator of the pharaoh's Egyptian language."[78] Curiously, though, the letter was found in Amarna—it had not been sent. Perhaps the tablet we have was a rough draft and the Hittite in the final version was more polished. Or perhaps word arrived that the power of Hatti was rising again so Amenhotep III scuttled his plans for an alliance with Arzawa. The court of the Hittite capital of Hattusa, like the court in Thebes, was home to a school that trained its scribes in Akkadian. The Egyptian relationship with the great king of Hatti would be one between equals, and it would be a lot easier to maintain. The king of Hatti, unlike the king of Arzawa, knew the rules.

Chapter 15
Gift Recipients and Royal In-Laws

The Amarna letters provide us with an insider's view of the royal courts and diplomacy in the Late Bronze Age, but many other cuneiform documents survive from this era. They provide glimpses of many people who were affected by the kings and the international spirit of the age.

Abi-hunni: Recipient of a House from the King of Hana

Abi-hunni was an individual for whom just one document survives. He lived a whole life in which, no doubt, he had a profession, a family, friends, neighbors, a house, some fields. He had favorite foods and perhaps he was an expert at the local board game, or perhaps he was known for his singing voice or his skill with numbers. But all that is gone. Everything we know about him is based on just the one text.[1] But the surprising thing is that this makes him incredibly fortunate. At least he left a tiny dent on history, unlike millions of other people who lived in the ancient Near East. His document was published in 1897,[2] and it remains the sole witness not just to Abi-hunni's life but to the time of a king named Ishar-Lim of Hana, in eastern Syria. Abi-hunni, King Ishar-Lim, and the fourteen other men named on the same tablet are the only individuals whose names survive, so far, from the entire reign. Ishar-Lim ruled sometime in the late fifteenth century or early fourteenth century BCE.[3] Given the international situation in that era, it's unlikely that Hana was independent. Even though the Hana kings issued their own year-names, they were probably vassals of one of the great powers—Babylonia or Mittani, or (later) Assyria.

The other kings who ruled Hana during this the same era had the same bad luck as Ishar-Lim in terms of their legacy. Although presumably thousands of documents were written during their reigns (each of which seems to have lasted an average of at least twenty years, since son followed father to the throne for generations), so far, just one or two tablets have shown up dated to each king.

Abi-hunni is interesting because he was the recipient of a generous gift from King Ishar-Lim: a small house in the city of Terqa. Their interaction was part of a trend in the Late Bronze Age, a trend seen from Hatti to Syria to Babylonia. Kings were granting more and more houses, fields, orchards, even whole towns, to their trusted friends, officials, vassals, and even, it seems, to normal citizens.

Abi-hunni's new house was just 2⅔ SAR in extent, or about 60 square meters (c. 650 square feet). But the gift was considered significant enough that the king seems to have been physically present at the ceremony when the contract for the gift was written. No royal gift was too small for the king's direct involvement. King Ishar-Lim rolled his own seal on the margin of the contract. It was an impressive cylinder seal, bearing gold caps on each end that were decorated with granulated triangles. A king's presence at the creation of a contract was a tradition not just in Hana, it was also becoming common across the Near East. Kings in this period showed up for ceremonies, seals in hand, in order to oversee a great many legal matters. We have already seen this in the case of Ilim-ilimma son of Tuttu in Alalakh; the scribes often noted specifically that such proceedings took place "in the presence of" the king. On the other hand, this phrase was not used on records of royal land grants. Something that took place "in the presence" of the king was a transaction to which he was a witness. In a royal land donation, he was one of the principal parties.

The scribe who recorded the gift to Abi-hunni carefully noted that Abi-hunni's house was on a town square called "the square of the land," and that the buildings on the other three sides of his house all belonged to the palace. A great deal of land everywhere belonged to the various palaces in the Late Bronze Age. The scribe also noted that the house could not be reclaimed by someone else, even in cases of an edict releasing borrowers from debt. This presumably meant that it had previously been home to another family who might have tried to get it back. Such a person would have to pay a huge fine of ten minas of silver, and the tablet notes that "his head will be smeared with hot asphalt."[4] This sounds horribly painful but, in Hana, it had been the standard penalty for challenging a real estate contract for centuries, and one has the sense that by now it was just a required legal clause, not an actual threat.

The scribe then listed the witnesses who had been present on what must have been a happy day for Abi-hunni. They seem almost ridiculously high-powered for the transfer of such a small house. The first witness was the crown prince. Then came another prince, followed by a "great judge," the overseer of the diviners, and the overseer of the ministers, and then four other men, including a priest. Admittedly, Hana was not a power the size of Mittani or Babylonia, and the royal court may have been located in the city of Terqa, where Abi-hunni's new house was located. So perhaps it wasn't that difficult to assemble the leaders of the kingdom when the contract was drawn up. Still, these types of distinguished men often served as witnesses for royal land donations, not just in Hana but elsewhere, and they—and the king—did often have to travel considerable distances in order to be present.[5] Donating land represents what was apparently a successful strategy for the kings of this era in many regions; in this way, the kings were accessible and visible to their subjects, and they rewarded loyal service with gifts that had an impact on lives: grants of real estate. It's unclear, though, how much of an impact this might have had on the poorer people in society, the ones actually working the fields. Were they transferred along with the land? Did they have the right to leave if they chose to? Did their lives change much at all when someone new came to power? Some of the royal land grants were surprisingly small and were made to people who are otherwise unknown, men like Abi-hunni, each of whom was identified by his father's name, not by his prestigious position. The engagement of royalty with the populace seems to have been not just among the elite.

Royal Land Grants and Loyalty

Fields and orchards still stood at the core of the Near Eastern economy, as had always been true. Ownership of agricultural land was important even to men whose official jobs completely precluded any possibility that they might work the land themselves. Likewise, owning a house, or having the right to live in one, created stability for a family. People generally didn't sell a family house unless forced to by crises beyond their control, so members of the same family often lived in a house for generations. Abi-hunni's gain of a new house probably also represented another family's tragic loss; perhaps they had been forced by debt to move out. In fact, in Hittite royal land grants, the person from whom the land had been taken was listed right along with the person to whom it was now being given.

What could endear an official more to his king than to be the recipient of a house or a field? In the Late Bronze Age, even vassals benefited from this system. In the region of Nuzi, near the eastern border of Mittani, the Mittanian king had donated whole towns to his vassals and their family members. At one point he needed to switch ownership of a district from one local leader to another. He wrote a letter commanding a local leader concerning his decision: "To Ithiya, speak. So says the king: [With regard to the district of] Paharrashe, which I previously gave to (Queen) Amminaia, now from its confines I have assigned a town to Ugi."[6] The man named Ugi obviously benefited from this, but Amminaia would be compensated. The king continued, regarding the man he was writing to, "Your own town I have assigned to the district of (Queen) Amminaia." The letter was impressed with the royal seal. This was necessary for any change that was made concerning the control of royal land. Land grants represented an ingenious, and apparently successful, way for a king to engender loyalty among his court, vassals, and officials.

Strikingly, the land grant contracts from across the region rarely mention what the recipient was supposed to do in exchange. These were not *ilku* lands that required military or corvée labor service. But these types of grants were not brand-new in the Late Bronze Age. Even in the Old Babylonian period, kings in the Middle Euphrates (in the region that later became known as Hana) sometimes granted land in the same way.[7] The royal grants seem to have been actual gifts, rewards for loyal service, something to spend a career working toward. Amazingly, they also had no end date. In Babylonia, most of the gifts made by kings specifically stated that they were forever and could be passed on to the recipient's descendants. The king "granted (the land) to (name of the recipient), his servant, for the distant future."[8]

Because the gifts of land and houses were so valuable, and because their descendants inherited them, the recipients wanted to keep the contracts that recorded them as safe as possible and for as long as possible. Real estate contracts had always been kept longer than any other legal documents. Some of the very first tablets from the Early Dynastic period were, remarkably enough, made of stone (into which the scribes had meticulously carved the cuneiform signs) just because they pertained to land.[9] Later on, you may remember that Ur-Utu, the lamentation priest in Sippar who was trying to rescue documents from his burning home, focused on those that recorded his rights to real estate. And land contracts show up in disproportionate numbers from the Late Bronze Age as well. In the city of Terqa in the land of Hana, for example, excavators found two jars containing records of royal land grants that went back about 200 years.[10] Long after other documents in a family archive had been scrapped or recycled, the ones that proved ownership or usage rights to fields, orchards, and houses needed to be kept safe.

Without the impression of the king's seal, though, the royal grants had no meaning.[11] In Hatti, the kings sealed such a contract right in the middle of the tablet, using their impressive, round stamp seals.[12] In the coastal city of Ugarit, the king rolled his seal at the top of the front of the tablet.[13] Kings of Mittani rolled theirs across the middle of the tablet's back.[14] And in Hana, as we have seen, the king rolled his seal in the margin on the left. No matter where the seal impression appeared, it was crucial and it was alone. No one else needed to seal the tablet once the king had done so.

In Babylonia, starting in the fourteenth century BCE,[15] some recipients of royal grants of land went a step further in preserving the records. They had stone carvers reproduce the text of the original sealed clay tablet on a polished stone boulder,[16] with the additions of curses on anyone who might take away the rights recounted in the text, along with symbols of the gods who would enforce the agreement and the curses. These small monuments are known as *kudurrus*, and almost all of them recorded royal gifts of agricultural land, or of other sources of perpetual income.[17] The *kudurru* was then set up in a temple.[18] Temples had become much more than places to worship and provide for the gods; they had become repositories for many different kinds of objects designed to remind the gods of requests that had been made of them. These included not just the *kudurrus* but also statues of royalty and other individuals that had been placed there to remind the gods to watch over them.

So Abi-hunni was not alone in being the recipient of the king's largesse, and he presumably benefited from the house he received. The contracts and *kudurrus* show that the great kings of Hatti, Mittani, and Babylonia, along with the lesser kings of Hana, Ugarit, and Alalakh, and probably other vassal states, all had become much more personally involved with their officials and subjects during this time, as seen in the appearance of the kings' seal impressions on what might otherwise seem to have been private transactions, and in the many documents drawn up in their presence. They had also claimed the right of controlling more land, even while also giving more of it away. Land sales became much less common than in the Old Babylonian period. If you received a grant of a field or house from the king, it seems that you could not then turn around and sell it. The royal land grants may well have helped to create internal stability within these great kingdoms during the fifteenth and fourteenth centuries BCE. One gets the impression that it was a time marked by fewer rebellions than in earlier eras.

The same emphasis on personal relationships pervaded international diplomacy. The kings may have never met one another, but their letters show that they felt deeply personal connections to one another anyway. This was partly because a visit from an envoy and translator became, in a way, a substitute for a visit from the king himself. The envoys showed up regularly, read their sovereign's letters and explained his ideas, received gifts, and were feted at banquets. The king might boast of how well he treated an envoy, that he "showed him very great honors."[19] The best of these ambassadors also seem to have been highly appreciated, singled out for praise by the allied king, as in the case of the translator Hane, whom you met in the previous chapter.[20] They made the brotherhood personal, not just something that existed in disembodied words on clay.

But perhaps more important, the marriages between the royal families across the Near East created powerful ties between the kings. Their alliances were not just based on treaties, trust, and gifts; the royal families in far-flung lands became actual kin. I have mentioned, throughout this book, how important family was as a fundamental building block on which the whole society was based, much more than social class, or citizenship, or any other way in which people can be divided or united in identity. Once kings had family members in other states, they had created an obligation that was hard to break. When Tushratta of Mittani stated, after his daughter married the Egyptian pharaoh, that "we, between us, are one, the Hurrian land and the land of Egypt . . . I am the k[ing] of Egypt and my brother is the ki[ng] of the Hurrian land,"[21] he was expressing a common perception. Their families and lands had been united. And just as the royal land grants were supposed to be held in perpetuity by the recipient's descendants, so too the alliances between the royal houses were supposed to be forever.

These secure ties between the great kings meant that Amenhotep III of Egypt never had to send troops out on campaign and, perhaps in consequence, he accumulated wealth beyond imagining. As his brother kings never tired of reminding him (with not-too-veiled envy), "In Egypt, gold is more plentiful than dirt."[22] But his allies were not suffering financially either. Tushratta of Mittani (mid-fourteenth century BCE) and Burna-Buriash II of Babylon (c. 1359–1333 BCE) both were able to put together truly enormous dowries for their daughters along with gifts for the pharaoh when the princesses married Egyptian kings,[23] and no doubt they did the same for other daughters who married other great kings.

The Children of Burna-Buriash II of Babylonia: Strengthening Alliances

We turn now to a remarkable example of the web of marriages that connected kings in the fourteenth century BCE.[24] It all revolved around the Babylonian king named Burna-Buriash II. He followed his father to the throne around 1359 BCE, as one in the long line of kings with Kassite names.[25] Although his own archives have not yet been found, documents mentioning him, or even written by him, have showed up at sites in Egypt, Turkey, Iraq, Iran, and even Greece![26] He had family members pretty much everywhere (though it must be admitted that they were probably not to be found in Greece).

Burna-Buriash II was a savvy diplomat. As a result of his efforts in marriage negotiation, he ended up being related to kings of four major states that dominated this period, and each of these kings had an outsize impact in Late Bronze Age history. Burna-Buriash II became the father-in-law of King Akhenaten of Egypt (c. 1353–1336 BCE), of King Suppiluliuma I of Hatti (c. 1344–1322 BCE), and of King Untash-Napirisha of Elam (c. 1340–1300 BCE), and he became the son-in-law of King Ashur-uballit I of Assyria (c. 1363–1328 BCE). Perhaps not until the time of Britain's Queen Victoria were the children and grandchildren of a monarch so entwined with the royal families of other states.

Burna–Buriash II notably excluded Mittani from his network, however. It seems that by Burna–Buriash's reign, Mittani's king Tushratta was gradually being shut out of the brotherhood of kings. Tushratta's daughter had married the Egyptian pharaoh Amenhotep III when that king was elderly, as we saw in the last chapter, and she had been taken on as a wife of the next pharaoh, Akhenaten, but Tushratta of Mittani seems not to have been related by marriage to any of the other great kings of the time. Even Akhenaten was less than friendly to him. Tushratta's letters to Akhenaten grew increasingly panicky; Mittani appeared to have been losing its standing among the great powers and Tushratta feared for its future.

It was a great advantage to Burna–Burniash II of Babylon to have daughters. Ever since the Early Dynastic period, daughters were important for any king. He hypothetically needed only one son to take over the throne after his death, but every adult daughter could marry and create a family tie to another monarch. It seems likely that the daughters were brought up to prepare for such a future. In fact, a school for princes, princesses, and children of court officials seems to have existed in the city of Nippur in Babylonia during the reign of Burna–Buriash II, educating children of high-ranking men from across the kingdom.[27] As in the time of Zimri-Lim of Mari, these elite girls, and in this case boys, seem to have been trained primarily in music. The school was mentioned in several letters from a physician concerning a bout of illness among the students.[28] He mentioned two girl singers who had become ill but had now recovered: "the daughters of Kuru and Ahuni are fine, their health is good. Should my lord so order, they can both leave and attend school again."[29] Among the other girls whom he had treated was the daughter of the Babylonian governor in the vassal state of Dilmun.[30] A second physician treated a "princess who suffered from repeated attacks of fever."[31] Perhaps this was one of the daughters of Burna–Buriash himself. In any event, the Babylonian princesses who ended up married to their three powerful husbands seem to have been well prepared to cope with their appointments as queens in foreign courts.

They were not alone when they arrived to be married; each would have taken hundreds of attendants and officials with her from home. The women no doubt wrote to their father, who in turn sent them gifts and messages whenever his envoys visited. Burna–Buriash II would also have expected them to send him gifts in return. The previous Babylonian king had written to the pharaoh about this: "As for my daughters who are married to kings that are my neighbors, if my envoys [go] there, they converse with the[m, and they se]nd to me a present."[32] It would be fascinating to know whether the women also maintained a correspondence among themselves. If so, perhaps they compared notes on their lives.

The Babylonian Wife of Akhenaten in Egypt

Amenhotep III of Egypt was still alive when Burna-Buriash II came to power, so one of the Babylonian king's first priorities was to send the pharaoh a letter confirming that he would continue to maintain the alliance that his father had enjoyed with Egypt. The letter was short, and Burna-Buriash got to the point quickly: "Just as previously you and m[y] father were friend[ly] to one another, you and I [should] now [be friendly] t[o one another]."[33] Unfortunately, Amenhotep III died soon afterward, but Burna-Buriash was undaunted. He was determined to continue his family's alliance with Egypt, so he continued to write regularly (though often rather coldly) to the new pharaoh, Akhenaten. Burna-Buriash's sister had been married to Amenhotep III,[34] and he soon sent a messenger and an interpreter to Egypt, proposing a new marriage to bind their lands together.[35] He suggested that one of his daughters, whose name we unfortunately don't know, might marry Akhenaten. The pharaoh consented and sent his own messenger and interpreter to formalize the engagement, by anointing the princess with oil.[36] The princess then wrote to the pharaoh—she is the only one of the sisters from whom a letter survives. She may well have been a teenager at the time. She didn't mention her name, or the name of Akhenaten, whom she would be marrying. The king was "my lord" and she was only "the princess."[37] The letter tells us little about her, her main point being her subordination to him: "In the pre[sence of my lord], thu[s,] I [prostrate myself], saying, 'Since . . . my envoy has brought colored cloth, to your cities and your house, may it be well. Do not murmur in your heart and impose darkness on me.'"[38] So far, things were going smoothly. They did not stay that way.

Burna-Buriash II was something of an expert in diplomatic marriages and he was inclined to see insults everywhere, even when they may not have been intended. So, when the Egyptian delegation arrived with just five chariots to transport his daughter to Egypt, he was not at all happy. This was not at all grand enough for Burna-Buriash's taste. He wrote to the pharaoh to protest: his sister had been accompanied by 3,000 soldiers when she left to marry Amenhotep III, he said, and that had been an appropriate escort.[39] But his hurt feelings were somehow assuaged, so he assembled a dowry[40] and sent his daughter off to marry Akhenaten. In turn, the pharaoh sent a gratifyingly extravagant collection of gifts to Burna-Buriash.[41]

If she later heard from her sisters after they had married the kings of Hatti and Elam, this Babylonian princess might have felt disappointed with her status in Egypt in comparison; she was a member of a large, fairly powerless, cadre of foreign wives, all of them completely overshadowed by Akhenaten's chief wife, Nefertiti, who was virtually his co-ruler.[42] The Babylonian princess's aunt had been in a similar situation a generation before: this woman had been so inconspicuous among the women of the palace that the pharaoh had been uncertain which wife she was. He was not even sure whether she was still alive when Burna-Buriash II had written to inquire about her.[43]

That woman's niece, the new Babylonian wife of Akhenaten, certainly didn't have a dull life. Akhenaten's court may have been the most international of any during this era, given the presence of his many foreign wives and the fact that each one of them may have brought more than 300 attendants with her from her homeland.[44]

During Akhenaten's reign, he changed the state religion, closed most of the temples, and built a new capital city at Amarna (where the diplomatic letters were later found), to which he moved his whole court, including all his wives and their entourages.[45] Burna-Buriash's daughter experienced this remarkable era firsthand, though it might have been traumatic to live through. She probably had no choice but to worship Akhenaten's beloved sun god, Aten, to the exclusion of other deities, even her gods of Babylon. Akhenaten required it.

Tawananna: The Babylonian Wife of Suppiluliuma in Hatti

Burna-Buriash's next daughter, who married the Hittite king Suppiluliuma I, played a much more prominent role in her adopted home, but at a cost: she was not at all popular. Her father had been ruling in Babylonia for at

least fourteen years when Suppiluliuma came to power in Hatti around
1344 BCE. Burna-Buriash must have recognized the need to have the warlike and impulsive Hittite king on his side, so he continued in his program
to unite all the great powers as members of his family. At some point, Burna-
Buriash was able to convince Suppiluliuma to agree to a peace treaty and a
diplomatic marriage between their two lands.

What is almost unbelievable is that Suppiluliuma also agreed to demote
his long-standing chief wife, Henti, so that the Babylonian princess could
assume her top position as queen.[46] Henti had been more than a wife to
Suppiluliuma—she seems to have been the very reason he was able to claim
the throne to begin with. Historians have been able to reconstruct what may
have happened. Henti's seal, when she was married to Suppiluliuma, bore
the following inscription: "Seal of Henti, Great Q[uee]n, daughter of the
Great King, Hero."[47] So Henti was a daughter of the previous Hittite king,
Tudhaliya III, and it was perhaps only by marrying her that Suppiluliuma
had any claim to the throne.[48] The previous king's choice of successor had
been his son, who was named for him, another Tudhaliya. This young man
duly took the throne after his father's death, and the members of the royal
family, all the courtiers, and the entire Hittite military swore an oath to
support him. Suppiluliuma, his brother-in-law, swore this oath, along with
the others.

But Suppiluliuma was not content with his status. Although he was
apparently not a prince, only the husband of a princess, he wanted to be king.
As his own son later put it, "[But when my father] mistreated Tudhaliya,
all [the princes, the noblemen], the commanders of the thousands, and the
officers of Hattusa [went over] to my [father]. Although he had sworn an
oath (to him), [they seized] Tudhaliya, and they killed [him]. Furthermore,
they killed those of his brothers who [stood by] him."[49] Although
Suppiluliuma later claimed to be the son of Tudhaliya III, he may have been
using the term "son" very loosely.

You might think that Queen Henti's support was crucial to Suppiluliuma's
acceptance as king. The couple had powerful sons, notably the crown prince
Mursili, who also was deeply attached to his mother. But Suppiluliuma seems
to have decided that he didn't need Henti, and her demotion and exile must
have rocked the Hittite court. The Babylonian princess arrived into what
must have been a political maelstrom. She would have immediately faced
anger and hostility from people she had never even met before. It can't have

helped that she was probably younger than many of her royal husband's children.

We don't know her original name, but she was given the title Tawananna, the traditional designation used for the great queen in Hatti. Tawananna's legacy is somewhat tarnished by the fact that the one person who wrote about her was her stepson, Suppiluliuma I's successor Mursili II (1321–1295 BCE), and he despised her. But, reading between the lines, it's clear that she was far from being cowed by her adversaries. She was appointed to a position as a priestess,[50] and she was given considerable control over resources.[51] Her enemies might have resented this, but they were unable to do anything about it as long as the king was alive.

Meanwhile, her husband, King Suppiluliuma, embarked on a much more militaristic career than those of his fellow great kings. He wrote to the pharaoh in Egypt in friendly terms about maintaining their alliance and initiating a new diplomatic marriage,[52] but he seems to have cared little for the peace that his brother kings had established and worked hard to maintain. Suppiluliuma campaigned with his army beyond the Hittite borders into Syria, destroying cities as he went. He clearly had his sights on King Tushratta and on taking over the lands controlled by Mittani.

Although Suppiluliuma was unsuccessful in conquering Mittani, Tushratta's long reign there did indeed come to an end during Suppiluliuma's reign. Tragically, the Mittanian king was assassinated by one of his own sons (though the records don't tell us which one). In what had been the eastern half of his kingdom, Assyria took advantage of the ensuing turmoil by reclaiming its independence. The remaining western half of the Mittanian Empire was claimed by at least two different sons of the assassinated king. One of them, whose name was Shattiwaza, sped, almost alone, to Babylonia to try to gain the support of its king Burna-Buriash II, the man who was so central to the network of great kings. Surely he would help restore stability to Mittani? But no, Burna-Buriash was completely uninterested in helping the prospective king.[53] In fact, the Mittanian prince had to flee for his life.

Shattiwaza turned instead to Suppiluliuma in Hatti for help against his brother and against the Assyrians. The Hittite king agreed and, ultimately, together they were victorious. But in exchange for his assistance, Suppiluliuma made sure that Shattiwaza, as the new king of Mittani, could no longer count himself among the brotherhood of great kings. Instead, Mittani became a dependent state of Hatti. Although their agreement ended with a diplomatic marriage, the Hittite princess was marrying a minor king, not an equal of her father.[54]

Suppiluliuma even raided Egyptian territory in the Levant during the 1320s BCE, perhaps during the reign of the young king Tutankhamun, after the death of Akhenaten. In doing so, Suppiluliuma was breaking the terms of his treaty with Egypt. Here again, as when he had killed his brother-in-law to become king of Hatti, he doesn't seem to have felt constrained by the rules and traditions followed by his fellow great kings. But, in the eyes of his contemporaries, he suffered for his hubris. The gods exacted their revenge on him.

After Suppiluliuma's campaign in Egyptian territory, a fatal plague began to spread across Hatti. Scholars believe that it might have been brought there by Egyptian prisoners of war, but Suppiluliuma's son was convinced that it was his father who had brought this disaster upon his land. After all, the Hittite king had broken the oath he had sworn to support his brother-in-law as Hittite king, and the gods always punished people who broke oaths. As if to prove this, one of the early casualties of the plague, around 1322 BCE, was King Suppiluliuma himself. Over subsequent years many people died, and no one knew how to prevent themselves from catching it. This was not a normal illness like the ones that had worried Zimri-Lim of Mari when they arose in his palace. This was terrifying.

But the Babylonian-born queen, Tawananna, the daughter of Burna-Buriash II, seems to have been unaffected; she lived on. By tradition, the Hittite queen had the right to keep her title and responsibilities until she died, so Tawananna continued to serve as a priestess after the death of Suppiluliuma. But this was too much for his son, the new king, Mursili II. Of course, he had hated Tawananna all along for replacing his mother, but that was not all. He accused her of squandering riches, introducing foreign Babylonian practices, and generally wreaking havoc on the orderly world of the Hittite court. He wrote, "Some things she brought in from the land of Sanhara (Babylon). Others in Hatti [. . .] to the populace she handed over(?). She left nothing. . . . My father's house she destroyed."[55] More traumatic for Mursili II was his belief that Tawananna had killed his own wife, whom he clearly loved very much. He wrote that "while she was queen, she kept [curs]ing [my wife] until she had killed her."[56] Did the Babylonian-born queen really hate her step-daughter-in-law so much that she called on the gods to kill her? We have no idea, but Mursili believed, deeply, that this was the cause of his wife's death. He lamented, "Because she killed her, throughout the days of life [my soul] goes down to the dark netherworld [on her account]. . . . Don't you gods [recognize] whose is the punishment?"[57]

Mursili II consulted the oracles and was told that he could, if he chose, rightfully have Tawananna executed. She may well have been aware of this and no doubt she feared for her safety. But the king settled instead for deposing her from her position as priestess,[58] putting her on trial, and banishing her from the capital.[59] He then composed a prayer to the gods to explain himself and to argue that, honestly, he had treated her well, considering her behavior. As he wrote, "I gave her a house. Nothing is lacking to her desire. She has food and drink. Everything stands at (her) disposal. Nothing is lacking to her. She is alive. She beholds the sun of heaven with her eyes."[60] So, he argued, the gods should not object to what he did. Hers had not been a very harsh punishment, after all. Mursili II had only removed Tawananna from her position as a priestess, and only after an oracle gave him permission to do so.

Still, the plague raged on. Mursili wrote, in one of several prayers to the gods, that "A plague broke out in Hatti, and Hatti has been beaten down by the plague. . . . This is the twentieth year."[61] He prayed for the gods to end the people's misery: "O gods, my lords. Send the plague [away]. . . . May you be well-disposed toward Hatti. Let [the plague] abate once more." Twenty years is a very long time for a country to suffer through a plague, but eventually it retreated. As for Tawananna, the daughter of Burna-Buriash II, unfortunately we have no record of what happened to her after she was banished.

Napir-Asu: The Babylonian Wife of Untash-Napirisha in Elam

The third daughter of Burna-Buriash II of Babylon to marry a powerful king might have believed herself to be in the best situation of any of her sisters. She did not disappear into a crowd of foreign wives, and she was not hated when she arrived in her new palace. For her we even have a name rather than a title: she was called Napir-Asu.[62] That was her Elamite name, anyway; we once again don't know the name she went by before she was married.

Elam, the land immediately to the east of Babylonia, extended from the Tigris River floodplain up into the Zagros Mountains in what is now Iran.[63] Although it had been a major power in previous centuries, it was not now a member of the great king brotherhood, at least not from the perspective of the king of Egypt. No letters from the king of Elam showed up among the Amarna letters. But Burna-Buriash II might still have considered neighboring Elam to be a great power; its king was his closest ally. Remarkably, Burna-Buriash II was already closely related to the Elamite royal family, even before his daughter married the king there. That king, Untash-Napirisha, was Burna-Buriash's first cousin: both were grandsons of a Babylonian king named Kurigalzu I (early fourteenth century BCE).[64] For generations, Elamite kings had married Babylonian princesses; Untash-Napirisha was at least the third Elamite king in his dynasty to do so (and two more kings did the same after him).[65] The woman he chose to marry was a daughter of his cousin Burna-Buriash II.

Untash-Napirisha seems to have come to power only seven years before the death of his Babylonian ally around 1333 BCE,[66] but Burna-Buriash's daughter, Queen Napir-Asu, may have been born when her father had been on the throne for many years. In any event, she must have been of the same generation as her husband, even though she married him at a time when her father was nearing the end of his twenty-seven-year reign.

The Elamite king probably spoke Akkadian in addition to his native language, having learned it from the Babylonian princess who was his mother, so Napir-Asu may have found her husband's palace more familiar and welcoming than would have been true for her sisters in Egypt and Hatti. She also had greater prestige than even her sister Tawananna; her son (unlike any sons of her sisters in Egypt and Hatti) eventually became a king—the king of Elam.[67] The relationship between the lands of Babylonia and Elam was profound and, for a long time, unwavering.

Almost nothing, however, is known about Napir-Asu's life in Elam other than that she was queen and that her son eventually became king. Her husband never seems to have mentioned her activities in any of his many inscriptions. She is, however, depicted on a tall stone stela that Untash-Napirisha dedicated to the gods, standing behind him with her arms folded. (Her name appears on one of her arms.)[68]

Napir-Asu did, however, leave behind something that we have from almost no one else in her family: an extraordinary free-standing statue of herself that she had commissioned (see Fig. 15.1). Surprisingly, no images at all survive of her father Burna-Buriash II, or of either of her sisters in Egypt and Hatti, or even of her self-aggrandizing brother-in-law Suppiluliuma I of Hatti. Napir-Asu's statue is one of the largest and heaviest bronze figures to survive from the ancient Near East, and it is said to be the best-known work of art from Elam.[69] It stands 1.29 meters high (4.23 feet) and would have been life-size, had her head survived, which, regrettably, it did not. The statue weighs an incredible 1,750 kilograms (3,860 pounds—almost 2 tons) and was discovered in 1903 during excavations in the ancient Elamite capital of Susa.[70]

Fig. 15.1 Bronze statue of Queen Napir-Asu of Elam, from Susa, mid to late fourteenth century BCE. (© RMN-Grand Palais/Art Resource, NY/Art Resource)

The ancient bronzeworkers cast the exterior of the statue in almost pure copper using the lost-wax technique, but the interior clay core over which it was cast is missing. For a reason that escapes us but that made sense to the bronze-workers, the clay was removed and the statue was filled with solid bronze (11 percent tin added to copper).[71] This represented a huge amount of effort and expense to create a solid core that not only was invisible to the viewer, it really wasn't necessary; her statue could just as well have been left hollow.[72] How many other solid bronze statues existed is impossible to know, because most metal objects had been melted down long before modern archaeologists came looking for them. What is clear, though, is that Napir-Asu was an important queen, deserving of an elaborate sculpture. The copper exterior may even have been coated in gold or silver.[73] Like the other royal statues that we have encountered so often, hers would have been set up in a temple to pray to the gods and to receive offerings. The inscription on it was written in Elamite, in the first person, and Napir-Asu didn't mince her words. She wanted this statue to survive:

> I, Napir-Asu, (am) wife of Untash-Napirisha. He who would seize my statue, who would smash it, who would destroy its inscription, who would erase my name, may he be smitten by the curse of (the god) Napirisha, of (the god) Kiririsha, and of (the god) Inshushinak, that his name shall become extinct, that his offspring be barren, that the forces of Beltiya, the great goddess, shall sweep down on him. This is Napir-Asu's offering.[74]

The curse didn't really work, since the head of her statue had indeed been "smashed" and removed long before the statue was found. But at least the body remains, and it is regal. Napir-Asu is dressed in what must have been some of the finest clothes produced in the Elamite palace. She wore three garments: a short-sleeved dress, which consisted of a top that was embroidered with small circles and a tiered skirt that was fringed along the bottom; a shawl around her shoulders; and an elaborately decorated flounce around her waist. She wore jewelry as well: four bracelets on each arm, and a ring on the fourth finger of her left hand. Although we are missing her head, it is safe to assume that she wore her hair in the Elamite fashion of the day, in a thick braided coil around her head.[75]

King Untash-Napirisha was ruling Elam at a time of great strength for his dynasty, when the former kingdoms of Susa, on the plain, and Anshan, in the highlands, were united under Elam's governance.[76] Envoys and messengers must have traveled regularly between the Babylonian court of

Burna-Buriash II and that of his son-in-law and cousin Untash-Napirisha. Only about 450 kilometers (280 miles) separated their capital cities: it took just a month to walk each way, and perhaps half that by chariot. So Burna-Buriash must have heard a lot about the building projects of the ambitious Elamite king. Untash-Napirisha didn't just build and rebuild many structures in the traditional Elamite capital of Susa (though he did that too), he decided to build a whole new capital city. He named it for himself: Al Untash-Napirisha, which meant "City of Untash-Napirisha." He even seems to have hoped that the city would replace Susa, not just as the political capital, but also as the center of worship for the Elamite gods of both the highlands of Anshan and the lowlands of Susa.[77] The city became home to twenty-five temples to different gods, all constructed pretty much simultaneously by architects and workmen during the time of Untash-Napirisha. He must have felt very strongly about his desire to unite the deities of the land in one place, and in doing so, to unite the land of Elam as well.

He shared the desire for a new political and religious capital not only with his Egyptian contemporary, Akhenaten (who had built his capital at Amarna), but also with his own (and Burna-Buriash II's) Babylonian grandfather, Kurigalzu I, who had constructed an impressive new capital in Babylonia and had also named it after himself: Dur-Kurigalzu. It boasted a huge ziggurat, the core of which still stands today near modern Baghdad.

Untash-Napirisha's choice of location for his new city was a site that is now called Chogha Zanbil, just 40 kilometers (25 miles) southeast of Susa. It was a dramatic spot on a high plateau, with views of a wide green river valley. When the city was excavated in the 1950s and early 1960s, by a French archaeological team, it proved to be in remarkable condition. Most ancient cities were continuously occupied for centuries or millennia, making it difficult to extract the details about a particular era from the many layers of occupation. Chogha Zanbil seems to have been dreamed up by Untash-Napirisha,[78] built at enormous expense, but then pretty much abandoned after his death. The same was true of Akhenaten's capital city. Both are frozen in time at the point when they were no longer of interest to the kings' successors. Just in case there might have been any doubt about who was responsible for the wonders of his new town, Untash-Napirisha subtly inserted his name all over the place. Brick inscriptions identifying him show up in the buildings; terracotta pommels glazed in blue and green that decorated the shrine at the top of the ziggurat bore his name (see Fig. 15.2).

That ziggurat was remarkable. Whereas most Mesopotamian ziggurats have eroded away over the millennia to just their lowest level (if that), four of the possible five stages of the ziggurat at Chogha Zanbil were still standing when excavated, encased inside the mound at the center of the site, like an insect preserved in amber. The archaeologists discovered staircases on which one could still climb, exterior ones for the first two levels and interior above that, along with the remains of a door decorated with a mosaic of black and white glass,[79] and even a doorway with its arch still intact.[80] At the top of the structure, a shrine to the great god of Susa, Inshushinak (his name literally means "god of Susa") would have shone in the sunlight, with glazed bricks flecked with silver and gold, and with those shiny terracotta pommels bearing the king's name.

The ziggurat stood more than 51 meters (165 feet) tall[81] and had been constructed in a surprising way. Before the tower went up, a large, square,

Fig. 15.2 Glazed pommel with the name of King Untash-napirisha of Elam, from Chogha Zanbil, 1340–1300 BCE. (Metropolitan Museum of Art)

one-story structure was built around a big courtyard. It incorporated two temples to Inshushinak and some storerooms.[82] The courtyard was later chosen as the location of the ziggurat. All the millions of bricks for the solid stepped tower[83] therefore must have been carried through the gates and doorways of the square building at the base. The interior doors of the square temple, which had previously led to the courtyard, now led just to the brick mass of the ziggurat, and many of these doors were blocked.

Like the earlier Mesopotamian ziggurats of the Ur III period, Untash-Napirisha's was made largely of sun-dried brick, but with a 2 meter (6.6 foot) thick façade of kiln-baked bricks. The bricks in every eleventh layer were inscribed to identify the king and the god Inshushinak.[84] Reed mats placed among the layers gave strength to the structure, and the unknown architect also incorporated thirty-eight drainage canals to prevent damage from rainfall.[85] It was a beautifully engineered building that weathered the elements until it eventually became entombed in a mound of dirt.

Untash-Napirisha fulfilled the role of king-as-builder better than almost any king in the Near East. Inscriptions survive attesting to his work on more than fifty buildings, many of which he initiated in Chogha Zanbil. He, like other kings of the era, seems to have benefited from the dearth of military conflicts; he had the time and money available to create spectacular edifices. He also had control over the necessary manpower. As in every period of widespread construction projects, men from across the land would have been called up for corvée labor duty and put to work in all the many jobs required in construction.

The excavators initially thought that the ancient city at Chogha Zanbil was only a place of pilgrimage, not a place where people lived, but that theory is now in doubt. Residential buildings certainly seem to have existed within the city's 100 hectare (c. 247 acre) extent, so people did live there. But it seems that Untash-Napirisha's administrators didn't share his enthusiasm for the new city. Apparently, as soon as word came that the king had died, the building materials that had been prepared for further construction were abandoned, unceremoniously, right where they were being stored. They were still there when the archaeologists arrived thousands of years later.

Underneath a palace-like building in the ceremonial complex of Chogha Zanbil, the archaeologists discovered five well-built, vaulted tombs that were reached by stairways.[86] These might possibly have housed the burials of the royal family.[87] One strange thing about the burials is that eight of the bodies were cremated, which does not seem to have previously been an Elamite tradition.[88] Just one of the bodies was undisturbed—that of a woman who was forty to sixty years old at the time of her death.[89] She had been carefully placed on a brick platform, lying on her left-hand side. Near her, on the same platform, were the cremated remains of two other individuals, accompanied by jewelry and weapons that seem to have been included in their cremations, with everything wrapped in red fabric.[90] It is tempting to agree with the interpretation of the excavators, who concluded that only members of the Elamite royal family were cremated, and that the body of the woman was that of a foreign princess whose culture prohibited cremation.[91] Since the foreign princesses known to have married Elamite kings were Babylonian, perhaps this was Napir-Asu herself, buried next to the remains of her husband Untash-Napirisha. If so, she was buried with the family she had acquired by marriage and she was still venerated at the time of her death.

The building above the tombs contained many goblets, dishes, and spoons.[92] Perhaps these were used during feasts in honor of the dead royals who were buried below.[93] The courtyard of the building may have been the location of animal sacrifices. In Elam at this time, as had been true in Mesopotamia for many thousands of years, past kings were not forgotten. They continued to be worshiped, remembered at festivals, and provided with gifts. Napir-Asu's bronze statue might originally have stood here above her tomb with the statues of other dead kings and queens, keeping their spirits and memories alive.

The era after the death of Untash-Napirisha of Elam was somewhat chaotic, but he was eventually succeeded by his son Kidin-Hutran II (early thirteenth century BCE). It seems that Kidin-Hutran must have been a boy when his father died, because two other relatives ruled before he took the throne.[94] The young king's mother was Napir-Asu, so he was Burna-Buriash II's grandson on his mother's side, and King Kurigalzu I's great-grandson on both sides of his family. Though he grew up in Elam and spoke Elamite as his native language, Kidin-Hutran II's genetic heritage was three-quarters (or more) Babylonian.

By now there were children and grandchildren of the Babylonian king Burna-Buriash II in almost every major royal family in the Near East, just as he had wanted.

You will not be surprised to hear that Kidin-Hutran II married yet another Babylonian princess. He may also have been the author of a remarkable letter, written by a king of Elam to a king of Babylonia (neither of whose names appear in the letter). After so many generations of intermarriage with Babylonia, this Elamite king felt that he had a right to rule not just his own land, but the land of his wife, mother, and grandmother as well: Babylon. He ranted that, as a "descendant of the eldest daughter of the mighty (Babylonian) King Kurigalzu, (why) do I not sit on the throne of the land of Babylonia?"[95] The royal families had become so intertwined, not just between Babylonia and Elam but across the Near East, that the old platitude that "my house is your house" (which was so often spoken after a diplomatic marriage) had come to seem like a promise. Why was a man like Kidin-Hutran II, with so many Babylonian kings among his ancestors, not in line for the Babylonian throne? Why should a minor detail, like the fact that he was already the king of Elam, get in the way?

This new sense of entitlement to the Babylonian throne on the part of Elamite kings created a rift between the old allies. In the next century, it led to war.

Muballitat-Sherua: The Assyrian Wife of Burna-Buriash II in Babylonia

While the three Babylonian princesses were negotiating their ways through the worlds into which they had married, their father Burna-Buriash II had made one more match with a foreign leader, but this time it did not involve one of his daughters. Burna-Buriash himself, probably well into middle age and already having sent grown daughters to other courts, decided to marry a foreign princess. Her name was Muballitat-Sherua, and she was the daughter of the Assyrian king Ashur-uballit I (1365–1330 BCE).[96]

Even before the disintegration of the land of Mittani, the Assyrian king (who was at that time still a vassal of Mittani) had been itching for independence and campaigning to join the great king brotherhood. Ashur-uballit had adopted the title "king of Assyria" (he was the first ruler to do so), apparently while King Tushratta of Mittani was still alive, and he had even sent messengers to Egypt with a short, tentative letter and some gifts for the pharaoh Akhenaten.[97] Burna-Buriash II of Babylon, who was protective of the privileges enjoyed by the great kings, was annoyed when he heard about this. He wrote to the pharaoh telling him to send the Assyrians away: "Now, as for my Assyrian vassals, I was not the one who sent them to you. Why on their own authority have they come to your country? If you love me, they will conduct no business whatsoever. Send them off to me empty-handed."[98] According to Burna-Buriash, Ashur-uballit had no business sending ambassadors to Egypt, he was not important enough. But that sentence about "my Assyrian vassals" is odd. If the Assyrians were the vassals of anyone at this point, it was of Mittani. Unless we are missing an episode in which the Babylonian king took over Assyria (which seems highly unlikely), Burna-Buriash II was bluffing. (See Fig. 15.3)

But after the collapse of Mittani, when Assyria really was independent, pharaoh Akhenaten apparently gave in and welcomed Assyria into the brotherhood as a new great power. In his next Amarna letter to the pharaoh, Ashur-uballit I of Assyria referred to himself as a "great king" and as the "brother" of Akhenaten.[99] He was also just as demanding as the other great kings, even including their common observation that "gold in your land is dirt,"[100] before asking for a vast amount of it.

At some point, perhaps soon after the death of Tushratta of Mittani, Ashur-uballit I also must have sent messengers to Babylonia to inquire about an alliance and a diplomatic marriage. It seems that Burna-Buriash II overcame his annoyance with the upstart king and relented. He certainly sought alliances with every other major power, and Assyria lay right across his northern border. He would not have wanted a hostile relationship with an aggressive, independent kingdom so close to home. Princess Muballitat-Sherua of Assyria moved to Babylonia and later she gave birth to at least one son.

When Burna-Buriash II died around 1333 BCE, the prince who succeeded him was Kara-hardash (1333 BCE), his young son with his Assyrian wife, Muballitat-Sherua.[101] Perhaps this son had jumped ahead in the line of succession, past his older brothers, because the Assyrian king had insisted upon it. We can't know for sure because very few documents survive.

The Babylonians were not pleased with this choice, however, and did not accept young Kara-hardash as king. He was overthrown within a year and replaced by a usurper.[102] We know this from a later chronicle called the Synchronistic History, which also tells us that Ashur-uballit I of Assyria was equally displeased with the Babylonians' decision to oust his grandson. He

Fig. 15.3 Letter from King Ashur-uballit I of Assyria to the king of Egypt, found at Amarna, Egypt, c. 1340 BCE. (Metropolitan Museum of Art)

decided to do something about it: he promptly sent troops into Babylonia. His Assyrian forces managed to depose the usurper and to replace him with another son of Burna-Buriash II. This son's reign was a success; he ruled in Babylonia for twenty-five years.[103] These events are described by a few terse phrases in the chronicle, but it's clear that within one year, 1333 BCE, the Babylonians were ruled by three successive, and mutually antagonistic, kings. It must have been a nerve-wracking time, very different from the calm years of Burna-Buriash II's reign.

The chaos of the year had also set a new precedent—Assyria had intervened militarily in Babylonian politics. This was not the last time that this would happen. The Assyrian kings who succeeded Ashur-uballit I wanted to create an empire. The polite diplomatic system of the previous Amarna period was not going to constrain them.

Chapter 16
Negotiators, Sea Traders, and Famine Sufferers

The mood across the Near East shifted a little in the mid-thirteenth century BCE. The generally peaceful stability of the Amarna period lived on in some places but faltered in others. With Mittani gone, old allies growled at one another across contested borders, or wrote anxious letters, worrying about aggression from unnamed enemies.

In Egypt, pharaoh Ramses II (1279–1213 BCE) dominated almost the whole thirteenth century BCE. He was probably born around 1303 BCE and lived for a remarkable ninety years; his twelve eldest sons predeceased him. He brought Egypt back to a pinnacle of wealth and power and took credit for more monuments than any king before him. Many of these he had indeed commissioned, but he also appropriated buildings of earlier kings by replacing their inscribed names with his own. He set up colossal stone statues of himself across Egypt, which were venerated by the population as intermediaries between the people and the gods.[1] Egyptian kings had always been considered at least somewhat divine, but Ramses II's cult was more visible than most. He must have come to seem almost immortal. By the time of his death almost no one alive in Egypt would have remembered a world in which he was not pharaoh.

But at the beginning of his reign, when no one had any idea that his reign would be so long and so dominant, his relationship with the Hittites was strained, as each empire tried to expand its control in the Levant. They went into battle against one another over their border, clashing at the contested city of Kadesh in Canaan in 1274 BCE. For what was apparently the first time, the great kings of both Egypt and Hatti were finally in the same place, but they were there facing one another as enemies, their chariots and infantry arrayed to kill. Ramses II claimed a great victory, but the border didn't move. The result was a stalemate.

Meanwhile, in Elam, kings became increasingly antagonistic to Babylonia, continuing to believe that the long line of Babylonian queens in their ancestry gave them the right to intervene there, and even to rule. In Assyria, imperialistic kings expanded the borders of their empire. The Assyrians conquered what was left of Mittani—already a shadow of its former self—around 1250 BCE. They created a new vassal kingdom there, ruled by the son of the king of Assyria and centered on a city called Dur-Katlimmu on the Habur River. During this era, known as the Middle Assyrian period, the government began deporting thousands of conquered people from one part of the empire to another. Military campaigns became ever more common, and the other great powers began to worry; Assyria was not playing by the old rules.

From its heartland in Anatolia, Hatti had extended its direct control south and east to the Euphrates, with a viceroy at the city of Carchemish controlling the region in Syria, creating a contested border between Hatti and Assyria that sometimes ran right along the Euphrates.

With the benefit of hindsight, we tend to view this era as careening toward catastrophe, with each of the great kingdoms heading for the collapse that occurred at the beginning of the twelfth century BCE. But the people alive at the time were blissfully ignorant of the future. They lived each day as it came. They were probably unaware that life had been more peaceful a century before. They were born into an uncertain and edgy world, and it was the only one they knew. In that era, some people were able to live full and pleasant lives, while others suffered deprivations and lived in fear.

Hattusili III and Puduhepa: A Hittite Royal Couple Continuing Diplomatic Traditions

In spite of these simmering hostilities of the mid-thirteenth century BCE, envoys kept on traveling between the capital cities, peace treaties continued to be forged, diplomatic marriages continued to be arranged, and luxury gifts exchanged. The international habits that had started in the Amarna period were deeply rooted by now, and they helped to keep the peace in some regions, even when battles were being fought elsewhere.

Letters were now being dictated and dispatched by new generations of kings and queens, almost 200 years after the first diplomatic overtures had taken place between the great kings of Egypt, Mittani, Hatti, and Babylonia. The leaders followed many of the old patterns of diplomatic address.[2] A collection of these letters was uncovered during the excavations in the Hittite capital city of Hattusa, and some of them reveal the worries of a thirteenth-century BCE Hittite king named Hattusili III (1267–1237 BCE).

Hattusili III had come to power in an unscrupulous way, not unlike his predecessor Suppiluliuma I, by usurping the throne from a relative who was the legitimate—if young and inexperienced—king.[3] In the case of Hattusili III, this was his nephew, not his brother-in-law, and the young man fled into exile, rather than being assassinated. But, more than had been true for Suppululiuma, Hattusili III seems to have worried about his legitimacy and about possible usurpers, so he needed all the support he could muster from any allies among the other great kings.

To judge from the letters, his wife Queen Puduhepa took the lead in much of the international diplomatic work. Hattusili III was often ill, and Puduhepa apparently had boundless energy and a keen interest in running the empire.[4] Unlike so many queens, she was not a princess by birth. She had been a priestess of the goddess Ishtar and had lived in the region around Kizzuwatna when Hattusili met and married her. Their match, unlike most, seems to have been for love rather than for political advantage. Hattusili wrote that "we joined (in matrimony), and the goddess (Ishtar) gave us the love of husband and wife."[5]

After overthrowing his nephew, Hattusili III was not able to convince the Assyrian king to support his shaky claim to the throne, but eventually the Babylonian king did so, as did the Egyptian pharaoh, Ramses II. This marked a dramatic improvement in relations between the two lands after their violent clash at Kadesh. In 1258 BCE, Hattusili and Ramses followed up by negotiating and confirming a peace treaty, which survives in both a Hittite and an Egyptian version.[6] Hattusili must have been very relieved to have such a powerful ally on his side, not just to secure his right to the Hittite throne, but also because both kings seem to have feared the growing power of Assyria.

The document they drew up is often referred to as the "world's first peace treaty," but that is a little misleading. Many other peace treaties had existed between ancient Near Eastern states before this, and some of them have survived—from the treaty between Ebla and Abarsal more than a thousand years earlier, to the treaty between Alalakh and Tunip in the fifteenth century BCE. It's also clear that peace treaties existed between all the major powers in the Amarna period, they just haven't been found.

So, just by chance, this one between Ramses II and Hattusili III is the earliest surviving peace treaty between major powers who recognized one another as equals (see Fig. 16.1). The fact that it wasn't actually the first doesn't diminish its importance, though. It's a powerful and inspiring document that clearly states that a lasting peace was the goal of both lands. The kings pledged to "establish good peace and good brotherhood in [the relations] of Egypt with Hatti forever. . . . From the beginnings of time and forever [by means of a treaty] the god has not allowed the making of war between them."[7] This commitment to eschewing warfare catches your breath—they presented it as absolute and eternal, and it was what the gods commanded.

Fig. 16.1 Peace treaty between King Ramses II of Egypt and King Hattusili III of Hatti, 1259 BCE. (Peter Horree/Alamy Stock Photo)

The specific clauses of the treaty included the kings' commitment to a continuing peaceful brotherhood, their agreement not to attack one another militarily, their pledges to support one another if either were to be attacked by an enemy or to face internal rebellions, and their support for one another's appointed successor if his position were to be threatened. The latter is a little disingenuous; when Hattusili III himself had usurped the throne, he had treated his nephew, the appointed successor of his brother the king, in just the way that the treaty condemned. That may, of course, be why he feared for his own son. Peaceful succession to the throne had been an ongoing problem in Hatti.

About half of the treaty was taken up with provisions for the treatment of fugitives and commitments to extradite them back to their homelands. This must have been a particularly vexing issue, to judge from the level of detail in the many clauses.

The peace treaty was to be followed, as always, by a diplomatic marriage. The Hittite queen Puduhepa took over these negotiations. A draft of a remarkable letter written by Puduhepa to Ramses II was found during the excavations at Hattusa.[8] Puduhepa, speaking in Hittite, had dictated her ideas for the letter to a scribe, and this is the draft that survives; the final version of the letter that was sent to Egypt would have been translated into Akkadian. It's clear that, at the time when the draft was written, the basic terms of the marriage between Ramses and the Hittite princess had been agreed upon. Several letters between Puduhepa and Ramses had clearly preceded this one. However, the Egyptian pharaoh and the Hittite queen had reached a sticking point.

Puduhepa was trying to sort things out. She noted that in an earlier letter she had written to Ramses, "I will give a daughter to you."[9] When, after some time, no princess appeared, Ramses must have written something abrupt in response, perhaps to try to speed up the process, but this upset Queen Puduhepa, who had clearly responded to him in some annoyance. So Ramses II tried again: "You have withheld her from me. And now you are even angry with me! Why have you not now given her to me?"[10]

The pharaoh was used to getting what he wanted, and I doubt that many people in his own court would have ventured to disagree with him in any way, let alone to get angry. This was the king who had built so many monuments to himself all over Egypt. He was, at that time, in the process of constructing the Abu Simbel temple on the Nile, the entrance of which was to be decorated with four colossal sculptures of himself carved out of the living rock. Each statue was 20 meters (66 feet) tall, so that carving the front of the temple represented a feat on the scale of the Mount Rushmore monument in the United States, but dedicated only to him. Ramses always got what he demanded—so why was Puduhepa delaying the arrival of his new queen?

He seems to have been thoroughly exasperated, noting, "I write to my sister (Puduhepa) that withholding the daughter is not right."[11] She in turn replied that she would be willing to make things move faster ("May I hurry!"), but she was not happy with the tone of Ramses' letters: "But my brother (Ramses) has not accepted in his own mind my status as a sister and my dignity." Pause for a moment to consider this; it's a remarkable statement. Rarely did any woman demand respect and equal status with men (at least in writing), but Puduhepa had no such qualms. She wanted Ramses to treat her as his "sister"—his equal—just as Hattusili III was his "brother," so she came right out and said so.

Puduhepa finally explained the reason for the delay in sending the princess. It was due to the fact that, although she was putting together an appropriate dowry for her daughter, times were tough. "What civilian captives, cattle and sheep should I give (as a dowry) to my daughter? In my lands I do not even have barley."[12] The barley she was missing was presumably the fodder needed for the cattle and sheep. This was a change from the old Amarna-era habit of never admitting weakness. It seems that goods were harder to come by than before. The shortage of barley that Puduhepa mentioned foreshadowed a famine that was to cripple much of the Near East by the end of the thirteenth century BCE.

Puduhepa promised that she would come up with a dowry for her daughter and that the pharaoh would approve. It would have been a mistake, she said, had she sent her daughter before everything was organized: "If I had sent the daughter to my brother precipitously, or if I had not given you (the gifts appropriate) for my brother <or for> his sister, what would my brother even have said?" She imagined (probably correctly) that Ramses would have viewed an inadequate dowry as a worse snub than a late-arriving bride.

Toward the end of the letter, Puduhepa assured Ramses II that the usual benefits would derive from the marriage: "And now I know that Egypt and Hatti will become a single country." This would happen because Ramses

II had no choice; the gods had willed it. In a commanding tone she wrote that "The Queen knows thereby how you will conclude it (the marriage) out of consideration for my dignity. The deity who installed me in this place does not deny me anything. . . . (The deity) has not denied me happiness. You, as son-in-law, will take my daughter in marriage."[13] One can't help but admire her self-confidence. The great Ramses II would do as she directed.

Eventually the dowry was ready, at which point Ramses II sent envoys to anoint the princess with oil (and thereby to formalize the marriage). In 1246 BCE, the princess set off with her entourage, guards, and dowry, just as so many princesses had done for so many centuries, each one following the command of her father or, in this case, her mother. Ramses wrote to both Puduhepa and Hattusili III that "The Sun God, the Storm God, the Gods of the Land of Egypt, the Gods of the Land of Hatti have granted that our two great countries will be united forever!"[14]

Once he met her, the pharaoh was thoroughly enamored of the Hittite princess, and she took the Egyptian name Maat-Hor-Neferure. The marriage was a success, and the alliance between Egypt and Hatti was back on firm ground.[15]

That drought in Hatti was worrying, though, and Hattusili III was also concerned about the threat from Assyria and the hostility of a group of people called the Arameans. At one point, he wrote to his "brother" king in Babylonia, complaining about the problems that the Babylonian king was having in getting his messengers through to Hatti. Without naming the enemy, he encouraged him to "Go to an enemy country and strike the enemy!"[16] No king in the earlier Amarna period had promoted armed aggression so transparently. Their world was changing.

The enemy to which Hattusili III referred might well have been the Assyrians, and in particular, the Middle Assyrian king Tukulti-Ninurta I (1243–1207 BCE). This king proved to be a real threat to his neighbors; Tukulti-Ninurta I was even able to seize control in Babylon and to take the Babylonian king captive. Ever since the time of the Assyrian king Ashur-uballit I, Babylonia had been a target of Assyrian interest and aggression, and it continued to be for hundreds of years. Tukulti-Ninurta's conquest set off a series of conflicts in Babylon, including attacks by the Elamites, Babylonian rebellions against the vassal king installed by the Assyrians, and a second attack by Tukulti-Ninurta I. This time he copied the strategy that the Hittites had used 400 years before: he kidnapped the statue of the city god Marduk and took it to Assyria. Another rebellion later freed southern Babylonia (the region that had once been Sumer), while the Assyrians still controlled northern Babylonia.[17]

The Kingdom of Ugarit

After the death of Hattusili III, his son took the Hittite throne, but Puduhepa still served as the queen of Hatti, and she maintained the same unflappable style in her correspondence. Like all Hittite queens, Puduhepa's title was unaffected by the death of her husband,[18] and she continued to be in charge of many aspects of the foreign relations of the Hittite government. The new king's wife would have to wait to become queen until Puduhepa passed away.

In the late 1220s BCE, Puduhepa was dealing with a problem in the vassal kingdom of Ugarit on the Mediterranean coast. In spite of the peace treaties of the Amarna period, Ugarit had been wrenched away from Egypt by the Hittites sometime around 1350 BCE, and it had been a jewel of a prize. The capital city extended over 30 hectares (74 acres),[19] was home to around 8,000 people,[20] and sat in an ideal spot for trade. It was right where the road from the Euphrates reached the Mediterranean, directly on a coastal road from Hatti to Egypt, and at the perfect spot for boats from Egypt, Alashiya (Cyprus), and the Aegean to dock in the Levant. In fact, the wider kingdom of Ugarit, stretching beyond the city, boasted eight ports.[21] To the north, Ugarit's green valley was dominated by the sacred mountain now known as Jebel al-Aqra. To the west was the blue horizon line of the Mediterranean. From a vantage point near the temples to Baal and Dagan on the city's high acropolis, one could watch the comings and goings of trading ships in the port.

Ugarit had already been prosperous for millennia—people had first settled there around 6000 BCE.[22] Like Alalakh, Ugarit was an attractive place to live, in a valley of olive trees, vines, and barley fields, and it had proved to be a magnet for people from many lands. From the fourteenth to the twelfth centuries BCE, Ugarit's diverse, multilingual population produced documents in five scripts (including the Cypro-Minoan script, which was used on the island of Cyprus and is still undeciphered).[23] These scripts recorded a host of different languages—the local Ugaritic (a west

Semitic language), Akkadian, Sumerian, Hittite, Hurrian, Egyptian, and even Mycenaean Greek. The innovative people of Ugarit developed one of the world's first alphabets to record their language. The signs were made up of the wedge shapes familiar from cuneiform, but each sign stood for a consonant or vowel rather than for a whole syllable. This made the Ugaritic script much easier to master than conventional cuneiform, having just thirty signs, rather than hundreds. The modern Latin, Greek, Arabic, and Hebrew alphabets have a different ancestor, a script created in Canaan around the same time, but the alphabetic principle was similar for both.

Like Ashur in the Old Assyrian period, the economy of Ugarit was dominated by merchants engaging in extensive trade. But, unlike Ashur, the local king was a powerful man. As the ostensible owner of all real estate, he awarded grants of fields, orchards, and houses to his civil servants and favorites, impressing his seal each time on the tablet that recorded the deed, as in Alalakh and many other kingdoms in the Late Bronze Age.[24] The system worked well and the town prospered. There was something that seemed very solid and permanent about Ugarit. The walls of the houses were constructed of finely cut stone and of rough stones that fit together like a jigsaw puzzle, with roofs made of wooden beams. Many of these walls still stood to a considerable height when they were excavated, even though the town had ultimately been conquered and burned by invaders.[25] After excavation of a neighborhood, visitors to the archaeological site could walk through the streets, noting the well-constructed stone sewer channels and narrow, neatly planned streets; they could even climb the stone staircases of the houses (though of course these no longer led to second floors).

The king and queen of Ugarit lived in a palace that extended over a whole hectare (3 acres)[26] and was built around six courtyards and a walled garden. It had ninety rooms on the ground floor alone and was famous among the local princes for its magnificence. The city had become rich as the middleman in trade between many lands, and from exploiting murex shells found in the sea in that area, which produced a vivid and valuable blue-to-purple dye. Ugarit's royal family, as you might imagine, lived in style.

During the Amarna period, the king of Ugarit had written to the Egyptian pharaoh almost as though they were equals; he was much more assertive in his tone than other Canaanite princes. It seems that this attitude hadn't changed among the later kings of Ugarit, and—to return to Queen Puduhepa—this was the problem she faced in Ugarit. She wanted King

Niqmaddu III of Ugarit (c. 1225–1215 BCE) to behave more like a vassal. After all, he was one.

Puduhepa (who must now have been quite elderly) deeply disapproved of the Ugaritic king's behavior and didn't hesitate to tell him so in a letter.[27] Vassals were supposed to visit the Hittite king and queen regularly but, she wrote, "to me you have not come [. . . and] your messenger-party you have not sent to me."[28] She didn't mention whether Niqmaddu had visited her son, the Hittite king. What troubled Puduhepa was that Niqmaddu was required specifically to see *her*, and he had not done so. Niqmaddu also was obliged by a treaty to send gold to his overlords, but only the king had received gold from him. Where was Puduhepa's gold? She wrote that "[you] have [not] remitted it (the gold) to me; (only) to the Sun (the king of Hatti) have [you] remitted [gold]." This may have become something of a diplomatic incident; one of Niqmaddu's officials was captured and put in fetters by Hittite authorities when traveling through Kizzuwatna, "because of the presents."[29] These, presumably, were the presents that the king of Ugarit had failed to send.

The rest of Puduhepa's letter pertained to caravans from Egypt that passed through Ugarit, with details about the routes that they took. Luxury gifts were still passing regularly between the great powers—many letters attest to this.

To judge from the letters exchanged between the kings of Ugarit and the kings and queen of Hatti, the kings of Ugarit made quite a habit of snubbing their overlords.[30] Niqmaddu III did not just make the one mistake that annoyed Puduhepa so much and provoked her letter. He did all kinds of things that annoyed the Hittite leaders. He prevented Hittite officials from returning home from Ugarit, sent paltry gifts to the king and queen of Hatti, missed his appointments to visit them, and on one occasion failed to send 200 men to Alalakh to assist with a building project, as he had been directed to do. Niqmaddu III seems to have willfully ignored the normal protocols. He acted more like a disenchanted great king than a subservient vassal. His successors did the same, and ever more blatantly.[31] The Hittite rulers constantly threatened these vassal kings of Ugarit with punishments. In the end, though, nothing happened; they seem to have decided not to bother. At least the kings of Ugarit were not actively rebelling, and the kingdom was an economic engine that benefited Hatti.

Urtenu: A Sea Trader

Surprisingly, some of the letters sent and received by the kings and queens of Ugarit showed up not in the royal palace but in a big private house in Ugarit. The house was excavated from 1986 to the 1990s and proved to belong to a man with the Hurrian name of Urtenu.[32] It's unclear why the king trusted him to store his correspondence. His archive included some letters from the queen of Ugarit to Urtenu, but it also included letters between the rulers of Ugarit and the kings of Hatti, Egypt, and Alashiya.[33] Why were they in Urtenu's house? He wasn't even a mayor, commander, or governor; he was a merchant.

His house was impressive in size: more than 250 square meters (2,691 square feet) in extent on the ground floor,[34] with stairs leading to more rooms on a second story. Urtenu's ancestors had been buried in a well-built, paved tomb beneath a room on the ground floor.[35] Unfortunately, the tomb was robbed at some point in antiquity, but the debris left by the robbers attested to the wealth of the family: fragments of imported pots from Greece and vases made of alabaster and serpentine lay scattered about. Elsewhere in the house, archaeologists found more pieces of imported ceramics and stone vases, along with metal objects,[36] and an impression of a scarab of Ramses II.[37] Urtenu even owned a chariot, which had been dismantled for storage in his house. As in Alalakh, ownership of a chariot was a sign of high social status.[38] And then there were the cuneiform tablets, more than 650 of them, including accounts, a few literary and scholarly works (including a fragment of the Epic of Gilgamesh),[39] and a great many letters. Eighty percent of them were written in Akkadian, but many others are in the local Ugaritic language.[40] They show that Urtenu was active in the late thirteenth and early twelfth century, a time of increasing difficulties in Syria and throughout the Near East.[41]

The tablets reveal that Urtenu was a powerful merchant, who was an associate of an equally powerful businessman named Shipti-Ba'al, son-in-law and agent for the queen of Ugarit.[42] Perhaps this connection accounts for how the royal correspondence somehow wound up in Urtenu's house. Indeed, Urtenu himself might have been a descendant of the daughter of a king; either way, he was closely associated with the royal family.[43]

At one point a queen of Ugarit wrote to Urtenu in strictest confidence. She was, for some reason, writing from a boat to let him know where she would be traveling next. One can imagine her dictating the letter from her cabin, or on the deck, as the scribe steadied himself to keep his handwriting legible. "I was on the sea when I gave this document (to be delivered) to you," she said.[44] She then told him where she had lodged the previous night, and where she would be staying for the next three nights. "You are now informed," she wrote. The rest of the letter is a little hard to follow, but it had something to do with a house, and with a woman who was to serve as a guarantee for Urtenu, and who was then to travel to the queen. Perhaps this was why the queen had included her itinerary—so that the woman could find her. This matter was of utmost secrecy. The queen warned Urtenu, "As for you, not a word must escape your mouth." And if the unnamed woman failed to come to the queen? Well, "she (the woman) will send a message to the king and you can kiss your head good-bye."

A second message had been added to the same tablet, from a man named Ilimilku; perhaps he had inscribed both letters on the tablet. He certainly was trusted by the queen, and he called Urtenu "my brother." He explained what Urtenu needed to do next: "What you must do is to seize the house for me. Moreover, you must recognize that the queen also has left." Then he reiterated the queen's message: "you must keep absolutely quiet (about all of this) at Ugarit."[45] What was going on here? Was the queen escaping? She clearly did not want the king to know of her plan.

A Hittite princess was, around this same time, married to a king of Ugarit and later divorced by him.[46] Perhaps the divorced Hittite princess was the queen who wrote the letter, and she was trusting Urtenu to get her affairs in order in Ugarit after she had fled.[47]

The queen of Ugarit (perhaps the same one, or an earlier or later queen) was actively involved in trade; she wrote and received many letters found in Urtenu's house. Unfortunately, she is only identified in the correspondence as "the queen," so her name is unknown. One letter from a governor to "the queen" included a report of goods that he had shipped to her, including barley, lamp-oil, vinegar, olives, and oil perfumed with myrrh.[48]

Urtenu and Shipti-Ba'al traded, often on behalf of the queen, all over the eastern Mediterranean, from the city of Emar on the Euphrates, to the island of Alashiya (Cyprus), to the provincial capital of Carchemish northeast of Ugarit, and even to Egypt.[49] Their connections and deals benefited the state, but also resulted in a nice profit for themselves. This doesn't seem to have been considered to be a conflict of interest.

A third man, named Dagan-belu, did a great deal of the actual traveling and trading for the firm, keeping Urtenu and Shipti-Ba'al apprised of his activities by letter. Dagan-belu often worked in the town of Emar, about 280 kilometers (174 miles) inland on the Euphrates. He had close ties there and may even originally have been a native of the region.[50] The sons of Dagan-belu, along with both Urtenu's son and sister, were also involved in their trading ventures.[51] Just as in Ashur centuries before, Urtenu's business was a family affair, though in this case it was also closely tied to the royal family.

The goods they exported ranged from purple-dyed wool, to alum, to oil. Olive oil was an important product in Ugarit; excavations there uncovered an oil workshop that could have produced large quantities, possibly for export.[52] One particular area of their expertise was in breeding and trading horses and also providing them for luxury gift exchanges instigated by the royal family. Urtenu's house adjoined a stable, where he may have housed the animals, and documents show that he helped manage horses for the palace.[53] In addition, the letters show that the men were in the business of exporting and importing copper and tin ingots, wood,[54] wine, beer, and barley.[55] Urtenu's house must have been a busy place, and during times when Ugarit was at peace, messengers and traders speaking any number of native languages must have passed through, perhaps checking on the foals in the stable, dropping off letters, or arranging to pick up purple cloth from a storehouse.

Several letters in Urtenu's archive pertain to men and goods that had traveled by ship. Seaborne traffic had been busy in the peaceful and stable era between the mid-fifteenth and the mid-thirteenth centuries BCE, dominated by ships carrying all the goods mentioned in Urtenu's archive, along with other materials such as glass. These ships sailed around a network of Mediterranean ports on a regular basis, with Ugarit serving as a crucial hub in the network.[56]

Earlier Old Babylonian traders in Ashur had stuck to land routes and goods carried on donkeys, but the merchants of the Late Bronze Age had taken to the Mediterranean. The crews of their ships played a vital (if anonymous) role in maintaining trade and diplomatic relationships among the great powers and among their vassals.

The queen of Ugarit was not, apparently, unusual in having a trading agent like Shipti-Ba'al working directly for her. The ships seem to have often been the property of royal families, and long-distance transactions fell under their purview.[57]

Boats in this era were sturdily built for sea travel. Even though the crews and captains could not avoid unexpected hazards such as bad weather and rough seas, sailors were adept at dealing with crises and could figure out their location even in the open sea; they didn't have to hug the coast.[58]

Not all the ships made it to their destinations, however. A shipwreck could represent the loss of a vast amount of wealth. Near a place called Ulu Burun, off the coast of Turkey, underwater archaeologists in the 1980s and 1990s discovered the wreck of a forty-five-foot-long ship that had been traveling from Cyprus, probably en route to the Aegean, around 1300 BCE.[59] Its hold was crammed with riches. Lying on the sea floor, still lined up on the ancient wooden boards of the hull, were more than 9,000 kilograms (10 tons) of copper ingots, more than 900 kilograms (one ton) of tin ingots, more than 300 kilograms (700 pounds) of glass ingots, and dozens of jars that had contained oils and other substances, along with many smaller luxury items.[60] To judge from their possessions, the crewmembers seem to have been Canaanite (though there's no way to know from which city-state), and two Mycenaean diplomats were on board as well. Many people must have been devastated at the news of the shipwreck: the Canaanite merchant firm and royal household who sponsored the ship, along with the king of Alashiya whose copper ingots were lost before being delivered, and the many prospective recipients of the goods in the cargo. If lives were lost as well, the tragedy represented by the disaster would have had a lifelong impact on the families of the victims.

Another shipwreck had a happier outcome. A number of ships had set off from Ugarit for Egypt, loaded with grain. This may seem like a case of carrying coals to Newcastle—Egypt was richer in grain than almost any other land—but, be that as it may, the ships "were wrecked near Tyre when they found themselves caught in a bad storm."[61] The port of Tyre was about 270 kilometers (168 miles) south of Ugarit. This message came from the king of Tyre in a letter to the king of Ugarit, his "brother" and ally. No doubt boats from Tyre had suffered similar crises in the past. Fortunately, the port of Tyre had experts on hand who were ready to help. The king of Tyre wrote that "The salvage master, however, was able to remove the ent[ire] (cargo of) grain in their possession." The grain, "as well as all the people and their food," had been recovered, and the boats "have been able to moor at Acco." Acco was a few more kilometers south. This must have been a great relief to the king of Ugarit. His boats could probably even be restored back to seaworthiness. "My brother should not worry" was the final, comforting message of the king of Tyre.

A century later, at the end of the thirteenth century BCE, those ships carrying grain would not have been sent off from Ugarit to Egypt. Grain was suddenly in short supply; any food produced would have been used to feed the local population. A letter found in Urtenu's house was written to the king of Ugarit by someone in dire need of help: "grain staples from you are not to be had! (The people of) the household of your servant will die of hunger!"[62] But the king of Ugarit was in no position to help. In desperation, he wrote to the Hittite king, but the Hittite king was not forthcoming, writing back, "Now, concerning the fact that you have sent a tablet to your Sun, your master"—this was the term used for the Hittite king, who referred to himself in the third person—"regarding food, to the effect that there is no food in your land: (know that) the Sun himself is perishing."[63] So the king of Ugarit tried asking for help from the king of Egypt instead: "[In] the land of Ugarit there is a severe hunger: May my Lord save [the land of Ugarit], and may the king give grain to save my life ... and to save the citizens of the land of Ugarit."[64] Egypt did have a more reliable supply of grain than its neighbors, because it didn't depend on Mediterranean-area rainfall. The Nile flooded every year as a result of the rains in central Africa, so the fields there were almost always productive. But the Egyptian king didn't send grain. His letter arrived with gold objects, textiles, and dried fish.[65]

Outside of Egypt, though, it seems that everyone in the region was suffering. The Hittite king and queen stopped badgering the king of Ugarit to visit their palace, send gold, and act more like an obedient vassal. They had too many other worries, as they struggled to cope with a growing famine.[66] Modern climate scientists doing research on the ancient Mediterranean region confirm the sense one gets from the ancient texts: "The whole of the east Mediterranean experienced arid conditions at 3000 ± 300 BP [before present], which may have been the driest time of the whole Holocene in this area."[67] This drought was devastating to areas dependent on rainfall to water their crops—areas like Greece, Anatolia, and coastal Syria. The place was a tinderbox ready to explode.

The Kingdom of Emar

More evidence for the mood of crisis in this era comes from the city of Emar, where Urtenu's business partner Dagan-belu seems to have been based. As we have seen, Emar was about a week's journey inland from Ugarit, on the Euphrates. It had already been a city of note a thousand years earlier, when it lay within the realm of the Early Dynastic kingdom of Ebla. The excavations at Emar have exposed levels dating from the fourteenth to the early twelfth centuries BCE, in which were found about 800 cuneiform tablets and fragments.[68] Many of these tablets reveal something of the uncertainty and fear that marked the end of the Late Bronze Age.

In the thirteenth century BCE, Emar was home to a dynasty of local kings, but they were not particularly powerful. A relatively small building that has been identified as their palace hardly seems palatial.[69] Either the actual palace was not found, or the kings lived very modestly. The tablets often mention a council of elders who held significant power. Sometimes the elders seem to have performed roles that were more important than those of the king, and the king often appeared as a witness to documents in which the main role was played by these town elders.

One of the most remarkable discoveries among the tablets at Emar was an account of a religious festival that was vital to the lives of the local people. Detailed descriptions of religious festivals are rare in the ancient Near East, but this one gives us a sense of how the townspeople sometimes had the chance to interact with the great gods. The festival was known as the *zukru*, and it took place once a year, with a longer and more elaborate version every seven years. At the center of the celebration was the great god of the region, Dagan, the god of grain.[70]

On the first day of the long version of the festival, people of Emar would have gathered in the streets in anticipation. The moment of Dagan's appearance must have been electric—there he was, among his people, probably as a life-size male statue made of polished stone or gold inlaid with gems, and clothed in colorful garments. The tablet notes that "his face (was) uncovered"; the god could look at his people, just as they looked at him. The people of Emar were invited to follow him to a place outside the city "in procession . . . at the gate of the upright stones."[71] These upright stones formed some kind of a shrine.

Once there, the priests performed rituals and offered sacrifices to Dagan and to other gods who (as statues) had joined the celebration. The temple provided food and drink for the people; this was a public occasion, a party of gods and citizens. It was nothing like the gods' day-to-day existence, which was private and hidden inside the walls of the temple. "After they sacrifice, eat, and drink, they cover his (the god's) face,"[72] the author notes. "Just before evening," when the light was dimming in the sky, the god returned to the city in "the wagon of Dagan," which "passes between the upright stones."[73] The term "wagon" probably doesn't do justice to what must have been an impressive carriage.

This passage in and out of the city for rituals and sacrifices took place four times over seven days, during which time the face of the statue was sometimes covered with a veil, but occasionally again uncovered for all to see, notably on his last return to the city on the seventh day of the festival.[74] The face of the statue was emphasized over and over in this ritual. To the people, as we have seen so often, the statue *was* the god and his ties to his people were reinforced when they could see his face directly.[75]

Religious rituals like this one strengthened the idea that life had a pattern, a predictability, and that the gods and humans worked together to keep the world in order. The *zukru* also symbolically emphasized Dagan's power over both the countryside (as he left to visit the shrine of stones) and the city.[76] Festivals at other cities no doubt had similar features. But, notwithstanding the regular performance of the *zukru* festival, by 1200 BCE life in Emar was becoming increasingly unpredictable.

During the late thirteenth century, Emar, like Ugarit, was a province within the Hittite Empire. A first intimation that their world was changing came when the local dynasty there collapsed, perhaps because of a revolt among the townspeople of Emar against their king. This crisis doesn't seem to have been caused by the Hittites, and Emar wasn't a particularly important place in the Hittite Empire, but as it was now lacking a local authority, the imperial administration stepped in.

In place of the old king of Emar and the council of elders, a man who held the title Overseer of the Land took charge.[77] He represented the king of the land of Carchemish, who was, in turn, a viceroy of the Hittite king himself. The Hittite officials' oversight in local affairs became much more obvious at this time, with their seals and names showing up on many documents.[78]

From what historians can tell from the documents, Emar struggled through something of a blur of political and economic crises. The words of the people of Emar let us know that they lived through difficult times. A great many documents were written during years that the writers referred to as "the year of distress" or "the year of distress and war."[79] The stories they tell reflect a chaotic time, in the late thirteenth and early twelfth centuries BCE, when not only were they suffering from the same region-wide famine that affected Ugarit and Hatti, but the town was also repeatedly under attack, and some of the people of Emar struggled just to survive.[80] Back in the fourteenth century BCE, Emar had been safely ensconced in the heart of the kingdom of Mittani but, by the late thirteenth century, with Mittani gone, the Euphrates marked the boundary between the Hittite Empire and the land of Assyria, and Emar was right on the Euphrates—right on that boundary. Those "years of distress and war" happened again and again, and the distress was very real.

A lot about the bigger picture of life at Emar is uncertain, but the tablets can take us very intimately into the lives of some people who lived there. In the midst of all the uncertainties, seven tablets provide a clear story, capturing vividly the hardships and impossible choices faced by one particular young family in this very difficult moment.

Ku'e, Zadamma, and Their Children: A Family Facing Starvation

The family's story started in a happier time, when a man named Zadamma and a woman named Ku'e got married. They were not among the elite of Emar—we don't know their professions, but they were far from rich. Zadamma's father was from a place called Shatappa, but the young couple didn't live there; they had settled in Emar.[81]

In time, Ku'e gave birth to a baby girl. The parents named her Ba'la-bia.[82] She presumably went through all the normal stages of babyhood, learning to crawl and then walk, smiling and babbling at her parents, and beginning to speak. Very soon after her birth, her mother was pregnant again. It must have been a difficult pregnancy this time, because she was carrying twins. The baby boys, named Ba'la-belu and Ishma'-Dagan, were born healthy and seem to have been little more than a year younger than their sister. But at that point, their mother Ku'e's life began to fall apart.[83]

We don't know why, but her husband left the family, and Ku'e had no way to support herself and her children. It was one of "the years of distress," and the distress was affecting everyone in Emar. One can imagine Ku'e's misery, nursing her baby boys, taking care of her barely toddler daughter, without enough money for food. Had this been a situation in which Ku'e was in debt and little Ba'la-bia was older, she might have given her daughter to her creditor to work for him until the debt was paid off. Had she been able to support two of her children but not all three, she might have given one of them up for adoption. But Ba'la-bia was far too young to work, and Ku'e needed money simply to live. She made what must have been a heartbreaking decision: she would sell her daughter. We've encountered this phenomenon before, in the Ur III period, when a family had to sell a child into slavery because that was the only way that the child would be able to be fed and to live, and that the parents could survive. But in Emar at this moment, almost everyone was suffering.

A woman named Anat-ummi agreed to buy little Ba'la-bia.[84] A contract was drawn up, and in it the scribe quoted the words of the mother, Ku'e: "My husband went away; [our children] (were all) babies [and I did not have (anyone)] who could feed (them). Therefore I have sold my daughter Ba'la-bia to be a daughter of Anat-ummi . . . and (thus) I could feed the (other) small children (of mine) during the year of the famine."[85]

The price of the baby was 30 shekels, which would have been enough for Ku'e to support herself and her twin boys for quite some time. For Anat-ummi, buying a baby was a risky proposition, given that at least 40 percent of children died in childhood (this was not just true in ancient Mesopotamia, it was true worldwide until the mid-eighteenth century of our own era).[86] But, as the contract specifies, Anat-ummi planned for Ba'la-bia to be her daughter. Perhaps the payment represented a kindness to Ku'e; Anat-ummi could have adopted the baby without paying for her. Unfortunately, though, Anat-ummi never came up with the money, and so Ku'e took Ba'la-bia back.[87]

The next we hear of Ku'e was written a year later. Her husband Zadamma had returned home. The financial situation had not improved for Ku'e's young family, however. She had given birth to yet another baby, a girl named Ba'la-ummi, and they were just as poor as before. The whole family may well have been starving.[88] Ku'e and her husband Zadamma came to the desperate decision to sell all four of their children. The contract for the sale lays it all out dispassionately:

> Zadamma and Ku'e, his wife, have sold their two sons and their two daughters–Ba'la-bia, Ba'la-belu, Ishma'-Dagan, and Ba'la-ummi, a daughter at the breast—into slavery for 60 shekels of silver, the entire price, to Ba'lu-malik, the diviner. If anyone sues to reclaim the four children of Zadamma, they must give ten other persons as compensation to Ba'lu-malik. And now Zadamma, their father, and Ku'e, their mother, have pressed their feet into clay.[89]

This time, the transaction did go through. The price of 60 shekels was not much, though, considering that the toddler Ba'la-bia alone was to have been sold for 30 shekels. By including a redemption clause, the buyer implicitly admitted that this was a low price. When people were purchased for what was considered to be a fair price, the scribe did not list a way for someone to "sue to reclaim" them.[90]

Then there is that clause that the parents have "pressed their (children's) feet into clay." That was not a metaphor—they had literally done so. The tiny clay footprints of the three oldest children were found by the archaeologists (see Fig. 16.2).[91]

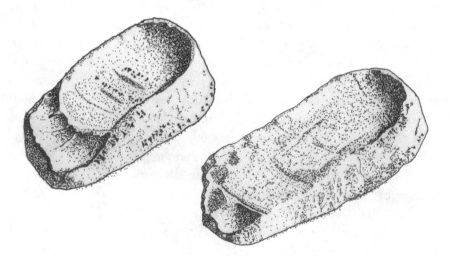

Fig. 16.2 Footprints of two of the children of Ku'e pressed into clay and sealed and inscribed by witnesses, from Emar, early twelfth century BCE (based on National Museum Aleppo M10561, M8649 in Fortin 1999, 286).

Two-year-old Ba'la-bia and one-year-olds Ba'la-belu and Ishma'-Dagan must have been held by their mother Ku'e as each child in turn placed his or her right foot on a lump of clay and stepped down hard. Baby Ba'la-ummi was too small at this point; she made no footprint in clay. The lumps of clay bearing the footprints were then handed around to the scribe and to the gathered witnesses and treated as though they were documents. The children's names were written on them. One reads, "The foot of Ba'la-belu, son of Zadamma, son of Karbu, the man from Shatappa," and the equivalent inscriptions were added for the other two children on their respective footprints.[92] Witnesses who were present for the transaction then rolled their seals on the clay around the footprints.[93]

One of these men was the Hittite Overseer,[94] which seems surprising. Why would such an important man as the Hittite Overseer have been present for the purchase of four impoverished children, the oldest of them no more than two years of age?[95] Perhaps it was because Ba'lu-malik, who was buying the children, was an important man in Emar. His family, known as the Zu-Ba'la family, from the name of an ancestor, lived and worked in a grand building called M-1 by the archaeologists.[96] One man in each generation of the family took the title "Diviner of the gods of Emar,"[97] but they seem to have served primarily as administrators.[98] Ba'lu-malik was a teacher and he was important enough to be of interest to the court in Carchemish.[99] Apparently even an intimate transaction like this adoption warranted the involvement of the Overseer.

Since the baby Ba'la-ummi was not yet weaned, she was presumably allowed to stay with her mother for a few more months; her footprint would not have been taken until she was delivered to Ba'lu-malik's household.[100] But the older children must have left their home for good once the contract was complete.

Who brought them up? Did Ba'lu-malik intend to raise them in his household as family (as Anat-ummi apparently had intended to do when proposing to buy the oldest girl), or was he going to put them to work as slaves? It's striking that no clause in the contract states what work the children would do. In adoption contracts the adoptive parents often pledged to teach their children a profession, thereby preparing them to live independently. Did Ba'lu-malik intend for the boys to become diviners like himself anyway? If not, were they put to work as soon as they could help in the household?

We don't know. We also don't know whether the children ever saw their parents Ku'e and Zadamma again. They had no hope of being manumitted. Reclaiming them would have cost their parents more than they could ever have accumulated—according to the contract, they would have been required to provide ten (enslaved) persons in exchange for their children. The sale of children was hardly considered normal at Emar; it was, in fact, condemned[101] and had to be justified as having been caused by extraordinarily difficult conditions.[102] But times were extremely hard at the end of the Bronze Age.

The End of the Late Bronze Age

The Hittite rulers seem to have lost control of Emar during the early years of the twelfth century; the last Overseer there was a man with the local name of Ahi-malik who seems not to have answered to Hittite officials.[103] The "years of distress and war" mentioned in the tablets culminated in the violent destruction of the city around 1180 BCE,[104] and evidently no Hittite forces arrived to fight off the invaders. Ultimately, the city was devastated. The population fled. It probably made little difference to the people of Emar themselves who attacked them. The tragedy was simply that it happened. Emar was not reoccupied.

Ugarit suffered the same fate at around the same time, between 1190 and 1185 BCE. There, too, the whole town burned. Although, as we have seen, plenty of texts had mentioned hunger and grain shortages in the final years before the attack, the inhabitants of Ugarit seem to have been able to continue to trade and to live, if in straitened circumstances. Then a few mentions of enemy ships suggest that something was amiss, followed by an urgent message. The king of Ugarit wrote to his overlord at Carchemish: "May my lord know that now the enemy forces are stationed at Ra'shu (one of the ports of Ugarit) and their avant-guard forces were sent to Ugarit."[105] It seems the letter was never sent. The enemies, who had come by sea, gave him no time. Suddenly the city of Ugarit was under attack.

Archaeologists found numerous arrowheads in the destruction level, but the people of the town had abandoned their homes before the end.[106] Like Emar, the city lay uninhabited for centuries. People like Urtenu never ventured back to their devastated community, even to retrieve important documents from their houses. One hopes that Urtenu and his family, along with the royal family of Ugarit and other citizens, moved elsewhere and managed to rebuild their lives. The people of Ugarit were not alone. A number of cities along the coast of the Mediterranean were attacked and destroyed, all within a few years of the destruction of Ugarit. Many people must have been on the move, searching for a safe place to live.

I have made it this far in this chapter without mentioning the Sea Peoples, and I hesitate to do so even now. For decades they provided a tidy explanation for the crises of the end of the Late Bronze Age. More recently their influence, and even their very existence, has been debated extensively.

The "Sea Peoples" is the modern name for a group of invaders and settlers who showed up in Egypt during the reign of Ramses III (1186–1155 BCE); they arrived in the mid-twelfth century BCE. The Egyptians didn't call them Sea Peoples, they simply named the constituent groups individually; they were known as Denyen, Ekwesh, Shekelesh, Sherden, and Weshesh. All these peoples were described as "of the sea" or "in their isles." Others, the Lukka, Peleset, and Tjeker, though not specifically from "the sea," were lumped in with them and have been included in the appellation "Sea Peoples." After Egypt experienced initial entanglements with the Sea Peoples in the thirteenth and early twelfth centuries BCE, in the reigns of Ramses II and his successor Merneptah, Ramses III claimed a great victory against seven of these groups. He commemorated this victory in detail in relief sculptures on the walls of his mortuary temple at Medinet Habu. The invaders are shown fighting (and dramatically losing to) the Egyptians during the course of a wild and claustrophobic sea battle. An inscription at Medinet Habu credits the Sea Peoples with having destroyed many other lands during the eighth year of Ramses III's reign: "No land could stand before their arms, from Hatti, Kode, Carchemish, Arzawa, and Alashiya on, being cut off at [one time]. . . . They laid their hands upon the lands as far as the circuit of the earth, their hearts confident and trusting: 'Our plans will succeed!'"[107]

So it seems likely that it was some contingent of the Sea Peoples who attacked Ugarit,[108] and also Alashiya (Cyprus), but Emar and Hatti faced different foes. The capital city of Hattusa was, indeed, attacked and destroyed around 1200 BCE, though it's unclear who was responsible. Hattusa was much too far inland to have fallen victim to the Sea Peoples. It was probably attacked by people situated to its north, though the city may have been largely abandoned before the attackers arrived.

Even some Mycenaean cities, far to the west, collapsed, and the Greeks may have recalled a distant folk memory of the disruptions of this chaotic time in the works of Homer. According to Homer in his epic poem the Iliad, the Trojan War was fought (in what was for them the distant past) between heroic Greeks and people of Troy, who lived on the coast of Anatolia. As in the Epic of Gilgamesh in Mesopotamia, Homer included interactions between humans and gods, and plenty of mythical elements in his tale (if Homer was a real person at all, but that's another issue). But there may be a kernel of historical truth in the story, because if ever there was a time when Greeks and Trojans might have been fighting in coastal Anatolia, it was during the disruptions at the end of the Late Bronze Age, when Greeks probably were swept up in the events.

Scholars have put forward numerous theories identifying who the Sea Peoples were and why they were on the move,[109] while some others have posited that no one was actually on the move at all. Recent theories suggest that what the Egyptians described as an invasion in the time of Ramses III actually was a migration of many peoples to many places on the eastern edge of the Mediterranean that took place over as many as fifty years.[110] For our purposes, what is important is that, in the context of a devastating drought and famine, the international system that had characterized two and half centuries of the Late Bronze Age came to a dramatic and messy end.

This was not just true in the eastern Mediterranean region. All the former great powers suffered. In Assyria, King Tukulti-Ninurta I's luck didn't last. After building the Middle Assyrian Empire to its largest extent, taking over Syria and conquering Babylon, he decided that he needed a new capital city. In this, he was emulating the earlier Late Bronze Age kings Kurigalzu of Babylon, Akhenaten of Egypt, and Untash-napirisha of Elam. He named the city for himself, Kar Tukulti-Ninurta, and, like Untash-napirisha's capital, it was intended to be "a dwelling place for the gods."[111] But before he could enjoy his city for long, the king was assassinated there, as a result of a conspiracy by his own sons. His death in 1207 BCE gave rise to a period of chaos and marked the beginning of an era of decline for Assyria; later kings proved to be unable to hold on to the empire.

Babylonia and Elam were affected by the instability of this era as well, as the Elamite kings continued their attacks on Babylonia, particularly dramatically in 1158 BCE, when the Elamite king Shutruk-Nahhunte brought some of Mesopotamia's most important statues and stelas back with him to Susa.[112] He proudly displayed his plunder across the citadel: statues of Akkadian kings, the law stela of Hammurabi, the victory stela of Naram-Sin, many *kudurru* stones and other stelas. On some of them he had masons chisel out the original inscription and replace it with one of his own.[113] The sculptures were still in Susa when they were discovered during excavations there in the early twentieth century of our era; the Babylonians never got them back. The Kassite dynasty lost power in Babylon soon after, replaced by a dynasty based in the city of Isin.

Even worse destruction was meted out in Babylonia by Elam under its next king, Kutir-Nahhunte, who plundered and burned temples across the land. To the horror of the Babylonians, he even stole the statue of Marduk, greatest of all the gods, and took it back to Susa with him.[114] The statue had not been home for long, since its return from Assyria where it had been taken by Tukulti-Ninurta I, and now the god was gone once again. It was only reclaimed when a Babylonian king named Nebuchadnezzar I in turn raided Susa in 1110 BCE and brought Marduk home.

Many cities in Babylonia were abandoned during the late twelfth and eleventh centuries. This may have been because the Euphrates seems to have shifted its course away from the cities. The plain was so flat in the south that, after a flood, there was always the chance that the river might not return to its original bed. Legions of flood mitigation workers had, in past centuries, worked to prevent this, maintaining levees, cutting flood channels, and maintaining reservoirs. But perhaps in this period the workforce simply didn't exist to keep the river in its normal course, leaving ancient cities deprived of water and fields impossible to irrigate.

Soon after the death of Tukulti-Ninurta I, not only did Assyria lose control of Babylon, but regions in central and northern Syria gained independence, and many of them became home to Aramean states. But, in all of this disarray, the Assyrian heartland benefited from a great advantage in comparison with the rest of the Near East. The same dynasty stayed on the throne, generation after generation through this era. The Assyrian kings continued to maintain a disciplined military force that had no equal. This ultimately gave Assyria an incomparable benefit, and even through the following century, when all of the great powers had collapsed, Assyria's kings never gave up on their goal to rule the whole world.

PART VII

The First Millennium, 1000–323 BCE

Chapter 17
Empire Builders, Sculptors, and Deportees

The year 1200 BCE is traditionally seen as the start of the Iron Age in the Near East, the third phase of the Stone-Bronze-Iron Age pattern to ancient history invented by scholars in the nineteenth century. But the moment of the division between the Bronze and Iron Ages is fairly arbitrary. The earliest known evidence for iron smelting has been found in Anatolia at a site that was occupied long before, during the Assyrian Colonies period, but it seems to have had little impact and the technology didn't spread at that time.[1] By about 1000 BCE, there's more evidence for iron smelting in Anatolia and in the Levant, but, even then, it didn't immediately change much of anything, even for the people who had access to it. Early iron was not necessarily superior to bronze in strength or availability, and it wasn't adopted instantly. Eventually, iron did replace bronze as the metal of choice for weapons and tools, but this change took many generations.[2]

Small Kingdoms in the Eleventh and Tenth Centuries BCE

During the first two centuries of the Iron Age, after the famine and destruction that marked the end of the Late Bronze Age, no great power dominated any part of the region—not in the Levant, Anatolia, Syria, Mesopotamia, or Elam (Map 4). If iron technology made any difference at all in people's lives, it's hard to detect. Small kingdoms continued to exist, but few of them produced many records. They probably didn't need written records in the same way as before, when vast administrations had been keeping track of taxes, corvée laborers, a military draft, and

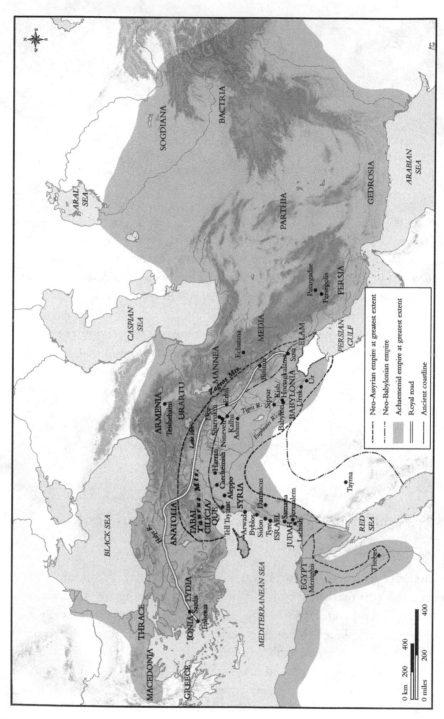

Map 4 The Near East from 1000 to 323 BCE

redistribution of resources, and when diplomatic letters had been written and delivered over long distances. The rulers of the smaller kingdoms of the eleventh and tenth centuries BCE had fewer uses for writing, and they left just a scattering of documents behind. Even Egypt slipped into a time of political disunity and economic weakness during the eleventh and the first half of the tenth centuries BCE. As in the sixteenth century BCE, this era is often referred to as a "Dark Age" simply because we know very little about it.

Three of the peoples that flourished between the eleventh and tenth centuries BCE ultimately did have a powerful influence on future events. None of them kept records in cuneiform, so they don't exactly fit the profile of the cultures discussed in this book, but they were too influential to leave out here.

One was the Arameans. Over the subsequent centuries, their language of Aramaic became the most widely spoken and written language in the Near East, even though they never ruled an empire or conquered other regions.

The origins of this group are rather obscure. Inscriptions by Middle Assyrian kings of the late twelfth century BCE include some of the first references to the Arameans, whose homeland seems to have been north of the Euphrates, between the Balikh and Habur Rivers.[3] It's possible that they had lived in this region for centuries, or it could be that they had arrived from elsewhere. We just don't know.

Although they spoke a common language, they were not, strictly speaking, one people. Several different Aramaic-speaking groups, often described as tribes, had spread out across a large area.[4] Most of the Aramean kingdoms in Syria and northern Mesopotamia were referred to as the "House of" some shared ancestor.[5] Like so many Mesopotamian groups, the Arameans' sense of kinship with some kind of larger household (whether real or mythical) seems to have been a principal source of their feelings of identity.

For reasons that are hard to explain, by the first millennium BCE, Aramaic had largely replaced Akkadian in Mesopotamia and Hurrian in Syria as the most common spoken language of the Near East. Aramaic only grew in influence through the middle of the first millennium BCE, and, although it was later replaced as the lingua franca in the region by Greek and then Arabic, it is still spoken in some communities today.[6]

Aramaic is a Semitic language, like Akkadian, and speakers of Aramaic and Akkadian could probably understand one another reasonably well without translation. Aramaic had an advantage, though—it was much easier to write. And that was thanks to the second group of people that flourished in this time—the Phoenicians.

The Phoenicians have a familiar name, but they were not actually referred to as Phoenicians during the eleventh century BCE. That term only came to be used for them much later. Josephine Quinn, a historian at Oxford University, has argued that the so-called Phoenicians didn't even have a sense of shared identity as a people.[7] The area identified as Phoenicia by the later Greeks and Romans was a strip of land on the coast of Canaan, only about 240 kilometers (150 miles) from north to south and barely 50 kilometers (30 miles) from west to east at its widest point. It wasn't united under a single government; in the eleventh century BCE, the area was home to four diminutive kingdoms: Arwad, Byblos, Sidon, and Tyre. The inhabitants of these cities specialized in seaborne trade, not unlike their entrepreneurial predecessors in Ugarit. They even traded in the same goods as the Ugaritians, especially purple dye and cedar. They had been subject to Egypt during the Late Bronze Age, but flourished as separate small kingdoms after the great powers collapsed. Like the people of Ugarit, they used an alphabetic script, and theirs is the one that was borrowed to write Aramaic, and also gave rise to all the subsequent European and Near Eastern alphabets.

Their alphabet had only twenty-two letters, all of them consonants, which made it a simpler script to learn than Akkadian cuneiform, for which one needed to learn at least 200 signs. The alphabetic signs themselves were also easier to write, consisting of fairly simple shapes that could be drawn by anyone, in contrast to cuneiform's complicated constructions of numerous wedges, each impressed separately with a stylus. Once the alphabet had developed, it was adopted in many of the regions the Phoenicians came in contact with. And because they were traders, they ended up being in contact with a great many regions around the Mediterranean.

The third people who flourished in the era of small kingdoms were the Israelites, southern neighbors to the Phoenicians, with whom they traded. Their history is known to us because the Israelites developed a tradition of writing about their past, resulting in the Hebrew Bible. It is one of the most remarkable sources for ancient history, written by many different authors over more than a thousand years. Some of the earliest passages of the Bible may have been written during this time, the eleventh century BCE, when the kingdom of Israel was first founded.

During most of the Late Bronze Age, no references to Israelites (outside the Bible) are known from Canaan or Egypt or anywhere else. The cities in the region, when the Amarna letters were written, for example, were clearly occupied by Canaanites. But the Egyptian pharaoh Merneptah (1213–1204 BCE) recorded, in a list of his Canaanite conquests, that "Israel is laid waste and his seed is not."[8] It seems therefore that the Israelites were, by the late thirteenth century BCE, living in Canaan. According to the Bible, the kingdom of Israel formed later, under a king named Saul, and remained unified under kings David and Solomon. It later split into two kingdoms. Israel, in the north, retained the land's original name, but eventually created a new capital at a city called Samaria, while Judah, in the south, maintained the Israelite capital at Jerusalem. This split took place around 925 BCE, just a few years before the Assyrians began an unprecedented military expansion, to which we will return.[9]

The Israelites, like the Arameans, adopted the Phoenicians' alphabetic script to write their own language of Hebrew. The early years of the Israelite kingdom are known from the Bible rather than from documents found on archaeological sites. In Israel (as in the Aramaic, Canaanite, and Phoenician kingdoms), day-to-day records, such as those written on clay tablets in much of the rest of the Near East, would have been written on perishable organic materials like papyrus and they haven't survived. Israel and Judah were small kingdoms in their time, especially in comparison with the great power of Assyria that grew to dominate them. But they have left a huge legacy: the Bible itself, of course, along with their monotheistic religion that lies at the roots of modern Judaism, Christianity, and Islam.

Assyrian Rebirth

As for the Assyrians—they became the greatest power the region had ever seen. Like all the other great powers of the Late Bronze Age, the Middle Assyrian Empire had gone into decline in the early twelfth century BCE, and from the mid-eleventh to the mid-tenth century the kingdom of Assyria was limited to its heartland, the area around Ashur. The kings continued to maintain records, and scribes continued to learn to write in cuneiform (the same was true in Babylonia), but in much smaller numbers than before.

When the Assyrian kings began to build up their military again, in the late tenth century, the world around Assyria was very different from the one of the Late Bronze Age. No other state had the resources to stand up to them. The old power balance that had maintained the brotherhood of great kings was gone. The Assyrians could sweep in and conquer pretty much any land they wanted to. And they did want to.

The Assyrians had honed and emphasized their military prowess in the Late Bronze Age and they continued to do so. Every king was a warrior, as were all his officials, no matter what other roles they held. Even a king's barber, his cupbearer, and his queen were in charge of troops. Assyrian kings simply had no choice but to lead the army out on campaign on a regular basis. Whereas Old Babylonian kings, for example, had plenty of different achievements by which they chose to mark their years— offerings to gods, canal constructions, dedications of priestesses, building renovations, and so on—almost every year in an Assyrian king's reign was remembered as being the occasion of a particular military expedition (or several). This new era of Assyrian aggression is known as the Neo-Assyrian period.

The Neo-Assyrian kings started out by "reclaiming" lands that they thought of as belonging to Assyria, lands that had been within the orbit of the Middle Assyrian Empire more than a century earlier, which were mostly to the north and west of the Assyrian heartland. The regions to the north, around Lake Van, were in a land known as Urartu,[10] whereas those to the west in Syria had largely been settled by Arameans. Later, the Assyrians expanded beyond there, into regions that had never been subject to Assyria, and they also reconquered their venerable southern neighbor, Babylonia.

For this Neo-Assyrian period (911–609 BCE), the choices of men and women that we could focus on are almost endless. Between the letters, administrative documents, royal inscriptions, and abundant other texts that survive, an absolute sea of names presents itself. Unlike for most earlier periods, one could fill an entire book just with the history of one particular king and his entourage (and authors have done so),[11] because so very much is known about them. Their queens, sons, daughters, officials, rivals, doctors, diviners, scribes, priests, priestesses—all were named and many of them wrote letters, as you will see in the next chapter, about king Esarhaddon.

For this chapter, though, I want to go in pursuit of two categories of people whose names rarely survive, but who are crucial to our understanding of this era. The first category is that of the artists and sculptors who created remarkable stone relief sculptures that lined the walls of Assyrian palaces. The second category is that of the people conquered by the Neo-Assyrian armies, some of them members of the foreign courts, but most of them normal everyday people, many of whom were uprooted from their homes and farms and deported hundreds of miles to start new lives somewhere else.

These two categories may seem unrelated, but that is not the case. It is only because of the artists that we really know much about the deportees. These people are almost invisible in Assyrian written documentation, where they were largely reduced to numbers and place-names, but they were portrayed with attention to detail by the Assyrian court sculptors. They may not have names that we know, but real individuals lie behind the representations on the walls of the palaces.

If you walk through the ancient Near Eastern galleries of the Iraq Museum in Baghdad, the British Museum in London, the Louvre in Paris, the Metropolitan Museum in New York, or many other museums around the world, you cannot miss the work of the extraordinary Assyrian sculptors. Their masterpieces were so abundant in the palaces in the Assyrian capitals at Kalhu, Dur-Sharrukin, and Nineveh that they can become almost overwhelming. You could sit and look at just one relief panel for hours and fail to take in all its detail, and there were acres of these panels lining the walls of the palaces. An army of sculptors must have been involved in carving them. But these men didn't sign their work and were never credited by the kings, so they remain anonymous to us.

Before looking for evidence for them, though, we need to meet Ashurnasirpal II, who was the first king to employ such sculptors to create a visual story of his achievements. He was also one of the many Assyrian kings who displaced thousands of people from one part of the empire to another.

Ashurnasirpal II: A Militaristic King

King Ashurnasirpal II (883–859 BCE) was not a modest man, but then, you would not expect him to be. He was one of the most prolific builders in Assyrian history, as well as being one of the kings most responsible for developing what we know as the Neo-Assyrian Empire. He ruled near the beginning of this new and dramatic era for Assyria, and for the whole Near East.

He created a model of a militaristic, untouchable, divinely appointed, and dangerous Neo-Assyrian king, a model that echoed for almost 300 years across the reigns of his successors. Throughout his annals—the annual records of his achievements—when he described what he thought of as "his" conquests and "his" building projects, he tended not to credit anyone else, not his army, and not his architects, builders, or artists. He did everything himself. He repeatedly wrote, concerning his victories, "I besieged the city and conquered it," or "I felled 600 of their combat troops," and so on, and of his constructions, "I rebuilt this city," and "I built its wall."[12] This, of course, had long been a common conceit in royal inscriptions. Ever since the Early Dynastic period, kings had used the first-person singular to take credit for actions that, in truth, had been organized and implemented by hordes of officials and workers. But in the case of Ashurnasirpal II, the achievements he took credit for were on a different scale, and the hyperbole of his claims could be breathtaking.

In his longest inscription, from a temple to the god Ninurta in the city of Kalhu, he used twenty-eight different epithets and titles to first introduce himself, starting with "(I,) Ashurnasirpal, strong king," and moving on (thirteen epithets later) to "valiant man who acts with the support of (the god) Ashur, his lord and has no rival among the princes of the four quarters." He continued the crescendo of self-adulation with the description of himself as a "mighty flood-tide which has no opponent ... who treads upon the necks of his foes, trampler of all enemies," and reached the blatantly false statement that he "has conquered all lands ... he who is victorious over all lands."[13] Ashurnasirpal certainly was aware that there were lands beyond Assyria that he had not conquered, but that was not the point. The god Ashur had made him the ruler of the world, so he could claim this as a fait accompli. It was inevitable.

The litany of self-praise continued for dozens more lines, including, "I am king, I am lord, I am praiseworthy, I am exalted, I am important, I am magnificent, I am foremost, I am a hero, I am a warrior, I am a lion, and I am virile." It went on and on, as though he was in such a frenzy of self-glorification that he found it hard to stop.

Finally, he reached the story of his first years on the throne, which comprised one long inventory of conquests. With almost every victory over a city or kingdom he noted that "I carried off prisoners and possessions from them, (and) burnt the cities."[14] The relentless descriptions of military victories continued for 300 lines before a brief pause for the one-line description of a wild animal hunt ("I killed 40 strong wild bulls on the other bank of the Euphrates . . .") and another line about founding two new cities, one on each bank of the Euphrates, and one of them (you will not be surprised to hear) called Kar-Ashurnasirpal. Then the tales of military campaigns, full of glorious conquests, elaborate tribute proffered by groveling vassals, and the unending support of the gods, started up again for another eighty-two lines.

It's been estimated that Ashurnasirpal II led an army of about 20,000 soldiers,[15] though in his time they were largely farmers called up seasonally for military service, as in all previous eras of Mesopotamian history. They probably were highly successful in battle, as the king claimed, but they couldn't campaign year-round.

Only at the very end of the inscription did Ashurnasirpal come to mention one of his biggest and most expensive projects: he had moved the capital city. This was a particularly radical idea in Assyria because the original and very ancient capital city, Ashur, was intimately bound to the kingdom and the state god: they all shared the same name. As we have seen, the god Ashur was embodied in the very landscape of the city of Ashur as the divine force of the rocky plateau on which the city was built.

Ashurnasirpal chose for his new capital a city that had fallen into ruin—Kalhu, which was to the north of Ashur and more centrally located in the kingdom. He wrote that "this city had become dilapidated; it lay dormant (and) had turned into ruin hills. I rebuilt this city."[16] He didn't want to build on top of the previous ruins, though, as had been the norm when other cities had been rebuilt in the past. Instead, "I cleared away the old ruin hill (and) dug down to water level; I sank (the foundation pit) down to a depth of 120 layers of brick." Imagine the manpower needed for this, before the new city even began to be built. And then the king commissioned the construction of a city wall, along with public buildings, nine temples,[17] and an immense palace. In his inscription in the Ninurta temple, in contrast to his detailed accounts of his wars, he included just a few lines about the new capital, a project that took years to complete by tens of thousands of workmen, to say nothing of all the engineers and supervisors.

Once the city was built, as he wrote, "I took people which I had conquered from lands over which I had gained dominion. . . . I settled (them) therein."[18] This effort to create a cosmopolitan capital was an innovation; Kalhu would be a microcosm of the empire. To celebrate the completion of his new city, Ashurnasirpal II threw a ten-day party, attended by 69,574 people from across his empire and beyond. The king described the menu in proud detail.[19] He fed his guests meat (18,300 oxen, sheep, and deer were slaughtered and cooked), and poultry (34,000 birds), along with vast quantities of fish, eggs, bread, cheese, beer, wine, fruits, nuts, and vegetables. He pampered his guests: "I gave them food, I gave them drink, I had them bathed, I had them anointed," he wrote.[20] He clearly anticipated that everyone would go home in awe of his wealth and largesse.

Of all the new buildings in Kalhu, Ashurnasirpal II was most proud of his palace. It's known to archaeologists as the Northwest Palace. He recounted its wonders in a different inscription that he had chiseled into many of the decorative alabaster slabs that lined the mudbrick walls.[21] He boasted of the many types of woods that had been used in the palace construction, presumably for reinforcing the brick walls, and for the ceilings and decoration: cedar, cypress, juniper, boxwood, terebinth, and tamarisk.[22] He noted the giant sculptures of fantastic animals that guarded its doorways: "I made (replicas of) beasts of mountains in white limestone and . . . alabaster (and) stationed (them) at its doors." These were known as *lamassu* figures (see Fig. 17.1). They were (and are) enormous, ranging from 3 meters (10 feet) to 4.25 meters (14 feet) tall, towering over anyone who walked through the doorways. Each had the body of a bull or lion, the wings of an eagle, and the head of a man. On their heads they wore horned crowns, revealing them to be gods.

Within the doorframes that were guarded by the *lamassus*, "I fastened with bronze bands doors of cedar, cypress, *dapranu*-juniper, boxwood, (and) *meskannu*-wood."[23] The wood that was used to make these doors has long since disintegrated, but the doors must have been beautifully crafted in

Fig. 17.1 Alabaster *lamassu* sculpture (human-headed winged lion) from the palace of King Ashurnasirpal II of Assyria at Kalhu, 865–860 BCE. (Metropolitan Museum of Art)

order to warrant being mentioned in several inscriptions. Some bronze bands survive from doors that Ashurnasirpal commissioned in another city—each one was decorated with intricate scenes of Ashurnasirpal's great achievements.[24]

Sculptors Working for Ashurnasirpal II

As for the sculpted alabaster panels, which are the most striking objects to survive from the palace, Ashurnasirpal noted only that "I depicted in greenish glaze on their walls my heroic praises, in that I had gone right across highlands, lands, (and) seas, (and) the conquest of all lands."[25] Who designed these sculptures? Who carved them? The king didn't say. The alabaster reliefs represented, in visual form, some of the same events that were commemorated in Ashurnasirpal's extensive written inscriptions. They represented a fascinating innovation. Previous stone reliefs commissioned by kings had usually shown just one scene, like Naram-Sin's victory stela, or at most a few scenes, in registers on a single block, like Ur-Namma's stela. Ashurnasirpal II wanted to tell a story on multiple blocks that lined the walls of a room, as though in a giant graphic novel on stone, advancing from plot point to plot point as one walked past them.

Although Ashurnasirpal's were the earliest of this type of narrative relief sculpture, the idea behind them may not have been entirely new. Perhaps earlier palaces had boasted similar narrative images, but in the form of wall paintings, which have disintegrated. (The fragmentary frescoes in Zimri-Lim's earlier Mari palace suggest this may have been the case, though his were images not of warfare, but of ceremonial processions.) If so, Ashurnasirpal II made such visual records more durable by having them carved and painted on stone instead of wall plaster. And the techniques and scale of the stone carving represented something brand new.

The stone slabs bearing the reliefs were to stand 2 meters (6 feet) tall, most of them with two horizontal registers of images on each slab. A lot of artisans must have been needed to realize the king's dream, and many of them must have been trained at one time to do stone carving on a different scale from before. Anyone learning a craft or profession did so by apprenticing to a master, and such skills often passed down from a man to his sons, or from a woman to her daughters. The unnamed sculptors of Ashurnasirpal's reliefs all had a sure hand by the time the final sculptures were carved, but they must have gone through many phases of training to reach that point. The apprentice sculptors learned to use the hammers, chisels, points, and drills that they would need; they learned to smooth the stone with abrasives, and to create shallow planes on the stone that created an illusion of much greater depth.

The relief sculptures of battle scenes and sieges were intended to show that Ashurnasirpal II and his army had traveled across the world (or at least the world that they knew), overcoming every difficulty, easily bringing every city into the empire. No mountain was too high, no river too deep or fast to be crossed; the army kept moving and kept conquering. No other land stood a chance of resisting.[26] More than that, the reliefs (like the royal inscriptions) needed to show that the world outside Assyria, which was seen as chaotic and strange, had been brought into a comforting order by becoming Assyrian.[27] Another message that was to be projected in the sculptures was that Ashurnasirpal was the gods' choice to lead the Assyrians in this inevitable (as he saw it) domination of the known world. This was a lot of propaganda for the sculptors to convey.

The process behind the creation of the reliefs must have been complex, and must have involved many people. First, the king, in consultation with his officials, diviners, and priests, had to decide what scenes he wanted and where in the palace he wanted them, for maximum effect on viewers and the most auspicious involvement of the gods.[28] The images needed to represent real achievements that had taken place while also creating the morality tale of Assyria's inevitable domination, for the edification of palace visitors. In addition to images of war, Ashurnasirpal II decided that he needed scenes of lion hunts and of the performance of rituals (both starring himself, of course).

His immense throne room, which was 45.5 meters (150 feet) long and 10.5 meters (almost 35 feet) wide,[29] would feature relief sculptures that fulfilled a different purpose, ones showing himself flanked by gods, genies, sacred trees, and other symbols that would be brought to divine life so as to actually protect him. Sculptures of this kind ended up being the most common reliefs in the palace; more than half of the stone slabs portray various kinds of religious scenes.[30] The sculptures were to be placed carefully to have the greatest effect on visitors, even taking into consideration the locations of doors and lines of sight.[31]

During the second stage, after planning, an artist (or several) began to design the reliefs, addressing in visual form all the components of the king's desired message. Who were these artists? How were the plans sketched out? What medium was used? Unfortunately, there are no easy answers to these questions. It seems likely that in the early planning stages, the artists incised sketches of the proposed scenes onto wax tablets mounted on wooden boards.[32] They may also have made small models, perhaps of clay.

We can get a glimpse of this process from the words of an artist named Nabu-ashared, who was commissioned to create a statue of a later Neo-Assyrian king (though it apparently was not a wall relief, in this case). He had been working on drafts for the sculpture with some other artists, but they were not in agreement on particular details. So Nabu-ashared sent some sketches and models to the king and wrote to him about them: "We have now sent two ro[yal im]ages to the king. I myself sketched the royal image which is an outline. They fashioned the royal image which is in the round. The king should examine them, and whichever the king finds acceptable we will execute accordingly."[33] Now he came to his particular concerns: "Let the king pay attention to the hands, the chin, and the hair." Nabu-ashared alerted the king about the disagreements among the artists regarding how the king's arm and scepter should be portrayed. He (not-too-subtly) campaigned for his own design and for some royal support: "As for the royal image which they are making, the scepter is lying across his arm and his arm is resting on his thighs. I myself do not agree with this and I will not fashion (it so). I could speak with them about features—about anything whatsoever—but they wouldn't listen to me."[34] No doubt if he got the king's approval, the other artists would do as Nabu-ashared wished.

Ashurnasirpal's artists might well have had similar disagreements and questions. Given the vast number of individual stone slabs that they were designing, the consultation process must have been long and possibly contentious. One can imagine one of Ashurnasirpal's artists leaning over a wax tablet, trying to come up with a way to show enough soldiers, horses, and chariots to indicate the might of the army, along with an imposing image of the king (who needed to appear on many panels), and a convincing representation of, for example, a besieged city and its defenders. People and animals had to seem to stand behind one another, though the reliefs would not be deeply incised. Perhaps the artist erased the image from his tablet many times before coming up with the solution for each composition.

In their designs, the artists followed the conventions of Assyrian relief sculpture. Bodies could be shown either frontally or from the side; the musculature beneath the skin should be carefully observed and represented, but faces were always in profile and expressionless. No one was ever shown smiling or frowning, no one had wrinkles or hollow cheeks, and no one ever looked out at the viewer. Also common to the Assyrian style was that artists included minute details—exact depictions of the jewelry and embroidery on clothing, for example—so that the closer you looked at the sculptures, the more you saw.[35]

The men who designed the religious scenes—the sacred trees, genies, libation scenes, divine figures, and so on—were probably not just artists, but priestly scholars as well.[36] They needed to have a great deal of knowledge about the divine world in order to create scenes that would have the power to protect the king.

Eventually the king (along with his advisors, diviners, and priests) must have approved a set of designs for the sculptures, so, in the third stage of the process, the actual manufacture got underway. Most importantly, the stone blocks had to be quarried and transported to the palace. The colossal *lamassu* bull-figures that guarded the doorways were roughly shaped at the quarry before transport. We know this because stone reliefs from the palace of a later king, Sennacherib (705–681 BCE), actually showed the (very difficult) process of quarrying and transporting an unfinished *lamassu*.

In the first scene, the alabaster was being chiseled into an oblong shape from the living rock, as dozens of prisoners of war with baskets on their backs climbed up and down the steep sides of the quarry (see Fig. 17.2). The baskets of the men struggling on their way up were full of rocky debris. The baskets of the men coming back down were empty, as they tripped and dislodged loose boulders in their hurry to return to the bottom to pick up more rocks. Their speed was no doubt influenced by the Assyrian armed guards posted around their work area.[37]

Once the basic shape of the *lamassu* had been separated from the native rock, it was hauled out of the quarry and across the countryside on a massive boat-shaped sled that rolled over logs. At the back of the sled, men manipulated a giant lever to gradually ease it forward. At the front, dozens more prisoners of war leaned forward, putting all their weight and effort into pulling the four ropes attached to the sled.[38] Foremen with sticks stood ready to lash any worker who was not pulling hard enough. The process must have been hot, exhausting, and loud, with men shouting at the workers, and punctuated by blasts from two men with trumpets who rode on top of the sculpture itself.

Finishing touches on the *lamassu* were added later. In a letter to a later king, an official wrote about this: "As to the bull colossi about which the king my lord wrote to me, I have worked out their positions at the . . . palaces and they are hewing them." He continued, noting that "they will trim the big ones and we shall place them before the middlemost gate."[39] Likewise, the limestone panels were probably carved to a rectangular shape

Fig. 17.2 Gypsum relief, and close-up, showing workmen removing stone from a quarry during the carving of a *lamassu* sculpture, from the palace of King Sennacherib of Assyria at Nineveh, 700–692 BCE. (© The Trustees of the British Museum)

at the quarry, but left blank to be finished later in situ. Transporting them to the palace was done by boat: "Let the king, my lord, send word that they bring (boats) [to me] . . . so that I can get the stone slabs across."[40]

Once the blocks were in place, the master artist transferred his drawings from the preliminary sketches to the surface of the stone,[41] after which all the sculptors, many of whom must have trained just for Ashurnasirpal's building program, began chiseling away, presumably following the drawn lines, to create the relief sculptures. The hands of different artists can sometimes be distinguished from one another, as some created thicker or thinner versions of the same basic image.[42]

They were masters at their art, carving away the background and creating a smooth, flat alabaster backdrop from which their figures stood out. They paid close attention to detail; so much so, that some studies of Assyrian textiles have been done based only on their representations in relief sculptures.[43] Details like the curls in hair and the embroidery on clothing were added with a sharp point, toward the end of the process.[44]

The artists worked with scribes who laid out inscriptions in cuneiform that accompanied the images, and whose words were carved into the stone by masons.[45] In Ashurnasirpal's palace, the inscription was written between the two horizontal scenes on each block, repeating over and over throughout the palace. In some other buildings, his choice of inscriptions varied. On one occasion an official hadn't been given instructions about inscriptions for a temple wall, but he knew they needed to be there. He wrote to the king, first quoting another man: "'Should we really not put any inscriptions in the walls of the temple?' I am now writing to the king, my lord: let one inscription be written and sent to me (as a model), and let them write the rest according to it and put them in the wall of the temple."[46]

After the reliefs had been carved, they would have been painted, presumably by artisans with different expertise from that of the sculptors. The painters used surprisingly bright colors, traces of which have survived. Trees were painted with black trunks and green leaves.[47] An attendant was dressed entirely in red.[48] The harness of one horse was found to have been painted in bright red and blue stripes.[49] The sculptures might even have looked almost gaudy to modern eyes, familiar as we are with the plain stone of Assyrian reliefs, stripped of their ancient color.

Every scene is a window onto the era. Admittedly they are all full of propaganda, but so are the royal inscriptions. And, unlike in the royal inscriptions, the battle scenes do not permit Ashurnasirpal II to take sole credit for every victory. They depict many other individuals who fought or helped with the campaigns. In some, the king dominates the picture, but in others he merges with the crowds. He is depicted as being of normal height but can always be distinguished by his distinctive headdress—a flat-topped conical hat with a small point on the top. Only the king could wear it. The images also include details that the king never thought to include in an inscription: the types of weapons used on campaign, the shapes of the chariots, the strategies for undermining city walls, and so much more, including representations of the treatment of the defeated enemies.

We tend to think of ancient warfare as being full of pitched battles on open fields, thousands of chariots and cavalry charging at one another, dirt flying from the horses' hooves, infantry engaged in one-on-one sword fights or lobbing showers of arrows toward the opposing army, a riot of violence resulting in a bloodied plain strewn with bodies. But such battles were actually very rare.[50] They were rare enough that the names of the battles were remembered and the events retold for centuries. The Battle of Kadesh, as we have seen, marked the only occasion when two of the great kings of the Late Bronze Age met on the same battlefield. And even when such confrontations did take place, they were planned in advance, organized by diplomats, and timed on the basis of propitious omens from the gods. The result of such a battle was also usually seen as definitive. One didn't need to have any more.[51]

Given the power and size of the Assyrian army, few of Assyria's adversaries had any desire to meet them on the battlefield. When Ashurnasirpal's army showed up, people were much more likely to retreat behind the high fortified walls of their city and to try to defend it. Small towns tended to fall easily, but a major city with strong defenses could hold out for months, even years.[52] Not every siege resulted in a violent conquest, though. The Assyrians could be effective at persuading the inhabitants of cities to surrender. They promised amnesty and were true to their word; populations that surrendered were not killed (though vast amounts of tribute were required of the local king and much of the population was still often deported). But if the city didn't give in, the Assyrians were expert at sieges, and likely to succeed. Siege warfare was much more common as the subject of palace wall reliefs than were pitched battles.

In one remarkable panel from Ashurnasirpal's palace, the artist and sculptors managed to depict, in an animated scene of troops battling for control of a city, just about every tactic the Assyrians utilized during a siege (see Fig. 17.3).[53] Three walls, one inside the other, protected the besieged inhabitants. The walls were topped with triangular crenellations and pierced

Fig. 17.3 Gypsum relief showing the troops of Ashurnasirpal II of Assyria besieging a city, with close-up of archers, from the palace at Kalhu, 865–860 BCE. (© The Trustees of the British Museum)

by arched doorways, with turreted towers flanking the main entranceway. From behind the walls, the local soldiers had their bows drawn, ready to rain arrows down upon the invading Assyrians. Some had thrown flaming torches. One man, though, had put down his bow and looked nervously behind him. Assyrian archers were never shown dropping their bows; this gesture showed that the enemy was not going to win.[54] In art commissioned for the palace, as in the king's inscriptions, the enemy never won.[55]

All was not going well for the city's defenders. A woman at the top of a tower raised her arms, perhaps in surrender or horror. One Assyrian soldier crouched on the ground, his bow drawn, ready to fire, as another held up a large shield to protect them both. The artist showed just the two soldiers in this pose but they represented any number of troops. That was a common convention in battle scenes. For every soldier and civilian depicted in the art, hundreds of real people had experienced the event, performing the same risky actions, and often dying in the process.

Other Assyrians in the scene were busily breaking a hole in the outside wall—the artist showed the bricks tumbling. The wall was barely standing; it was shown, frozen, just before its collapse. Another soldier had created a tunnel and was already crawling through the outer wall. To the right of the scene we see that the Assyrians had rolled in a huge battering ram, covered in armor and positioned to attack. An archer and his shield bearer were positioned on its turret, and the crown prince and his shield bearer stood behind it. The battering ram even bore a decorative plaque at the front, showing a helmeted soldier, or perhaps the king himself, in miniature, launching himself forward, his bow drawn. Throughout the scene, the artist included the figures of enemy soldiers falling from the ramparts, their limbs flailing, their hair in disarray.

Ever since the Early Dynastic period, enemy soldiers had been portrayed lying on the ground beneath the wheels of the chariots and the hooves of the donkeys or horses of the victors. This was true in the scenes from Ashurnasirpal's palace as well, and the weakness of the enemy in comparison to the Assyrian army was a constant theme. Art historians have argued that every detail of the reliefs was designed to show the Assyrians as inevitably victorious and divinely ordained to dominate their enemies.[56]

Be that as it may, and without breaking the no-facial-expression rule that applied to every person in the scenes, the artists managed to portray the enemies of Assyria with humanity. In one scene, a soldier, whose back had been pierced by two Assyrian arrows, struggled to raise himself onto his hands and knees, his left leg bent, his right leg stretched out behind him, his body a study in futile effort, as the horses pulling the king's chariot heedlessly galloped over him.[57] What did the king want the viewer to think by including individuals like these? That they were inferior and deserved to die? Perhaps, but by emphasizing their suffering, the artist seems to have given the viewer permission to feel for them, or perhaps to worry that he or she might *become* one of them. Fear this king, says the image; he kills indiscriminately. You too could lose your home and family. You too could become food for vultures.

Deportees

The wall panels in Ashurnasirpal's palace also reveal a lot about the fate of the people who ended up on the wrong side of all those arrows and daggers after the Assyrian battles were over, the fate of those who died and those who didn't die. The many images of beheaded bodies, of Assyrian soldiers carrying severed heads, and of scribes counting piles of heads—these could not have been fictional. They were battlefield realities, confirmed by Ashurnasirpal's own inscriptions. When his troops conquered a city named Nishtun, for example, he wrote that "I felled 260 of their combat troops with the sword. I cut off their heads and formed (therewith) a pile."[58] The same was true in the descriptions of many other Assyrian conquests. Representations of captives and deportees also ring true. Certainly they were included as propaganda, but they were based on real people and can be interpreted like any primary source.

Ashurnasirpal II, like many kings before him, used deportation as a means to quell rebellions. Inhabitants of conquered cities were rounded up and forced to march to new lands where they would begin new lives, far from their homelands. The Assyrians might have rationalized deportation in many ways—perhaps the people needed to be punished for their resistance; or the new land needed cultivation and the government would benefit from the taxes on newly farmed land; or the people were less likely to rebel if far from home; or they would culturally become Assyrians by being compelled to live with others. It could be simply that the god Ashur had willed that they should move—but, whatever the rationale, deportations caused great suffering to those forced to move.

The officials chose which individuals to deport and which to allow to remain; we don't know how. Royal family members and officials often were led away, along with professionals who had valuable expertise, such as singers and physicians. But many manual laborers and farmers were chosen for deportation as well. Relief sculptures show that armed guards led separate groups of male and female prisoners to King Ashurnasirpal II, who stood under a canopy, attended by more armed men, along with an all-important servant waving a fan to swat away the flies.[59] The captives might have been powerful leaders of the conquered city, humiliated now, and forced to grovel before the Assyrian king. From there, the deportees were sent off across the empire, while the people left in the city were obligated to pay crippling amounts of tribute.

But Ashurnasirpal II's approach to maintaining his empire, described in his inscriptions and seen in his reliefs, doesn't seem to have worked for long. Without a clear imperial structure, it was fear alone that initially kept tribute payments coming. But after a while, subsequent, less fearsome, kings watched the river of wealth from conquered lands dry up. By the early eighth century BCE, governors who supposedly ruled on behalf of Assyrian kings were inheriting their positions and behaving like independent rulers. Some of them commissioned inscriptions that give no clue that they even had an overlord. Many lands that were nominally subject to Assyria stopped paying tribute.

At this point Assyria was no longer the great behemoth that Ashurnasirpal II had created; it was now matched, in its power, by the neighboring lands of Babylonia to the south, Elam to the east, and Urartu to the north, and by more distant Egypt far to the southwest. A number of smaller kingdoms even managed to exist independently of these larger states. This era, the late ninth and early eighth centuries BCE, is often described as a time of "Assyrian decline," almost as though this was a bad thing. But the respite from Assyrian attacks was no doubt welcomed by the lands that had been on the receiving end of the assaults and on the giving end of the precious metals, textiles, horses, and other riches that the Assyrian kings had demanded. People in these lands perhaps thought, with relief, that the worst of the Assyrian aggression was over. If so, they were wrong.

A king named Tiglath-Pileser III (744–727 BCE) reformed and restructured the Assyrian government so that he could not just reconquer the empire; he could hold onto to it. His reforms successfully gave the empire new life; it was to last for over 120 more years. Tiglath-Pileser III replaced all those almost-independent governors by appointees of his own choosing, beholden to him for their power. He divided up big provinces so that the new governors controlled less territory, and had less power, than their predecessors. He split high official positions so that each man had half the responsibilities and authority of someone who had held that position in the past. He chose eunuchs for many government and military jobs; these men had no sons, no one who could inherit their position. He created a network of spies, traveling through the empire, who would inform him of any treachery, and any possible rebellions before they broke out. And he no longer depended on farmers called up for military service; he seems to have created a vast standing army, recruiting and training men from across the empire to fight for Assyria. It may have included as many as 60,000 men.

The new army was unrelenting; soldiers campaigned throughout his reign, expanding the borders of the empire farther and farther, beyond lands that had been subject to Assyria during the Late Bronze Age to regions with no previous history of submission to Assyria. A conquered king might become a vassal at first. If he paid the required tribute on time, he might keep his throne. If not, Tiglath-Pileser replaced him with a puppet king, who often was replaced, in turn, by an Assyrian governor. A vassal kingdom had at that point become an Assyrian province. Through all of this, the Assyrian king increased deportations, moving hundreds of thousands of people from one end of the empire to the other. Provinces were no longer occupied mostly by people with centuries of ancestral connections to their land, but by newly arrived groups of deportees, forced there from somewhere else, or from several other places.

Tiglath-Pileser III was even able to take control of Babylonia. He seems to have been seen by the Babylonians, initially, as something of an ally in their struggle against Arameans and a new population group known as the Chaldeans. Later, Tiglath-Pileser III deposed a Chaldean man who had taken the throne of Babylon and, in 728 BCE, the Assyrian king proclaimed himself to be king of Babylonia as well. This was a first. It marked the beginning of more than a century of rocky, often antagonistic relations between Assyria and Babylonia. Right at the start, Tiglath-Pileser III deported hundreds of thousands of Chaldeans from Babylonia, according to the king's inscriptions.

Tiglath-Pileser III's successor, Sargon II (722–705 BCE), continued his same practices, especially with regard to imperial expansion and deportation. But he emulated King Ashurnasirpal II as well, in deciding that he needed a new capital city. Kalhu had been the capital for 150 years; Sargon wanted to live in a place of his own, in a palace decorated with relief sculptures of his own achievements. He called the new city Dur-Sharrukin (Fort Sargon). It was as ambitious a building project as any that we've encountered before, the city extending over 288 hectares (712 acres) and surrounded by a massive city wall, with an administrative complex that was dominated by an immense palace. Remarkably, the entire city was constructed within eleven years, from 717 to 706 BCE.[60] Like Ashurnasirpal II, Sargon II must have had a great many artists and sculptors on his staff, and they worked fast to meet his needs for relief sculptures and giant *lamassu* figures. Unfortunately, the sculptures from Dur-Sharrukin fared much less well in modern times than those from Kalhu. They were in poor condition when excavated by a French team in the mid-nineteenth century, and many of them (more than 200 crates full) were lost forever in the Tigris River in 1855 when being shipped to Paris.[61]

We do know, though, that some of the reliefs commemorated Sargon's campaign to the Levant in 721 BCE to quash a rebellion by a coalition of kingdoms there. One of the troublesome kingdoms was Israel, which had ceased to pay its required tribute to Assyria. In several of the inscriptions set up in his palace, Sargon II mentioned the conquest of Israel's capital city, Samaria (among many Levantine cities), claiming that he "conquered the city Samaria and all of the land Bit-Humria."[62] (Bit-Humria or "House of Omri" was the Assyrian term for Israel, named for a king named Omri whom the Assyrians viewed as Israel's founder.) In more detail Sargon II noted that "I surrounded and conquered the city Samaria. I carried off as booty 27,290 of its inhabitants, conscripted fifty chariots from them, and allowed the remainder to practice their (normal) occupations."[63] This conquest is corroborated in the Bible (though attributed to the brief reign of Shalmaneser V [727–722 BCE], Sargon's immediate predecessor who began the actions against the Levantine rebellion). After Israel's defeat, according to the author of the book of 2 Kings in the Bible, "The king of Assyria brought people from Babylon, Cuthah, Avva, Hamath, and Sepharvaim and settled them in the towns of Samaria to replace the Israelites."[64] This marked the end of the northern kingdom of Israel; the land had become an Assyrian province. Judah and its capital of Jerusalem were spared conquest and deportation at that time, though Judah was required to pay tribute to the Assyrian king.

Sargon II had only occupied his grand new capital city for one year before he led his troops out on an ill-fated campaign to the land of Tabal far away in south-central Anatolia. He was about sixty years old. In the course of the campaign, in 705 BCE, "the king was killed, the camp of the king of Assyria was pl[undered]."[65] This was a shock. Assyrian kings were rarely killed in battle, and subsequent kings seem to have been careful to avoid actual combat.

Sargon II's son Sennacherib took the throne in 705 BCE and decided that his father's capital of Dur-Sharrukin—even though it had cost a fortune, was newly occupied, and was still incomplete—wouldn't meet his needs. So Sennacherib set about construction of yet another capital city, this one at Nineveh, only 20 kilometers (12 miles) to the south of Dur-Sharrukin. He built another new palace for himself there. He, too, decorated the walls with many alabaster panels, carved by his artists with scenes of his victories and other proofs of his divine appointment to rule the world. One imagines that the sculptors, though perhaps happy to have the work, might have been astonished to find they were needed again, so soon after creating so many relief panels and *lamassus* for Sargon II. It was Sennacherib who commissioned the reliefs showing the quarrying and transport of a *lamassu* sculpture.

He devoted one room of his palace to the commemoration of a specific siege, that of Lachish in Judah, which took place in 701 BCE—the images he commissioned of the event extended along 26.85 meters (88 feet) of the walls of the room.[66] As far as Sennacherib was concerned, his successful attack on Judah was a highlight of his reign.

For as long as Judah had been paying the required tribute, the Assyrian kings had pretty much left the country alone, as was the usual practice.[67] But when the Judeans decided to withhold tribute, hoping for support from the neighboring kingdom of Egypt, Sennacherib paid attention. The region was no longer "submitting to the heavy yoke of Ashur," to use a favorite expression of the Assyrian kings. The Assyrian army marched on Judah to crush its rebellious tendencies. Once again, many of the people would be dispatched elsewhere.

Sennacherib emphasized the victory not just in relief sculptures but also in his inscriptions and annals, though, curiously, he didn't mention the city of Lachish by name. One of the inscriptions reads as follows:

> (As for) Hezekiah of the land Judah, I surrounded (and) conquered forty-six of his fortified walled cities and small(er) settlements in their environs, which were without number, by having ramps trodden down and battering rams brought up, the assault of foot soldiers, sapping, breaching, and siege engines. I brought out of them 200,150 people, young (and) old, male and female, horses, mules, donkeys, camels, oxen, and sheep and goats, which were without number, and I counted (them) as booty.[68]

Judah was not alone in its suffering. Scholars have calculated that as many as 4,500,000 people are likely to have been deported from regions across the Neo-Assyrian Empire during the periods when mass deportations were at their height, including during the reign of Sennacherib.[69] To get a sense of the scale of that migration, note that about 13.3 million Syrians have been displaced during their civil war, with devastating effects on the region.[70] The modern population of the Middle East is many times greater than it was in the first millennium BCE, so the impact of Assyrian deportations would have been extreme. The roads and rivers—wide stretches of the countryside—must have been packed with families and livestock on the move.

And, as was true everywhere, just as people were being rounded up and moved away from Judah, other populations were moved in to replace them. Everyone involved would have been unsettled by this, thrown into a limbo in which all the ties to land, tradition, and ancestors had been severed. Everyone had to find their way in a new place, around new people, while also being required to continue to pay their taxes to the state. It is not surprising that the people of the northern state of Israel, who had been much more completely conquered and displaced by the Assyrians than was true of Judah, simply disappeared from the records, becoming the "ten lost tribes of Israel."

The Assyrian campaign against Judah in 701 BCE also features in the Bible, in one of the few episodes for which both Assyrian and biblical accounts survive. For this reason, as you might imagine, it has been the subject of many studies for a very long time. Concerning the wider conflict in Judah, beyond Jerusalem, the writer of the biblical book of 2 Kings simply stated that "King Sennacherib of Assyria came up against all the fortified cities of Judah and captured them."[71] The author of 2 Chronicles added that "while King Sennacherib of Assyria was at Lachish with all his forces, he sent his servants to Jerusalem."[72] Neither author recorded anything about the Judean deportees who were counted in Sennacherib's annals and represented in his reliefs, though the biblical authors did acknowledge that the Assyrian sieges of Judean cities were successful. Only Jerusalem was miraculously spared, according to the Bible, and Hezekiah, its king, still had to send vast amounts of tribute to Assyria.

The site of Lachish (modern Tell ed-Duweir in Israel) has been excavated, which has allowed historians to compare historical accounts (Sennacherib's inscriptions, the relief sculptures in his palace, and the biblical accounts of the campaign in Judah), with the physical remains in the ground.[73]

At the time of the Assyrian attack, the city of Lachish extended over 12.5 hectares (31 acres) and was surrounded by a strong city wall. The archaeologists discovered evidence of a huge ramp that the Assyrians had built up against the wall in order to be able to move their siege machines into place (this is the only such ramp to survive anywhere). It had been constructed with heavy boulders and topped by mortar so that soldiers and wheeled vehicles could mount it more easily. The ramp was made up of between 13,000 and 19,000 tons of stone.[74] A major siege was, in many ways, as much a building project as it was a battle, though the process of building the ramp must have been more dangerous than most, probably taking place under a shower of arrows, rocks, and flaming torches thrown down by the inhabitants of the city. Just such a ramp is shown in Sennacherib's scenes of the siege of Lachish (though the angle of the ramp in the relief defies gravity, being much steeper than could ever have been possible). The Assyrian artists depicted five siege machines in the process of attacking the city walls from the ramp (see Fig. 17.4).

The Assyrian forces had also constructed an armed camp for the soldiers near the city. This wasn't found during the excavations but was shown in the reliefs. Its oval enclosure wall boasted towers and crenellations, like a scaled-down version of a city wall. Inside, the artists depicted the tents and huts of the Assyrian soldiers.

The excavators found other clues about the violent destruction of the city, such as hundreds of iron arrowheads, many slingstones, and some metal scales from armor. The dead may have been laid to rest in a mass burial of about 1,500 people that was found in some caves nearby.[75]

Many Judeans were forced to leave Lachish, and, among all those millions of anonymous deportees across the Assyrian Empire, we can see them vividly represented on Sennacherib's reliefs. The families were allowed to take bags of possessions with them, along with some of their cattle. Although their situation was impossibly hard, at least they had not died in the siege, and at least they could hold out hope that perhaps a new home lay at the end of their march, if they managed to survive it. They were portrayed walking out of the city, past the end of the siege ramp, leaving their homes forever. Assyrian soldiers carrying booty from the campaign joined the deportees, and eventually they all passed in front of the king,

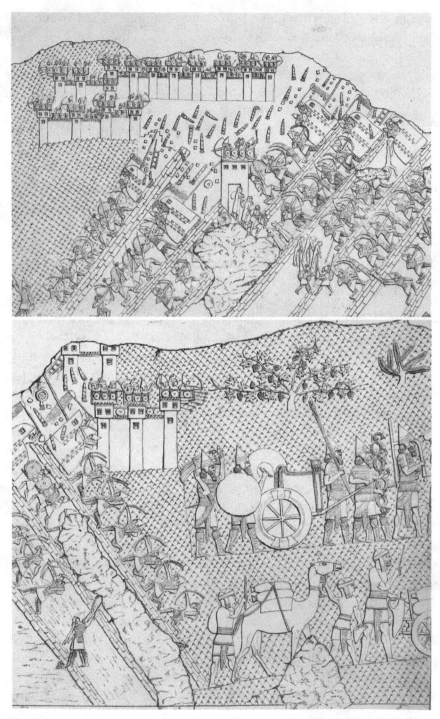

Fig. 17.4 Two details from a drawing by Austin Henry Layard of the relief of the siege of Lachish from the palace of King Sennacherib of Assyria at Nineveh, 700–692 BCE. (© The Trustees of the British Museum)

who was seated in a throne on a hill.[76] (In this sculpture and just about every other depiction of him, Sennacherib's face has since been chiseled away by attackers who conquered Nineveh itself almost a century later, in 612 BCE. Their treatment of the Assyrian capital was just as violent as the Assyrian treatment of Lachish had been, as you will see in Chapter 19.) The figure of the king was provided with a label: "Sennacherib, king of the world, king of Assyria, took (his) place on the *nemedu* throne, and the booty of Lachish passed before him."[77]

The artist showed two women of Lachish walking together, wearing shawls over their hair, followed by two girls, all of them apparently holding flasks of drinking water (see Fig. 17.5, bottom left of the close-up image). A small child reached up as though to take the hand of his father, but the man was using both hands to manage a large sack across his shoulders, perhaps containing all the possessions the family could take with them. Next to them, a woman sat on top of two full sacks of family possessions on a wagon. One of her children sat behind her with his arms around her waist, another sat on her lap, her face right up against that of her mother as though about to kiss her (see Fig. 17.5, top right of the close-up image).[78]

Some of the inhabitants of Lachish were treated very differently from the deportees. A group of men, probably the leaders of the rebellion, were singled out for torture and execution. These men carried no possessions; they were not going to live to need them. The artists showed their treatment in gruesome detail, as they were being impaled on stakes, stabbed, or flayed by Assyrian soldiers.[79] All the deportees seem to have been marched past these men, people they must have known and perhaps followed in life. Sennacherib was clearly sending a message about what would happen to leaders of rebellions against his regime.[80]

Deportees from another of Sennacherib's campaigns were captured in the same detail by the artists. In this sculpture we see a mother leaning down to give her child a drink from a full skin of water, as they paused in the shade of a date palm tree (see Fig. 17.6). The thirsty child rushed toward her. A woman beside the mother and child had a basket on her head and a woman in front of them had a large bag on her back. These two were straight-backed, proud, continuing on their march in their long robes and bare feet.[81] The journey to a new land was not intended to kill the deportees, according to Assyrian records. They were provided with provisions by the government, who wanted them to survive in order to settle in new places.

Fig. 17.5 Gypsum relief, with a close-up showing deportees from Lachish after the Assyrian victory, from the palace of King Sennacherib of Assyria at Nineveh, 700–692 BCE. (© The Trustees of the British Museum)

Fig. 17.6 Gypsum relief showing a group of deportees, including a woman giving a child a drink, from the palace of King Sennacherib of Assyria at Nineveh, 700–692 BCE. (© The Trustees of the British Museum)

And whatever the Assyrian king might have intended, the deportees were not shown by the Assyrian artists as hated enemies but as struggling families, heading off to an unknown future in a land that had been chosen for them by their Assyrian conquerors.

The Assyrians kept track of the people who had been deported. One tablet lists 977 people from Que, the land in the northeast corner of the Mediterranean that had previously been called Kizzuwatna.[82] None of the deportees were named, but all the children had been counted in groups based on height. Since the ancient people of the Near East never kept track of ages or birthdays, a child's height provided a way of determining how ready he or she might be for work. Behind the statistics on this tablet one can envision a process—someone, or a group of people, gathered this vast crowd of people together, perhaps at the beginning of their trek, perhaps at the end, to count and classify them. Was the crowd quiet and nervous or clamorous and unruly? Did the children stay with their parents, or were they separated out? Families were not split up in the course of deportation, so the children would have been reunited with their parents after being measured. The officials must have had each of the 293 children (172 boys and 121 girls), stand against some sort of measuring post, which was marked with lines at 3 spans, 4 spans, and 5 spans, in order to roughly categorize them by height. Children taller than that were considered to be adults. Among the youngest children, forty-five were toddlers, while fifty babies were still nursing. Some of their mothers must have given birth to them shortly before undertaking the grueling march to their new home.

Once they had been documented and their long journey was complete, not all deportees were treated alike. A very small number of them became officials in the Assyrian government, holding the title of "guide" or "translator" and assigned to help the king negotiate his way through his dealings with their homeland and people.[83] Others were provided with farms in previously uncultivated areas of the empire, or in regions that themselves had been subject to deportation. Yet others were chosen to live in Ashurnasirpal's new city of Kalhu or, later, in Sennacherib's rebuilt city of Nineveh. The later kings asserted that these deportees were free, were considered to be Assyrians, and could continue to work in the same professions they had held in their homelands.[84] It's hard to know if there was any truth to this. We do know that some served in the Assyrian military as charioteers.[85] But yet others, as we have seen, toiled in the quarries under the lash of Assyrian soldiers.

The attacks on Samaria and Israel and the displacement of Israelites across the empire were bemoaned by biblical authors. Their treatment at the hands of the Assyrians struck a chord with readers of the Bible for hundreds of years. But, as we have seen, the Israelites and Judeans were far from alone, they just happen to be the one group that left a record of their treatment that has survived. Deportation had become a standard strategy of imperial control, one that the kings extolled in their inscriptions and depicted on their reliefs.

Ever since the time of Sargon of Akkad, more than 1,500 years before Ashurnasirpal II, the idea of empire had existed as a dream in the minds of ambitious leaders in the Near East, but the Neo-Assyrian kings, starting with Tiglath-Pileser III, were the first to turn it a long-lasting reality. They came up with a system that maintained control over far-flung regions as well as their own populations. They built roads so that messages and troops could travel quickly. They stationed garrisons in forts across the empire. They appointed governors over provinces. They maintained a professional military. They punished, tortured, and killed rebel leaders in extreme ways to deter would-be rebels from following their lead. They imposed taxes and tribute so that wealth flooded into the capital and other Assyrian cities. And they moved whole populations from one region to another, not, as we have seen, with the goal of killing them (though many died),[86] but, in a way, to pull the ground out from under their feet. The deportees had to build whole new lives; they had little energy left for rebellion. The palace artists gave these anonymous people a human face and showed us their tragic situations in a way that still can tug at our hearts, even though centuries have passed since their lifetimes.

Once this imperial system had been invented, it never went away. Each subsequent empire in turn, in the Near East, Europe, and South Asia, adopted many of the same practices, and for people in those regions, living under an empire became the norm. Given the reputation of Neo-Assyrian kings as tyrants, it is surprising to remember that their distant predecessors had been the kings of second-millennium Ashur, with its merchant colonies and town councils, who were among the least autocratic rulers in any era of Near Eastern history.

Chapter 18
Conspirators, Diviners, and Officials

It would be hard to imagine a worse way to come to the throne than the one endured by Esarhaddon (681–669 BCE).[1] He was far from being his father Sennacherib's obvious successor; he was the youngest of the royal princes, in his early thirties,[2] and had only recently been appointed crown prince. Sennacherib, who had ruled Assyria for twenty-four years, had just been brutally assassinated at the age of fifty-nine or sixty.[3] In a horrifying twist, this murder had been executed not by a usurper but by one of the king's own sons—one of Esarhaddon's older brothers. This disastrous sequence of events haunted Esarhaddon throughout his reign, giving rise to conspiracies and assassination plots, and to a matching, almost debilitating, fear of such conspiracies and assassination plots on the part of the king. The story of his worries involves not just the anxiety-ridden king himself, but a number of other fascinating individuals as well: the diviner Bel-ushezib, an enslaved female prophet, the dream interpreter Nabu-ushallim, the captured Babylonian scribe Kudurru, and several men who schemed to replace Esarhaddon as king, including a mayor named Abda, a powerful eunuch, and Sasi, the apparent mastermind behind several conspiracies. Esarhaddon's search for answers and his reactions to what he learned will guide us on a tour of how the Mesopotamians tried, in many different ways, to fathom the will of the gods.

Esarhaddon: An Unlikely Heir to the Throne

But first we need to go back to the source of Esarhaddon's power and also his grief: his eleventh-hour appointment as heir to the throne. In 683 BCE, just two years before King Sennacherib was murdered, he had changed his mind about the royal succession. He decided against an older prince and suddenly wanted his youngest son Esarhaddon to be the next king, and so, he said, did the gods.

At around the same time, Sennacherib appointed Esarhaddon's mother, Naqi'a (who had until then been one of the king's secondary wives), to the powerful position of *segallu*, or queen (see Fig. 18.1).[4] Sennacherib's previous queen (the mother of the former crown prince) had either died or been deposed. No matter which, this would have been a great loss for many in the court. Sennacherib had written of her, ten or twelve years before, that she was "my beloved wife, whose features (the goddess) Belet-ili has made perfect above all women."[5] She had a long career in the palace and must have been loved by many other loyal family members and servants.

Fig. 18.1 Bronze plaque of King Esarhaddon of Assyria and his mother Naqi'a, from Hillah, Iraq. seventh century BCE. (© RMN–Grand Palais/Art Resource, NY/Art Resource)

Obviously, when the king made these two big decisions about Esarhaddon and Naqi'a, he had no idea that he was two years away from being assassinated. But we have the benefit of hindsight and can see why the older princes reacted badly to these two big changes. Their mother was no longer queen, a former minor wife had abruptly replaced her as the most important woman in the land, and that woman's son had inexplicably become the king's appointed successor. All the older sons had been unceremoniously bypassed for the most powerful position in Assyria, which was arguably the most powerful position in the whole world at that time. Assyria certainly had the largest empire on Earth in the seventh century BCE (though of course its kings knew nothing about most of the kingdoms and empires in the rest of the world). The vengeful prince who eventually led the assassins was the man who had been the original crown prince, until he was toppled from the position by Sennacherib's choice of Esarhaddon.[6]

Esarhaddon explained the crisis this way, in his most confessional inscription: "I am my older brothers' youngest brother (and) by the command of the gods Ashur, Sin, Shamash, Bel, and Nabu, Ishtar of Nineveh (and) Ishtar of Arbela, (my) father, who engendered me, elevated me firmly in the assembly of my brothers, saying 'This is the son who will succeed me.'"[7] Esarhaddon continued by describing how his father had consulted the gods "and they answered him with a firm 'yes,' saying: 'He is your replacement.'"

Throughout his account of his selection for the throne and the events that followed, Esarhaddon repeated over and over that the gods had given him that "firm 'yes'" vote, that they were on his side. He kept consulting diviners to be certain. He desperately needed to be reassured of the gods' support because, right from that moment when he was chosen to be the next king, he gained a whole pack of enemies.

King Sennacherib must have known that changing his heir would be an unpopular move. To try to keep the peace in his family and kingdom, he required all his sons, along with "the people of Assyria, young and old," to swear an oath to support Esarhaddon's succession. Sennacherib, too, consulted with the gods about every step in this process. Accordingly, he chose "a favorable month, on a propitious day" for Esarhaddon to go through the ceremony in which he became the heir to the throne. Esarhaddon writes that he "joyfully entered the House of Succession, an awe-inspiring place within which the appointing to kingship (takes place)." One suspects that his joy was tinged with more than a hint of terror. His fate had changed completely and, to judge from his later correspondence, he spent much of the rest of his life in a state of high anxiety.

The older princes were clearly furious about Esarhaddon's promotion. "Persecution (and) jealousy fell over my brothers and they forsook (the will) of the gods," wrote Esarhaddon. "They trusted in their arrogant deeds, and they were plotting evil." This evil, he wrote, included spreading rumors, slander, and lies about him, and even turning his father against him. But, of course, their worst act of all (which he didn't specifically mention) was plotting to kill their father the king. Sennacherib perhaps didn't suspect that he himself was in danger, but he feared for his heir and convinced Esarhaddon to flee west from the capital.[8] Esarhaddon wrote that the gods "settled me in a secret place away from the evil deeds" and kept him safe in a tower, somewhere in Syria.

One version of the story of the assassination recorded that the princes stabbed their father, but a more graphic tale had them toppling one of the huge stone *lamassu* statues in the palace and crushing him to death. It's unclear which was true. After the murder, the land was in an uproar. Loyal advisors found ways to inform Esarhaddon, in his place of hiding, that he was next on the hit list of his murderous older brothers, which honestly cannot have come as a surprise. But Esarhaddon knew that he had to return to the capital—he alone had the right to be king. He just had to overcome the seemingly impossible odds against him: the hatred of his brothers toward him, the antipathy of many in the court and across the empire, and the not particularly secret plots against his life.

Meanwhile, not all the news was bad. Esarhaddon's brothers discovered that they were less popular than they had anticipated. Esarhaddon did have his defenders. After all, the "people of Assyria . . . swore by oil and water to the treaty, an oath bound by the great gods"[9] to support Esarhaddon's succession. (This was an important point; he reminded the reader twice in his inscription about this oath that the people had sworn.) And Sennacherib's blood was on the hands of the brothers; killing a relatively popular king was not a great way to gain followers. But although Esarhaddon was pleased to claim that the population "did not come to their aid," that wasn't entirely true. His brothers certainly had some support.

While spending time in hiding, Esarhaddon assembled an army of his own and, when he was ready, fought his way back to Nineveh in order to take the throne. On the day of his victorious entry into the capital, two

months after his father's death,[10] he wrote that he "joyfully entered Nineveh
... and I sat happily on the throne of my father."[11] He had survived; he was
now the official king. And once again he consulted the diviners: "Favorable
signs came in good time to me in heaven and on earth. They (the gods)
continually and regularly encouraged me with oracles through ecstatics, the
message(s) of the gods and goddess(es)."

The Mesopotamians believed that the gods and goddesses hid such
messages in many places in the heavens and on earth. They could be found
in the actions of the sun, moon, stars, and planets, in dreams, in animal
behaviors, in plants, in the messages of prophets, and in the internal organs
of sacrificed animals.[12] It was as though the gods had inscribed their plans
for the future right across the natural world, but only diviners had the
expertise to read this sacred writing. Esarhaddon made use of almost all the
techniques of divination as he tried to hold onto his power, and as he tried
to root out later plots against him.

Just to be sure that the rebels and their supporters were crushed, Esarhaddon
got rid of the security forces who protected the palaces in Nineveh and in
the old capital of Kalhu and replaced them with loyal followers.[13] He also
sought out the "guilty soldiers who incited my brothers." He calmly noted
that he "imposed a grievous punishment on them: I exterminated their
offspring."[14] He didn't say, however, whether the soldiers themselves, or for
that matter his brothers, were killed. In fact, the assassins had escaped north
into exile in the land of Urartu, Assyria's longtime enemy, and continued to
cause Esarhaddon difficulties for years.[15]

Urartu (called Biainili by its inhabitants) had always been a region that
was difficult for invaders to conquer, as it lay in mountainous territories,
and its communities spread out across a number of fertile valleys with no
obvious routes of communication with the lowlands. In winter, when the
snowstorms were fierce, even the Urartian valleys could be cut off from one
another. Urartu had become a unified land only during the ninth century,
when Assyrian kings had repeatedly sent military campaigns into the region
and the people had joined together in defense. Once the heartland was
unified, the rulers of Urartu had conquered many neighboring regions,
expanding their kingdom during annual military campaigns to incorporate
a vast area north of Assyria and south of the Caucasus Mountains. It was
one of the only great powers able to hold out against Assyrian imperial
ambitions, though the Assyrians did manage periodically to conquer parts

of the region, only to lose them again. Like the Hittites before them, the Urartians had adopted cuneiform, and (also like the Hittites) seem to have been trained by Assyrian scribes, since they initially wrote not in their own language, but in Akkadian. Later they adapted cuneiform to write in Urartian, and scribes composed royal inscriptions attesting to the kings' military successes.[16]

In Esarhaddon's time, the Urartian ruler Rusa II (c. 673 BCE) constructed some of the largest fortresses in Urartian history. The administrative center of a fortress city called Teishebaini was a massive mudbrick structure on stone foundations that extended over 4 hectares (10 acres) and incorporated 150 rooms.[17] It was more than simply a palace for the governor—it contained warehouses, granaries, workshops, and a brewery. A place like this might have safely housed fugitives from Assyria, such as the princes who killed Sennacherib.

Bel-ushezib and Sasi: An Astronomer and a Suspected Conspirator

One of the diviners who had lifted Esarhaddon's spirits during his exile was named Bel-ushezib.[18] This man later took credit for reading the signs that had predicted Esarhaddon's successful succession to the throne. He wrote to Esarhaddon to remind him that it was he who had reported "the omen of the kingship of my lord, the crown prince Esarhaddon."[19] Bel-ushezib had brought this uplifting message from the gods when Esarhaddon's morale might have been at its lowest point, when he was living in exile, hiding in fear for his life. Bel-ushezib "[we]nt to pay homage to the crown prince my lord, who evaded execution [by fleeing] to the Tower, whose murder along with your servants [was plotted] every day."[20] Bel-ushezib didn't specify here which omens he observed, but they were probably astronomical observations; that was his area of specialization. His other letters to Esarhaddon were full of such sightings, and he often gave incredibly detailed suggestions for what the king should do based on what he had seen.

For example, another letter from Bel-ushezib, written later, when Esarhaddon was king, provided guidance in the planning of an invasion of the land of Mannea, in what is now northwestern Iran. The diviner started with two astronomical observations, both pertaining to shooting stars or meteors. (The first was "If a star flashes like a torch from the east and sets in the west: the main army of the enemy will fall."[21]) From these he continued on to make very specific and apparently well-informed recommendations about the invasion, such as, "the whole army should not invade; (only) the cavalry and the professional troops should invade," and "[the cha]riots and wagons should stay side by side [in] the pass." He reassured Esarhaddon that his words came directly from the god Marduk himself: the god "[has ordered] the destruction of the Manneans and is for the second time [delivering] them into the hands of the king, my lord. If on this 15th day the moon [is seen] with the sun, it will be on account of them."

In spite of the specificity of the messages from Marduk, Bel-ushezib was aware of the limitations of his own knowledge, in this case of geography. He acknowledged that the countryside in Mannea was unknown to him, and that the king needed to get practical advice, in addition to the messages from the gods. "The lord of kings should ask an expert of the country, and the king should (then) write to his army as he deems best," he wrote. Bel-ushezib's final message from Marduk was that "I (Marduk) will deliver all countries into his hands." But the diviner also wrote, humbly, at the end of the letter, as he almost always did when advising the king: "The king may happily do as he deems best."

Diviners who specialized in astronomy, like Bel-ushezib, made their observations of the sky every night, probably from the highest platforms of ziggurats, way above the house walls of the city that would have obstructed their view. The night sky in ancient Nineveh was much darker than it is in modern cities; they had no light pollution. The stars were innumerable, the Milky Way a bright ribbon across the heavens, the patterns of the constellations strikingly clear. They named the stars and the constellations, and some of these identifications have come down to us, almost unchanged.[22] For example, they saw in the sky a sheep (Aries), the Bull of Heaven (Taurus), twins (Gemini), a crab (Cancer), a lion (Leo), and a snake (Hydra).[23] They recorded some unmistakable descriptions of the constellations. For example, this is "the Wagon" (the Big Dipper): "[4 s]tars are drawn at its fore. Its pole (is) towards the heel of Eru. 3 stars on its pole—1 bright star at the head of the pole and 2 lower stars side by side <in front> on the pole—are drawn."[24] Sometimes the astronomers went beyond describing the simple positions of the stars and added imaginative details that had come to seem real, perhaps, as they stared into the night sky, just as one can sometimes see faces in clouds. One of the twins of Gemini, for example, "carries a . . . large jug in his right hand; [in] his left [hand] he carries a whip; he holds a lightning bolt with the whip."[25]

The visible planets, Mercury, Venus, Mars, Jupiter, and Saturn, stood out from the stars not just in their brilliance but also in their eccentric travels across the sky. Every astronomical detail revealed some message from the gods, if you just knew how to read it. The diviners watched for shooting stars and lunar eclipses, noted the movements of the planets among the constellations and around the sun and moon, and paid attention to where the sun and moon stood with respect to one another and the stars. Observations of the weather were included—clouds, too, were in the sky and were controlled by the gods.

Starting in the eighth century BCE, astronomers started keeping detailed daily records of what they saw, and, incredibly, generations more continued to do the same for 700 years.[26] Alongside the highlights of the night sky, they listed political and social events, and disease outbreaks. They seem to have been looking for patterns and correlations between them—for example, could eclipses or particular movements of planets reliably predict epidemics or famines?[27] Although the diviners had different priorities from those of modern astronomers—they believed that their observations provided messages from the gods—they were astute observers and interpreters nonetheless. They eventually got to the point of being able to predict astronomical events, such as eclipses.[28] Some of their notes have allowed modern scholars to assign exact dates to ancient events based, for example, on observed eclipses or appearances of the planet Venus that are known to have happened on specific dates.

Bel-ushezib didn't only write to the king about divine omens; he also had warnings for him about treacherous schemes brewing around the empire. For these, he didn't need to consult oracles; he simply watched what was going on, listened to what he was told by informants, and let the king know. He had his eye, especially, on a man named Sasi. In one letter, Bel-ushezib mentioned a powerful hostage who had been smuggling gold and luxuries to this man, and noted that one of Sasi's friends "may have been induced to join the conspiracy. . . . The king should be wary of them."[29]

Sasi is a puzzling character. He had a very public career, serving as the mayor of a city at one point,[30] and later as the superintendent for

Esarhaddon's crown prince, Ashurbanipal.[31] He certainly was deeply involved in the conspiracies against Esarhaddon, but it's unclear which side he was working for. His story is fascinating.[32] Some ancient letters suggest that Sasi had fostered a widespread ring of dissidents who planned to overthrow Esarhaddon, and even that Sasi believed he, himself, was destined to rule Assyria, but others, curiously, suggest that Sasi was loyal to Esarhaddon.

An Enslaved Female Prophet

The king heard from a lot of informants during the first decade of his reign, some of their letters more damning than others. One is particularly vivid. It was written by an official who was loyal to the king,[33] who started his letter with a series of alarmed imperatives that would have all been marked with exclamation points, that is, if cuneiform had punctuation. This man wrote that he had discovered the names of the conspirators. Before revealing them, though, he pleaded, "Destroy their [peopl]e, name and seed from your palace!" and he repeated, "Let [the people] die! [Rescue] your life and the life of your family! . . . Do not destroy your life. . . !"[34]

The source of his inside information was, surprisingly, an enslaved girl in the Syrian city of Harran, who had related a message from the god Nusku. The writer unfortunately (though not surprisingly) didn't provide her name, only that of her owner, a man named Bel-ahu-usur. He noted that the girl spoke the god's words directly, as though she were just his mouthpiece. In this, prophecy was different from other types of divination—the girl had, they believed, been taken over by the god and the words she spoke were beyond her control. But this girl's message was crucial for the king to hear. She had been in some way "enraptured" for three months, which was perhaps a sign of divine possession. Her message? A treasonous one, even if it was in the words of a god: "The kingship is for Sasi. I will destroy the name and seed of Sennacherib!"

People trusted prophets, male and female, and their utterances were taken seriously. Esarhaddon later specifically required that any words spoken by a prophet, an ecstatic, or someone who questioned oracles had to be reported to him. He included this clause in an oath that people were obligated to swear, namely that they would support his son as his successor.[35] Prophets tended to shout their messages in public, and sometimes their revelations voiced the gods' support of the king. But this girl was different. Yes, she was shouting a message from a god, but she was not a professional prophet and she was denouncing the king. Could her words be believed? Presumably Esarhaddon thought not, especially since the girl had asserted that the god Nusku planned to destroy him ("the seed of Sennacherib") and to place another man, Sasi, on the throne. Sasi, though, might have been thrilled with this message and its promise of great power.

The letter writer revealed that the girl had been taken to the house of Sasi himself; the aspiring usurper must have been protecting her. The letter writer suggested to Esarhaddon that he should question the man who owned the enslaved girl, and that the guards who took her to Sasi's house should "bring her here, and let the king perform an (extispicy) ritual on her (account)." This was how they could check on the truth of her prediction.

Extispicy was one of the few techniques available to the Mesopotamians by which they could pose questions to the gods and receive prompt answers. Most omens simply appeared spontaneously and had to be interpreted— like the signs in the night sky, or births of deformed animals, or movements of birds. The gods sent those whenever they felt like it, not on demand. But at this point, Esarhaddon needed to ask them whether the girl prophet was actually speaking for the god Nusku. Not everyone who claimed to have a message from the gods was telling the truth, after all.

When the girl arrived at the palace for the validity of her prophecy to be tested by the diviner, the process would have taken an entire day. Four young rams were procured, for reasons that I will come to shortly. The diviner would then have posed the question to the sun god Shamash and the storm god Adad as to whether the girl's prophecy was false. He might have whispered this into the ear of one of the rams, or written the question on a tablet that he placed in front of the statues of the gods, for them to read.[36] After asking the question, he finished by making a standard request: "Be present in this ram; place an affirmative answer, favorable, propitious omens of the flesh of the query by the command of your great divinity, so that I may see them."[37]

At this point the four rams were slaughtered as sacrifices to the gods, two for Shamash and Adad, and one each for the goddess Aya (the divine wife of Shamash) and the god Bunene (the divine vizier of Shamash). The diviner slashed the veins in the rams' necks. One of the rams that had been sacrificed to Shamash and Adad was then disemboweled, its internal organs carefully examined. Most important was the liver, along with, sometimes, the lungs and intestines. Hidden in the naturally occurring lumps on the liver or lungs, or in the bends of the intestine, the expert would find the gods' response to the question that he had posed. Often the shapes even looked, to the diviner, like cuneiform signs, as though the gods had taken a stylus to the internal organs of the ram and written on them.[38] The diviner had to check and list each part of the organs in turn, in order to come up with the gods' yes or no answer. A "firm yes" was usually the desired outcome. In this case he hoped that the gods would say, yes, the girl had faked her prophecy. Sometimes, back in the Old Babylonian period, scribes had even created and archived clay copies of livers, bearing notes about the meanings of the topography of the liver's surface.

The author of the letter to Esarhaddon was sure that the extispicy would reveal that the girl prophet had been lying. He wrote fervently, "May the name and seed of Sasi, Bel-ahi-usur (the slave owner), and their accomplices perish, and may (the gods) Bel and Nabu establish the name and seed of the king, my lord, until far-off [days]!"[39]

Finally, the letter writer advised that a particular colleague of Sasi's should be interrogated. He even suggested a whole series of questions that should be used in the cross-examination, including "Did Sasi speak with you . . . on the following day? Why have you [not reported] what you sa[w and heard]?" And he advised the king to "stay in safety in your palace." The conspiracy that had been uncovered represented a major threat to the king. Unfortunately, we don't know the result of the liver-reading.

A second letter to Esarhaddon from the same writer is harder to make out because many breaks interrupt the text, but it is clearly full of the same warnings to the king and curses on his enemies, and was written in the same state of agitation. In this case, rather than reporting the ranting of a prophet, the writer wanted to let the king know that he himself "had a vision" that pertained to the conspiracy,[40] though it's a little hard to make out the rest of his message. Sasi was mentioned again, this time in reference, alarmingly, to preparations for an ambush. Apparently Sasi had concrete plans to kill Esarhaddon.

Nabu-ushallim: A Dream Interpreter

Esarhaddon received messages like this from others as well. Another one of his loyal followers, a man named Nabu-ushallim, wrote to say that he had

Fig. 18.2 Letter from Nabu-ushhallim to King Esarhaddon of Assyria about a conspiracy, 681–669 BCE. This image shows that the scribe wrote on all six sides of the tablet. The message began at the top left of the front side. (Yale University, Peabody Museum)

been held captive for the past three months in a man's house as retribution for his support of Esarhaddon (see Fig. 18.2).[41] He wrote that "because of what I see and hear and betray to the king my lord, because of this, many people hate me and are plotting to kill me." Clearly this was not his first contact with the king; he had reported to him before and had suffered for it. His enemies had even tried to prevent his letters getting through. Once again, the treacherous Sasi was involved: "All this is done to me at the orders of the overseer of the city of . . . (Ashur) and at the orders of Sasi," but, to the frustration of the writer, Nabu-ushhallim, he realized that "the king does not know it."

On this occasion, however, it seems that Sasi was not the one who wanted to become king. Abda, the overseer of the city of Ashur, had dreams of overthrowing Esarhaddon, and this time they were, literally, dreams. Nabu-ushallim, the author of the letter, had a reputation as a dream interpreter, so the overseer Abda had consulted with him. In his letter, Nabu-ushallim described Abda's dreams in detail. One involved a small boy who handed a staff to Abda and said, "Under the protection of this . . . staff you will become mighty and powerful." Dreams had always held great meaning for Mesopotamians. If a god appeared in a dream and spoke, just as when a prophet proclaimed a vision, the dreamer or a witness had an obligation to let someone in power know—this was another way that gods sent messages to humans, and anyone could be the medium through which a deity spoke. In this case the speaker in the dream was a small boy rather than a god, but perhaps it was clear to Esarhaddon whom the small boy represented. The message definitely seemed to indicate that a god had chosen Abda for the throne.

Nabu-ushallim was dealing with powerful, dangerous men here. Abda had recruited 120 elite soldiers to his side, all of whom had sworn their allegiance to him in a formal ceremony that had included the sacrifice of an ox. Some of the soldiers had even approached Nabu-ushallim, asking him to join them: "Come and swear with us!" they said. But Nabu-ushallim stayed loyal to the king, in spite of the perils of doing so when surrounded by rebels. He told Esarhaddon that "I did not obey."

At this point the conspirators, Abda and Sasi, hired two men and sent them to Nineveh to try to convince King Esarhaddon that it was Nabu-ushallim who was the one plotting against him, rather than Abda and Sasi themselves. Then, someone claiming to be on Nabu-ushallim's side, a fellow loyal supporter of King Esarhaddon, had asked Nabu-ushallim to write a letter in which he laid out everything that had happened, as evidence against Sasi and Abda. Nabu-ushallim trustingly did so and gave it to his would-be friend. But this supposed ally turned around and handed his letter to Sasi instead. Sasi now knew everything that Nabu-ushallim had heard and, what was more damning, everything he believed the king should know.

By the time Nabu-ushallim wrote his letter to Esarhaddon, he was desperate, and he probably feared that Sasi would have him killed. Plus, the coup against the king might be about to happen at any time, so he wanted Esarhaddon to realize the gravity of the situation. On the other hand, since he had been maligned by the conspirators, he feared that Esarhaddon might not believe his account. He might be mistaken for a traitor. He was in an impossible situation and hoped that his loyalty would come through in his letter.

Kudurru and the Chief Eunuch: An Oil Diviner and a Pretender to the Throne

Sasi was not just a city mayor. He also worked in King Esarhaddon's library. He was put in charge of two captured scribes, men named Kudurru and Kunaya, who had been brought (against their will) with a group of other scribes from Babylon to Nineveh to copy tablets for the Assyrian royal library.[42] This was not a collegial situation. One of their Babylonian colleagues who had finished his work had "been put in irons . . . (because) there is no work for him at present."[43]

Given the general atmosphere of suspicion that surrounded Sasi, you will not be surprised to hear that King Esarhaddon directed his son, the crown prince Ashurbanipal, as follows: "Send word that Sasi be interrogated."[44] But, strangely, he was being interrogated not about his own activities, but about his prisoners in the tablet-copying department, Kunaya and Kudurru. Were they, too, in some way involved in a plot against the king? Incredibly, yes. Well, perhaps not Kunaya, but Kudurru had been swept up into the investigation of yet another man's aspirations to overthrow Esarhaddon and rule Assyria. This new pretender to the throne was not Kudurru's boss Sasi, nor was it Abda, the overseer of the city of Ashur. This time it was the chief eunuch, a man with wide-ranging powers.

Ever since the reign of Ashurnasirpal II more than 200 years before, and especially since the reign of Tiglath-Pileser III, eunuchs—men who had been castrated, probably in childhood—had been serving in some of the highest positions in the Assyrian administration and military. Perhaps they were trusted by the kings because they couldn't father children and therefore presumably had no dynastic ambitions. People now tend to assume that eunuchs were largely employed in the women's quarters of the palace because they didn't pose a sexual threat, but in fact they were appointed to pretty much any administrative role you can think of.

They were shown in many Assyrian relief sculptures, often right at the side of the king, which indicated their high status (see Fig. 18.3). They are easily recognizable—they had no beards, in contrast to almost all other Assyrian men—and were generally shown as having soft features and being of a somewhat short stature.[45] Many of the eunuchs' roles were just as traditionally "masculine" as those of high officials throughout Mesopotamian history,

Fig. 18.3 Gypsum relief showing larger-than-lifesize figures of King Ashurnasirpal II of Assyria and a courtier, who was a eunuch, from the palace of King Ashurnasirpal II at Kalhu, 865–860 BCE. (Metropolitan Museum of Art)

including fighting in battle and leading troops. On many occasions during his reign, Esarhaddon asked diviners to perform extispicies to determine whether he should "send Sha-Nabu-shu, chief eunuch, and the army at his disposal" to fight in various regions, or to besiege particular cities.[46] Sha-Nabu-shu was one of Esarhaddon's most trusted and valued generals.

Esarhaddon's chief eunuch, at the time when this plot to usurp the king was uncovered, was named Ashur-nasir.[47] This was a man who might well have had his eye on gaining even more power, as the captured Babylonian scribe Kudurru was to discover.

We know about the chief eunuch's role in this plot because Kudurru wrote a letter to King Esarhaddon, recounting a shocking experience that he went through. It is one of the most evocative letters to survive from the Assyrian archives, full of specific and almost literary details about the incident. Perhaps he wanted the king to feel that he had been right there in the room with him.

After the traditional blessing for the king that introduced every letter, Kudurru began his shocking tale. "[Ever si]nce the day when the king my lord [dep]orted me (from Babylon), I have sat in confinement, praying to the king, my lord, [every day], until . . . the chief cupbearer sent [a cohort commander] to release me."[48] He seems to have been imprisoned in Nineveh (where he had been working for Sasi in the library). Was he kept in irons during his confinement, like his unfortunate colleague? It must have been a relief to have been released, but why was he wanted?

It turned out that the chief cupbearer, a very high official in the palace, needed Kudurru for his expertise. The cohort commander asked him, as they walked together, "You are an expert in [scrib]al lore? [Someone] tells me [you] are an expert in scribal lore." Kudurru no doubt assured him, that, yes, that was his specialty. They kept walking until they got to the temple of the god Bel of Harran, where someone powerful was waiting to cross-examine him. In the letter, Kudurru didn't name his questioner. He stood and waited in the temple, until "the cohort commander re-emerged and took me to an upper room into his presence." Five powerful men were in the room with him, including the cohort commander who had escorted him, the chief cupbearer who had summoned him, and his unnamed questioner. The chief eunuch was not there, however. "In addition," Kudurru wrote, "the overseer of the city kept entering and leaving his presence." It's tempting to see this as Sasi; he was indeed an overseer of a city.

Kudurru continued, "They tossed me a seat and I sat down, drinking wine until the sun set. Moving my seat closer, he (the unnamed official) started speaking to me . . . saying: 'You are an expert in divination?'" One can imagine the six men, seated in the upper room of the temple as the room grew darker with the coming of twilight, drinking wine together. Kudurru might have been disoriented by it all. Here he was, a prisoner, suddenly thrust into the company of some of the most powerful men in Assyria, getting light-headed from the wine, wondering why he was there. And then his powerful questioner had pulled him closer and asked him to perform a divination for them. The bottom of the letter is unfortunately broken, but when the text resumes on the other side of the tablet, the questioner had come to his point. He said to Kudurru: "'Go and perform the (following) divination before Shamash: "Will the chief eunuch take over the kingship?"'"

What a question! And what answer did they want? Were these high officials supporters of Esarhaddon or not? If they had been loyal to the king, surely they would have asked one of the temple diviners to do the job. They were, instead, asking a captive prisoner from Babylon who happened to have divining skills. Sasi, Kudurru's overseer in the library, might well have suggested him for the work.

Kudurru continued his letter: "I washed myself with water in another upper room, donned clean garments and, the cohort commander having brought up for me two skins of oil, performed (the divination)." Oil divination was an alternative to reading animal entrails that provided a quicker answer from the gods. Oil would be poured on the surface of a dish of water, and the shapes it assumed could be "read" by a diviner with expert knowledge of such things.[49] Similar techniques included sprinkling flour on water, or burning cedar and interpreting the shapes taken by the smoke. The gods left clues about their plans all over the place.

It's interesting to learn that the temple had upper rooms where the procedure could take place, and that the procedure required cleanliness on the part of the diviner. The clean garments for Kudurru must have been procured from the temple; he certainly wouldn't have brought them with him.

Kudurru examined the oil and discerned the gods' reply, announcing: "He will take over the kingship." So, yet another pretender to the throne seemed to have the gods' support. Fortunately for Kudurru, this was the response that his interrogators had wanted. The next day was one long party. He wrote, they "made [merry] until the sun was low." This, no doubt, involved more wine. The officials even made outlandish (probably drunken) promises to Kudurru—that he would be returned to his home and even that they would make him king of Babylonia.

But there is a reason that this account was found in a letter to King Esarhaddon. Kudurru had been performing a charade. He was not, in fact, on the side of the conspirators and, by writing to the king, he had revealed their plot and identified them as traitors. At last, he confessed to the king that his "divination" had been performed under great duress. Kudurru wrote that the whole thing was "but a colossal fraud! (The only thing) [I was th]inking of (was), 'May he not kill me.'" The last section of the letter that can be made out is a plea for mercy: "I am writing to the king, lest [the king my lord] hear about it and kill me." Kudurru might have feared that the cupbearer and chief eunuch would kill him if they found out that he had identified them and divulged their scheme, but he seems to have feared even more that the king would kill him if he found out about the divination that Kudurru had performed and if he therefore believed that Kudurru was a conspirator.

Esarhaddon Reacts to the Conspiracies

Esarhaddon might well have been uncertain, when he received all these letters, whom to believe. The astronomer and diviner Bel-ushezib, the unnamed girl prophet, the dream interpreter Nabu-ushallim, and the scholar Kudurru had all received or interpreted messages from the gods, and they were not in agreement. The men who wrote to the king all claimed to be on his side, but they reported about oracles and prophecies that implied that the gods may have been against him.

Did the gods want Sasi to be king, as the prophet had proclaimed? Or did they want Abda, as that man's dreams implied? Or did they support Esarhaddon himself, as Bel-ushezib maintained? The king could see that divinations could be faked—Kudurru had admitted to exactly that. And was Nabu-ushallim, who had accused Abda and Sasi, really on the king's side or just trying to save himself from punishment after Sasi's attempts to defame him to the king? How many people right there in King Esarhaddon's court were against him? If he trusted Kudurru (who, admittedly, was keen not to be killed and might have been less loyal than he seemed), then five or six of his closest advisors were supporting his chief eunuch's aspirations.

Esarhaddon, who had spies in many places, seems to have rounded up many of the accused conspirators and brought them to Nineveh. The king's chief physician wrote a letter to him, approving of his actions. The physician wrote that "(the god) Ashur and the great gods bound and handed over to the king these criminals who plotted against (the king's) goodness."[50] What struck the physician most was that the conspirators had broken the sacred oath they had taken to support Esarhaddon when he was first made crown prince. They had "concluded the king's treaty together with his servants before Ashur and the great gods, (but they) broke the treaty." He noted, though, that the gods prevailed: "The goodness of the king caught them up."

All of the spreading corruption and betrayal had left a bad taste in Esarhaddon's mouth. Whom could he trust? As the physician put it, the conspirators "made all other people hateful in the eyes of the king, smearing them like a tanner with the oil of fish." This expression is brilliant—it evokes beautifully how conspiracies can begin to stick to everything, making every person a suspect.

But this was not the main reason for the physician's letter. He was sending a healer to the king, and two plants that "are good for counterspells." Esarhaddon was often ill, and in need of the attention of his physician. His growing fear of people close to him can't have helped either his physical or mental health.

Adad-shumu-usur: A Physician Dealing with Royal Illness and Substitute Kings

King Esarhaddon's life was not easy, and he seems to have felt his losses acutely. In a single year (673 BCE), his wife and a young son both died. He mourned them deeply, and he never promoted another wife to become queen (*segallu*) after that. Instead, his mother, Naqi'a, took over the responsibilities and title of queen.[51] She seems to have assumed the role energetically, making up for her son's hesitancy with her own competence. She received reports from across the empire, and sometimes she and Esarhaddon together were addressed as "my lords."[52]

The letters from Esarhaddon's personal physician and exorcist Adad-shumu-usur reveal a worried, frail king who preferred his own company.[53] The doctor sent Esarhaddon various medicines and told him which incantations were effective against such things as vomiting, dizziness, and "cough with phlegm."[54] He also worried sometimes that the king was making his illnesses worse by isolating himself. On one occasion, Esarhaddon shut himself away in a dark room and refused to eat for two days. The physician wrote, in worried tones, that "The king, the lord of the world, is the very image of (the sun god) Shamash. He (should) keep in the dark for half a day only!"⁵⁵ And he really did need to eat. "[Eating of b]read and [drinking of w]ine [will soon re]move [the illness of the king]. G[ood ad]vice is to be heeded: restlessness, not eating and not drinking disturbs the mind and adds to illness."

Medicine and exorcism were intertwined in Mesopotamia, because they believed that illnesses were sent by the gods as a form of punishment for actions that the sick person had performed, or, in some cases, failed to perform. A physician did not just prescribe medicines; he was also responsible for exorcising any demons that might be causing the illness by reciting prescribed incantations. Although diviners could determine the will of the gods, they were not trained in exorcism; that required a specialist. An ill king was vulnerable not only because his sickness made him weak, but because it could be interpreted as a sign that the gods didn't support him. One of Esarhaddon's many maladies seems to have been a skin condition on his face that would have been hard to disguise, and that might have looked to others like a clear vote of no confidence from the gods. No wonder he sometimes retreated to a room where he would not be seen.

Adad-shumu-usur was a member of an "inner circle" of about fifteen scholars on whom Esarhaddon depended: astrologers, exorcists, physicians, diviners, and lamentation priests.⁵⁶ All of them had a surprisingly close relationship with the king and all were literate. Adad-shumu-usur, for example, had to be able to consult the many medical and religious texts that would direct him to the right substances to cure his patient, in his role as physician (asu in Akkadian), along with the correct ritual actions and incantations to perform in his role as exorcist (ashipu in Akkadian).⁵⁷ Both types of treatment were considered to be necessary and effective, and both probably worked in many cases, thanks to the doctors' knowledge of herbs, honey, minerals, and other natural products, many of which were indeed effective, and to the patients' trust in the exorcists' ability to cure them. This no doubt resulted from what is now recognized as the placebo effect, which has always helped people recover if their condition allowed it.

As Esarhaddon became increasingly worried for his own safety, several times he supposed that his own demise was imminent; it had been foretold by the gods. His diviners and his physician were not necessarily convinced. The king believed fervently, at one point, that an eclipse of the sun was about to happen, which would have presaged his death. Accordingly, he stepped down and appointed a peasant to take the throne in his place as a substitute king. For a hundred days Esarhaddon became a "farmer" while the substitute king ruled in his place, living in the palace and being served by the courtiers. The arrangements for this substitute were the concern of Adad-shumu-usur, in his role as exorcist. He determined that the substitute should have not just "the clothes of the king, my lord," but the "necklace [of go]ld, the scepter and the throne." Remarkably, a "statue of the substitute king" had even been created, which needed garments of its own.[58] Nothing could look less than real. The substitute king had to be given every luxury and privilege that Esarhaddon normally enjoyed. When everything was ready, the physician wrote to Esarhaddon that "the order should be given to enthrone (the substitute king)." Meanwhile, the real king sloped off into obscurity for a while. For more than three months he didn't have to make decisions, he didn't have to appear in public, he could live quietly and invisibly so that the gods were clear about which king had to die. It seems to have suited Esarhaddon well.

In spite of all the preparations, Esarhaddon worried about the forthcoming eclipse anyway, and he wrote to his physician (carefully using his assumed identity so that the gods wouldn't know that it was him): "An order of the 'farmer' [to] Adad-shumu-usur . . . : I am well. Speak again with the comman[der-in]-chief (as follows): 'Will you assume responsibility for the eclipse of the sun? . . . Surely there will be an eclipse of the sun? Send me definite word!'"[59]

As you may recall, this same strategy of appointing a substitute king had been used by King Erra-imitti of Isin in the Old Babylonian period more than a thousand years earlier, but it had backfired when he died anyway and the gardener Enlil-bani, who had been in the temporary position of substitute king, stayed on the throne. Esarhaddon's substitute was not so lucky. At the end of the hundred days, the substitute king was killed and buried in an appropriately ornate tomb, so that the predicted death of the king had taken place and Esarhaddon could breathe a little easier, at least for a while. Given that at least four substitute kings "ruled" at various times during his reign, the relief doesn't seem ever to have lasted long. And one pities the men sacrificed for eclipses that never happened or for other omens that would never normally have justified the expense and complications of a substitute king.

Many more than four men suffered for Esarhaddon's paranoia, though. In 670 BCE the king purged his court. He never mentioned this in his royal inscriptions; we know about it only because the authors of a later Babylonian chronicle mention the executions in a single sentence: "Eleventh year: The king in Assyria killed his many officials with weapons."[60] This was the ultimate outcome of all those worried letters from people like the astronomer Bel-ushezib, the Babylonian scribe Kudurru, and the loyalist Nabu-ushallim. We don't know whom he targeted, but it seems likely that informers ended up dead, right along with the men and women they had accused.[61] Everyone seems to have been suspect, in Esarhaddon's eyes.

But there was a surprising survivor of Esarhaddon's purge: Sasi. This man—identified by so many as the ultimate conspirator, the mastermind of several schemes against the king—was, amazingly, still alive in the reign of the next ruler, Esarhaddon's son Ashurbanipal. Some scholars have proposed that Sasi could have been a double agent, a spy for Esarhaddon who infiltrated the underground circles of conspirators and reported back to his king, naming names and keeping himself safe from royal fear and fury.[62] Or perhaps he survived the purge by switching sides, accusing others, and pretending to have been loyal to Esarhaddon all along.

The Succession Treaty and Imperial Expansion: Enlisting the Gods' Support

Esarhaddon's reign lasted only twelve years, but in that short time he and his government achieved much more than you might expect, especially given his distrust of pretty much everyone. He built himself a fortified (perhaps coup-proof) palace at Nineveh and strengthened the defenses of the palace at Kalhu. But he didn't just close himself inside his towers; he also looked outward across the wide empire. He was even able to expand its limits to their greatest extent, and to finally reach a treaty agreement with Elam.

The king fathered at least eighteen children and selected his son Ashurbanipal to succeed him as king of Assyria. Another son was to serve as the king of Babylon after Esarhaddon's death. In 672 BCE he drew up a "treaty" between himself and the people of the empire concerning the future succession. He decided to have a rare gathering of his vassals so that he could see them in person and witness their oaths to support his plan for Ashurbanipal's succession, just as they had sworn to support Esarhaddon when he had been appointed crown prince eleven years earlier.

Tablets inscribed with the treaty have been found at several sites across the Near East, from Turkey to Iran. Each vassal seems to have taken a copy home with him and to have overseen his people swearing to be governed by it. The treaty was epic in length: 670 lines.[63] It would have taken a long time to read aloud, which must have happened in order for the populations to understand their obligations. Learning from his father's mistakes, Esarhaddon included clauses to try to prevent the kinds of treacherous conspiracies and assassination plots that had plagued his own reign. He also added almost a hundred lines of complex curses on anyone who damaged the tablet on which the treaty was written, followed by more than 150 lines of yet more (and fiercer) curses on anyone who broke the oath. A lot of them called for vivid and horrible disasters to happen to the oath-breaker and his family. But the writer of curses seems to have run out of steam at some point, coming up with this slightly nihilist wish: "Just as the inside of a hole is empty, may your inside be empty."[64]

The text was so long that the clay tablets on which it was written are bigger than almost any other cuneiform tablet from any era. A copy that was recently discovered at a site called Tell Tayinat in Turkey is typical in size, measuring 40 × 28 centimeters (16 × 11 inches).[65] Each copy of the treaty had four columns of text on each side and was sealed at the top of the front with three seals belonging to the god Ashur. The tablets were designed to be displayed in temples across the empire,[66] and they were, indeed, found in temples by modern archaeologists. Esarhaddon even seems to have made the oath document itself a divine object, so that the tablet in each temple could be worshiped as though it were a god.[67] He was clearly preoccupied, even obsessed, with the idea that his choice of successors would be respected.

With the succession settled, Esarhaddon was back to fighting to expand the empire. He was particularly taken by what must have seemed an almost impossible goal: the conquest of Egypt. Egypt had been the star of its own separate universe (at least in the minds of the Egyptians) for close to three millennia by this time—not very far away from Mesopotamia but never remotely vulnerable to Mesopotamian military attack before. No previous Mesopotamian army had been strong enough.

Egypt was now controlled by the Twenty-fifth Dynasty, whose kings had originated in Nubia (modern Sudan). They had unified Egypt for the first time since the end of the Late Bronze Age and had even tried to regain control of the Levant. It had been a Twenty-fifth Dynasty king, Taharqa, who had come to the aid of the Judeans when they tried to rebel against Assyria during the reign of Sennacherib.

Esarhaddon's first attempt to take Egypt was not a success; in fact, his army completely failed that time to bring Egypt into the Neo-Assyrian Empire. This marked the first major defeat of the Assyrian army in hundreds of years. The Babylonian Chronicle comments dispassionately, "Seventh year. On the fifth day of the month of Adar, the army of Assyria was defeated in the land of Egypt."[68] Behind that sentence lay months of preparations; untold numbers of troops who marched for hundreds of miles carrying heavy armor and supplies, and who fought hard in a very hot, distant, and unfamiliar land; the many deaths that resulted; and an ignominious return to Assyria of those who survived, without the usual spoils of war to enrich the Assyrian treasury. It was an expensive war and a humiliating outcome.

But Esarhaddon was undeterred. He was determined to conquer Egypt. Three years later, in 671 BCE, his troops were back on the march across Syria with their sights on the Egyptian capital of Memphis. During this journey, Esarhaddon received another message from the gods. Unlike all the prophesies of doom that he received in letters, this one was entirely positive.

The king had stopped in the Syrian city of Harran, which had been growing in importance and influence. It was one of the cities where the moon god, Sin, had a great temple. During the time that Esarhaddon was there, for some reason, "a temple of cedar was bu[ilt] outside the city of Harran." This sounds as though it was a temporary structure, not like the monumental mudbrick and stone temples where the gods normally resided. The statues of two gods were placed inside: Sin, the moon god, wearing two crowns, and, in front of him, Nusku, the god of fire and light. Esarhaddon entered the cedar temple and "placed [the crown(s)] on (his) head, (and it was said to him) 'You will go and conquer the world with it.'"[69] Who spoke these words? It sounds like a prophecy spoken by the god Sin himself, but, given that statues don't actually speak, someone—a priest or priestess perhaps—must have relayed the message.

The gods had once more provided the king with a view of his future, and it may have motivated him to pursue his surprisingly aggressive policy of expansion. He had been promised the whole world.

When the Assyrian forces arrived in Egypt, this time they managed to take control of the northern capital of Memphis. "Memphis was turned into booty," wrote the author of the Chronicle, "its people taken as plunder; and its property carried off."[70] Although Esarhaddon crowed about his victory, the destruction must have represented an inexpressible tragedy for the Egyptians who were captured and marched off to live somewhere in the Assyrian Empire. Like all the people deported by the Assyrians, the exiled Egyptians were forced to settle in a land foreign to them, far, in their case, from the wide Nile and its rich, dark soil, far from the ancient pyramids that stood near Memphis, already almost 2,000 years old, perpetual reminders of the power of their early kings.

The truth of this campaign belied Esarhaddon's image of himself bravely leading his troops to Memphis, however. During this period, he was going through one of his many substitute king phases; for months during this time, he was "the farmer" who was not really in power and could not appear in public. His chief eunuch probably led the successful attack on Egypt.[71]

It was in the wake of this victory in Egypt, once the army had returned home, that Esarhaddon turned on his officials and executed so many of them. But Egypt grabbed his attention again, soon enough. The Egyptians were unhappy with the Assyrian governors and their demands, and the people there rebelled again. For a third time in six years, the Assyrian army gathered weapons, supplies, and armor and headed back to Egypt.

Esarhaddon did not return alive. "The king of Assyria went to the land of Egypt. He became ill during the campaign and on the tenth day of the month of Arahsamni, he died."[72] After a lifetime of fearing assassination plots, Esarhaddon seems to have died of natural causes.

Chapter 19
Gardeners, Artisans, and a Centenarian Priestess

By the mid-seventh century BCE Harran, in Syria, had been an important place for longer than anyone could remember. No doubt the people living there sometimes came across tablets from almost 2,000 years before, when Harran had been within the kingdom of Ebla, or from 1,200 years before, when it had provided a rest stop for the caravans of traders and donkeys traveling from Ashur to Kanesh in Anatolia with their loads of textiles and tin.

The main temple in the city, the Ehulhul (which means "the house which gives joy"), had stood on the same spot at least since the time of Hammurabi of Babylon a thousand years before, and probably long before that. The temple was dedicated to the moon god Sin, who was the patron deity of Harran and was worshiped along with his divine family: his wife, the goddess Ningal (also called Nikkal), his son Nusku, and his daughter-in-law Sadarnunna. The other great temple to Sin was, of course, in Ur, near the Persian Gulf, where priestesses had taken care of the moon god and his estates for thousands of years. But Ur was very far away from Harran, more than 1,100 kilometers (680 miles) to the southeast. To travel from Harran to Ur, one had to follow first the Balikh River south to the Euphrates, and then the Euphrates River downstream almost to its mouth. For the Assyrians, it was Harran that was Sin's home. During the reign of Esarhaddon, the moon god of Harran had become one of Assyria's most important deities, and this continued to be true in the reign of his son Ashurbanipal.[1]

A major road from the Assyrian capital of Nineveh to Carchemish in Syria passed right through Harran, and another road led southwest from Harran to Damascus. Harran helped link the major cities of the Neo-Assyrian

Empire to one another, and, even though it lay 500 kilometers (310 miles) from Nineveh, it was considered a thoroughly Assyrian city. It had been part of the empire throughout most of the Middle Assyrian period in the Late Bronze Age, and had been brought back into the Neo-Assyrian Empire in the ninth century BCE.[2] You may remember that a conspiracy against Esarhaddon had hatched there when a girl prophet claimed to speak for the god Nusku, and Harran was also where Esarhaddon had received his prophecy of world domination. Later, in fact, Esarhaddon had died there when he was on his way to Egypt. Ultimately, Harran proved to be one of the final strongholds of the Neo-Assyrian Empire, even after Nineveh was lost. We'll come back to that later in this chapter.

In any event, Harran, like Aleppo, Damascus, and a number of other cities in the region, has been occupied for so many thousands of years that the remains from ancient times are deeply buried and have not been recovered. Somewhere beneath the modern streets and buildings lies the Neo-Assyrian city. But archaeologists haven't reached it.

Adad-guppi's Early Life

In Harran, in 649 BCE, the twentieth year of the reign of King Ashurbanipal of Assyria (668–630/627 BCE), a person was born who would change history, someone who lived to grand old age and experienced, and brought about, incredible changes in the Near East. This was a baby girl named Adad-guppi. In a world where life expectancy at birth was about thirty-five, she ended up living for an astonishing 102 years, dying in 547 BCE. Near the end of her life, she wrote a short autobiography (or, more likely, one was written for her by her son after her death), which is how we know about her.[3] This chapter will cover her tumultuous century. Most of it is not directly about Adad-guppi, but over her lifetime she had a surprising number of connections to the major events that took place.

Adad-guppi seems to have been appointed as a high priestess of the moon god Sin in his temple at Harran. It's unclear why she was chosen for this role, but in her autobiography she described herself as "a worshipper of Sin, Ningal, Nusku, and Sadarnunna, my gods, for whose divinity I have cared since my youth."[4] Centuries after the poet Enheduana devoted her life to the moon god (then called Nanna), priestesses still took on some of the most vital responsibilities when it came to human relationships with the gods. Young Adad-guppi was stepping into a venerable role, one that her community depended upon. They would have trusted her to keep the gods provided for.

Adad-guppi was thirty-nine years old before anything dramatic happened to her, according to her autobiography. She spent those first decades of her life devoted to the gods, not just the moon god and his family but to all the great gods. She wrote that "I . . . have been piously devoted all my lifetime to Sin, Shamash, Ishtar, and Adad, who are in heaven and in the nether world."[5] At some point she married a high Assyrian official or a prince, about whom we know very little,[6] and she had one child, a boy named Nabu-na'id.

Harran was a sacred place to the Assyrian kings; with regard to the gods it was second only to Ashur, and its priestesses and priests were among the elite of the empire. Harran's people had once been exempted from taxes, but at some point that privilege had been taken away. About sixty years before the birth of Adad-guppi, King Sargon II (722–705 BCE, father of Sennacherib) had decided to reinstate it. He wrote in an inscription that "I restored the exemption (from obligations) of (the city) Baltil (i.e., Ashur) and the city Harran, [which] had fallen into oblivion [in the distant past], and their privileged status that had la[psed]."[7]

In order to be sure to implement this policy fairly, King Sargon II, with typical Mesopotamian thoroughness, commissioned a census to list all the properties and families in Harran that, from then on, would be exempt from paying taxes and other obligations.[8] Fifteen tablets from this census were found by archaeologists in the capital of Nineveh, listing 101 families, almost all of them tenant farmers.[9] Originally the full census would have included many more people. Like an ancient Near Eastern version of the British Domesday Book, the census reveals details about these workers and their families that are otherwise invisible.[10] The lives of tenant farmers would have changed little by Adad-guppi's time. So we'll pause for a moment to visit the farms and vineyards around Harran to understand more about the world in which she lived.

Se'-idri and His Family: Tenant Vineyard Gardeners

One of the men interviewed for the census was named Se'-idri.[11] He worked as a gardener and lived with his family in a house outside Harran,[12] where they tended a plot of land planted with 5,000 grapevines. Their house would have been built of mudbrick, modest in size, and probably situated out in the hilly countryside, surrounded by the vineyard that the family managed. Like almost all the farmers and gardeners surveyed in the census, his land didn't belong to him. Se'-idri and his family worked it on behalf of a landowner. The family paid a proportion of the crop each year to their landlord, but the rest was theirs to keep, to trade, or to sell, so that they could afford all the other expenses of their lives. There was a crucial difference in their situation when compared with farmers who paid a fixed rent. It's true that in a year with a good harvest, Se'-idri's family had to pay more to the landowner than usual, but in a bad year, paying that same percentage resulted in a much lower rent. They could survive without having to go into debt in order to pay the landowner his portion. Owner and tenant both tightened their belts if the crop was poor, but when things were good, both benefited from Se'-idri's careful maintenance of the vines and treatment of the grapes.

The family was listed in the census like this: "Se'-idri, gardener, Nashuh-idri, his son, adolescent; 1 woman; 1 daughter, adolescent: a total of 4 people."[13] Unlike in some earlier eras, women and girls were rarely named in the Neo-Assyrian census records. Generally, the names of men and adolescent boys were the only ones considered to be important enough to write down. Nashuh-idri was the only boy in the family who was living at home during the census, but he may have had older brothers.

A scholar named Galil Gershon has used the Harran census to examine the lives of families in the lower stratum of Assyrian society, and he notes that most sons probably left their parents' home and the lands they had been working when they reached adulthood to become tenants on other lands and to take on their own gardening or farming obligations.[14] Once a man had his own land tenancy, he could afford to marry and have children. There was no shortage of land at the time; if anything, the Assyrian government faced a shortage of farmers for the land available to be cultivated.[15] (This was another driving force behind mass deportations: a keen desire on the part of the government to get potential farmland cultivated and to extract taxes from the farmers.) So Se'-idri and his wife might well have had other sons who lived and worked on lands nearby. Since the census doesn't list the fathers' names of almost any of the residents, there's no way to know.

Likewise, the couple may also have had older daughters who had already left home to get married. A woman in the census was identified by the name of her husband (not even by her own name, let alone those of her parents), so there would be no way to know if any of the other women in the census was a daughter of Se'-idri and his wife. The daughter who was still at home was adolescent, like her brother Nashuh-idri, and her parents probably were already making plans for her future marriage. Boys were more commonly listed than girls in census households. In fact, only 40 percent of the children listed in the census families were girls. This was not for any unsavory reason such as female infanticide. Overall, males and females were equally represented in the census. The lower number of teenage girls than boys in individual households was probably because women generally married at a younger age than men.[16] A boy in his late teens might still be living at home with his parents, but a girl of the same age had probably married and moved away.

Surprisingly, Se'-idri's household of four people wasn't a small one. Four was the average size of a household of tenant farmers in the Harran census.[17] Their family was also typical in the fact that Se'-idri had just one wife. It seems that none of the Harran tenant farmers was married to more than one woman.[18] Throughout ancient Near Eastern history, polygamy was rare, except among the upper classes. Even then, a man generally only married a second wife if his first wife had been unable to have children. Kings could have multiple secondary wives, but even a king had only one queen.

One might assume that ancient Near Eastern people lived in extended families full of aunts, uncles, grandparents, nieces, and nephews—after all, the concept of family was so pervasive and elemental in their world. Allied kings were "brothers" (even when they weren't), adult siblings witnessed one another's legal contracts and expected support from one another, and even the gods were related to one another by complicated family ties. But only about one in twenty of the lower-stratum households of this era included anyone outside the nuclear family—perhaps an unmarried aunt or a grandmother.[19] Presumably, if the elderly parents of Se'-idri or his wife had still been alive, they would have lived with one of their adult children. For example, a household listed a few lines before that of Se'-idri on the same tablet included "Ahunu, gardener; his mother: a total of 2 people."[20] But Ahunu's mother was unusual. Most poor people died long before reaching old age; very few lived to see their grandchildren.[21] Only a fraction of the (already tiny) number of extended families who lived together included more than two generations—adults and their children. Although richer people seem to have lived longer (if they survived childhood diseases), Adad-guppi's lifespan of 102 years must have seemed so long as to be almost incomprehensible.

The property occupied by Se'-idri's family is described as follows:"5,000 stalks of (grape) vine; 1 house; 1 vegetable garden."²² The garden was a common feature of many houses; the family would have used it to grow the vegetables they enjoyed for their meals.

The Mesopotamians had a fondness for all kinds of onions and garlic, and their meals were also flavored with herbs such as cilantro and mustard. These would have grown well in the garden, alongside greens such as arugula, lettuce, and cress; root vegetables like radishes, beets, and turnips; and legumes, including beans, chickpeas, peas, and lentils.²³ Stews were popular, such as one called Tuh'u. The ancient recipe reads as follows: "Leg meat (probably lamb or goat) is used. You prepare water. You add fat. You sear. You fold in salt, beer, onion, arugula, cilantro, Persian shallot, cumin, and red beet, and [you crush] leek and garlic. You sprinkle coriander on top. [You add] kurrat (a type of leek) and fresh cilantro."²⁴ Obviously the cook was expected to know the quantities and the cooking times, but modern chefs have experimented and come up with an excellent version of this dish, which they recommend serving with steamed bulgur, chickpeas, and naan bread (which is very similar to Mesopotamian flat bread).²⁵ The recipe is just as delicious without meat. In fact, Se'-idri's family probably didn't eat a lot of meat, since they don't seem to have owned sheep or goats (and even if they had, the animals would have been more useful alive than eaten).

Cooking was the responsibility of women and girls; Se'-idri's unnamed wife and daughter might well have cooked wild birds and fish for protein. The family didn't manage any barley fields, so the large amounts of grain that every family consumed, in the form of bread, beer, and porridge, must have been supplied by another farmer or family member, in exchange, perhaps, for the grapes or wine from their vineyard.

Se'-idri's vineyard, with its 5,000 vines, was a relatively small one. The average number of vines in a vineyard in the census records was 11,000. Most of the grapes that the family harvested probably went to make wine.

Mesopotamians had been drinking wine for millennia, but it could not be produced in Babylonia, where the weather was too hot and dry for the vines. There, wine represented an expensive import.²⁶ Back in the eighteenth century BCE, the king of Mari had boasted of his ice house and the iced wine that he served guests, and, around the same time, wine mixed with honey was used as a treatment for a bad cough.[27] But the vast majority of references to alcoholic beverages in that era were to beer.

In the first millennium BCE, the Assyrian rulers, who had acquired a taste for wine, had expanded the wine-growing region of their empire right across the foothills that surrounded northern Mesopotamia, from Iran to northern Syria and southern Turkey—including the areas near Harran where Se'-idri's family managed their vineyard. Some of the wine was for local consumption, not just by people but also by gods in the temples. Adad-guppi would no doubt have offered local wines in her libations to the god Sin.

But a lot of wine made its way to the capital city of Nineveh. Sometime between 645 and 635 BCE, at the same time that Adad-guppi was a child in Harran, King Ashurbanipal of Assyria commissioned a relief sculpture for his palace showing himself seated with his wife, Queen Liballi-sharrat, under a grape arbor (see Fig. 19.1). They were depicted drinking what must have been wine, from shallow cups, to the accompaniment of music played by a harpist.[28] (Somewhat alarmingly, the head of Ashurbanipal's recently defeated enemy, the king of Elam, was shown hanging from the branch of a nearby tree, breaking the serene mood a little.)

Fig. 19.1 Gypsum relief showing King Ashurbanipal of Assyria and Queen Liballi-sharrat in a garden, attended by women, with the head of the defeated Elamite king hanging from a tree. From the North Palace at Nineveh, 645–635 BCE. (© The Trustees of the British Museum)

So Se'-idri's family and the other vineyard gardeners around Harran probably found a good market for the grapes they grew. And thanks to Sargon II's proclamation and the census, none of them had to pay taxes.

Ashurbanipal of Assyria: Scholar and War Leader

King Ashurbanipal, in the middle of whose reign Adad-guppi had been born, was the son of the perpetually worried Esarhaddon. It's worth noting here that Ashurbanipal's name is so similar to that of Ashurnasirpal II that the two kings are easily confused. But they were very different men. Their reigns were more than 200 years apart, as distant from one another as the administrations of the American presidents George Washington and George H. W. Bush.

Unlike many of his predecessors, there was a side to Ashurbanipal that was scholarly and contemplative. He boasted not just that he could read and write, but that he also engaged in academic debates with diviners and scribes and could read ancient scripts. He sometimes had himself depicted in relief sculptures with a stylus tucked into his belt. This was true even in a lion hunt scene, as though, after killing the lion, he might have been inspired to sit down and write a few lines about it.[29] His wife Libbali-sharrat was also literate. At one point, before her husband became king, she received a letter from her sister-in-law (a daughter of King Esarhaddon), reprimanding her for neglecting her studies: "Why don't you write your tablet and do your homework?"[30] It was unusual for a king to claim to be a scholar, and even more unusual for a royal couple to both show an interest in mastering cuneiform. Ashurbanipal was passionate about it.

His father Esarhaddon had employed (or forced) a number of scribes, like the Babylonian captive Kudurru, to copy tablets for his collection, and Ashurbanipal took this a step further. He wanted a copy of every important literary work produced in the empire for his library—and his scribes set about fulfilling this goal with meticulous care. When British excavator Austin Henry Layard and Iraqi scholar Hormuzd Rassam uncovered Ashurbanipal's palace at Nineveh during the mid-nineteenth century, they found thousands of these tablets. Most of them were beautifully written on tablets made of very fine clay, often in extraordinarily minute and precise handwriting. The scribes often signed the tablets and even included notes about where they had encountered breaks in the original that they were copying from.

As for the works included in the library, Ashurbanipal's main concern seems to have been with texts that he and others could consult to help him understand the will of the gods as he ran the empire. In some cases, the library included multiple copies of the same work. The shelves were lined with myths, epic poems, hymns, medical texts, ritual programs, and divination records, along with long lexical texts and dictionaries of the type that scribal students learned in school. Vast numbers of oracles had been kept and copied, listing questions that had been posed to the gods, along with the gods' responses (as seen, for example, in the livers of sacrificed animals or in patterns of smoke or oil). Alongside these were records of natural events that had been interpreted as omens, and what each represented as a message from the gods. The library also included archival tablets, such as letters, contracts, and administrative documents.[31] It was the largest library yet accumulated and, remarkably, it was one of the first collections of cuneiform tablets ever found. This was as though some future archaeologists were to discover the US Library of Congress during their first excavations in North America. Ashurbanipal didn't create his library for us, but it has been enormously helpful to historians.

On the other hand, you will not be surprised to hear that Ashurbanipal was also a war leader, like his father Esarhaddon and pretty much all the Neo-Assyrian kings before him. The decapitated Elamite king's head hanging from a tree during Ashurbanipal's wine party was not the kind of garden decoration you would expect from a man interested only in his library.

He had inherited a complicated relationship with both Elam and Babylonia. His father Esarhaddon and grandfather Sennacherib had more difficulties in those regions than in any others. We need to go back in time for a moment in order to understand what Ashurbanipal was facing with regard to his southern province. During the early seventh century BCE, King Sennacherib had been confronted with repeated rebellions in Babylonia and had campaigned there six different times, eventually appointing his eldest son to rule as Babylon's king. The Babylonians were unimpressed with this development; they kidnapped the Assyrian prince and gave him over to the Elamites, who almost certainly executed him. A Babylonian then claimed the throne, denouncing Assyrian rule. Sennacherib was furious; in his desire for vengeance for the death of his son he ended up ignoring Assyria's long tradition of respect for Babylonia and venting his rage on the whole land.

After a war against the Elamites and Babylonians, Sennacherib laid siege to the city of Babylon for fifteen long months, during which time the Babylonians must have increasingly realized that they had run out of options. In 689 BCE the city finally fell, after which the Assyrian troops went on a rampage of murder and destruction, killing people, rich and poor, most of whom had nothing to do with the rebellion against Assyria. Untold numbers of Babylonians died. The Assyrians defied the usual sacred rule of respecting the temples and gods of other lands. As Sennacherib put it, "The hands of my people laid hold of the gods dwelling there and smashed them; they took their property and goods." Read that again. The Assyrians had *smashed the statues* of the Babylonian gods, the very images in which the gods lived. These were the Assyrians' gods, too. The frenzy of violence incited the troops to actions that no one on either side could later justify. It's interesting to note that here, for once, Sennacherib didn't claim that he committed the destruction himself. Perhaps recognizing just how egregious the crime had been, he claimed that it was his people who smashed the gods, not him.[32] I doubt this would have made any difference to the Babylonians; they would still have blamed the king for the unforgivable desecration.

He continued, "I destroyed the city and its houses, from foundation to parapet; I devastated and burned them. I razed the brick and earthenwork of the outer and inner wall (of the city), of the temples, and of the ziggurat; and I dumped these into the Arahtu canal." Worse yet, he tried to make the city uninhabitable by inundating it with water: "I dug canals through the midst of that city, I overwhelmed it with water, I made its very foundations disappear, and I destroyed it more completely than a devastating flood."[33]

The Assyrians even captured the statue of Marduk, the state god of Babylonia, from his home in the Esagil temple, and, like Tukulti-Ninurta I centuries before, apparently took him away to the city of Ashur.[34] All of this, to put it mildly, did not endear the Babylonians to their Assyrian overlords.

Later, after the murder of Sennacherib, his son Esarhaddon inherited a toxic situation in the south. He attempted to assuage Babylonian feelings by rebuilding many of the structures that his father's army had destroyed in Babylon, but Marduk was still missing from his home, and many festivals, most notably the New Year's Festival, could not be conducted until the god returned.

Esarhaddon decided to solve the Babylonian problem by dividing his empire in two, so that, after his death, his son Ashurbanipal would assume the throne as king of Assyria, and another, older, son named Shamash-shumu-ukin would serve as king of Babylonia. But this plan, ultimately, did not work. Although Shamash-shumu-ukin did finally return the statue of Marduk to Babylon, and the early years of the brothers' joint reign were uneventful, they were never really equals. Ashurbanipal controlled much more land, and he made sure that Shamash-shumu-ukin had less power than him. Shamash-shumu-ukin's hands were increasingly tied—he needed his brother's permission to do any number of things, and Ashurbanipal took charge of several building projects that definitely should have been his brother's to direct.

In the spirit of Sasi and the other men who had conspired against Esarhaddon, Shamash-shumu-ukin secretly plotted against his brother Ashurbanipal. His plot found wide support. He convinced leaders from all across the Neo-Assyrian Empire and beyond to side with him, from Amurru in the west, to Gutium and Elam in the east, to Arabia in the south.[35] By 652 BCE, civil war had broken out between the brothers and their respective allies, and by 650 the exhausted city of Babylon was once again under siege, this time by Ashurbanipal's forces. Perhaps the hungry, desperate Babylonians wondered why the battles, sieges, and destruction always took place in their land, never in Assyria. The siege of Babylon continued for two years, until 648 BCE, when Shamash-shumu-ukin died in a fire and Ashurbanipal's army entered Babylon unopposed. This was within a year, as it happens, of Adad-guppi's birth in Harran.

For the next twenty years, relations between Assyria and Babylonia finally calmed, though the Babylonians certainly weren't about to forget how they had been treated. And they can't have missed the fact that, after almost three centuries, the Neo-Assyrian Empire was beginning to show signs of weakness. Ashurbanipal may have been victorious over Babylonia, as well as over the Elamites and the Arabs, but he had been unable to maintain control in Egypt. People must have realized that it was, therefore, at least possible to successfully rebel against Assyria; the god Ashur was not always, inevitably victorious. Hope might well have stirred among the peoples under Assyrian domination.

For some reason, documents simply dry up toward the end of Ashurbanipal's reign, and it's unclear how and even exactly when he died. He was succeeded by one son, Ashur-etel-ilani, who ruled for about four years, and then by another, Sin-shar-ishkun, who took the throne in 624 BCE and who, over the course of his ill-fated reign, witnessed the collapse of the Neo-Assyrian Empire.

The End of the Assyrian Empire

In 626 BCE, during the short reign of Ashur-etel-ilani, a former general in the Assyrian army named Nabopolassar (626–605 BCE) seized power in Babylon and led yet another Babylonian revolt against Assyria.[36] This one was ultimately successful. At this point, Adad-guppi was twenty-two years old and certainly, by now, serving as Sin's devotee or priestess in Harran. Her city was still within the Assyrian Empire, but perhaps some people there were rooting for Nabopolassar, whose rebellion was taking place far to the south. She mentioned in her autobiography that she lived through the reign of the Assyrian king Ashur-etel-ilani, but she didn't list his brother Sin-shar-ishkun at all. Instead, she noted that, after the reign of Ashur-etel-ilani, she lived through twenty-one years of the reign of Nabopolassar of Babylon. Maybe her allegiance had already shifted to support the Babylonians, or maybe, by the time the autobiography was written, she felt obliged to mention the Babylonian conqueror from the beginning of his reign, long before he controlled Harran.

Adad-guppi would have heard stories about the constant battles and sieges taking place in Babylonia and would have realized that the Assyrian king Sin-shar-ishkun, unlike his father and great-grandfather, was proving unable to stop the rebellions. Fourteen years after the civil war began, long-awaited and almost unbelievable news spread across the lands of the Neo-Assyrian Empire: Nineveh had fallen. Nabopolassar had been able, at last, to move the battles and sieges out of Babylonia and into Assyria itself. A group of people called the Medes, who lived in western Iran, had joined in the attack on Assyria a couple of years before. It was the Medes who managed to conquer the city of Ashur in 614 BCE, and the alliance they formed with Babylonia proved to be fatal for Assyria. After a siege of just three months, the combined armies were able to conquer Nineveh in

612 BCE. The Assyrian capital hadn't been built for defense; perhaps when Sennacherib had enlarged and rebuilt Nineveh as his capital no one had envisioned a time when it would even need to be defended. Assyria had fought innumerable offensive, aggressive wars, but almost never defensive ones. For hundreds of years no war had reached the center of Assyria, because its military had been unmatched.

Excavations all across Assyria have revealed just how violently the invaders attacked the main cities. Assyrian palaces burned, tombs were looted, and other buildings torn down. This was the moment when Sennacherib's face was chiseled from his relief sculptures in his former palace. Copies of Esarhaddon's supposedly divine treaty of succession, identifying his sons as his heirs, were smashed to pieces. The treaties had been set up in temples, where the Assyrian king had required his subjects to worship them as divine objects; now they lay on the floor, nothing more than piles of broken clay. The Medes had even thought to bring the copies of the treaty from their own temples so that they could be vengefully destroyed in the temple to Nabu in the city of Kalhu.[37] The treaty had no power as a divine object once it had been smashed. The curses Esarhaddon had included would no longer work.[38]

According to a later text by the Babylonian king Nabonidus, it was the Median forces, not those of the Babylonians, who did all the major damage, especially to Assyrian temples:

> The king of the Umman-manda (Medes), who was impudent (i.e. without reverence for the holy) destroyed their sanctuaries. He also desecrated the cultic rites of all the gods of Assyria and the cities of the territory of the land of Akkad (Babylonia) that had rebelled against the king of the land of Akkad and had not gone to his assistance. He spared no one. He utterly laid waste their cult centers.[39]

The Babylonian king would never have done these sacrilegious things, according to Nabonidus: "The king of Babylon, the creation of Marduk, to whom blasphemy is abhorrent, did not lay a hand on the cult of any of the gods, (rather) he wore the unkept hair (of mourning), slept on the ground."

The Assyrian king Sin-shar-ishkun died with the fall of Nineveh and it might have seemed, in 612 BCE, that the Neo-Assyrian Empire was over. But one last man, probably a son of Sin-shar-ishkun, claimed the Assyrian throne.[40] He chose, as his capital, Adad-guppi's city of Harran and set up an Assyrian government in exile there. By doing so, in a way he put a target on Harran. The Babylonians and Medes arrived two years later and by 609 BCE they had taken control. The Neo-Assyrian Empire was at an end. Adad-guppi wrote that "Sin, the king of the gods, became angry with his city (i.e. Harran) and temple and went up to heaven, the city and the people inside it became ruins."[41] The statue of Sin, along with those of Ningal, Nusku, and Sadarnunna, must have been taken out of their temples in Harran at this time, and either taken to Babylon or, more likely, destroyed by the Median attackers.[42] They "went up to heaven," as Adad-guppi put it.

In the minds of the Mesopotamians, this was an act akin to murder. The gods were immortal, but they needed their original statues in order to dwell on Earth. A new statue could not simply be fashioned, set up in the temple, and thereby become the god. The bodies of the gods were gone and could not be recovered. A new statue could only be made if an image of the old one existed and could be replicated,[43] after which specific rituals had to take place to bring the god's presence back into his or her new image.

An eerie silence fell over Assyria after this. Suddenly, no one was writing anything there. At least, no one was writing in cuneiform.[44] It's possible that some documents were written in Aramaic, on papyrus, but they have left no trace. Excavators find almost no evidence for people living on in the once-great cities, which became ghost towns. Skeletons of people killed defending Nineveh were left beneath the rubble, unburied. The cities of the Assyrian heartland seem to have been abandoned, mourned by almost no one. The Babylonians took control there,[45] but faced no more resistance.

When the Neo-Assyrian Empire fell in 609 BCE, Adad-guppi was about thirty-nine years old. Her son Nabu-na'id must have still been a child.[46] Mother and son faced the same fate that had been suffered by so many conquered leaders and officials during the Neo-Assyrian Empire: they were removed from their home and taken as captives to the city of their conquerors. In this case their destination was Babylon, capital of the new empire, known to us as the Neo-Babylonian Empire, and home to its king Nabopolassar.

In her autobiography, Adad-guppi described a trying time, during which she attempted to convince the moon god to return to Harran. She visited the shrines of her beloved gods in Babylon, where she "constantly sought out Sin, Ningal, Nusku, and Sadarnunna, worshipping their godheads."[47] Clearly, she was not imprisoned in Babylon, and she was given access to the shrines. Her status as a priestess of the god Sin must have been acknowledged by the Babylonian authorities. One can envision her, in the stillness of the shrine to the moon god (in her words), "continually beseeching Sin. Gazing at him prayerfully and in humility, I knelt before them. Thus (I said): 'May your return to your city take place. May the black-headed people worship your great divinity.'"[48] The "black-headed people" was a common term for all of humanity.

Nebuchadnezzar II of Babylon: The King and His Capital City

The city of Babylon, meanwhile, found a new lease on life. Nabopolassar had won, the Assyrian authorities were gone, and the Babylonian king now ruled more than half of what had been the Neo-Assyrian Empire. The northern part of the empire, including Adad-guppi's home city of Harran, was now ruled by the Medes.[49] The people of the provinces might have hoped that they would become independent after Nineveh fell, but they discovered that this was not to be; they had traded one imperial power for another. And that was to be the pattern for centuries. One enormous empire after another ruled the entire Near East (and often quite a bit of the rest of Eurasia as well). For much of the sixth century BCE, the ruling empire was that of the Babylonians.

Just four years after the end of the Neo-Assyrian Empire, in 605 BCE, the Babylonian king Nabopolassar died, and the throne passed to his son, Nebuchadnezzar II (604–562 BCE). The new king was already well known as a popular and respected general, and he went on to enjoy a long reign of forty-three years, a period that proved to be the height of the Neo-Babylonian Empire. Strictly speaking, we should probably call him Nebuchadrezzar; there was no second "n" sound in his Akkadian name, Nabu-kudurru-usur. But Nebuchadnezzar is his name in the Bible, and, like all such names of Assyrian and Babylonian kings, this is just an approximation of what the Judean authors heard and not his real name at all.

Nebuchadnezzar II probably imagined himself to be ruling at the start of a long period of Babylonian dominance of the Near East, and he wanted a capital city to match his empire's greatness. In many ways, Nebuchadnezzar modeled his kingdom, and his very sense of what it meant to be a king, even of what a state could be, not on the Neo-Assyrians but on his predecessors in his own region—the Babylonians of Hammurabi's era, and the Sumerians of the Early Dynastic period, in what was already the very distant past. Hammurabi had lived 1,200 years before Nebuchadnezzar. Unlike the Neo-Assyrian kings, Nebuchadnezzar had no interest in glorifying his military deeds in inscriptions and relief sculptures.[50] He didn't use the warlike titles of the Assyrian kings. Instead he emphasized his reverence for the gods, his humility, and the order he brought to his kingdom.[51] He "put the land in order, and made the people prosper." He also, like Hammurabi, promoted justice: "From the people, I drove away the criminals and villains."[52]

His father Nabopolassar had begun embellishing Babylon, and Nebuchadnezzar was determined not just to complete his father's projects but to go far beyond what had been planned. A whole new building program was to be developed, encompassing the entire city. We have seen this so often, from the temples of the Eanna in Uruk 3,000 years before, to the ziggurats constructed by the kings of the Ur III dynasty, to Untash-Napirisha's new capital city in Elam, to three different new capital cities in Assyria during the Neo-Assyrian Empire. Every time, the relevant kingdom devoted phenomenal amounts of wealth, natural resources, manpower, and engineering expertise to create the most impressive structures imaginable.

Nebuchadnezzar went all out. Over the course of his long reign he (or rather, thousands of workers, under his direction) doubled the size of the city to 800 hectares (1,977 acres), so that it was bigger even than Nineveh (see Fig. 19.2). It was, as far as we know, the largest city in the world at the time (though the population is difficult to estimate because much of the area inside the walls remains unexcavated).[53] He surrounded it with a double city wall, 18 kilometers (11 miles) long, with a street running between the inner and outer wall. This double wall was later deemed one of the wonders of the world by Greek authors. Beyond it, he commissioned the construction of a moat, 80 meters (262 feet) wide.[54]

Another of the supposed wonders of the ancient world was the Hanging Garden of Babylon, but there is no contemporaneous evidence for its existence; the Greek historian Herodotus did not mention it when he visited, nor, sadly, was it found during excavations in Babylon (though not for lack of trying). Historian Stephanie Dalley has proposed that this might be because of a dramatic mix-up: perhaps later Greek and Roman writers confused Babylonia and Assyria (which was not uncommon for them) and the Hanging Garden had in fact been in Nineveh, where Sennacherib's

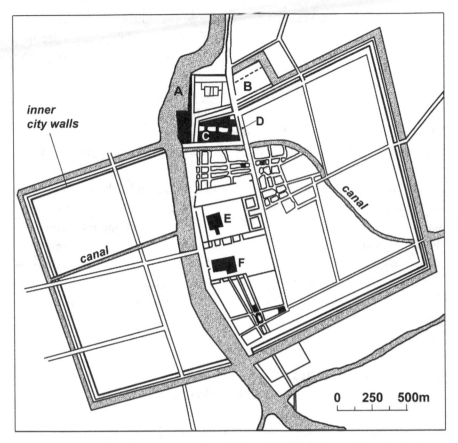

Fig. 19.2 Plan of Babylon in the time of King Nebuchadnezzar II, early sixth century BCE. Key: A – Euphrates; B – Ishtar Gate; C – Palace; D – Processional Way; E and F – Esagila temple complex of Marduk (E – ziggurat, F – temple) (based on Oates 1979, 148, Fig. 100).

engineers had constructed and developed an irrigation system for remarkable gardens on manmade terraces, which he proudly depicted in reliefs on his palace walls.[55] These would truly have been a technological wonder at a time when plants grew only on the ground, not several stories up, on top of a building.

Notwithstanding the missing Hanging Garden, everything about the city of Babylon inspired superlatives. Nebuchadnezzar II had the immense royal palace completely rebuilt in baked brick (marked as C in Fig. 19.2), with more than 250 rooms arranged around five courtyards. By the end of his reign, Babylon's main gateway, the Ishtar Gate (B in Fig. 19.2), stood 15 meters (49 feet) high. With its new façade of glazed blue bricks, it seemed almost to be built out of solid lapis lazuli, a shining blue vision. Gleaming lions strode along the walls of the main processional way (D in Fig. 19.2), created out of glazed bricks and molded in relief, brightly colored and seemingly ready to step right out from the walls. The Esagila temple (E and F in Fig. 19.2), home to Marduk, was dominated by its rebuilt ziggurat (E in Fig. 19.2), the base of which extended for about 91.5 meters (300 feet) on each side. It rose in six giant steps, with a shrine to Marduk on the top that was covered in glazed blue bricks.[56]

A century later, Herodotus proclaimed Babylon, as it had been transformed by Nebuchadnezzar, to be the most impressive city he had ever seen. He wrote that "in magnificence there is no other city that approaches to it."[57] This remarkable place was where Adad-guppi and her young son Nabuna'id had been brought to live. For four decades, corvée laborers, deportees, and slaves must have been working in all parts of the city pretty much all the time in order to realize Nebuchadnezzar's dream. How could one not be caught up in the excitement?

Washermen, Weavers, Goldsmiths, and Perfume-Makers

Adad-guppi, however, seems to have taken no pleasure in this renaissance for Babylon. She was in mourning. Sin's image was gone from Harran's Ehulhul temple, which had itself been tragically destroyed in the fighting. She doesn't seem to have blamed the Medes for destroying the image of the god, or the Assyrians for making Harran a target of the attackers by setting up their capital there. Instead, she attributed Sin's disappearance to the moon god's own anger. Her job, as she saw it, was to calm him and to find a way to convince him and his divine spouse to return. She started by depriving herself of luxuries. "In order to appease the heart of my god and my goddess, I did not put on a garment of excellent wool, silver, gold, a fresh garment," she wrote. "I did not allow perfumes (or) fine oil to touch my body."[58] To show her devotion, she was going to live as an ascetic. "I was clothed in a torn garment. My fabric was sackcloth." She devoted herself entirely to the deities, apparently in the forms of their Babylonian statues: "I proclaimed their praises . . . I stood their watch. I served them food."[59]

The list of the luxuries that Adad-guppi renounced reveals a lot about how she had lived in Harran before her world changed: wearing fine clothes made of "excellent wool," adorning herself with jewelry, and using perfume and fine oil for her skin. Since she was a high priestess, her clothing may have resembled that of Ashurbanipal's queen, Liballi-sharrat, which you can see in the relief of the royal couple sitting under the grape arbor, sipping wine (see Fig. 19.3).

Her robe would have been made of a length of wide cloth that she wrapped around herself, somewhat like a sari; the borders were decorated with four strips of delicate embroidery and a fringe. Libbali-sharrat's gown was decorated all over with small circles, probably gold disks. There were parallels for this. Fortunately for us, the pillaging troops who brought an

Fig. 19.3 Close up of Queen Liballi-sharrat of Assyria from the garden scene, North Palace at Nineveh, 645–635 BCE. (© The Trustees of the British Museum)

end to the Neo-Assyrian cities failed to find four royal tombs when they were ransacking everything in sight. These tombs lay hidden under the floor of the palace in Kalhu.[60] They were excavated by Iraqi archaeologists between 1985 and 2001 and proved to be the burial places of several queens of Assyria, still with their treasures intact. Some of the women wore clothing that would have sparkled with small gold appliqués.[61]

Libbali-sharrat wore a dress with three-quarter-length sleeves (also decorated with many rows of patterns, probably in bright colors) underneath the wrapped garment and, on her feet, slippers that covered her toes. Elaborate jewelry adorned her wrists, neck, and ears. The queen's hair was shoulder-length and carefully arranged, and on her head was a "mural" crown, shaped like a city wall. This crown would probably not have been an option for a priestess like Adad-guppi; it seems to have been reserved for royalty.[62] Interestingly, the small mural crown eventually transformed into the stereotypical pointed crown—the type that children now draw to indicate a king. Adad-guppi probably wore a headband of some kind, in place of a crown; almost every high-ranking Assyrian did so.

Behind the formal attire of queens and eminent women, helping to create it, one has to imagine innumerable artisans, craftsmen, and laborers, many of them in the direct employ of the palace or temple. In the Neo-Assyrian and Neo-Babylonian administrative and legal records we can even learn some of their names and the nature of their work.

The manufacture of textiles and clothing had continued to be a defining Mesopotamian art in the Neo-Assyrian and Neo-Babylonian periods. Almost 2,000 years and about eighty generations after the weaving women in Lagash and Ebla had perfected their woolen fabrics, their successors still lived up to their high standards. Female weavers had always been attested in the records, along with men, as producers of such garments.[63] Many of the same procedures that we encountered among earlier textile workers were practiced, but some changes had been made as well. Wool was still generally plucked from sheep and hair from goats, rather than being sheared.[64] It was spun into thread and dyed, but the colors might have been brighter than in the past; the Neo-Assyrian scribes had words for wools that had been dyed in many shades of blue, purple, green, yellow, and red; red wool was mentioned the most often and seems to have been popular. Dyers used alum to set the colors.[65] The textile workers also had a new type of fabric to weave, in addition to linen and wool. This was cotton, though it seems to have been rare. A fragment of it was found in the queens' tombs at Kalhu,[66] and, in recounting the wonders of his gardens and agricultural projects, King Sennacherib claimed that workers "picked trees bearing wool (and) wove (it) into clothing."[67] Since cotton wasn't native to the region, it must have been imported either from South Asia or the Sudan. New styles of fabric had also probably been introduced; the royal weavers came from across the empire, even from as far away as Egypt.[68]

Weavers were organized into teams under a leader known (in rather military fashion) as the "cohort commander of the weavers."[69] One of these "commanders" in the time of Sennacherib was a man named Nabuti.[70] Actually, we know the names of several weavers and "chief weavers," and they were almost all men. They were mentioned not in association with their work, but often because they served as witnesses to legal contracts. One of the few named women from the textile workshops was a supervisor named Damqa.[71]

Royal weavers had access to wools and dyes from many different lands across the empire, and they were understood to be experts on the best raw materials. In one letter written by Sennacherib (before he became king), he mentioned that a shipment of red wool had arrived from one of the provinces. Some local merchants surveyed the wool and chose seven talents (190 kilograms or 420 pounds) of it that they thought good, but the emissaries from the province retorted, "Who do you think you are? You are not to make the selection. Let them take it over and let the king's (female) weavers make the selection over there."[72] The female weavers clearly knew more about the quality of wool than did the merchants.

Creating the intricate borders on clothing was the work of high-ranking specialists, called "weavers of multicolored trim."[73] One such man, Urdaya, witnessed a contract for the sale of a house and was listed first among some very eminent witnesses, including the brother of the mayor and the chief shepherd.[74] He was evidently an important person.

Clothes had to be washed, of course, and, to address this need, washermen ran successful businesses, serving the richest people in the Babylonian cities.[75] The clothes that adorned the sacred statues of the deities themselves were laundered within the temples,[76] but people working in temples (like others in the city) would have needed to have their clothes cleaned as well. Adad-guppi initially pledged to eschew new garments, but presumably she still had to have her clothes cleaned, no matter how simply she was living.[77]

Surprisingly, domestic slaves of the rich didn't do the laundry for the households in which they worked. Washing clothes seems to have been a complicated and specialized process that was best left to professionals.[78] So Adad-guppi would have hired a washerman (they were apparently all men) and set terms with him for a year. Once the agreement had been made, she would have followed millennia-old Mesopotamian legal practice and hired a scribe, brought in some reliable witnesses, and made sure that everything was set down in writing. Afterward, she held on to the contract, in case the washerman failed to complete the work. He presumably had a copy of the contract as well, in case she failed to pay him. Either one of them could have taken the other to court, and some contracts specified the fine that would have to be paid in that case.

For example, late in Adad-guppi's life, a man named Ina-teshi-etir had a business in which he would "clean and whiten the whites" of a Babylonian family for one shekel of silver per year.[79] Several contracts specified this same amount, which seems to have been the going rate for washermen, and this was true for decades,[80] though some were willing not just to clean the whites but "all the laundry and whites" for the same price.[81] Other clients paid the washermen in barley or dates, rather than silver. Some contracts also specified the turnaround time for bringing the laundry back. A tailor who also did washing wrote that "I will clean the dirty clothes by the 10th day of the month . . . and return them."[82] Dealing with "whites" was a big concern. One contract required that the washerman "will make the whites really white."[83]

The washermen came from several different classes in society: enslaved, free but without family names, and free with family names (only people of higher status used family names). The washerman Ina-teshi-etir had a family name; he was described as "son of Iddina of the Hulamishu family."[84] All the washermen, no matter what their status, engaged with their clients in much the same way, drew up similar contracts, and were paid about the same amount, but their businesses might have varied in size.[85] A washerman would have needed at least 12 shekels of silver per year to support a family, so each man must have had at least 12 clients.[86]

Adad-guppi's jewelry, when she lived in Harran, might also have resembled that of Queen Libbali-sharrat. Jewelry of the Neo-Assyrian period was astonishing in its craftsmanship. The royal women buried in Kalhu had been provided with jewelry of extraordinary quality for use in the afterlife: necklaces, earrings, fibulas, finger rings, bracelets, collars, pendants, anklets, and crowns (see Fig. 19.4). The goldsmiths incorporated patterns of granulation, micro-mosaics, gold basketwork, chains, openwork, and several other techniques, all on a miniature scale, in order to create their masterpieces.

Some of the earrings worn by the queens were composed of gold crescent shapes with dangling conical objects looking a little like pine cones.[87] They look exactly like the ones worn by Libbali-sharrat when seated under the grape arbor. The goldsmiths would have been highly trained and, as a result, regarded as higher in status than many other types of artisans.[88] Although the items of jewelry in the tombs at Kalhu were manufactured a couple of centuries before Adad-guppi's lifetime, as a high-ranking priestess she might well have owned similar items.

Goldsmiths in Neo-Assyrian times often worked professionally for a temple or palace, but they could also be hired privately to make jewelry for elite clients.[89] When she was a priestess in Harran, Adad-guppi probably would have been provided with jewelry by the temple goldsmiths, who

Fig. 19.4 Examples of Assyrian bracelets from the Nimrud royal tombs, ninth century BCE. (Barry Iverson/Alamy Stock Photo)

were considered to be consecrated to the god.[90] In Neo-Assyrian palaces as well, the goldsmiths were singled out in the records as directly serving the royal family; they were considered some of the most important of all craftsmen.[91]

The "perfumes" and "fine oil" that Adad-guppi gave up using in Babylon were probably one and the same thing—perfumes at the time were oil-based. The oils were scented with such substances as lavender, rosemary, pine, anise, coriander, juniper, and cinnamon.[92] They were largely made by women,[93] and their manufacture might have been controlled by the Babylonian palace.[94]

Several years after Adad-guppi had arrived in Babylon, during the reign of Nebuchadnezzar II, a scribe created a list of people receiving rations of sesame oil from the palace. It included rations provided for six women described as perfume-makers.[95] The oil was allocated to their supervisor, a man named Nabu-dur-maki. Individuals from across the known world appear on the same tablet along with the perfume-makers, apparently because they were all receiving rations from the palace. There were carpenters and desert patrolmen from Ionia (Greek Asia Minor), messengers "of Daradani," a courtier from Egypt, captives from Elam and Cilicia, 126 people from Tyre, a gardener, an alphabetic scribe, and even a "warden of monkeys."[96] It's a safe guess that the perfumers might also have been foreign to Mesopotamia, even though the text doesn't say so specifically.[97] In fact, an Egyptian perfumer is known from another, earlier document.[98]

For Adad-guppi, personal luxuries were in her past. She had renounced such things and presented herself to the god in sackcloth, unadorned.

Jehoiakin of Judah: Exiles in Babylon

That oil ration list that included the perfumers is of interest for another reason, because it reflects something else that was happening in Babylon: the city had become incredibly cosmopolitan. All those people from Elam, Egypt, Tyre, Ionia, and so on were living side by side in the city. They had arrived as deportees (like Adad-guppi), or immigrants, mercenaries, or traders, some of them employed or supported by the king's court, some not. Presumably they encountered one another in the hallways and streets, talked with one another, and, in the process, learned about one another's cultures. Curiously, though, in its physical structures, Babylon itself remained stubbornly Babylonian. Archaeologists found little evidence of influence from outside. No temples to gods from other lands seem to have been constructed there.[99]

Several people on the oil ration list were described as "Ya'uda," which was the Akkadian spelling of "Judean." Eight of the Judeans were unnamed, one was named Ur-milki, and one was actually their king, Ya'u-kinu, which was the Akkadian spelling of the biblical king Jehoiakin. This is not the only document that listed oil rations for him; three others have also been found. One reads "1 *seah* (of oil) to Jehoiakin, king of J[udah]. 2½ *qu* to 5 sons of the king of Judah. 4 *qu* to 8 Judeans."[100] This represented a substantial amount of oil, and probably meant that Jehoiakin was using his rations to provide for his household as well as himself. The date was preserved on one of the tablets; it was written during Nebuchadnezzar II's thirteenth year.[101] Each time, the female perfume-makers were listed on the same tablets. They seem to have belonged to the same administrative unit in the palace as the exiled Judeans.

Finding references to Jehoiakin and other Judeans living in Babylon during the reign of Nebuchadnezzar II is not a surprise. The Babylonian Chronicles and the biblical book of 2 Kings both explain how the Judeans got there. Early in his reign, Nebuchadnezzar II ran into difficulties with the provinces at the very western edge of his empire, along the Mediterranean coast. In earlier times, these lands had rebelled against their former overlords, the Neo-Assyrian kings, and, finding themselves once again being asked to pay tribute to a very distant emperor, they rebelled again. You remember how the people of Judah had anticipated help from Egypt during the reign of Sennacherib, when the Assyrians laid siege to Lachish? They did the same thing this time. At first, Egypt came to their aid. In 601 BCE, Nebuchadnezzar's fourth year on the throne, according to Babylonian records, he led his troops to the west where they "marched toward Egypt. The king of Egypt heard (of it) and sent out his army; they clashed in an open battle and inflicted heavy losses on each other."[102] This doesn't sound much like a victory for Babylon; the Levantine kings could continue to hope that they could successfully change allegiance.

Nebuchadnezzar II made the same march with his troops two years later, during his sixth year on the throne, and this time he fought in Arabia as well as in the Levant. The army seems to have been more successful than before.

Again, to quote Babylonian records, they "took much booty from the land of the Arabs, (also) their herds and divine images in great number."[103] But Egypt wasn't mentioned again; the pharaohs had apparently given up in their attempt to take over control in the Levant.

Nebuchadnezzar's seventh year, according to Babylonian records, was the decisive moment for Judah. In December 598 BCE, "The king of Akkad moved his army into Hatti land"—Hatti was by now the name used for the Levant, rather than for Anatolia—"laid siege to the city of Judah (Jerusalem) and the king took the city on the second day of the month Addaru." This was March 16, 597 BCE. "He appointed in it a (new) king of his liking, took heavy booty from it and brought it into Babylon."[104] That's all the detail provided in the chronicle; to the Babylonians, Judah was just another western kingdom that needed to be brought back into obedient vassaldom. Two sentences in the chronicle took care of it.

For the Judeans, though, the experience was much more traumatic than those laconic words suggest. As the author of 2 Kings put it: "Nebuchadnezzar himself came up to the city while his officers were besieging it. Jehoiakin king of Judah, his mother, his attendants, his nobles and his officials all surrendered to him."[105] After surrendering, Jehoiakin and the members of his court were taken away as prisoners. Along with much of the population of Judah—10,000 people in all—they were then deported to Babylon.[106] The biblical author noted that "Only the poorest people in the land were left."[107] The author also enumerated the "heavy booty" that had been mentioned in the Babylonian records: "all the treasures from the temple of the Lord and from the royal palace" were seized, along with "all the gold articles that Solomon king of Israel made for the temple of the Lord."[108] These losses must have been devastating to the Judeans.

This was how Jehoiakin and his sons ended up in Babylon, receiving rations from the king alongside other foreigners in the court. The imprisonment of the Judean court seems to have been relatively benign, however. They were well provided for.

The Bible and the Babylonian Chronicles agree that, in the meantime, another king had been appointed to take over from Jehoiakin as the vassal king of Judah—his name was Zedekiah, according to the Bible. Nine years later, Zedekiah also rebelled and once again Nebuchadnezzar and his troops showed up in Judah. This time, his army besieged Jerusalem for eighteen months (though this isn't mentioned in the Babylonian Chronicles).

When the Babylonians finally succeeded in taking Jerusalem, they executed Zedekiah's sons right in front of him, after which the Babylonian commanders blinded and imprisoned the Judean king. The Babylonian army looted all the remaining metal objects from the temple, and then burned down every major building in Jerusalem, including the temple. They "carried into exile the people who remained in the city, along with the rest of the populace."[109] With that, in the summer of 587 BCE, Judah "went into captivity, away from her land."[110]

A similar sequence of events probably happened to any number of cities and kingdoms in the Neo-Babylonian Empire, and the same had been true during the Neo-Assyrian Empire. This particular conquest had a lasting impact on the world, however. The Judean people practiced a singular religion that was focused on the worship of one god, and that was unlike the faiths of the other peoples in the bustling city in which they found themselves. During their exile in Babylonia, the Judeans didn't adopt the worship of Marduk or Nabu or any of the other gods of Mesopotamia, but held on to their belief in one god, and sought to understand their history by assembling the books that became the Hebrew Bible (the Christian Old Testament). Ultimately, of course, the Jewish faith became one of the world's major religions and the earliest of the Abrahamic faiths, later giving rise to Christianity and Islam.

The stories told in the Bible about the Neo-Assyrian and Neo-Babylonian kings provided most of what anyone knew about the ancient Near East for thousands of years, because the ancient cuneiform records had disappeared into the ground, and even those still visible could not be read. This is why we still refer to these kings by their biblical names—Sargon instead of Sharru-ukin, Sennacherib instead of Sin-ahhe-eriba, Nebuchadnezzar instead of Nabu-kudurri-usur, and so on. Even though the kings' actual names were deciphered from cuneiform more than a century and a half ago, the tradition of using the more familiar biblical versions continues.

Jehoiakin lived in Babylon for the rest of his life, as did the other people in exile from Judah. Even the author of the book of 2 Kings acknowledged that Jehoiakin was treated well in the end, though the author's timing of events differs from the evidence supplied by the tablets found in Babylon. The biblical author wrote that Jehoiakin was eventually released from prison, and that the Babylonian king "spoke kindly to him and gave him a seat of honor," that Jehoiakin "for the rest of his life ate regularly at the king's table," and that "the king gave Jehoiakin a regular allowance as long as he lived."[111] The difference is that the Bible puts this release in the thirty-seventh year of Jehoiakin's exile, after the death of Nebuchadnezzar, whereas the ration texts suggest that Jehoiakin's "regular allowance" had been provided by Nebuchadnezzar all along.

Nabu-na'id: An Official Becomes King

Through all of this, Adad-guppi continued to pray to the moon god Sin, though perhaps she relaxed her ascetic strictures after a while. Meanwhile, her son Nabu-na'id received an education and trained to serve as an official.[112] Historian Paul-Alain Beaulieu has drawn some fascinating conclusions about how his education may have had an impact on Nabu-na'id's later career.[113] The curriculum hadn't changed a great deal since the Old Babylonian period when students had studied at schools such as the one in House F at Nippur. Nabu-na'id would have copied a lot of lists— lexical lists, lists of personal names, and syllabaries, among other things— and would have learned some basic mathematics.[114] He then moved on to copying proverbs and, most important, a canon of five specific literary works, which all apprentice scribes in this period seem to have studied.[115] They included a birth legend about Sargon of Akkad, a legend about Naram-Sin, and two letters that purported to be historical but were actually written much later. They all reinforced the idea that kings experienced their successes and their failures as a direct result of the extent to which they obeyed the gods' commands, and several of them did so in the form of kings instructing others about the best way to rule.[116] This was also a theme of the last of the classics that the students studied, one that is much more familiar to us: the Epic of Gilgamesh, the story of the ancient king of Uruk who went on a journey in search of immortality. He, like the other kings in the canonical school texts, ended up recognizing his dependence on the power of the gods and the futility of going against their wishes.

The Gilgamesh Epic that he read was similar to the one that we've already encountered, which was studied by scribal students in the Old Babylonian period.[117] Sometime between 1300 and 1000 BCE, a new version of the epic poem had been compiled, one that, even today, remains stunning in its subtlety and wisdom. A scribe named Sin-leqi-unnini is credited with refining this classic Standard Babylonian version of the epic, but, like his fellow poet Homer, we know little about him. The epic was studied, copied, and translated into different languages. Writing out parts of it became a common assignment in scribal schools.[118]

After finishing his education, Nabu-na'id began working in Nebuchadnezzar's administration and he became a career official, continuing in his position into the reigns of kings who succeeded Nebuchadnezzar. Adad-guppi took credit for her son's success in obtaining the position. She wrote that "I have made Nabu-na'id, the son whom I bore, serve Nebuchadnezzar, son of Nabopolassar, and Neriglissar, king of Babylon, and he performed his duty for them day and night by doing always what was their pleasure."[119] Nabu-na'id, in turn, found some sort of official role for his mother, as she acknowledged: "He also made me a good name before them and they gave me an elevated position as if I were their real daughter."[120] By the time king Nebuchadnezzar II died in 562 BCE, Adad-guppi was eighty-six years old. But she was still going strong, and all this time she had been praying to the moon god Sin to "become reconciled with the temple Ehulhul, the temple of Sin in Harran,"[121] and to return.

The three kings who followed the death of Nebuchadnezzar II all had short reigns. Nebuchadnezzar's son Amel-Marduk ruled for two years (561–560 BCE) before being overthrown by that king's brother-in-law Neriglissar (a general from an Aramean tribe, who was married to a princess, 559–556 BCE).[122] He died after four years on the throne and in turn was succeeded by his son Labashi-Marduk (556 BCE), who ruled for, at most, three months. Labashi-Marduk was killed in a coup, led by a man named Bel-shar-usur. After forty-three years of stability, the Neo-Babylonian Empire had now spent more than six years in turmoil.

And this is where the political history in this chapter meets up with the tale of Adad-guppi, because Bel-shar-usur, the leader of the coup, was her grandson. He didn't personally gain from overthrowing and executing Labashi-Marduk; instead he put his father Nabu-na'id on the throne. You may recognize this king better by the name that the Greeks later gave him: Nabonidus (556–539 BCE). His mother Adad-guppi was now ninety-five years old, according to her own reckoning. After a lifetime of service to the gods, she was suddenly the queen mother and finally in a position to have her dream realized: her son could authorize the creation of new statues of Sin and his divine family, and could commission the restoration of the Ehulhul temple in Harran.

King Nabonidus must have been at least sixty years old. It's surprising that his son Bel-shar-usur (better known as the biblical Belshazzar) didn't take the throne himself. He was probably in his thirties, a much more reasonable age for a new king. But Nabonidus claimed to have experienced a vivid dream in which Sin revealed that he was the one the gods wanted to be king. Dreams provided direct messages from the gods, as we have seen. "Sin called me to kingship," he wrote in an inscription found in Harran. The kingship came with an order: "At midnight he (Sin) made me have a dream and said (in the dream) as follows: 'Rebuild speedily Ehulhul, the temple of Sin in Harran, and I will hand over to you all the countries.'"[123] His mother had a similar revelation, but in her telling, the elderly Nabonidus owed his position exclusively to *her* and her steadfast devotion to the god Sin. She wrote that "Sin, the king of the gods, looked with favor upon me and called Nabonidus, my only son, whom I bore, to kingship and entrusted him with the kingship of Sumer and Akkad, (also of) all the countries from the border of Egypt, on the Upper Sea, to the Lower Sea."[124]

Once he was king, Nabonidus focused a lot of his attention on the gods, and especially on Adad-guppi's patron god, Sin, just as she wanted. He set about the reconstruction of the Ehulhul temple in Harran and the re-creation of statues of the gods. Beaulieu has made the interesting point that the course of Nabonidus's reign bore an uncanny resemblance to the ideal image of a king he would have encountered in the five canonical works from the school curriculum.[125] He seems to have followed the advice of the literary versions of the kings, from Gilgamesh to Naram-Sin to Samsu-iluna, the supposed author of one of the letters the scribes studied. Naram-Sin advised in the mythical text to avoid warfare and live a contemplative life; Nabonidus did the same. He responded to the gods' requests sent through dreams, as in one of the alleged letters between kings. And, as Samsu-iluna had requested in one of the fake letters, Nabonidus restored proper images of the gods to their rightful places and accused others (in his case the Babylonians) of misbehavior and desecration of the gods (in his case, the moon god Sin).[126] His actions were often unpopular, but he may have felt that they were entirely in keeping with the behavior of kings in the past because he had learned these stories in school.

Adad-guppi's Funeral

When Nabonidus had been on the throne for nine years, Adad-guppi finally died, at the age of 102. Before her death, another dream from Sin had reassured her that her life's mission would be accomplished. "In a dream Sin, the king of all the gods, put his hands on me, saying: 'The gods will return on account of you! I will entrust your son, Nabonidus, with the divine residence of Harran; he will restore and make Harran more (beautiful) than it was before! He will lead Sin, Ningal, Nusku, and Sadarnunna in solemn procession into the temple Ehulhul!'"[127]

What a life she had lived. From her days as a priestess in Harran, living in style and dressed in the finest of clothes, to witnessing the destruction of her city and of the gods she loved, to being deported to Babylon, to living as an ascetic in her new city, to taking an official position, and finally to seeing her son become king, it was a tale of grit and devotion. Was it true that Nabonidus became king because of her? It could be. He certainly felt absolutely compelled to restore the Ehulhul temple and its gods. And he gave her a funeral worthy of a woman of her power and influence. A postscript to her autobiography describes it. Nabonidus "laid her body to rest [wrapped in] fine [wool garments and] shining white linen. He deposited her body in a hidden tomb with splendid [ornaments] of gold [set with] beautiful stones . . . expensive stone beads, [containers with] scented oil."[128] In the last years of her life, she had certainly enjoyed all these luxuries, the same ones that she had given up for the gods during her early years in Babylon. She would continue to enjoy the use of them in the afterlife as well, content in the knowledge that Sin, "the king of the gods" (at least to her mind), would be receiving his appropriate recognition and veneration.

Her funeral lasted days. Nabonidus invited guests from across the empire to attend. For the first seven days they mourned, "heads hung low." But after that, everyone present was provided with food and drink, fine oil, "chests with (new) attire," and provisions for their journeys home. Everything seemed to be going just as the gods had willed.

Chapter 20
Brewers, Rebels, and Exorcists

A lot that was written about Nabonidus was penned by his enemies, so he often comes off badly in histories. He was later blamed for the end of the Neo-Babylonian Empire and described as a heretic or even as a madman. I think he would have been surprised and perhaps saddened had he known this. In his own inscriptions he comes off as an earnest and pious man, someone who felt that he was on a mission from the god who had chosen him—the moon god Sin—to ensure Sin's place at the head of the pantheon. Nabonidus wasn't a monotheist; he believed in all the gods. He showed himself in an image on a stone stela venerating the symbols of three deities: Sin, Ishtar, and Shamash (see Fig. 20.1). He did, though, seem to see Sin as embodying the characteristics of several gods. He had a sense of himself not as a revolutionary but as a traditionalist, drawing his inspiration from very ancient practices. He just deeply believed that Sin was the king of all the gods. Had he been successful in persuading his fellow Babylonians about this, perhaps he would have been lauded in the chronicles and described as a prophet who had received and conveyed the true message of the moon god. Nabonidus's problem was that, in Babylonia, Marduk had a very ancient claim to the title of king of the gods, and the Babylonians were not about to change centuries of belief on the basis of the visionary dreams of an elderly king (who was not even a member of the existing royal family) and his even more elderly mother.

Nabonidus of Babylon: The King and the Moon God

One of Nabonidus's first acts was to appoint an *en*-priestess, the high priestess of the moon god, in the city of Ur. He was walking in the steps of

Fig. 20.1 Basalt stela, probably of King Nabonidus of Babylon, with symbols of the gods Sin, Ishtar, and Shamash, 554–539 BCE. (© The Trustees of the British Museum)

Sargon of Akkad in doing so, only Sargon's appointment of Enheduana to that same role had taken place about 1,750 years beforehand. Like Sargon (and after several consultations with diviners), Nabonidus chose one of his daughters for the position and gave her a Sumerian name: En-nigaldi-Nanna, meaning "the high priestess requested by Nanna" (Nanna being the Sumerian name for the moon god, Sin). Imagine if a leader today were to appoint someone to be a Vestal Virgin in Rome or a Grand Preceptor in China, reviving a position that had not existed for centuries. Imagine if he also gave that person a name in an old, dead language and excavated the ancient palace that was the traditional home for someone in that role. You might think this leader was pretty eccentric. But Nabonidus believed it to be the will of the moon god. A text called *Enuma Anu Enlil*, which was already very ancient in his time, included the following omen: "If there is an eclipse of the moon in the month Ululu, (this means that) the god

Sin requests a high-priestess."[1] A lunar eclipse did indeed occur—and in the month of Ululu—during Nabonidus's second year on the throne. A miracle! Nabonidus had no choice; the appointment had to happen. He believed that the moon god was sending him signs confirming his divinely ordained mission.

In an inscription about this appointment he wrote that "I was attentive towards the word of the god Sin, the supreme lord, the god who created me, (and) the command(s) of the gods Shamash and Adad, the lords of divination, and elevated (my) daughter, my own offspring, to the office of *entu*-priestess and (then) I named (her) En-nigaldi-Nanna, as her (new, official) name."[2] En-nigaldi-Nanna had no choice in this matter, but she made the most of her new role.

She could not live in the traditional Gipar palace of the *en*-priestess—it was uninhabitable. As Nabonidus put it, "its site was in ruins and had turned into rubble. Date palms and fruit orchards were growing inside it."[3] One can imagine Nabonidus picking his way among the palms and fruit trees, his eyes scanning the ground, looking for the remnants of the ancient walls of the palace. As a result of the love for antiquity that he shared with his predecessor Nebuchadnezzar, Nabonidus often expressed his excitement about finding ancient objects during rebuilding projects.

When reconstructing the Ebabbar temple in Sippar, he wrote that he "discovered inside it an inscription of Hammurabi, a king of the past who came before me, <who> for the god Shamash had built Ebabbar and the ziggurat (precisely) on the original foundation(s) 700 years before Burna-Buriash."[4] Nabonidus saw himself as the successor to these Babylonian kings of the past—Hammurabi whose laws were still studied, and Burna-Buriash, one of the great kings of the brotherhood of the Late Bronze Age. To have found an actual inscription of Hammurabi? That was a thrill. He wrote, "Then, my heart was happy (and) my face beamed." Showing immense respect for the ancient architecture and the kings who had commissioned it, he made sure that his own architects followed the exact footprint of the ancient walls. He had the new walls built "not a fingerbreadth outside or inside" the foundations constructed by Hammurabi.

As he searched for the walls of the ancient Gipar palace, he was no doubt looking for old inscriptions and objects there as well. To his delight, he found them. "I discovered inside it inscription(s) of ancient kings of the past. I (also) discovered an ancient inscribed object of Enanedu, *entu*-priestess of

Ur, daughter of Kudur-mabuk, sister of Rim-Sin, king of Ur, who had renewed the Gipar palace and restored it."⁵ This object confirmed that the priestesses had indeed lived here, and in fact that Enanedu herself (not her brother, surprisingly) had restored the palace in the time of King Rim-Sin I of Larsa in the early eighteenth century BCE. "Then," he wrote proudly, "I rebuilt the Gipar palace anew as (it had been) in ancient times."

When Woolley was excavating in Ur, he found yet more evidence for the antiquarian passions of Nabonidus and his family. In a building that seems to have been the new Gipar, built by Nabonidus for his daughter En-nigaldi-Nanna, Woolley uncovered some surprising objects, all lying together: a stone *kudurru* from the Kassite period, an arm of a statue with an inscription of King Shulgi from the Ur III period, a foundation cone from the Old Babylonian period, and a very ancient stone mace head.

Near them was a small clay cylinder, 10.8 centimeters (4.25 inches) high, inscribed with copies of an Old Babylonian period inscription written in Sumerian followed by a Neo-Babylonian explanation written in Akkadian: "Copy of a baked brick from the rubble in Ur, deeds of Amar-Suen, King of Ur"⁶ (see Fig. 20.2). It went on to explain that the copied brick had been found "in the search for the ground plan of the Ekishnugal (temple) by Sin-balassu-iqbi, governor of Ur." After Sin-balassu-iqbi found the brick, he had given it to a lamentation priest of the moon god, who "has inspected and written (it) out for observation." Woolley concluded that these objects had been curated by the priestess En-nigaldi-Nanna as a kind of ancient museum display.⁷ If you search for En-nigaldi-Nanna's name online you will find her listed on several sites as the founder of the "first museum." Clearly though, if these objects were indeed gathered for display, this wouldn't have been a museum that was open to the public. It was a private collection of ancient objects that had been found during the renovation of the Ekishnugal temple—the temple to the god Sin. It was more a "cabinet of curiosities" than a museum in the modern sense.

Even if it wasn't exactly a museum, its existence fits well with Nabonidus's enthusiasm for ancient objects. He would have loved the chance to look over the artifacts and ponder his connection to their age-old makers. It was Nabonidus who had preserved the statue of Enmetena, the Early Dynastic king of Lagash, that we encountered in Chapter 3. The Mesopotamians had always wanted ancient objects to be preserved and displayed, especially when the ancient objects were statues of former kings. For example, Zimri-Lim

Fig. 20.2 Clay cylinder with a copy of a Sumerian brick inscription, found in Ur, 556–539 BCE. (© The Trustees of the British Museum)

at Mari had been joined in his throne room by the statues of kings going back hundreds of years. And scribes had copied inscriptions from ancient stelas and tablets at least since the time of Sargon of Akkad, adding notes about where the original inscriptions were to be found (just like the label to Amar-Suen's brick inscription in the Gipar) and keeping the clay copies that they had made. Their efforts, as we have seen repeatedly in this book, were largely responsible for the preservation of any number of texts that would otherwise have been lost.

In the same inscription in which Nabonidus described the appointment of En-nigaldi-Nanna as priestess and the restoration of the Gipar palace, he also listed the staff of the moon god's temple in Ur (and other temples in the city) and boasted that he had released these workers from corvée labor and service obligations.[8] They would be free to focus on taking care of the moon god. To his mind they deserved this, given that Sin was the greatest of all gods. The list of workers provides a fascinating window into a temple's personnel, the people who were present in the building daily in service to the deity.

A number of different types of priests head the list: the *ramku*-priests, the *enu*-priest, the purification priest, and the *zabarbaddu* official. (This man held an archaic title that had not been used since the Old Babylonian period—even in naming the positions of his temple administrators, Nabonidus was looking back in time for his inspiration.)[9] They were followed by a mix of officials and people working in service positions. Helping to run the temple every day and to provide for the gods were "the brewer, the cook, the miller, . . . the builder, the courtyard sweeper, the head doorkeeper."[10] These men prepared the food and drink for the temple, maintained the property, and provided security. The list also included "the singers who please the heart(s) of the gods." As in the Early Dynastic period and the kingdom of Mari, where we have encountered such singers before (and, for that matter, in all eras of ancient Near Eastern history), music was as important to the happiness of the gods as food and drink.

Those food and drink preparers—the brewer, the cook, the miller—they were practicing culinary professions that, by Nabonidus's time, had a pedigree of at least 2,500 years, if not longer. You may remember Kushim, the controller of the barley warehouse in Uruk, way back when syllabic writing had first developed, around 3100 BCE.[11] He too worked for a temple, managing the ingredients for beer making, while also distributing jars of beer.

Beer had always been essential to life in this region. In the Neo-Babylonian period, a list of the basic necessities of life consisted of "bread, beer, salt, cress, oil, and garments."[12] By the time of Nabonidus, barley beer, of the kind that had been a staple in earlier times, was mostly consumed by the deities (and their temple staffs). At this point, most people outside the temples drank beer made of fermented dates.[13] They drank at home and at work, because beer was still a vital part of the Babylonian diet, but they also drank in inns and taverns. It was expected that an adult would consume a lot of beer: from one to three liters a day.[14] Although drunkenness was mentioned sometimes, it was not common; their beer must not have had a high alcohol content.

The Sahit-gines and the Egibis: Rich Temple Families in Sippar and Babylon

By the sixth century BCE, a powerful person in Babylonia often had the equivalent of a surname, which was usually the name of a long-past founder of the family. Just as behind every modern O'Reilly there was some original man named "Reilly," and behind every "Fernandez" an original "Fernando," so a whole lot of people in Babylon had, for example, the family name Egibi, because they shared an ancestor who bore that name. There were many other such families. High positions in the temples were dominated by these powerful families, and for their incomes they owned "prebends"—entitlements to particular roles within a temple that assured a continued income and association with that temple. Often a specific named family monopolized the prebends for one role, such as that of the bakers or brewers, or for a higher role such as the head of the bakers or head of the brewers. Lists were drawn up of the people who owned particular prebends and the rights to the income that came from them. But a prebend had, over time, become something you could sell, lend, sublet, or swap, so that you could make money from a prebend without actually having to do the job associated with it.[15] This system also provided these elite families with even more opportunities to gain wealth.

The temple families tended to have Babylonian names and they were proud of their local roots. They seem to have resisted adopting Aramaic, which was fast becoming the main spoken and written language of much of the Near East. Instead, they probably spoke Akkadian and they continued to write in Akkadian using cuneiform on clay tablets. This means that many of their records survive.

People who worked outside the temples and who weren't involved in the vast undertakings of the gods' estates tended not to have family names, they came from many different places, and they almost certainly used Aramaic as a lingua franca, no matter what their native languages might have been. Although they probably wrote many documents on papyrus or leather, which have since disintegrated, they still had a lot of their contracts and other records set down in the traditional way, in Akkadian on clay (though sometimes they added notes in Aramaic on the edges).[16]

I mentioned the Egibi family because members of that family went into business and ended up dominating the beer trade (along with several other enterprises). Beer was profitable and was one of the major businesses of the era, both for local consumption and probably for external trade as well.[17] Another powerful family, this one in Sippar, was named not for an ancestor but for their traditional vocation. They were the Sahit-gine family; Sahit-gine meant "oil presser of the regular offerings."[18] As the name suggests, they owned the prebends for pressing oil to be used in offerings in the

Ebabbar temple.[19] The family had migrated to Sippar from Babylon, but they kept close ties to their ancestral home city.[20] They were unusual in that they were able to move up into an elite level of the temple hierarchy without losing their ties to the Sippar business district. Like the Egibis, they got involved in the making and selling of beer.

A powerful man usually had three names—a personal name, a patronym (the name of his father), and a family name, each of which was (as always) a short sentence or clause. One of the men we will be meeting was known as Bel-uballit, son of Iqisha, of the Sahit-gine (oil pressers) family. The other was Itti-Marduk-balatu, son of Nab-ahhe-iddin, of the Egibi family. Both of these men began their business careers during the reign of Nabonidus and both made money from beer. These two men do seem to have been aware of one another, even though they lived in different cities and came from different families.[21]

Bel-uballit: Oil Presser, Brewer, and Temple Functionary

Soon after he married a woman named Bu'itu, Bel-uballit's business was thriving in his family's adopted city of Sippar, and at that point he seems mostly to have been involved in the oil and textile industries.[22] It was the middle of the reign of Nabonidus. Sippar, as you may recall, was upstream from Babylon, on the road to the north from Ur and other southern cities. Textile traders had passed through there on their way to Ashur more than a thousand years earlier, when Sippar had been home to the entrepreneurial *naditum* women, with their trading connections to Susa in Iran. In Nabonidus's time it was still a center for trade between Mesopotamia and the rest of the Near East.

The harbor on the river at Sippar buzzed with activity; merchants from all over the Neo-Babylonian Empire and beyond lived and worked there. There were people from Iran, Judah, Syria, and Egypt as well as from Mesopotamia, some of them travelers, others merchants, brewers, and entrepreneurs, many of them storing and selling their goods in warehouses near the river.[23] You might see a donkey caravan loading up with a shipment of cloth caps for the army, ready to be transported to the town of Humadeshu (near Persepolis) in Iran,[24] or a boat returning with a batch of old beer vats (proudly described as being "without damage or leaks") to a brewer.[25] Every transaction required witnesses, whose names were listed on the tablets that scribes drew up by the hundreds. The community was clearly close-knit. They engaged in the same kinds of transactions as one another, witnessed one another's contracts, and shared storage locations for their archives.[26] Their names generally didn't include a family name; most of the merchants and traders were not from the elite families.[27]

Bel-uballit and his family members could be frequently spotted at the harbor, conducting business, but they also owned significant amounts of real estate and were members of the rarefied world of the Ebabbar temple.[28] Bel-uballit was able to move up in Sippar society, partly because of his prebend as an oil presser for the temple, and partly because he married a woman from an influential family. His wife Bu'itu had been born into the highest ranks of the Sippar temple community—men in her family held the prestigious position of "head of the temple enterers."[29] A son from Bel-uballit's marriage to Bu'itu later inherited a prebend from his grandmother on his mother's side: he too became a "temple enterer." Unusually for someone with such a role, this son continued to participate actively in the trade of the Sippar harbor.[30]

But long before this, in 547 and 546 BCE (the ninth and tenth years of Nabonidus's reign) Bel-uballit spent a fortune on wool. On one occasion he bought c. 900 kilograms (c. 2,000 pounds) of wool for 4 minas 33⅓ shekels of silver.[31] This was a huge investment, but presumably he knew that it would pay off. He would have hired women, who worked in their homes, to spin and weave the wool into textiles that he then sold. We know that the wife of one of Bel-uballit's relatives ran this type of operation, so it's entirely possible that women in Bel-uballit's family did the same.[32] (A few decades later, in 520 BCE, Bel-uballit owned a herd of sheep and goats of his own, so at that point he probably didn't need to purchase the wool for his textile operation.)[33]

Bel-uballit may already have been exploring opportunities in the beer brewing business, even during the reign of Nabonidus. We know that he was trading in large amounts of dates, and the main reason for buying or selling dates at this point was for making beer.[34] Later in his life, he was definitely in the beer business: he went into partnership with two other men to run a brewery. One man, a professional merchant, provided a house in which the business would have its home, as a brewery and warehouse, and perhaps as a tavern or inn as well. A second man contributed dozens of beer vats and invested five minas of silver—a significant sum. He also pledged the women of his family to be employees of the firm: his wife, daughters, and female slaves. Bel-uballit contributed 100 more beer vats than his partner, along with another five minas of silver.[35] They had what they needed to make the enterprise a success. Beer could be a big money-maker. Everyone drank it.

Nabu-utirri, Mizatu, and Itti-Marduk-balatu: Brewers and a Businessman

In order to learn more about the social world surrounding beer, we need to move south to the capital city, Babylon. Around the time that Bel-uballit was beginning his business career, starting in the fourteenth year of the reign of Nabonidus, two slaves belonging to the businessman Itti-Marduk-balatu (of the Egibi family) were busy setting up a lucrative business, brewing and selling beer in Babylon.[36]

These slaves were a married couple: the husband, Nabu-utirri, took on many responsibilities as an agent working for Itti-Marduk-balatu—dealing with his master's business associates and also engaging in transactions of his own.[37] His wife Mizatu worked with him in the brewery, but enslaved women like her almost never worked as agents for their owners in this era.[38] Nabu-utirri and Mizatu were regularly referred to as slaves in the documents, but they had considerable autonomy. They lived in their own house, for which they paid rent, and they controlled most of the profits from their brewing business. The couple may have produced both date beer for customers and barley beer for religious purposes.

Babylonian date beer probably tasted very different from modern beer. Not only was it not made from grain, it also wasn't flavored with hops (which were not introduced into beer until the Middle Ages in Europe). In fact, although the Babylonians used the same term for both barley and date beer, the version made from dates was probably more like hard cider.[39]

The closest thing that survives to a Mesopotamian beer recipe is a hymn to Ninkasi, the goddess of beer. Just as beer was one of the most ancient inventions of the Sumerians, so was Ninkasi one of the most ancient goddesses.[40] As always, we are indebted to scribes for making copies of the hymn in school. They weren't particularly reverent as they wrote—they paired the hymn, in their exercises, with a drinking song dedicated to a woman innkeeper.[41] The hymn was written hundreds of years before Nabu-utirri and Mizatu opened their brewery, and it's about the brewing of barley beer. (Several enterprising modern brewers have tried reproducing Mesopotamian beer from the description in the hymn.)[42]

The hymn lists the stages in making barley beer, each time noting "(Goddess) Ninkasi you are the one who" takes care of each step. First the dough (bappir) was made, and mixed "in a pit . . . with sweet aromatics."[43] The aromatics were herbs of various kinds.[44] Then the dough was baked "in a big oven."

Meanwhile, "piles of hulled grain" were created, covered in earth, and watered in order to make them germinate. These were then soaked in a jar, and presumably heated (though this isn't mentioned in the hymn as a specific step). The resulting "cooked mash" was spread "on large reed mats" to be cooled and dried. This was the malt.

The wort was then brewed "with honey (and) wine" and fermented in a fermenting vat. "The fermenting vat . . . makes a pleasant sound; you place (it) appropriately on (top of) a large collector vat." This suggests that the liquid from the fermenting vat could filter down into the collecting vat—the fermenting vat must have had holes in its base. Finally, the beer was ready. The author of the hymn wrote, appreciatively, that when "the filtered beer . . . (pours out) of the collector vat, it is (like) the onrush of the Tigris and the Euphrates." The beer must have been a lot sweeter than modern beer, given the honey that was incorporated into the recipe.

Date beer would have been simpler. Scholars who tried making it, following a later Greek recipe from the first century CE, used nothing but water and dates. They found that the resulting drink had a pleasant acidic taste and, surprisingly, wasn't sweet.[45]

In 541 BCE, Nabu-utirri and Mizatu were able to earn 5.5 minas of silver as a result of their brewery—a very healthy profit—of which they paid one-sixth to their master.[46] Nabu-utirri used the rest of the profits to finance other operations, including lending silver, dates, and barley to other slaves and to free individuals, and, in one instance, renting a boat and hiring a pilot for it.[47] Boats were almost always associated with trade, so perhaps he needed the boat to ship some of his beer to another city to sell it there. Nabu-utirri, himself a slave, had even purchased two slaves during Nabonidus's thirteenth year—a woman and her son.[48] We know nothing else about them, but perhaps they came to be involved in the beer business as well. Most of the tablets pertaining to Nabu-utirri show him acting almost completely independently. He was not legally free, but he had the kinds of responsibilities taken on by free businessmen and also had the opportunity to make and keep his own money. Sometimes, though, he did need his master's help, for example when a man died who still owed him money. Itti-Marduk-balatu imposed some control that way, setting limits on what Nabu-utirri could do.[49]

Nabu-utirri also rented several properties.[50] One of these houses, perhaps the one in which he and his wife ran their beer business, was owned by a man and two women from a wealthy family. Nabu-utirri, according to his contract, was required to "build a reed hut in front of the gate, together (?) with an exit (?), and must spread clay on the roof."[51] His construction work was considered to be worth four shekels and was put toward the year's rent. It's tempting to see the reed hut in front of the gate of the house as a place where they sold beer, though that's just a guess.

In this contract scholars have found a distant connection between Bel-uballit in Sippar and Itti-Marduk-balatu in Babylon: the owners of the house that Itti-Marduk-balatu's slaves rented in Babylon were members of the Sippar family of Bel-uballit (the Sahit-gines). It makes you wonder if the two men were aware of one another, if, perhaps through mutual friends, the men knew that they were both venturing into the beer trade, in different cities—Bel-uballit on his own in Sippar, Itti-Marduk-balatu, through the efforts of Nabu-utirri and Mizatu, in Babylon.

Ina-qate-Nabu-bultu: A Baker

Itti-Marduk-balatu might have had trouble keeping track of all his ventures and investments. He was a very rich man. He ran many businesses and owned sixteen houses and about 100 slaves, who constituted as many as eighteen different families.[52] Most of his slaves had probably been born into slavery, and specifically into his household.[53] Generations of enslaved people worked for generations of the same family. But Itti-Marduk-balatu had also purchased slaves on occasion, sometimes whole families of individuals, who had often been captured as prisoners of war. In one instance another wealthy man "sold to Itti-Marduk-balatu . . . his slave woman Nana-ittiya and her daughter of three months, an Egyptian from the booty of the bow, for two minas of silver as the full price."[54] Nana-ittiya and her baby daughter, already so far from their home in Egypt, now joined a new household. They almost certainly never saw their homeland again.

Itti-Marduk-balatu didn't just buy slaves, he traded them as well. There's little evidence for professional slave traders in this era,[55] but a wealthy man like Itti-Marduk-balatu sometimes used his slaves the way he used some of his other possessions, at one point paying a seller for a house not with silver but with an enslaved family of a woman and her two daughters.[56] The Egyptian woman Nana-ittiya and her baby could have been in this situation, shuffled from one household to another, like so many bushels of barley.

So, what was life like for enslaved people? It's a little hard to tell, because they didn't write about it, and experiences would have varied considerably from one person to another. But we can reconstruct some details from the contracts that survive.

A baby boy born to an enslaved couple belonging to Itti-Marduk-balatu (or any other rich man like him) grew up knowing no other life. The baby probably had siblings, and he lived in a house in Babylon, perhaps a house rented by his parents (like the one rented by the brewers Nabu-utirri and Mizatu). It's unlikely that he saw his owner often as he was growing up—a whole hierarchy of members of the enslaved community separated him from the family that controlled his fate. Between the ages of two and four, his parents settled on a name for him. One such boy was given the name Ina-qate-Nabu-bultu (this was quite a mouthful; he probably had a nickname).[57] At some point, he went through the (presumably painful) process of having his owner's name tattooed on his hand.[58] Ina-qate-Nabu-bultu was someone's property, that was something he could never forget; it was right there on his skin. He would have lived with his mother until he reached an age when he could be put to work.[59]

There must have been endless jobs that needed to be done within the sixteen households owned by Itti-Marduk-balatu. Food and drink had to be made, clothes to be sewn, rooms to be cleaned (though, still, laundry seems to have been sent out to washermen). Although the family owned fields and date orchards, few of the slaves were involved in agriculture. That was still the realm of tenant farmers, as it had been during the Neo-Assyrian Empire.[60] It was decided that Ina-qate-Nabu-bultu was to be trained for a specific profession. Some of his friends and relatives in the household might have been apprenticed to weavers, shoemakers, or other craftsmen.[61] Ina-qate-Nabu-bultu would become a baker. Slavery was so pervasive in the society that the experienced baker under whom he trained was also a slave. The contract for his apprenticeship was drawn up in the year 534 BCE: "Ina-qate-Nabu-bultu, the slave belonging to Itti-Marduk-balatu, has been placed at the disposal of Reheti, the slave of Basya, to be taught the baker's trade. . . . He must teach him the baker's trade in its entirety before the month of Arahsamnu."[62] If Reheti failed to train the boy within fifteen months, he had to pay a fine.

And, from then on, Ina-qate-Nabu-bultu had a profession. He probably baked bread throughout his whole life and may periodically have been hired out to other families.[63] Unlike the beer made by the brewers Nabu-utirri and Mizatu, the breads made by Ina-qate-Nabu-bultu weren't for sale. Most people who worked as slaves produced goods only for the household in which they worked.[64]

Were they unhappy? The fact that enslaved people ran away, just as they had in the Ur III period, suggests that freedom was always preferred. But, surprisingly, there is little evidence for slaves rebelling in this era,[65] and there's no indication that runaway slaves were punished, or that any slaves were physically restrained.[66] Enslaved workers were contracted for their labor and benefited to some extent from the profits they realized, which may have made life bearable.[67] Of course, it could be that records of mistreatment just didn't survive. But based on the lack of evidence, one can hope that they were treated humanely.

Ishunnatu: An Innkeeper

In 524 BCE, a decade after Ina-qate-Nabu-bultu started his apprenticeship as a baker, an enslaved woman from his same household was put in charge of a new venture by their owner Itti-Marduk-balatu. Her name was Ishunnatu. I wonder what it was about her that made her stand out from the rest of the household, that made her seem like the exact person for Itti-Marduk-balatu to invest in. Whatever it was, she proved him right.

His family, the Egibis, had been expanding their operations for some time into Kish, the ancient city just 15 kilometers (9 miles) to the east of Babylon. Kish had benefited from Nebuchadnezzar II's urban beautification campaign—many buildings there had been restored and improved at the same time that the king had been focusing on Babylon. The city had two main tells. One was known as Kish proper; the other, adjacent to it, was Hursagkalama. The latter was where the Egibi family began to invest. Itti-Marduk-balatu owned a house there, and in the sixteenth year of Nabonidus (540 BCE) he rented it to his brother, who used it as a base for his business.[68] Sixteen years later, the enslaved woman Ishunnatu moved to Hursagkalama to open a brewery and inn.

The inn wasn't new. Another man had been running it and, to help with the transition in ownership, he lent all the furniture and equipment to Ishunnatu for two and a half months. On the eleventh day of the month Kislimu (late November to us), Ishunnatu met with the previous innkeeper right there in the inn in Hursagkalama, along with three male witnesses (all from influential families) and a scribe named Kalbaia, who wrote down the contract between them. It was in Ishunnatu's name; her owner Itti-Marduk-balatu wasn't even mentioned, though he does seem to have been present.[69]

There were three parts to the inn, and the contents of each were listed. Perhaps the group walked from room to room as she inspected the items that she would be using, and the scribe wrote them all down. In the bar, an intimate place that seated just a few people, were three tables, ten chairs, and a lampstand. This was where customers gathered to drink beer and talk. In the mid-sixth century BCE, to judge from the documents that survive, bars seem to have been no more dangerous or notorious than pubs are today in Britain, or coffee shops around the world. They were social gathering spots.

In the second part of the establishment, the brewery, the previous innkeeper left Ishunnatu a fermenting vat, a vessel stand, and a decanting vat.[70] Here she would be brewing the beer for her customers. The dates, water, and *kasu* flavoring would be left to stand for perhaps eleven days in the fermenting vat,[71] after which she would filter it into the decanting vat. She also received an iron hoe, probably for her vegetable garden,[72] along with a kettle, an ax, and three knives, perhaps for cooking.

And in the third part, the inn, the former proprietor let her use his five beds for her guests. Exactly what a bed looked like at this point is unclear.

In the late sixth century, kings had wooden beds, but a "bed" for someone outside the palace might simply have been a rug.[73]

Many stories have been spun from the mention of these five beds. Some earlier scholars jumped to the conclusion that Ishunnatu ran a brothel, and even that she was, herself, a prostitute. But nothing at all in the documentation backs that up. Had she been a sex worker, they had a term that would have been used to describe her, and the scribe would have used it. He didn't. There's no more reason to assume that an inn was a brothel than would be true of a small hotel today.[74] Travelers needed places to stay; this had always been true. And an inn providing food and beer was an ideal place to also provide beds for travelers to spend the night. Innkeepers were sometimes women and sometimes men. There is no reason to project modern stereotypes about the past onto Ishunattu's venture.

In addition to the furniture and equipment lent by the previous innkeeper, on that same day, in front of the same witnesses and recorded by the same scribe, Ishunnatu also received a valuable gift from Itti-Marduk-balatu: "50 vats of fine beer," "10,800 liters of dates" for brewing more of it, and "720 liters of kasu" for flavoring the beer. Kasu was only used in beer making and was probably the term for a type of the herb dodder called cuscuta, which grew wild, creeping like a weed around other plants.[75] He also gave her bronze kettles, cups, and bowls for serving.[76] Each vat held 180 liters of beer, so she could have opened her inn that very day if she wanted to. She already had 9,000 liters of beer ready for customers before she even began fermenting the dates to make more.[77]

After the first few months she had to return the prior innkeeper's furniture and equipment to him. By that time she had presumably earned enough from her own enterprise to be able to afford to buy replacements for them. But perhaps some of her friends or customers pitched in to help. A third, undated contract, lists items that were "made available to Ishunnatu" (though the donor isn't listed) in the presence of different witnesses. They were just the things she needed: beds, chairs, a table, a vat for beer, a vat for water, a fermentation vat, and a rack, perhaps for holding jars.[78]

In any event, Ishunnatu would have been experienced in brewing and ready to serve beer to her customers, to put them up for the night if they needed a place to stay, and perhaps also to serve simple meals. She had to pay Itti-Marduk-balatu some of her profits, but he mostly seems to have left her alone to her entrepreneurial success. And after he died, Ishunnatu continued to run her business, now overseen by Itti-Marduk-balatu's son, who had a typically long Babylonian name but went by the nickname Shirku.[79] In 520 BCE Ishunnatu received a payment of 1,800 liters of dates that she used, in turn, to pay for a new decanting vat,[80] and at some other time she borrowed 10,800 liters of dates for some unspecified reason that had to be brought back, perhaps to Babylon "on the canal."[81] She agreed to pay the transportation costs.

Ishunnatu's inn seems to have been a success. Like Nabu-utirri and Mizatu, several decades earlier, her status as a slave seems to have had little impact on her business or her ability to manage it independently. Itti-Marduk-balatu gave the proprietors of both of these beer establishments plenty of freedom, contenting himself with taking some of the profits.

Cyrus of Persia: Empire Builder and Propagandist

One has the impression that life stayed very much the same in Babylon, Kish, and Sippar between around 545 and 520 BCE. The archives of Itti-Marduk-balatu and Bel-uballit continued through the decades as their businesses grew. Sometimes they experienced small setbacks and recovered, and gradually their sons took over more of the work, but, to judge from the archives that they kept of their business activities, their world hadn't changed.

Except that, in fact, it had. Falling right in the middle of those years of brewing beer, making loans, serving customers, and renting houses, was one of the Big Years in world history: 539 BCE. That was when the Persian Empire conquered Babylonia, the Neo-Babylonian Empire came to an end, and Mesopotamia, for the first time ever, began to be ruled by a king who had not been born there, who didn't even live there. This was Cyrus II, and he, in turn, is one of the Big Names of world history. His story is told in almost every survey of ancient history. He was the king of a dynasty known as the Achaemenids (from the name of the founder, Achaemenes), who started building the Persian Empire, which became the largest empire that had ever been known on Earth. Cyrus styled himself as a kind and tolerant man and drew contrasts between himself and the supposedly extremist king of Babylon who had preceded him, namely Nabonidus.

Cyrus was featured in the book on the Persian Wars written by Herodotus, the Greek "father of history," and he was viewed favorably by writers in the Bible, who asserted that Cyrus had been chosen by God. He was the only person from outside the Judean community to receive the title of "messiah" from any biblical author. He reversed the practice of deporting conquered peoples and instead allowed former deportees to return to their homelands. Among these were the Jews, who were permitted to leave Babylon and to return to Jerusalem to rebuild their temple. An inscription that Cyrus commissioned, known as the Cyrus Cylinder, has sometimes been described as the first statement of human rights (though the abstract concept of human rights did not develop for a long time after this).[82] A replica of the Cylinder is displayed at the headquarters of the United Nations.

But, to Itti-Marduk-balatu, Cyrus seems to have been just another king, another reason for the dating system to go back to year one; in the business documents written in Babylon and Kish, "Cyrus year 1" followed "Nabonidus year 17" without so much as a comment. In the past, the collapses of some ancient states in the Near East had left great swaths of devastation that affected almost everyone. This was true when the Late Bronze Age powers came to an end in the twelfth century BCE and when the Neo-Assyrian Empire was conquered in 609 BCE. But when the Third Dynasty of Ur was replaced by the First Dynasty of Isin, for example, people living under its rule could have been forgiven for not noticing it at all. The same seems to have been true of the switch from rule by the Neo-Babylonian kings to rule by the Persian kings, at least at first. To the average person living in Babylon, Ur, or Sippar, Cyrus's takeover may even have seemed like a return to stability after the uncertainties of Nabonidus's somewhat erratic regime.

We should go back in time in order to understand why this might have been true. Nabonidus, as you know, was singularly obsessed with restoring the temple in his hometown of Harran. In 556 BCE, once he had become king, just one obstacle stood in his way of completing this project, but it was a big one. He didn't actually control Harran. It was in the region of the former Assyrian Empire that was now ruled by the Medes. He couldn't send construction teams to a city in another state, or command the king of the Medes to follow his directions. The temple would remain unrestored unless he gained control of Harran.

The Medes were clearly a major power—they had, after all, made an important contribution to the fall of Assyria—but we can see them only through the texts written by others; not a single Median document has ever been recovered. They always seem to be out of focus, just beyond our line of sight. They spoke an Indo-European language and had been mentioned in Assyrian records since the ninth century BCE. Their capital city was at Ecbatana, modern Hamadan, in a mountainous region of western Iran. But how big was their empire during the reign of Nabonidus? How powerful an army did their king command? How difficult would it have been for Nabonidus to take them on? We don't know. And he was in no mood to attack the Medes, anyway.

As it happened, an ambitious young king named Cyrus (559–530 BCE) had recently come to the throne in Persia. This land adjoined the eastern shores of the Persian Gulf and comprised what had previously been called Anshan in Elam, to the south and east of Mesopotamia. Like the Medes, the Persians spoke an Indo-European language. They ended up playing such a huge role in history that it's hard to remember that around 550 BCE Persia was not a powerful kingdom at all. The apparently nomadic Persians had arrived in Anshan only about a century before, and they didn't displace the local population. Most people living in Persia continued to speak their own language of Elamite, though Aramaic was gaining speakers, as it had across the Neo-Assyrian Empire. The land wasn't even called Persia right away, Cyrus was "king of Anshan."[83]

When Cyrus became king, his land, like Harran, was subject to the Medes, and perhaps Nabonidus sent envoys to his court to encourage him to lead a force against his overlords. An alliance may even have developed between the elderly Babylonian king and the upstart Persian.[84] Whether inspired by Nabonidus or not, Cyrus did rebel and, by 550 BCE, he had replaced the king of the Medes as ruler of their empire, at which point Harran fell into Nabonidus's hands, and both men were presumably happy with the outcome. Nabonidus commissioned the construction to begin on the temple to the moon god Sin. Cyrus, meanwhile, now ruled all the lands that had been subject to the Medes, including the northern lands of Urartu and central Anatolia.

When Croesus, the king of Lydia, in western Anatolia, tried to claim some lands beyond the river Halys, Cyrus marched his troops there, to his far western border, to fight back. They were successful and, in 547 BCE, the

Persians took control of Lydia as well. Lydia was a rich place, with gold mines and an opulent capital city called Sardis. Lydia is also notable as the place where coins were first minted. Once coinage had developed it spread widely, not least through the Persian Empire that Cyrus was building.[85] People had paid for goods with silver for more than a thousand years before this, but the silver had to be weighed each time. A stamped coin was much easier to manage. Although it took Cyrus's troops several years to fully subdue rebellions in Lydia, the region became a source of considerable wealth for the growing empire.

You might think that all this would have worried Nabonidus. His Neo-Babylonian empire lay just to the south of Cyrus's growing empire, and Cyrus was showing no signs of feeling that he had done enough expanding.

Here's the odd thing, though. Through all of this, Nabonidus was away from Babylon. He wasn't on campaign; he was just living somewhere else. He'd been gone since 553 BCE, just three years into his reign. He was away when he made the agreement with Cyrus (if indeed that is what happened), away when Cyrus conquered the Medes, away when he himself authorized construction of a new temple in Harran (apparently not even going there to visit his mother's beloved home city), away when his mother Adad-guppi died during his ninth year on the throne, away when her elaborate burial took place, away when Cyrus conquered Lydia.

This was not something that Babylonian kings were in the habit of doing. They normally lived in Babylon, maintaining their administrations in the fortress-like palace there, close to Marduk, their god, and available to participate in all the rituals that marked the seasons. The Akitu festival, which took place in spring at the celebration of the new year, was particularly important. Babylonians believed that its enactment helped ensure the continued order of the universe. Year after year, though, in the absence of Nabonidus, the Babylonian Chronicles noted that the Akitu festival did not take place. Nabonidus had left his thoroughly competent son Belshazzar in charge in Babylon when he left, but Belshazzar wasn't the king. He could run the government, but he couldn't enact the Akitu festival. And, given the amount of military activity going on beyond the Babylonian borders, Nabonidus had even more reason to be present and visible in his city.

So, where was Nabonidus all this time? In his inscriptions he wrote that he was in northern Arabia, mostly in a city called Tayma. Archaeological excavations there have backed up his claim; the great king of the Neo-Babylonian Empire really did decide to spend a whole decade in a distant town in the Arabian desert. There are many theories as to why he did so. It didn't hurt that Tayma was a city devoted to the moon god. Perhaps Nabonidus felt uncomfortable in Marduk-centric Babylon and wanted to live in a place where he could express his passion for the moon god without restraint. He could also avoid the tensions that had erupted in his court. He was also elderly; he didn't know how long he was going to live. Perhaps he thought that Belshazzar would soon be inheriting the throne anyway and would do a better job, even now, at running the empire. There was no tradition of abdication in the Near East; a king left the throne either by dying or by being overthrown. Nabonidus had created a limbo for himself—not exactly out of royal office, not dead, not required to defer and cower before Marduk at the Akitu festival, not in easy smiting distance of his enemies.

As you might imagine, a pretty vocal anti-Nabonidus faction started growing in Babylon. What was wrong with this king? Marduk couldn't possibly be happy about being so rudely ignored by him. Later writers, including Cyrus himself, piled on the recriminations, making it difficult to discern the man Nabonidus from the heretic portrayed by his enemies. Even the author of the biblical book of Daniel, writing much later, in the second century BCE, reported stories of the king's madness. He wrote that a Babylonian king, the father of Belshazzar, "was driven away from his people and ate grass like cattle"[86] for seven years. It was only later, after his exile that his "sanity was restored."[87] (In the intervening centuries the king's name had been mixed up—the author of Daniel called this king Nebuchadnezzar, but it was Nabonidus who was the father of Belshazzar, who went into exile, and who acquired a reputation for insanity.)

Nabonidus did, indeed, return from Tayma to Babylon around 543 BCE, apparently finally worried about the threat that Cyrus posed to Babylonian autonomy. Three years later, for reasons that must have made sense to him but didn't add to his popularity, he summoned the gods of much of Mesopotamia to Babylon. Indeed, the actual statues of many gods departed from their home cities to live for a while in exile in the capital. Nabonidus may have been protecting the gods in case of Persian attack, or hoping that their combined power would protect the empire (or at least its capital), but it seems to have been a thoroughly unpopular move. Residents of other cities could no longer enact their usual rituals and festivals and must have felt that they were no longer protected by their local deities. Later, Cyrus wrote that "The gods living inside them abandoned their shrines, angry that he (Nabonidus) had made (them) enter Shuanna (Babylon)."[88]

In the end, Cyrus was able to take over Babylonia with very little destruction or disturbance to the land's usual routines. He arrived so quickly that some northern cities had not yet dispatched the gods who had been summoned by Nabonidus, though apparently they had made plans to do so.[89] A battle did take place between Persian and Babylonian forces at Opis, north of Babylon, near the Tigris River, in late September 539 BCE, and it proved to be a victory for the Persians. A few days after that, Sippar, where Bel-uballit and his family were living, surrendered to Cyrus without a fight, without even a siege.[90] According to Cyrus, the same thing happened shortly afterward in Babylon itself, and with the blessing of the city god Marduk, no less:

> Without a fight, he (Marduk) allowed him (Cyrus) to enter Shuanna (Babylon). . . . The people of Babylon, all of them, the entirety of the land of Sumer and Akkad, (as well as) the nobles and governor(s), bowed down before him (and) kissed his feet. They were happy at him being king (and) their faces shone.[91]

This sounds a bit exaggerated, but perhaps the relentless anti-Nabonidus propaganda put out by his enemies in Babylonia and magnified by Cyrus in his own campaign for the hearts of the Babylonians had worked. They had become convinced that they would be better off with a Persian ruler who claimed to have been chosen by Marduk than with a usurper from Harran who continued in his mission to prove that the moon god was the greater power. Nabonidus was arrested and exiled far from the city about which he seems to have been so ambivalent.

Rebellions and Changes in Babylonia

Initially, life in Babylonia was comfortable under the Achaemenid Persian kings. Cyrus did not allow his troops to loot the cities. He returned the gods to their home cities, allowed his new subjects plenty of autonomy and freedom of movement, proclaimed his love for Marduk, rebuilt damaged shrines and constructed new buildings in Babylon,[92] and even participated in the Akitu festival. He put out a statement, on the Cyrus Cylinder, concerning his relationship with Babylonia. It was written in Akkadian, in cuneiform, and was so like a traditional Mesopotamian royal inscription, and so reverent toward Marduk, that one would be hard pressed to tell, from reading it, that Cyrus was Persian.[93] He did not, however, choose to live in Babylon. Cyrus commissioned a brand-new capital city, Pasargadae—a place of columned halls and lush gardens—but he had it constructed in his homeland of Persia.[94]

When Cyrus died, nine years after taking control in Mesopotamia, his son Cambyses II (530–522 BCE) succeeded him. But there were grumblings now in Babylonia about Persian rule. The Babylonians had little experience being ruled from outside. The Assyrian kings had left a thoroughly bad impression, and now the Persian kings seemed less attractive than before. When Cambyses died in 522 BCE, some of the Babylonians rebelled, supporting first one local would-be king (calling himself, optimistically, Nebuchadnezzar III) and then another (Nebuchadnezzar IV).

They were not successful. The next Persian king, Darius I (522–486 BCE) made a point not just of executing both of the rebel Nebuchadnezzars but of boasting about it on public monuments. Darius's most ostentatious monument (though also the one that was hardest to read, being halfway up a mountain on a steep cliff face) was at Bisitun in Iran. Under a huge image of himself, victorious over a number of rebels, he had the account inscribed in three different languages—Elamite, Old Persian (now written in a new cuneiform alphabet that bore no real connection to Akkadian cuneiform), and a rather clunky Akkadian (see Fig. 20.3). No human could have read the tiny script at such a distance, so presumably it was written for the gods and for the future. The future—our modern era—actually made good use of it, but not in the way Darius could have intended or even imagined. Since the Persian version could be understood without too much difficulty once the basic alphabetic code was broken, the Bisitun inscription provided the key to the decipherment of Akkadian in the early nineteenth century of our era, not unlike the Rosetta Stone for Egyptian hieroglyphs.

In Sippar, Bel-uballit's family's fortunes began to change at this point. The political crises finally started having an impact on daily life at the harbor and in the Ebabbar temple. The two pretenders, the rebel Nebuchadnezzars, had been popular in Sippar and supported by the family that controlled the position of high priest there, so Darius punished the city by putting his own

Fig. 20.3 Relief sculpture showing King Darius I of Persia, with a trilingal inscription, on a rock face in Bisitun, Iran. Early fifth century BCE. (HIP/Art Resource, NY)

nominee into the role of high priest of the Ebabbar temple.[95] Bel-uballit had died shortly before this, but his son still managed to profit from his businesses, in spite of the changed mood of the city. He even ended up as what was called a College Scribe of the Ebabbar temple—one of the most important people in the community.[96]

Life in Babylonia got worse under the rule of Darius's son Xerxes (485–465 BCE). The Babylonians were thoroughly done with Persian rule, but the Persians were not even vaguely inclined to cut them free from the empire. Babylonia was proving to be a valuable source of income. Xerxes no longer made any pretense of being a Babylonian king. He didn't worship Marduk, nor did he participate in the Akitu festival. Darius had built another beautiful new capital city at Persepolis in the heart of Persia, and Xerxes had every intention of living there while embellishing it further.

His only reason to come to Babylon was to crush another rebellion, which broke out in his second year, with two more local pretenders claiming the throne. Xerxes made it clear that this type of behavior was unacceptable. Babylonia was a Persian province, not an independent state.

You remember the beautiful ziggurat for Marduk that Nebuchadnezzar II had so carefully restored in the heart of Babylon, with its shining blue shrine at the top? Xerxes had his troops destroy its staircases.[97] No one could now climb up to reach the shrine. Marduk was snubbed, dishonored; no longer the king of all gods, he was, in the eyes of the Persian king, a non-entity.

Old commercial families like the Egibis went out of business; their archives came to an end. Right up through the reign of Darius they had continued to trade, lend money, go to court, invest in businesses, and so on. Ishunnatu's inn had still been in business in 520 BCE, during the first years of Darius's reign. But the power of those old families came to an end. Cuneiform largely went out of use in the area around Babylon, an event known to scholars as the "end of archives." Commerce, along with positions of power in the temples, switched to new individuals who would be more supportive of Persepolis. Only in the south, in the areas closer to the Persian Gulf, like Uruk, which had not rebelled, did cuneiform continue to be used to any extent.

Persia, Mesopotamia, Greece, and Alexander

Throughout this period, Darius and Xerxes had been preoccupied with many details of their empire besides coping with rebellions in Babylon. Darius had sent his armies out across thousands of miles as he continued to expand the borders of the Persian Empire in all directions. Egypt had already been conquered by Persia in the reign of Cambyses, but Darius went farther south, so that Nubia was now under Persian control. His forces drove east all the way to western India, and west all the way to Libya in Africa, and to Thrace in Europe. The Persians must have seemed unstoppable. Their empire was now wildly bigger than anything the Assyrians had achieved. More than two dozen modern countries lie at least partly within its ancient boundaries at their greatest extent. In 490 BCE, the Persians confronted the Greeks at the Battle of Marathon. It must have been a shock to Darius when his army lost the battle, and a great morale boost to the Greeks. Their city-states weren't unified under a single government and the idea that they could possibly fight off the fearsome Persian army must have seemed quixotic beforehand.

Whether Darius cared much about this loss is hard to tell. He was busy with a great many other things. He was constructing his new capital at Persepolis and rebuilding the ancient city of Susa; organizing the empire into provinces, all of which paid tribute to the king; creating military garrisons to respond to rebellions; building roads across the empire (notably the Royal Road, which covered 2,500 kilometers [1,550 miles] from Susa to Sardis); gathering information from a network of spies; and maintaining diplomatic relations with innumerable leaders inside and outside the borders of the empire. Darius must have been deluged with letters; his scribes were no doubt constantly at work keeping up with his correspondence. He took the model of empire created by the Assyrians and made it more efficient and, initially at least, less terrifying to its subjects.

During the reign of Xerxes, the Persians again tried to conquer Greece and to bring it into their empire, and again they failed. This seems to have made a much greater impression on the Greeks than it did on the Persians. Herodotus devoted his extensive "Histories" to the Persian War and all that led up to it, with the result that the war has been studied in the West ever since. The Persians didn't continue to send troops to Greece; perhaps it didn't seem worth the expense.

You may be wondering about the fate of cuneiform and the scribes, whose careers we have been following, in all this. The Persians had written some documents in cuneiform after they conquered Babylonia, but starting in the reign of Xerxes their kings made the decision to adopt Aramaic as their lingua franca. It was already spoken over much of the empire, after all. And Aramaic was written not on clay but mostly on leather and papyrus.[98] No one at the time contemplated the fact that cuneiform documents, even documents written thousands of years earlier, would outlive the new Aramaic ones by millennia. We don't look at stone inscriptions today and think, those will be here forever, whereas books in our libraries will disintegrate, and digital files will simply vanish when technology changes. Most of us don't get the mad urge to write essays on clay tablets or stone stelas just so that the future has some record of us. Nor did they. Cuneiform was harder to learn and more time-consuming to write than the Aramaic script, and it recorded languages that were no longer spoken. The later Achaemenid kings had no interest at all in supporting cuneiform scholarship.[99]

The Persian Empire continued to thrive after the reign of Xerxes, but surviving sources become much less abundant after the switch to the use of Aramaic. Meanwhile the Greeks turned to fighting one another, while always glancing over their shoulders to check on Persia, and sometimes even appealing to Persia to help.

The man who brought an end to the Achaemenid Persian Empire, and the stages in his conquest, seem like inevitabilities in retrospect. Alexander of Macedon—"Alexander the Great" (336–323 BCE)—tore across the empire with his armies and engraved his name across the conquered lands and across history. Following in the footsteps of many Near Eastern kings who had built cities that they named for themselves, Alexander founded (or at least renamed) more than twenty cities, calling them all Alexandria. Some of these cities—Alexandria in Egypt, Kandahar in Afghanistan, Iskandariya in Iraq—still bear his name today. (Kandahar derives from Iskander, the local pronunciation of Alexander.) But it must have been a strange time to live through, and his victory may have seemed far from inevitable at the beginning.

It was Alexander's father, Philip II of Macedon (359–336 BCE), who had conceived the idea of conquering Persia. He managed to unify Greece—far from an easy task, given the perpetual wars that had divided it—but was assassinated in 336 BCE, before he had been able to venture out eastward. His son Alexander, twenty years old, took the throne and launched into fulfilling his father's plans. By the age of thirty-two, Alexander was dead, in Babylon, having brought the whole Persian Empire under his control in the course of ten years of almost constant military campaigns.

From here, this book could take a deep breath and embark on the discovery of this whole transformed world that had developed between the time of Darius and the conquest of the region by Alexander. We could stop and knock at the doors of many more individuals and eavesdrop on their lives. But we are not going to do that. This book has been held together by cuneiform records. We began with the invention of proto-cuneiform writing in the Uruk period, and we are now coming close to the end of the use of cuneiform, other than for esoteric scholarly purposes.

Once the Persians lost interest in using cuneiform for administration, the only people still using the script were in Mesopotamia, and there weren't many of them. But some very dedicated scribes seem to have been determined not to let the ancient system of writing die. Generation after generation of scribal students learned to write the complicated signs in order to record texts in languages that no one spoke natively anymore.

With Alexander's conquests and Macedonian rule over the Near East, Greek was introduced as a new language of administration, while Aramaic was still spoken on the streets. But as late as 61 BCE, scholars still, remarkably, continued to stare at the night sky and to record their astronomical observations in Akkadian, in cuneiform, continuing to add to the series of texts that had started 700 years earlier. Next to notes about the locations of planets, the moon, and so on, they recorded current political events. They were still looking for messages from the gods—the same gods who had been worshiped for thousands of years. But they lived in a time when Mesopotamia was under Parthian rule and the Roman Empire was the great power in the west. They lived in a time far beyond the world of this book, far beyond the world that was bound together by the use of cuneiform for communication and shared memory.

Rimut-Anu: Exorcist and Scholar in Uruk

Let's travel, then, back to Uruk, where we began this journey. It had been abandoned a couple of times when life got bad in southern Mesopotamia, but was always resettled. Even when Alexander conquered Mesopotamia, Uruk stood in exactly the same place where it had been founded, atop the tell that included the remains of the city from every previous era.

It had changed a great deal over 3,000 years. After the rebellions during the reign of Xerxes, in the fifth century BCE, and after the "end of archives" in the north, the great Eanna complex was no longer dedicated to the goddess Ishtar (Inana). The main temple of Uruk had been renamed the Bit-Resh and it was dedicated entirely to the god of the heavens, Anu. Of course, Anu had been there all along—he had been the resident of an important temple in the Uruk period as well—but now he was the only great god of Uruk. The gods Marduk and Nabu, introduced by the Neo-Babylonian kings and even worshiped in the magnificent shrines of the city gods, had been removed. Prominent Babylonian families who had been living there lost their influence too. Uruk was looking backward to its origins, and Marduk had no place there.[100] In fact, just as Nabonidus had believed that Sin was the greatest of the gods, so the priests in Uruk may have believed the same about Anu, even that Anu embodied gods who had previously been considered to be distinct deities. The Persians worshiped a great god named Ahuramazda who encompassed all virtuous gods. The Jews worshiped a single god named Yahweh. Their ideas were circulating across the Near East and may well have influenced new ideas about the Mesopotamian gods as well.

It is time for us to knock on one last door. Fittingly, it was a house of scribes. In the sixth and fifth centuries BCE, a family of scribes lived in a house in a residential neighborhood southeast of the temple to Anu in Uruk. They were the Shangu-Ninurta family.[101] The section of their house that archaeologists were able to excavate included three rooms grouped around a big courtyard, and the size of the courtyard suggests that there was a lot more to the house that extended beyond the area that the archaeologists uncovered. The Shangu-Ninurtas weren't the only scholarly family to live in the house; a later family of cuneiform-writing professionals occupied it in the late fourth century BCE, after Alexander had conquered the Persian Empire.[102]

The Shangu-Ninurta family probably took a lot of their cuneiform tablets with them when they moved out, around 420 BCE, but about 160 of their tablets remained in the house for archaeologists eventually to find. Some of them had been abandoned or scattered by later residents, but some had been put into clay jars by the Shangu-Ninurtas and carefully buried, as though the family intended to return to get them (though they never did). Reading their tablets, we are once again in the company of a family, and of a group of scribes who consciously copied documents that they felt were important to keep, important to study, important to pass down to the future. They could have had no idea just how far into the future their efforts would reverberate. Scribes like those of the Shangu-Ninurta family have been our guides to so much of their world. But there were fewer such scribes now, and they were increasingly isolated in their use of cuneiform. The types of contracts, administrative lists, letters, and memos on which so much of this book has been based were still being written, but, as we have seen, usually in the easier alphabetic scripts, in languages that people actually spoke, and on more ephemeral materials.

Three generations of men in the family served as priests known as *ashipu*s, or "exorcists." You may recall that we encountered an *ashipu* who worked for Esarhaddon. They were scholars who focused on healing people, largely through incantations, prayers, and rituals, though they could also use medicine as well.[103] The men of the family were highly educated and respected, continuing a tradition that went back for eons. One of them was named Rimut-Anu. He was in the middle generation, son of the patriarch Shamash-iddin, brother to a third *ashipu*, and uncle to a fourth.[104] They all seem to have lived and worked in the house. There must have been women in the family as well, but unfortunately they aren't mentioned in the tablets. Given how many women we have met along the way, I was hoping to end the book with a family that included prominent women, but it was not to be. Perhaps it's fitting, though; women's roles outside the household had become more limited over time.

The library of the Shangu-Ninurtas included, as you might expect, plenty of incantations, along with prescriptions and rituals that the men used in their work, but they also owned omen texts, lexical lists, hymns, and even astronomical and mathematical documents—the kinds that scribes had learned in school for as long as there had been schools. The library also included a handful of tablets that had come from Babylon.[105] They received documents that moved among a network of scholars; in spite of the decline in cuneiform scholarship in the north, the scribes in Uruk were not alone.

One document is known as the "*Ashipu's* Handbook," and the version of it in the household library had been copied by Rimut-Anu. This was a well-known work at the time, among *ashipu*s, one that included a catalog of about 200 texts that were important to their work. Rimut-Anu had access to about fifty of these, to judge from what was found in the house. It's possible, though, that more of them might have been kept on wax-covered wooden boards,[106] and others might have been taken by the family when they left. The handbook laid out the rituals and responsibilities of the *ashipu*, including "the totality of wisdom (and) the secret of exorcism."[107] It noted that an exorcist performed treatments against ten specific ailments, including those called "falling sickness . . . Hand of a god . . . Evil spirit, Hand of a curse, and Hand of humanity." All of these would have been familiar to Rimut-Anu. He recognized their symptoms and knew the secret ways to bring the person back to health. But his training extended far beyond that. An *ashipu* understood how to treat "the whole range of affliction(s) of a sick person, against seizure of fever and against women's afflictions." If a person was sick, an *ashipu* understood how to restore him or her to health, how to manage the very gods or demons who caused the sickness. This was still absolutely real to the Mesopotamians. It was not some sort of laughable superstition or magic. They were intelligent people and they had seen patients get well as a result of the ministrations of the *ashipu*. The gods controlled everything, in their eyes; it would have been foolish not to bring in the man who knew the right words to speak, the right actions to take, to get the gods' attention and to give the patient the best chance at recovery.

Rimut-Anu's knowledge, and that of his father, brother, and nephew, included more than just what they needed for their profession. They copied and studied classic texts in order to master ancient knowledge, some of it not practical at all. The handbook acknowledged this, noting that "you will interpret the commentaries, the glosses and the compositions in Emesal, you will learn to research the rituals in Sumerian and Akkadian."[108] Sumerian had been a dead language for about 1,500 years, and Emesal was a dialect of Sumerian, one that had long ago been used by the lamentation priests. As Akkadian, too, was going out of use, these scholars of ancient knowledge may have felt that they were fighting a tide of ignorance, holding on to ancient wisdom in a modern age that was losing track of these important ideas. The handbook assured the *ashipu* that he would be "wise, erudite" and that "the gods of exorcism will give expanded intelligence." The world in which Rimut-Anu lived was full of new ideas that were being written down in other languages and other scripts, while the study of ancient cuneiform wisdom was a dying art, practiced by fewer and fewer scholars who had decreasing access to one another and to their classic texts.[109]

The last few lines of the handbook tablet are touching. Rimut-Anu was finishing up his careful copy, coming to the benediction—the blessing on himself, in fact, that had been penned by an earlier scholar. "May . . . his tutelary god, be good! His name will be pronounced until distant days." Did this mean the name of the tutelary god, or the name of the exorcist? Rimut-Anu may have hoped that it would be his own name that would be kept alive into the unknown future, as a result of his careful efforts. He wasn't wrong.

As he sat in the room of his house in Uruk, he looked back over the original tablet that he was copying and put it next to his clean new version. Was everything correct? Had he missed any signs? It looked good. He picked up his stylus and added the colophon, the only lines that he did not copy from the original document. He wrote, "In accordance with the (original) tablet. Duplicate written and checked and properly executed." Anyone using the tablet in their work as an *ashipu*, and anyone who came across this tablet in the future, could be assured that he had done it carefully.

Then he signed his name:"Rimut-Anu, [son of] Shamash-iddin, descendant of Shangu-Ninurta."

All that was left was the date and the place. "Uruk," he wrote. He must have known that he was living in the oldest city on Earth. His education had taught him that. Modern archaeologists have confirmed it. He certainly did not think of himself as living in the ancient world. He knew about the ancient world—he studied it every day. His world, his life, were in the modern new era of the Persian kings. For better or worse, they seemed to be in Mesopotamia to stay. He wouldn't have dreamed that a century later his city would be ruled by a dynasty from Greece. Greece! Impossible, not even in the realm of imagining. Greece was a tiny, unimportant, blip of a place at the edge of the mighty Persian Empire, a land not even ruled by a single government. Uruk, its gods, its language, and its literature would surely live on forever. Rimut-Anu put down his stylus.

Cast of Main Characters

Individual	Profession and location	Date (all BCE)	Chapter
Abi-eshuh	king of Babylon	1711–1684	13
Abi-hunni	recipient of a house in Terqa (m)	late 15th or early 14th century	15
Adad-guppi	priestess of Sin in Harran, official, and mother of the king in Babylonia	649–547	19
Adad-shumu-usur	physician and exorcist in Assyria (m)	early 7th century	18
Akhenaten	king of Egypt	1353–1336	15
Alexander	king of Macedon	336–323	20
Amat-Shamash	*naditum* in Sippar (f)	mid-18th century	12
Ashur-idi	merchant in Ashur (m)	20th–19th century	9
Ashur-nada	merchant in Ashur and Anatolia (m)	20th–19th century	9
Ashur-uballit I	king of Assyria	1363–1328	15
Ashurbanipal	king of Assyria	668–630/628	19
Ashurnasirpal II	king of Assyria	883–859	17
Awat-Aya	*naditum* initiate in Sippar (f)	mid-18th century	12
Ba'la-bia	child in Emar (f)	late 13th century	16
Ba'la-belu	child in Emar (m)	late 13th century	16
Ba'la-ummi	child in Emar (f)	late 13th century	16
Baranamtara	queen of Lagash	c. 2400	4
Bazatum	musician in Mari (f)	mid-18th century	10
Bel-uballit	oil presser, brewer, and temple functionary in Sippar (m)	mid-6th century	20
Bel-ushezib	diviner and astronomer in Assyria (m)	early 7th century	18

Individual	Profession and location	Date (all BCE)	Chapter
Beltum	princess of Qatna, queen in Mari	early 18th century	10
Burna–Buriash II	king of Babylonia	1359–1333	15
Cyrus	king of Persia	559–530	20
Dimtur	queen mother in Lagash	c. 2400	4
Dusigu	queen mother in Ebla	c. 2300	5
Eannatum	king of Lagash	25th century	3
Elletum	scribal student in Nippur (m)	mid-18th century	12
Emete	head of female royal servants in Lagash (f)	mid-24th century	4
Enar–Lim	merchant and envoy in Ebla (m)	c. 2300	5
Enheduana	*en*-priestess of Nanna in Ur	c. 2300–2250	6
Enlil-bani	gardener, substitute king, and king of Isin	1860–1837	8
Enlil-mansum	temple official and slave trader in Dur-Abi-eshuh (m)	late 17th century	13
Enmetena	king of Lagash	c. 2450	3
Erra–imitti	king of Isin	1868–1861	8
Esarhaddon	king of Assyria	681–669	18
Geme-Suen	lender in Umma (f)	mid-21st century	7
Gimil-Ninkarrak	chief barber in Terqa (m)	c. 1710–1680	13
Gudea	king of Lagash	2144–2124	7
Hammurabi	king of Babylon	1792–1750	11
Hane	translator in Egypt and Mittani (m)	mid-14th century	14
Hattusili I	king of Hatti	1650–1620	13
Hattusili III	king of Hatti	1267–1237	16
Ibni–Sin	commander in Babylon	early 17th century	13
Igi-bar	weaving supervisor in Lagash (f)	mid-24th century	4
Ilim-ilimma	charioteer, lender in Alalakh (m)	early 15th century	14
Ina-qate-Nabu-bultu	enslaved baker in Babylon (m)	mid-6th century	20
Ishar-damu	king of Ebla	c. 2300	5

Individual	Profession and location	Date (all BCE)	Chapter
Ishar-Lim	king of Hana	late 15th or early 14th century	15
Ishbi-Erra	king of Isin	2017–1985	8
Ishma'-Dagan	child in Emar (m)	late 13th century	16
Ishunnatu	enslaved innkeeper in Kish (f)	mid-6th century	20
Itti-Marduk-balatu	businessman in Babylon	mid-6th century	20
Jehoiakin	king of Judah, exile in Babylon	mid-6th century	19
Kitushdu	scribe in Ur (m)	c. 2300	6
Ku'e	woman in Emar	late 13th century	16
Kudurru	scribe in Babylonia and Assyria and oil diviner (m)	early 7th century	18
Kushim	*sanga* and controller of the barley warehouse in Uruk (m)	late 4th millennium	2
Lu-Nanna	escaped slave in Umma (m)	21st century	7
Lugalanda	king of Lagash	c. 2400	4
Lugalzagesi	king of Uruk	late 24th century	6
Marduk-lamassashu	vizier in Babylon	early 17th century	13
Mashum	soldier and farmer in Larsa (m)	mid-18th century	11
Mizatu	enslaved brewer, wife of Nabu-utirri in Babylon	mid-6th century	20
Muballitat-Sherua	princess of Assyria, queen of Babylonia, wife of Burna-Buriash II	mid-14th century	15
Nabu-naid/ Nabonidus	scribal student, official, and king of Babylonia	ruled 556–539	19 and 20
Nabu-utirri	enslaved brewer, husband of Mizatu in Babylon	mid-6th century	20
Nabu-ushallim	dream interpreter in Assyria (m)	early 7th century	18
Napir-Asu	princess of Babylonia, queen of Elam, wife of Untash-Napirisha	mid-14th century	15
Naram-Sin	king of Akkad	2254–2218	6

Individual	Profession and location	Date (all BCE)	Chapter
Nebuchadnezzar II	king of Babylonia	604–562	19
Nefertiti	queen of Egypt	mid-14th century	15
Pihatni-ipiq	possible governor in Larsa	mid-19th century	8
Puabi	queen of Ur	c. 2500	3
Puduhepa	queen of Hatti	mid-13th century	16
Rimut-Anu	scribe and exorcist in Uruk (m)	5th century	20
Rishiya	chief musician at Mari (m)	mid-18th century	10
Ruzi-malik	merchant and envoy in Ebla (m)	c. 2300	5
Samsu-ditana	king of Babylon	1625–1595	13
Samsu-iluna	king of Babylon	1749–1712	13
Sargon	king of Akkad	2334–2279	6
Sasi	official and possible conspirator in Assyria (m)	early 7th century	18
Se'-idri	tenant vineyard gardener in Assyria (m)	late 8th century	19
Shamash-hazir	land overseer in Larsa	mid-18th century	11
Shamshi-Adad	king of Upper Mesopotamia	1807–1776	10
Shara-igizi-Abzu	esh-a in Umma, daughter of Ushumgal	early 3rd millennium	3
Shulgi	king of Ur	2094–2046	7
Sin-idinnam	governor general of Larsa	mid-18th century	11
Sumu-El	king of Larsa	1894–1866	8
Sumu-la-El	king of Babylon	1880–1845	8
Suppiluliuma I	king of Hatti	1344–1322	15
Tabur-damu	queen of Ebla	c. 2300	5
Tawananna	princess of Babylonia, queen of Hatti, wife of Suppiluliuma I	mid-14th century	15
Tushratta	king of Mittani	mid-14th century	14 and 15
Unnamed Babylonian princess	princess of Babylonia, wife of Akhenaten	mid-14th century	15
Unnamed brickmaker	brickmaker in Ur (m)	early 21st century	7

Individual	Profession and location	Date (all BCE)	Chapter
Unnamed children	child laborers who worked for the temple in Girsu (m, f)	21st century	7
Unnamed deportees	deportees in the Assyrian Empire (m, f)	9th and 8th centuries	17
Unnamed eunuch	chief eunuch and conspirator in Assyria	early 7th century	18
Unnamed girl	enslaved girl and prophet in Harran	early 7th century	18
Unnamed goldsmiths	goldsmiths in Assyria (m)	9th–7th centuries	19
Unnamed perfume-makers	perfume-makers in Babylonia (f)	mid-6th century	19
Unnamed priest-king/*en*	leader of Uruk	late 4th millennium	1 and 2
Unnamed sculptors	sculptors in Assyria (m)	early 9th century	17
Unnamed traveler	visitor to the Stone Cone Temple, Uruk	mid-4th millennium	1
Untash-Napirisha	king of Elam	1340–1300	15
Ur-Namma	king of Ur	2112–2095	7
Ur-Nanshe	king of Lagash	mid-3rd millennium	3
Urtenu	merchant in Ugarit (m)	late 13th century	16
Urukagina	king of Lagash	mid-24th century	4
Ushumgal	*pab-shesh* priest in Umma, father of Shara-igizi-Abzu	early 3rd millennium	3
Various *naditums*	*naditums* in Sippar (f)	mid-18th century	12
Various washermen	washermen in Babylonia	mid-6th century	19
Various weavers	weavers in Assyria (m, f)	9th–7th centuries	19
Wife of Ur-lugal	borrower in Umma (f)	mid-21st century	7
Yasmah-Addu	viceroy in Mari	early 18th century	10
Zadamma	man in Emar	late 13th century	16
Zimri-Lim	king of Mari	1774–1762	10
Zum	weaving supervisor in Lagash (f)	mid-24th century	4

Timeline

Dates are all BCE and are approximate.

Individuals are in italics; dates given for kings are regnal years.

Uruk period	4000–2900
First city in Uruk	3500
Uruk colonies begin	3500
Stone Cone Temple constructed	3500
Beginning of proto-cuneiform	3300
Early Dynastic period	**2900–2300**
Cuneiform develops from proto-cuneiform	2900
Beginning of kingship	2900
Ur-Nanshe, king of Lagash	mid-3rd millennium
Royal tombs of Ur	mid-3rd millennium
Earliest kings of Ebla	2525
Lagash-Umma border conflict	2500–2350
Eannatum, king of Lagash	25th century
Enmetena, king of Lagash	2450
First evidence of diplomacy in Sumer	2450
Baranamtara, queen of Lagash	2400
Urukagina, king of Lagash	2350
Ebla archives	2350–2300
Tabur-damu and Ishar-damu of Ebla	2300
Akkadian period	**2300–2200**
Sargon, king of Akkad	2316–2277
Enhuduana, en-priestess in Ur, daughter of Sargon	2300–2250
Naram-Sin, king of Akkad	2253–2218
Naram-Sin deified after putting down rebellions	2230
End of Akkadian Empire	2150

Gudea, king of Lagash	2144–2124
Ur III period	**2112–2000**
Ur-Namma, king of Ur	2112–2095
Construction of ziggurats	early 21st century
Shulgi, king of Ur	2094–2046
Creation of *bala* system by Shulgi	2070
Ibbi-Sin, king of Ur	2028–2004
End of Ur III period	2004
Isin–Larsa period/Old Assyrian period	**2017–1792**
Ishbi-Erra king of Isin	2017–1985
Assyrian merchants trading in Anatolia	2000–1775
Erishum, king of Ashur	1974–1935
Gungunum, king of Larsa	1932–1906
Sumu-El, king of Larsa	1894–1866
Sumu-la-El, king of Babylon	1880–1845
Erra-imitti, king of Isin	1868–1861
Sumu-El fights Erra-imitti	1860s
Enlil-bani, gardener and king of Isin	1860–1837
Sin-magir king of Isin	1827–1817
Rim-Sin, king of Larsa	1822–1763
Old Babylonian period	**1800–1595**
Shamshi-Adad, king of Upper Mesopotamia	1807–1776
Shamshi-Adad unites Upper Mesopotamia	1792
Siruk-tuh, king of Elam	early 18th century
Hammurabi, king of Babylon	1792–1750
Zimri-Lim, king of Mari	1774–1762
Hammurabi unites Mesopotamia	1766–1761
Hammurabi promulgates laws	1755
Naditums at Sippar	mid-18th century
School at House F in Nippur	mid-18th century
Samsu-iluna, king of Babylon	1749–1712
Rebellions against Babylon in southern Mesopotamia	late 18th century
First Dynasty of the Sealand begins	late 18th century
Abi-eshuh, king of Babylon	1711–1684
Ili-ma-ilu, king of the Sealand	early 17th century
Ammi-ditana, king of Babylon	1683–1647

Expansion of the Hittite Empire	mid–17th century
Hattusili I, king of Hatti	1650–1620
Ammi-saduqa, king of Babylon	1646–1626
Samsu-ditana, king of Babylon	1625–1595
Mursili I, king of Hatti	1620–1590
End of the First Dynasty of Babylon	1595
Dark Age	**1595–1500**
Late Bronze Age	**1550–1000**
Agum, king of Babylon	mid–16th century
Mittani founded in Syria	1500
Battles for northwest Syria between Egypt, Hatti, and Mittani	1500–1418
Idrimi, king of Alalakh	early 15th century
Babylonian conquest of the Sealand	1475
Kingdom of Hana begins in Syria	late 15th century
Saushtatar, king of Mittani	late 15th century
Diplomatic relations start between great powers	1418
Amenhotep III, king of Egypt	1386–1349
Kurigalzu I, king of Babylon	early 14th century
Amarna letters	mid–14th century
Tushratta, king of Mittani	mid–14th century
Ashur-uballit I, king of Assyria	1363–1328
Burna-Buriash II, king of Babylon	1359–1333
Akhenaten, king of Egypt	1353–1336
Suppilulima I, king of Hatti	1344–1322
Untash-Napirisha, king of Elam	1340–1300
Shattiwaza, king of Mittani	late 14th century
Dissolution of Mittani and independence of Assyria	1335
Plague in Hatti	late 14th century
Kara-hardash, king of Babylon	1333
Mursili II, king of Hatti	1321–1295
Ulu Burun shipwreck	1300
Sin-leqi-unnini composes the Gilgamesh Epic	13th century?
Kidin-Hutran II, king of Elam	early 13th century
Ramses II, king of Egypt	1279–1213
Battle of Kadesh between Egypt and Hatti	1274

Hattusili III, king of Hatti	1267–1237
Puduhepa, queen of Hatti	mid-13th century
Egypt–Hatti peace treaty	1259
Final end of Mittani	1250
Growth of Middle Assyrian Empire	mid-13th century
Tukulti-Ninurta I, king of Assyria	1243–1207
Niqmaddu III, king of Ugarit	1225–1215
Widespread drought and famine	late 13th/early 12th century
Ramses III, king of Egypt	1186–1155
Destruction of Ugarit	1185
Destruction of Emar	1180
Attacks on Egypt by Sea Peoples	early 12th century
Aramean kingdoms founded in Syria	12th century
Shutruk-Nahhunte, king of Elam	1160
Elamite attack on Babylon, capture of Babylonian objects	1158
End of Kassite dynasty in Babylon	1155
Kutir-Nahhunte, king of Elam	mid-12th century
Nebuchadnezzar I, king of Babylon	1126–1105
Nebuchadnezzar I raids Susa	1110
Israelite kingdom founded	11th century
Phoenician alphabet invented	11th century
Iron technology spreads	11th century
First millennium	**1000–323**
Expansion of Neo-Assyrian Empire begins	911
Ashurnasirpal II, king of Assyria	883–859
Unification of Urartu	mid-9th century
Tiglath-Pileser III, king of Assyria	744–727
Shalmaneser V, king of Assyria	727–722
Assyrian defeat of Israel	722–720
Sargon II, king of Assyria	722–705
Sennacherib, king of Assyria	705–681
Taharqa, Nubian king of Egypt	690–664
Sennacherib sacks Babylon	689
Hezekiah, king of Judah	early 7th century
Esarhaddon, king of Assyria	681–669
Rusa II, king of Urartu	673
Esarhaddon's attack on Egypt	671

Ashurbanipal, king of Assyria	668–630 or 627
Adad-guppi, priestess of Sin in Harran	649–547
Shamash-shumu-ukin, Assyrian king of Babylon	668–648
Civil war between Ashurbanipal and Shamash-shumu-ukin	652–648
Ashurbanipal sacks Susa	647
Ashur-etel-ilani, king of Assyria	630/627–625
Nabopolassar, king of Babylon	626–605
Neo-Babylonian period begins	626
Sin-shar-ishkun, king of Assyria	624–612
Civil war between Assyria and Babylonia	624–609
Conquest of Nineveh	612
Conquest of Harran, end of the Neo-Assyrian Empire	609
Nebuchadnezzar II, king of Babylon	604–562
Nebuchadnezzar II conquers Judah	587
Jehoiakin, king of Judah, and Judean exiles living in Babylon	early to mid-6th century
Amel-Marduk, king of Babylon	561–560
Neriglissar, king of Babylon	559–556
Cyrus II, king of Persia	559–530
Achaemenid Persian Empire begins	559
Labashi-Marduk, king of Babylon	556
Nabu-na'id/Nabonidus, king of Babylon	556–539
Cyrus's conquest of Babylonia	539
Cambyses II, king of Persia	530–522
Nebuchadnezzar III, rebel king of Babylon	late 6th century
Nebuchadnezzar IV, rebel king of Babylon	late 6th century
Darius I, king of Persia	522–486
Greeks defeat Persians at Battle of Marathon	490
Xerxes, king of Persia	485–465
Xerxes puts down Babylonian rebellion	484
Herodotus, Greek historian	484–425
Greeks defeat Persian forces of Darius I	480–479
Philip II, king of Macedon	359–336
Alexander, king of Macedon	336–323
Alexander conquers Persian Empire	331

Acknowledgments

I began writing this book on a hot day in July 2019. I was in New York City at the start of a sabbatical, and I had settled at the end of a long table in a reading room of NYU's Bobst Library, seated next to big windows looking out on Washington Square. I was utterly content. The books stacked in front of me were full of recently published documents peopled with ancient individuals, along with studies of ancient lives. Pieces of what was to become Chapter 8 began to emerge that very day. I finished writing the book on an equally hot day, two years later almost to the day, in a house in Houston where I was staying with my daughter's family, waiting for the imminent arrival of her baby twins. Those two years witnessed quite a journey, both personally for me as I wrote, and for us all as we experienced the turmoil of the global pandemic.

Throughout the writing of this book I have been keenly aware of the sufferings of people in many regions in the Middle East in recent years, people whose lives have been turned upside down by invasion, civil war, and terrorism. In the face of incredible danger, the bravery and determination of so many to not only defend themselves and to save the lives of others, but also to protect and save the cultural heritage of their lands, is truly inspiring. Their ancestors gave the world justice, diplomacy, writing, and so many other extraordinary gifts; theirs is a civilization of deep and enduring power.

The completion of this book would not have been possible without the help of a great many people. I am grateful for my sabbatical leave, which was awarded by my university, Cal Poly Pomona, as a result of the kind support of Eileen Wallis, my department chair, Iris Levine, my dean, the professional leave committee, and Sylvia Alva, the provost. I also deeply appreciate the support of my wonderful colleagues in the history department.

Daniel Fleming at NYU generously sponsored my position as a visiting scholar at NYU, Alexander Jones allowed me to use the resources at the Institute for the Study of the Ancient World, and David Ratzen and Gabriel

McKee made me feel very welcome at the ISAW library, where I did most of my research in 2019. The library was an extraordinary resource. While in New York I appreciated the community of scholars, including Joan Aruz, Anastasia Amrhein, Lorenzo d'Alfonso, Dan Fleming, Aure Ben-Zvi Goldblum, Elizabeth Knott, Liat Naeh, Beate Pongratz-Leisten, Marc Van De Mieroop, and many others with whom I had fascinating conversations that stimulated my thinking about this book.

Soon after I arrived back in Los Angeles, the pandemic shut everything down and I wondered how I would be able to proceed with my research, having no access to a physical library. At that point, my days in the library at ISAW seemed worlds away. But the librarians at Cal Poly Pomona and at libraries connected through Document Delivery provided online access and digital files of various materials and images I needed, as did many generous colleagues, including Yigal Bloch, Yoram Cohen, Janine Pibal, Samantha Rainford, Osama Shukir Muhammed Amin, Giorgio Buccellati, Sebastian Hageneuer, Luma Juda, Jean-Michel Margot, Paolo Matthiae, and Davide Nadali. Jack M. Sasson is a hero for his constant and generous efforts to keep the Assyriological community in touch with recent developments in the field through his Agade mailing list. The cuneiform databases, Oracc, CDLI, Archibab, and ETCSL, have completely transformed how one can do research in this field, and I know that each one is a labor of love for its administrators.

I am particularly grateful to Eleanor Robson, Steven Garfinkle, Seth Richardson, and Sidney Babcock who read and critiqued some chapters of the book, and to the anonymous external reviewers of the book proposal and the completed manuscript for their helpful suggestions. Huge thanks also to my editor Stefan Vranka at OUP for his support throughout this process. Please be assured, though, that if you find mistakes, they are all my own.

Students in my upper division classes on the ancient Near East were terrifically helpful as they read and commented on drafts of some of the chapters, first History 3310 in spring 2020 and then History 3312 in spring 2022. I promised them I would thank them in print—so thank you, all! History 3310 was the last class I taught in a classroom in March 2020 before everything went online. I missed my students' friendly banter when we switched to virtual learning—encumbered as it was by "mute" buttons and screens full of squares—though the students have continued to inspire me.

In writing this book I have drawn on the research and insights of a great many scholars, to whom I am indebted, and of whom I am in awe. They are listed in the notes and bibliography, and I encourage you to read their work.

My fellow members of the Oracc advisory board and members of the Oracc steering committee helped keep me sane during the pandemic, as our monthly conference calls—while still Assyriological at heart—transformed into a friendly support group. Many thanks, Steve Tinney, Eleanor Robson, Niek Veldhuis, Jamie Novotny, Matthew Rutz, Enrique Jiménez, and Miller Prosser. Other, non-Assyriological, friends—especially Vicki Peterson, Rachel Van, Georgia Mickey, and Jill Watts—made my pandemic-isolated writing process less lonely and they kept me laughing, as we got together frequently by phone and on videocalls.

My family has been extraordinary. I love them all and am so grateful to them. My son Nick was home for several months of the pandemic, and, as I wrote, he kept me supplied with lattes from the local coffee shop, along with moral support. (He also roped me into being a voiceover actor in his one-man YouTube series, but that's a different story.) My daughter Emily and son-in-law Nate had their first child right before I started writing this book, and their twins were born days after I finished it. Through all that time (as Emily was also completing her medical residency, no less), she and I talked daily. My husband Jerry listened to every chapter (several of them multiple times) as I read them aloud to catch mistakes that I could no longer see on my computer screen. He was a source of great advice, and he produced bottles of champagne at various big moments in the book's progress. He also drafted the plans of buildings in Babylon, Mari, Sippar, Kanesh, and Nippur that I have used as illustrations (though I should note that the drawing of the clay feet is mine). I could not have written this book without him.

Finally, my mother, Margaret Hills, at 93 years of age, read the entire manuscript twice through, with the eagle eye of a copy-editor. Her marked-up hard copy is next to me here as I write. After an early career with the Royal Ballet School, she taught ballet until she was 90 years old, and, in her well-earned retirement, she continues to be a joy to all her friends and family. She phoned whenever she read a section that she particularly enjoyed, just to let me know. I'm dedicating the book to her with my heartfelt love and thanks; she has been a fabulous partner on this journey, as has my whole family.

Abbreviations

A	Registration numbers for texts found at Mari
AbB	*Altbabylonische Briefe in Umschrift und Übersetzung* (Leiden, 1964 ff.)
ActaSum	*Acta Sumerologica*
AfO	*Archiv für Orientforschung*
AHK	Edel, E. *Die ägyptisch-hethitische Korrespondenz aus Boghazköi in babylonischer und hethitischer Sprache* (Opladen, 1994)
AJA	*American Journal of Archaeology*
AlT	Wiseman, D. J. *The Alalakh Tablets* (London, 1953)
AnOr	*Analecta Orientalia* (Rome 1931 ff.)
AO	Museum numbers for antiquités orientales at the Louvre
AOAT	*Alter Orient und Altes Testament* (Kevelaer/Neukirchen-Vluyn, 1969 ff.)
Archibab	Archives babyloniennes (XXe–XVIIe siècles av. J.-C.): https://www.archibab.fr/
ARET	*Archivi Reali di Ebla, Testi* (Rome, 1985 ff.)
ARET XI	Fronzaroli, Pelio. *Testi rituali della regalità* (ARET XI), 1993
ARET XX	Archi, A. *Administrative Texts: Allotments of Clothing for the Palace Personnel (Archive L. 2769). With the Collaboration of Gabriella Spada.* (Wiesbaden: Harrassowitz, 2018).
ARM	*Archives royales de Mari*
AuOr	*Aula Orientalis* (Barcelona, 1983 ff.)
AUWE	*Ausgrabungen in Uruk-Warka. Endberichte* (Mainz, 1987 ff.)
B	Museum numbers for the Penn Museum
Bab	*Babyloniaca: Études de philologie assyrobabylonienne* (Paris, 1906–1937)
BASOR	*Bulletin of the American Schools of Oriental Research*
BCT	Watson, Philip J. *Catalogue of Cuneiform Tablets in Birmingham City Museum*, 2 vols. (Warminster: Aris and Phillips 1986, 1993)
BE	*The Babylonian Expedition of the University of Pennsylvania* (Philadelphia, 1893 ff.)
BM	Museum numbers for the British Museum, London

BM   *Bibliotheca Mesopotamica* (Malibu)

BOQ   Lambert, W. G. *Babylonian Oracle Questions*. Mesopotamian
            Civilizations 13 (Winona Lake, IN: Eisenbrauns, 2007)

BPOA   *Biblioteca del Proximo Oriente Antiguo* (Madrid, 2006ff.)

CAD   *The Assyrian Dictionary of the University of Chicago* (Chicago, 1956 ff.)

Camb.   Strassmaier, J. N. *Inschriften von Cambyses, König von Babylon* (1890)

CANE   Sasson, Jack M. (ed.) *Civilizations of the Ancient Near East*, 4 vols.
            (New York: Charles Scribner's Sons, 1995)

CCT   *Cuneiform Texts from Cappadocian Tablets in the British Museum*
            (London, 1921–1975)

CDLI   Cuneiform Digital Library Initiative: http://cdli.ucla.edu/

CH   Laws of Hammurabi

CRRAI   *Compte rendu de la Rencontre Assyriologique Internationale*

CTH   Laroche, L. *Catalogue des textes hittites* (Paris, 1966; repr. 1971)

CTMMA   Corpus of Cuneiform Texts in the Metropolitan Museum of Art

CUNES   *Cornell University Near Eastern Studies*

CUSAS   *Cornell University Studies in Assyriology and Sumerology* (Bethesda, MD,
            2007ff.)

Cyr.   Strassmaier, J. N. *Inschriften von Cyrus, König von Babylon*, 1890

DP   Allotte de la Fuÿe, M. F. *Documents présargoniques* (Paris, 1908–1920)

EA   Knudtzon, J. A. *Die El-Amarna-Tafeln* (Leipzig, 1915)

EKI   König, F. W. *Die elamischen Königsinschriften*, AfO 16 (Graz, 1965).

Emar   Arnaud, D. *Recherches au pays d'Astata: Emar 6/1-4, Textes sumeriens et
            accadiens* (Paris, 1986).

ETCSL   The Electronic Text Corpus of Sumerian Literature: https://etcsl
            .orinst.ox.ac.uk/

FAOS   *Freiburger Altorientalische Studien* (Freiburg, 1975 ff.)

FM   *Florilegium Marianum*

HCCT   Hirayama Collection Cuneiform Texts (Japan)

HDT   Beckman, Gary M. *Hittite Diplomatic Texts*, 2nd ed. (Atlanta: Scholars
            Press, 1999)

ICAANE   *International Congress on the Archaeology of the Ancient Near East*

IM   Museum numbers of the Iraq Museum in Baghdad

ITT   Inventaire des tablettes de Tello

JANEH   *Journal of Ancient Near Eastern History*

JAOS   *Journal of the American Oriental Society*

JCS   *Journal of Cuneiform Studies*

JESHO   *Journal of the Economic and Social History of the Orient*

JNES   *Journal of Near Eastern Studies*

KBo   *Keilschrifttexte aus Boghazköi* (Bd. 1–22 in WVDOG, Leipzig/Berlin, 1916 ff.)

KUB   *Keilschrifturkunden aus Boghazköi* (Berlin, 1921 ff.)

LAPO   *Littératures anciennes du Proche-Orient*

LH   Podany, Amanda H. *Land of Hana: Kings, Chronology, and Scribal Tradition* (2002).

M   Registration number of texts found at Mari

MEE   *Materiali epigrafici di Ebla* (Naples, 1979 ff.)

MHEM   *Mesopotamian History and Environment, Memoirs*

MLC   Morgan Library Collection, tablet numbers of the Yale Babylonian Collection, New Haven

MSL   *Materialien zum sumerischen Lexikon/Materials for the Sumerian Lexicon* (Rom 1937 ff.); SS = Supplementary Series (1, 1986)

MSVO   *Materialien zu den frühen Schriftzeugnissen des Vorderen Orients* (Berlin, 1991 ff.)

NABU   *Nouvelles assyriologiques brèves et utilitaires* (Paris, 1987 ff.)

Nbn.   Strassmaier, J. N. *Inschriften von Nabonidus, König von Babylon* (Leipzig, 1889)

NEA   *Near Eastern Archaeology*

NINO   Nederlands Instituut voor het Nabije Oosten

OEANE   Meyers, Eric M., ed. *The Oxford Encyclopedia of Archaeology in the Near East*, 5 vols. (Oxford and New York: Oxford University Press, 1997)

OECT   *Oxford Editions of Cuneiform Texts* (Oxford, 1923 ff.)

OIMP   *Oriental Institute Museum Publications*

OIS 6   Frahm, Eckart. "Reading the Tablet, the Exta, and the Body: The Hermeneutics of Cuneiform Signs in Babylonian and Assyrian Text Commentaries and Divinatory Texts." In *Divination and Interpretation of Signs in the Ancient World*, Oriental Institute Studies 6, edited by Amar Annus, 93–141 (Chicago: Oriental Institute of the University of Chicago, 2010)

OLA   *Orientalia Lovaniensia analecta* (Leuven, 1975 ff.)

Oracc   Open richly annotated cuneiform corpus: http://oracc.museum.upenn.edu/

PBS   *University of Pennsylvania, Publications of the Babylonian Section* (Philadelphia, 1911 ff.)

PG   Excavation number for graves at Ur

RA   *Revue d'assyriologie et d'archeologie orientale*

RAI   Rencontre Assyriologique Internationale

RIMA   *The Royal Inscriptions of Mesopotamia, Assyrian Periods* (Toronto, 1987 ff.)

RIMB   *The Royal Inscriptions of Mesopotamia, Babylonian Periods*

RIME   *The Royal Inscriptions of Mesopotamia, Early Periods* (Toronto, 1990 ff.)

RINAP   *The Royal Inscriptions of the Neo-Assyrian Period*

RLA   *Reallexikon der Assyriologie und vorderasiatischen Archäologie* (Berlin: de Gruyter)

RS   Museum numbers of the Louvre and Damascus (Ras Shamra)

RTC   Thureau-Dangin, F. *Recueil des tablettes chaldéennes* (Paris, 1903)

SAA   *State Archives of Assyria* (Helsinki, 1987 ff.)

SAA 1   Parpola, S. *The Correspondence of Sargon II. Part I: Letters from Assyria and the West.* State Archives of Assyria 1. (Helsinki, 1987)

SAA 2   Parpola, S., and K. Watanabe, *Neo-Assyrian Treaties and Loyalty Oaths.* State Archives of Assyria 2. (Helsinki, 1988)

SAA 4   Starr, I. *Queries to the Sungod: Divination and Politics in Sargonid Assyria.* State Archives of Assyria 4. (Helsinki, 1990)

SAA 6   Kwasman, T., and S. Parpola. *Legal Transactions of the Royal Court of Nineveh. Part I: Tiglath-Pileser III through Esarhaddon.* State Archives of Assyria 6. (Helsinki, 1991)

SAA 8   Hunger, H. *Astrological Reports to Assyrian Kings.* State Archives of Assyria 8. (Helsinki, 1992)

SAA 10   Parpola, S. *Letters from Assyrian and Babylonian Scholars.* State Archives of Assyria 10. (Helsinki, 1993)

SAA 11   Fales, F. M., and J. N. Postgate. *Imperial Administrative Records. Part II: Provincial and Military Administration.* State Archives of Assyria 11. (Helsinki, 1995)

SAA 13   Cole, S., and P. Machinist. *Letters from Priests to Kings Esarhaddon and Assurbanipal.* State Archives of Assyria 13. (Helsinki, 1999)

SAA 14   Mattila, R. *Legal Transactions of the Royal Court of Nineveh. Part II: Assurbanipal through Sin-šarru-iškun.* State Archives of Assyria 14. (Helsinki, 2002)

SAA 15   Fuchs, A., and S. Parpola. *The Correspondence of Sargon II. Part III: Letters from Babylonia and the Eastern Provinces.* State Archives of Assyria 15. (Helsinki, 2001)

SAA 16   Luukko, M., and G. Van Buylaere, *The Political Correspondence of Esarhaddon.* State Archives of Assyria 16. (Helsinki, 2002)

SAA 18   Reynolds, F. *The Babylonian Correspondence of Esarhaddon.* State Archives of Assyria 18. (Helsinki, 2003)

SAAB   *State Archives of Assyria. Bulletin* (Padua, 1987 ff.)

SAAS   *State Archives of Assyria Studies*

SANER   *Studies in Ancient Near Eastern Records* (De Gruyter 2012 ff.)

SARI   *Sumerian and Akkadian Royal Inscriptions*, I (= American Oriental Society. Translation Series, I): J. Cooper, Presargonic Inscriptions (New Haven, 1986)

SCCNH   *Studies on the Civilization and Culture of Nuzi and the Hurrians* (Winona Lake, IN, 1981ff.)

SMEA   *Studi Micenei ed Egeo-Anatolici* (Rome, 1966 ff.)

SpTU 5   von Weiher, E. *Spätbabylonische Texte aus Uruk*, V: (= AUWE 13, 1998)

Tab   Tablet numbers from Tell Taban

TC   Contenau, G. *Tablettes Cappadociennes* (Paris, 1920) = TCL 4

TCL   *Textes cunéiformes, Musée du Louvre* (Paris, 1910 ff.)

TFR   Tablet numbers from *Terqa Final Reports* (Malibu)

TM   Object numbers from Tell Mardikh/Ebla

TMH NF   *Texte und Materialien der Frau Professor Hilprecht Collection, Neue Folge* (Leipzig, 1937; Berlin, 1961 ff.)

VAT   Museum numbers of the Vorderasiatisches Museum, Berlin (Vorderasiatische Abteilung. Tontafeln)

VS   *Vorderasiatische Schriftdenkmäler der (Königlichen) Museen zu Berlin* (Berlin, 1907 ff.)

YBC   Tablet numbers from the Yale Babylonian Collection (New Haven)

YPM BC   Tablet numbers from the Yale Peabody Museum, Babylonian Collection (New Haven)

ZA   *Zeitschrift für Assyriologie und vorderasiatische Archäologie*

Notes

INTRODUCTION

1. Killgrove 2018.
2. Killgrove 2018.
3. Thomsen 1931.
4. Oppenheim 1967, 82–83.
5. Woolley 1929.
6. Kramer 1959.
7. Jacobsen 1976.
8. In scholarly literature about the ancient Near East it is conventional to use italics when writing out words in Akkadian but not for Sumerian, but I am not making that distinction here. All untranslated ancient words are in italics.
9. This web of interconnections from approximately 2300 to 1300 BCE was the topic of one of my previous books: Podany 2010.

CHAPTER 1

1. http://www.catalhoyuk.com/site/rise_and_fall_of_a_neolithic_town.
2. Jotheri et al. 2018, 66.
3. These are known as crevasse splays: Jotheri et al. 2018, 67.
4. Jotheri et al. 2018, 67.
5. Nissen 2003, 12.
6. Selz 2020, 167.
7. Charvát 2002, 128.
8. Algaze 2013, 68.
9. Charvát 2002, 119.
10. Boehmer 1997, "Uruk-Warka," 294.
11. See, for example, the plan of contemporary Habuba Kabira, which was an Uruk-period city: Kohlmeyer 1997, 446.
12. Sołtysiak 2017.
13. Eichmann 2019, 97–99.
14. Eichmann 2019, 102.
15. The mosaic on the enclosure wall was made of clay cones with glazed ends, whereas the cones on the temple itself were made of stone: Boehmer 1990, 64.
16. Charvát 2002, 121.
17. Charvát 2002, 121, 146–147.

18. This period of construction was referred to as Level VI; Charvát 2002, 121. A detailed and carefully researched 3D video about the construction of the Stone Cone Temple can be seen at "(Re-)Constructing the Stone-Cone building in Uruk—Exhibition Version": https://vimeo.com/54015188. This was created by the company called Artefacts, with the guidance of R. Eichmann.

19. See Eichmann 2007 for architectural details about the Eanna during this period.

20. The plaster pots are known as "White Ware" and were made starting in the eighth millennium BCE, in the Levant: Akkermans and Schwartz 2003, 81. Plaster sculptures of human figures from the eighth and seventh millennia are particularly well known from the site of 'Ain Ghazal in Jordan: Tubb 2001; Bahrani 2017, 33.

21. Selz 2020, 172; Charvát 2002, 121; Eichmann 2019, 102.

22. Hageneuer and Schmidt 2019, 295.

23. Sebastian Hageneuer and Sophie C. Schmidt conducted a detailed analysis of the building materials of Uruk Period temples: Hageneuer and Schmidt 2019.

24. Hageneuer and Schmidt 2019, 295.

25. Hageneuer and Schmidt 2019, 303.

26. Boehmer 1990, 64.

27. Boehmer 1990, 65.

28. These observations about the use of water in the temple, and possible rituals there, were made by Rainer Michael Boehmer: Boehmer 1990.

29. Boehmer 1990, 64–65.

30. Boehmer 1990, 61.

31. Boehmer 1990, 54–59.

32. Eichmann 2019, 102.

33. Boehmer 1990, 64 and plates 6a–c.

34. Selz 2020, 173.

35. Charvát 2002, 123–124.

36. This is known as the Riemchen building, from the German term for the bricks used in its construction: Selz 2020, 173.

37. A reconstruction of the building can be seen at "The Riemchen-Building" from the Uruk Visualization Project: http://www.artefacts-berlin.de/portfolio-item/the-riemchen-building/.

38. Charvát 2002, 123.

39. Hageneuer and Schmidt 2019, 300.

40. These calculations were made by Hageneuer and Schmidt: Hageneuer and Schmidt 2019.

41. Hageneuer and Schmidt 2019, 300.

42. Selz 2020, 173.

43. Hageneuer and Schmidt 2019, 293.

44. Steinkeller 2017, 347.

45. Charvát 2002, 121.

46. Selz 2020, 196.

47. Charvát 2002, 175.

48. Notably, sealings were found by the hundreds in the Burnt Village layer dating to around 6000 BCE at Tell Sabi Abyat: Bennison-Chapman 2018, 311.

49. Selz 2020, 180.

50. Selz 2020, 170.

51. Pollock 2017, 209–210.

52. Selz 2020, 170.
53. Wright, Miller, and Redding 1981, 273–274.
54. Damerow and Englund 1987, 153–154.
55. Charvát 2002, 148.
56. Selz, 2020, 170.
57. Charvát 2002, 120.
58. Charvát 2002, 147.
59. Though some blocks of a similar concrete were found at Ur: Charvát 2002, 147.
60. Selz 2020, 180; Topçuoğlu 2010, 30.
61. Topçuoğlu 2010, 32.
62. McMahon 2007, 29.
63. BM 116722: https://www.britishmuseum.org/collection/object/W_1925-0110-20.
64. YPM BC 005552.
65. Topçuoğlu 2010, 30.
66. Steinkeller 2017, 88. E.g., BM 116721, https://www.britishmuseum.org/collection/obj ect/W_1925-0110-19.
67. Steinkeller 2017, 82.
68. Topçuoğlu 2010, 31.
69. Piotr Steinkeller has been particularly responsible for increasing our understanding of this shadowy individual: Steinkeller 2017, 82–104.
70. Miller et al. 2017, 57.
71. Miller et al. convincingly argue for these identifications: Miller et al. 2017, 57–65.
72. Steinkeller 2017, 86–87.
73. This theory was proposed by Jason Ur: Ur 2014, 264.

CHAPTER 2

1. Kohlmeyer 1997, 446–448.
2. Selz 2020, 175.
3. Collins 2016, 28.
4. Algaze 1993, 15, Fig. 3.
5. E.g., at Hacinebi in southeastern Turkey: Stein 1999, 16–19.
6. Lawler 2006.
7. Lawler 2006, 1458.
8. Midant-Reynes 2000b, 219.
9. Midant-Reynes 2000a, 66–67.
10. Van de Mieroop 2016, 40.
11. Collins 2016.
12. This is now Level IV. C[14] dates suggest it started around 3500 BCE: Boehmer 1997, 295.
13. Nissen 2013, 90.
14. Boehmer 1997, 294.
15. See Figures 2.1 and 2.2B in Salje 2019, 16–17.
16. Damerow 1999.
17. Woods 2010, 34.
18. Schmandt-Besserat 1992.
19. Bennison-Chapman 2018, 335.
20. Englund 2004, 26.

21. Englund 2004, 28–30.
22. See especially Nissen, Damerow, and Englund 1993.
23. Friberg 1999, 119–122; 134–135.
24. Friberg 1999, 125–126.
25. Johnson 2019.
26. Völling 2019, 242.
27. Pollock 2017, 217.
28. Pollock 2017, 217.
29. Engelbert Kämpfer: https://www.britishmuseum.org/collection/term/BIOG11220.
30. Woods 2010, 43.
31. Damerow 1999.
32. Damerow 1999.
33. Englund 2004, 32.
34. Englund 2004, 32–33.
35. Nissen, Damerow, and Englund 1993, 36–46.
36. Paulette 2020, 66.
37. Damerow 2012, 4.
38. Paulette 2020, 67.
39. Mittelman 2008, 9.
40. Damerow 2012, 18.
41. Paulette 2020, 68.
42. MSVO 3 29: Nissen, Damerow, and Englund 1993, 36.
43. Nissen, Damerow, and Englund 1993, 43.
44. Nissen, Damerow, and Englund 1993, 46.
45. Nissen 2019, 150–151.
46. Englund 2004, 28.
47. VAT 15003: Woods 2010, object 46, p. 74.
48. Woods 2010, 42.
49. Englund 2004, 28.
50. "The 10 Most Important Cuneiform Objects": https://cdli.ox.ac.uk/wiki/doku.php?id=objects1to10.
51. Liverani 1996, 12.
52. MSVO 1, 2: https://cdli.ucla.edu/search/archival_view.php?ObjectID=P005069.
53. Pedde 2019, 270–271.
54. Frayne and Stuckey 2021, 143.
55. Steinkeller 2017, 92.
56. See, e.g., the discussion in Potts 2020.
57. See Chapter 18.
58. Potts 2020, 20.

CHAPTER 3

1. Bartash 2020, 539.
2. Jotheri et al. 2018, 67.
3. Hansen 2003, 22.
4. Woods 2010, 43.

5. Bartash 2020, 535.
6. Kingsbury 1963, 7–8, n. 28.
7. Stela of Ushumgal at the Metropolitan Museum of Art, object 58.29, https://www. metmuseum.org/art/collection/search/329079.
8. Gelb 1991, 44.
9. Gelb 1991, 46.
10. This suggestion was made by Irene Winter: Gelb 1991, 46.
11. Balke 2016, 90.
12. Aruz 2003, 78.
13. The cities of Umma were Gesha, Zabalam, and Umma: Bartash 2020, 540.
14. The "Figure aux Plumes" at the Louvre: AO 221, http://cartelfr.louvre.fr/cartelfr/vis ite?srv=car_not_frame&idNotice=11372.
15. Bartash 2020, 548.
16. The inscription was published and analyzed by Piotr Steinkeller: Steinkeller 2013a.
17. Steinkeller 2013a, 133. The inscription can be seen at https://cdli.ucla.edu/dl/photo/ P453401.jpg.
18. For a discussion of the dispute between Umma and Lagash, see Cooper 1981.
19. Frayne 2008, RIME 1, 81.
20. Orthmann 1975, pl. 85.
21. Frayne 2008, RIME 1, 84.
22. Frayne 2008, RIME 1, 84.
23. Frayne 2008, RIME 1.9.1.20.
24. Frayne 2008, RIME 1.9.1.17.
25. Frayne 2008, RIME 1: E1.9.1.6b, p. 92.
26. Frayne 2008, RIME 1, 82.
27. Bartash 2020, 545.
28. Jerry Cooper was responsible for an influential analysis of the battles between Umma and Lagash: Cooper 1981.
29. Bartash 2020, 566.
30. "Sumerian King List" translated by Piotr Michalowski, in Chavalas 2006, 82.
31. "Sumerian King List" translated by Piotr Michalowski, in Chavalas 2006, 83.
32. See Chapter 12.
33. Frayne 2008, RIME 1: E1.9.1.6a, pp. 87–89.
34. Frayne 2008, 125.
35. Stela of the Vultures: Frayne 2008, RIME 1: E1.9.3. 1, p. 129.
36. Stela of the Vultures: Frayne 2008, RIME 1: E1.9.3. 1, p. 133.
37. "Enmetena" translated by Glenn Magid, in Chavalas 2006, 14.
38. "Enmetena" translated by Glenn Magid, in Chavalas 2006, 14.
39. "Enmetena" translated by Glenn Magid, in Chavalas 2006, 14.
40. Frayne 2008, RIME 1: E1.9.5.3, p. 200.
41. Frayne 2008, RIME 1: E1.9.5.4, p. 204.
42. Bartash 2020, 579.
43. Frayne 2008, RIME 1: E1.9.5.12, pp. 213–215.
44. Frayne 2008, RIME 1: E1.9.5.17, pp. 220–221. For an account of the discovery and modern history of the statue, see Collins 2021, 70.
45. Frayne 2008, RIME 1: E1.9.5.17, pp. 220–221. For the reading of Shul-utul's name, see Ragavan 2010, 2–3.

46. See Chapter 20.
47. Iraq Museum IM 5; Evans 2012. The statue was looted from the Iraq Museum in Baghdad in 2003, discovered at Kennedy Airport in New York, and returned to Iraq from the United States in 2006.
48. Zettler and Horne 1998, 22.
49. Zettler and Horne 1998, 22.
50. See Marchesi 2004 for compelling arguments in favor of the royal nature of the tombs. He also includes a discussion of the alternate suggestions.
51. Zettler and Horne 1998, 30–31.
52. Tombs PG 779 and PG 1236. Woolley 1934, 58; Marchesi 2004, 181.
53. This was building PG 779.
54. "Standard of Ur": Aruz 2003, 97–100.
55. Room A: Woolley 1934, 59.
56. Room C: Woolley 1934, 59.
57. Woolley 1934, 59.
58. Chamber C: Woolley 1934, 60.
59. Chamber D: Woolley 1934, 60.
60. Dietrich Sürenhagen noted the similarities to the Ur burials: Sürenhagen 2002.
61. Sürenhagen 2002, 331.
62. Sürenhagen 2002, 332.
63. PG 777, 789, 800, 1054, 1618, 1631, 1648, 1050.
64. The team of researchers was led by Aubrey Baadsgaard of the University of Pennsylvania Museum: Baadsgaard et al. 2011.
65. Baadsgaard et al. 2011, 38.
66. PG 337, 580, 1232, 1237, 1332: Marchesi 2004, 154.
67. E.g., PG 1237 in Ur Online: http://www.ur-online.org/location/931/.
68. This was PG 1237.
69. Hafford 2019a, 218.
70. Hafford 2019a, 218.
71. Min-bara-Abzu is depicted on a stela from the reign of Ur-Nanshe: Romano 2014, 185. The stratum that sealed the royal tombs included seal impressions of Mesannepada, who was probably contemporary with Eannatum of Lagash: Zettler and Horne 1998, 21. Puabi therefore lived before Eannatum.
72. Zettler and Horne 1998, 30.
73. PG 755: Zettler and Horne 1998, 24–25; Woolley 1934, 155–160. Marchesi reads his name as Mes-uge-idu and notes that he may have been the grandson of a better-known king with the same name: Marchesi 2004, 183–185. Ur Online: http://www.ur-online.org/location/1089/.
74. Woolley 1934, 156.
75. Woolley 1934, 158.

CHAPTER 4

1. Frayne 2008, 237.
2. Frayne 2008, 239.
3. E.g., Tablet VS 14 no. 30 was written in the first year that Lugalanda was king, but Dimtur was still the active queen: Lambert 1953, 60–61.

4. SARI 8.3, Louvre AO 13222.
5. Van de Mieroop 1989, 55.
6. Van de Mieroop 1989, 55.
7. Bartash 2020, 568–569.
8. Bartash 2020, 568–569.
9. Van de Mieroop 1989, 63.
10. Maekawa 1996, 171.
11. See Frayne 2008, 241.
12. Emelianov 2017, 292.
13. Emelianov 2017.
14. These diplomatic relationships have been studied by Rosemary Prentice: Prentice 2010.
15. Prentice 2010, 163. His name was Aneda-numea. His name never appears in the Lagash corpus except in this context.
16. One of these gift-giving moments was recorded on a clay tablet that may have originally been from the king's palace archive rather than from the E-Mi: Prentice 2010, 171.
17. RTC 19, Lambert 1953, 58–59. For a detailed discussion of this tablet, see Prentice 2010, 162–164.
18. Prentice 2010, 162–163.
19. His name was Malga-sud or Malga, which was a fairly common name in Lagash.
20. Published in Marchesi 2011.
21. Prentice 2010, 164; Marchesi 2011, 194–195.
22. RTC 26.
23. VS 14 30; VS 14 194; VS 14 38. In DP 518 a different merchant took goods for Baranamtara to Dilmun: Lambert 1953, 62–63.
24. Tablets mentioning the trade done by Urenki: RTC 26; VS 14 no. 30; VS 14 no. 194: Lambert 1953, 60–61.
25. Boucharlat 1995, 1341.
26. Evans 2012, 146–178.
27. Evans 2012, 158.
28. DP 53, XIX, translated in Kobayashi 1983, 43.
29. Kobayashi 1984, 45; A. C. Cohen 2005, 109.
30. This description of the festival draws from a 1983 analysis by Toshiko Kobayashi: Kobayashi 1983.
31. DP 53 includes the details about the festival: Kobayashi 1983, 45–47.
32. A. C. Cohen 2005, 110.
33. The recently excavated site of Tell Zurghul was the site of ancient Nigin: Nadali and Verderame 2021.
34. DP 53 II, 13, in Kobayashi 1984, 45.
35. DP 54, XV 3–7, in Kobayashi 1984, 46.
36. A. C. Cohen 2005, 109.
37. A. C. Cohen 2005, 110.
38. These documents have been studied by Andrew C. Cohen: A C. Cohen 2005.
39. A. C. Cohen 2005, 54–55.
40. A. C. Cohen 2005, 54–55.
41. Cooper 1986, 88.
42. Feldman 2007, 313.

43. A. C. Cohen 2005, 56.
44. See Chapters 7 and 20.
45. A. C. Cohen 2005, 58.
46. DP 75, see A. C. Cohen 2005, 164–166, for a translation.
47. The first three are fairly common. Erekagina: Bartash 2020, 553; Eri'enimgennak: Marchesi 2011, 193.
48. Frayne 2008, 246.
49. Hallo and Younger 2003, 2:408.
50. Hallo and Younger 2003, 2:408.
51. Three scholars who have devoted considerable attention to the weaving women of Lagash are Rosemary Prentice (Prentice 2010), and Fumi Karahashi and Agnès Garcia-Ventura (Karahashi and Garcia-Ventura 2016).
52. Larsen 2015, 196. Vertical looms requiring loom weights were introduced later: Peyronel 2014: 130–132.
53. Prentice 2010, 57.
54. Prentice 2010, 68.
55. Postrel 2020, 49.
56. This may have been Queen Shasha's first year running the palace.
57. Karahashi and Garcia-Ventura 2016, 10.
58. Text DP 442: Karahashi and Garcia-Ventura 2016, 10.
59. Karahashi and Garcia-Ventura 2016, 11.
60. Prentice 2010, 63.
61. Bartash 2020, 569.
62. Her name was Shasha: Prentice 2010, 55.
63. This was Shesh-eanak: Prentice 2010, 55.
64. Karahashi and Garcia-Ventura 2016, 7.
65. Prentice 2010, 56; Karahashi and Garcia-Ventura 2016, 7.
66. She held this role from the third year of King Lugalanda to the sixth year of Urukagina: Karahashi and Garcia-Ventura 2016, 9.
67. Karahashi and Garcia-Ventura 2016, 9; Karahashi 2016a, 67.
68. Karahashi and Garcia-Ventura 2016, 9.
69. Bartash 2020, 575.
70. Prentice 2010, 60–62.
71. Prentice 2010, 62.
72. Bartash 2015.
73. Bartash 2020, 578.
74. Hallo and Younger 2003, 2:407.
75. Hallo and Younger 2003, 2:408.
76. These are all attested among the personnel of the E-Mi: Karahashi 2016b.

CHAPTER 5

1. The excavations were led by Paolo Matthiae of the University of Rome, La Sapienza.
2. Room L 2769.
3. Matthiae 1997.
4. Archi 2012.
5. Bartash 2020, 541.
6. Biga 2011.

7. Maria Giovanna Biga and Alfonso Archi have devoted their careers to studying the Ebla texts. I am drawing a great deal from their analyses.
8. Archi 2017, 299.
9. Matthiae 1997.
10. Archi 2017, 304.
11. Archi 2017, 301, for name of the queen.
12. Archi 2018, ARET XX 6, p. 33.
13. Biga 2016, 74.
14. Biga 2016, 82.
15. Biga 2016, 74.
16. Biga 2016, 75.
17. Archi 2017, 304.
18. Biga 2016, 75.
19. Biga 2016, 77.
20. Biga 2016, 74.
21. Biga 2016, 75–76; Archi 2002, 177.
22. ARET XI 1.
23. ARET XI 2.
24. Ristvet 2011, 9.
25. Biga 2016, 72.
26. Biga 2016, 85.
27. Tonietti 2005, 246.
28. Biga 2016, 85; Archi 2018, 33.
29. The evidence concerning the wedding has been analyzed by Mario Bonechi: Bonechi 2016.
30. Bonechi 2016, 55–56.
31. Biga and Steinkeller 2021, 38.
32. Biga and Steinkeller 2021, 30.
33. ARET XX 16; Archi 2018, 116.
34. Archi 2018, 179.
35. ARET XX 24.
36. Bonechi 2016, 55.
37. Pasquali 2005, 175.
38. Bonechi 2016, 56; Pasquali 2005, 171–172.
39. Bonechi 2016, 56.
40. Bonechi 2016, 64.
41. Bonechi 2016, 57. Ristvet believes it was the southeast gate: Ristvet 2011, 9.
42. Bonechi 2016, 59.
43. Archi 2017, 304.
44. This was called a *mashdabum mariatum*: Archi 2017, 301.
45. Parentheses and square brackets removed; 1939+=XI2, obv IV:4–V:6, in Bonechi 2016, 58.
46. Pasquali 2005, 173.
47. Bonechi 2016, 59.
48. Ristvet 2011, 9; Bonechi 2016, 57.
49. Biga 2014, 99.
50. Biga 2016, 83.

51. Biga 1998, 20.
52. Biga 1998, 20, Archi 1993, text 4: TM.84.G.201.
53. Peyronel et al. 2014, 35.
54. Biga 1998, 19, Archi 2002, 172.
55. Ristvet 2011, 9.
56. Archi 2005, 82, 96; Matthiae 2009.
57. Ristvet 2011, 12.
58. Ristvet 2011, 9.
59. Possibly Nenash—it's a little unclear how the first sign in the name was pronounced: Ristvet 2011, 9.
60. Archi 2017, 301.
61. Archi 2017, 301.
62. TM 74.G.120; Archi 2001; Matthiae 1997.
63. Biga 2010, 148; Biga 2016, 71.
64. Ristvet 2011, 9.
65. Archi 2001, 5.
66. Biga 2010, 148.
67. Archi 2002, 184.
68. ARET XI 1, in Ristvet 2011, 10.
69. Archi 2001, 5; Ristvet 2011, 10.
70. Parentheses and square brackets omitted, Archi 2005, 91 n. 34, from ARET XI 2.
71. TM.75.G.1730 (+) in Archi 2005, 91.
72. Ristvet 2011, 10.
73. Bonechi 2016, 69.
74. Archi 2017, 301.
75. MEE 7.34 in Archi 2017, 301.
76. Ristvet 2011, 11.
77. Archi 2001, 5.
78. ARET XX, Archi 2018, 164; ARET XI 2.
79. Biga 2016, 74.
80. Archi 2018, 45.
81. Matthiae 2009, 308.
82. Archi 2002, 174–184.
83. Archi 2017, 294.
84. Matthiae 2009.
85. Matthiae 2009, 311.
86. Pinnock 2015, 21.
87. Archi 2017, 304.
88. Biga 2010, 149.
89. Biga 2010, 152.
90. Biga 2010, 151, 152; Peyronel 2014, 128.
91. 75.G/1741: Biga 2010, 152.
92. Breniquet 2010, 55.
93. Biga 2010, 55.
94. Biga 2010, 153.
95. "The Hamazi Letter," Michalowski 1993, 13–14.

96. "The Hamazi Letter," Michalowski 1993, 13–14.
97. TM 75.G.2040, Milano 1995, 1228.
98. Biga 2014, 98; Biga and Steinkeller 2021.
99. Biga and Steinkeller 2021, 31–45.
100. Biga 2014, 99.
101. Dugurasu may have been even farther away than Egypt. Thomas Schneider has argued that the name might be a variation of the Egyptian name for Kerma, which was a powerful kingdom to the *south* of Egypt during the Sixth Dynasty: Schneider 2015, 447.
102. Biga 2014, 99.
103. Schneider 2015, 440.
104. ARET XX, text 21, Archi 2018, 150, 154.
105. Biga and Steinkeller 2021, 14.
106. Biga and Steinkeller 2021, 13.
107. Biga and Steinkeller 2021, 15.
108. Archi 2018, 150, 154; Biga and Steinkeller 2021, 18.
109. Biga and Steinkeller 2021, 18.
110. Biga and Steinkeller 2021, 16.
111. Biga and Steinkeller 2021, 19.
112. Archi 2017, 305.
113. Biga 2010, 164.
114. Biga 2016, 73.
115. Archi 2017, 299.
116. Archi 2018, 45; Biga 2016, 79.
117. Archi 2017, 302, list in 75.2022.
118. Archi 2017, 299, 303.
119. Ristvet 2011, 11.
120. Archi 2017, 302.
121. Biga 2016, 76.

CHAPTER 6

1. His actual name was longer than this—a sign or two is missing at the beginning of the line where his name was written. The name was unusual; a man with a similar name lived in the later Ur III period and is known from one administrative tablet. His name started with the name of the city Ur; he was Ur-kitushdu: Marcel Sigrist, *Documents from Tablet Collections in Rochester, New York* (Bethesda, MD: CDL Press, 1991). No. 91, obv 3: PN Uri$_5$^{ki}-ki-tuš-du$_{10}$; https://cdli.ucla.edu/search/archival_view.php?ObjectID=P128196.
2. https://www.britishmuseum.org/collection/image/1613190825.
3. CDLI, Seals 021025 (composite), https://cdli.ucla.edu/search/search_results.php?CompositeNumber=Q001411.
4. Michalowski 1993, 19.
5. "The Birth Legend of Sargon of Akkad," trans. Benjamin R. Foster, in Hallo and Younger, vol. I, 2003, 461.
6. "The Birth Legend of Sargon of Akkad," 461.
7. "The Birth Legend of Sargon of Akkad," 461.

8. One of the later Sargons made it into the Bible (though not as a hero—he was one of the Assyrian kings who were much hated by the people of Israel and Judah) and, as a result, we have his name wrong. In their own language of Akkadian, both kings were named Sharru-ukin. The writers of the Bible called him Sargon. There was no "o" sound in Akkadian, so his name was certainly not pronounced Sargon. But it has stuck and therefore we continue to use it, even for the earlier Sharru-ukin, who wasn't mentioned in the Bible at all.

9. Foster 2016, 245.

10. This was Nabonidus; we will return to him and his fascination with ancient objects in Chapter 20. Foster 2016, 271–272.

11. Wagensonner 2020, 40–41; https://www.britishmuseum.org/collection/object/W_1 928-1009-55; Frayne 1993, RIME 2.1.1.2003, 38: http://oracc.museum.upenn.edu/etc sri/corpus.

12. Westenholz 1989, 546; Wagensonner 2020, 41; Frayne 1993, RIME 2.1.1.2004, 38–39: http://oracc.museum.upenn.edu/etcsri/corpus.

13. Frayne 1993, RIME 2.1.1.2001, 36–37: http://oracc.museum.upenn.edu/etcsri/corpus.

14. Frayne 1993, RIME 2.01.01.2006 and RIME 2.01.01.2007.

15. Foster 2016, 317; Frayne 1993, 26–27.

16. Louvre, Sb 1: https://collections.louvre.fr/en/ark:/53355/cl010123451; Michalowski 2020, 708–709.

17. See Chapter 12.

18. Studevent-Hickman and Morgan 2006, 18, text 14.

19. ABW II, Luzag. 1 in Maeda 2005, 5–9.

20. ABW II, Luzag. 1 in Maeda 2005, 5–9.

21. Maeda 2005, 11–12.

22. Sargon inscriptions 1, 2, and 8, in Foster 2016, 321–322; Frayne 1993, RIME 2.1.1.1, 9–12; RIME 2.1.1.2; 13–15; RIME 2.1.1.13, 32.

23. Sargon inscription 1, in Foster 2016, 321; Frayne 1993, RIME 2.1.1.1, 9–12.

24. Sargon inscription 1, in Foster 2016, 321; Frayne 1993, RIME 2.1.1.1, 9–12.

25. Schrakamp 2020, 614.

26. Sargon inscription 2, in Foster 2016, 321; Frayne 1993, RIME 2.1.1.2, 13–15.

27. Sargon inscription 2, in Foster 2016, 321; Frayne 1993, RIME 2.1.1.2, 13–15.

28. Sargon inscription 7, in Foster 2016, 322; Frayne 1993, RIME 2.1.1.10, 27–29.

29. Sargon inscription 2, in Foster 2016, 322; Frayne 1993, RIME 2.1.1.2, 13–15.

30. Benjamin R. Foster makes a good case for this: Foster 2016, 3–6.

31. Sargon inscriptions 8 and 9, in Foster 2016, 322; Frayne 1993, RIME 2.1.1.13 and RIME 2.1.1.15, 32–34.

32. Sargon inscription 1, in Foster 2016, 321; Frayne 1993, RIME 2.1.1.1, 9–12.

33. Sargon inscription 7, in Foster 2016, 322; Frayne 1993, RIME 2.1.1.10, 27–29.

34. Sargon inscription 2, in Foster 2016, 321; Frayne 1993, RIME 2.1.1.2, 9–12.

35. "The Curse of Agade," in Foster 2016, 351, from ETCSL 2.1.5.

36. "The Curse of Agade," in Foster 2016, 351, from ETCSL 2.1.5.

37. Reade 2002, 269.

38. https://www.britishmuseum.org/collection/object/W_1903-1012-7.

39. Reade 2002, 265.

40. See Bahrani 2017, 133, Fig. 5.18, for a similar depiction of a water buffalo from later in the Akkadian period, also on a cylinder seal belonging to a scribe.

41. Collon 1987, 32.

42. Herrmann and Moorey 1980, 490.

43. Sargon inscription 7, in Foster 2016, 322; Frayne 1993, RIME 2.1.1.10, 27–29.
44. Year-names of Sargon: https://cdli.ox.ac.uk/wiki/doku.php?id=sargon_year-names.
45. Year e: Year-names of Naram-Sin: https://cdli.ox.ac.uk/wiki/doku.php?id=naram-sin_year-names.
46. Year s: Year-names of Naram-Sin: https://cdli.ox.ac.uk/wiki/doku.php?id=naram-sin_year-names.
47. YBC 02191: Frayne 1993, RIME 2.01.01.2001, ex. 01: https://cdli.ucla.edu/search/archival_view.php?ObjectID=P217642.
48. E.g., "Biography of Sargon," https://cdli.ox.ac.uk/wiki/doku.php?id=biography_sargon, from Joannès 2001, 755.
49. "Creation of the Akkadian Empire," Studevent-Hickman and Morgan (trans.), in Chavalas 2006, 18.
50. Year s, Year-Names of Naram-Sin, https://cdli.ox.ac.uk/wiki/doku.php?id=naram-sin_year-names.
51. See Chapter 18.
52. Westenholz 1989, 544.
53. Westenholz 1989, 545.
54. Hafford 2019a, 218.
55. Konstantopoulos 2021, 58, based on Frayne 1993, 35, RIME 2.1.1.16, and Westenholz 1989, 540; Gadotti 2011, 197, writes, "The inscription on the disk is damaged but has been reconstructed from Old Babylonian parallels"; Frayne 1993, RIME 2, 35 f.
56. Westenholz 1989, 544; Konstantopoulos 2021, 59.
57. Stol 2016, 558.
58. Winter 2009, 69.
59. Ninmeshara 120, quoted in Stol 2016, 572.
60. Stol 2016, 564.
61. E.g., Gibson and McMahon 1997, 11.
62. Westenholz 1989, 545–546.
63. Gina Konstantopoulos notes that Enheduana's popular acclaim arose only after the publication of a 1978 article by folklorist Marta Weigle: Weigle 1978. See Konstantopoulos 2021, 63–65.
64. Enheduana is, for example, the only Mesopotamian woman named in *National Geographic*'s special issue on "The Most Influential Figures of Ancient History" (though admittedly only in a sidebar to an article about her father, Sargon): National Geographic 2021, 12.
65. Westenholz 1989, 540.
66. Wagensonner 2020, 42.
67. Wagensonner 2020, 42.
68. See Zgoll 1997; Glassner 2009, 224.
69. YBC 4656, YBC 7169, YBC 7167: Wagensonner 2019, 58–59.
70. Konstantopoulos 2021, 62.
71. The exaltation of Inana: https://etcsl.orinst.ox.ac.uk/section4/tr4072.htm.
72. The Great Revolt was recorded in an inscription from the time of Naram-Sin (Frayne 1993, RIME 2.1.4.6) and was elaborated in literary accounts from later centuries. See Tinney 1995 for an interpretation of these later Old Babylonian literary tales.
73. The rebel kings were Iphur-Kish of Kish and Amar-Girid of Uruk: Frayne 1993, 84. See also Foster 2016, 12; Schrakamp 2020, 632.
74. Frayne 1993 RIME 2.1.4.7; Foster 2016, 207.

75. The Exaltation of Inana: http://etcsl.orinst.ox.ac.uk/section4/b4072.htm.
76. Wagensonner 2020, 44; Haul 2009, 38.
77. The Exaltation of Inana: http://etcsl.orinst.ox.ac.uk/section4/b4072.htm.
78. Westbrook 2008, 318.
79. The Exaltation of Inana: http://etcsl.orinst.ox.ac.uk/section4/b4072.htm.
80. Schrakamp 2020, 632–633.
81. Frayne 1993 RIME 2.1.4.7; Foster 2016, 207.
82. Schrakamp 2020, 624.
83. Lassen 2020, 30–31.
84. Lassen 2020, 31.
85. Michalowski 2008, 34.
86. Michalowski 2008, 34; Schrakamp 2020, 633.
87. Schrakamp 2020, 667.
88. Feldman 2007, 315–317; https://www.louvre.fr/en/oeuvre-notices/victory-stele-naram-sin.
89. Kerr 1998.

CHAPTER 7

1. "Sumerian King List," lines 266–296: https://etcsl.orinst.ox.ac.uk/section2/tr211.htm.
2. Edzard 1997, RIME 3.1.1.7.StB.
3. Edzard 1997, RIME 3.1.1.7.StB.
4. Edzard 1997, RIME 3.1.1.7.StB.
5. Edzard 1997, 26.
6. Edzard 1997, RIME 3.1.1.7.StB.
7. Flückiger-Hawker 1999, 4.
8. Ur-Namma, year-name k: https://cdli.ox.ac.uk/wiki/doku.php?id=year_names_ur-namma.
9. See Canby 2001 for a detailed discussion of the stela.
10. Hafford 2019b, 93; Bahrani 2017, 164.
11. Bahrani 2017, 164.
12. Winter 2003, 404.
13. Bahrani 2017, 165.
14. Sauvage 1998, 49.
15. TMH NF I/II 311, cited by Sauvage 1998, 60.
16. These details come from texts from a different place, Garshana, which have also been analyzed by Sauvage, in Sauvage 2011, 3.1.2 "Bricks."
17. See Richardson 2015, 305–311 for a detailed breakdown of the stages in brickmaking and building.
18. Sauvage 2011, 3.1.2 "Bricks."
19. Sauvage 1998, 55.
20. Sauvage 1998, 56. Robson notes that mathematical problems pertaining to bricks also make a distinction between square baked bricks and rectangular sun-dried bricks: Robson 1996, 182.
21. Ur-Namma brick inscription: Frayne 1997, RIME 3/2.1.1.2, p. 24.
22. Ur-Namma brick inscription: Frayne 1997, RIME 3/2.1.1.4, p. 26.
23. Driscoll et al. 2009, 9972.
24. B16461: Tinney 2019, Fig. 4.8, p. 97.

25. These calculations represent the work of Martin Sauvage: Sauvage 1998, 56.
26. Kleinerman and Owen 2009; Heimpel 2009.
27. Kleinerman and Owen 2009, 423, 486, 551.
28. Adams 2010, 3; Heimpel 2009, 46–47.
29. Adams 2010, 3–4; Heimpel 2009, 67–70, 121.
30. Sauvage 1998, 60.
31. Adams 2010, 3–4.
32. Robson 1996.
33. Sauvage 1998, 60–61.
34. Sharlach 2017, 214.
35. Frayne 1997, notes to RIME 3.2.1.1.4.
36. Lafont and Westbrook 2003, 183.
37. Civil 2011.
38. Laws of Ur-Namma, Roth 1997, 16.
39. Laws of Ur-Namma, Roth 1997, 15–16.
40. Laws of Ur-Namma, Roth 1997, 16.
41. Van de Mieroop 2013, 287.
42. Civil 2011, 246–252.
43. Civil 2011, 247.
44. Ur-Namma's Law 20: Civil 2011, 247.
45. Ur-Namma's Law 18: Civil 2011, 247.
46. Ur-Namma's laws 1, 2, 6, and 34: Civil 2011, 246, 248.
47. Respectively, Ur-Namma's laws E5, E6, and C6: Civil 2011, 252, 250.
48. Yang 1991, 243–244.
49. Van de Mieroop 2013, 278.
50. BM 106451: Molina 2010, text 1, pp. 201–203; Culbertson 2009, text 308, pp. 206–207.
51. Many of these records from Umma have been studied by Laura Culbertson (2009) and Manuel Molina (2010).
52. https://www.britishmuseum.org/collection/object/W_1913-0416-1283.
53. Englund 2012, 443.
54. Steinkeller 2013b, 370.
55. Lafont and Westbrook 2003, 213.
56. Molina 2010, 202.
57. Culbertson 2009, 129.
58. Culbertson 2009, 236.
59. Culbertson 2009, 130.
60. Molina 2010, 202.
61. Lafont and Westbrook 2003, 193; Van de Mieroop 2013, 279.
62. Molina 2010, 202.
63. These clauses are in the wrong order in the original text, perhaps because the oath had to be last.
64. Lafont and Westbrook 2003, 194.
65. Lafont and Westbrook 2003, 194.
66. Van de Mieroop 2013, 279.
67. Van de Mieroop 2013, 279.
68. Ur-Namma's Law 38: Civil 2011, 248.
69. Lafont and Westbrook 2003, 194.

70. Ur-Namma's Law 14: Civil 2011, 247.
71. Lafont and Westbrook 2003, 196.
72. NG 205: 27–42: Lafont and Westbrook 2003, 196.
73. John Nicholas Reid has studied Ur III fugitive slaves, including the record pertaining to Lu-Nanna: Reid 2015.
74. BM 110379: Reid 2015, 585.
75. Lafont and Westbrook 2003, 199.
76. Lafont and Westbrook 2003, 199.
77. There were surprisingly few such escapes in the documents, however, perhaps because they went unrecorded, rather than that they were rare: Snell 2001, 48, 54.
78. Local slaves were probably more likely to run away: Adams 2010, 2.
79. Reid 2015, 585.
80. Reid 2015, 584.
81. Ur-Namma's Law 16: Civil 2011, 247.
82. Reid 2018, 84.
83. Reid 2015, 589, 600.
84. Ur-Namma's Laws 3: Civil 2011, 246; Reid 2015, 595.
85. See the entry for "Manun-gal, Nun-gal, Magala, Manuna": Frayne and Stuckey 2021, 200.
86. Sjöberg 1973, 19.
87. Miguel Civil published and analyzed this hymn: Civil 1993.
88. The Nungal Hymn, line 44: Civil 1993, 73.
89. The Nungal Hymn, line 52: Civil 1993, 73.
90. The Nungal Hymn, line 55: Civil 1993, 73.
91. The Nungal Hymn, lines 50–51: Civil 1993, 73.
92. The Nungal Hymn, line 56: Civil 1993, 73.
93. The Nungal Hymn, lines 104–105: Civil 1993, 74.
94. The Nungal Hymn, line 106: Civil 1993, 74.
95. The Nungal Hymn, line 109-111: Civil 1993, 74.
96. Reid 2015, 585.
97. Reid 2015, 585.
98. Adams 2010, 6.
99. Lafont and Westbrook 2003, 198.
100. Englund 1991, 257.
101. Reid 2015, 600.
102. Heimpel 2010, 159.
103. Wolfgang Heimpel analyzed the "waifs" in these texts: Heimpel 2010.
104. Heimpel 2010, 160.
105. Heimpel 2010, 160.
106. Heimpel 2010, 160.
107. BM 26191: Maekawa 1998, 81–88.
108. Klein 1995, 843; Flückiger-Hawker 1999, 7.
109. "Ur-Namma A," lines 18–21: Flückiger-Hawker 1999, 104.
110. Melville 2007, 240.
111. Klein 1995, 846.
112. "About CDLI": https://cdli.ucla.edu/?q=about. Michael P. Streck calculates that 533,800 cuneiform-inscribed objects have been found: Streck 2010, 58.
113. https://cdli.ucla.edu/.

114. Transliterations represent the values of the Sumerian and Akkadian signs written out in our script.
115. "About CDLI": https://cdli.ucla.edu/?q=about.
116. For example, 308 tablets from the reign of Shulgi mention an official named Ur-e'e in Umma. These tablets have contributed to many studies, concerning, for example, the renting of fields (Steinkeller 1981), the structure and size of institutional arable agriculture (Van Driel 1999/2000, 88), and dairy productivity (Englund 1995, see especially 402, n. 52).
117. Diakonoff 1971, 20.
118. Cripps 2014, 206.
119. This research was done by Xiaoli Ouyang: Ouyang 2013, 94.
120. Garfinkle 2008, 56.
121. Garfinkle 2008, 60.

CHAPTER 8

1. "A praise poem of Shulgi (Shulgi A)": https://etcsl.orinst.ox.ac.uk/section2/tr24 201.htm.
2. Banks 1904, 143.
3. Seri 2006, 33–34.
4. Ishbi-Erra year-names: https://cdli.ox.ac.uk/wiki/doku.php?id=year_names_ishbi-erra. Ishbi-Erra's years in which priestesses were installed and the deities to whom they were dedicated 7: Ninurta; 11: Ishkur; 13: Inana; 22: An; 23a: Lugal-marda; 24a: Enlil; 30: Nin-kilim; 32: Lugal-girra.
5. Ishbi-Erra year 22: https://cdli.ox.ac.uk/wiki/doku.php?id=year_names_ishbi-erra.
6. Cohen 2019, 246.
7. These were Eshnunna and Der.
8. Liverani 2014, 187.
9. "Laws of Lipit-Ishtar": Roth 1997, 23–35.
10. Beaulieu 2018, 63.
11. Abî-sarê year-names: https://cdli.ox.ac.uk/wiki/doku.php?id=year_names_abi-sare.
12. De Boer 2019a, 244.
13. "Kisurra," in Bryce 2009, 391.
14. See the texts published in Goddeeris 2009 and Kienast 1978, along with analysis in Goddeeris 2007.
15. Goddeeris 2009, 72.
16. Tyborowski 2012; Goddeeris 2009, 72.
17. Charpin 1982, 157.
18. Goddeeris 2009, 72.
19. De Boer 2019a, 242
20. George 2018, CUSAS 36 text 1, p. 11.
21. George 2018, CUSAS 36 text 1, p. 11.
22. George 2018, CUSAS 36, texts 7, 11, 12, pp. 17, 21, 22.
23. George 2018, CUSAS 36, text 7, p. 17.
24. George 2018, CUSAS 36, text 11, p. 21.
25. George 2018, CUSAS 36, text 12, p. 22.
26. George 2018 CUSAS 36, text 26, p. 32.
27. George 2018, CUSAS 36, text 24, pp. 30–31.

28. George 2018, CUSAS 36, text 25, pp. 31–32
29. George 2018, CUSAS 36, text 6, p. 16.
30. Puzur-Numushda was one of the recipients of letters 22 (p. 29), 23 (p. 30), 24 (pp. 30–31), and 25 (pp. 31–32). He was also mentioned in letters 7 (p. 17), 10 (p. 20), and 12 (p. 22): George 2018, CUSAS 36.
31. E.g., George 2018, CUSAS 36, letter 7, p. 17.
32. De Boer 2019b, 313.
33. George 2018, CUSAS 36, text 8, p. 18.
34. De Boer 2019b, 310.
35. De Boer 2019b, 311.
36. Rost 2017, 11.
37. De Boer 2019b, 312.
38. George 2018, CUSAS 36, text 29, p. 34.
39. Charpin NABU 2002/39, 42. Sealing is found on two tablets, OECT 13: 7 and 12: https://cdli.ucla.edu/search/archival_view.php?ObjectID=P385537; https://cdli.ucla.edu/search/archival_view.php?ObjectID=P385542.
40. FAOS 2, 148: Goddeeris 2007, 60–61.
41. De Boer 2019a, 242.
42. Fitzgerald 2002, 64.
43. Frayne RIME 4, 107–109.
44. Fitzgerald 2002, 31.
45. Frayne RIME 4, 130–137.
46. Sûmû-El year-names: https://cdli.ox.ac.uk/wiki/doku.php?id=year_names_sumu-el.
47. Sumu-el, year 23: https://cdli.ox.ac.uk/wiki/doku.php?id=year_names_sumu-el.
48. Erra-imitti year-names: https://cdli.ox.ac.uk/wiki/doku.php?id=year_names_erra-imitti.
49. Goddeeris 2002, 316.
50. Goddeeris 2002, 317.
51. Sumulael year-names: http://cdli.ox.ac.uk/wiki/doku.php?id=sumulael.
52. Grayson 1975, 155, lines 31–36.
53. Grayson 1975, 155.
54. All quotes from this inscription: Frayne RIME 4, E4.1.10.1, p. 78.
55. Enlil-bani year-names aa and ab: https://cdli.ox.ac.uk/wiki/doku.php?id=year_names_enlil-bani.
56. Enlil-bani years m and p: https://cdli.ox.ac.uk/wiki/doku.php?id=year_names_enlil-bani.
57. "A praise poem of Enlil-bani (Enlil-bani A): https://etcsl.orinst.ox.ac.uk/section2/tr2581.htm.
58. Frayne 1990, RIME 4.1.10.9, and E4.1.10.10, p. 85.
59. Frayne 1990, RIME 4.1.10.11, p. 86.
60. Sumu-El and the last Larsa king, Rim-Sin (1822–1763).
61. Michalowski, in Chavalas 2006, 81.

CHAPTER 9

1. Hallo 1964.
2. Hallo 1964, 64.

3. Larsen 2015, 197–199.
4. Frayne and Stuckey 2021, 34.
5. Palmisano 2018, 19.
6. Michel 2008, 78.
7. Palmisano 2018, 17.
8. Larsen 2002, xiii.
9. Michel 2008, 73.
10. "Ilu-šumma 2": http://oracc.org/riao/Q005620/.
11. Michel 2008, 74.
12. Marchesi and Marchetti 2019, 15–16.
13. Larsen 2015, 196.
14. Derckson 2004, 26.
15. Palmisano 2018, 31.
16. LAPO 19 2: Michel 2008, 78.
17. Özgüç 1997, 266.
18. Özgüç 1997, 266.
19. Larsen 2015, 138.
20. Palmisano 2018, 20.
21. Larsen 2015, 137.
22. Larsen 2015, 141–145.
23. Waal 2012.
24. Larsen 2002, xv.
25. Larsen 2002.
26. Larsen 2002.
27. Hertel 2014, 37–38.
28. Their names were Ili-alum and Ashur-taklaku.
29. Larsen 2002, xxi.
30. Larsen 2002, xix.
31. Larsen erred on the side of caution and only included in his study documents that very clearly referred to the same family: Larsen 2002. See also Larsen 2015 for a detailed account of Kanesh and the Assyrian merchants who lived and worked there.
32. Michel 2010, 130, quoting Michel 2001, no. 303.
33. Larsen 2002, xxv.
34. CCT 3, 6b: Larsen 2002, text 22, pp. 35–36.
35. Larsen 2002, 147.
36. TC 3, 88: Larsen 2002, text 40, pp. 56–57.
37. Derckson 2004, 278.
38. Derckson 2004, 283.
39. Larsen 2002, xxi–xxii.
40. See Chapter 13.
41. Günbatti 2004.
42. Günbatti 2004.
43. Larsen, 2002, xxv.
44. Michel 2010, 125.
45. TC 1, 15: Larsen 2002, text 48, pp. 68–69.
46. Larsen 2002, 52.
47. Larsen 2002, xxii.

CHAPTER 10

1. Hallo 1964, 72; Villard 2013.
2. Hallo 1964, 86: Hallo proposes a date in the reign of Zimri-Lim of Mari.
3. Shamshi-Adad's name might have been read in the language of Amorite, in which case it would have been Samsi-Addu, but he is better known by the Akkadian reading, as Shamshi-Adad, so I will use that here.
4. Westenholz 2004, 12 and n. 76.
5. Westenholz 2004, 12–13 and n. 76.
6. Veenhof 2017, 58–59.
7. Liverani 2014, 225–226.
8. This observation was made by Mario Liverani: Liverani 2014, 224.
9. Hallo 1964, map on 71.
10. Ristvet 2012, 37.
11. This is the modern site of Tell Leilan: Weiss 1997, 345.
12. The excavations were directed by Harvey Weiss, a professor at Yale University. Size of the tell: Weiss et al. 1990, 581.
13. Weiss 1985.
14. Grayson 1987 RIMA A.0.39.5, p. 57.
15. Tablets from Mari have been published in the series *Archives royales de Mari*. Dominique Charpin and Jean-Marie Durand, of the French team of Mari specialists, have written extensively on the Mari archives, as has Jack M. Sasson, who has made hundreds of the Mari letters more accessible to general readers by publishing them in a single volume called *From the Mari Archives*: Sasson 2015.
16. ARM 1 77: Sasson 2015, 104 n. 196; Charpin 2019, 226.
17. ARM 1 46: Sasson 2015, 104.
18. ARM 1 46: Sasson 2015, 104.
19. A. 3158: Sasson 2015, 104.
20. ARM 5 15: Sasson 2015, 105.
21. Uerpmann and Uerpmann 2002.
22. Sasson 2008, 97.
23. Sasson 2015, 105.
24. Sasson 2015, 106 n. 207.
25. ARM 26 298: Sasson 2015, 106.
26. ARM 26 298: Sasson 2015, 106.
27. Stol 2007; Sasson 2019, 935.
28. ARM 10 92: Sasson 2015, 320.
29. Margueron 1997, 415.
30. Parrot 1945, 158–159.
31. This description is based on the plan and narrative by Kohlmeyer 1985, 195–197 and Fig. 41.
32. Matthiae et al. 1995, 173.
33. Parrot 1945, 156.
34. Bahrani 2017, 188–189.
35. Parrot 1945, 164.
36. M. 10337: Sasson 2015, 306–307 n. 31.
37. ARM 5 13: Dalley 1984, 34.
38. Ziegler 2011, 295.
39. E.g., Grayson 1987 RIMA A.0.39.1

40. Zimri-Lim called himself the son of Yahdun-Lim, but his father was actually Yahdun-Lim's brother: Ziegler 1999, 68.

41. Ziegler 2011, 292.

42. Ziegler 2011, 295.

43. Her name was Dam-hurasi.

44. See especially Ziegler 1999 and Ziegler 2007.

45. Ziegler 1999, 75 n. 488.

46. Ziegler 2016, 306.

47. Ziegler 1999, 6.

48. Ziegler 1999, 73.

49. The total number of women in the palace who were involved in some way in making music increased from around 175 at the start of Zimri-Lim's reign to around 200 by the end: Ziegler 2011, 289–290.

50. Ziegler 1999, 94.

51. FM 4 3, discussed in Ziegler 1999, 94.

52. Ziegler 1999, 69.

53. Ziegler 1999, 58–59.

54. Stol 2016, 353

55. Stol 2016, 357.

56. Ziegler 2011, 290.

57. It was called the "*mummu*" in Akkadian.

58. All quotes from ARM 10 125 are from Sasson 2015, 44.

59. Ziegler 1999, 69.

60. ARM 10 129: Sasson 2015, 331.

61. ARM 10 130: Sasson 2015, 331 n. 112.

62. ARM 1 115: Sasson 2015, 330.

63. Dialog between Enkihegal and Enkitalu, lines 94–99: Michalowski 2010, 201.

64. This was a school exercise, not an actual contract, but Michalowski notes that it probably represented some real aspects of music education: Michalowski 2010, 204–205.

65. Michalowski 2010, 223.

66. Frayne 1990, RIME E4.6.12.3, p. 625.

67. Sasson 2015, 309–310.

68. Bahrani 2017, 165, Fig. 7. 9.

69. This was true in the reigns of Old Babylonian kings of King Yawium in Kish and King Manana in Sippar: Shehata 2014, 110.

70. Shehata 2014, 109.

71. Old Babylonian kings of Isin, Kish, Kisurra, and Sippar all named years after the dedication of kettledrums, called *lilissum* drums: Shehata 2014, 115–116.

72. A. 3165, translated in Sasson 2015, 243–245; discussed in Ziegler 2011, 300–301.

73. The instrument was called a "*balag*." Sasson 2015, 243, calls Ninigizibara "the Lyre goddess," as does Ziegler 2011, 300, but Shehata 2014, 121, describes the *balag* as being a membranophone.

74. E.g., Tuttul, Sippar, Isin, and Larsa: Shehata 2014, 118.

75. A. 3165. All quotes from the ritual are from the translation in Sasson 2015, 243–254. The Dingirgubbu gods seem only known from this ritual; their name means "deities of the left": Frayne and Stuckey 2021, 73.

76. Sasson 2015, 244 n. 26.

77. Ziegler 2011, 299.

78. Ziegler 1999, 58–59.
79. Ziegler 1999, 75 n. 488.
80. Sasson 2012, 530.
81. Sasson 2012, 530 n. 13.
82. Sasson 1993, 43.
83. Van Koppen 2002, 295.
84. The town in which they lived was called Zurubban.
85. ARM 9 97: Van Koppen 2002, 296; Michel 2016, 6–7.
86. Reculeau 2010, 205.
87. Stol 2016, 165.
88. M. 8555, ARM 25, 748; ARM 32, 467–468. Transliteration available on Archibab: http://www.archibab.fr/4DCGI/recherche1.htm.
89. Ziegler 1999, 75 n. 488.
90. The archive at Mari didn't keep letters sent to the lower-ranking wives of the king.
91. ARM 25 353: Ziegler 1999, 75; Van Koppen 2002, 296.
92. ARM 26 276: Van Koppen 2002, 296.
93. ARM 26 277: Sasson 2015, 336.
94. Van Koppen 2002, 303–305.
95. Van Koppen 2002, 313.
96. Van Koppen 2002, 296, 302.
97. Van Koppen 2002, 312.
98. Van Koppen 2002, 307–308.
99. Ziegler 1999, 56.
100. ARM 10 137: Sasson 2015, 311.
101. ARMT 13 22: Sasson 2015, 158–159.

CHAPTER 11

1. CH 196, 197, 200: Roth 1997, 121.
2. "The Kaiser Right in Lauding Hammurabi," *New York Times*, April 26, 1903.
3. Van De Mieroop 1993, 55.
4. De Graef 2018, 136.
5. Potts 2012, 43–44; Charpin 2012a, 352.
6. These are by Marc Van De Mieroop (Van De Mieroop 2005) and Dominique Charpin (Charpin 2012b).
7. Sasson 1998, 461.
8. ARM 2 87.
9. Van De Mieroop 1993, 58.
10. https://cdli.ucla.edu/tools/yearnames/HTML/T12K6.htm.
11. The lands and year-names in which they were mentioned are as follows: Uruk (7), Isin (7), Malgium (10, 30, 33, 35), Rapiqum (11), Shalibi (11), Elam (30), Subartu (30, 33, 37, 39, 43), Gutium (30, 32, 37), Eshnunna (30, 32, 38), Emutbal (Larsa) (31), Eshnunna (32), Mankisum (32), Mari (33, 35), Sutum (37), Turukkum (37), Kakmum (37), Cutha (39), Ekallatum (43), Burunda (43), and Zamlash (43): Horsnell 1999, 112–166 and CDLI year-names, https://cdli.ucla.edu/tools/yearnames/HTML/T12K6.htm.
12. Sasson 1998, 461.

13. CDLI year names: Hammurabi year 33: https://cdli.ucla.edu/tools/yearnames/HTML/T12K6.htm.

14. Sasson 1998, 461.

15. This was the later name of the kingdom in this region: Podany 2002, 32–56.

16. Fiette 2018, 323.

17. Ishikida 1999, 71, 82.

18. Baptiste Fiette has analyzed their correspondence, especially that of Shamash-hazir, focusing on his role and relationship to Hammurabi: Fiette 2018.

19. Yokoyama 1997, 4.

20. Fiette 2018, 48.

21. AbB 13 8: van Soldt 1994, p. 13; Fiette 2018, 49.

22. Breckwoldt 1995/96, 72 n. 23.

23. Rothman and Brumfiel 1994, 153.

24. Stol 1982, 141.

25. Stol 1982, 141.

26. Rothman and Brumfiel 1994, 153.

27. Renger 1995, 296.

28. Renger 1995, 296.

29. Charpin 1987, 113. Fiette 2018, Chapter 2, 101–238.

30. Fiette 2018, 14.

31. De Boer 2016, 140.

32. De Boer 2016, 139.

33. Charpin 1987, 114–115.

34. Charpin 1987, 116.

35. Charpin 2012b, 186.

36. TCL 7, 16, AbB 4 16: Kraus 1968, pp. 10–11.

37. AbB 9 198: Stol 1981, pp. 128–129.

38. See Fiette 2018, Chapter 2, for a detailed account of Shamash-hazir's responsibilities.

39. Fiette 2018, 323.

40. De Boer 2016, 148.

41. Rost 2017, 2.

42. Rost 2017, 13.

43. Rost 2017, 13: AbB 9 194.

44. AbB 4 85; AbB 4 109: Kraus 1968; Rost 2017, 13.

45. AbB 4 19: Kraus 1968; Wu 1998, 94.

46. AbB 4 19: Kraus 1968; Wu 1998, 94.

47. AbB 9 190: Stol 1981, pp. 122–123.

48. Van de Mieroop 2005, 90.

49. Fiette 2018, 237.

50. Brenquiet 2010, 55.

51. Yokoyama 1997, 2.

52. Charpin 2012b, 187.

53. AbB 9 195: Stol 1981, pp. 124–127.

54. Yokoyama 1997, 5.

55. https://www.louvre.fr/en/oeuvre-notices/law-code-hammurabi-king-babylon#:~:text=The%20Law%20Code%20of%20Hammurabi,earlier%20than%20the%20Biblical%20laws.

56. "Laws of Hammurabi": Roth 1997, 76–142.
57. Roth 1997, 77.
58. Roth 1997, 77–80.
59. Roth 1997, 80–81.
60. CH 266: Roth 1997, 130.
61. Ishikida 1999, 64.
62. AbB 4 89: Kraus 1968, p. 61; discussed by Ishikida 1999, 67.
63. Widell 2013, 60.
64. The other is AbB 4 94: Kraus 1968. The other two soldiers were Ṣilli-ishum and Ahu-kinum.
65. CH 26: Roth 1997, 85–86.
66. CH 36: Roth 1997, 88.
67. CH 34, Roth 1997, 87.
68. CH 28: Roth 1997, 86.
69. CH 29: Roth 1997, 86.
70. CH 32, Roth 1997, 87.
71. CH 32, Roth 1997, 87.
72. CH 32, Roth 1997, 87.
73. CH 32, Roth 1997, 87.
74. Ishikida 1999, 65, 67.
75. For example, a recent special issue of the *National Geographic* magazine included the statement that "The code (of Hammurabi) certainly favored people of wealth and rank, who were required to only pay a fine if they injured commoners": "Hammurabi," in *National Geographic* 2021, 14.
76. CH 196–198: Roth 197, 121.
77. CH 274: Roth 131.
78. CH 221, 222: Roth 1997, 124.
79. E.g., CH 175, 176a, 176b: Roth 1997, 115–116.
80. Epilogue to "Laws of Hammurabi," in Roth 1997, 133.

CHAPTER 12

1. Veldhuis 2011, 71.
2. Veldhuis 2011, 72.
3. Charpin 2010, 66–67.
4. Van de Mieroop 1999, 166; Mahmood 2006. Sippar-Yahrurum is modern Abu Habbah, Sippar-Amnanum is modern Tell ed-Der.
5. Mahmood 2006, 17.
6. Al-Rawi and Dalley 2000, 18.
7. Al-Rawi and Dalley 2000, 19.
8. All year-names of Hammurabi: https://cdli.ucla.edu/tools/yearnames/HTML/T12K6.htm.
9. Frayne 1990, RIME 4.5.6.1.
10. ARM 10 43 = LAPO 18 1202: quoted in Harris 1989, 155.
11. Rassam 1897.
12. Gasche and Janssen, 1997.
13. Al-Jadir 1986, 52.
14. Al-Rawi and Dalley 2000, 3.

15. De Graef 2018, 102.
16. LH 110: Roth 1997, 101.
17. Katrien De Graef of Ghent University came up with this new interpretation of the law: De Graef 2018, 99.
18. De Graef 2018, 110.
19. Area V 108, see Al-Rawi and Dalley 2000, iv, Fig. 4.
20. Al-Jadir 1986, 54.
21. Farouk Al-Rawi of the School of Oriental and African Studies in London and Stephanie Dalley of Oxford University published and analyzed this material: Al-Rawi and Dalley 2000, 3–4.
22. Al-Rawi and Dalley 2000, texts 117–130. Four of them definitely came from this neighborhood—texts 118, 119, 121, and 125—and the others all have excavation numbers close to these in sequence, which suggests a nearby provenance.
23. Al-Rawi and Dalley 2000, texts 117, 126, 129.
24. Al-Rawi and Dalley 2000, text 118.
25. Al-Rawi and Dalley 2000, text 130.
26. Al-Rawi and Dalley 2000, texts 119, 120.
27. Al-Rawi and Dalley 2000, text 128.
28. Al-Rawi and Dalley 2000, texts 121, 125.
29. Al-Rawi and Dalley 2000, text 121, found in room 164.
30. This area was dubbed U 106 by the excavators.
31. Al-Rawi and Dalley 2000, 15.
32. Al-Rawi and Dalley 2000, 15–16; though in n. 62 Al-Rawi disagrees and thinks the excavated areas were near but not in the *gagum*.
33. Harris 1989, 155.
34. De Graef 2018, 101.
35. De Graef 2018.
36. Al-Rawi and Dalley 2000, 20.
37. De Graef 2018, 88.
38. This theory was proposed by Elizabeth Stone, of Stony Brook University: Stone 1962, 65.
39. Stol 2016, 601.
40. Harris 1964, 110–116.
41. Rivkah Harris analyzed text PBS 8/2 183 to re-create the events. Quotations from the text are from Harris 1964, 111–115.
42. PBS 8/2 183, in Harris 1964, 111.
43. Harris 1989, 154; Harris 1964, 115.
44. Kraus 1985, AbB 10 4:7–12, quoted in Stol 2016, 591.
45. Harris 1989, 153.
46. Harris 1964, 114.
47. Lion 2018, 159–160.
48. Al-Rawi and Dalley 2000, 16–17.
49. House 11, see Al-Rawi and Dalley 2000, iv Fig. 3.
50. Al-Rawi and Dalley 2000, 16.
51. All quotes from this letter: Dalley et al. 1976, text 134, pp. 108–109, translation from Stol 2016, 596.
52. Note that this Amat-Shamash was the daughter of Sumu-Addu, and Iltani was also the daughter of Sumu-Addu, according to her seal, so they were sisters—see Stol 2000, 461 n. 27.

53. Stol 2016, 598.
54. Dalley et al. 1976, text 134, pp. 108–109, translation from Stol 2016, 596.
55. Stol 2016, 154.
56. Stone 1987, 24.
57. Stone 1987, 129.
58. Robson 2001, 40.
59. Robson 2001, 44; town plan in Fig. 2 and 3, Robson 2011, 41; Proust 2014, 73.
60. Stone 1987, 56–59. Robson 2001, 40.
61. Robson 2001, 41–42.
62. Eleanor Robson has published about the tablets from House F on several occasions: e.g., Robson 2001; Robson 2008, 85–124; Robson 2009.
63. Robson 2001, 44.
64. Shulgi Hymn E, in Charpin 2010, 25.
65. Charpin 2010, 33.
66. George 2001, 5.
67. Robson 2001, 62–63.
68. MSL 12 157: http://oracc.museum.upenn.edu/dcclt/corpus. My thanks to Eleanor Robson for alerting me to this text and the colophon naming Elletum (personal communication).
69. Stone 1987, 125.
70. "Schooldays": Kramer 1963, 238.
71. Stone 1987, 57.
72. Robson 2009, 202, Fig. 3.1.2.
73. "Schooldays": Kramer 1963, 238.
74. The elementary curriculum was reconstructed by Veldhuis 1997, 63.
75. Charpin 2010, 33; Veldhuis 2011, 83.
76. Robson 2009, 206, Table 3.1.1, provides the stages of the noun lists studied.
77. Robson 2001, 48.
78. Proust 2014, 86.
79. Veldhuis 2000, 387.
80. Veldhuis 2011, 77.
81. The list was called Lu-azlag: Gadotti and Kleinerman 2021, 51.
82. Charpin 2010, 30, and Fig. 7.
83. "Schooldays," translated in George 2001, 1.
84. Robson 2009, 206–208.
85. Robson 2009, 203.
86. Robson 2001, 49.
87. Proust 2014, 86.
88. Robson 2008, 85.
89. See Chapter 2.
90. Robson 2008, 16.
91. Robson 2008, 123–124.
92. Robson 2008, 274–284.
93. Robson 2008, 284–288.
94. Tinney 2011, 584.
95. Veldhuis 2000, 385; Tinney 2011, 583.
96. Proust 2014, 75.
97. Veldhuis 2011, 83.

98. Charpin 2010, 43.

99. Veldhuis 2011, 85; Robson 2011, 562.

100. Stone 1987, text 74. Thanks to Eleanor Robson for this observation (private communication).

101. Tinney 2011, 579.

102. Tinney 2011, 582.

103. Proust 2014, 72.

104. Robson 2001, 53.

105. Robson 2001, 53, 54, 56, 60.

106. "Bilgames and Huwawa": George 1999, 149–166; quote on 151.

107. "Bilgames and the Bull of Heaven": George 1999, 166–175.

108. Robson 2001, 60.

109. George 1999, xxi.

110. George 1999, 111.

111. Part of the section about Huwawa was in the segment of the epic found in House F: George 1999, 116–118.

112. George 1999, 124.

113. Veldhuis 2011, 79–80.

114. Veldhuis 2011, 71.

115. Veldhuis 2011, 72.

CHAPTER 13

1. All from Boivin 2018, 86.

2. Boivin 2018, 87.

3. Frayne 1990, RIME 4.3.7.3, pp. 376–377.

4. Frayne 1990, RIME 4.3.7.7, p. 387.

5. Boivin 2018, 88.

6. Charpin 2004, 360.

7. Van Lerberghe et al. 2017 on water deprivation, section 20.

8. Van Lerberghe et al. 2017 on water deprivation, section 20.

9. Van Lerberghe et al 2017 on water deprivation, section 20.

10. CDLI year names https://cdli.ucla.edu/tools/yearnames/HTML/T12K7.htm.

11. In the region where Yadih-Abum ruled, the "m" at the end of his name was optional.

12. CDLI year names: https://cdli.ucla.edu/tools/yearnames/HTML/T12K7.htm.

13. Buccellati 1984.

14. Rouault 2006; Podany 2019a.

15. Podany 2019a, 130–131.

16. Podany 2019a, 127.

17. These assertions about barbers are based on the work of Alexandra Kleinerman, who has studied barbers in the Ur III period. Her conclusions about that era are almost certainly also valid for the Old Babylonian period: Kleinerman 2013.

18. Kleinerman 2013, 306–307.

19. Adamson 1991, 431.

20. LH 226–227; Roth 1997, 124.

21. Geller 2018, 260; Kleinerman 2013, 303.

22. Kleinerman 2013, 304.

23. Kleinerman 2013, 306.
24. TFR2 5-17: Rouault 2011, 19.
25. TFR2 5-6, discussed in Podany 2019a.
26. Podany 2019a, 130, 132.
27. Abraham and Van Lerberghe 2017, CUSAS 29, 5–6.
28. CDLI year-names: https://cdli.ucla.edu/tools/yearnames/HTML/T12K6.htm.
29. CDLI year-names: https://cdli.ucla.edu/tools/yearnames/HTML/T12K6.htm.
30. George 2013, CUSAS 18, 15. Richardson 2019a argues for the basic historical reliability of these sources, BOQ 3 and BOQ 1 (Lambert 2007), in spite of their distance in time from the late Old Babylonian period.
31. George 2013, CUSAS 18, 15.
32. Abraham and Van Lerberghe 2017, CUSAS 29, 5.
33. See Chapter 18.
34. George 2013, CUSAS 18, 14.
35. George 2013, CUSAS 18, 14.
36. Abraham and Van Lerberghe 2017, CUSAS 29, 1.
37. Boivin 2018, 99.
38. Abraham and Van Lerberghe 2017, CUSAS 29, 7.
39. Richardson 2019b, 32.
40. Karel Van Lerberghe, Gabriella Voet, and Kathleen Abraham of the University of Leuven published and analyzed these documents in CUSAS 8 (Van Lerberghe and Voet 2009) and CUSAS 29 (Abraham and Van Lerberghe 2017).
41. Abraham and Van Lerberghe 2017, CUSAS 29, 7.
42. CUNES 51-03-290, Abraham and Van Lerberghe 2017, CUSAS 29, text 27, p. 52.
43. Richardson 2019a, 226.
44. Abraham and Van Lerberghe 2017, CUSAS 29, 7; e.g., text 39, pp. 9–73.
45. This research is by Seth Richardson: Richardson 2005, 284; Richardson 2019a, 232–233; Richardson 2019b, no. 21.
46. Abraham and Van Lerberghe 2017, CUSAS 29, texts 6, 7, 14, 15, 16, 20.
47. CUNES 51-03-155, Abraham and Van Lerberghe 2017, CUSAS 29, text 13.
48. Abraham and Van Lerberghe 2017, CUSAS 29, text 38.
49. BM 96152, Grayson 1975, 156, quoted in George 2013, CUSAS 18, 15.
50. Van Lerberghe and Voet 2009, CUSAS 8, 1.
51. CUNES 51-02-138, Abraham and Van Lerberghe 2017, CUSAS 29, text 205, pp. 166–167.
52. CUNES 51-02-138, Abraham and Van Lerberghe 2017, CUSAS 29, text 205, pp. 166–167.
53. CUNES 51-02-138, Abraham and Van Lerberghe 2017, CUSAS 29, text 205, pp. 166–167.
54. Van Lerberghe and Voet 2009, CUSAS 8, 1.
55. Van Lerberghe and Voet 2009, CUSAS 8. Text 16, seal inscription in Van Lerberghe and Voet 2009, p. 189; translation in Van Lerberghe et al. 2017, section 14.
56. CAD, N vol. 2, pp. 190–191: most people with this title were associated with Enlil at Nippur in the Old Babylonian period.
57. His career lasted from Ammi-saduqa year 5 to Samsu-ditana year 4.
58. Van Lerberghe and Voet 2009, CUSAS 8, 1–2.
59. Richardson 2019a, 225.
60. CTMMA I 69: Richardson 2019a, 225.

61. Van Lerberghe and Voet 2009, CUSAS 8: 9, pp. 26–27.
62. Van Lerberghe and Voet 2009, CUSAS 8, 15.
63. Westbrook 1994, 1663.
64. Van Lerberghe and Voet 2009, CUSAS 8, 2.
65. Richardson 2020, 56–57.
66. Van Lerberghe and Voet 2009, CUSAS 8, 20.
67. Richardson 2005, 283.
68. Van Lerberghe and Voet 2009, CUSAS 8, 20.
69. Van Lerberghe and Voet 2009, CUSAS 8, 50.
70. Van Lerberghe and Voet 2009, CUSAS 8, 53.
71. Bryce 2005, 69.
72. Kloekhorst 2021, 572–573.
73. KBo x 2: Bryce 2005, 76.
74. Bryce 2005, 83.
75. KUB xxix 1: Bryce 2005, 85.
76. Weeden 2016, 158.
77. Bryce 2002, 98–118.
78. Richardson 2016 lists thirteen documents that provide clues to the destruction of Babylon.
79. Landsberger 1954, 64–65; Richardson 2016, 108.
80. YBC 2242: Paulus 2014, 296–304; translation from Richardson 2016, 111.
81. This theory was proposed by Seth Richardson: Richardson 2005.
82. Richardson 2005, 284.
83. Janssen 1996, 245.
84. Van Lerberghe and Voet 1991.
85. Janssen 1996, 246.
86. Gasche 1989, 44.
87. Of course, it might not have been Ur-Utu himself who dropped the tablets, but the choice of which tablets to take must have been made by someone literate, and he seems the most likely candidate.
88. This is also a theory put forward by Seth Richardson: Richardson 2005, 286.
89. Boivin 2018, 117–118.
90. Richardson 2016, 125.
91. Boivin 2018, 122–123; Dalley 2009.
92. Podany 2002, 57–60.
93. Paulus has shown decisively that the later inscription was copied from a real Kassite document: Paulus 2018.

CHAPTER 14

1. He was a contemporary of King Niqmepa of Alalakh who was in turn a contemporary of Saushtatar of Mittani. Dates for these kings are from Maidman 2018, 22.
2. This discussion of Ilim-ilimma is largely based on research by Eva von Dassow and Guy Bunnens: von Dassow 2008; von Dassow 2014; Bunnens 1978.
3. Bunnens 1978, 5–6.
4. Bunnens 1978, 2.
5. AlT 330: Rowe 2002, 13 n. 41; von Dassow 2008, 297, 444.
6. Darnell and Manassa 2007, 63–65.

7. Woolley 1953, 17, 19.

8. Woolley 1953, 20.

9. von Dassow 2008, 12–13.

10. This king of Mittani was Parattarna I (c. 1500–1480 BCE). Autobiography of Idrimi: Oller 1977.

11. The spellings used by the kings were "Maitani," from the seal of king Saushtatar: Grayson, 1987, *RIMA* I, N.O.1001, p. 333; "Mittanni," used in letters by king Tushratta EA 17, Rainey 134–135; EA 19, Rainey 2014, 140–141; EA 24, Rainey 2014, 274–275; EA 28, Rainey 2014, 296–297; and "Mitanni," also used in letters by king Tushratta: EA 21, Rainey 2014, 156–157; EA 22, Rainey 2014, 182–183; EA 23, Rainey 2014, 184–185.

12. "Mittani": e.g., EA 75, Rainey 2014, 460–461; and "Mitana": e.g., EA 76, Rainey 2014, 462–463.

13. The capital is likely to be at a Habur site called Tell Fakhariyah, but excavations have been halted there for years because of the Syrian civil war.

14. von Dassow 2014, 12.

15. von Dassow 2014, 13.

16. Potts 2006, 116.

17. This theory of the conscious implementation of a formal class system in Alalakh and elsewhere in Mittani was developed by Eva von Dassow: von Dassow 2014, 26–28.

18. AlT 128: Wiseman 1953, 11; Bunnens 1978, 4; von Dassow 2008, 148.

19. Von Dassow 2014, 27. See also von Dassow 2008, 233–366, for an extensive discussion of social class at Alalakh during this period.

20. von Dassow 2014, 27.

21. The word *ilku* was the same as the earlier *ilkum*; by this time the "m" sound at the end of nouns in Akkadian had largely been dropped.

22. Von Dassow 2014, 26.

23. von Dassow 2014, 26–28.

24. AlT 2: Wiseman 1953, 26–31; von Dassow 2008, 53.

25. AlT 47: a man and a wife borrowed 60 shekels and would serve him in his house until the debt was paid; AlT 49: another man borrowed 30 shekels and also became his indentured servant.

26. AlT 70: Bunnens 1978, 11–12.

27. AlT 66.

28. Bunnens 1978, 8.

29. AlT 16; see von Dassow 2008, 295 and n. 91.

30. Bunnens 1978, 7.

31. Bunnens 1978, 4.

32. AlT 13, AlT 14.

33. AlT 48: Bunnens 1978, 10–11; and see von Dassow 2008, 296 and n. 92.

34. AlT 48: Bunnens 1978, 11.

35. von Dassow 2008, 62.

36. von Dassow 2008, 61.

37. For a discussion of the creation of the international system, see Podany 2010, 163–187.

38. "The Memphis and Karnak Stelae of Amenhotep II": Hallo and Younger 2003, vol. 2, 22.

39. EA 7: Moran 1992, 13.

40. EA 4: Moran 1992, 8.

41. Fischer 2001, 37.

42. EA 21: Rainey 2014, 156–159; Moran 1992, 50.
43. These were all listed on various documents that were sent with her. See Podany 2010, 217–231 for the stages of Tadu-Hepa's marriage and a discussion of the bridal gifts.
44. EA 21: Moran 1992, 50.
45. EA 21: Rainey 2014, 157.
46. EA 21: Moran 1992, 50.
47. EA 21: Moran 1992, 50.
48. E.g., EA 1, in which Amenhotep III accuses the messengers of the Babylonian king of being dishonest and lying to their king: Moran 1992, 1–3; Rainey 2014, 58–65.
49. EA 21: Rainey 2014, 159.
50. The meanings of *nahra* and *maninnu* are uncertain.
51. EA 21: Rainey 2014, 159.
52. Meier 1988, 196, 198.
53. Meier 1988, 198.
54. Meier 1988, 165.
55. EA 24 II: 101–105, cited in Meier 1988, 172.
56. EA 24: Rainey 2014, 188–241.
57. Cohen 2009, 47.
58. Izre'el 1997, 2, 12.
59. Van Soldt 2000, 105.
60. Tarawneh 2011, 276. The myths included Adapa and the South Wind (EA 356); Nergal and Ereshkigal (EA 357); and the Epic of the King of Battle (EA 359).
61. Van Soldt 2000, 105.
62. Izre'el 1997, 12.
63. Izre'el 1997, 79.
64. EA 368: Izre'el 1997, 77–78.
65. Izre'el 1997, 81, notes on line 16.
66. EA 21: Moran 1992, 50.
67. Podany forthcoming.
68. EA 17: Rainey 2014, 134–135.
69. Podany forthcoming.
70. CAD Vol. R, 136–145.
71. This was fairly common in the Old Babylonian period, see, e.g., *Sumer* 14, no. 18 (IM 51238A), Pl. 11
72. EA 9, Moran 1992, 18.
73. Podany, forthcoming.
74. EA 32: Hoffner 2009, 270.
75. EA 32: Hoffner 2009, 272.
76. In EA 1, Amenhotep III quotes the Babylonian king as suggesting that the pharaoh's wives included a Kaskan.
77. EA 31: Hoffner 2009, 273–277.
78. Hoffner 2009, 270.

CHAPTER 15

1. LH 10: Podany 2002, 122–125.
2. Thureau-Dangin 1897.

3. Podany 2014, 54–55.
4. LH 10: Podany 2002, 124.
5. Hittite royal grants often listed where they were drawn up; not all were in the capital city, so the officials would have traveled some distance in order to witness the contracts: Beal 2016, 176.
6. Source of this quote and the next: Speiser 1929, 270–271.
7. E.g., in the region of Hana, an Old Babylonian–era document found at Tell Taban records that a king gave two fields and a small house to a man named Yasim-Mahar: Tab T06-4: Yamada 2008, 156–160. See Podany 1997 for parallels between Hana and Kassite land grants.
8. Slanski 2003, 115.
9. Tinney and Sonik 2019, 45 (image of a stone tablet), 46 (caption).
10. Rouault 1992; Podany 2014, 54–55: the relevant tablets are listed under "Texts from Terqa" and their numbers begin with the designation TQ12.
11. Slanski 2003, 116.
12. Easton 1981; for a study of the Hittite royal land grants, see Rüster and Wilhelm 2012.
13. E.g., RS 16.250, Nougayrol 1955, Plate 13.
14. E.g., Bazi 1 and Bazi 2: Sallaberger et al. 2006, 78–79, 81–82.
15. Slanski 2003, 287.
16. Slanski 2003, 118–121.
17. Slanski 2003, 288.
18. Slanski 2003, 288.
19. EA 20: Moran 1992, 48.
20. See, e.g., EA 21: Moran 1992, 50.
21. EA 24: Moran 1992, 65.
22. E.g., EA 20: Moran 1992, 48.
23. Gifts from Tushratta to Amenhotep III when his daughter married the pharaoh: EA 22: Moran 1992, 51–61; dowry for Tushratta's daughter: EA 25: Moran 1992, 72–81; dowry for Burna-Buriash's daughter: EA 13: Moran 1992, 24–27. Discussed in Podany 2010, 219–224.
24. The international relationships between great kings of the Late Bronze Age have been addressed in several books, including Cohen and Westbrook 2000, Liverani 2001, Bryce 2003, and Podany 2010.
25. By this time, kings with Kassite names had ruled the region of southern and central Mesopotamia for more than 200 years. Burna-Buriash II's relationship to his dynasty's original Kassite origins was as tenuous as Hammurabi's had been to those of his Amorite forebears. The kings and their families had adopted Mesopotamian culture thoroughly, and no longer seem to even have spoken Kassite. No documents at all have been found in the Kassite language. The kings were as Babylonian as anyone else, notwithstanding their names. Although their dynasty was Kassite in origin, we can simply call them Babylonian.
26. The Greek object is a cylinder seal found in Thebes, owned by a man named Kidin-Marduk who was an official of Burna-Buriash II: Brinkman 1976, E.2.23, p. 111.
27. Potts 1986, 170; Ritter 1965, 317–318.
28. The physician was named Shumu-libshi. For the reading of his name (which was originally read as Mukallim) and a discussion of these letters, see Plantholt 2014.
29. BE 17 47: Oppenheim 1967, 118.

30. BE 17 47: Oppenheim 1967, 118; Potts 1986.

31. PBS I 2 Ritter 1965, No. 72, p. 318.

32. EA 1: Rainey 2014, 60–63. This letter is from the time of Burna-Buriash II's father, Kadashman-Enlil I.

33. EA 6: Moran 1992, 12.

34. EA 1: Moran 1992, 1–5.

35. EA 11: Moran 1992, 21.

36. This interpreter was a man named Mihuni, taking the same role played by Hane in Mittani.

37. EA 12: Rainey, 106–107.

38. EA 12: Rainey, 106–107.

39. EA 11: Moran 1992, 21.

40. Items in the dowry are listed in EA 13: Moran 1992, 24–26.

41. EA 14: Moran 1992, 27–37.

42. Nefertiti is famous for her sculpture now in the Berlin Museum: https://www.smb. museum/en/museums-institutions/aegyptisches-museum-und-papyrussammlung/ collection-research/bust-of-nefertiti/the-bust/.

43. EA 1: Moran 1992, 1–5.

44. The princess of Mittani, Tadu-Hepa, had a "dowry personnel" of 270 women and 30 men: EA 25: Moran 1992, 81. Her aunt Kilu-Hepa had brought 317 attendants to Egypt, according to a scarab distributed by Amenhotep III: "Marriage with Kirgipa": Breasted 1906, vol. 2: 347–348.

45. The new capital, Akhetaten, was located at the modern site of Amarna, where the diplomatic letters were found.

46. Bryce 2003, 103.

47. Stavi 2011, 229.

48. Stavi 2011, 229–230; Mladjov 2016, 23.

49. First plague prayer of Mursili II: Hallo and Younger 2003, vol. 1, 156.

50. Her position was as a *shiwanzanni* priestess.

51. Hoffner 1983, 191.

52. EA 41: Moran 1992, 114–115; Rainey 358–361.

53. The prince was named Shattiwaza. For his subsequent treaty with the Hittites, in which this history is recounted, see HDT 6B: Beckman 1999, 48–54.

54. For a more detailed account of these events, see Podany 2010, 293–301.

55. KUB 14.4 ii 3–12: Hoffner 1983, 191.

56. KBo 4.8: Hoffner 1983, 189.

57. Kbo 4.8: Hoffner 1983, 188.

58. Bryce 2002, 21.

59. Beckman 2012, 489.

60. Kbo 4.8: Hoffner 1983, 188.

61. "Plague Prayers of Muršili II": Hallo and Younger, vol. 1 2003, 156.

62. Untash-Napirisha is known to have married a Babylonian princess as his chief wife, and the inscription on the statue of Napir-Asu calls her the wife of Untash-Napirisha, so it seems almost certain that they were the same person: Potts 2016, 212.

63. These developments are analyzed by Daniel T. Potts in a comprehensive book called *The Archaeology of Elam*: Potts 2016.

64. Potts 2016, 198.

65. Potts 2016, 198.
66. Harper et al. 1992, 121.
67. Potts 2016, 223. This was King Kidin-Hutran II.
68. Harper et al. 1992, 127–130.
69. Potts 2016, 212.
70. Potts 2016, 211.
71. Meyers 2000; Harper et al. 1992, 134.
72. Harper et al. 1992, 134.
73. Harper et al. 1992, 134.
74. EKI §16: Harper et al. 1992, 132.
75. E.g., Harper et al. 1992, object 84, p. 136.
76. Harper et al. 1992, 121.
77. Harper et al. 1992, 121.
78. Potts 2016, 214.
79. Ghirshman 1961, 72.
80. Ghirshman 1961, 71–72.
81. Some scholars have suggested that it was 200 feet tall, e.g., Harper et al. 1992, 121.
82. Mofidi-Nasrabadi 2015, 38.
83. For the "millions of bricks": Potts 2016, 215.
84. Ghirshman 1961, 71.
85. Mofidi-Nasrabadi 2015, 50.
86. Carter 2011, 53–56.
87. This is based on Elizabeth Carter's analysis of the tombs and the structure that had been built over them: Carter 2011.
88. See, e.g., Carter 2011.
89. Carter 2011, 56.
90. Carter 2011, 56.
91. Ghirshman et al. 1968, 73–74.
92. Carter 2011, 54.
93. Carter 2011, 56.
94. Potts 2016, 223.
95. Potts 2016, 223.
96. Melville 2007, 241. Some scholars have proposed that it was Burna-Buriash's son, not the king himself, who married the Assyrian princess.
97. EA 15: Moran 1992, 37–38; Rainey 2014, 128–129.
98. EA 9: Moran 1992, 18.
99. EA 16: Moran 1992, 39–41; Rainey 2014, 130–133.
100. EA 16: Rainey 2014, 130–131.
101. Brinkman 1976, 167 n. 3.
102. Brinkman 1976, 166.
103. This was Kurigalzu II: Brinkman 1976, 31.

CHAPTER 16

1. Price 2011.
2. See Mynářová 2007 for a discussion of the diplomatic language used in Amarna letters, and particularly 147–164 for the introductory formulas.
3. The young king's name was Urhi-Teshub.

4. Silver 2010.

5. "The Apology of Ḫattušili III," translated by Harry A. Hoffner Jr., in Chavalas 2006, 268.

6. Hittite version of the treaty: CTH 91: Beckman 1999, no. 15, pp. 96–100.

7. CTH 91: Beckman 1999, no. 19, 97.

8. KUB 21.38: Hoffner 2009, text 98, 282–289. This letter is also quoted extensively and analyzed in Van de Mieroop 2007, 223–226.

9. KUB 21.38: Hoffner 2009, text 98, 282.

10. KUB 21.38: Hoffner 2009, text 98, 282.

11. This was a quote from Ramses in Puduhepa's letter: KUB 21.38: Hoffner 2009, text 98, 285.

12. KUB 21.38: Hoffner 2009, text 98, 283.

13. KUB 21.38: Hoffner 2009, text 98, 289.

14. AHK 51, translation from Bryce 2003, 109.

15. For a detailed account of the marriage, see Bryce 2003, 106–111.

16. "A letter from the Hittite King Hattušili III to Kadašman-Enlil II, King of Babylonia," translated by Kathleen R. Mineck in Chavalas 2006, 275–279.

17. Yamada 2003, 166–168.

18. van Soldt 2010, 250.

19. Akkermans and Schwartz 2003, 336.

20. Cline 2014, 109.

21. Sauvage 2012, 41, 83.

22. Yon 1997, 258.

23. Atwood 2021.

24. van Soldt 2010, 249.

25. Excavations have taken place at Ugarit, fairly continuously, since 1929.

26. Akkermans and Schwartz 2003, 337. See Yon 2006, 37 Fig. 20 for a plan of the palace.

27. RS 17.434+: Pardee 2003, text 10, pp. 96–97. See discussion in Devecchi 2019, 125–126.

28. RS 17.434+: Pardee 2003, text 10, pp. 96–97.

29. RS 34.136: Devecchi 2019, 126. This was a later letter, reflecting back on events in Niqmaddu III's reign.

30. This is an argument made by Elena Devecchi: Devecchi 2019.

31. Devecchi 2019, 127–133.

32. Urtenu's ownership of the house is not entirely certain (see Lackenbacher and Malbran-Labat 2016), but there is no doubt that he was closely associated with the house because of the many documents and letters found there that were written to him.

33. Cline 2014, 106–107.

34. Álvarez García 2021, 24.

35. Calvet 2000, 210.

36. Calvet 2000, 210.

37. Y. Cohen 2021, 50; Álvarez García 2021, 24.

38. Yon 2006, object 53, p. 161.

39. Calvet 2000, 211.

40. Yon 2006, 87; Y. Cohen 2021, 50.

41. Y. Cohen 2021, 51.

42. Bordreuil and Malbran-Labat 1995, 444; Malbran-Labat 1999, 240.

43. Bordreuil and Malbran-Labat 1995, 448.

44. All quotes from this letter: RS 94.2406: Pardee 2003, text 18, pp. 102–103.

45. RS 94.2406: Pardee 2003, text 18, pp. 102–103.

46. This section is based on analysis of the letters by Dennis Pardee (Pardee 2003) and Gary Beckman (Beckman 2007).
47. Pardee 2003, 102 n. 107.
48. RS 94.2479: Pardee 2003, text 26, p. 107.
49. Beckman 2007, 167–168.
50. Beckman 2007, 168–170.
51. Urtenu's sister: RS 94.2284: Pardee 2002, text 38, pp. 113–114; Urtenu's son: RS 31.134: Beckman 2007, 169; Dagan-belu's son: RS 31.141: Beckman 2007, 170.
52. Sauvage 2012, 130.
53. Álvarez García 2021, 25–26.
54. Atwood 2021.
55. Bordreuil and Malbran-Labat 1995, 445; Calvet 2000, 211. Malbran-Labat 1999, 238–239.
56. Sauvage 2012, Chapter 2, 85–138.
57. This is the argument made by archaeologist Caroline Sauvage: Sauvage 2012, 156.
58. Sauvage 2012, 292–293.
59. Pulak 2008.
60. See Podany 2010, 255–258, for a reconstruction of the journey and wreck of the Ulu Burun ship.
61. RS 18.031: Pardee 2003, text 8, pp. 93–94.
62. RSO 23: 184–185, no. 107: translation by Y. Cohen 2021, 53.
63. RS 18.038: Devecchi 2019, 131.
64. Devecchi 2019, 131; Atwood 2021; Y. Cohen 2021, 54.
65. Y. Cohen 2021, 55.
66. Devecchi 2019, 133.
67. Finné et al. 2019, 859.
68. Huehnergard 1997, 240.
69. Fleming 2000, 4.
70. This festival was described in texts Emar 373 and 375 and has been extensively analyzed by Daniel E. Fleming: Fleming 2000, 48–140; Fleming 2015. See also Michel 2014 and Thames 2020.
71. Fleming 2015, 201.
72. Fleming 2015, 201.
73. Fleming 2015, 201.
74. Fleming 2015, 204.
75. Fleming notes that the unveiling provided "a two-way exchange, a meeting of the eyes" providing "a world of non-verbal communication": Fleming 2015, 209.
76. Fleming 2000, 139.
77. Démare-Lafont and Fleming 2015, 68.
78. Y. Cohen 2012, 14.
79. Adamthwaite 2001, 133, 229.
80. Adamthwaite 2001, 232.
81. The first part of this story was reconstructed by Carlo Zaccagnini (Zaccagnini 1994) and Lena Fijałkowska (Fijałkowska 2014).
82. The baby's name includes the name of a god, written with the cuneiform signs ᵈIM. This always represented the storm god in cuneiform. The name or divine title that was intended by this sign varied depending on region and seems to have been read as Ba'la or Ba'lu, meaning "lord" in Emar.
83. Fijałkowska 2014, 390.

84. Emar 216: Fijałkowska 2014, 390.
85. Emar 216: Zaccagnini 1994, 1.
86. Johnson 2021, 16.
87. Zaccagnini 1994, 2.
88. Fijałkowska 2014, 390 n. 54.
89. Emar 217, Arnaud 1986, translation from Wells 2007, 207.
90. Fijałkowska 2014, 391.
91. Emar 218 and 219, found in Building M-1 and Emar 220, found in Building M-2: Thames 2020, 11.
92. Emar 219 and 220: Y. Cohen 2005, 166.
93. Zaccagnini 1994, 3.
94. Thames 2020, 263 n. 124.
95. For the ages of the babies: Zaccagnini 1994, 4.
96. Fleming 2000, 6.
97. Fleming 2000, 34.
98. Fleming 2000, 35.
99. Thames 2020, 264.
100. Zaccagnini 1994, 3.
101. Fijałkowska 2014, 394.
102. Fijałkowska 2014, 396.
103. Y. Cohen 2012, 21.
104. Fleming 2015, 199.
105. RSO 23: 33–35, no. 12: translation by Y. Cohen 2021, 58.
106. Cline 2014, 109.
107. "The War against the Peoples of the Sea," translated by John A. Wilson: Pritchard 1969, 262.
108. Y. Cohen 2021, 58–59.
109. See Cline 2014 for a book-length discussion of these issues.
110. Cline 2014, 158.
111. Grayson 1972, 117.
112. Potts 2016, 225.
113. Potts 2016, 226–227.
114. Potts 2016, 229.

CHAPTER 17

1. Erb-Satullo 2019, 564, 574, Fig. 6. The site was Kaman-Kalehöyük IIIb.
2. Erb-Satullo 2019, 566–572.
3. Younger 2016, 37.
4. Younger 2016,
5. Younger 2016, 45. This was not true in southern Mesopotamia, where Aramean tribes were not called "House of" someone.
6. Younger 2016, 33.
7. Quinn 2017, 201.
8. Pritchard 1969, 378.
9. See Miller and Hayes 1986, 220–221, Chart IX, for a timeline of the kings of Israel and Judah.
10. Urartu was the name used by the Assyrians for the land; it seems to have been called Biainili by the people who lived there.

11. See, e.g., Melville 2016 on Sargon II and Elayi 2018 on Sennacherib. The British Museum created an entire exhibit and catalogue devoted to Ashurbanipal in 2018: Brereton 2018.

12. Ashurnasirpal II 001: http://oracc.museum.upenn.edu/riao/Q004455/.

13. Ashurnasirpal II 001: http://oracc.org/riao/Q004455/.

14. Ashurnasirpal II 001: http://oracc.org/riao/Q004455/.

15. Liverani 2017, 131.

16. This and subsequent quotes from this inscription: Ashurnasirpal II 001: http://oracc.museum.upenn.edu/riao/Q004455/.

17. These temples are listed in the Banquet Inscription in lines 55–59: Ashurnasirpal II 030: http://oracc.museum.upenn.edu/riao/Q004484/.

18. Ashurnasirpal II 001, iii 110–113: http://oracc.museum.upenn.edu/riao/Q004455/.

19. http://oracc.museum.upenn.edu/nimrud/livesofobjects/standardinscription/.

20. Ashurnasirpal II 030, "Banquet Inscription": http://oracc.museum.upenn.edu/riao/Q004484/.

21. This is known as the "Standard Inscription": http://oracc.org/riao/Q004477/.

22. Ashurnasirpal II 023, "Standard Inscription": http://oracc.org/riao/Q004477/.

23. Ashurnasirpal II 030, "Banquet Inscription": http://oracc.museum.upenn.edu/riao/Q004484/.

24. Curtis and Tallis 2008.

25. Ashurnasirpal II 030, "Banquet Inscription": http://oracc.museum.upenn.edu/riao/Q004484/.

26. Collins 2016, 44.

27. Feldman 2014, 100.

28. Bahrani 2017, 232.

29. Winter 1981, 6.

30. Collins 2010, 181.

31. Winter 1981. See discussion of other scholarship in Fales 2009, 244–246.

32. Such wax tablets were in common use, but the wood panels rarely survive and the wax never does.

33. SAA 13 34: http://oracc.org/saao/P313456/.

34. SAA 13 34: http://oracc.org/saao/P313456/.

35. Feldman 2014, 82.

36. Collins 2010, 186.

37. BM 124821: https://www.britishmuseum.org/collection/object/W_1851-0902-5.

38. BM 124820: https://www.britishmuseum.org/collection/object/W_1851-0902-6; and BM 124822: https://www.britishmuseum.org/collection/object/W_1851-0902-4. See Collins 2016, 46, regarding the use of prisoners of war for this work.

39. SAA 1 110: http://oracc.org/saao/P224487/.

40. SAA 1 139: http://oracc.org/saao/P334912/.

41. Bahrani 2017, 232.

42. Bahrani 2017, 232.

43. E.g., Canby 1971 on the garments in Ashurnasirpal's relief sculptures.

44. Albenda and Guralnick 1986, 240.

45. Bahrani 2017, 232.

46. SAA 15 4: http://oracc.org/saao/P334103/.

47. Albenda and Guralnick 1986, 240.

48. Albenda and Guralnick 1986, 233–234.

49. Verri et al. 2009.
50. This was observed by Mario Liverani: Liverani 2017, 125–126.
51. Liverani 2017, 125.
52. Liverani 2017, 126.
53. BM 124554: https://www.britishmuseum.org/collection/object/W_1849-1222-23. See also the excellent photographs in Amin 2017. The relevant panel images are of Panels 4 and 5.
54. Cifarelli 1998, 224.
55. Cifarelli 1998, 223.
56. Fales 2009, 245.
57. "Fallen foe of Assyrians": Amin 2017. BM 124540: https://www.britishmuseum.org/collection/object/W_1849-1222-16.
58. Ashurnasirpal II 1: http://oracc.museum.upenn.edu/riao/Q004455/.
59. Seen in BM 124685 and 124687, described in Curtis and Tallis 2008, 35, Figs. 17 and 18, and 38, Figs. 23 and 24.
60. Melville 2016, 16.
61. Melville 2016, 16.
62. Sargon II 013: http://oracc.museum.upenn.edu/rinap/rinap2/corpus/.
63. Sargon II 007: http://oracc.museum.upenn.edu/rinap/rinap2/corpus/#rinap/rinap2:Q006488_project-en.1.
64. 2 Kings 17:24.
65. Millard 1994, 60, cited in Melville 2016, 187.
66. Ussishkin 1997, 321.
67. See Liverani 2017, 188–190, for details about tribute in the Assyrian Empire.
68. Prism of Sennacherib: Sennacherib 004, http://oracc.org/rinap/Q003478/.
69. Liverani 2017, 192.
70. UNHCR, "Syria Emergency": https://www.unhcr.org/en-us/syria-emergency.html.
71. 2 Kings 18:13. An almost identical account is found in Isaiah 36:1.
72. 2 Chronicles 32:9.
73. Uelinger 2003, 223.
74. Ussishkin 1997, 321.
75. Ussishkin 1997, 321.
76. Ussishkin 2003, 207.
77. Uelinger 2003, 240.
78. BM 124907: https://www.britishmuseum.org/collection/object/W_1856-0909-14_3.
79. Ussishkin 2003, 209.
80. Ussishkin 2003, 210.
81. BM 124954: https://www.britishmuseum.org/collection/object/W_1856-0909-1_6.
82. SAA 11 167: http://oracc.org/saao/P335907/.
83. Dalley 2017, 528.
84. Dalley 2017, 528.
85. Dalley 2017, 531.
86. Oded 1979.

CHAPTER 18

1. Esarhaddon's name in Akkadian was Ashur-ah-iddin. The writers of the Bible called him Esarhaddon.
2. Esarhaddon was born between 715 and 710 BCE: Frahm 2014, 191.

3. Sennacherib was born around 740 BCE: Frahm 2014, 176.

4. Svärd 2015, 43. Note though that it is possible that Naqi'a took the title of Sennacherib's queen only after her husband's death, though I find that argument less persuasive: Svärd 2015, 46.

5. Svärd 2015, 187: Appendix A, text 44. Date of the text: Frahm 2014, 190.

6. The son who assassinated Sennacherib was named Arda-mullissi or Urdu-Mullisu, see Parpola 1980 and Brereton 2018, 14. He probably had help from one of his brothers. Other scholars have proposed that Esarhaddon might have been behind the assassination himself: Dalley and Siddall 2021.

7. This and the rest of the quotes from this text are found in Esarhaddon 1: Leichty 2011, 11.

8. Eph'al-Jaruzelska 2016, 133.

9. Esarhaddon 1: Leichty 2011, 13.

10. Eph'al-Jaruzelska 2016, 133.

11. Esarhaddon 1: Leichty 2011, 14.

12. Frahm 2010b, 98.

13. Radner 2003b, 167.

14. Esarhaddon 1: Leichty 2011, 14.

15. Radner 2003b, 167; Eph'al-Jaruzelska 2016, 134.

16. Zimansky 2006, 263.

17. Piotrovsky 1974–1977, 50.

18. Bel-ushezib is sometimes described as a "scholar" rather than as a diviner, e.g., Eph'al-Jaruzelska 2016, 128, but he was clearly involved in reading omens and oracles and interpreting them for the king.

19. SAA 10 109: http://oracc.org/saao/P334798/.

20. SAA 10 109: http://oracc.org/saao/P334798/.

21. All quotes from the letter from Bel-ushezib about the Mannean campaign are from SAA 10 111: http://oracc.org/saao/P237234/.

22. Beaulieu et al. 2017, 1.

23. Beaulieu et al. 2017, 71–76.

24. Beaulieu et al. 2017, 9.

25. MLC 1866, Section C: Beaulieu et al. 2017, 40.

26. Rochberg 2011, 621. These are called the Babylonian Astronomical Diaries: Sachs and Hunger 1988.

27. Rochberg 2011, 631.

28. Rochberg 2011, 622.

29. SAA 10 112: http://oracc.org/saao/P238052/.

30. Frahm 2010a, 121.

31. SAA 16 69: http://oracc.org/saao/P334309/.

32. Three scholars in particular have tried to solve the riddle of Sasi: Karen Radner (2003b); Martti Nissinen (1998, 109–153); and Eckart Frahm (2010a, 120–126; 2015, 9–10).

33. His name was Nabu-rehtu-usur.

34. SAA 16 59: http://oracc.org/saao/P313533/; all quotes from this letter are at this link. Stökl 2012, 105.

35. Jean 2010, 270.

36. Koch 2011, 462–463.

37. Koch 2011, 462.

38. Frahm 2010a, 100–101.
39. SAA 16 59: http://oracc.org/saao/P313533/.
40. SAA 16 60: http://oracc.org/saao/P313432/.
41. All quotes from this letter are from YBC 11382, YPM BC 025176: Frahm 2015, 9–10. Commentary in the same citation, also in Podany 2019b, 69–71; Lassen et al. 2019, object no. 40, pp. 225–226.
42. Frahm 2010a, 121. The tablet listing them is SAA 11 156: http://oracc.org/saao/P334311/.
43. SAA 11 156: http://oracc.org/saao/P334311/.
44. SAA 16 18: http://oracc.org/saao/P334819/.
45. N'Shea 2016, 215.
46. See, e.g., SAA 4, texts 9, 63, 78, 79, 80, 88. All in http://oracc.museum.upenn.edu/saao/corpus.
47. N'Shea 2016, 219.
48. This quote and others from this letter: http://oracc.org/saao/P237270/. Frahm 2010a, 121–122, includes a discussion of this letter.
49. Veldhuis 2010, 78; Winitzer 2010, 186–189.
50. This quote and others from this letter: SAA 10 316: http://oracc.org/saao/P313436/.
51. Svärd 2015, 46.
52. E.g., SAA 18 10: http://oracc.org/saao/P237817/; Svärd 2015, 204.
53. On Adad-shumu-usur's close relationship to Esarhaddon: Šašková 2018, 61.
54. SAA 10 229: http://oracc.org/saao/P333960/.
55. This quotation and the next: SAA 10 196: http://oracc.org/saao/P333957/.
56. Šašková 2018, 55.
57. Biggs 1995, 1918–1921; Šašková 2018, 64.
58. This quotation and the next: SAA 10 189: http://oracc.org/saao/P334453/.
59. SAA 10 216: http://oracc.org/saao/P334906/.
60. Chronicle 1, translated by Bill T. Arnold and Piotr Michalowski: Chavalas 2006, 411.
61. See Frahm 2010a, 113–123, for a detailed analysis of this.
62. Frahm 2010a, 124–126; Nissinen 1998, 144–150. Note that Radner, writing in 2003, believed that Sasi was probably executed with the other high officials. The later Sasi would, in that case, not be the same man: Radner 2003b, 176.
63. SAA 2 6: http://oracc.org/saao/Q009186/.
64. SAA 2 6 paragraph 98: http://oracc.org/saao/Q009186/.
65. Lauinger 2012, 90.
66. Taylor 2015.
67. Fales 2012.
68. Chronicle 1, translated by Bill T. Arnold and Piotr Michalowski: Chavalas 2006, 411.
69. SAA 10 174: http://oracc.org/saao/P334626/. See also Fales 2009, 257.
70. Chronicle 1, translated by Bill T. Arnold and Piotr Michalowski: Chavalas 2006, 411.
71. Radner 2003b, 172.
72. Chronicle 1, translated by Bill T. Arnold and Piotr Michalowski: Chavalas 2006, 411.

CHAPTER 19

1. Beaulieu 2007, 139.
2. Radner 2003a, 228.

3. Beaulieu 1995, 972.

4. "The Adad-guppi Autobiography," translated by Tremper Longman III, in Hallo and Younger 2003, vol. 1, 477–478.

5. "The Mother of Nabonidus," translated by A. Leo Oppenheim: Pritchard 1969, 560–562.

6. Beaulieu 1995, 972; Melville 2006, 390; Razmjou 2013, 105. Adad-guppi's husband was named Nabu-balatsu-iqbi.

7. Sargon II 84: http://oracc.museum.upenn.edu/rinap/corpus/#Q006565.2.

8. Postgate 1974.

9. Gershon 2007, 14, 345. The tablets can be found at http://oracc.museum .upenn.edu/saao/saa11/corpus under Chapter 9 (Harran Census).

10. Gershon 2007.

11. SAA 11 201: http://oracc.org/saao/P334934/.

12. His house was in the town of Hamede, which is otherwise almost completely unknown.

13. SAA 11 201: http://oracc.org/saao/P334934/. The translation there has the girl described as "nubile," but the term used for her in the census, batussu, is just the feminine version of the general term for "adolescent."

14. Gershon 2007, 347–348.

15. Gershon 2007, 348.

16. Gershon 2007, 351.

17. The exact average was 4.08 people: Gershon 2007, 346.

18. Gershon 2007, 350. Among all the lower-stratum families Gershon studied, only 1.5 percent were polygamous.

19. Gershon 2007, 351.

20. SAA 11 201: http://oracc.org/saao/P334934/.

21. Gershon 2007, 352.

22. SAA 11 201: http://oracc.org/saao/P334934/.

23. Barjamovic et al. 2019, 111.

24. Barjamovic et al. 2019, 124.

25. It can be found in one version in Barjamovic et al. 2019, 125, and another at https:// www.biblicalarchaeology.org/daily/ancient-cultures/daily-life-and-practice/bar-test-kitchen-tahu-stew/.

26. Renfrew 2003, 58.

27. Norrie 2003, 22.

28. The Banquet Scene: https://www.britishmuseum.org/collection/object/W_1 856-0909-53.

29. E.g., BM 124872–124878: https://www.britishmuseum.org/collection/object/W_1 856-0909-47.

30. SAA 16 28: http://oracc.org/saao/P334196/. Discussed in Taylor 2018, 94–95.

31. Finkel 2018, 80–82.

32. Brinkman 1973, 94–95.

33. OIP 2 83: Brinkman 1973, 94.

34. Brinkman 1973, 95 and n. 31.

35. Novotny 2018, 203.

36. His actual name was Nabu-aplu-usur.

37. Scurlock 2012.

38. Scurlock 2012, 182.

39. Nab. 8, translation by Thomas G. Lee: Lee 1993, 133–134.

40. This was Ashur-uballit II.
41. "Funerary Stele of Adad-guppi," translated by Paul-Alain Beaulieu: Beaulieu 2007, 146.
42. Melville believes the statues were taken to Babylon: Melville 2006, 390.
43. Lee 1993, 132.
44. Beaulieu 2017, 550.
45. Beaulieu 2017, 551.
46. Adad-guppi may have given birth to her son in her thirties, because he lived for another seventy years, until 539 BCE, and it's unlikely that he survived to be more than about eighty years old.
47. Autobiography of Adad-guppi, translation by Thomas G. Lee: Lee 1993, 134.
48. "The Adad-guppi Autobiography," translated by Tremper Longman III, in Hallo and Younger 2003, vol. 1, 477–478.
49. Beaulieu 1995, 976.
50. Beaulieu 2008, 9.
51. Beaulieu 2008, 9.
52. Nebuchadnezzar II 2: http://oracc.org/ribo/Q005473/.
53. Pedersén 2011, 20.
54. Pedersén 2011, 13.
55. Dalley 2015.
56. Statistics are from Klengel-Brandt 1997 and Pedersén 2011.
57. Herodotus, *The History of the Persian Wars*, I.178.
58. "The Adad-guppi Autobiography," translated by Tremper Longman III, in Hallo and Younger 2003, vol. 1, 477–478.
59. "The Adad-guppi Autobiography," translated by Tremper Longman III, in Hallo and Younger 2003, vol. 1, 477–478.
60. Hussein 2016.
61. Álvarez-Mon 2009, 153–154.
62. Álvarez-Mon 2009, 148, 152.
63. Gross and Garcia-Ventura 2018, 381.
64. Salvatore Gaspa did a study of weaving in the Neo-Assyrian period: Gaspa 2013, 226.
65. Gaspa 2013, 226–227.
66. Álvarez-Mon 2009, 153.
67. Sennacherib 17: http://oracc.museum.upenn.edu/rinap/rinap3/corpus/#rinap/rinap3:Q003491_project-en.68.
68. Gaspa 2013, 231–232.
69. Gaspa 2013, 235.
70. SAA 6 91: http://oracc.org/saao/P335011/.
71. SAA 8 305: http://oracc.org/saao/P238716/.
72. SAA 1 33: http://oracc.org/saao/P334141/, discussed by Gaspa 2013, 230.
73. Gaspa 2013, 232.
74. SAA 6 42: http://oracc.org/saao/P335270/.
75. Waerzeggers 2006, 95.
76. Bongenaar 1997, 305–307.
77. Caroline Waerzeggers has reconstructed the workings of the laundry business in Babylonia from a number of contracts written during the sixth and early fifth centuries BCE: Waerzeggers 2006.
78. Waerzeggers 2006, 95.

79. BM 29228: Waerzeggers 2006, 83–84.
80. Waerzeggers 2006, 94.
81. E.g., BE 8 119: Waerzeggers 2006, 91–92.
82. BM 96390: Waerzeggers 2006, 85–86.
83. VS 6 86: Waerzeggers 2006, 90–91.
84. BM 29228: Waerzeggers 2006, 83–84.
85. Waerzeggers 2006, 94.
86. Waerzeggers 2006, 95.
87. Hussein 2016, 7–8, and Plate 16a.
88. Gross and Garcia-Ventura 2018, 383.
89. Radner 2007, 192–193.
90. Gross and Garcia-Ventura 2018, 379.
91. Gross and Garcia-Ventura 2018, 378.
92. Cousin 2016, 521.
93. Cousin 2016.
94. Cousin 2016, 520.
95. Bab 28122, Melanges Dussaud A: http://oracc.museum.upenn.edu/ctij/corpus; discussed in Cousin 2016, 518.
96. Bab 28122, Melanges Dussaud A: http://oracc.museum.upenn.edu/ctij/corpus. See Beaulieu 2008, 6–7, for a discussion of the foreigners listed in these tablets.
97. Cousin 2016, 521–522.
98. SAA 14 161: http://oracc.org/saao/P335252/; discussed in Cousin 2016, 522.
99. Beaulieu 2008, 10–11.
100. Melanges Dussaud B: http://oracc.museum.upenn.edu/ctij/corpus.
101. http://cojs.org/cojswiki/Babylonian_Ration_List:_King_Jehoiakhin_in_Exile,_592/1_BCE.
102. BM 21946, translated by A. Leo Oppenheim: Pritchard 1969, 563–564.
103. BM 21946, translated by A. Leo Oppenheim: Pritchard 1969, 563–564.
104. BM 21946, translated by A. Leo Oppenheim: Pritchard 1969, 563–564.
105. 2 Kings 24:11–12.
106. 2 Kings 24:15.
107. 2 Kings 24:14.
108. 2 Kings 24:13.
109. 2 Kings 25:1–17.
110. 2 Kings 25:21.
111. 2 Kings 25:27–30.
112. Beaulieu 2007, 142.
113. Beaulieu 2007.
114. Beaulieu 2007, 140.
115. Beaulieu 2007, 140.
116. Beaulieu 2007, 142.
117. See Chapter 12.
118. Excellent translations of the Epic are available, such as those by Andrew George (1999, 1–100), Stephanie Dalley (2009, 39–135); and Benjamin Foster (2019, 3–100).
119. "The Mother of Nabonidus," translated by A. Leo Oppenheim: Pritchard 1969, 561.
120. "The Mother of Nabonidus," translated by A. Leo Oppenheim: Pritchard 1969, 561.
121. "The Mother of Nabonidus," translated by A. Leo Oppenheim: Pritchard 1969, 561.

122. His real name was Nergal-sharru-usur.
123. "Nabonidus and his God," translated by A. Leo Oppenheim: Pritchard 1969, 562–563.
124. "The Mother of Nabonidus," translated by A. Leo Oppenheim: Pritchard 1969, 561.
125. Beaulieu 2007, 140–148.
126. Beaulieu 2007, 140–144.
127. "The Mother of Nabonidus," translated by A. Leo Oppenheim: Pritchard 1969, 561.
128. "The Mother of Nabonidus," translated by A. Leo Oppenheim: Pritchard 1969, 561.

CHAPTER 20

1. Beaulieu 2018b, 239.
2. Nabonidus 34: http://oracc.org/ribo/Q005431/.
3. Nabonidus 34: http://oracc.org/ribo/Q005431/.
4. This quote and subsequent ones about the Ebabbar are from Nabonidus 27: http://oracc.org/ribo/Q005424/.
5. This quote and the next: Nabonidus 34: http://oracc.org/ribo/Q005431.
6. This quote and the next two: BM 119014: https://www.britishmuseum.org/collection/object/W_1927-1003-9.
7. Moorey 1982, 251–252.
8. Nabonidus 34: http://oracc.org/ribo/Q005431/.
9. CAD Z, 6.
10. This quote and the next: Nabonidus 34: http://oracc.org/ribo/Q005431/.
11. See Chapter 2.
12. AnOr 8 14, discussed in Stol 1994, 180.
13. Still and Sonnevelt 2020, 105 n. 33.
14. Stol 1994, 180.
15. Bongenaar 2000, 82.
16. Still and Sonnevelt 2020.
17. Still and Sonnevelt 2020, 105.
18. Bongenaar 2000, 84; Pirngruber and Waerzeggers 2011.
19. Waerzeggers 2014, 32.
20. Waerzeggers 2014, 119.
21. Caroline Waerzeggers has done extensive research on the world of Bel-uballit and his family, especially his son Marduk-remanni: Waerzeggers 2014.
22. Waerzeggers 2014, 41.
23. Still and Sonnevelt 2020, 107.
24. Jursa 2010, 220.
25. LB 1743: Still and Sonnevelt 2020, 103.
26. Waerzeggers 2014, 91.
27. Still and Sonnevelt 2020, 108.
28. Waerzeggers 2014, 33.
29. Bongenaar 2000, 84–85.
30. The son's name was Marduk-remanni.: Waerzeggers 2014.
31. BM 63940: discussed in Waerzeggers 2014, 77 and n. 12.
32. NBC 6189: Jursa 2010, 221.
33. MR 18: Waerzeggers 2014, 77.
34. MR 6: Waerzeggers 2014, 76.

35. Waerzeggers 2014, 76–77.
36. Jursa 2010, 223; Dromard 2017, 231–237.
37. Many scholars have written about Itti-Marduk-balatu and his slaves, but I am drawing here especially from the works of Muhammad A. Dandamaev (1984), Michael Jursa (2010), Gauthier Tolini (2013), and Benjamin Dromard (2017).
38. Tolini 2013, 2.
39. Alstola 2017.
40. "Ninkasi": Frayne and Stuckey 2021, 259–260.
41. Damerow 2012, 15.
42. See, e.g., the efforts of Patrick McGovern and Dogfish Head brewery to re-create ancient beers: McGovern 2017.
43. Quotes from the Hymn to Ninkasi are all from Civil 1964.
44. Damerow 2012, 15.
45. Alstola 2017.
46. Dandamaev 1984, 323.
47. Nbn. 1019: Dandamaev 1984, 324.
48. Nbn. 681: Dandamaev 1984, 322; Dromard 2017, 234.
49. Dromard 2017, 237.
50. Dromard 2017, 236.
51. Nbn. 845: Dandamaev 1984, 323; discussed in Dromard 2017, 232.
52. Baker 2001, 20.
53. Jursa 2010, 225.
54. Camb. 334: Dandamaev 1984, 107.
55. Jursa 2010, 226.
56. Dandamaev 1984, 197.
57. Cyr. 248: Dandamaev 1984, 282.
58. Baker 2001, 22.
59. Wunsch 2012, 50.
60. Baker 2001, 23.
61. Dandamaev 1984, 117, 120.
62. Cyr. 248: Dandamaev 1984, 282.
63. Wunsch 2012, 50.
64. Baker 2001, 25.
65. Wunsch 2012, 51.
66. Baker 2001, 24.
67. Wunsch 2012, 51.
68. Tolini 2013, 9.
69. Camb. 330: Joannès 1992a; Tolini 2013, 3.
70. See Stol 1994, 170–174, for a discussion of the brewing utensils.
71. Alstola 2017: this was the amount of time the scholars fermented their experimental date beer.
72. Tolini 2013, 6.
73. Abouali et al. 2019, 51, 53.
74. Tolini 2013, 7–8.
75. Stol 1994, 176; Alstola 2017.
76. Camb. 331: Joannès 1992b; Tolini 2013, 4.
77. Tolini 2013, 6.

78. OECT 10, 239:Tolini 2013, 4–5.
79. His full name was Marduk-nasir-apli.
80. CTMMA 3, 65:Tolini 2013, 5.
81. BM 30948:Tolini 2013, 6.
82. Razmjou 2013, 122.
83. Razmjou 2013, 111.
84. Beaulieu 2018a, 241–242.
85. Davies 2002, 66.
86. Daniel 4:33.
87. Daniel 4:34.
88. Cyrus Cylinder, translated by Irving Finkel: http://oracc.org/ribo/Q006653/.
89. Sandowicz 2015.
90. Razmjou 2013, 116.
91. Cyrus Cylinder, translated by Irving Finkel: http://oracc.org/ribo/Q006653/.
92. Razmjou 2013, 117.
93. Cyrus Cylinder, translated by Irving Finkel: http://oracc.org/ribo/Q006653/.
94. Razmjou 2013, 112–113.
95. Waerzeggers 2014, 116.
96. Waerzeggers 2014, 118–119.
97. George 2010.
98. Clancier 2011, 756.
99. Robson 2019, 176.
100. Frahm 2019, 293.
101. Robson, 2008, 227; Robson 2019, 229.
102. Eleanor Robson has written about this house and analyzed the documents found there: Robson 2008, Robson 2019.
103. Arbøll 2021, 7.
104. Robson 2018.
105. Robson 2019, 238.
106. Robson 2019, 238.
107. SpTU 5, 231: http://oracc.org/cams/gkab/P348818; Robson 2008, 232.
108. SpTU 5, 231: http://oracc.org/cams/gkab/P348818; Robson 2008, 232.
109. Robson 2019, 244.

Bibliography

Aboualil, Ladan, Jianlin Ni, and Jake Kaner. 2019. "A Study of the Interior Furniture and Decorative Motifs of Achaemenid and Sassanid." *American Journal of Art and Design* 4 (4): 48–57.

Abraham, Kathleen, and Karel Van Lerberghe. 2017. *A Late Old Babylonian Temple Archive from Dūr-Abiešuḫ, The Sequel.* CUSAS 29. Bethesda, MD: CDL Press.

Adams, Robert McC. 2010. "Slavery and Freedom in the Third Dynasty of Ur: Implications of the Garshana Archives." *Cuneiform Digital Library Journal* 2: 1–8.

Adamson, P. B. 1991. "Surgery in Ancient Mesopotamia." *Medical History* 35 (4): 428–435.

Adamthwaite, Murray R. 2001. *Late Hittite Emar: The Chronology, Synchronisms, and Socio-Political Aspects of a Late Bronze Age Fortress Town.* London: Peeters.

Akkermans, Peter M. M. G., and Glenn M. Schwartz. 2003. *The Archaeology of Syria: From Complex Hunter-Gatherers to Early Urban Societies (c. 16,000–300 bc).* Cambridge and New York: Cambridge University Press.

Albenda, Pauline, and Eleanor Guralnick. 1986. "Some Fragments of Stone Reliefs from Khorsabad." *JNES* 45 (3): 231–242.

Algaze, Guillermo. 1993. *The Uruk World System: The Dynamics of Expansion of Early Mesopotamian Civilization.* Chicago: University of Chicago Press.

Algaze, Guillermo. 2013. "The End of Prehistory and the Uruk Period." In *The Sumerian World*, edited by Harriet Crawford, 68–94. London and New York: Routledge.

Al-Jadir, Walid. 1986. "Sippar: Ville du dieu soleil." *Dossiers histoire et archéologie* 103: 52–54.

Al-Rawi, Farouk N. H., and Stephanie Dalley. 2000. *Old Babylonian Texts from Private Houses at Abu Habbah Ancient Sippir.* É-DUB-BA-A 7. London: Nabu Publications.

Alstola, Tero. 2017. "Date Beer: Brew It Like the Ancient Babylonians." Academy of Finland Centre of Excellence: Changes in Sacred Texts and Traditions. https://blogs.helsinki.fi/sacredtexts/2017/12/22/date-beer-brew-it-like-the-ancient-babylonians/.

Álvarez García, Juan. 2021. "La Maison d'Urtenu. A Functional Study of a 'Great House' from Ugarit." In *Bridging the Gap: Disciplines, Times, and Spaces in Dialogue–Volume 1: Sessions 1, 2, and 5 from the Conference Broadening Horizons 6 Held at the Freie Universität Berlin, 24–28 June 2019*, edited by Christian W. Hess and Federico Manuelli, 22–36. Oxford: Archaeopress Publishing Ltd.

Álvarez-Mon, Javier. 2009. "Ashurbanipal's Feast: A View from Elam." *Iranica Antiqua* 44: 131–180.

Amin, Osama Shukir Muhammed. 2017. "Wall Reliefs: Ashurnasirpal II's War Scenes at the British Museum." *World History Encyclopedia.* Last modified September 13, 2017. https://www.worldhistory.org/article/1118/wall-reliefs-ashurnasirpal-iis-war-scenes-at-the-b/.

Arbøll, Troels Pank. 2021. *Medicine in Ancient Assur: A Microhistorical Study of the Neo-Assyrian Healer Kiṣir-Aššur.* Leiden: Brill.

Archi, Alfonso. 1993. "Trade and Administrative Practice: The Case of Ebla." *Altorientalische Forschungen* 20 (2): 43–58.

Archi, Alfonso. 2001. *The King Lists from Ebla.* Bethesda, MD: CDL Press.

Archi, Alfonso. 2002. "Jewels for the Ladies of Ebla." *ZA* 92 (2): 161–199.

Archi, Alfonso. 2005. "The Head of Kura—The Head of 'Adabal." *JNES* 64 (2): 81–100.

Archi, Alfonso. 2012. "Ebla." In *The Encyclopedia of Ancient History.* https://doi.org/10.1002/9781444338386.wbeah01051.

Archi, Alfonso. 2017. "Religious Duties for a Royal Family: Basing the Ideology of Social Power at Ebla." *JNES* 76 (2): 293–306.

Archi, A. 2018. *Administrative Texts: Allotments of Clothing for the Palace Personnel (Archive L. 2769). With the Collaboration of Gabriella Spada. ARET* XX. Wiesbaden: Harrassowitz.

Archibab. N.d. http://www.archibab.fr/Accueil.htm.

Arnaud, Daniel. 1986. *Emar: Recherches au pays d'Aštata. VI.3, Les textes sumériens et accadiens.* Paris: Éditions Recherche sur les Civilisations.

Aruz, Joan. 2003. *Art of the First Cities: The Third Millennium bc from the Mediterranean to the Indus.* New York: Metropolitan Museum of Art, 2003.

Atwood, Roger. 2021. "The Ugarit Archives." *Archaeology,* July/August 2021. https://www.archaeology.org/issues/430-2107/features/9752-ugarit-bronze-age-archive.

Baadsgaard, Aubrey, Janet Monge, Samantha Cox, and Richard L. Zettler. 2011. "Human Sacrifice and Intentional Corpse Preservation in the Royal Cemetery of Ur." *Antiquity* 85 (327): 27–42.

Bahrani, Zainab. 2017. *Art of Mesopotamia.* New York: Thames and Hudson.

Baker, Heather D. 2001. "Degrees of Freedom: Slavery in Mid-First Millennium bc Babylonia." *World Archaeology* 33 (1): 18–26.

Balke, Thomas E. 2016. "The Interplay of Material, Text, and Iconography in Some of the Oldest 'Legal' Documents." *Materiality of Writing in Early Mesopotamia* 13: 73–94.

Banks, E. J. 1904. "Impressions from the Excavations by the Germans at Fara and Abu Hatab." *Biblical World* 24: 138–146.

Barjamovic, Gojko, P. Jurado Gonzalez, Chelsea Graham, Agnete W. Lassen, Nawal Nasrallah, and Pia M. Sörensen. 2019. "Food in Ancient Mesopotamia. Cooking the Yale Babylonian Culinary Recipes." In *Ancient Mesopotamia Speaks: Highlights from the Yale Babylonian Collection,* edited by A. W. Lassen, E. Frahm, and K. Wagensonner, 108–125. New Haven: Yale University Press.

Bartash, Vitali. 2015. "Children in Ancient Sumer: How Much Do We Know?" *The Ancient Near East Today* III, no. 6 (June): http://www.asor.org/anetoday/2015/06/children-in-ancient-sumer-how-much-do-we-know/.

Bartash, Vitali. 2020. "The Early Dynastic Near East." In *Oxford History of the Ancient Near East,* vol. 1, edited by Karen Radner, Nadine Moeller, and D.T. Potts, 531–611. Oxford and New York: Oxford University Press.

Beal, Richard H. 2016. Review of *Landschenkungsurkunden hethitischer Könige* by Christel Rüster and Gernot Wilhelm. *JAOS* 136 (1): 174–177.

Beaulieu, Paul-Alain. 1995. "King Nabonidus and the Neo-Babylonian Empire." In *CANE,* 2:969–979.

Beaulieu, Paul-Alain. 2007. "Nabonidus the Mad King: A Reconsideration of His Stelas from Harran and Babylon." In *Representations of Political Power: Case Histories from Times of Change and Dissolving Order in the Ancient Near East,* edited by Marlies Heinz and Marian H. Feldman, 137–168. Winona Lake, IN: Eisenbrauns.

Beaulieu, Paul-Alain. 2008. "Nebuchadnezzar's Babylon as World Capital." *Canadian Society for Mesopotamian Studies Journal* 3: 5–12.

Beaulieu, Paul-Alain. 2017. "Assyria in Late Babylonian Sources." In *A Companion to Assyria*, edited by Eckart Frahm, 547–555. Malden, MA: John Wiley & Sons.

Beaulieu, Paul-Alain. 2018a. *A History of Babylon, 2200 bc–ad 75*. Malden, MA: John Wiley and Sons.

Beaulieu, Paul-Alain. 2018b. "Uruk before and after Xerxes: The Onomastic and Institutional Rise of the God Anu." In *Xerxes and Babylonia: The Cuneiform Evidence*, edited by Caroline Waerzeggers and Maarja Seire, 189–206. Leuven: Peeters.

Beaulieu, Paul-Alain, Eckart Frahm, Wayne Horowitz, and John Steele. 2017. "The Cuneiform Uranology Texts: Drawing the Constellations." *Transactions of the American Philosophical Society*, n.s., 107 (2): 1–121.

Beckman, Gary M. 1999. *Hittite Diplomatic Texts*. 2nd ed. Atlanta: Scholars Press.

Beckman, Gary M. 2007. "Ugarit and Inner Syria during the Late Bronze Age." In *La royaume d'Ougarit de la Crète á l'Euphrate: Nouveaux axes de recherche*, edited by Jean-Marc Michaud, 163–174. Sherbrooke: Éditions GGC.

Beckman, Gary M. 2012. "Tawan(n)anna." *RLA* 13 (5/6): 488–490.

Bennison-Chapman, Lucy E. 2018. "Clay Objects as 'Tokens'? Evidence for Early Counting and Administration at Late Neolithic Tell Sabi Abyad, Mesopotamia." *Levant* 50 (3): 305–337.

Biga, Maria Giovanna. 1998. "The Marriage of Eblaite Princess Tagriš-Damu with a Son of Nagar's King." In *About Subartu: Studies Devoted to Upper Mesopotamia, Subartu IV/2*, edited by Marc Lebeau, 17–22. Turnhout: Brepols.

Biga, Maria Giovanna. 2007. "Buried among the Living at Ebla? Funerary Practices and Rites in a XXIV Cent. b.c. Syrian Kingdom." *Scienze dell'Antichità* 14: 125–151.

Biga, Maria Giovanna. 2010. "Textiles in the Administrative Texts of the Royal Archives of Ebla (Syria, 24th Century bc) with Particular Emphasis on Coloured Textiles." In *Textile Terminologies in the Ancient Near East and Mediterranean from the Third to the First Millennia bc*, edited by C. Michel and M.-L. Nosch, 146–172. Ancient Textiles Series 8. Oxford and Oakville: Oxbow.

Biga, Maria Giovanna. 2011. "An Angry Scribe of the Third Millennium bc." *Scienze dell'Antichità* 17: 281–282.

Biga, Maria Giovanna. 2014. "Inherited Space—Third Millennium Political and Cultural Landscape." In *Constituent, Confederate, and Conquered Space. The Emergence of the Mittani State*, edited by E. Cancik-Kirschbaum, N. Brisch, and J. Eidem, 93–110. Berlin: De Gruyter.

Biga, Maria Giovanna. 2016. "The Role of Women in Work and Society in the Ebla Kingdom (Syria, 24th century bc)." In *The Role of Women in Work and Society in the Ancient Near East (SANER 13)*, edited by Brigitte Lion and Cécile Michel, 71–89. Berlin: De Gruyter.

Biga, Maria Giovanna, and Piotr Steinkeller. 2021. "In Search of Dugurasu." *JCS* 73: 9–70.

Biggs, Robert D. 1995. "Medicine, Surgery, and Public Health in Mesopotamia." In *CANE*, 3:1911–1924.

Boehmer, R. M. 1990. "Zur Funktion des Steinstifttempels in Uruk nach Befunden der Kampagne 39." *Baghdader Mitteilungen* 21: 49–65.

Boehmer, R. M. 1997. "Uruk-Warka." In *OEANE*, 5:294–298.

Boivin, Odette. 2018. *The First Dynasty of the Sealand in Mesopotamia*. Berlin: de Gruyter.

Bonechi, Marco. 2016. "A Passive, and Therefore Prized, Bride: New Proposals for the Queen's Wedding in the Ebla Royal Rituals." *RA* 110 (1): 53–78.

Bongenaar, Arminius Cornelius Valentinus Maria. 1997. *The Neo-Babylonian Ebabbar Temple at Sippar: Its Administration and Its Prosopography*. Istanbul: Nederlands Historisch-Archaeologisch Instituut.

Bongenaar, Arminius Cornelius Valentinus Maria. 2000. "Private Archives in Neo-Babylonian Sippar and Their Institutional Connections." In *Interdependency of Institutions and Private Entrepreneurs: Proceedings of the Second MOS Symposium (Leiden 1998)*, edited by A. C.V. M. Bongenaar, 73–94. Leiden: Nederlands Historisch-Archaeologisch Instituut te Istanbul.

Bordreuil, Pierre, and Florence Malbran-Labat. 1995. "Les archives de la maison d'Ourtenou." *Comptes rendus des séances de l'Académie des Inscriptions et Belles-Lettres* 139 (2): 443–451.

Boucharlat, Rémy. 1995. "Archaeology and Artifacts of the Arabian Peninsula." In *CANE*, 2:1335–1353.

Breasted, James Henry. 1906. *Ancient Records of Egypt*. 5 vols. New York: Russell and Russell.

Breckwoldt, Tina. 1995/1996. "Management of Grain Storage in Old Babylonian Larsa." *AfO* 42/43: 64–88.

Breniquet, Catherine. 2010. "Weaving in Mesopotamia during the Bronze Age: Archaeology, Techniques, Iconography." In *Textile Terminologies in the Ancient Near East and Mediterranean from the Third to the First Millennia bc*, edited by C. Michel and M.-L. Nosch, 52–67. Ancient Textiles Series 8. Oxford and Oakville: Oxbow.

Brereton, Gareth, ed. 2018. *I Am Ashurbanipal: King of the World, King of Assyria*. London: Thames & Hudson.

Brinkman, John Anthony. 1973. "Sennacherib's Babylonian Problem: An Interpretation." *JCS* 25 (2): 89–95.

Brinkman, John. 1976. *Materials and Studies for Kassite History*. Vol. 1: *A Catalogue of Cuneiform Sources Pertaining to Specific Monarchs of the Kassite Dynasty*. Chicago: Oriental Institute of the University of Chicago.

Bryce, Trevor. 2002. *Life and Society in the Hittite World*. New York and Oxford: Oxford University Press.

Bryce, Trevor. 2003. *Letters of the Great Kings of the Ancient Near East: The Royal Correspondence of the Late Bronze Age*. London and New York: Routledge.

Bryce, Trevor. 2005. *The Kingdom of the Hittites*. New ed. New York and London: Oxford University Press.

Bryce, Trevor. 2009. *The Routledge Handbook of the Peoples and Places of Ancient Western Asia: The Near East from the Early Bronze Age to the Fall of the Persian Empire*. London and New York: Routledge.

Buccellati, Giorgio. 1984. *Terqa Preliminary Reports*. 10: *The Fourth Season: Introduction and the Stratigraphic Record*. BM 10. Malibu: Undena Publications.

Bunnens, Guy. 1978. "Ilim-ilimma, fils de Tuttu 'bourgeois-gentilhomme' d'Alalakh au XVe s. av. n.e." *Akkadica* 10: 2–15.

Calvet, Yves. 2000. "The House of Urtenu." *NEA* 63 (4): 210–213.

Canby, Jeanny Vorys. 1971. "Decorated Garments in Ashurnasirpal's Sculpture." *Iraq* 33 (1): 31–53.

Canby, Jeanny Vorys. 2001. *The "Ur-Nammu" Stela*. University Museum Monograph 110. Philadelphia: University of Pennsylvania Museum.

Carter, Elizabeth. 2011. "Landscapes of Death in Susiana during the Last Half of the 2nd Millennium B.C." In *Elam and Persia*, edited by Javier Álvarez-Mon and Mark B. Garrison, 45–58. University Park: Penn State University Press.

CDLI year names. N.d. https://cdli.ox.ac.uk/wiki/doku.php?id=year_names.

Charpin, Dominique. 1982. Review of *Die Altbabylonischen Briefe und Urkunden aus Kisurra*, by Burkhart Kienast. *JAOS* 102 (1): 156–160.

Charpin, Dominique. 1987. "Le rôle économique du palais en Babylonie sous Hammurabi et ses successeurs." In *Le système palatial en Orient, en Grèce et a Rome*, edited by Edmond Lévy, 111–126. Strasbourg: Université des sciences humaines de Strasbourg.

Charpin, Dominique. 2002. "Ibni-šadûm, roi de Kisurra, fils de Manna-balti-El et gendre de Sûmû-El de Larsa." *NABU* 2002 (2): 41–42.

Charpin, Dominique. 2004. "Histoire politique du Proche-Orient amorrite (2002–1595)." In *Mesopotamien: Die altbabylonische Zeit*, edited by D. Charpin, O. E. Dietz, and S. Marten, 25–480. Orbis Biblicus et Orientalis 160/4. Fribourg: Academic Press; Göttingen: Vandenhoeck & Ruprecht.

Charpin, Dominique. 2010. *Reading and Writing in Babylon*. Cambridge, MA: Harvard University Press.

Charpin, Dominique. 2012a. "'Ainsi parle l'empereur' à propos de la correspondance des sukkal-mah." In *Susa and Elam. Archaeological, Philological, Historical and Geographical Perspectives: Proceedings of the International Congress Held at Ghent University, December 14–17, 2009*, edited by Katrien De Graef and Jan Tavernier, 341–353. Leiden: Brill.

Charpin, Dominique. 2012b. *Hammurabi of Babylon*. London and New York: I. B. Tauris.

Charpin, Dominique. 2019. *"Tu es de mon sang": Les alliances dans le Proche-Orient ancien*. Paris: Les Belles Lettres.

Charvát, Petr. 2002. *Mesopotamia before History*. New York: Routledge.

Chavalas, Mark W., ed. 2006. *Ancient Near East: Historical Sources in Translation*. Oxford and Malden, MA: Wiley-Blackwell.

Cifarelli, Megan. 1998. "Gesture and Alterity in the Art of Ashurnasirpal II of Assyria." *The Art Bulletin* 80 (2): 210–228.

Civil, Miguel. 1964. "A Hymn to the Beer Goddess and a Drinking Song." In *From the Workshop of the Chicago Assyrian Dictionary: Studies Presented to A. Leo Oppenheim*, edited by Martha T. Roth, Walter Farber, Matthew W. Stolper, and Paula von Bechtolsheim, 67–89. *AS* 27. Chicago: University of Chicago Press.

Civil, Miguel. 1993. "On Mesopotamian Jails and Their Lady Warden." In *The Tablet and the Scroll: Near Eastern Studies in Honor of William W. Hallo*, edited by Mark E. Cohen, Daniel C. Snell, and David B. Weisberg, 72–78. Bethesda, MD: CDL Press.

Clancier, Philippe. 2011. "Cuneiform Culture's Last Guardians: The Old Urban Notability of Hellenistic Uruk." In *The Oxford Handbook of Cuneiform Culture*, edited by Karen Radner and Eleanor Robson, 752–773. Oxford: Oxford University Press.

Cline, Eric H. 2014. *1177 bc: The Year Civilization Collapsed*. Princeton: Princeton University Press.

Cohen, Andrew C. 2005. *Death Rituals, Ideology, and the Development of Early Mesopotamian Kingship: Toward a New Understanding of Iraq's Royal Cemetery of Ur*. Leiden: Brill.

Cohen, Raymond, and Raymond Westbrook, eds. 2000. *Amarna Diplomacy: The Beginnings of International Relations*. Baltimore: Johns Hopkins University Press.

Cohen, Yoram. 2005. "Feet of Clay at Emar: A Happy End?" *Orientalia* 74 (2): 165–170.

Cohen, Yoram. 2009. *The Scribes and Scholars of the City of Emar in the Late Bronze Age*. Winona Lake, IN: Eisenbrauns.

Cohen, Yoram. 2012. "Aḫi-malik: The Last 'Overseer of the Land' in the City of Emar." In *Looking at the Ancient Near East and the Bible through the Same Eyes. Minha LeAhron, A Tribute to Aaron Skaist*, edited by Kathleen Abraham and Joseph Fleishman, 13–23. Bethesda, MD: CDL Press.

Cohen, Yoram. 2016. "The Scribal Traditions of Late Bronze Age Emar." In *Cultures and Societies in the Middle Euphrates and Habur Areas in the Second Millennium bc, I: Scribal Education and Scribal Traditions*, edited by Shigeo Yamada and Daisuke Shibata, 119–131. Wiesbaden: Harrassowitz, 2016.

Cohen, Yoram. 2019. "Cuneiform Writing in Bronze Age Canaan." In *The Social Archaeology of the Levant: From Prehistory to the Present*, edited by A. Yasur-Landau, E. H. Cline, and Y. M. Rowan, 245–264. Cambridge: Cambridge University Press.

Cohen, Yoram. 2021. "The 'Hunger Years' and the 'Sea Peoples': Preliminary Observations on the Recently Published Letters from the 'House of Urtenu' Archive at Ugarit." In *Ve-'Ed Ya'aleh (Gen. 2:6): Essays in Biblical and Ancient Near Eastern Studies Presented to Edward L. Greenstein*, edited by Peter Machinist et al., 47–61. Atlanta: SBL.

Collins, Paul. 2010. "Attending the King in the Assyrian Reliefs." In *Assyrian Reliefs from the Palace of Ashurnasirpal II: A Cultural Biography*, edited by Ada Cohen and Steven E. Kangas, 181–197. Hanover, NH: Hood Museum of Art.

Collins, Paul T. 2016. "The Face of the Assyrian Empire: Mythology and the Heroic King." In *Assyria to Iberia: Art and Culture in the Iron Age*, edited by Joan Aruz and Michael Seymour, 42–53. New York: Metropolitan Museum of Art.

Collins, Paul. 2021. *The Sumerians: Lost Civilizations*. London: Reaktion Books.

Collon, Dominique. 1987. *First Impressions: Cylinder Seals in the Ancient Near East*. London: British Museum Publications.

Cooper, Jerrold S. 1981. *Reconstructing History from Ancient Inscriptions: The Lagash-Umma Border Conflict*, Malibu: Undena.

Cooper, Jerrold S. 1986. *Sumerian and Akkadian Royal Inscriptions*. New Haven: American Oriental Society.

Cousin, Laura. 2016. "Beauty Experts: Female Perfume-Makers in the 1st Millennium BC." In *The Role of Women in Work and Society in the Ancient Near East*, edited by Brigitte Lion and Cécile Michel, 512–525. Berlin: Walter de Gruyter.

Cripps, Eric L. 2014. "Money and Prices in the Ur III Economy of Umma." Review of *Monetary Role of Silver and Its Administration in Mesopotamia during the Ur III Period (c. 2112–2004 bce). A Case Study of the Umma Province*, by Xiaoli Ouyang. *Wiener Zeitschrift für die Kunde des Morgenlandes* 104: 205–232.

Crüsemann, Nicola, Margarete van Ess, Markus Hilgert, and Beate Salje, eds. 2019. *Uruk: First City of the Ancient World*. Translated by Timothy Potts. Los Angeles: Getty Publications.

Culbertson, Laura E. 2009. "Dispute Resolution in the Provincial Courts of the Third Dynasty of Ur." PhD diss., University of Michigan.

Curtis, John, and Nigel Tallis, eds. 2008. *The Balawat Gates of Ashurnasirpal II*. London: British Museum Press.

Dalley, Stephanie. 1984. *Mari and Karana: Two Old Babylonian Cities*. Piscataway, NJ: Gorgias Press.

Dalley, Stephanie, trans. 1989. *Myths from Mesopotamia: Creation, the Flood, Gilgamesh, and Others*, Rev. ed. Oxford and New York: Oxford University Press.

Dalley, Stephanie. 2009. *Babylonian Tablets from the First Sealand Dynasty in the Schøyen Collection*. CUSAS 9. Bethesda, MD: CDL Press.

Dalley, Stephanie. 2015. *The Mystery of the Hanging Garden of Babylon: An Elusive World Wonder Traced*. New York and Oxford: Oxford University Press.

Dalley, Stephanie. 2017. "Assyrian Warfare." In *A Companion to Assyria*, edited by Eckart Frahm, 525–533. Malden, MA: John Wiley & Sons.

Dalley, Stephanie, and Luis R. Siddall. 2021. "A Conspiracy to Murder Sennacherib? A Revision of SAA 18 100 in the Light of a Recent Join." *Iraq* 83: 45–56.

Dalley, Stephanie, C. B. F. Walker, and J. D. Hawkins. 1976. *The Old Babylonian Tablets from Tell Rimah*. London: British School of Archaeology in Iraq.

Damerow, Peter. 1999. "The Origins of Writing as a Problem of Historical Epistemology." Invited lecture at the symposium "The Multiple Origins of Writing: Image, Symbol, and Script." University of Pennsylvania, Center for Ancient Studies. March 26–27, 1999. https://pure.mpg.de/rest/items/item_2273744/component/file_2273742/content.

Damerow, Peter. 2012. "Sumerian Beer: The Origins of Brewing Technology in Ancient Mesopotamia." *Cuneiform Digital Library Journal* 2012 (2). http://www.cdli.ucla.edu/pubs/cdlj/2012/cdlj2012_002.html.

Damerow, Peter, and Robert Englund. 1987. "Die Zahlzeichensysteme der Archäischen Texte aus Uruk." In *Zeichenliste der Archäischen Texte aus Uruk*, edited by Margaret W. Green and Hans J. Nissen, 117–166. Archäische Texte aus Uruk 2. Berlin: Gebr. Mann Verlag.

Dandamaev, Muhammad A. 1984. *Slavery in Babylonia: From Nabopolassar to Alexander the Great (626–331 bc)*. DeKalb: Northern Illinois University Press.

Darnell, John Coleman, and Colleen Manassa. 2007. *Tutankhamun's Armies: Battle and Conquest during Ancient Egypt's Late Eighteenth Dynasty*. Hoboken, NJ: John Wiley & Sons.

Davies, Glyn. 2002. *A History of Money*. Cardiff: University of Wales Press.

De Boer, Rients. 2016. "From the Yaḫrūrum Šaplûm Archives: The Administration of Harvest Labor Undertaken by Soldiers from Uruk and Malgium." *ZA* 106 (2): 138–174.

De Boer, Rients. 2019a. "New Insights from the Early Babylonian Period, Especially Concerning the Isin-Larsa Wars between Erra-Imittī and Sumu-El (ca. 1870–1865 BCE)." *Bibliotheca Orientalis* 76 (3–4): 241–251.

De Boer, Rients. 2019b. "Pīhatni-ipiq, an Official in the Service of King Sumu-El of Larsa." In *De l'argile au numérique: Mélanges assyriologiques en l'honneur de Dominique Charpin*, Vol. 1, edited by Grégory Chambon, Michaël Guichard, and Anne-Isabelle Langlois, 307–314. Leuven: Peeters.

De Graef, Katrien. 2018. "*In Taberna Quando Sumus*: On Taverns, *Nadītum* Women, and the *Gagûm* in Old Babylonian Sippar." In *Gender and Methodology in the Ancient Near East: Approaches from Assyriology and Beyond,* edited by Stephanie Lynn Budin et al., 77–115. Barcino monographica orientalia 10. Barcelona: University of Barcelona.

Démare-Lafont, Sophie, and Daniel Fleming. 2015. "Emar Chronology and Scribal Streams: Cosmopolitanism and Legal Diversity." *RA* 109 (1): 45–77.

Dercksen, J. G. 2004. *Old Assyrian Institutions*. MOS Studies 4. Leiden: Nederlands Instituut voor het Nabije Oosten.

Devecchi, Elena. 2019. "A Reluctant Servant: Ugarit under Foreign Rule during the Late Bronze Age." In *The Crossroads III—A Stranger in the House. Foreigners in Ancient Egyptian and Near Eastern Societies of the Bronze Age*, edited by Jana Mynářová, Marwan Kilani, and Sergio Alivernini, 121–136. Prague: Charles University, Faculty of Arts.

Diakonoff, I. M. 1971. "On the Structure of Old Babylonian Society." In *Beiträge zur sozialen Struktur des alten Vorderasien*, edited by H. Klengel, 15–32. Berlin: Akademie-Verlag.

Driscoll, Carlos A., David W. Macdonald, and Stephen J. O'Brien. 2009. "From Wild Animals to Domestic Pets, an Evolutionary View of Domestication." *Proceedings of the National Academy of Sciences* 106 (S1): 9971–9978.

Dromard, Benjamin. 2017. "Esclaves, dépendants, deportés: Les frontières de l'esclavage en Babylonie au premier millénaire avant J.-C." PhD diss., Université Panthéon-Sorbonne-Paris I.

Easton, Donald F. 1981. "Hittite Land Donations and Tabarna Seals." *JCS* 33 (1): 3–43.

Edzard, Dietz Otto. 1997. *Gudea and His Dynasty. RIME* 3/1. Toronto: University of Toronto Press.

Eichmann, Ricardo. 2007. *Uruk. Architektur I. Von den Anfängen bis zur frühdynastischen Zeit. AUWE* 14. Rahden/Westf: Marie Leidorf.

Eichmann, Ricardo. 2019. "Uruk's Early Monumental Architecture." In *Uruk: First City of the Ancient World*, edited by Nicola Crüsemann et al., 97–107. Los Angeles: Getty Publications.

Elayi, Josette. 2018. *Sennacherib, King of Assyria*. Atlanta: SBL Press.

Emelianov V. V. 2017. "First Account of a Birthday in Human History." *Asian and African Studies* 9 (3): 281–294.

Englund, Robert K. 1991. "Hard Work—Where Will It Get You? Labor Management in Ur III Mesopotamia." *JNES* 50 (4): 255–280.

Englund, Robert K. 1995. "Regulating Dairy Productivity in the Ur III Period." *Orientalia,* n.s., 64 (4): 377–429.

Englund, Robert K. 2004. "Proto-Cuneiform Account-Books and Journals." In *Creating Economic Order: Record-keeping, Standardization and the Development of Accounting in the Ancient Near East*, edited by Michael Hudson and Cornelia Wunsch, 23–46. Bethesda, MD: CDL Press.

Englund, Robert K. 2012. "Equivalency Values and the Command Economy of the Ur III Period in Mesopotamia." In *The Construction of Value in the Ancient World*, edited by John K. Papadopoulos and Gary Urton, 427–458. Los Angeles: Cotsen Institute of Archaeology Press.

Eph'al-Jaruzelska, Izabela. 2016. "Esarhaddon's Claim of Legitimacy in an Hour of Crisis: Sociological Observations." *Orient* 51: 123–142.

Erb-Satullo, Nathaniel L. 2019. "The Innovation and Adoption of Iron in the Ancient Near East." *Journal of Archaeological Research* 27 (4): 557–607.

Evans, Jean M. 2012. *The Lives of Sumerian Sculpture: An Archaeology of the Early Dynastic Temple*. Cambridge and New York: Cambridge University Press.

Fales, Frederik M. 2009. "Art, Performativity, Mimesis, Narrative, Ideology, and Audience: Reflections on Assyrian Palace Reliefs in the Light of Recent Studies." *KASKAL Rivista di storia, ambienti e culture del Vicino Oriente Antico* 6: 237–295.

Fales, Frederick Mario. 2012. "After Ta'yinat: The New Status of Esarhaddon's *adê* for Assyrian Political History." *RA* 106 (1): 133–158.

Fales F. M., and J. N. Postgate. 1985. *Imperial Administrative Records, Part II: Provincial and Military Administration. SAA* 11. Helsinki: Helsinki University Press.

Feigin, Samuel I. 1934. "The Captives in Cuneiform Inscriptions." *American Journal of Semitic Languages and Literatures* 50 (4): 217–245.

Feldman, Marian H. 2007. "Mesopotamian Art." In *A Companion to the Ancient Near East*, edited by Daniel C. Snell, 304–324. Malden, MA: Blackwell.

Feldman, Marian H. 2014. *Communities of Style: Portable Luxury Arts, Identity, and Collective Memory in the Iron Age Levant*. Chicago and London: University of Chicago Press.

Fiette, Baptiste. 2018. *Le palais, la terre et les hommes: La gestion du domaine royal de Larsa d'après les archives de Šamaš-hazir*. Archibab 3. Memoires de NABU 20. Paris: Sepoa.

Fijałkowska, Lena. 2014. "Family in Crisis in Late Bronze Age Syria: Protection of Family Ties in the Legal Texts from Emar." In *La famille dans le Proche-Orient ancien: réalités, symbolismes et images: Proceedings of the 55e Rencontre Assyriologique Internationale, Paris*, edited by Lionel Marti, 383–396. Winona Lake, IN: Eisenbrauns.

Finkel, Irving. 2018. "Ashurbanipal's Library: Contents and Significance." In *I Am Ashurbanipal: King of the World, King of Assyria*, edited by Gareth Brereton, 80–87. London: Thames & Hudson.

Finné, Martin, Jessie Woodbridge, Inga Labuhn, and C. Neil Roberts. 2019. "Holocene Hydro-Climatic Variability in the Mediterranean: A Synthetic Multi-Proxy Reconstruction." *The Holocene* 29 (5): 847–863.

Fischer, Steven R. 2001. *A History of Language*. London: Reaktion Books.

Fitzgerald, Madeleine André. 2002. "The Rulers of Larsa." PhD diss., Yale University.

Fleming, Daniel E. 1992. *The Installation of Baal's High Priestess at Emar: A Window on Ancient Syrian Religion*. Atlanta: Scholars Press.

Fleming, Daniel E. 2000. *Time at Emar: The Cultic Calendar and the Rituals from the Diviner's Archive*. Winona Lake, IN: Eisenbrauns.

Fleming, Daniel E. 2015. "Seeing and Socializing with Dagan at Emar's *zukru* Festival." In *The Materiality of Divine Agency*, edited by Beate Pongratz-Leisten and Karen Sonik, 197–210. Berlin: De Gruyter.

Flückiger-Hawker, Esther. 1999. *Urnamma of Ur in Sumerian Literary Tradition*. Fribourg: University Press; Göttingen: Vandenhoeck und Ruprecht.

Fortin, Michel. 1999. *Syria: Land of Civilizations*. Quebec: Musée de la civilization.

Foster, Benjamin R. 2016. *The Age of Agade: Inventing Empire in Ancient Mesopotamia*. London and New York: Routledge.

Foster, Benjamin R., trans. 2019. *The Epic of Gilgamesh*. 2nd ed. New York and London: W. W. Norton.

Frahm, Eckart. 2010a. "Hochverrat in Assur." In *Assur-Forschungen. Arbeiten aus der Forschungsstelle "Edition literarischer Keilschrifttexte aus Assur" der Heidelberger Akademie der Wissenschafter*, edited by S. M. Maul and N. P. Heeßel, 89–138. Wiesbaden: Harrassowitz.

Frahm, Eckart. 2010b. "Reading the Tablet, the Exta, and the Body: The Hermeneutics of Cuneiform Signs in Babylonian and Assyrian Text Commentaries and Divinatory Texts." In *Divination and Interpretation of Signs in the Ancient World*, edited by Amar Annus, 93–141. Chicago: Oriental Institute of the University of Chicago.

Frahm, Eckart. 2014. "Family Matters: Psychohistorical Reflections on Sennacherib and His Times." In *Sennacherib at the Gates of Jerusalem: Story, History, and Historiography*, edited by I. Kalimi and S. Richardson, 163–222. Leiden and Boston: Brill.

Frahm, Eckart. 2015. "Some Like It Hot: Reflections on the Historical 'Temperature' of Letters from Mesopotamian Royal Archives." In *Official Epistolography and the Language(s) of Power, Proceedings of the First International Conference of the Research Network Imperium and Officium*, edited by Stefan Procházka, Lucian Reinfandt, and Sven Tost, 3–14. Papyrologica Vindobonensia 8. Vienna: Verlag der Österreichischen Akademie der Wissenschaften.

Frahm, Eckart. 2019. "Cuneiform-Savvy Princesses and Literate Brewers: Three Millennia of Intellectual Life in Uruk." In *Uruk: First City of the Ancient World*, edited by Nicola Crüsemann et al., 290–297. Los Angeles: Getty Publications.

Frayne, Douglas R. 1990. *Old Babylonian Period (2003–1595 bc)*. RIME 4. Toronto: University of Toronto Press.

Frayne, Douglas R. 1993. *Sargonic and Gutian Periods (2234–2113 bc)*. RIME 2. Toronto: University of Toronto Press.

Frayne, Douglas R. 1997. *Ur III Period (2112–2004 bc)*. RIME 3/2. Toronto: Toronto University Press.

Frayne, Douglas R. 2008. *Pre-Sargonic Period (2700–2350 bc)*. RIME 1. Toronto: University of Toronto Press.

Frayne, Douglas R., and Johanna H. Stuckey. 2021. *A Handbook of Gods and Goddesses of the Ancient Near East: Three Thousand Deities of Anatolia, Syria, Israel, Sumer, Babylonia, Assyria, and Elam.* University Park: Penn State University Press.

Friberg, Jöran. 2011. "Counting and Accounting in the Proto-Literate Middle East: Examples from Two New Volumes of Proto-Cuneiform Texts." *JCS* 51 (1): 107–137.

Gadotti, Alhena. 2011. "Portraits of the Feminine in Sumerian Literature." *JAOS* 131 (2): 195–206.

Gadotti, A., and A. Kleinerman. 2021. *Elementary Education in Early Second Millennium bce Babylonia.* CUSAS 42. University Park: Penn State University Press.

Garfinkle, Steven J. 2008. "Was the Ur III State Bureaucratic?" In *The Growth of an Early State in Mesopotamia: Studies in Ur III Administration: Proceedings of the First and Second Ur III Workshops at the 49th and 51st Rencontre Assyriologique Internationale, London July 10, 2003 and Chicago July 19, 2005,* edited by Steven J. Garfinkel and J. Cale Johnson, 55–61. BPOA 5. Madrid: Editorial CSIC-CSIC Press.

Gasche, H. 1989. *La Babylonie au 17e siècle avant notre ère: approche archéologique, problèmes et perspectives. MHEM* II/1. Ghent: University of Ghent.

Gasche, Hermann, and Caroline Janssen. 1997. "Sippar." in *OEANE,* Vol. 5. https://www.oxfordreference.com/view/10.1093/acref/9780195065121.001.0001/acref-9780195065121-e-990?rskey=5Q8oFG&result=1.

Gaspa, Salvatore. 2013. "Textile Production and Consumption in the Neo-Assyrian Empire." In *Textile Production and Consumption in the Ancient Near East: Archaeology, Epigraphy, Iconography,* edited by M.-L Nosch, H. Koefoed, and Strand E. Andersson, 224–248. Oxford and Oakville: Oxbow Books.

Gelb, Ignace J., Piotr Steinkeller, and Robert M. Whiting Jr. 1991. *Earliest Land Tenure Systems in the Near East: Ancient Kudurrus.* Chicago: Oriental Institute Publications.

Geller, M. J. 2018. Review of *Sourcebook for Ancient Mesopotamian Medicine,* by JoAnn Scurlock. *Journal of Semitic Studies* 63 (1): 259–264.

George, Andrew R., trans. 1999. *The Epic of Gilgamesh.* London: Penguin.

George, Andrew. R. 2001. "In Search of the é.dub.ba.a: The Ancient Mesopotamian School in Literature and Reality." Transcript of paper given at the conference on the Fifth Millennium of the Invention of Writing, Baghdad. https://eprints.soas.ac.uk/1618/1/GeorgeEdubbaa.pdf.

George, Andrew R. 2010. "Xerxes and the Tower of Babel." In *The World of Achaemenid Persia: History, Art and Society in Iran and the Ancient Near East,* edited by J. Curtis and S. Simpson, 471–480. London: I. B. Tauris.

George, Andrew R. 2013. *Babylonian Divinatory Texts Chiefly in the Schoyen Collection.* CUSAS 18. Bethesda, MD: CDL Press.

George, Andrew R. 2018. *Old Babylonian Texts in the Schøyen Collection, Part One, Selected Letters.* CUSAS 36. Bethesda, MD: CDL Press.

Gershon, Galil. 2007. *The Lower Stratum Families in the Neo-Assyrian Period.* Leiden and Boston: Brill.

Ghirshman, Roman. 1961. "The Ziggurat of Tchoga-Zanbil." *Scientific American* 204 (1): 68–77.

Ghirshman, Roman, Paul Auberson, and T. Ghirshman. 1968. *Tchoga Zanbil (Dur-Untash).* Vol. 2: *Temenos, temples, palais, tombes.* Paris: P. Geuthner.

Gibson, McGuire, and Augusta McMahon. 1997. "The Early Dynastic-Akkadian Transition Part II: The Authors' Response." *Iraq* 59: 9–14.

Glassner, Jean-Jacques. 2009. "En-hedu-Ana, une femme auteure en pays de Sumer au IIIe millénaire?" *Topoi. Orient-Occident* 10 (1): 219–231.

Goddeeris, Anne. 2002. *Economy and Society in the Early Old Babylonian Period (ca. 2000–1800 bc)*. OLA 109. Leuven: Peters.

Goddeeris, Anne. 2007. "The Economic Basis of the Local Palace of Kisurra." *ZA* 97 (1): 47–85.

Goddeeris, Anne. 2009. *Tablets from Kisurra in the Collections of the British Museum*. Wiesbaden: Harrassowitz.

Grayson, A. Kirk. 1972. *Assyrian Royal Inscriptions*. Vol. I. Wiesbaden: Harrassowitz.

Grayson, A. Kirk. 1975. *Assyrian and Babylonian Chronicles*. Texts from Cuneiform Sources V. Locust Valley, NY: J. J. Augustin.

Grayson, A. Kirk. 1987. *Assyrian Rulers of the Third and Second Millennia bc (to 1115 bc)*. RIMA 1. Toronto: University of Toronto Press.

Gross, M. M., and A. Garcia-Ventura. 2018. "Craftsmen in the Neo-Assyrian Empire." In *What's in a Name? Terminology Related to the Work Force and Job Categories in the Ancient Near East*, edited by Agnès Garcia-Ventura, 369–395. AOAT 440. Münster: Ugarit Verlag.

Günbatti, Cahit. 2004. "Two Treaty Texts Found at Kültepe." In *Assyria and Beyond: Studies Presented to Mogens Trolle Larsen*, edited by Jan Gerrit Dercksen, 249–268. Leiden: NINO.

Hafford, William B. 2019a. "The Royal Cemetery of Ur." In *Journey to the City: A Companion to the Middle East Galleries at the Penn Museum*, edited by Steve Tinney and Karen Sonik, 196–234. Philadelphia: University of Pennsylvania Museum of Archaeology and Anthropology.

Hafford, William B. 2019b. "The Ur-Namma Stele." In *Journey to the City: A Companion to the Middle East Galleries at the Penn Museum*, edited by Steve Tinney and Karen Sonik, 93–96. Philadelphia: University of Pennsylvania Museum of Archaeology and Anthropology.

Hageneuer, Sebastian, and Sophie C. Schmidt. 2019. "Monumentality by Numbers." In *Size Matters: Understanding Monumentality across Ancient Civilizations*, edited by Federico Buccellati et al., 291–308. Berlin: De Gruyter.

Hallo, William W. 1964. "The Road to Emar." *JCS* 18: 57–88.

Hallo, William W., and K. Lawson Younger Jr. 2003. *The Context of Scripture*. 3 vols. Leiden and Boston: Brill.

Halvgaard, Christian, and Christina Johansen. 2004. "Ur III Texts in the Danish National Museum." *RA* 98: 1–12.

Hansen, Donald P. 2003. "Art of the Early City-States." In *Art of the First Cities: The Third Millennium b.c. from the Mediterranean to the Indus*, edited by Joan Aruz and Ronald Wallenfels, 21–37. New Haven and London: Yale University Press.

Harper, Prudence Oliver, Joan Aruz, and Françoise Tallon, eds. 1992. *The Royal City of Susa: Ancient Near Eastern Treasures in the Louvre*. New York: Metropolitan Museum of Art.

Harris, Rivka. 1964. "The *nadītu* Woman." In *From the Workshop of the Chicago Assyrian Dictionary: Studies Presented to A. Leo Oppenheim*, edited by Martha T. Roth, Walter Farber, Matthew W. Stolper, and Paula von Bechtolsheim, 106–135. AS 27. Chicago: University of Chicago Press.

Harris, Rivka. 1989. "Independent Women in Ancient Mesopotamia?" In *Women's Earliest Records from Ancient Egypt and Western Asia*, edited by Barbara S. Lesko, 145–156. Atlanta: Scholars Press.

Haul, M. 2009. *Stele und Legende, Untersuchungen zu den keilschriftlichen Erzählwerken über die Könige von Akkade*. Göttinger Beiträge zum Alten Orient 4. Göttingen: Universitätsverlag Göttingen.

Heimpel, Wolfgang. 2009. *Workers and Construction Work at Garšana*. CUSAS 5. Bethesda, MD: CDL Press.

Heimpel, Wolfgang. 2010. "Left to Themselves. Waifs in the Time of the Third Dynasty of Ur." *Why Should Someone Who Knows Something Conceal It: Cuneiform Studies in Honor of David I. Owen on His 70th Birthday*, edited by A. Kleinerman and Jack M. Sasson, 159–166. Bethesda, MD: CDL Press.

Herrmann, G., and P. R. S. Moorey. 1980. "Lapislazuli.B.Archäologisch." *RLA* 6: 489–492.

Hertel, Thomas Klitgaard. 2014. "The Lower Town of Kültepe: Urban Layout and Population." In *Current Research at Kültepe-Kanesh: An Interdisciplinary and Integrative Approach to Trade Networks, Internationalism, and Identity*, edited by Levent Atici et al., 25–54. *JCS* supplemental series number 4. Atlanta: Lockwood Press.

Hoffner, Harry A., Jr. 1983. "A Prayer of Muršili II about His Stepmother." *JAOS* 103: 187–192.

Hoffner, Harry A., Jr. 2009. *Letters from the Hittite Kingdom*. Atlanta: Society of Biblical Literature.

Horsnell, Malcolm John Albert. 1999. *The Year-Names of the First Dynasty of Babylon*. Vol. 2. Hamilton, ON: McMaster University Press.

Huehnergard, John. 1997. "Emar Texts." In *OEANE*, 2:239–240.

Hussein, Muzahim Mahmoud. 2016. *Nimrud: The Queens' Tombs*. Translated by Mark Altaweel. Baghdad: Iraqi State Board of Antiquities and Heritage.

Ishikida, Miki Yokoyama. 1999. "The *ilkum* Institution in the Provincial Administration of Larsa During the Reign of Hammurapi (1792–1750 B.C.)." *Orient* 34: 61–88.

Izre'el, Shlomo. 1997. *The Amarna Scholarly Tablets*. Groningen: Brill.

Jacobsen, Thorkild. 1976. *Treasures of Darkness: A History of Mesopotamian Religion*. New Haven: Yale University Press.

Janssen, Caroline. 1996. "When the House Is on Fire and the Children Are Gone." In *Houses and Households in Ancient Mesopotamia. Papers Read at the 40th Rencontre Assyriologique Internationale, July 5–8, 1993*, edited by K. R. Veenhof, 237–246. Leiden and Istanbul: Nederlands Historisch-Archaeologisch Instituut te Istanbul.

Jean, Cynthia. 2010. "Divination and Oracles at the Neo-Assyrian Palace: The Importance of Signs in Royal Ideology." In *Divination and Interpretation of Signs in the Ancient World*, edited by Amar Annus, 267–275. Chicago: Oriental Institute of the University of Chicago.

Joannès, F. 1992a. "Inventaire d'un cabaret." *NABU*, item no. 64: 48–50.

Joannès, F. 1992b. "Inventaire d'un cabaret (suite)." *NABU*, item no. 89: 69.

Joannès, F. 2001. "Sargon Ier (d'Akkad)." In *Dictionnaire de la civilisation mésopotamienne*, 755. Paris: Bouquins.

Johnson, J. Cale. 2019. "Meat Distribution in Late Uruk Diacritical Feasts: Second-Order Bookkeeping Techniques and their Institutional Context in Late Fourth Millennium bce Mesopotamia." In *Culture and Cognition: Essays in Honor of Peter Damerow*, edited by Jürgen Renn and Matthias Schemmel, 75–86. Berlin: Max Planck Institute for the History of Science. Online version at http://mprl-series.mpg.de/proceedings/11/.

Johnson, Steven. 2021. "The Living Century." *New York Times Magazine*, May 2, 2021.

Jotheri, Jaafar, Mark Altaweel, Akihiro Tuji, Ryo Anma, Benjamin Pennington, Stephanie Rost, and Chikako Watanabe. 2018. "Holocene Fluvial and Anthropogenic Processes in the Region of Uruk in Southern Mesopotamia." *Quaternary International* 483: 57–69.

Jursa, M. 2010. *Aspects of the Economic History of Babylonia in the First Millennium bc: Economic Geography, Economic Mentalities, Agriculture, the Use of Money and the Problem of Economic Growth*. AOAT 377. Münster: Ugarit Verlag.

Karahashi, Fumi. 2016a. "Women and Land in the Presargonic Lagaš Corpus." In *The Role of Women in Work and Society in the Ancient Near East*. SANER 13, edited by Brigitte Lion and Cecile Michel, 57–70. Berlin: De Gruyter.

Karahashi, Fumi. 2016b. "Some Professions with Both Male and Female Members in the Presargonic E2-MI2 Corpus." *Orient* 51: 47–62.

Karahashi, Fumi, and Agnès Garcia-Ventura. 2016. "Overseers of Textile Workers in Presargonic Lagash." *Kaskal* 13: 1–19.

Kerr, Richard A. 1998. "Sea-Floor Dust Shows Drought Felled Akkadian Empire." *Science* 279, no. 5349 (January 16, 1998): 325–326.

Kienast, Burkhart. 1978. *Die altbabylonischen Briefe und Urkunden aus Kisurra*. Vols. I and II. Wiesbaden: Franz Steiner Verlag.

Kingsbury, Edwin C. 1963. "A Seven Day Ritual in the Old Babylonian Cult at Larsa." *Hebrew Union College Annual* 34: 1–34.

Klein, Jacob. 1995. "Shulgi of Ur: King of a Neo-Sumerian Empire." In *CANE*, 2:842–857.

Kleinerman, Alexandra. 2013. "The Barbers of Iri-Saĝrig." In *From the 21st Century b.c. to the 21st Century a.d.: Proceedings of the International Conference on Sumerian Studies Held in Madrid, 22–24 July 2010*, edited by Steven Garfinkle and Manuel Molina, 301–312. Winona Lake, IN: Eisenbrauns.

Kleinerman, Alexandra, and David I. Owen. 2009. *Analytical Concordance to the Garšana Archives*. CUSAS 4. Bethesda, MD: CDL Press.

Klengel-Brandt, Evelyn. 1997. "Babylon." In *OEANE*, 1:251–256.

Kloekhorst, Alwin. 2021. "A New Interpretation of the Old Hittite Zalpa-Text (CTH 3.1): Neša as the Capital under Ḫizziia I, Labarna I, and Ḫattušili I." *JAOS* 141 (3): 557–575.

Kobayashi, Toshiko. 1983. "Miscellanea of ᵈlugal-é-muš." *Orient* 19: 29–50.

Kobayashi, Toshiko. 1984. "On the Meaning of the Offerings for the Statue of Entemena." *Orient* 20: 43–65.

Koch, Ulla Susanne. 2011. "Sheep and Sky: Systems of Divinatory Interpretation." In *The Oxford Handbook of Cuneiform Culture*, edited by Karen Radner and Eleanor Robson, 447–469. Oxford and New York: Oxford University Press.

Kohlmeyer, Kay. 1985. "Mari (Tell Hariri)." In *Ebla to Damascus, Art and Archaeology of Ancient Syria*, edited by Harvey Weiss, 194–197. Seattle and London: University of Washington Press.

Kohlmeyer, Kay. 1997. "Habuba Kabira." In *OEANE*, 2:446–448.

Konstantopoulos, Gina. 2021. "The Many Lives of Enheduana: Identity, Authorship, and the 'World's First Poet.'" In *Powerful Women in the Ancient World: Perception and (Self)Presentation. Proceedings of the 8th Melammu Workshop, Kassel, 30 January–1 February 2019*, edited by Kerstin Droß-Krüpe and Sebastian Fink, 57–76. Münster: Zaphon.

Kramer, Samuel Noah. 1959. *History Begins at Sumer*. Garden City, NY: Doubleday.

Kramer, Samuel Noah. 1963. *The Sumerians*. Chicago: University of Chicago Press.

Kraus, F. R. 1968. *Breife aus dem Archive des Šamaš-Ḫazir in Paris und Oxford (TCL 7 und OECT 3)*. AbB 4. Leiden: Brill.

Kraus, F. R. 1985. *Briefe aus kleineren westeuropäischen Sammlungen*. AbB 10. Leiden: Brill.

Lackenbacher, S., and F. Malbran-Labat. 2016. *Lettres en Akkadien de la "Maison d'Urtenu."* Fouilles de 1994, Ras Shamra Ougarit 23. Paris: Peeters.

Lafont, Bertrand, and Raymond Westbrook. 2003. "Mesopotamia: Neo-Sumerian Period (Ur III)." In *A History of Ancient Near Eastern Law*, edited by Raymond Westbrook, 183–226. Leiden: Brill.

Lambert, W. G. 1953. "Textes commerciaux de Lagash (époque présargonique)." *RA* 47: 57–69.

Lambert, Wilfred. 2007. *Babylonian Oracle Questions*. Mesopotamian Civilizations 13. Winona Lake, IN: Eisenbrauns.

Landsberger, B. 1954. "Assyrische Königsliste und 'Dunkles Zeitalter' (Continued)." *JCS* 8 (2): 47–73.

Larsen, Mogens Trolle. 2002. *The Aššur-nādā Archive*. Leiden: Nederlands Instituut voor het Nabije Oosten.

Larsen, Mogens Trolle. 2015. *Ancient Kanesh: A Merchant Colony in Bronze Age Anatolia*. Cambridge and New York: Cambridge University Press.

Lassen, Agnete W. 2020. "Women and Seals in the Ancient Near East." In *Women at the Dawn of History*, edited by Agnete W. Lassen and Klaus Wagensonner, 25–37. New Haven: Yale Babylonian Collection.

Lassen, Agnete W., Eckart Frahm, and Klaus Wagensonner, eds. 2019. *Ancient Mesopotamia Speaks: Highlights of the Yale Babylonian Collection*. New Haven: Yale University Press.

Lauinger, Jacob. 2012. "Esarhaddon's Succession Treaty at Tell Tayinat: Text and Commentary." *JCS* 64: 87–123.

Lawler, A. 2006. "North versus South, Mesopotamian Style." *Science* 312: 1458–1463.

Lee, Thomas G. 1993. "The Jasper Cylinder Seal of Aššurbanipal and Nabonidus' Making of Sîn's Statue." *RA* 87 (2): 131–136.

Leichty, Erle. 2011. *The Royal Inscriptions of Esarhaddon, King of Assyria (680–669 bc)*. RINAP 4. University Park: Penn State University Press.

Lion, Brigitte. 2018. "Une (ou quatre?) tablette(s) rédigée(s) par une *nadītum*." *NABU* 2018 (101): 159–160.

Liverani, Mario. 1996. "Reconstructing the Rural Landscape of the Ancient Near East." *JESHO* 39 (1): 1–41.

Liverani, Mario. 2001. *International Relations in the Ancient Near East, 1600–1100 bc*. Basingstoke: Palgrave.

Liverani, Mario. 2014. *The Ancient Near East: History, Society and Economy*. London: Routledge.

Liverani, Mario. 2017. *Assyria: The Imperial Mission*. Winona Lake, IN: Eisenbrauns.

Luukko, M., and G. Van Buylaere. 2002. *The Political Correspondence of Esarhaddon*. SAA 16. Helsinki: Helsinki University Press.

Maeda, Tohru. 2005. "Royal Inscriptions of Lugalzagesi and Sargon." *Orient* 40: 3–30.

Maekawa, Kazuya. 1996. "The Governor's Family and the 'Temple Households' in Ur III Girsu." In *Houses and Households in Ancient Mesopotamia, Papers Read at the 40e Rencontre Assyriologique Internationale, Leiden, July 5–8, 1993*, edited by Klaas R. Veenhof, 171–179. CRRAI 40. Istanbul: Nederlands Historisch-Archaeologisch Instituut.

Maekawa, Kazuya. 1998. "Ur III Records of Labor Forces in the British Museum (1)." *Acta Sumerologica* 20: 63–110.

Mahmood, Lina. 2006. "Two Cities of Sippar: Tell Abu-Habbah and Tell ed-Der." MA thesis, Stony Brook University.

Maidman, Maynard L. 2018. "Mittanni Royalty and Empire: How Far Back?" *Canadian Society for Mesopotamian Studies* 11/12: 15–28.

Malbran-Labat, F. 1999. "Les textes akkadiens découverts à Ougarit en 1994." In *Languages and Cultures in Contact: At the Crossroads of Civilizations in the Syro-Mesopotamian Realm; Proceedings of the 42th [sic] RAI*, edited by Karel Van Lerberghe and Gabriela Voet, 237–244. Leuven: Peeters.

Marchesi, Gianni. 2004. "Who Was Buried in the Royal Tombs of Ur? The Epigraphic and Textual Data." *Orientalia* 73 (2): 153–197.

Marchesi, Gianni. 2011. "Goods from the Queen of Tilmun." In *Akkade Is King—A Collection of Papers by Friends and Colleagues Presented to Aage Westenholz on the Occasion of His 70th Birthday 15th of May 2009*, edited by J. G. Dercksen, J. Eidem, K. van der Toorn, and K. R. Veenhof, 189–200. Leuven: Peeters.

Marchesi, Gianni, and Nicolò Marchetti. 2019. "A Babylonian Official at Tilmen Höyük in the Time of King Sumu-la-el of Babylon (Tab. I–XII)." *Orientalia* 88 (1): 1–36.

Margueron, Jean-Claude. 1997. "Mari." In *OEANE*, 3:413–417.

Matthiae, Paolo. 1997. "Ebla." In *OEANE*, 2:180–183.

Matthiae, Paolo. 2009. "The Standard of the *maliktum* of Ebla in the Royal Archives Period." *ZA* 99 (2): 270–311.

Matthiae, Paolo, Frances Pinnock, and Gabriella Scandone Matthiae, eds. 1995. *Ebla: Alle origini della civiltà urbana*. Milan: Electra.

McGovern, Patrick E. 2017. *Ancient Brews: Rediscovered and Re-created*. New York: W. W. Norton.

McMahon, Augusta. 2007. "From Sedentism to States, 10,000–3000 BCE." In *A Companion to the Ancient Near East*, edited by Daniel C. Snell, 20–33. Malden, MA: John Wiley & Sons, 2007.

Meier, Samuel A. 1988. *The Messenger in the Ancient Semitic World*. Atlanta: Scholars Press.

Melville, Sarah C. 2006. "The Autobiography of Adad-guppi." In *The Ancient Near East*, edited by Mark Chavalas, 389–393. Malden, MA: Blackwell.

Melville, Sarah C. 2007. "Royal Women and the Exercise of Power in the Ancient Near East." In *A Companion to the Ancient Near East*, edited by Daniel C. Snell, 235–244. Malden, MA: John Wiley & Sons.

Melville, Sarah C. 2016. *The Campaigns of Sargon II, King of Assyria, 721–705 bc*. Norman: University of Oklahoma Press.

Meyers, Pieter. 2000. "The Casting Process of the Statue of Queen Napir-Asu in the Louvre." In *From the Parts to the Whole: Acta of the 13th International Bronze Congress, Cambridge, Massachusetts, May 28–June 1, 1996*, edited by Carol C. Mattusch, Amy Brauer, and Sandra E. Knudsen, 11–18. Portsmouth, RI: Journal of Roman Archaeology.

Michalowski, Piotr. 1993. *Letters from Early Mesopotamia*. Atlanta: Scholars Press.

Michalowski, Piotr. 2008. "The Mortal Kings of Ur: A Short Century of Divine Rule in Ancient Mesopotamia." In *Religion and Power: Divine Kingship in the Ancient World and Beyond*, edited by N. M. Brisch, 33–45. University of Chicago Oriental Institute Seminars 4. Chicago: Oriental Institute of the University of Chicago.

Michalowski, Piotr. 2010. "Learning Music: Schooling, Apprenticeship and Gender in Early Mesopotamia." In *Musiker und Tradierung: Studien zur Rolle von Musikern bei der Verschriftlichung und Tradierung von literarischen Werken*, edited by Regine Pruzsinszky and Dahlia Shehata, 199–240. Vienna: LIT Verlag.

Michalowksi, Piotr. 2020. "The Kingdom of Akkad in Contact with the World." In *Oxford History of the Ancient Near East*, edited by Karen Radner, Nadine Moeller, and D. T. Potts, 1:686–764. Oxford and New York: Oxford University Press.

Michel, Cécile. 2001. *Correspondance des marchands de Kanish*. Paris: Les éditions du Cerf.

Michel, Cécile. 2008. "The Old Assyrian Trade in the Light of Recent Kültepe Archives." *Journal of the Canadian Society for Mesopotamian Studies* 3: 71–82.

Michel, Cécile. 2010. "Women of Aššur and Kaniš." In *Anatolia's Prologue, Kültepe Kanesh Karum, Assyrians in Istanbul*, edited by F. Kulakoğlu and S. Kangal, 124–133. Kayseri: Avrupa Kültür Baskent.

Michel, Cécile. 2016. "Textile Workers in the Royal Archives of Mari (Syria, 18th Century bc)." *10th ICAANE*: 127–138. https://halshs.archives-ouvertes.fr/halshs-02995804/document.

Michel, C. , and M.-L. Nosch, eds. 2010. *Textile Terminologies in the Ancient Near East and Mediterranean from the Third to the First Millennia bc*. Ancient Textiles Series 8. Oxford and Oakville: Oxbow.

Michel, Patrick Maxime. 2014. *Le culte des pierres à Emar à l'époque Hittite*, Orbis Biblicus Orientalis No. 266. Fribourg, Göttingen: Academic Press.

Midant-Reynes, Béatrix. 2000a. "The Naqada Period." In *The Oxford History of Ancient Egypt*, edited by Ian Shaw, 44–60. Oxford and New York: Oxford University Press.

Midant-Reynes, Béatrix. 2000b. *The Prehistory of Egypt*. Oxford and Malden, MA: Blackwell Publishers.

Milano, Lucio. 1995. "Ebla: A Third-Millennium City-State in Ancient Syria." In *CANE*, 3:1219–1230.

Millard, Allan. 1994. *The Eponyms of the Assyrian Empire 910–612 b.c. SAAS* 2. Helsinki: Helsinki University Press.

Miller, J. Maxwell, and John H. Hayes. 1986. *A History of Ancient Israel and Judah*. Philadelphia: Westminster Press.

Miller, Naomi F., Philip Jones, and Holly Pittman. 2017. "Sign and Image: Representations of Plants on the Warka Vase of Early Mesopotamia." *Origini* 39: 53–73.

Mittelman, Amy. 2008. *Brewing Battles: A History of American Beer*. New York: Algora.

Mladjov, Ian. 2016. "Ammuna, Ḫuzziya, and Telipinu Reconsidered." *NABU* 2016 (1): 21–24.

Mofidi-Nasrabadi, Behzad. 2015. "Reconstruction of the Ziqqurrat of Chogha Zanbil." *Elamica* 5: 37–51.

Molina, Manuel. 2010. "Court Records from Umma." In *Why Should Someone Who Knows Something Conceal It: Cuneiform Studies in Honor of David I. Owen on His 70th Birthday*, edited by A. Kleinerman and Jack M. Sasson, 201–218. Bethesda, MD: CDL Press.

Moorey, P. R. S. 1982. *Ur "of the Chaldees": A Revised and Updated Edition of Sir Leonard Woolley's Excavations at Ur*. Ithaca, NY: Cornell University Press.

Moran, William L. 1992. *The Amarna Letters*. Baltimore: Johns Hopkins University Press.

Mynářová, Jana. 2007. *Language of Amarna—Language of Diplomacy: Perspectives on the Amarna Letters*. Prague: Czech Institute of Egyptology.

Nadali, D., and L. Verderame. 2021. "Fragments of the Third Millennium bc from Nigin." *Iraq* 83: 105–118.

National Geographic. 2021. *The Most Influential Figures of Ancient History*. Reissue.

Nissen, Hans J. 2003. "Uruk and the Formation of the City." In *Art of the First Cities: The Third Millennium bc from the Mediterranean to the Indus*, edited by Joan Aruz, 11–20. New York: Metropolitan Museum of Art.

Nissen, Hans J. 2013. "Uruk." In *The Encyclopedia of Ancient History*. https://doi.org/10.1002/9781444338386.wbeah01203.pub2.

Nissen, Hans J. 2019. "Uruk's Beginnings and Early Development." In *Uruk: First City of the Ancient World*, edited by Nicola Crüsemann et al., 87–93. Los Angeles: Getty Publications.

Nissen, Hans, Peter Damerow, and Robert Englund. 1993. *Archaic Bookkeeping: Writing and Techniques of Economic Administration in the Ancient Near East*. Chicago: University of Chicago Press.

Nissinen, M. 1998. *References to Prophecy in Neo-Assyrian Sources. SAAS* 7. Helsinki: Neo-Assyrian Text Corpus Project.

Norrie, P. A. 2003. "The History of Wine as Medicine." In *Wine: A Scientific Exploration*, edited by Merton Sandler and Roger Pinder, 21–55. London and New York: Taylor and Francis.

Nougayrol, J. 1955. *Le palais royal d'Ugarit III: Textes accadiens et hourrites des archives est, ouest et centrales*. Paris: Imprimerie Nationale.

Novotny, Jamie. 2018. "A Previously Unrecognized Version of Esarhaddon's 'Annals.'" *ZA* 108 (2): 203–208.

N'Shea, Omar. 2016. "Royal Eunuchs and Elite Masculinity in the Neo-Assyrian Empire." *NEA* 79 (3): 214–221.

Oates, Joan. 1979. *Babylon*. London: Thames and Hudson.

Oded, Bustenay. 1979. *Mass Deportations and Deportees in the Neo-Assyrian Empire*. Wiesbaden: Harrassowitz.

Oller, Gary Howard. 1977. "The Autobiography of Idrimi: A New Text Edition with Philological and Historical Commentary." PhD diss., University of Pennsylvania. Ann Arbor, MI: University Microfilms.

Oppenheim, A. Leo. 1967. *Letters from Mesopotamia: Official, Business, and Private Letters on Clay Tablets from Two Millennia*. Chicago and London: University of Chicago Press.

Orthmann, Winfried. 1975. *Der alte Orient*. Berlin: Propyläen Verlag.

Ouyang, Xiaoli. 2013. *Monetary Role of Silver and Its Administration in Mesopotamia during the Ur III Period, c. 2112–2004 bce: A Case Study of the Umma Province*. Madrid: Consejo Superior de Investigaciones Científicas.

Özgüç, Tahsin. 1997. "Kaneš." In *OEANE*, 3:266–268.

Palmisano, Alessio. 2018. *The Geography of Trade: Landscapes of Competition and Long-Distance Contacts in Mesopotamia and Anatolia in the Old Assyrian Colony Period*. Oxford: Archaeopress Archaeology.

Pardee, D., 2003. "Ugaritic Letters." In *The Context of Scripture*. Vol. III: *Archival Documents from the Biblical World*, edited by W. W. Hallo and K. Lawson Younger, 88–114. Leiden: Brill.

Parpola, Simo. 1980. "The Murderer of Sennacherib." In *Death in Mesopotamia: Papers Read at the XXVIe Rencontre assyriologique internationale*. Mesopotamia: Copenhagen Studies in Assyriology 8, edited by B. Alster, 171–182. Copenhagen: Akademisk Forlag.

Parrot, Andre. 1945. *Mari: Une ville perdue*. Paris: Société Commerciale d'Edition et de Librairie.

Pasquali, Jacopo. 2005. "Remarques comparatives sur la symbolique du vêtement à Ébla." In *Memoriae Igor M. Diakonoff*, edited by L. Kogan et al., 165–185. Babel und Bibel 2. Winona Lake, IN: Eisenbrauns.

Paulette, Tate. 2020. "Archaeological Perspectives on Beer in Mesopotamia: Brewing Ingredients." In *After the Harvest: Storage Practices and Food Processing in Bronze Age Mesopotamia*, edited by Noemi Borrelli and Giulia Scazzosi, 65–89. Turnhout: Brepols.

Paulus, Susanne. 2014. *Die babylonischen Kudurru-Inschriften von der kassitischen bis zur frühneubabylonischen Zeit*. AOAT 51. Münster: Ugarit-Verlag.

Paulus, Susanne. 2018: "Fraud, Forgery, and Fiction: Is There Still Hope for Agum-Kakrime?" *JCS* 70: 115–166.

Pedde, Friedhelm. 2019. "Metals in Uruk." In *Uruk: First City of the Ancient World*, edited by Nicola Crüsemann et al., 270–271. Los Angeles: Getty Publications.

Pedersén, Olof. 2011. "Work on a Digital Model of Babylon Using Archaeological and Textual Evidence." *Mesopotamia: Rivista di archeologia, epigrafia e storia orientale antica* 46: 9–22.

Peyronel, Luca. 2014. "From Weighing Wool to Weaving Tools. Textile Manufacture at Ebla during the Early Syrian Period in the Light of Archaeological Evidence." In *Wool Economy in the Ancient Near East and the Aegean: From the Beginning of Sheep Husbandry to Institutional Textile Industry*, edited by Catherine Breniquet and Cécile Michel, 124–138. Oxford and Philadelphia: Oxbox Books.

Peyronel, Luca, Agnese Vacca, and Claudia Wachter-Sarkady. 2014. "Food and Drink Preparation at Ebla, Syria. New Data from the Royal Palace G (c. 2450–2300 BC)." *Food and History* 12 (3): 3–38.

Pinnock, Frances. 2015. "The King's Standard from Ebla Palace G." *JCS* 67 (1): 3–22.

Piotrovsky, Boris. 1974–1977. "Excavations of Kamir-Blur, Armenian SSR Gouv. Eriwan." *IPEK* 24: 50–53.

Pirngruber, Reinhard, and Caroline Waerzeggers. 2011. "Prebend Prices in First-Millennium B.C. Babylonia." *JCS* 63: 111–144.

Plantholt, Irene Sibbing. 2014. "A New Look at the Kassite Medical Letters, and an Edition of Šumu-libši Letter N 969." *ZA* 104 (2): 171–181.

Podany, Amanda H. 1997. "Some Shared Traditions between Ḫana and the Kassites." In *Crossing Boundaries and Linking Horizons: Studies in Honor of Michael C. Astour on His 80th Birthday*, edited by Gordon D. Young, Mark W. Chavalas, and Richard E. Averbeck, 417–432. Bethesda, MD: CDL Press.

Podany, Amanda H. 2002. *The Land of Hana: Kings, Chronology, and Scribal Tradition*. Bethesda, MD: CDL Press.

Podany, Amanda H. 2010. *Brotherhood of Kings: How International Relations Shaped the Ancient Near East*. New York and Oxford: Oxford University Press.

Podany, Amanda H. 2014. "Hana and the Low Chronology." *JNES* 73 (1): 49–71.

Podany, Amanda H. 2019a. "Family Members, Neighbors, and a Local Shrine in Terqa, Syria, in the Late Old Babylonian Period." In *Ina ᵈmarri u qan ṭuppi. Par la bêche et le stylet! Cultures et sociétés syro-mésopotamiennes. Mélanges offerts à Olivier Rouault*, edited by P. Abrahami and L. Battini, 125–134. Oxford: Archaeopress.

Podany, Amanda H. 2019b. "Kings and Conflict." In *Ancient Mesopotamia Speaks: Highlights of the Yale Babylonian Collection*, edited by A. W. Lassen, E. Frahm, and K. Wagensonner, 56–71. New Haven: Yale University Press.

Podany, Amanda H. forthcoming. "Affection among the Brotherhood of Kings in the Amarna Letters." In *Handbook of Emotions in the Ancient Near East*, edited by Karen Sonik and Ulrike Steinert. Milton Park: Routledge / Taylor & Francis (in press, forthcoming).

Pollock, Susan. 2017. "Working Lives in an Age of Mechanical Reproduction: Uruk-Period Mesopotamia." In *The Interplay of People and Technologies. Archaeological Case Studies on Innovations*, edited by Stefan Burmeister and Reinhard Bernbeck, 205–224. Berlin Studies of the Ancient World 43. Berlin: Edition Topoi.

Postgate, J. Nicholas. 1974. "Some Remarks on Conditions in the Assyrian Countryside." *JESHO* 17: 225–243.

Postrel, Virginia. 2020. *The Fabric of Civilization: How Textiles Made the World*. New York: Basic Books.

Potts, Daniel T. 1986. "Nippur and Dilmun in the 14th Century bc." In *Proceedings of the Seminar for Arabian Studies* 16: 169–174.

Potts, Daniel T. 2006. "Elamites and Kassites in the Persian Gulf." *JNES* 65 (2): 111–119.

Potts, Daniel T. 2012. "The Elamites." In *The Oxford Handbook of Iranian History*, edited by Touraj Daryaee and Tūrağ Daryāyī, 43–44. New York and Oxford: Oxford University Press.

Potts, Daniel T. 2016. *The Archaeology of Elam: Formation and Transformation of an Ancient Iranian State*. New York and Cambridge: Cambridge University Press.

Potts, Daniel T. 2020. "Accounting for Religion: Uruk and the Origins of the Sacred Economy." In *Religion: Perspectives from the Engelsberg Seminar 2014*, edited by Kurt Almqvist, 17–24. Stockholm: Stolpe.

Prentice, Rosemary. 2010. *The Exchange of Goods and Services in Presargonic Lagash*. Münster: Ugarit Verlag.

Price, Campbell. 2011. "Ramesses, 'King of Kings': On the Context and Interpretation of Royal Colossi." In *Ramesside Studies in Honour of K. A. Kitchen*, edited by Mark Collier and Steven R. Snape, 403–411. Bollton: Rutherford Press.

Pritchard, James B., ed. 1969. *Ancient Near Eastern Texts Relating to the Old Testament*. Princeton: Princeton University Press.

Proust, Christine. 2014. "Does a Master Always Write for His Students? Some Evidence from Old Babylonian Scribal Schools." In *Scientific Sources and Teaching Contexts throughout History: Problems and Perspectives*, edited by Alain Bernard and Christine Proust, 69–94. Heidelberg: Springer Dordrecht.

Pulak, Cemal. 2008. "The Uluburun Shipwreck and Late Bronze Age Trade." In *Beyond Babylon: Art, Trade, and Diplomacy in the Second Millennium b.c.*, edited by Joan Aruz, 289–305. New York: Metropolitan Museum of Art, 2008.

Quinn, Jennifer Crawley. 2017. *In Search of the Phoenicians*. Princeton and Oxford: Princeton University Press.

Radner, Karen. 2003a. Review of *Aššur Is King! Aššur Is King! Religion in the Exercise of Power in the Neo-Assyrian Empire*, by Steven W. Holloway. *JESHO* 46 (2): 226–230.

Radner, Karen. 2003b. "The Trials of Esarhaddon: The Conspiracy of 670 bc." *Isimu: Revista sobre Oriente Proximo y Egipto en la antiguedad* 6: 165–184.

Radner, Karen. 2007. "Hired Labour in the Neo-Assyrian Empire." *SAAB* 16: 185–226.

Ragavan, Deena. 2010. "Cuneiform Texts and Fragments in the Harvard Art Museum/ Arthur M. Sackler Museum." *Cuneiform Digital Library Journal* 1: 1–17.

Rainey, Anson F. 2014. *The El-Amarna Correspondence: A New Edition of the Cuneiform Letters from the Site of El-Amarna Based on Collations of All Extant Tablets*. 2 vols. Boston: Brill.

Rassam, Hormuzd. 1897. *Asshur and the Land of Nimrod*. Cincinnati: Curts and Jennings.

Razmjou, Shahrokh. 2013. "The Cyrus Cylinder: A Persian Perspective." In *The Cyrus Cylinder: The King of Persia's Proclamation from Ancient Babylon*, edited by Irving Finkel, 104–126. London: I.B. Tauris.

Reade, Julian. 2002. "Early Monuments in Gulf Stone at the British Museum, with Observations on some Gudea Statues and the Location of Agade." *ZA* 92: 258–295.

Reculeau, Hervé. 2010. "The Lower Ḫābūr before the Assyrians: Settlement and Land Use in the First Half of the Second Millennium bce." In *Dūr-Katlimmu 2008 and Beyond*, edited by Hartmut Kühne, 187–215. Wiesbaden: Harrassowitz.

Reid, John Nicholas. 2015. "Runaways and Fugitive-Catchers during the Third Dynasty of Ur." *JESHO* 58 (4): 576–605.

Reid, John Nicholas. 2018. "The Birth of the Prison: The Functions of Imprisonment in Early Mesopotamia." *JANEH* 3 (2): 81–115.

Renfrew, J. M. 2003. "Archaeology and Origins of Wine Production." In *Wine: A Scientific Exploration*, edited by Merton Sandler and Roger Pinder, 56–69. London and New York: Taylor and Francis.

Renger, Johannes M. 1995. "Institutional, Communal, and Individual Ownership or Possession of Arable Land in Ancient Mesopotamia from the End of the Fourth to the End of the First Millennium B.C." *Chicago-Kent Law Review* 71 (1): 269–320.

Richardson, Seth. 2005. "Trouble in the Countryside *ana tarṣi* Samsuditana: Militarism, Kassites, and the Fall of Babylon I." In *Ethnicity in Ancient Mesopotamia, 48th Rencontre Assyriologique Internationale*, edited by W. H. van Soldt, 273–289. Leiden: NINO.

Richardson, Seth. 2015. "Building Larsa: Labor-Value, Scale and Scope-of-Economy in Ancient Mesopotamia." In *Labor in the Ancient World*, edited by Piotr Steinkeller and Michael Craig Hudson, 237–328. Dresden: Islet.

Richardson, Seth. 2016. "The Many Falls of Babylon and the Shape of Forgetting." In *Envisioning the Past through Memories: How Memory Shaped Ancient Near East Societies*, edited by Davide Nadali and Martin Bommas, 101–142. New York: Bloomsbury.

Richardson, Seth. 2019a. "The Oracle BOQ 1, 'Trouble,' and the Dūr-Abiešuḫ Texts: The End of Babylon I." *JNES* 78 (2): 215–237.

Richardson, Seth. 2019b. "Updating the List of Late OB Babylonian Fortresses." *NABU* 2019/I (March): 32.

Richardson, Seth. 2020. "The Origin of Foreign Slaves in the Late Old Babylonian Period." *Kaskal* 17: 53–73.

Ristvet, Lauren. 2011. "Travel and the Making of North Mesopotamian Polities." *BASOR* 361 (1): 1–31.

Ristvet, Lauren. 2012. "Resettling Apum: Tribalism and Tribal States in the Tell Leilan Region, Syria." In *Looking North: The Socioeconomic Dynamics of the Northern Mesopotamian and Anatolian Regions during the Late Third and Early Second Millennium bc*, edited by Nicola Laneri, 37–50. Wiesbaden: Harrassowitz.

Ritter, Edith K. 1965. "Magical-Expert (= *Āšipu*) and Physician (= *Asû*): Notes on Two Complementary Professions in Babylonian Medicine." In *Studies in Honor of Benno Landsberger on His Seventy-fifth Birthday, April 21, 1965*, edited by Hans G. Güterbock and Benno Landsberger, 299–321. Assyriological Studies 16. Chicago: University of Chicago Press, 1965.

Robson, Eleanor. 1996. "Building with Bricks and Mortar: Quantity Surveying in the Ur III and Old Babylonian Periods." In *Houses and Households in Ancient Mesopotamia. Papers Read at the 40th Rencontre Assyriologique Internationale, July 5–8, 1993*, edited by K. R. Veenhof, 181–190. Leiden and Istanbul: Nederlands Historisch-Archaeologisch Instituut te Istanbul.

Robson, Eleanor. 2001. "The Tablet House: A Scribal School in Old Babylonian Nippur." *RA* 93 (1): 39–66.

Robson, Eleanor. 2008. *Mathematics in Ancient Iraq: A Social History*. Princeton and Oxford: Princeton University Press.

Robson, Eleanor. 2009. "Mathematics Education in an Old Babylonian Scribal School." In *The Oxford Handbook of the History of Mathematics*, edited by Eleanor Robson and Jacqueline Stedall, 199–227. Oxford and New York: Oxford University Press.

Robson, Eleanor. 2011. "The Production and Dissemination of Scholarly Knowledge." In *The Oxford Handbook of Cuneiform Culture*, edited by Karen Radner and Eleanor Robson, 557–576. Oxford, New York: Oxford University Press.

Robson, Eleanor. 2018. "Scholars of the Šangu-Ninurta Family and Their Associates in Late Achaemenid Uruk." *Ancient Knowledge Networks Online*. http://oracc.museum.upenn. edu/cams/akno/babylonianscholars/b8anguninurtafamilyofuruk/.

Robson, Eleanor. 2019. *Ancient Knowledge Networks: A Social Geography of Cuneiform Scholarship in First-Millennium Assyria and Babylonia.* London: UCL Press. https://library.oapen.org/handle/20.500.12657/23632.

Rochberg, Francesca. 2011. "Observing and Describing the World through Divination and Astronomy." In *The Oxford Handbook of Cuneiform Culture*, edited by Karen Radner and Eleanor Robson, 618–636. Oxford and New York: Oxford University Press.

Romano, Lisa. 2014. "Urnanshe's Family and the Evolution of Its Inside Relationships as Shown by Images." In *La famille dans le Proche-Orient ancien: Réalités, symbolismes, et images: Proceedings of the 55th Rencontre assyriologique internationale at Paris, 6–9 July 2009*, edited by Lionel Marti, 183–192. Winona Lake, IN: Eisenbrauns.

Rost, Stephanie. 2017. "Water Management in Mesopotamia from the Sixth till the First Millennium bc." *Wiley Interdisciplinary Reviews: Water* 4 (5): e1230.

Roth, Martha T. 1997. *Law Collections from Mesopotamia and Asia Minor.* 2nd ed. Atlanta: Scholars Press.

Rothman, M., and E. Brumfiel. 1994. "Palace and Private Agricultural Decision-Making in the Early 2nd Millennium bc City-State of Larsa, Iraq." In *The Economic Anthropology of the State*, No. 11, edited by Elizabeth M. Brumfiel, 149–167. Lanham, MD: University Press of America.

Rouault, Olivier. 1992. "Cultures locales et influences extérieures: Le cas de Terqa." *SMEA* 30: 247–256.

Rouault, Olivier. 2006. "Le barbier de Terqa et ses voisins." In *Les espaces syro-mésopotamiens: Dimensions de l'expérience humaine au Proche-Orient ancien. Volume d'hommage offert à Jean-Claude Margueron*, Subartu XVII, edited by P. Butterlin et al., 473–475. Brepols: Turnhout.

Rouault, Olivier. 2011. *Terqa Final Reports 2: Les texts des saisons 5 à 9. BM 29.* Malibu: Undena Publications.

Rowe, Ignacia Márquez. 2002. "The King's Men in Ugarit and Society in Late Bronze Age Syria." *JESHO* 45 (1): 1–19.

Rüster, Christel, and Gernot Wilhelm. 2012. *Landschenkungsurkunden hethitischer Könige.* Studien zu den Boğazköy-Texten 4. Wiesbaden: Harrassowitz.

Rutz, Matthew. 2013. *Bodies of Knowledge in Ancient Mesopotamia: The Diviners of Late Bronze Age Emar and Their Tablet Collection.* Leiden: Brill.

Sachs, Abraham J., and Hermann Hunger. 1988. *Astronomical Diaries and Related Texts from Babylonia*, Vol. 1. Vienna: Verlag der Österreichischen Akademie der Wissenschaften.

Salje, Beate. 2019. "Uruk and the Vorderasiatisches Museum." In *Uruk: First City of the Ancient World*, edited by Nicola Crüsemann et al., 16–17. Los Angeles: Getty Publications.

Sallaberger, W., et al. 2006. "Schenkungen von Mittani-Königen an die Einwohner von Basiru. Die zwei Urkunden aus Tall Bazi am Mittleren Euphrat." *ZA* 96: 69–104.

Sandowicz, Małgorzata. 2015. "More on the End of the Neo-Babylonian Empire." *JNES* 74, no. 2: 197–210.

Šašková, Kateřina. 2018. "'Place in My Hands the Inexhaustible Craft of Medicine!' Physicians and Healing at the Royal Court of Esarhaddon." *Chatreššar* 2: 51–73.

Sasson, Jack M. 1993. "Mariage entre grandes familles." *NABU* 1993 (2): 43–44.

Sasson, Jack M. 1998. "The King and I: A Mari King in Changing Perceptions." *JAOS* 118 (4): 453–470.

Sasson, Jack M. 2008. "Texts, Trade, and Travelers." In *Beyond Babylon: Art, Trade, and Diplomacy in the Second Millennium b.c.*, edited by Joan Aruz, 95–100. New York: Metropolitan Museum of Art.

Sasson, Jack M. 2012. "'Nothing So Swift as Calumny': Slander and Justification at the Mari Court." In *The Ancient Near East, A Life! Festschrift Karel Van Lerberghe*, edited by Tom Boiy et al., 525–542. Leuven: Peeters.

Sasson, Jack M. 2015. *From the Mari Archives*. University Park: Penn State University Press.

Sasson, Jack M. 2019. "Vile Threat: Rhetoric of a Marital Spat." In *De l'argile au numérique: Mélanges assyriologiques en l'honneur de Dominique Charpin*, edited by Grégory Chambon, Michaël Guichard, and Anne-Isabelle Langlois, 923–941. Leuven: Peeters.

Sauvage, Caroline. 2012. *Routes maritimes et systèmes d'échanges internationaux au Bronze récent en Méditerranée orientale*. Lyon: Maison de l'Orient et de la Méditerranée Jean Pouilloux.

Sauvage, Martin. 1998. "La construction des ziggurats sous la troisième dynastie d'Ur." *Iraq* 60: 45–63.

Sauvage, Martin. 2011. "Construction Work in Mesopotamia in the Time of the Third Dynasty of Ur (End of the Third Millennium bc): Archaeological and Textual Evidence." In *TerrAsia 2011. 2011 International Conference on Earthen Architecture in Asia*, edited by Heyzoo Hwan, Soowun Kim, Hubert Guillaud, and David Gandreau, 55–65. Seoul: TERRAKorea.

Schmandt-Besserat, Denise. 1992. *Before Writing*. Vol. I: *From Counting to Cuneiform*. Austin: University of Texas Press.

Schmidt, Michael. 2019. *Gilgamesh: The Life of a Poem*. Princeton and Oxford: Princeton University Press.

Schneider, Thomas. 2015. "The Old Kingdom Abroad: An Epistemological Perspective: With Remarks on the Biography of Iny and the Kingdom of Dugurasu." In *Towards a New History for the Egyptian Old Kingdom*, edited by Peter Der Manuelian and Thomas Schneider, 429–455. Leiden: Brill.

Schrakamp, Ingo. 2020. "The Kingdom of Akkad: A View from Within." In *Oxford History of the Ancient Near East*, edited by Karen Radner, Nadine Moeller, and D. T. Potts, 1:612–685. Oxford and New York: Oxford University Press.

Scurlock, JoAnn. 2012. "Getting Smashed at the Victory Celebration, or What Happened to Esarhaddon's So-Called Vassal Treaties and Why." In *Iconoclasm and Text Destruction in the Ancient Near East and Beyond*, edited by Natalie Naomi May, 175–186. Chicago: Oriental Institute of the University of Chicago.

Selz, Gebhard J. 2020. "The Uruk Phenomenon." In *Oxford History of the Ancient Near East*, edited by Karen Radner, Nadine Moeller, and D. T. Potts, 1:163–244. Oxford and New York: Oxford University Press.

Seri, Andrea. 2006. *Local Power in Old Babylonian Mesopotamia*. London: Equinox.

Sharlach, Tonia. 2017. "Šulgi, Mighty Man, King of Ur." *Fortune and Misfortune in the Ancient Near East: Proceedings of the 60th Rencontre Assyriologique Internationale Warsaw, 21–25 July 2014*, edited by Olga Drewnowska and Małgorzata Sandowicz, 211–220. University Park: Penn State University Press.

Shehata, Dahlia. 2014. "Sounds from the Divine: Religious Musical Instruments in the Ancient Near East." In *Music in Antiquity: The Near East and the Mediterranean (Yuval 8)*, edited by Joan Goodnick Westenholz, Yossi Maurey, and Edwin Seroussi, 102–128. Berlin: Walter de Gruyter.

Sigrist, Marcel. 1991. *Documents from Tablet Collections in Rochester, New York*. Bethesda, MD: CDL Press.

Silver, Carly. 2010. "From Priestess to Princess." *Archaeology Archive*. archive.archaeology.org/online/features/iron_ladies/puduhepa.html.

Sjöberg, Åke W. 1973. "Nungal in the Ekur." *AfO* 24: 19–46.

Slanski, Kathryn E. 2003. *The Babylonian Entitlement narûs (kudurrus): A Study in Their Form and Function*. Boston: American Schools of Oriental Research.

Snell, Daniel C. 2001. *Flight and Freedom in the Ancient Near East*. Leiden: Brill.

Sołtysiak, Arkadiusz. 2017. "Antemortem Cranial Trauma in Ancient Mesopotamia." *International Journal of Osteoarchaeology* 27 (1): 119–128.

Speiser, E. A. 1929. "A Letter of Saushshatar and the Date of the Kirkuk Tablets." *JAOS* 49: 269–275.

Stavi, Boaz. 2011. "The Genealogy of Suppiluliuma I." *Altorientalische Forschungen* 38 (2): 226–239.

Stein, G. J. 1999. "Material Culture and Social Identity: The Evidence for a 4th Millennium bc Mesopotamian Uruk Colony at Hacinebi, Turkey." *Paléorient* 25 (1): 11–22.

Steinkeller, Piotr. 1981. "The Renting of Fields in Early Mesopotamia and the Development of the Concept of 'Interest' in Sumerian." *JESHO* 24 (1): 113–145.

Steinkeller, Piotr. 2013a. "An Archaic 'Prisoner Plaque' from Kiš." *RA* 107: 131–157.

Steinkeller, Piotr. 2013b. "Corvée Labor in Ur III Times." In *From the 21st Century b.c. to the 21st Century a.d.: Proceedings of the International Conference on Sumerian Studies Held in Madrid 22–24 July 2010*, edited by Steven Garfinkle and Manuel Molina, 347–424. Winona Lake, IN: Eisenbrauns.

Steinkeller, Piotr. 2017. "Appendix 1: The Priest-King of Uruk Times." In *History, Texts and Art in Early Babylonia: Three Essays by Piotr Steinkeller*, 82–104. Berlin: De Gruyter.

Still, Bastian, and Rieneke Sonnevelt. 2020. "On Sippar's Quay: Cuneiform Tablets with Aramaic Inscriptions from the Böhl Collection in Leiden." *ZA* 110 (1): 94–110.

Stökl, Jonathan. 2012. *Prophecy in the Ancient Near East: A Philological and Sociological Comparison*. Leiden: Brill.

Stol, Marten. 1981. *Letters from Yale*. *AbB* 9. Leiden: Brill.

Stol, Marten. 1982. "State and Private Business in the Land of Larsa." *JCS* 34: 127–230.

Stol, Marten. 1994. "Beer in Neo-Babylonian Times." In *Drinking in Ancient Societies: History and Culture of Drinks in the Ancient Near East*, edited by Lucio Milano, 155–183. Padua: Sargon.

Stol, Marten. 2000. "Titel altbabylonischer Klosterfrauen." In *Assyriologica et Semitica: Festschrift für Joachim Oelsner anläßlich seines 65. Geburtstages am 18. Februar 1997*, edited by Joachim Marzahn and Hans Neumann, 457–512. *AOAT* 252. Munich: Ugarit-Verlag.

Stol, M. 2007. "Suicide in Akkadian." *NABU* 2007 (1): 13.

Stol, Marten. 2016. *Women in the Ancient Near East*. Translated by Helen Richardson and Mervyn Richardson. Berlin and Boston: De Gruyter.

Stone, Elizabeth C. 1962. "The Social Role of the *Nadītu* Women in Old Babylonian Nippur." *JESHO* 25 (1): 50–70.

Stone, Elizabeth C. 1987. *Nippur Neighborhoods*. *SAOC* 44. Chicago: Oriental Institute of the University of Chicago.

Streck, Michael P. 2010. "Großes Fach Altorientalistik: Der Umfang des keilschriftlichen Textkorpus." *Mitteilungen der Deutschen Orient-Gesellschaft zu Berlin* 42: 35–58.

Studevent-Hickman, Benjamin, and Christopher Morgan. 2006. "Old Akkadian Period Texts." In *The Ancient Near East*, edited by Mark Chavalas, 17–44. Malden, MA: Blackwell.

Sürenhagen, Dietrich. 2002. "Death in Mesopotamia: The 'Royal Tombs' of Ur Revisited." In *Of Pots and Plans. Papers of the Archaeology and History of Mesopotamia and Syria presented to David Oates in Honour of his 75th Birthday*, edited by Lamia Al-Gallani Werr, 324–338. London: Nabu Publications.

Svärd, Saana. 2015. *Women and Power in Neo-Assyrian Palaces*. *SAAS* 23. Helsinki: Neo-Assyrian Text Corpus Project.

Tanret, Michel. 2011. "Learned, Rich, Famous, and Unhappy: Ur-Utu of Sippar." In *The Oxford Handbook of Cuneiform Culture*, edited by Karen Radner and Eleanor Robson, 270–287. Oxford and New York: Oxford University Press.

Tarawneh, Hanadah. 2011. "Amarna Letters: Two Languages, Two Dialogues." In *Egypt and the Near East—the Crossroads: Proceedings of an International Conference on the Relations of Egypt and the Near East in the Bronze Age Prague, September 1–3, 2010*, edited by Jana Mynářová, 271–284. Prague: Czech University, Czech Institute of Egyptology.

Taylor, Jonathan. 2015. "The Succession Treaty in Detail." *Nimrud: Materialities of Assyrian Knowledge Production*. The Nimrud Project at Oracc.org. http://oracc.museum.upenn. edu/nimrud/livesofobjects/successiontreaties/treatyindetail/.

Taylor, Jon. 2018. "Knowledge: The Key to Assyrian Power." In *I Am Ashurbanipal: King of the World, King of Assyria*, edited by Gareth Brereton, 88–97. London: Thames & Hudson.

Thames, John Tracy, Jr. 2020. *The Politics of Ritual Change: The Zukru Festival in the Political History of Late Bronze Age Emar*. Leiden: Brill.

Thomsen, Peter. 1931. "Ausgrabungen und Forschungsreisen." *Archiv für Orientforschung* 7: 129–143.

Thureau-Dangin, F. 1897. "Tablettes chaldéennes inédites." *RA* 4 (3): 69–78, Pl. XXXII.

Tinney, Steve. 1995. "A New Look at Naram-Sin and the 'Great Rebellion.'" *JCS* 47: 1–14.

Tinney, Steve. 2011. "Tablets of Schools and Scholars: A Portrait of the Old Babylonian Corpus." In *The Oxford Handbook of Cuneiform Culture*, edited by Karen Radner and Eleanor Robson, 577–596. Oxford and New York: Oxford University Press.

Tinney, Steve. 2019. "Religion and the Gods." In *Journey to the City*, edited by Steve Tinney and Karen Sonik, 75–100. Philadelphia: University of Pennsylvania Press.

Tinney, Steve, and Karen Sonik, eds. 2019. *Journey to the City: A Companion to the Middle East Galleries at the Penn Museum*. Philadelphia: University of Pennsylvania Museum of Archaeology and Anthropology.

Tolini, Gauthier. 2013. "Between Babylon and Kiš: The Economic Activities of Isḫunnatu, a Slave Woman of the Egibi family (Sixth Century bc)." Paper given at REFEMA—"The Economic Role of Women in the Public Sphere in Mesopotamia," 24–25 June 2013, Chuo University (Tokyo). https://refema.hypotheses:org/766.

Tonietti, Maria Vittoria. 2005. "Symbolisme et mariage à Ebla. Aspects du rituel pour l'intronisation du roi." In *Memoriae Igor M. Diakonoff*, edited by L. Kogan et al., 245–261. Babel und Bibel 2. Winona Lake, IN: Eisenbrauns.

Topçuoğlu, Oya. 2010. "Iconography of Protoliterate Seals." In *Visible Language: Inventions of Writing in the Ancient Middle East and Beyond*, edited by Christopher Woods, 29–32. OIMP 32. Chicago: Oriental Institute of the University of Chicago.

Tubb, K. W. 2001. "The Statues of 'Ain Ghazal: Discovery, Recovery and Reconstruction." *Archaeology International* 5: 47–50.

Tyborowski, Witold. 2012. "New Tablets from Kisurra and the Chronology of Central Babylonia in the Early Old Babylonian Period." *ZA* 102: 245–269.

Uehlinger, Christoph. 2003. "Clio in a World of Pictures: Another Look at the Lachish Reliefs from Sennacherib's Southwest Palace at Nineveh." In *Like a Bird in a Cage: The Invasion of Sennacherib in 701 bce*, edited by Lester L. Grabbe, 221–305. New York: Bloomsbury.

Uerpmann, Hans-Peter, and Margarethe Uerpmann. 2002. "The Appearance of the Domestic Camel in South-East Arabia." *Journal of Oman Studies* 12: 235–260.

Ur, Jason. 2014. "Households and the Emergence of Cities in Ancient Mesopotamia." *Cambridge Archaeological Journal* 24 (2) (June): 249–268.

Ur Online. N.d. http://www.ur-online.org.

Ussishkin, David. 1997. "Lachish." In *OEANE*, 3:317–323.

Ussishkin, David. 2003. "Symbols of Conquest in Sennacherib's Reliefs of Lachish: Impaled Prisoners and Booty." In *Culture through Objects: Ancient Near Eastern Studies in Honour of P. R. S. Moorey*, edited by Timothy Potts, Michael Roaf, and Diana Stein, 207–217. Oxford: Griffith Institute.

Van De Mieroop, Marc. 1989. "Women in the Economy of Sumer." In *Women's Earliest Records: From Ancient Egypt and Western Asia: Proceedings of the Conference on Women in the Ancient Near East; Brown University, Providence, Rhode Island, November 5–7, 1987*, edited by Barbara S. Lesko, 53–66. Atlanta: Scholars Press.

Van De Mieroop, Marc. 1993. "The Reign of Rim-Sin." *RA* 87 (1): 47–69.

Van De Mieroop, Marc. 1999. *Cuneiform Texts and the Writing of History*. London: Routledge.

Van De Mieroop, Marc. 2005. *King Hammurabi of Babylon: A Biography*. Oxford: Blackwell.

Van De Mieroop, Marc. 2007. *The Eastern Mediterranean in the Age of Ramesses II*. Malden, MA: Blackwell.

Van De Mieroop, Marc. 2013. "Democracy and the Rule of Law, the Assembly and the First Law Code." In *The Sumerian World*, edited by Harriet Crawford, 277–289. London and New York: Routledge.

Van De Mieroop, Marc. 2016. *A History of the Ancient Near East, ca. 3000–323 bc*. 3rd ed. Oxford and Malden, MA: Wiley Blackwell.

Van Driel, Govert. 1999/2000. "The Size of Institutional Umma." *AfO* 46/47: 80–91.

van Koppen, Frans. 2002. "Seized by Royal Order. The Households of Sammêtar and Other Magnates at Mari." In *Florilegium marianum VI: Recueil d'etudes à la mémoire d'André Parrot*, edited by Dominique Charpin and Jean-Marie Durand, 289–372. Paris: SEPOA.

Van Lerberghe, Karel, David Kaniewski, Kathleen Abraham, Joël Guiot, and Elise Van Campo. 2017. "Water Deprivation as Military Strategy in the Middle East, 3.700 Years Ago." *Méditerranée*. https://journals.openedition.org/mediterranee/8000#text.

Van Lerberghe, Karel, and Gabriella Voet. 1991. *Sippar-Amnānum: The Ur-Utu Archive*. MHET III/1. Ghent: University of Ghent.

Van Lerberghe, Karel, and Gabriella Voet. 2009. *A Late Old Babylonian Temple Archive from Dur-Abieshuh*. CUSAS 8. Bethesda, MD: CDL Press.

van Soldt, W. H. 1994. *Letters in the British Museum*, Part 2. AbB 13. Leiden: Brill.

van Soldt, Wilfred. 2000. Review of *The Amarna Scholarly Tablets* by Shlomo Izre'el. *JAOS* 120 (1): 105–106.

van Soldt, Wilfred. 2010. "The City Administration of Ugarit." In *City Administration of the Ancient Near East, Proceedings of the 53e Rencontre Assyriologique Internationale*, Part 2, edited by L. Kogan et al., 247–261. Winona Lake, IN: Eisenbrauns.

Veenhof, Klaas R. 2017. "The Old Assyrian Period (20th–18th Century BCE)." In *A Companion to Assyria*, edited by Eckart Frahm, 57–79. Malden, MA: John Wiley & Sons.

Veldhuis, Niek. 1997. "Elementary Education at Nippur: The Lists of Trees and Wooden Objects." PhD diss., Rijksuniversiteit Groningen.

Veldhuis, Niek. 2000. "Sumerian Proverbs in Their Curricular Context." *JAOS* 120: 383–399.

Veldhuis, Niek. 2010. "The Theory of Knowledge and the Practice of Celestial Divination." In *Divination and Interpretation of Signs in the Ancient World*, edited by Amar Annus, 77–91. Chicago: Oriental Institute of the University of Chicago.

Veldhuis, Niek. 2011. "Levels of Literacy." In *The Oxford Handbook of Cuneiform Culture*, edited by Karen Radner and Eleanor Robson, 68–89. Oxford and New York: Oxford University Press.

Verri, Giovanni, Paul Collins, Janet Ambers, Tracey Sweek, and St. John Simpson. 2009. "Assyrian Colours: Pigments on a Neo-Assyrian Relief of a Parade Horse." *Technical Research Bulletin* 3: 57–62.

Villard, Pierre. 2013. "Ekallatum." In *The Encyclopedia of Ancient History*. Wiley Online Library. https://onlinelibrary.wiley.com/doi/epdf/10.1002/9781444338386.wbeah24065.

Völling, Elisabeth. 2019. "Sheep, Wool, and Textiles in the Sumerian Economy." In *Uruk: First City of the Ancient World*, edited by Nicola Crüsemann et al., 242–243. Los Angeles: Getty Publications.

von Dassow, Eva. 2008. *State and Society in the Late Bronze Age: Alalaḫ under the Mittani Empire.* SCCNH 17. Bethesda, MD: CDL Press.

von Dassow, Eva. 2014. "Levantine Polities under Mittanian Hegemony." In *Constituent, Confederate, and Conquered Space. The Emergence of the Mittani State*, edited by Eva Cancik-Kirschbaum, Nicole Brisch, and Jesper Eidem, 11–32. Topoi 17. Berlin: Walter de Gruyter.

Waal, Willemijn. 2012. "Writing in Anatolia: The Origins of the Anatolian Hieroglyphs and the Introductions of the Cuneiform Script." *Altorientalische Forschungen* 39 (2): 287–315.

Waerzeggers, Caroline. 2006. "Neo-Babylonian Laundry." *RA* 100 (1): 83–96.

Waerzeggers Caroline. 2014. *Marduk-rēmanni. Local Networks and Imperial Politics in Achaemenid Babylonia.* Ghent: Peeters.

Wagensonner, Klaus. 2019. "Larsa Schools: A Palaeographic Journey." In *Current Research in Cuneiform Palaeography*, edited by Elena Devecchi, Jana Mynářová, and Gerfrid G. W. Müller, 2:41–86. Gladbeck: PeWe Verlag.

Wagensonner, Klaus. 2020. "Between History and Fiction—Enheduana, the First Poet in World Literature." In *Women at the Dawn of History*, edited by Agnete W. Lassen and Klaus Wagensonner, 38–45. New Haven: Yale Babylonian Collection.

Weeden, Mark. 2016. "Hittite Scribal Culture and Syria: Palaeography and Cuneiform Transmission." In *Cultures and Societies in the Middle Euphrates and Habur Areas in the Second Millennium bc.* Vol. I: *Scribal Education and Scribal Traditions*, edited by Shigeo Yamada and Daisuke Shibata, 157–191. Wiesbaden: Harrassowitz, 2016.

Weigle, Marta. 1978. "Women as Verbal Artists: Reclaiming the Sisters of Enheduanna." *Frontiers: A Journal of Women Studies* 3 (3): 1–9.

Weiss, Harvey, ed. 1985. *Ebla to Damascus: Art and Archaeology of Ancient Syria.* Seattle and London: University of Washington Press.

Weiss, Harvey. 1997. "Leilan, Tell." In *OEANE*, 3:341–347.

Weiss, Harvey, Peter Akkermans, Gil J. Stein, Dominique Parayre, and Robert Whiting. 1990. "1985 Excavations at Tell Leilan, Syria." *AJA* 94: 529–581.

Wells, Bruce. 2007. "Law and Practice." In *A Companion to the Ancient Near East*, edited by Daniel C. Snell, 199–211. Malden, MA: John Wiley & Sons.

Werner, Peter. 1994. *Die Entwicklung der Sakralarchitektur in Nordsyrien und Südostkleiasien.* Munich and Vienna: Profil Verlag.

Westbrook, Raymond. 1994. "Slave and Master in Ancient Near Eastern Law." *Chicago-Kent Law Review* 70: 1631–1676.

Westbrook, Raymond. 2008. "Personal Exile in the Ancient Near East." *JAOS* 128 (2): 317–323.

Westenholz, Joan Goodnick. 1983. Review of *Die Altbabylonischen Briefe und Urkunden aus Kisurra*, by Burkhart Kienast. *JNES* 42 (3): 219–228.

Westenholz, Joan Goodnick. 1989. "Enheduana, En-Priestess, Hen of Nanna, Spouse of Nanna." In *Dumu é. dub. ba. a.: Studies in Honor of A. Sjöberg*, edited by H. Behrens, D. Loding, and M. Roth, 539–556. Occasional Publications of the Samuel Noah Kramer Fund 11. Philadelphia: University Museum of Archaeology and Anthropology.

Westenholz, Joan Goodnick. 2004. "The Old Akkadian Presence in Nineveh: Fact or Fiction." *Iraq* 66: 7–18.

Widell, Magnus. 2013. "Sumerian Agriculture and Land Management." In *The Sumerian World*, edited by Harriet Crawford, 55–67. London: Routledge.

Winitzer, Abraham. 2010. "The Divine Presence and Its Interpretation in Early Mesopotamian Divination." In *Divination and Interpretation of Signs in the Ancient World*, edited by Amar Annus, 177–197. Chicago: Oriental Institute of the University of Chicago.

Winter, Irene J. 1981. "Royal Rhetoric and the Development of Historical Narrative in Neo-Assyrian Reliefs." *Studies in Visual Communication* 7 (2): 2–38.

Winter, Irene J. 2003. Review of *The "Ur-Nammu" Stele*, by Jeanny Vorys Canby. *JAOS* 123 (2): 402–406.

Winter, Irene J. 2009. "Women in Public: The Disk of Enheduana, the Beginning of the Office of En-Priestess, and the Weight of Visual Evidence." In *On Art in the Ancient Near East*. Vol. II: *From the Third Millennium bce*, edited by Irene J. Winter, 65–83. Leiden: Brill.

Wiseman, D. J. 1953. *The Alalakh Tablets*. London: British Institute of Archaeology at Ankara.

Woods, Christopher. 2010. "Visible Language: The Earliest Writing Systems." In *Visible Language: Inventions of Writing in the Ancient Middle East and Beyond*, edited by Christopher Woods, 15–25. OIMP 32. Chicago: Oriental Institute of the University of Chicago.

Woolley, Charles Leonard. 1929. *Ur of the Chaldees*. Harmondsworth: Penguin Books.

Woolley, Charles Leonard. 1934. *Ur Excavations.* Vol. 2: *The Royal Cemetery*. Oxford: Oxford University Press.

Woolley, Charles Leonard. 1953. *A Forgotten Kingdom: Being a Record of the Results Obtained from the Excavations of Two Mounds, Atchana and Al Mina in the Turkish Hatay*. Harmondsworth: Penguin.

Wright, H. T., N. F. Miller, and R. Redding. 1981. "Time and Process in an Uruk Rural Center." In *L'archéologie de l'Iraq: Perspectives et limites de l'interpretation anthropologique des documents*, 265–284. Colloques Internationaux du C.N.R.S. 580. Paris: Centre national de la recherche scientifique.

Wu, Yuhong. 1998. "The Earliest War for Water in Mesopotamia: Gilgamesh and Agga." *NABU* 1998, no. 4 (December): 93–95.

Wunsch, Cornelia. 2012. "Neo-Babylonian Entrepreneurs." In *The Invention of Enterprise: Entrepreneurship from Ancient Mesopotamia to Modern Times*, edited by David S. Landes, Joel Mokyr, and William J. Baumol, 40–61. Princeton: Princeton University Press.

Yamada, Shigeo. 2003. "Tukulti-Ninurta I's Rule over Babylonia and Its Aftermath: A Historical Reconstruction." *Orient* 38: 153–177.

Yamada, Shigeo. 2008. "A Preliminary Report on the Old Babylonian Texts from the Excavation of Tell Taban in the 2005 and 2006 Seasons: The Middle Euphrates and Habur Areas in the Post-Hammurabi Period." *al-Rāfidān* 29: 153–168.

Yang, Zhi. 1991. "King of Justice." *AuOr* 9: 243–249.

Yokohama, Miki. 1997. "The Administration of Public Herding in the First Dynasty of Babylon during the Reigns of Hammurapi and His Successors (1792–1595 B.C.)." *Orient* 32: 1–8.

Yon, Marguerite. 1997. "Ugarit." In *OEANE*, 5: 255–262.

Yon, Marguerite. 2006. *The City of Ugarit at Tell Ras Shamra*. Winona Lake, IN: Eisenbrauns.

Younger, K. Lawson, Jr. 2016. *A Political History of the Arameans: From Their Origins to the End of Their Polities*. ABS 13. Atlanta: Society of Biblical Literature.

Yuhong, Wu. 1998. "The Earliest War for the Water in Mesopotamia: Gilgamesh and Agga." *NABU* 1998 (4): 93–95.

Zaccagnini, C. 1994. "Feet of Clay at Emar and Elsewhere." *Orientalia* 63: 1–4.

Zettler, Richard L., and Lee Horne. 1998. *Treasures from the Royal Tombs of Ur*. Philadelphia: University of Pennsylvania Museum of Archaeology.

Zgoll, Annette. 1997. *Rechtsfall der En-ḫedu-Ana im Lied nin-me-šara*. AOAT 246. Münster: Ugarit Verlag.

Ziegler, Nele. 1999. *Le harem de Zimrî-Lîm*. *FM IV.* Mémoires de NABU V. Paris: SEPOA.

Ziegler, Nele. 2007. *Les musiciens et la musique d'après les archives de Mari*. *FM* IX. Paris: SEPOA.

Ziegler, Nele. 2011. "Music, the Work of Professionals." In *The Oxford Handbook of Cuneiform Culture*, edited by Karen Radner and Eleanor Robson, 288–312. Oxford and New York: Oxford University Press.

Ziegler, Nele. 2016. "Economic Activities of Women According to Mari Texts (18th Century BC)." In *The Role of Women in Work and Society in the Ancient Near East*, edited by Brigitte Lion and Cécile Michel, 269–309. *SANER* 13. Berlin: De Gruyter.

Zimansky, Paul. 2006. "Writing, Writers, and Reading in the Kingdom of Van." In *Margins of Writing, Origins of Cultures*, edited by Seth L. Sanders, 263–282. Chicago: Oriental Institute of the University of Chicago.

Index

For the benefit of digital users, indexed terms that span two pages (e.g., 52–53) may, on occasion, appear on only one of those pages.

Figures are indicated by an italic *f* following the para ID.